Textbook on Land Law

Textbook on

Land Law

....

Fourteenth edition

Judith-Anne MacKenzie

LLM, AKC, Barrister

and

Mary Phillips

MA, LLM, Barrister

OXFORD
UNIVERSITY PRESS

Great Clarendon Street, Oxford, OX2 6DP,
United Kingdom

Oxford University Press is a department of the University of Oxford.
It furthers the University's objective of excellence in research, scholarship,
and education by publishing worldwide. Oxford is a registered trade mark of
Oxford University Press in the UK and in certain other countries

Eleventh Edition Published 2006
Twelfth Edition Published 2008
Thirteenth Edition Published 2010

Impression: 1

British Library Cataloguing in Publication Data
Data available

Library of Congress Cataloging in Publication Data
Data available

ISBN 978-0-19-969927-8

Printed in Great Britain by
Ashford Colour Press Ltd, Gosport, Hampshire

CONTENTS

PREFACE

Once again, the text has been updated to take account of changes to the land law of England and Wales which have occurred since the previous edition. We include two significant decisions of the Supreme Court: *Jones v Kernott* [2011] 3 WLR 1121, the latest instalment in the *Stack v Dowden* story, and *Berrisford v Mexfield Housing Co-operative Ltd* [2011] 3 WLR 1091, which re-opens the debate about the application of the rule in *Lace v Chantler* to periodic tenancies. In the chapter on registered land, we note several new cases on the rights of a person in 'actual occupation', and in particular consider the observations of the Court of Appeal in *Link Lending Ltd v Bustard* [2010] EWCA Civ 424 about the duration of a temporary absence from the property. In Chapter 24 we cover the Mortgage Repossessions (Protection of Tenants, etc) Act 2010, which provides limited protection to tenants affected by repossession actions against their landlords. We also provide, in the relevant chapters, a full consideration of the proposals from the Law Commission for reform of the law of Easements, Covenants and Profits à Prendre. In response to feedback from lecturers and students, we have increased the use of diagrams and tables, and in particular now include a table of our imaginary characters and the roles that they play in our running story of Trant Way.

When looking along the shelves of libraries and bookshops, it is only too obvious that all law textbooks grow in size and weight from one edition to another. We are determined to keep this text to a reasonable size, and so have continued our practice of transferring full coverage of certain topics to the Online Resource Centre (**www.oxfordtextbooks.co.uk/orc/landlaw14e**) while dealing with them more briefly in the book.

Both of us have been fascinated by land law ever since our first encounters with the subject as undergraduates and were disappointed to discover that many law students and practitioners regarded the subject with dislike. We felt that one source of confusion, and often boredom, in the student was produced by the traditional method of teaching land law, in which the historical background to the subject was heavily emphasised. As a result, during the years in which we taught together we developed a new approach to the subject, which concentrated on its modern and practical aspects. However, we found our efforts hampered by the lack of a text which suited our methods, and were therefore pleased to be offered the opportunity to present our style of teaching in book form in our earlier book, *A Practical Approach to Land Law*, which first appeared in 1986. Over the years we have been pleased to see that many other teachers have come to approach this subject in a more accessible way. We hope that this text will continue to encourage an interest in a lively and important subject and that it will, perhaps, prove to be a comfort to the confused and faint-hearted.

Some have queried our decision to leave the question of what constitutes land to the end of the book, rather than dealing with it at the start. Notwithstanding these comments, we remain of the view that this is the most technical aspect of the subject and consider it unhelpful to expect students to understand the concept of an incorporeal hereditament before they have even grasped the basics of estates and interests in land. Accordingly, the more detailed material on this topic remains in the last chapter of the book but we have included an introduction to the concepts involved in Chapter 1. There is, of course, nothing to stop you reading the detailed chapter on this subject at an early stage, if your teachers do not agree with us.

In case there is any doubt about it, we should emphasise that Trant Way, Mousehole, in the country of Stilton is a purely fictional street and so are its inhabitants, and the other characters and institutions in this book are all inventions and bear no relation to any real persons or bodies, living or dead.

Judith-Anne MacKenzie retired from the Civil Service at the end of 2010. She continues to advise and support Bar students at Lincoln's Inn and law students at her *alma mater,* King's College, London. She is also taking a professional embroiderers' course at the Royal School of Needlework and was recently appointed as a broderer at Southwark Cathedral. Mary Phillips, following her retirement from the post of Dean at the Inns of Court School of Law, for some years continued her interest in the teaching of land law at City University and later at the University of Surrey. However she is now simply enjoying retirement, spending time with granddaughters Sophie and Emma and 'dog-sitting' with Foxy, who lives with Alex and Martin in their country cottage with its flying bedroom.

We hope that this new edition will prove as popular as its predecessors. As always, we are happy to receive any comments and suggestions for improvements; which may be sent to us via our publishers.

Finally, we must express our gratitude to the staff of the Land Registry for the advice which they always give so readily, and in particular for providing the copy of the register of title for 1 Trant Way, which appears on p. 93. We are also grateful for permission to reproduce the transfer form on pp. 128–30.

The law is stated as at 1 March 2012.

Judith-Anne MacKenzie
Mary Phillips

WHO'S WHO

WHO'S WHO				
Property	Characters	Estates, interests etc	Topics considered	Chaps
TRANT HOUSE	**Victor Venables**	Freehold owner and prospective vendor	*Introduction to basic concepts of land law, including the multiplicity of estates and interests in land*	1, 2
	Victor's wife			
	Victor's mother			
	Penelope Price	Possible purchaser		
	Ted Topling	Tenant of flat in stables		
	Un-named owner of neighbouring cottage			
	Another neighbour who owns a pony			
	Victor's bank or building society			
		TRANT WAY		
1.	**Victor Venn**	Freehold owner and vendor	*Registered title—sale and purchase of freehold house*	4
	Mr and Mrs Armstrong	Purchasers	*Investigation of title; transfer and registration*	7
			Co-ownership	16
	Double Gloucester Building Society	Mortgagees, after purchase by the Armstrongs	*Mortgages and charges*	24

(continued)

WHO'S WHO				
Property	**Characters**	**Estates, interests etc**	**Topics considered**	**Chaps**
3.	**Victoria Ventnor**	Freehold owner and vendor	*Unregistered title—sale and purchase of freehold house*	4
	Barbara Bell	Purchaser	*The contract* *Investigations of title; conveyance* *First registration*	5 6 7
	Bob Bell: Barbara's father	Occupier of top floor 'granny flat'	*Licences; enforcement of licences; protection from molestation*	Intro. to Part V; 23; 27
4.	**Oscar Oregano**	Former freehold owner, now dead	*Adverse possession*	8
	Nicholas Oregano: Oscar's nephew	Has inherited the freehold		
	Sidney Sorrell	Adverse possessor or 'squatter'		
5.	**David Derby**	Freehold owner	*Fee simple absolute in possession*	9
	David's nephews: **Eric, Frank and Hal**			
	David's friend: **George**			

2.	**Fingall Forest**	Freehold owner and landlord of Gerald Gruyere and James Harding	*Leasehold estate; obligations of landlord and tenant; running of covenants on assignment of lease and reversion*	10, 11, 12
	Gerald Gruyere	Weekly tenant of basement flat		
	James Harding	Tenant of maisonette under 99 yr. lease granted in 2012 (a 'new' lease for purposes of L&T (Covs) Act, 1995)		
	Wensleydale Bank plc	Mortgagee of James Harding's 99 year lease	*Mortgages*	24
	Gerald Gruyere keeps dustbin in landlord's garden	Easement of storage	*Easements*	25
6.	**Irene Ivy**	Former freehold owner and landlord of John Jarlsberg	*Obligations of landlord and tenant; running of covenants on assignment of lecse and reversion*	11, 12
	John Jarlsberg	Former tenant under 40 yr. lease, granted in 1979 (an 'old' lease for purposes of L&T (Covs) Act, 1995)		
	Liam Lyle	Current freehold owner		
	Keith Kale	Current tenant		

(continued)

WHO'S WHO				
Property	Characters	Estates, interests etc	Topics considered	Chaps
7.	**Martin Mount**	Freehold owner and landlord of Nigel Norman	*Enforcement of leasehold covenants in head leases and subleases; remedies for breach*	12, 13
	Nigel Norman	Tenant under 90 yr. lease, and landlord of Olav Orion and Paula Primrose		
7A	**Olav Orion**	Monthly periodic tenant of 7A		
7B	**Paula Primrose**	Monthly periodic tenant of 7B		
12.	**Alice, Brian, Colin, David, Eric and Fanny**	Co-owners	*Co-ownership, severance of joint tenancy; disputes between co-owners; TOLATA 1996, s.14*	16, 17
13.	**Sidney Search** and **Frederick Find**	Partners in firm of chartered surveyors, tenants under 99 yr. lease	*Co-ownership*	16
20.	**John Brown,**	Freehold owner	*Trusts of land under TOLATA, 1996*	17
	his wife, **Janet Brown** and their two daughters			
11.	**Mark Mould**	Freehold owner	*Resulting and constructive trusts; property rights on divorce*	20
	his wife, **Sally Mould**		*Home rights*	27

8.	**Mildred Mumps**	Freehold owner and mortgagor	*Cohabitants' property rights at end of relationship; home rights; protection from molestation*	Intro. to Part V, 27
	Henry Mumps: Mildred's unmarried partner			
	Red Leicester Building Society	Mortgagee		24
	Royal Windsor Bank	Prospective second mortgagee		24
8A	**Laura Lymeswold**	Occupier of the basement flat	*Nature of a licence; 'lease or licence?'; enforcement of licences*	Intro to Part V, 22, 23
14	**Nigel Neep**	Freehold owner		
		Grazes his goat on Fieldy Farm	*Easements and profits*	25
	Nigel's bank	Possible mortgagee	*Grant of informal mortgages*	24
15	Un-named past freehold owner (in 1947)		*Easements; their grant and transmission*	25
	Charles Chive	Current freehold owner		
16	Un-named past freehold owner (in 1947)		*Easements; their grant and transmission*	25
	Marjorie Marjoram (until 1980)	Former freehold owner		
	Dan Dill	Current freehold owner		

(continued)

WHO'S WHO				
Property	Characters	Estates, interests etc	Topics considered	Chaps
16A	**Marjorie Marjoram**	Freehold owner until 1980, when she divided the then 16 and sold the part which became 16A to Basil Borage	*Easements; their grant and transmission*	25
	Basil Borage	Purchased freehold in 1980		
Fieldy Farm (behind 14–16 Trant Way)	**Farmer George**	Freehold owner of a large farm, which neighbours some of the properties towards the end of Trant Way	*Easements and profits*	25
		Maintains fence separating farm from 14 Trant Way		
17	**Olive Orange** (died 1995)	Freehold owner in 1988 and covenantee	*Freehold covenants: grant and running of covenants*	26
	Paul Peach	Current freehold owner		
18	**Olive Orange**	Freehold owner in 1988	*Freehold covenants: grant and running of covenants*	26
	Robert Raspberry	Purchaser of freehold in 1988 and covenantor		
	Silvia Strawberry	Current freehold owner		

19	**Daniel Date**	Freehold owner in 1988	*Freehold covenants: grant of covenants*	26
20 Also called "The Old Rectory"	**Big Builders Ltd**	Freehold owner in 1999 Divided property and constructed the new Rectory Crescent on the land forming part of the old 20 Trant Way	*Freehold covenants: building schemes*	26
		RECTORY CRESCENT (formerly 20 Trant Way)		
1 2 3 4 5 6	**Alfred Alpha** **Bertie Beta** **Gail Gamma** **Dolly Delta** **Ewan Epsilon** **Oscar Omega**	Freehold owners	*Freehold covenants: building schemes*	26

TABLE OF CASES

TABLE OF STATUTES

European Union Legislation

International Treaties and Conventions

TABLE OF STATUTORY INSTRUMENTS

PART I

Introduction

In this part, we will introduce you to Trant Way, a road in the fictitious town of Mousehole in the county of Stilton, which we use throughout the book to illustrate the application of land law rules in practical situations. Most of the properties in Trant Way are occupied as houses or flats, but the basic land law covered in this book is just as relevant to non-residential property.

A very important fact about the whole neighbourhood is that the county of Stilton became an area of compulsory land registration on 1 December 1990. We know that this will not mean a lot to you at the moment, but we will explain it in Chapter 4.

In our first two chapters, we follow a prospective purchaser who is viewing a house in Trant Way and explain:

- what is meant by 'owning land' (in Chapter 1); and
- how one person may have rights over land owned by another (in Chapter 2).

In these two chapters we are, as it were, getting the chess pieces up on the board, and telling you what they are called and how they move. Some of the material in these two chapters may seem rather theoretical but, if you can get a basic understanding of the concepts we describe, we are sure that it will make the rest of your study of land law much easier. In Chapter 3 we consider very briefly some of the provisions of the Human Rights Act 1998 which may be relevant to land law.

Looking ahead, you may like to know that in Part II we work through the process of acquiring title to a piece of land, and then spend the rest of the book looking at some of the rights over land in more detail. We leave discussion of the question 'What is land?' to the end of the book. It is one of the more technical areas of the subject, and we think you will find it easier to follow at a later stage, although we do include a brief introductory section about this topic in Chapter 1.

We have not included any general introduction to equity because students often study land law and equity (or trusts) at the same time, and in such a case your studies in equity will provide the background knowledge which is needed for land law. If, however, land law precedes equity in your course, or if you are not required to study equity in detail or you are not a law student, we do advise you to read some outline introduction to its history and nature. Some suggested references are given at the end of Chapter 2.

1925 property legislation

Finally, this is a convenient place in which to mention the property legislation which was passed in 1925 and which came into force on 1 January 1926. This legislation consolidated earlier amendments to land law, put into statutory form some common law rules and introduced further reforms. This turning-point in land law was contained in the following statutes:

Settled Land Act 1925

Trustee Act 1925

Law of Property Act 1925

Land Registration Act 1925

Administration of Estates Act 1925

Land Charges Act 1925

These statutes have been amended by later enactments and in some cases are largely superseded by later statutes. For convenience we have used the following abbreviations throughout the book, giving the year in each case, in order to avoid confusion where there are two or more statutes with similar names:

SLA—Settled Land Act

LPA—Law of Property Act

LRA—Land Registration Act

More recently, the Trusts of Land and Appointment of Trustees Act 1996 has introduced major changes to the important area of trusts of land. You will find that Act referred to here as TOLATA 1996.

Note on Bibliography

You will find a Bibliography at p. 587, but may like to note now the abbreviations we use for four main textbooks, which are as follows:

Cheshire and Burn's Modern Law of Real Property, 18th edn., Oxford University Press, 2011: Cheshire and Burn.

Gray and Gray, *Elements of Land Law*, 5th edn., Oxford University Press, 2009: Gray and Gray.

Megarry and Wade, *The Law of Real Property*, 8th edn., Sweet & Maxwell, 2012: Megarry and Wade.

Smith, *Property Law*, 7th edn., Pearson Longman, 2011: Smith.

1

Estates in land

1.1 Introducing Trant Way—and Trant House

Since Trant Way exists only in our imagination, we must explain that we visualise it as a road on the outskirts of an old country town. The town has grown considerably over the past 50 years (although so far it has avoided a ring road), and many of the outlying houses have been built on land which was once farmland. Thus the houses in Trant Way which are nearest to the centre of the town stand in a typically suburban environment, whereas the houses at the further end of the road are in more countrified surroundings.

One of these more rural properties, Trant House, has just come onto the market, and the house agent's particulars include the following details:

> ... a freehold property, offering spacious accommodation.... set in delightful grounds of approx. 2 acres, with open views to rear..... property includes converted stables containing two self-contained flats, suitable for permanent occupation or for use as holiday lets....

Penelope Price is looking for a house in the area in which she can run a bed-and-breakfast business. She likes the sound of Trant House and arranges to view it.

1.2 Viewing Trant House

When Penelope arrives at the property she finds that a long drive leads from the gate to the house. Half-way up it, a smaller drive branches off and runs through a boundary wall towards a small cottage. Penelope notes that she must find out more about this.

She is shown around the property by Vernon Venables, who explains that he has lived here with his wife and family for over 30 years, having bought the house in 1979.

Their children are now grown up, with families of their own, and he and his wife no longer need such a large house. After going all over the house, which seems comfortable and well maintained, Penelope is taken out to look at the additional accommodation in the converted stables. It is obvious that both flats are currently occupied, and Vernon explains that one of them is let to a mature student, Ted Toppling, who is following a three-year course in Applied Astrology at Mousehole University. Vernon tells Penelope that the other flat was specially converted into a 'granny annexe' for his mother, who came to live with the family when his father died a few years ago. He mentions that converting the stables was a very expensive job. Fortunately for him, his mother contributed towards the cost of fitting out her flat, but he had to get quite a large loan to finance the rest of the work and intends to pay this off when he sells Trant House. He adds that his mother will be moving with them when they find a new house.

The grounds around the house prove to be most attractive. The part nearest to the house has been landscaped as a formal garden. Beyond this there are flower beds and a shrubbery, and then a large area of rough grassland, which the house agent's details describe as 'the orchard'. Penelope is rather surprised to see a pony grazing here, and Vernon tells her that it belongs to one of his neighbours, 'who has always grazed his ponies here'.

Vernon asks Penelope if she has any questions, and she takes the opportunity to ask about the drive at the front, which appears to be shared with the neighbouring property. She is told that the cottage used to belong to Trant House, and was approached by the main drive. When the cottage was sold off many years ago (before Vernon bought the property), the new owner was allowed to continue to use the Trant House drive, and occupants of the cottage have done so ever since. Talking about this reminds Vernon that, when the previous owner of Trant House sold the cottage, there was some agreement between him and the buyer that neither of them would carry on any sort of business or trade on their respective properties. He is rather vague about the details, but is sure that 'the lawyers will know'.

Penelope asks if she can have another look around the inside of the house, and having done so, goes away to think it all over. For her, as for most purchasers, thinking it over will involve all sorts of questions about how she will use the property, what sort of alterations she might make and, most important of all, how she will finance her purchase. One question that she probably will not ask herself is: what am I buying? The answer seems obvious: I'm buying a house and some land. For a lawyer, however, the answer is rather different and in the next section we will tell you what someone who is 'buying a house' is really buying.

1.3 What am I buying?

Under the system of landholding which operates in England and Wales, all land belongs to the Crown and the only person who is capable of owning land is the sovereign. This is an idea which dates from the Norman Conquest in 1066 and which persists even today. As a result, an individual cannot own the land on which he lives or runs his business, but he is allowed the use of the land by the Crown. What he does in fact own is a collection of rights and duties in relation to the land, one of the most important rights being to take and retain possession of the land and to make use of it. The technical name for the individual's interest in the property is *'an estate in land'*, and thus a person who buys a house becomes the owner of *an estate* in it but does not own the land itself.

1.4 Tenure

When the new system of landholding was introduced in the eleventh century, the king gave rights over large areas of land to each of his most powerful supporters, in exchange for an oath of loyalty and the performance of services (which very often involved fighting for the king when necessary). In turn, each lord would grant to his followers similar rights over parts of the land he had received, again in exchange for loyalty and services. The relationship between the grantor (the king or lord who granted the rights) and the grantee (the tenant who received them) is called 'tenure' (from the Latin word '*tenere*' which means 'to hold'), and various forms of tenure developed, according to the nature of the services to be performed by the tenant. These forms of tenure came to be described as '*freehold tenures*', because rights in land could be held in this way only by free men (i.e., not by the unfree serfs or villeins, who were obliged to remain in the area in which they had been born and to work for the local lord).

Over the centuries, changes in society meant that the services due from the tenant were no longer performed and the link between lord and tenant was forgotten. However, the underlying theory that land is held from the Crown remained, and although most forms of tenure have been abolished a 'landowner' is still said to hold his land from the Crown by the one remaining form of tenure ('free and common socage'). Nevertheless, for all practical purposes the doctrine of tenure has little modern significance, and it is very likely that the owner of Trant House is completely unaware of his tenurial relationship with the Crown.

1.5 Estates in land

Throughout the book, we will be talking about freehold and leasehold estates, and we need to look briefly at how these developed.

1.5.1 The freehold estates

An estate in land which could be held by a free man on free tenure came to be known as a freehold estate, and over the years three main types of freehold estate developed.

1.5.1.1 The life estate

At the outset, it was usual to grant the right to possess and use land only for the life of the tenant, who accordingly could be said to have a life estate. The king or lesser noble who granted the estate depended on the loyalty of his tenants and would make grants only to those personally known to him.

1.5.1.2 The fee simple

As time went by, grants to a tenant 'and his heirs' became more common, with the result that the right to possession would last longer than the lifetime of the original tenant. In a further development, it became possible for the tenant to transfer the estate (i.e., on a sale or by gift) and the right to possession of the land would continue as long as there was an heir to inherit on the death of the current owner. The heading to this section describes this estate as a '*fee simple*' and we need to explain the meaning of this term.

The word 'fee' denoted an inheritable interest in land and the word 'simple' meant that the estate could be inherited by the 'general heirs'. On the death of the current tenant, the estate would pass to his heir—a single individual who was identified according to complicated rules. If the deceased had children, the heir would be his eldest son. If the eldest son had died before his father but had himself left a son, that grandson would be his grandfather's heir. If there were no sons to inherit, any daughters inherited the estate jointly. If the deceased had no descendants, his heir would be one of his blood relations, found among his brothers or sisters (or their descendants), or more remotely among his uncles, aunts or cousins, At a later stage, one of the deceased's ancestors, such as his father or grandfather, might be entitled to inherit. It was therefore possible for a fee simple estate to pass to a fairly distant relation.

1.5.1.3 The fee tail

As we explained above, the fee simple estate was inheritable by general heirs, the heir being drawn from a wide range of relatives of the deceased. In the case of a fee tail, however, the estate was still inheritable (denoted by the word 'fee'), but the heir had to come from a more limited class. This class was the 'heirs of the body', meaning the lineal descendants of the original tenant in tail. Sometimes this class was limited even further, to the 'heirs of the body male' (or, rarely, 'female'). In such a case, the estate could not pass to an heir of the wrong gender, nor could it pass to the ascendants or siblings of the original tenant. It would pass only to his direct descendants of the correct gender. The fact that the estate was limited or 'cut down' in this way led to it being described as a fee 'tail' (from the French word *'tailler'*—to cut down).

If no heir of the right sort existed, the estate would come to an end and the property reverted to the fee simple owner who had originally created this more limited estate (or, if he had already died, would pass to his general heir). The person who had the right to recover the property should the entail come to an end was said to have a 'reversion'.

1.5.2 The leasehold estate

Once the owner of a freehold estate was free to deal with his estate as he chose, the practice developed of permitting another person to take possession of the land for a fixed time, usually in exchange for rent. In modern terms, we would say that the freehold owner 'let' the land or 'granted a lease' of it. This was in essence a commercial development, and although the relationship between landlord and tenant is also one of tenure (i.e., the tenant 'holds' from the landlord), the tenant usually paid for his use of the land with money, rather than by the performance of services.

Originally, letting the land in this way was regarded as creating only a contractual relationship between the parties. Over time, however, the tenant's position improved and the courts treated him as having a right to possession of the land which he could enforce against the landlord and also against any other person who dispossessed him. Recognition of this right meant that a tenant holding under a lease could be said to have an estate in the land.

1.6 Reducing the number of legal estates

In the past, the freehold and leasehold estates we have described above were recognised and protected in the common law courts and so were described as 'legal' estates (as opposed to the equitable interests which were protected by the Chancellor). Today, however, only two of those estates retain their legal status, and the other former legal estates take effect only in equity.

This change was introduced by the 1925 property legislation (see p. 2), as one of the measures designed to further its aim of simplifying the process of buying and selling land. Dealings with land were complicated by the existence of the three freehold legal estates. This was because it was possible for a fee simple owner to create a number of smaller legal estates out of the fee simple, so as to give successive interests in the property to current and later generations of his family. He could, for example:

- give a life estate to some elderly relative;
- create a fee tail in favour of his eldest son, which would entitle the son and his direct descendants to possession of the land when the previous life estate ended; and
- dispose of the reversion on the fee tail which would arise if the direct line died out (see 1.5.1.3).

This process was known as 'making a settlement', and we will tell you more about it in Chapter 15. At the moment all you need to know is that this practice of dividing up the legal fee simple could cause difficulties on a later sale of the estate, even if the settlement had come to an end. Any prospective purchaser would want to satisfy himself that the seller owned the estate he offered for sale, and the fact that the fee simple could be fragmented into smaller estates made the process of investigating the seller's title more complicated.

The solution to this problem which was adopted in 1925 was to provide that in future the smaller freehold estates should take effect only in equity, leaving one freehold estate (the fee simple) and the leasehold estate to continue as the two remaining legal estates. As a result, there are today only two estates in land which are recognised at law.

1.7 The two modern legal estates

The two legal estates which exist today are set out in LPA 1925, s. 1(1):

> The only estates and interests in land which are capable of subsisting or of being conveyed or created at law are –
>
> (a) an estate in fee simple absolute in possession;
>
> (b) a term of years absolute.

Section 1(3) of the Act provides:

> All other estates, interests, and charges in or over land take effect as equitable interests.

1.7.1 Estate in fee simple absolute in possession ('freehold estate')

This is now the only freehold estate which can exist at law, and it is becoming increasingly common to refer to it as 'the freehold estate' rather than using its technical name. You may remember that the particulars of Trant House describe it as 'a freehold property', and this tells us that Vernon owns a fee simple absolute in possession. Although for practical purposes one may speak of 'a freehold estate', it is important to understand the precise meaning of the older term, which you will certainly encounter throughout the 1925 legislation. Each part of the term has a technical meaning, which we will consider briefly.

1.7.1.1 Fee simple

We have already explained that originally this term indicated that the estate was inheritable by 'the general heirs' of the current tenant (see 1.5.1.2). Rather confusingly, the 1925 legislation retains this term, although it abolished the old concept of the heir and introduced new statutory rules of inheritance, with the result that one cannot really define a fee simple today by describing it as an estate 'inherited by the general heirs'. What remains true is that the fee simple is an estate which can last indefinitely, as long as there are persons entitled to take the property under the provisions of the will of the previous owner, or under the statutory rules relating to an intestacy. Very occasionally no person entitled to the estate can be discovered after the rules have been applied. In such cases the estate will at this point come to an end and the land will revert to the Crown.

1.7.1.2 'Absolute'

The explanation of the word 'absolute' gives rise to further complications. The word indicates that the fee simple should not be subject to any restriction which would prevent it lasting as long as there are persons entitled to inherit. So, if I try to give Fred a fee simple estate 'until he qualifies as a solicitor', the gift cannot be of a fee simple estate. The estate will not necessarily last forever (as long as there is someone to inherit) because it will end earlier should Fred ever become a solicitor. This sort of arrangement is called a 'determinable fee' and, together with its relative the 'conditional fee', it now takes effect as an equitable interest. (For further details of determinable and conditional fees, see Chapter 9.)

1.7.1.3 'In possession'

The final words in the legal term for a freehold estate are 'in possession'. This means that the estate must be current, rather than being one which is to give the owner the use of the land at some time in the future. Thus, if I give Paul an estate to start in five years' time, I have not given him a legal estate and he will have only an equitable interest. Future interests in land are dealt with in more detail in Chapters 15, 17 and 18.

It should be noted that the estate owner does not have to be in physical possession of the land itself in order to have a legal estate. For example, the property may be let to a tenant, in which case the tenant will be in physical possession of the land, whilst the landlord has the right to receive the rent payable under the lease. In this case the landlord still has a legal estate because LPA 1925, s. 205(1)(xix), provides that:

> 'Possession' includes receipt of rents and profits or the right to receive the same, if any.

1.7.1.4 Former legal estates which become equitable interests under LPA 1925, s. 1(3)

It will be obvious that there are many kinds of arrangement which one may wish to make concerning a piece of land, but which now cannot amount to a legal estate in fee simple. Examples of arrangements which fall into this category include: an interest for life; an interest to start at some time in the future—a future interest; and a determinable or conditional fee simple. Arrangements of this sort can still be made, but they create equitable interests which have to operate by means of a trust. In such a case, the legal fee simple is held by trustees on trust for those entitled to the equitable interests (see 2.5.2 and Part IV).

For some 60 years after the 1925 property legislation, an entailed interest (formerly the fee tail estate) was one of the equitable interests which operated behind a trust. However, major changes in this area of law were introduced by the TOLATA 1996, and it is no longer possible to create an entailed interest, even in equity (see 17.10.3).

1.7.2 Term of years absolute ('leasehold estate')

The 'term of years absolute' is the lawyers' name for what is more commonly called a lease. It has remained as a legal estate but it is inferior to the fee simple estate because it is of limited duration. The essential requirement is that a lease must be for a fixed 'term of years', though this can include periods of less than a year (LPA 1925, s. 205(1)(xxvii)) and can include arrangements such as weekly or monthly tenancies. The word 'absolute' does not seem to add anything to the meaning because a lease does not cease to be a legal estate merely because it will terminate on the occurrence of some event (e.g., if the rent is unpaid).

Section 1(1)(b) of LPA 1925 does not require that the term of a legal lease should start at the date of grant (i.e., unlike the freehold estate, it does not have to be 'in possession'). Thus, subject to certain rules (for which, see 10.1.3.4), it is possible to grant a lease now, to take effect at some time in the future.

It should be noted that the owner of a term of years does not hold the land of the Crown. The leaseholder derives his title from that of his landlord, who will be either the owner of a fee simple estate or of a longer leasehold estate.

The lease is of considerable importance in land law and it is considered in greater detail in Chapters 10–13.

1.7.3 Legal estates in Trant House

In this section, we simply want to draw your attention to the fact that both of the two modern legal estates can be found in the Trant House property. We have already noted that the description of the property as 'freehold' tells us that Vernon holds the fee simple absolute in possession in the property. In addition, one of the flats in the converted stables has been 'let' to the student, Ted. Provided that this letting satisfies the legal requirements for a lease and has been made in the correct form (which we will tell you about in Chapter 10), a legal term of years absolute will have been created, which Ted will hold as a tenant from Vernon as his landlord.

1.8 What is land?

When Penelope was looking over Trant House, she was particularly impressed by the very lovely gardens. She has always dreamt of having gardens like these and thinks that they will also be a great attraction to possible guests for her business. She noticed that a major feature of the gardens is the presence of a number of statues, which appear to be antiques and to have been part of the gardens for some considerable time. She also noticed that the gardens contain a stunning display of scented roses and Vernon Venables explained that rose growing had been his main hobby for some time and that he had won prizes for his champion roses, some of which he had cultivated himself. She is also very interested in some of the tapestries that seem to have been used as wall coverings in some of the rooms of the house, in place of wallpaper. Penelope is now worried that Vernon may want to move or sell the statues and tapestries (which seem very valuable) and that he is certainly likely to want to remove some or all of the roses.

Penelope is starting to ask herself questions about what she is actually buying. The estate agent's particulars just mention the house, gardens and orchard: they say nothing about statues, tapestries or plants. She wonders whether, if nothing is said in the conveyancing documents about these items, she will get them if she buys the property. In essence, she is starting to wonder what actually constitutes land.

Unfortunately, the answer to Penelope's concern is one of the most complex and technical aspects of land law. Indeed, it is quite difficult to understand this issue fully until you have learnt a great deal about the estates and interests in land. Accordingly, we think it best to consider this issue at the end of the book (see Chapter 28). However, we realise that you will need a working concept of 'land' from the start of your studies, so we will give some basic ideas here. Also, in some courses this issue is tackled at an early stage. If that is true for you, we suggest that you read the first three chapters of this text and then Chapter 28.

The traditional answer to what constitutes land is that land is the physical land down to the centre of the earth and up to the 'heavens' (skies). 'Land' also includes everything physically attached to the land. Thus the house and its foundations are also land. Since the roses are necessarily embedded in the land, they are also land. As far as the tapestries are concerned, the issue of whether they are part of the land may depend on the degree to which they are fixed to the walls and the purpose of that fixing. Is it just to display the tapestries conveniently or is it to incorporate them more fully into the design of the house? The statues may well just be placed on top of the land, rather than fixed to it. In that case they may not constitute land. However, if they can be regarded as forming part of the integral design of the garden, they may be taken to have become part of the land. We discuss the cases on this important topic in Chapter 28 and you should look there if you need more detailed answers.

The whole issue of what is land is, however, made even more complex by the fact that not only physical things fixed to land are regarded by the law as being land. Thus the legal estates and most interests in land are also 'land'.

It is, of course, always possible for a document to provide its own definition of land for the purpose of that document. Thus the document transferring Trant House to Penelope could specifically exclude the roses. If it does not, they will transfer without being mentioned because they are certainly affixed to the land. If Vernon removed them, he could be sued successfully by Penelope. This can be important because vendors often forget to tell their conveyancer that they want to take such items with them. In most cases it is not worth bringing a court action but, where what is removed is significant, it may be, particularly if the items removed can be restored to the property.

As we have seen already, in fact only the monarch owns land; others can only own an estate or interest in land. Thus, part of the answer to the question, 'What is land?' is that estates and interests can be regarded as land.

For most of your work on land law, the most important definition of land will be that provided by s. 205 of the LPA 1925 because that definition applies to the 1925 legislation as a whole (see para. 28.1.1 for this provision). If you look at it, you will see that, as we have explained above, it mixes together physical things which are land (such as buildings) with the estates and interests that can also be land. Do not worry; we explain all of this in much more detail in Chapter 28.

1.9 Who else may have rights over Trant House?

In this chapter we have told you about the two legal estates in land and explained that the house agent's description of Trant House as 'a freehold property' means that the vendor, Vernon, holds the 'fee simple absolute in possession' in the property.

In addition to Vernon, a number of other people may have rights over the property. We will tell you about some of these rights in the next chapter, but suggest that before you go any further you may like to look back at the account of Penelope's visit to the property, and see if you can identify some of the other people who might claim to have rights over it.

FURTHER READING

Cheshire and Burn, *Cheshire and Burn's Modern Law of Real Property*, 18th edn., Oxford University Press, 2011, Chapter 2 (The Common Law System) (history of tenures and estates—very detailed—for reference only).

Cooke, *Land Law*, Oxford University Press, 2006, Chapter 2 (Property Rights in Land) pp. 13–22.

2

Interests in land

2.1 Introduction

If you did as we suggested at the end of the last chapter, and looked back at the description of Penelope's visit to Trant House, you have probably identified a number of people, other than Vernon, who might have rights over the property.

They include:

- the owner of the neighbouring cottage;
- the neighbour who has always grazed his ponies in the orchard;
- Vernon's wife;
- Vernon's mother;
- Ted, the student who rents one of the flats; and
- the person or institution from whom Vernon borrowed the money to pay for the stable conversion.

It is possible that any or all of these people could have rights over Trant House, and that such rights could be enforced not only against Vernon, the fee simple owner, but also against anyone who acquires the property from him.

2.2 Rights which others may have over Trant House

In this section, we will look at the people we have identified and tell you about the rights which each might have. On what we know at present, we will not be able to say whether anyone does in fact have rights over Trant House, but the information gathered by Penelope provides an opportunity to introduce you to some of the rights which can exist over another's land and which we will be studying in detail later on in this book.

If Penelope does decide to buy Trant House, she (or her legal adviser) will have to find out much more about these possible rights, because if they do exist and can be enforced against her they could have a considerable effect on her use and enjoyment of the land.

2.2.1 The owner of the neighbouring cottage

Penelope has learnt two things about the owner of the cottage: he appears to have a right to use part of the Trant House drive and he may have a right to prevent the property being used for trade or business purposes.

2.2.1.1 Right to use the drive

This could mean that the neighbouring property has a right of way over part of Trant House. In more general terms, such a right would be known as an easement. Easements are rights attached to one piece of land, entitling its occupants to do something on another's property, or preventing the owner of that property from interfering with the passage of some benefit to the first piece of land. Thus one may have a right to walk or drive over one's neighbour's land (a right of way), or perhaps the right to prevent the neighbour building so as to block the passage of light to one's windows (a right to light). In each case there is a piece of land which is benefited by the easement and a piece of land which is burdened with it. There are many types of easement, such as rights to storage or drainage, the right to water, and a great number of others. A list of common examples is given in Chapter 25, in which we will tell you more about the characteristics of easements and how they are created.

2.2.1.2 Right to prevent the use of Trant House for business or trade

Such a right, if it exists, would have arisen from an undertaking by the former owner of Trant House, made in the document ('the conveyance' or 'the transfer') by which he transferred the legal estate in the cottage to its new owner. Such an undertaking is known as a *'restrictive covenant'* and, subject to certain rules, it can be enforced not only against the estate owner who made it, but also against later owners of his land. We will tell you a little more about these covenants later in this chapter (see 2.5.5) and will then look at them in greater detail in Chapter 26. It is obvious that if such a restriction did exist and could be enforced against Penelope, she would not be able to carry out her plan of running a bed-and-breakfast business at Trant House, and so would probably decide not to buy the property.

2.2.2 The neighbour who has always grazed his ponies in the orchard

It is possible that this neighbour has a right very similar to an easement, known as a 'profit à prendre' (from the French word 'prendre', which means 'to take'). This is a right to take something from land which belongs to another estate owner: for example, to cut wood or to dig gravel. The right to take grass or other plants from land by grazing is a well-established profit, and if the practice of grazing ponies in the Trant House orchard satisfies the relevant rules for the recognition and creation of profits à prendre (considered in Chapter 25) Penelope, or any other future owner of the property, might find that she could not prevent this use of her land.

2.2.3 Vernon's wife

Penelope did not meet Vanessa Venables, but learned of her existence from Vernon. Without knowing more about the couple's circumstances, there is no way of knowing what, if any, rights Vanessa may in fact have over Trant House, but there are several possibilities.

2.2.3.1 Rights of a co-owner

When the property was bought, the legal estate may have been conveyed to both Vernon and Vanessa, so that they hold it as joint legal owners. Co-ownership of property, especially of the family home, has become increasingly common during the last 60 years and we will tell you how it works in Chapter 16.

2.1.3.2 Rights of a beneficiary under a trust

Even if Vanessa is not a co-owner of the legal estate, she may have rights to the property arising under a trust. This could have been created formally, or have arisen informally, either by agreement between the couple or as a result of financial contributions made by Vanessa to the cost of buying or improving Trant House.

Trusts play a very important part in land law. We will explain briefly how they work later in this chapter (2.5.2), and then consider trusts relating to land in detail in Part IV.

2.2.3.3 Rights of occupation

If Vanessa does not own the legal estate jointly with her husband, she will have statutory rights of occupation, known as 'home rights', which arise in cases of marriage and civil partnership. The rights prevent the partner who owns the property from excluding the other partner as long as the marriage or civil partnership lasts, and in some cases can be enforced against anyone who buys the property (see 27.3.3).

2.2.4 Vernon's mother

For a number of years now, Vernon's mother has been allowed to occupy one of the flats in the old stables as her home. In legal terms, she appears to be a 'licensee', that is, someone who is on another's property with his permission or licence, and is therefore not a trespasser. Family arrangements of this sort, although usually made with the best of intentions, can cause problems because the parties to them often give little or no thought to the legal implications of what they are doing. If relationships break down, the licensee may claim to have a right to remain in the property and/or to be entitled to a share in its value. We will look at cases in which this has occurred in Chapters 22 and 23, but for the moment simply want you to be aware that it could happen. Vernon says that his mother will be moving out with him and his wife, but if she changed her mind she might claim that she has a right to continue to live in the flat:

- because the arrangements with her son gave her a lease of the flat, so that she is a tenant, not a licensee; or
- because her son promised her that she could live there for the rest of her life and, relying on this, she spent all her money on fitting out the flat.

Further, even if she is willing to move out, she could claim to be a beneficiary under a trust arising from her financial contributions, and therefore to have a right to a share in the value of Trant House.

Any of these claims could give rise to rights which might be enforceable against a purchaser of the property and, if Penelope decides to buy the house, the presence of the vendor's elderly mother living in self-contained accommodation at Trant House might very well ring alarm bells with her legal adviser.

2.2.5 Ted, the student who occupies the other flat

In the previous chapter, we noted that Ted holds a leasehold estate in part of the Trant House property. This means that as far as Penelope is concerned he is another person who has rights which might be enforceable against her. In Chapter 10, we will see that a lease can be granted for a fixed term (for example, for 10 years) or it may be a periodic tenancy, which will run on from one period to another, such as from week to week or from month to month, until one party ends it by giving notice to the other. Without knowing more about the arrangements between Vernon and Ted, we cannot say whether Ted would be able to stay on in the flat when the whole property is sold, but it is certainly possible that his lease might bind Penelope if she buys Trant House.

2.2.6 The lender who provided the money for the stable conversion

We know that Vernon borrowed a considerable amount of money for the conversion of the stables and that he has not yet repaid the loan. It is almost certain that the lender (most probably a bank or building society) would have required Vernon to provide security for the loan by granting a mortgage over Trant House. Under a mortgage the lender acquires rights over the property and is entitled to sell it if the borrower fails to repay the loan. We know that Vernon is planning to repay his debt out of the money which he will get when he sells Trant House. If he did this, the mortgage would be 'discharged' and would not affect Penelope, but if Vernon did not repay the money Penelope would take the property subject to the mortgage and would be at risk of losing it to the lender. In practice, it is very unlikely that Penelope's legal adviser would allow her to pay over the purchase money before he had ensured that the mortgage would be discharged—but unlikely things sometimes happen in exam questions!

2.3 Interests in land

In the previous section, we noted a number of rights which benefit someone other than the estate owner, and which can be enforced against him and possibly against anyone who acquires the estate from him. In the terminology adopted by the 1925 property legislation, such rights are known as *'interests in land'*, but they are often referred to more informally as *encumbrances* (because they burden or 'encumber' the land), and they can also be described as *'third-party rights'*. All three terms are used interchangeably in this book, and we want to emphasise that to us they are just three different ways of describing the same sort of rights.

Whatever terminology is used, the important thing to notice about these rights is that they are divided into two main categories:

- rights recognised by law: legal interests in land;
- rights recognised by equity: equitable interests in land.

In the rest of this chapter, we will tell you about the most important legal and equitable interests, and explain why the distinction between them is important.

2.4 Legal interests

2.4.1 Reducing the number of legal interests

A number of the rights described earlier in this chapter, such as easements, profits à prendre and mortgages, were developed by the common law courts and so were classified as *legal* rights. We saw in Chapter 1 that the 1925 property legislation reduced the number of legal estates in order to facilitate the sale of land, and a similar process was applied to legal third-party rights.

Section 1(2) of LPA 1925 provides:

> The only interests or charges in or over land which are capable of subsisting or of being conveyed or created at law are—
>
> (a) An easement, right, or privilege in or over land for an interest equivalent to an estate in fee simple absolute in possession or a term of years absolute;
>
> (b) A rentcharge in possession issuing out of or charged on land being either perpetual or for a term of years absolute;
>
> (c) A charge by way of legal mortgage;
>
> (d) [Land tax, tithe rentcharge] and any other similar charge on land which is not created by an instrument;
>
> (e) Rights of entry exercisable over or in respect of a legal term of years absolute, or annexed, for any purpose, to a legal rentcharge.

Thus today an interest in land takes effect as a *legal* interest only if it is of a type listed in s. 1(2) and has been granted for a period equivalent to one of the two legal estates. This means that such rights must be capable of lasting forever (i.e., for a period equivalent to a fee simple absolute in possession or, as s. 1(2)(b) puts it, 'perpetual') or for a fixed period (i.e., equivalent to a term of years absolute).

Any interest which does not satisfy the requirements of s. 1(2) takes effect as an *equitable* interest (s. 1(3)). Thus for example, a right of way given to a neighbour 'until the new road is constructed' cannot be a legal easement, because it is for an uncertain period and accordingly exists only in equity.

We have already told you a little about easements and profits à prendre (see 2.2.1.1 and 2.2.2) and will not say any more about them at this point, but we do need to look at the other legal interests listed in s. 1(2).

2.4.2 Rentcharges (s. 1(2)(b))

The first thing to note about the term 'rentcharge' is that it does not refer to rent which is payable under a lease, but to other arrangements whereby land is charged with the payment to someone of an annual or periodic sum. If the money is not paid, the person with the benefit of the rentcharge is entitled to enter upon the land in order to enforce payment.

At one time, and in certain parts of the country, it was rare for an estate in fee simple to be sold for a single payment of money; instead the vendor took a lump sum plus a rentcharge securing an annual payment. However the Rentcharges Act 1977 prevented the creation of any new rentcharges of this type, provided that any existing ones are to end 60 years after the Act came into force, and gave the estate owner of the charged land the right to redeem the rentcharge earlier on the payment of compensation.

The 1977 Act did not, however, abolish rentcharges altogether and they may still be created for certain purposes. Thus it is still possible to leave a property to a person, subject to a rentcharge obliging him to make a periodical payment to your widow or widower, or to some other member of your family, in order to provide for the maintenance of such person. This sort of rentcharge gives rise to a trust of the land and is considered at 17.10.2.

It is also still possible to create 'estate rentcharges', which are used to ensure that the estate owner of the charged land makes a payment towards the upkeep of facilities on other land. An example of this type is the rentcharge obliging the estate owner to pay an annual sum towards the maintenance of a road on his neighbour's property. These rentcharges are a means of providing for the enforcement of positive covenants in freehold land and they are considered further in Chapter 26.

For a rentcharge to be a legal interest in land it must last for the same period as one of the two legal estates; that is, either in perpetuity or for a fixed period.

2.4.3 Charge by way of legal mortgage (s. 1(2)(c))

As we explained earlier in this chapter, a mortgage is used to charge an estate in land with the repayment of a debt (or the performance of some other obligation). For example, the borrower, who grants the mortgage over his estate and is called the 'mortgagor', provides security for a loan by granting a mortgage to the lender, who is known as the 'mortgagee'. The grant of a mortgage gives the mortgagee an estate or interest in the property, and if the borrower fails to repay the loan, the mortgagee may take the mortgagor's property and sell it to satisfy the debt.

Granting a charge by way of legal mortgage is one of the three ways in which a legal mortgage may be created after 1925 (LPA 1925, ss. 85–87). The other two methods of mortgaging property are not mentioned in LPA 1925, s. 1(2), because they operate by giving the mortgagee a legal estate in the property (in fact, a very long lease), and are therefore legal by virtue of s. 1(1). The charge by way of legal mortgage does not create an estate in the land but takes effect as a legal interest under s. 1(2). The mortgagee acquires the same rights over the mortgaged property irrespective of which method of creation is used.

We will tell you much more about mortgages in Chapter 24.

2.4.4 ...and any other similar charge on land which is not created by an instrument (s. 1(2)(d))

The rather peculiar wording of this section is due to the repeal of the first four words, which originally referred to 'land tax' and 'tithe rentcharge'. The charges in this category are all created by statute and are rarely encountered.

2.4.5 Rights of entry (s. 1(2)(e))

This heading includes rights of entry included in leases or attached to rentcharges. It is usual to include in a lease a clause which allows the landlord to recover, or 're-enter', the property (i.e., to forfeit the lease), should the tenant be in breach of any of his obligations under the lease. This right is a legal right in itself under s. 1(2)(e) and is regarded as an interest in land. A similar right is usually included in a rentcharge, so that the owner of the rentcharge may enter and recover the land should the owner of the charged estate fail to pay the sums due.

2.5 Equitable interests

2.5.1 Introduction

Historically, equitable interests in land were developed by the Chancellor and his court in circumstances in which the common law courts were not able to provide a remedy. However, the range of equitable interests was enlarged considerably in 1926 by the addition of a number of rights which until then had been legal but ceased to be so as a result of the statutory reforms (LPA 1925 s. 1(2) and (3)). We have already explained this change in the previous section, noting, for example, that the grant of an easement or profit à prendre for an uncertain period no longer creates a legal interest and takes effect only in equity. Nothing more needs to be said about this newer type of equitable interest, and in what follows we will concentrate on the 'traditional' equitable interests, which continue to be of great importance today.

2.5.2 The interest of a beneficiary under a trust of the legal estate

Trusts are extremely important in land law and are considered further in Part IV. However, it is not possible to proceed very far with a study of this subject without having a basic idea of what a trust is, and so a brief explanation will be included here.

A trust arises when property is held by a person or persons 'upon trust' for another person or persons. Thus, Teresa may hold property upon trust for Bob. Teresa is called a 'trustee', whilst Bob is called a 'beneficiary'. It is the trustee's job to hold the property for the benefit of the beneficiary. It is the beneficiary who is entitled to the benefits of the property (called 'the *beneficial interest*'), whilst the trustee is a bare owner and must not use the estate for his own benefit. It may be easier to understand this idea if one compares the estate with a banana: the trustee is regarded as the owner of the banana-skin, whereas the beneficiary is the owner of the banana inside!

Historically, common law did not recognise such a separation of ownership and enjoyment and would not help the beneficiary if the trustee used the estate for his own benefit. Equity did, however, protect the beneficiary, who accordingly came to have an enforceable right to the property. Thus even today the rights of the beneficiary are enforceable only in equity and not at law.

Where there is a trust of the legal estate in land there are therefore effectively two owners:

- the trustee owns the legal estate; and
- the beneficiary owns an equitable interest (i.e., the beneficial interest).

When thinking about a trust, you may find the following diagram helpful:

LAW **Legal estate**	EQUITY **Beneficial interest**
Trustee	Beneficiary
(Teresa)	(Ben)

In addition to trusts which are created expressly by the owner of property, there are situations which the courts will interpret as giving rise to a trust, sometimes to give effect to the presumed intention of the owner, but on other occasions very much against his will. It is this sort of trust which we suggested might have arisen at Trant House, if Vanessa Venables had contributed to the cost of acquiring or converting the property. Trusts which are recognised by the courts in this way, without express creation, are said to be 'implied', 'resulting' or 'constructive' trusts. We deal with them in more detail in Chapter 20.

2.5.3 Interests under estate contracts and options

2.5.3.1 Estate contracts

Equitable interests also arise from the special way in which equity treats estate contracts (i.e., contracts to create or transfer legal estates or interests). If, for example, a contract is made between Vernon and Penelope for the sale and purchase of the freehold estate in Trant House, different remedies for breach of that contract are available at law and in equity.

The legal remedy is that of damages for breach of contract. Equity, however, goes further and may give an order for specific performance of the contract. Specific performance is an order which will make the parties to a contract perform their promises—in our example Vernon can be compelled to convey the estate and Penelope can be made to pay the purchase price. Specific performance is, of course, a remedy which lies in the discretion of the court, because it is equitable in origin and all equitable remedies are discretionary (see further at 2.6.1).

The application of an equitable maxim, that 'Equity regards as done that which ought to be done', produces the result that a contract which can be specifically enforced is regarded as creating an interest in equity. The operation of this rule can best be explained by reference to our example of the sale by Vernon to Penelope. 'That which ought to be done' is the conveyance of the estate to Penelope. From the time that the contract is made, therefore, equity acts as though that conveyance had already been completed. As a result, Penelope is treated as being the owner in equity from the date that the contract is made, whilst Vernon remains the legal owner until the deed conveying the legal estate is made. Until that time, Vernon is regarded by equity as holding the legal estate upon trust for Penelope (see further at 5.7).

2.5.3.2 Options

Under an agreement for an option, an estate owner gives the other party the right to acquire an estate in the property as some time in the future. For example, Vera, the fee simple owner of a bungalow, may agree that if Peter wishes to buy the property, he may do so at any time within the next 10 years. Peter thus acquires an option in respect of the bungalow. He is under no obligation to buy it, but has the right to do so if he wishes. By contrast, Vera is bound by the agreement and is under a contractual duty to sell to Peter if asked to do so. The agreement between them creates a sort of half-way situation, in which the prospective vendor is bound but the prospective purchaser remains free.

If Vera later refuses to sell the bungalow to Peter, equity will compel her to do so by means of the remedy of specific performance. This is another situation in which equity 'regards as done that which ought to be done', and as a result Peter is regarded as having an equitable interest in the property from the time when he acquired the option.

This special way in which equity treats contracts to create or convey estates or interests in land leads us on to the third type of equitable interest.

2.5.4 Interests which are not created formally

2.5.4.1 Formal requirements

Usually, in order to create or transfer a legal estate or interest in land it is necessary to use a deed (for cases in which a deed is *not* required, see 10.3.1.1). LPA 1925, s. 52(1) provides:

> All conveyances of land or any interest therein are void for the purpose of conveying or creating a legal estate unless made by deed.

Additional requirements for the creation or transfer of certain legal estates or interests are imposed by LRA 2002, but we will postpone consideration of these until Chapter 7, and will concentrate here on the nature of a deed.

A deed is a document which has been executed in accordance with certain formalities in order to ensure that its validity can be proved. The nature of the formalities required depends on the date at which the deed was executed.

(a) *Deeds executed before 31 July 1990* Deeds made before this date are subject to the traditional rules which required a deed to be signed, SEALED, and delivered. At one time it was a person's seal that was essential in order to prove the authenticity of a document, but for many years the habit of using sealing wax and a real seal had been abandoned and the seal was represented by a red sticker on the document, or even by a printed circle containing the letters 'LS' (from the Latin phrase '*locus sigilli*'—'the place of the seal'). It should be noted that in relation to these older documents no witness was necessary though most deeds were in fact witnessed.

(b) *Deeds made on or after 31 July 1990* Since 31 July 1990, the Law of Property (Miscellaneous Provisions) Act 1989, s. 1, has required that to be a deed a document must:

- make it clear on the face of the document that it is intended to be a deed; and
- be signed by the person executing the deed in the presence of a witness who attests the signature (this means that the witness sees the deed being signed and then signs the deed himself as a witness), and
- be delivered by the person executing or by someone else on his behalf.

So basically the document must be signed, witnessed and delivered.

Delivery
In the case of both the old and the new rules it is technically necessary for the deed to be delivered formally. Correctly this used to be done by the person concerned placing his hand on the seal on the document and saying, 'I deliver this as my act and deed'. Today formal delivery is usually dispensed with, a practice which was approved in *Stromdale & Ball Ltd v Burden* [1952] Ch 223.

How do you know if a document is a deed?
The changes introduced by the Law of Property (Miscellaneous Provisions) Act 1989 have simplified the creation of deeds for the parties involved, but seem to have made the concept of a deed more difficult for law students to understand! The difference between a deed and a document which is merely 'in writing' is less obvious now, but the distinction between the two is essential because, as we have said, most legal estates and interests cannot be created or transferred unless a deed is used. Since 31 July 1990 the distinguishing characteristics of a deed are that the signature of the party executing it is witnessed and the document is stated to be a deed (for example, by some phrase such as 'This Deed of Conveyance is made the first day of September 1999', or by the party executing it saying that he is signing it 'as a deed'—see pp. 82 and 128–30). A written document which does not satisfy these requirements is not a deed, and in general will not create or transfer a legal estate or interest.

2.5.4.2 Help from equity when formal requirements not observed

At law an attempt to create an estate or interest without a deed will be totally ineffective. It may be, however, that the attempted grant can be treated as a contract to create the estate or interest. Contracts relating to land are now subject to strict formalities (see Chapter 5), but in the earlier law less formality was required and frequently the courts were able to deduce the existence of a contract from the circumstances surrounding the ineffective grant.

Where such a contract could be identified, specific performance of that contract might be available in equity to compel the creation of a legal estate or interest in the proper form, by requiring one party to make a grant by deed. Moreover, as we explained above, the maxim that equity regards as done that which ought to be done might enable equity to treat the person entitled to the grant as already having the interest in equity.

We may illustrate this principle with the following example:

- If Len purports to grant a lease of a flat to Tom for 10 years without using a deed, Tom does not obtain a legal lease.
- If Tom could satisfy the court that a valid contract for a lease exists, he could seek an order for specific performance to compel Len to grant the lease by deed.
- If specific performance could be granted, equity would 'regard as done that which ought to be done', i.e., it would act as though Len had complied with an order for specific performance and had granted the lease in the correct form.
- As a result, equity would regard Tom as having an equitable lease in the property for 10 years.

An example of such an equitable lease may be found in *Walsh v Lonsdale* (1882) 21 ChD 9 (considered further at 10.3.4).

A similar process operates to give rise to other rights, such as equitable easements and equitable mortgages, where the correct formalities for granting these interests have not been observed, but the court is able to identify a contract to grant such an interest.

2.5.5 Interests arising under restrictive covenants

A further example of equity's willingness to provide a remedy when the law would not do so relates to restrictive covenants. These are promises made in a deed by which the promisor, or 'covenantor', undertakes not to do certain things on his land. If, for example, Pip is buying a house he might covenant with the vendor not to carry on a business on the premises. Law will enforce this promise against Pip, the original covenantor, as a matter of contract. If Pip later sells the property to Quentin, law will not enforce the covenant against Quentin, because he was not a party to the original contract. This is the ordinary contractual rule which requires 'privity of contract'.

However, in certain circumstances, which are explained in Chapter 26, equity will enforce the covenant against Quentin. The person who is seeking to enforce the covenant will therefore have a right which is enforceable in equity against the owner for the time being of the property, and so has an equitable interest in that land. Thus if the owner of the cottage next to Trant House does indeed have such an interest (2.2.1.2), it is likely that he or she could prevent Penelope from using the property as bed-and-breakfast accommodation.

2.5.6 Other rights to equitable relief

Having told you about some equitable interests, we must mention briefly some more rights which have on occasion been described by the courts as 'mere' equities. A party is sometimes said to have an 'equity' when he has a right to some form of equitable remedy, such as a right to have a transaction set aside for fraud or undue influence, or to have a document rectified for mistake. In some cases, most notably those involving estoppel (see below), the courts regard themselves as having a wide discretion to choose the form of relief most appropriate to the circumstances. In the past, these rights to relief appeared to operate only between the parties personally concerned, but increasingly now they are regarded as enforceable against successors in title (that is, against the current owner of land formerly owned by the person subject to the equity).

2.5.7 Equitable estoppel

Before leaving this introductory account of equitable developments, we must refer briefly to equitable estoppel, which in recent years has come to play an important part in many areas of land law. In general, rules of estoppel operate to prevent a party denying matters which he has previously asserted or represented. The doctrine is used by both law and equity, and we shall see some examples of legal estoppel when we come to consider leases (tenancy by estoppel—10.10.4; and surrender by operation of law—10.5.2.3(2)). At law, the representation must relate to existing fact, but equity, in its traditional role of restraining unconscionable behaviour, applies the concept more widely.

In a particular form of equitable estoppel, called 'proprietary estoppel', equity may prevent an estate owner denying representations made by him which have led the representee to believe that he has, or will have, some rights in the representor's land and to act to his detriment in reliance on that belief. In some cases the equity (right to relief) which arises from such an estoppel is enforceable not only against the representor, but also against anyone who acquires the land from him. Thus it is just possible that if Vernon's mother wants to remain in her flat after Trant House is sold (see 2.2.4), she might claim that her son represented to her that she could live there for the rest of her life. This, coupled with her expenditure on the property (arguably a 'detriment') might give her a right to some relief in equity which could bind Penelope or any other purchaser of Trant House.

We will deal with equitable estoppel in more detail in Chapters 21 and 23. However, you will come across other references to estoppel in the course of reading this book, and in particular should note a possible new application of the principle as a replacement for the old doctrine of part performance of a contract (see 5.4 and 5.5).

2.6 Legal interests and equitable interests compared

2.6.1 Discretionary nature of equity

The fact that a right is recognised only in equity and not at law is of practical significance, since all equitable rights are enforceable only at the discretion of the court. Thus although, since the Supreme Court of Judicature Acts 1873 and 1875, the rules of law and equity have both been administered by the same courts, it is still important to know whether one is dealing with a legal interest or an equitable interest.

There is no absolute right to the protection by the courts of an equitable interest—remedies are at the discretion of the court. In this context the old equitable maxim, that 'He who comes to equity must come with clean hands', is of great importance. A person may be able to show that he has an equitable interest in land, but this would be of little use to him if he has 'dirty hands' and accordingly would be refused any remedy by the courts. For example, if he claims to have an equitable easement entitling him to walk across another estate owner's land, he may find that he is refused a remedy to enforce his right of way if he has behaved improperly himself (perhaps by exceeding the limits of his right or by causing damage).

Legal rights, however, are enforceable as of right, and once the existence of the right is established it is not really open to the court to consider the merits of the situation before giving a remedy. Thus, if a person with a legal easement causes damage, the land owner may be able to claim compensation but the easement will still be enforced by the courts.

2.6.2 Enforcement against third parties

A major difference between legal and equitable rights used to be found in the rules governing the enforceability of those rights against a third party, for example, against the purchaser of the estate which is subject to the rights. Thus while a legal easement over a piece of land could be enforced against a purchaser of any estate in that land, an equitable easement over the same piece of land might not be enforceable against certain purchasers.

This was a rule which had its origins in the separate evolution of law and equity. Legal rights were said to be rights *in rem*; that is, rights in the land itself ('in the thing', from the Latin word *res*, meaning 'thing') and hence generally could be enforced against any person who acquired an estate or interest in the land. This was expressed by saying that legal rights were 'good against the world'.

By contrast, equitable rights were only rights *in personam*; that is, rights which were enforceable against certain categories of person, because it was considered to be fair or equitable that they should take subject to them. The rule which applied to equitable interests was that they bound everyone who took the legal estate except a bona fide purchaser for value of that legal estate without notice of the equitable interest. This rule is commonly referred to as the 'notice rule'.

In studying the notice rule, you may find it helpful to note Maitland's brief but memorable explanation (see Maitland, *Equity* (1936) at pp. 112–15). The Court of Chancery is pictured as working through the list of people who might acquire the legal estate from a trustee: which of them, in fairness, should be bound by the beneficiary's rights? Over the years, the court decides that it would be fair to enforce such rights against:

- those who inherit from the trustee;
- those who take the property from him as a gift ('donees' or 'volunteers'); and
- those who buy the property from him, either knowing about the beneficiary's rights or deliberately closing their eyes to them.

At the end of this development, there is just one person against whom it would not be fair to enforce the beneficiary's rights: someone who buys the legal estate in ignorance of the fact that it is trust property, despite having made all the appropriate enquiries, i.e., to use the technical phrase, the bona fide purchaser of the legal estate for value without notice. You should note, of course, that although Maitland explains the doctrine of notice by reference to the trust, the courts applied it to all equitable interests.

As a result of major changes introduced by the 1925 legislation, the doctrine of notice is of less importance today, but it can still be of some significance (see 6.5.2 and 7.11.3) and so we need to tell you a little more about it here.

2.6.3 The equitable doctrine of notice

2.6.3.1 The purchaser must be bona fide

This means that the purchaser must act in good faith. This part of the rule seems to be duplicated by the requirement that the purchaser should not have notice of the right, and it is difficult to see what is added by this phrase. However, Lord Wilberforce in *Midland Bank Trust Co. Ltd v Green* [1981] AC 513 at p. 528 considered that:

> it would be a mistake to suppose that the requirement of good faith extended only to the matter of notice...good faith is a...separate test which may have to be passed even though absence of notice is proved.

We cannot point to any cases in which a purchaser without notice has failed the good faith test, but you may like to note the comment in Smith at p. 218 that 'the role of bona fides remains obscure, as it seems that deception practised on the vendor is irrelevant' (see *Corbett v Halifax Building Society* [2003] 1 WLR 964—considered further at 24.10.3).

2.6.3.2 The purchaser must give value

It is necessary for the person who acquires the estate to give value if he is to rely on the notice rule. Thus a donee (or 'volunteer') takes a gift of land subject to any equitable interests that there may be. 'Value' includes money, money's worth and some other forms of consideration, such as marriage.

A person who acquires an estate for value is described as a 'purchaser for value'. This may seem unnecessarily long-winded, since in ordinary speech 'purchaser' means 'buyer' and so includes the notion of taking for value. However, for the lawyer, 'purchaser' has the technical meaning of 'one who takes by act of the parties rather than by operation of law'. This means that he has had the property transferred to him in the appropriate way by the previous owner, rather than having it vested in him automatically by operation of some rule of law, such as that which vests a bankrupt's property in his trustee in bankruptcy or the deceased's property in his personal representatives. In this sense then, even a donee is a purchaser and so in a context like this it is necessary to state specifically that the person acquiring the estate is a purchaser for value.

2.6.3.3 The purchaser must acquire a legal estate

The purchaser must buy a legal estate, rather than an equitable interest in the land. Thus, if the purchaser is to be safe, he must have acquired the legal estate before he discovers the equitable interest.

2.6.3.4 The purchaser must not have notice of the equitable interest

There are three types of notice: actual notice; constructive notice; and imputed notice.

- *Actual notice.* This is quite straightforward and applies where the purchaser has actual knowledge of the existence of the equitable interest. It is not necessary for the purchaser to obtain this information from any particular source and he may even discover the truth from a complete outsider (*Lloyd v Banks* (1868) LR 3 Ch App 488).
- *Constructive notice.* When the notice rule was first created by the courts of equity, clever purchasers soon realised that they could obtain an advantage if they declined to make any investigations which might lead to the discovery of equitable interests. Equity was quick to extend the rule to prevent purchasers deliberately 'turning a blind eye' in this way, as such behaviour was evidence of a lack of good faith on the part of the purchaser. The means used was to say that the purchasers would be deemed to know of interests which they would have discovered if they had asked the usual questions about the property and so were bound by such interests. This rule is preserved in modern law by LPA 1925, s. 199(1)(ii).
- *Imputed notice.* A purchaser is also deemed to have notice of an equitable interest if his agent has either actual or constructive notice of it. This rule is essential, since most purchasers do not conduct their own conveyancing. Thus if a conveyancer obtains actual notice of an equitable interest, the purchaser, as his client, is also regarded as having notice of it (*Jared v Clements* [1903] 1 Ch 428).

2.7 A multiplicity of rights

It will be obvious from what we have said so far that one piece of land may be subject to a large number of interests all at the same time. Indeed the doctrine of estates may be responsible for encouraging the development of such multiple interests, because it encourages one to think in terms of owning rights in land rather than of owning the land itself. As we shall see, in England and Wales land law is not really concerned with absolute rights but rather with balancing the relative claims to land which may be made by a number of people. Thus one piece of land could be subject to all the following rights at the same time:

- a fee simple owned by Amy;
- a 99-year lease granted by Amy to Bob;

- a weekly tenancy granted by Bob to Carol;
- a legal mortgage of the freehold granted by Amy to a building society;
- an equitable mortgage of the 99-year lease granted by Bob to his bank;
- a right of way over the property granted in perpetuity to David, the owner of the house next door (a legal easement);
- an estate rentcharge granted by Amy to Eric, a neighbouring owner, to ensure that Amy contributes to the cost of maintaining a shared drive;
- a restrictive covenant enforceable by another neighbour, Fred, which prevents the land from being used for business purposes.

2.8 Classification of property

Although we are leaving questions about the statutory definition of land, and other technical matters, until the last chapter, we must make a brief mention here of the lawyers' classification of property and a few of the technical terms connected with it.

2.8.1 Real and personal property

Property is divided into two main categories: 'real' property and 'personal' property (or 'realty' and 'personalty'). Real property consists of all the estates and interests in land which we will be considering in this book, with the exception of leases which, for historical reasons, are regarded as a form of personal property. The reason for this is explained in Chapter 28, but we must mention here that 'real property' got its name from the fact that in early law it was protected by a 'real action' (i.e., an action to recover the '*res*' or 'thing').

2.8.2 Personal property

Personal property is divided into three categories: choses in possession, choses in action and chattels real.

2.8.2.1 Choses in possession

Tangible objects other than land which can be physically possessed (such as cars, books and clothes) are called 'choses in possession'. 'Chose' is another word which, like 'res', means 'thing' but this time lawyers use French rather than Latin.

2.8.2.2 Choses in action

Intangible rights, other than those relating to land, of which one cannot take physical possession and which depend for their existence on enforcement by the courts are called 'choses in action'. In this category are placed debts, copyrights and patents, amongst other rights.

2.8.2.3 Chattels real

Leases, which are estates in land, but were classified as personal property, are known technically as 'chattels real', because although they are chattels (another name for personal property) they became very like real property, as we explain in Chapter 28.

FURTHER READING

Generally

Cheshire and Burn, *Cheshire and Burn's Modern Law of Real Property*, 18th edn., pp. 83–91 (doctrine of notice).

Cooke, *Land Law,* Oxford University Press, 2006, Chapter 2 (Property Rights in Land) pp. 22–32.

Hanbury and Martin, *Modern Equity,* 19th edn., Sweet & Maxwell, 2012, paras. 1-039–1-046 (doctrine of notice).

On origins and nature of equity

Hanbury and Martin, *Modern Equity*, 19th edn., Sweet & Maxwell, 2012, Chapter 1 (History and Principles—in particular paras. 1–001–1–008 and 1–024–1–038).

Lawson and Rudden, *The Law of Property*, 3rd edn., Oxford University Press, 2002, pp. 82–8 (equitable rights and remedies).

Maitland, *Equity*, Cambridge University Press, 1936, Lectures 1 and 11 (The Origins of Equity).

Pearce and Stevens, *The Law of Trusts and Equitable Obligations*, 5th edn., Oxford University Press, 2010, Chapter 2.

Smith, *Property Law*, 7th edn., Pearson Longman, 2011, Chapter 4.

3

Land law and human rights

3.1 Introduction

In this chapter we want to tell you briefly about aspects of the European Convention for the Protection of Human Rights and Freedoms ('the Convention') and the Human Rights Act 1998 ('HRA 1998'), both of which are relevant to your study of land law. The long title of HRA 1998 describes the purpose of the Act as being 'to give further effect to rights and freedoms guaranteed under the European Convention on Human Rights' and the Act has the effect of incorporating the Convention into our domestic law.

3.2 The Convention rights

HRA 1998, s. 1 describes the rights it protects as 'Convention rights' and these are defined in s. 1 by reference to the Articles of the Convention and of the First and Sixth Protocols to it (you will find the text of the Convention in Sch. 1 of the Act). Of the 16 Articles included in this definition, the four which are most likely to be of significance in a land law context are:

Art. 6—right to a fair trial;

Art. 8—right to respect for private and family life;

Art. 14—prohibition of discrimination; and

Art. 1 of the First Protocol—protection of property.

We cannot look at the Convention provisions in any detail here, but we do need to explain that although the first part of each article appears to give an absolute right, in each case (except that of the prohibition of discrimination) the opening statement is qualified by further provisions which set out the circumstances in which the right may be limited or excluded by individual states.

3.2.1 Right to a fair trial

The opening words of Art. 6 provide that:

> In the determination of his civil rights and obligations or of any criminal charge against him, everyone is entitled to a fair and public hearing within a reasonable time by an independent and impartial tribunal, established by law....

Thus the requirement of a fair trial applies to civil matters just as much as to the criminal ones with which we more usually associate it. From a land law perspective this provision raises concerns about some 'self-help' remedies, which in certain circumstances allow a landlord or a mortgagee to take physical possession of property without the need for any court authorisation, and similarly allow a landlord to seize property belonging to a tenant in arrears with the rent (see further 13.3.1, 13.4.4.1, 24.7.2 and 24.8.1.3).

3.2.2 Right to respect for private and family life

Art. 8 (1) provides that:

> Everyone has the right to respect for his private and family life, his home and his correspondence.

It is important to note that this Article protects the privacy of an individual and his family and home life from invasion or interference by the state: it does not create a right to a home or impose a duty on governments to deal with homelessness (see *Chapman v UK* (2001) 33 EHRR 399 at para. 99).

The concept of 'home' has been given a wide interpretation by the European Court of Human Rights ('ECHR'), so that the right to respect of a person's home extends also to other property occupied by him, such as his office or business premises (see *Niemietz v Germany* (1992) 16 EHRR 97 at paras. 29–31). At one time the effect of Art. 8 seemed likely to be limited in the United Kingdom by the suggestion that it applied only to cases in which the claimant had a legal right to occupy the property, which would of course have prevented any trespasser relying on the Article in eviction proceedings. This view was rejected in the ECHR in *Buckley v United Kingdom* (1996) 23 EHRR 101, in which the Court stated that:

> The concept of 'home' within the meaning of article 8 is not limited to those which are lawfully occupied...'Home' is an autonomous concept which does not depend on classification under domestic law. Whether or not a particular habitation constitutes a 'home' which attracts the protection of article 8(1) will depend on the factual circumstances, namely, the existence of sufficient and continuous links.

As a result of this interpretation, it is accepted that the process of evicting an occupier from his home can amount to a prima facie infringement of his rights under Art. 8 (which may however be justified under Art. 8(2)), and a number of human rights cases both in this jurisdiction and before the ECHR have arisen from possession proceedings by a landowner against a trespasser or a landlord against a tenant. In addition, there are concerns that the self-help remedies we noted above, which involve entering premises without a court order, could be said to violate rights under Art. 8, as well as under Art. 6.

3.2.3 Prohibition of discrimination

Art. 14 provides that:

> The enjoyment of the rights and freedoms set forth in this Convention shall be secured without discrimination on any ground such as sex, race, colour... [etc].

The Article continues by setting out a long list of grounds on which discrimination is not permitted, and it is clear from the phrase 'such as' that this is merely illustrative and not intended to be an exhaustive list. A further point to note is that the provision is concerned with discrimination in recognising and protecting Convention rights: it does not create a general right to be free from discrimination.

3.2.4 Protection of property

Art. 1 of the First Protocol provides that:

> Every natural or legal person is entitled to the peaceful enjoyment of his possessions. No one shall be deprived of his possessions except in the public interest and subject to the conditions provided for by law and by the general principles of international law.
>
> The preceding provisions shall not, however, in any way impair the right of a state to enforce such laws as it deems necessary to control the use of property in accordance with the general interest or to secure the payment of taxes or other contributions or penalties.

In considering this Article, which we will return to in Chapter 8 (see 8.7), you may find it helpful to note the following passage in Megarry and Wade at para. 1-024:

> The Court of Human Rights has frequently stated that the Article comprises three distinct but related rules:
>
> (i) a general principle of peaceful enjoyment of property: in substance it guarantees the right of property;
>
> (ii) a rule that is concerned with the deprivation of possessions and which subjects it to certain conditions; and
>
> (iii) a rule that recognises that the contracting states are entitled to control the use of property in accordance with the general interest, by enforcing such laws as they deem necessary for the purpose.

3.3 HRA 1998

The Convention is designed to protect rights and freedoms of individual citizens against the power of the state in those countries which are signatories to it, and it is the government of each country (rather than any private individual) which is answerable in the ECHR for violation of such rights.

In the United Kingdom, this protection against state power is incorporated into domestic law by two major provisions of the 1998 Act: one relating to public authorities and the other to the interpretation of legislation.

3.3.1 Public authorities

Section 6(1) of the Act provides:

> It is unlawful for a public authority to act in a way which is incompatible with a Convention right.

The Act does not provide a complete definition of 'a public authority', merely stating in s. 6(3) that the term includes:

- a court or tribunal; and
- any person certain whose functions are of a public nature.

If you are studying the law of human rights you will need to look in detail at the debate about the different types of public authority and the possible need for a more satisfactory definition. However, for our purposes we only need to note the inclusion of courts and tribunals by s. 6(3) and to tell you that local authorities are, as you would expect, recognised as a type of public authority.

3.3.2 Interpretation of legislation

Section 3 (1) provides that:

> So far as it is possible to do so, primary and subordinate legislation must be read and given effect in a way which is compatible with the Convention rights.

Where a court is satisfied that a provision is incompatible with a Convention right and is unable to adopt any compatible interpretation 'it may make a declaration of that incompatibility' (s. 4(2)). Such a declaration does not affect the operation of the provision between the parties to the proceedings, nor does it invalidate the provision for the future. Its effect is to identify a problem with the legislation, and it is then for government to decide whether any amendment should be made.

3.3.3 Does HRA 1998 have 'horizontal' effect?

A major uncertainty about HRA 1998 is whether it has 'horizontal' effect: that is, whether the Convention rights are enforceable between private individuals. On the face of it the Act, like the Convention, protects the individual's rights against the state (the 'vertical' effect) and does this through the provisions about public authorities and the interpretation of legislation which we have noted above. However, as we have seen, courts and tribunals are themselves public authorities and so are subject to the provision in s. 6(3) which makes it unlawful for them to act in a way incompatible with a Convention right. Some writers suggest that this imposes a duty on the courts to enforce Convention rights in all proceedings, including those between private individuals. Although the Act has now been in force for over 10 years, there has been very little discussion of the question by the courts, at least in cases arising from land law issues. In *J. A. Pye (Oxford) Ltd v Graham* [2001] Ch 804 (at para. 42) Mummery LJ referred to:

> the very difficult and important questions, which have been extensively debated elsewhere, concerning the effect of s. 6(1) of the 1998 Act on private law issues arising between one citizen and another

He considered, however, that it was 'neither necessary nor appropriate' to express a view on them in the present case. By contrast, Lord Bingham was at pains to emphasise in *Harrow LBC v Qazi* [2004] 1 AC 983 (at para. 23), a case involving a local authority landlord, that:

> Nothing I have said in this opinion should be understood as applying to any landlord or owner which is not a public authority.

More recently, the Supreme Court has adopted the same approach in *Manchester City Council v Pinnock* [2011] 2 AC 104, stressing that its conclusions in that case related to:

> possession proceedings brought by local authorities...nothing which we say is intended to bear on cases where the person seeking the order for possession is a private landowner.

Thus all we can tell you on this question is that the courts are clearly aware of the debate but so far do not appear to regard themselves as bound to give effect to Convention rights between private individuals except, as we shall see, in cases involving statutory interpretation.

3.4 Significance of HRA 1998 in land law cases

The fact that HRA 1998 is not as yet regarded as having a horizontal effect may make you wonder how significant the Act can be in the land law context, where so many of the cases before the courts are between private individuals. However, it must be remembered that a good deal of land is owned by public authorities (local authorities for example having a major role as landlords of social housing), and issues about Convention rights have been raised in a number of cases involving such landowners. In general, these cases have been concerned with details of statutory codes and procedures, often for the protection of tenants, which are beyond the scope of this book. However there are some more general land law concepts which could raise human rights issues where a public authority owner is involved and we will note these in the appropriate chapters.

Furthermore, as you are probably beginning to realise, a good deal of land law is now in statutory form. The s. 3(1) requirement that, as far as possible, legislation should be interpreted in a way compatible with Convention rights applies to all cases before the courts, regardless of whether the parties are private individuals or public authorities. A recent example of this is to be found in *J. A. Pye (Oxford) Ltd v Graham*, a case between private individuals which involved consideration of the human rights implications of the statutory rules about adverse possession (i.e., the process by which a landowner can lose his title to land as a result of dispossession by a 'squatter'). In fact, the owner's loss of his beneficial interest in the property had occurred before HRA 1998 had come into force, with the result that the court was not required to apply the Act, but nevertheless the case is a good illustration of a situation in which s. 3(1) could have a major impact on the outcome between private individuals. We will tell you about the various stages of this case, and the subsequent application to ECHR by the dispossessed owner, in Chapter 8 (see 8.2.1.3 and 8.7).

3.5 Domestic anti-discrimination law

When thinking of human rights considerations, you should also bear in mind that a number of the forms of discrimination listed in Art. 14 of the Convention are the subject of anti-discrimination legislation in the United Kingdom. The relevance of this to the study of land law is that the legislation includes provisions which make it unlawful to discriminate on specified grounds in any dealings with premises. These provisions used to be found in separate statutes specific to each form of discrimination, but are now all contained in Part 4 of the Equality Act 2010.

FURTHER READING

Howell, 'The Human Rights Act 1998: the "Horizontal Effect" on Land Law', *Modern Studies in Property Law, Vol.1: Property 2000*, Hart Publishing, 2001, p. 149.

Megarry and Wade, *The Law of Real Property*, 8th edn., Sweet & Maxwell, 2012, paras. 1-021—1-031 (Human Rights and Property Law).

Smith, *Property Law*, 7th edn., Pearson Longman, 2011, Chapter 3 (Human Rights).

PART II

Acquisition of estates in land

Introduction

In this part we intend to concentrate on the acquisition of a fee simple estate in land. Most of what we say will also be relevant to acquiring an existing long lease from the current leaseholder, but details of how such leases are originally created will be dealt with in detail in Chapter 10, in which the term of years absolute is further discussed. Although estates and interests in land may be acquired by way of gift, either in the lifetime of the donor or on his death, we are primarily concerned here with acquisitions for value, and will, in the main, be describing the process by which a purchaser buys an estate in land from a vendor.

Although land law and conveyancing are normally taught separately, they are in fact inextricably linked: the law relating to conveyancing is unintelligible without an understanding of the underlying structure of land law, and land law seems pointless unless one has an appreciation of how the theory of the law is applied in practice. In this book we are concentrating on the rules of land law rather than those of conveyancing but we will set the land law rules in their conveyancing context as this will make it easier to appreciate their purpose. To this end we will consider in Chapters 4–7 the steps necessary to purchase two properties, Nos. I and 3 Trant Way.

We will also discuss another manner of acquiring an estate, which may occur in circumstances in which the owner of the estate has no intention of transferring the estate to another person. This may happen when the other person takes possession of the land and remains upon it for a prescribed period of time; the title so acquired is commonly known as 'squatter's rights' but is more technically called 'title by adverse possession' and is further explained in Chapter 8.

4

Buying a house

4.1 The properties and the parties

Two freehold properties are currently for sale in Trant Way, Mousehole, Stilton.

4.1.1 1 Trant Way

This property is a large Victorian house with a garden. The current owner of the fee simple is Victor Venn. Mr Venn bought the property in 1992 but is now obliged to move to another part of the country. Mr and Mrs Armstrong (Arnold and Arriety) are interested in buying the property for £350,000.

4.1.2 3 Trant Way

Number 3 is another large house but it has been divided up so that the top floor provides a separate 'granny flat', with its own internal front door but sharing the street door with the rest of the house and using the internal stairs for access. The current fee simple owner is Victoria Ventnor who bought the property in 1988. Barbara Bell is interested in buying the house for £360,000. Barbara has an elderly father, Bob Bell, and she hopes that he will agree to come and live in the top-floor flat so that she can 'keep an eye on him'.

4.2 Two systems of title

4.2.1 What the buyer wants to know

As we saw in Chapters 1 and 2, a prospective purchaser of any property (or normally his legal adviser) has two main concerns.

First, he must be sure that the vendor of the property is really entitled to sell it. Thus the buyer must insist that the vendor proves that his title to the land is good and that he can pass to the purchaser the estate which he is offering to sell.

Secondly, the purchaser will want to know whether any third parties have rights to the land which might interfere with his intended use of it. These third-party rights might include covenants restricting use, rights of way, tree preservation orders or even mortgages obliging the owner of the estate to make payments to a creditor.

Concern about these matters will lead the purchaser, or his representatives, to make extensive enquiries before the purchase of the estate is finally concluded.

4.2.2 Registered and unregistered systems

Unfortunately for the student of English land law, there are two totally separate systems of proving title to land and investigating third-party rights in it. The newer (and now more common) system is the registered land system; the older system is usually called the unregistered system of conveyancing. The enquiries to be made by a purchaser differ depending on whether the title to the property he wishes to buy is registered or unregistered. For the student this means learning two totally different sets of laws: one governed by statute, the Land Registration Act 2002, which repealed and replaced the earlier Land Registration Act 1925 (see Chapter 7); the other governed by the old rules of common law and equity as amended by statute, chiefly now the Law of Property Act 1925 and the Land Charges Act 1972 (see Chapter 6).

4.2.3 Which system applies?

The first thing which you must ascertain when dealing with any piece of land is which system of conveyancing is to be applied to it. In other words you must find out whether the estate in the land is (or should be) registered or not. It may surprise you to find that the old unregistered system of title is still in operation more than 80 years after the introduction of compulsory registration. This is a result of the policy of phased introduction, which we explain below, but undoubtedly the whole process has taken far longer than was expected in 1925, and recent statutory changes are designed to extend registration of title more quickly.

4.2.3.1 Areas of compulsory registration

Although there had been some limited registration of title before 1926, it was LRA 1925 which provided that in future registration of title to land was to become compulsory in areas designated as areas of compulsory registration by central government. As it was not possible to introduce the registration system to the whole country immediately (largely due to cost), the practice was adopted of making only certain places areas of compulsory registration and gradually increasing those areas as time went on. Originally it was thought that the whole country would soon be covered, but economic depression, followed by a war and further recession, held up the extension of the system. *However, the last areas, including our imaginary town of Mousehole, became compulsory registration areas on 1 December 1990.* Accordingly, now all land in England and Wales stands in an area of compulsory registration and any person dealing with a property simply needs to ask the Land Registry whether the title has in fact been registered.

4.2.3.2 Has the title to the estate been registered?

One has to ask this question because estates did not have to be registered as soon as the area in which the land stands became an area of compulsory registration. To require this would have involved estate owners in unexpected costs, for Land Registry fees are payable on all registrations. Instead, estates had to be registered at the time of the first dealing for value with the estate (usually the sale of the freehold or a grant of a long lease) after the area became a compulsory area. Thus in Mousehole all estates which have been dealt with since 1990 should have been registered at the Land Registry. Accordingly the title to 1 Trant Way will be registered (dealing in 1992), whilst the title to 3 Trant Way will not be registered (last dealing in 1988).

Triggering registration
From 1997 onwards, the occasions which give rise to compulsory registration have been considerably extended, so that the duty to apply for first registration now arises not only on dealings for value, but on dispositions by way of gift and on those made by personal representatives (who pass property to those entitled to it on the death of the previous owner), and by trustees (on transfers to beneficiaries or on the appointment of new trustees). In addition, a legal estate becomes registrable if the owner creates over it a first legal mortgage protected by the deposit of the title deeds (as to which, see 6.4.2.2(1)), even though the owner is not transferring the estate itself.

We will consider the requirements for first registration more fully in Chapter 7, but you should note now that the extension of events inducing registration must lead to a very real increase in the number of titles coming on to the register.

Voluntary registration
While most registered land has been entered on the register in compliance with the requirements for compulsory registration, there are also cases in which registration is appropriate on a voluntary basis. For example, a developer planning to build a large housing estate on land which is currently unregistered may choose to register the title to the whole estate voluntarily. He can then agree an estate plan for all the new properties with the Land Registry before he starts to sell the individual plots. This makes conveyancing of each plot of land easier once purchasers are found and is convenient for the developer, the purchasers and the Registry. Voluntary registration is also sometimes used to solve a problem which has arisen in relation to the property, for example, if the title deeds have been destroyed in a fire or due to an accident. In these cases voluntary registration can avoid many difficulties when the estate owner comes to sell, because the registry entry will replace the missing deeds.

As we shall see in Chapter 7, it is now considered desirable to extend registration of title as rapidly and thoroughly as possible. The Land Registry encourages landowners to seek voluntary registration by offering reduced fees for the process and by drawing attention to the advantages of registered title which, under LRA 2002, include improved protection against squatters (see Chapter 8).

How to find out if title has been registered
At present, the result of the gradual introduction of registration is that the title to some pieces of land will be registered, whilst the title to others will not. If you are not sure whether a registration has been made you can find out by making an 'index map search', which will tell you whether the estate has been registered (but which will not reveal any other information, such as the name of the estate owner). Further details may be obtained by making a full search of the register, which, since 3 December 1990, can be done without the consent of the estate owner.

4.2.3.3 **Unregistered land**

Any land which is not shown as being registered on the Land Registry index map is necessarily unregistered land, even though it is in an area of compulsory registration. As such it is covered by the older system of conveyancing rules which are substantially different, particularly as regards the protection of third party rights. According to a Law Commission Consultative Document published in 1998 (*Land Registration for the Twenty-First Century*, 1998, Law Com No. 254, para. 1.6) more than 80 per cent of the estimated number of titles to land in England and Wales was registered at that date and the increase in registrations in recent years means that unregistered land is rapidly becoming even less common. In an announcement made in October 2011, the Land Registry noted that 'more than three quarters of England and Wales is registered'. Nevertheless, it remains necessary to have an understanding of how the older system works, because it is still far from being redundant.

4.3 Outline of the conveyancing process

4.3.1 A two-stage process

Conveyancing is usually conducted in two stages. Following an informal agreement between vendor and purchaser (which has no legal effect) the parties will enter into a contract, in which the purchaser agrees to buy, and the vendor agrees to sell, the property. After a period of time, the contract will be performed or completed by the transfer or conveyance of the legal estate by the vendor to the purchaser.

The interval between contract and completion used to be quite long, and was the stage at which the main investigation of the vendor's title took place. Nowadays, however, a full investigation of title usually precedes the exchange of contracts, and as a result the period between contract and completion is often shortened. The consequence of this change, however, has been to lengthen the period between the informal agreement to buy the property and the formal making of the contract. Until the contract is concluded neither party is legally bound to continue with the transaction and either of them can withdraw from the negotiations without liability. It is this freedom from obligation which leads to the practice of 'gazumping', in which the vendor accepts a higher offer from another purchaser. Although the vendor is legally free to do this, the original purchaser may well feel aggrieved, especially if he or she has already incurred the expense of surveyors' and solicitors' fees. On the other hand, it may be the purchaser who withdraws, for a variety of reasons which could include receiving an unfavourable surveyor's report, finding a cheaper property or simply changing his or her mind. (A threat of withdrawal, with the object of obtaining a reduction in price, is sometimes described as 'gazundering'.)

For the purposes of this book, we still find it convenient to deal with questions relating to the contract before going on to matters of title, but you should remember that this is not necessarily the order in which these topics will present themselves in real life!

4.3.2 Steps before a contract is concluded

Before they enter into contracts to buy 1 and 3 Trant Way, Mr and Mrs Armstrong and Miss Bell will want confirmation of certain information about the properties: they will want to know how much the council tax is, whether the price includes any fittings, such as carpets, whether there have been any disputes in respect of the land (e.g., boundary disputes) and, no doubt, a good deal else. In addition, their solicitors may wish to query portions of the draft contract which each will have received from the vendor's solicitor.

At this stage, it is also usual to make a search about the property in the local land charges register.

4.3.2.1 Local land charges

These registers are maintained by the local authorities for the properties in their areas under the Local Land Charges Act 1975. They contain details of a variety of 'charges' (burdens) on the land. Thus you might discover from searching the register that the property is in a smoke control zone, or that a tree in the garden is the subject of a tree preservation order, or that the local authority has a claim against the land because the council tax has not been paid. You might also discover planning restrictions or that the building is listed as being of outstanding architectural or historical importance. As all these matters might have a considerable effect upon the use to which the land can be put, it is essential that a purchaser should know about them.

Oddly, a purchaser of an estate will be bound by any charge which exists, even if it has not been registered. However, a search is still worthwhile because, if a purchaser obtains an official search certificate, compensation can be claimed under the Local Land Charges Act 1975, s. 10 if later a charge is discovered which was not revealed by the certificate. This right to compensation arises whether the search was clean because the charge had not been registered or because the local authority made a mistake when issuing the certificate. The compensation is paid by the local authority, even if the loss is due to the mistake of some third party who has failed to register a charge (the authority may seek to recover from the third party any sums so paid).

In addition to providing an official search of the local land charges register, the local authority will also provide, if asked, a wide range of other information about the property (including, for example, details of any planned local road alterations).

4.3.3 The contract

Once a purchaser is satisfied with the answers to whatever enquiries he is making at this stage, has made any necessary arrangements to finance the transaction, and has had a surveyor's report on the property (if he so wishes), the point will have been reached at which the parties are ready to conclude a legally binding contract. Once this has been done, each party is legally obliged to give effect to the transaction, unless the other party is in breach of the terms of the contract. The detailed requirements for the creation of contracts relating to land will be considered in Chapter 5.

4.3.4 Investigating title

At some stage in the process of selling his house the vendor must show that he does have the title to the land which he intends to sell to the purchaser. The means by which this is done varies depending upon whether the title to the land is registered or unregistered. Basically, if the title is registered the purchaser will investigate the register, whilst if the title is unregistered he will need to see the title deeds to the property. The methods used to protect third-party rights also differ between the two systems and the searches to be made by the purchaser will accordingly be different.

Thus there are two very different processes ahead of Barbara Bell and the Armstrongs, who respectively are buying 3 Trant Way (unregistered title), and 1 Trant Way (registered title) (see 4.2.3.2) and we will follow their progress and consider the two systems in more detail in Chapters 6 and 7.

4.3.5 Completing the transaction

Once both parties have made all the necessary arrangements, the time will have arrived for the purchaser to pay the purchase price and the vendor to transfer the legal estate in the land to the purchaser. The vendor will also be obliged to give possession of the property to the purchaser. This transfer is usually called 'completion'. Obviously it requires a further document, and you will recall from Chapter 2 (see 2.5.4.1) that the document used to dispose of a legal estate must be a 'deed', a document which is signed, witnessed and delivered (Law of Property (Miscellaneous Provisions) Act 1989, s. 1). If the land is *unregistered* the deed is called a 'conveyance' and it has the effect of conveying the legal estate to the purchaser without the need for further formalities. If the title to the land is *registered* the deed used is called a 'transfer' and the transfer must be completed by being registered at the Land Registry: the legal title will not transfer to the purchaser until registration. The Land Registry is currently developing systems which will replace the paper transfer and subsequent registration with an electronic transfer and simultaneous registration, and we will tell you more about this in Chapter 7.

5

The contract

5.1 Introduction

To some extent, a contract for the sale of an estate or an interest in land is just like any other contract. It must comply with the basic requirements for a contract not made by deed: there must have been an offer and an acceptance, there must be consideration, and the parties must have intended to create a legal relationship. However, due to the considerable value of land, it is not surprising that for many centuries there have been additional rules relating to these contracts which require certain formalities to be observed.

The nature of these formalities will depend upon the date at which the contract was made:

- contracts made on or after 27 September 1989 are governed by the new rules introduced by the Law of Property (Miscellaneous Provisions) Act 1989, s. 2;
- contracts made before 27 September 1989 are governed by the old rules contained in the LPA 1925, s. 40, which was repealed by the 1989 Act.

You might think that most contracts made under the old law would by now either have been performed or have come before the courts, but in fact cases could continue to arise for some years yet. One of the reasons for this is that, as we explained in Chapter 2, equity may regard an ineffective grant of a legal estate or interest as a contract to make that grant, giving rise to an equitable interest in the property. Parties who rely on informal arrangements of this type, made before 27 September 1989, may continue to enjoy rights under them for many years before any dispute arises. An example of this is to be found in *Lloyds Bank plc v Carrick* [1996] 4 All ER 630, in which the defendant relied upon a contract with her brother-in-law, entered into in the early 1980s. In such a case, it will be necessary to show that the alleged contract satisfied the requirements of the law in force at the date of its creation, and accordingly it seems likely that, for some time to come, one will have to be familiar with the old rules as well as with the new ones.

We will start by looking at the new rules, and will then consider the old ones more briefly.

5.2 Contracts made on or after 27 September 1989

5.2.1 Law of Property (Miscellaneous Provisions) Act 1989, s. 2

Any contract relating to land which is made on or after 27 September 1989 must:

- be made in writing;
- contain all the terms agreed between the parties; and
- be signed by each of the parties.

These requirements are imposed by s. 2 of the Law of Property (Miscellaneous Provisions) Act 1989 (which we will refer to hereafter as 'the 1989 Act').

Section 2(1)–(3) provides:

> (1) A contract for the sale or other disposition of an interest in land can only be made in writing and only by incorporating all the terms which the parties have expressly agreed in one document or, where contracts are exchanged, in each.
>
> (2) The terms may be incorporated in a document either by being set out in it or by reference to some other document.
>
> (3) The document incorporating the terms or, where contracts are exchanged, one of the documents incorporating them (but not necessarily the same one) must be signed by or on behalf of each party to the contract.

We will now look at the provisions of s. 2 in some detail.

5.2.2 Requirements of s. 2

5.2.2.1 Contracts for the sale or other disposition of an interest in land

The effect of this phrase is that s. 2 applies to a wide range of transactions. Obviously the words would cover the sale of a fee simple and of an existing lease, but they also include a contract for the original grant of a lease, and contracts to grant a wide range of other interests in land, such as mortgages and easements. However, questions have arisen about its application to certain other agreements, and we note these in the following paragraphs.

Options

In 2.5.3.2 we explained that a property owner may give another person an option to acquire an estate in his property at a later date. Although it is clear that the option is enforceable by the contractual remedy of specific performance, there has always been some debate about the point at which the contract arises.

Some authorities describe the option to purchase as a conditional contract, because the vendor is bound to sell the property if the purchaser performs certain conditions (such as giving notice). Other authorities reject this view, relying on the fact that only one party, the vendor, is bound, and prefer to describe the option as an irrevocable offer, with the contract only coming into existence when the option is exercised.

This debate about the nature of an option formed the background to the case of *Spiro v Glencrown Properties Ltd* [1994] Ch 537. The purchaser here had given notice that he wished to exercise his option and buy the property, but he did not complete the transaction and wished to avoid being compelled to do so. He therefore argued that it is the exercise of the option which is to be regarded as the making of the contract, and which therefore has to satisfy the requirements of s. 2.

The trial judge, Hoffmann J (at p. 544), took the view that:

> An option is not strictly speaking either an offer or a conditional contract. It does not have all the incidents of the standard form of either of these concepts. To that extent it is a relationship sui generis ['of its own type']. But there are ways in which it resembles each of them. Each analogy is in the proper context a valid way of characterising the situation created by an option. The question in this case is not whether one analogy is true and the other false, but which is appropriate to be used in the construction of s. 2.

In the view of the judge:

> Section 2 . . . was intended to prevent disputes over whether the parties had entered into a binding agreement or over what terms they had agreed. It prescribes the formalities for recording their mutual consent. But only the grant of the option depends upon consent. The exercise of the option is a unilateral act. It would destroy the very purpose of the option if the purchaser had to obtain the vendor's counter-signature to the notice by which it was exercised (at p. 541).

The court therefore held that the grant of the option, which satisfied the requirements of s. 2, was a valid contract, which became enforceable against the purchaser when he gave notice to exercise the option. (We shall see later at 6.4.2.2(4) that a similar question about the stage at which an option gives rise to a contract was considered in *Armstrong and Holmes Ltd v Holmes* [1993] 1 WLR 1482 in connection with registering the option as a land charge.)

While you are considering options, you may like to note that an option to surrender a lease is within the terms of s. 2 (*Commission for the New Towns v Cooper (Great Britain) Ltd* [1995] Ch 259), and that a lockout agreement, by which a vendor agrees with a prospective purchaser not to negotiate with anyone else for a specified time, falls outside them (*Pitt v PHH Asset Management Ltd* [1994] 1 WLR 327).

Contracts to sell to a third party

In two first-instance cases (*Jelson Ltd v Derby County Council* [1999] 3 EGLR 91 and *RG Kensington Co Ltd v Hutchinson IDH Ltd* [2003] 2 P&CR 195) the High Court appears to have accepted that a contract between A and B which provides that A shall sell land to C falls within s. 2 and must satisfy its requirements. Discussion in both cases turned on whether s. 2 requires C to sign the contract (see further 5.2.2.5), thus by implication accepting that the section does apply to such a contract, but there was no express consideration of this wider question.

In *Nweze v Nwoku* [2004] 2 P&CR 33 the Court of Appeal referred briefly to contracts to transfer land to a named third party, saying merely that 'it may be' that s. 2 would apply (para. 24). By contrast, the court had no doubt on the facts before it that an agreement between A and B that A would market his property with a view to selling it to a buyer (who was as yet unknown) did not fall within the terms of the Act. The case before the court arose from an oral compromise agreement between the parties (i.e., an agreement made in settlement of an earlier dispute) that Nwoku would sell his house and, having discharged a mortgage on it, would pay the balance of the proceeds of sale to the Nwezes. He did not, in fact, sell the property. When the Nwezes sought to enforce the compromise agreement, Nwoku claimed that it fell within s. 2 and was void for non-compliance.

The court had little difficulty in rejecting this suggestion. Although the words of the section ('contract for the sale or disposition of an interest in land') could 'as a matter of language' (para. 29) bear the meaning claimed by Nwoku, the court could find no case in which the provisions of s. 2 (or of its predecessors, dating back to the Statute of Frauds in 1677) had been given this wider meaning. In the court's view, s. 2 relates to a contract which *effects* (or brings about) the sale or disposition of an interest in land, rather than to a contract which merely *results* in such a sale or disposition (per Sedley LJ at paras. 29–31). In other words (per Waller LJ at para. 16) the statutory provisions relate to a contract

> under which there is a vendor on the one side and a purchaser on the other, and with the terms of [the] sale or... disposition.

Here the contract did not bring about the sale or disposition of any interest in the land; it was merely an agreement that the property would be marketed with a view to a resulting sale. Such an agreement did not have to comply with s. 2 and was therefore enforceable against Nwoku.

5.2.2.2 The contract must be made in writing

We want to emphasise here that there is no alternative to this requirement. The only way in which a contract relating to land can be made on or after 27 September 1989 is in writing: an oral agreement between the parties will not create a contract.

We will see later on that equitable concepts such as estoppel or the constructive trust may assist a party who relies on an agreement which does not satisfy the Act's requirements (see 5.5) but, even so, this does not give the agreement the force of a valid contract.

5.2.2.3 The written contract must incorporate all the terms which the parties have expressly agreed

This requirement is set out in s. 2(1), and s. 2(2) then goes on to provide that the terms agreed by the parties may be incorporated in the contract either by setting them out in it, or by referring to some other document which contains them. Failure to do this will invalidate the contract.

Since the 1989 Act has been in operation, a number of cases have come before the courts in which it has been alleged that a term which forms part of the agreement has not been incorporated in the written contract and that the contract is accordingly void. The attempt by one party to escape from his agreement often appears to be somewhat unmeritorious, and occasionally the court has succeeded in holding him to his bargain.

In some cases the court has done this by treating the missing terms as a separate contract, the omission of which does not invalidate the contract relating to an interest in land. By contrast, there have been other decisions in which the court has refused to adopt this approach, and has treated the whole contract as void because certain terms have been omitted.

Missing terms treated as separate contract

This approach was first adopted by the High Court in *Record v Bell* [1991] 1 WLR 853, where a purchaser failed to complete his purchase and then argued that the contract for sale was invalid because it did not include a condition, agreed between the parties' solicitors, about proof of title.

It was held that in this transaction there had been two contracts: one for the sale of the estate in land and the other a collateral contract that the title to the property would be revealed as described when the necessary paperwork was produced. The collateral contract was not in itself a contract for the sale of an estate or interest in land and thus was not subject to s. 2 and could be concluded orally. The collateral contract had been fulfilled and there was no defect in the contract for sale, which accordingly could be enforced.

The possibility of two separate contracts was also accepted by the Court of Appeal in *Tootal Clothing Ltd v Guinea Properties Management Ltd* [1992] 2 EGLR 80. Here the agreements were: (1) for the grant of a lease; and (2) that the tenant would carry out shopfitting works at the premises within 12 weeks and that for this work the landlord would pay £30,000. The contract to grant the lease was fulfilled by the formal grant of a lease and the tenant thereafter carried out the work. However, when the work was done the landlord refused to pay. In this case the Court of Appeal held that s. 2 could not continue to apply to the agreement to grant the lease after the transaction had been completed by the making of the grant and that, in any event, there were two separate contracts here. Thus the agreement for the work did not have to be included in the same document as the agreement for the lease in order to be enforceable. Scott LJ said:

> If parties choose to hive off parts of the terms of their composite bargain into a separate contract distinct from the written land contract that incorporates the rest of the terms, I can see nothing in section 2 that provides an answer to an action for enforcement of the land contract, on the one hand, or of the separate contract on the other hand. Each has become, by the choice of the parties, a separate contract.

Thus, in two cases at least, attempts to invalidate a contract by reference to s. 2 have been met by the device of treating the omitted terms as constituting a separate agreement.

Refusal to treat missing terms as separate contract

Despite its decision in *Tootal Clothing Ltd*, the Court of Appeal adopted a stricter approach in *Wright v Robert Leonard (Developments) Ltd* [1994] NPC49. In this case the purchaser agreed to buy both a show flat and its furnishings, but the furnishings were not mentioned in the written contract. After completion, the purchaser found that the furnishings had been removed and, when he sought damages for breach of contract, was met with the argument that there was not sufficient writing to satisfy s. 2. It would have been relatively easy for the court to adopt the approach taken in *Record v Bell*, construing the agreement as creating two separate contracts. The Court of Appeal, however, declined to do this, taking the view that 'if the contract is all one arrangement, there is no collateral contract, and all the terms in it must be in writing, even those which do not refer to the land'. Here there was only one contract with two elements, and both should have been included in the written document (and note the similar approach adopted by the Court of Appeal in *Godden v Merthyr Tydfil Housing Association* [1997] NPC 1).

In *Wright v Robert Leonard (Developments) Ltd* the court nevertheless found itself able to assist the purchaser, holding that the case was one in which it was appropriate to grant the equitable remedy of rectification, and awarding the purchaser damages for breach of the rectified contract. It should be noted here that s. 2(4) makes express reference to the possibility of rectification, and it appears from *Joscelyne v Nissen* [1970] 2 QB 86 that, as long as there is a pre-existing *agreement*, it is not necessary to establish that there was a pre-existing *contract* in order to obtain rectification. (If this were not so, it would of course be impossible to obtain rectification of a document which failed to satisfy s. 2 and so in consequence was not a valid contract.)

McCausland v Duncan Lawrie Ltd [1997] 1 WLR 38 was another case in which the Court of Appeal favoured a strict interpretation of s. 2. Here a written contract which complied with the requirements of s. 2 specified a date for completion which was subsequently varied by agreement in correspondence between the parties. When the purchaser failed to complete on the new date, the vendor issued a notice requiring him to complete and, when this did not happen, sought rescission of the contract. The purchaser, who still wished to buy the property, sought specific performance, and the case turned on whether the variation of the original completion date was effective. The purchaser relied upon s. 2, claiming that the variation was ineffective because it did not satisfy the requirements of the Act. The Court of Appeal accepted this argument, holding that a variation of a material term in the contract had to comply with the requirements of s. 2 if either party was to be able to enforce the contract as varied.

Court of Appeal reviews earlier decisions

The most recent decision on this matter is *Grossman v Hooper* [2001] 2 EGLR 82, which concerned an agreement for the transfer of a property from a man to a woman on the breakdown of their relationship. He subsequently claimed that she had undertaken to pay off a debt owed to a third party and that the omission of this from the written agreement invalidated the contract for transfer. The Court of Appeal held that the agreement about the debt was not part of the contract for transfer.

The interest of this decision lies in the court's observations about earlier decisions, and its attempt to explain the process of deciding whether or not an agreed term should be included in the written contract. Schiemann LJ commented (at para. 19), in relation to s. 2(1) of the 1989 Act that:

> the terms which the parties have expressly agreed means the terms... upon which the parties to the sale or other disposition have agreed that the relevant interest in land shall be sold or otherwise disposed of. The words do not refer to terms upon which the parties have agreed (albeit contemporaneously) that some other transaction should be entered.

The judge illustrated this statement by reference to a hypothetical agreement that a purchaser should take over a vendor's carpets and curtains. Whether or not a provision to this effect is a term of the contract of sale is a matter of fact in each case. It is for the court to decide whether the parties agreed that the sale of the house was conditional on the sale of the furnishings, in which case the term is part of the contract, or whether the agreement was for the sale of the house independently of the furnishings, in which case the agreement about carpets and curtains is *not* a term.

In the court's view, its task of interpreting agreements of this type was not assisted by the notion of 'collateral contracts', which Sir Christopher Staughton described as 'elusive'. He also disagreed with the view expressed in *Tootal Clothing Ltd v Guinea Properties Management Ltd* [1992] 2 EGLR 80 (see above) that parties could 'hive off' part of their composite bargain into a separate contract:

> If the parties are allowed, by a simple device, to avoid the effects of s. 2..., what was the point of Parliament enacting it? (at para. 35).

It can be seen from the above that the apparently simple requirement that all the terms of the agreement should be incorporated in the written contract has given rise to some difficulties in practice, and it remains to be seen whether the courts will continue to treat the omitted terms as forming separate contracts, or will follow the stricter approach adopted by the Court of Appeal in more recent decisions.

5.2.2.4 The written contract may take the form of one document, which both parties sign, or of identical documents, each signed by one party and then exchanged

This requirement is derived from s. 2(1) and (3). The provision for the exchange of contracts perpetuates the method which conveyancers have developed over the years for concluding contracts for the sale of estates in land. The normal procedure is for two identical copies of the contract to be prepared. One copy is signed by the vendor and the other by the purchaser, and when the time comes to create a binding contract the parties exchange their copies. As a result of the exchange, each party holds a copy of the contract signed by the other.

Contracts by correspondence

The terms of s. 2(1) and (3) appear to produce the result that it is no longer possible to create what are known as 'contracts by correspondence'. Under the old rules, an enforceable contract could come into existence as a result of a written offer and a written acceptance contained in letters passing between the parties, or through correspondence between them confirming the terms of a previously made oral agreement. There have so far been two cases in which the Court of Appeal has had to consider the effect under the 1989 Act of such 'contracts by correspondence'.

In *Hooper v Sherman* [1994] NPC 153 an unmarried couple agreed that the man would transfer his interest in the family home to the woman in return for being released from his mortgage obligations. This arrangement was confirmed by letters between the parties' solicitors, but some delay in proceeding was caused by the mortgagees and eventually the man refused to complete. The Court of Appeal held that, while neither letter by itself constituted a contract, a bilateral contract came into existence through the exchange of the letters. Morritt LJ, in a dissenting judgment, took the view that the letters were no more than confirmation of the oral agreement, and were not enough for the purposes of s. 2 of the 1989 Act.

In *Commission for the New Towns v Cooper (Great Britain) Ltd* [1995] Ch 259 the documents in question again took the form of letters passing between the plaintiff and the defendant, purporting to record and confirm an oral agreement reached at a meeting between the parties. The facts of the case are complicated because the defendant had deliberately planned to mislead the plaintiff and had engineered the discussions at the meeting in such a way that the plaintiff was not aware of the true effect of the proposals to which it agreed. The Court of Appeal found for the plaintiff on a number of grounds, one of them being that the correspondence between the parties did not constitute an exchange of contracts for the purpose of s. 2. In the view of the court the exchange of documents contemplated by the Act cannot take place until agreement between the parties has been concluded by offer and final acceptance; in other words, the parties must agree on the sale and then reduce that agreement to writing, in the form of either one document signed by both parties, or in two documents which are to be exchanged between them. Written offers and acceptances can no longer give rise to a written contract: they are merely the process by which the agreement is reached.

It was only at a late stage of the proceedings in *Commission for the New Towns v Cooper (Great Britain) Ltd* that the Court of Appeal was reminded of its decision in *Hooper v Sherman*. The court was, however, able to find reasons for not following this earlier decision, and held on the facts of the case before it that the exchange of letters did not satisfy s. 2.

5.2.2.5 **The written contract must be signed by both parties**

This requirement of s. 2(3) can be satisfied either by both parties signing the same document, or by each party signing a copy and then exchanging them.

The requirement for signature was considered in *Firstpost Homes Ltd v Johnson* [1995] 1 WLR 1567. Here the purchaser prepared a letter to himself from the vendor, in which she agreed to sell him land which was identified 'on the enclosed plan'. The purchaser signed the plan but not the letter, and sent both plan and letter to the vendor, who signed both of them. After the vendor's death, the purchaser sought to enforce the contract against the vendor's personal representatives, but the Court of Appeal held that the requirements of s. 2(3) as to the signature were not satisfied, and accordingly there was no valid contract. The court regarded the letter and the plan as two documents, not one ('Something enclosed with the letter is not…the same document as the letter'—per Peter Gibson LJ at p. 1573); it was the letter which set out the terms of the agreement, incorporating the details of the plan by referring to it; and accordingly it was the letter which should have been signed by both parties. The purchaser sought to meet this point by arguing that he was identified as the addressee on the letter and that earlier authorities showed that the typing or printing of the name of a party as addressee, in a document prepared by that party, was a sufficient signature. The Court of Appeal, however, rejected this argument, saying that it was an artificial use of language to describe the typing or printing of a name in this way as a signature, and quoting with approval the words of Denning LJ in *Goodman v J. Eban Ltd* [1954] 1 QB 550:

> In modern English usage, when a document is required to be 'signed' by someone, that means that he must write his name with his own hand upon it.

In consequence, the court held that the relevant document, the letter, was not signed in accordance with s. 2(3), and accordingly there was no written contract within the provisions of s. 2.

Although it may seem self-evident from the wording of s. 2(3), we need to draw your attention to the fact that it is the parties to the contract who are required to sign it. The reason for emphasising this is to be found in two High Court decisions, *Jelson Ltd v Derby County Council* [1999] 3 EGLR 91, and *RG Kensington Co Ltd v Hutchinson IDH Ltd* [2003] 2 P&CR 195. In *Jelson*, a developer, seeking permission to develop a site, entered into a written agreement with the local authority that it would allocate part of the site for affordable housing and, when work was completed, would transfer that area to a housing association. Later, the developer successfully challenged that part of the agreement, the court holding that it was void under s. 2 because it had not been signed by the housing association as the prospective purchaser.

A similar point arose in the *Kensington* case, in which a developer contracted with the first claimant, Caan, that it would sell the developed site to the second claimant, Kensington Management Co. Again, the developer argued that this contract was unenforceable because it had not been signed by the prospective purchaser, but this was rejected by Neuberger J:

> The closing words of s. 2(3) require the contract to be signed by 'each party to the contract', not by 'each party to the prospective conveyance or transfer'.... Kensington is not a party to the... agreement and, as it is not a party to that contract, it seems there is no reason to require it to sign it (at para. 57).

In reaching his decision that s. 2 did not require Kensington's signature and that therefore the contract was valid, the judge departed from the interpretation adopted in *Jelson*, saying that in his view it could not be supported. Although these two decisions are of equal weight, the later one seems more in accordance with the terms of the statute and, as Neuberger J commented, the interpretation relied on by the developer:

> would involve an impermissible re-writing and extension... of s. 2(3) [and] would also involve giving s. 2 a greater degree of interference with Common Law rights and freedom to contract than it naturally bears.

More recently, the decision in *Jelson* has been described by the Court of Appeal as being 'open to criticism' on the signature point (see *Nweze v Nwoku* [2004] 2 P&CR 33 at paras. 21 and 35).

5.2.3 Contracts which do not have to satisfy s. 2

Section 2(5) specifies certain types of contract which do not have to comply with the main provisions of s. 2, and which accordingly may be made without a written contract.

5.2.3.1 Contracts to grant short leases

While most leases have to be granted by deed, certain leases for not more than three years may be granted more informally: in writing or even by word of mouth (LPA 1925, s. 54(2)); see 10.3.1.1. In these circumstances, it would seem inappropriate to require a written contract to grant a lease when the actual grant does not need to be in writing, and accordingly s. 2(5)(a) excludes contracts for such leases from the general requirements of s. 2.

5.2.3.2 Contracts made in the course of a public auction

These contracts have always had their own rules, and we will say no more about them here, other than that essentially the contract is concluded on the fall of the hammer.

5.2.3.3 Contracts regulated under the Financial Services Act 1986

This exclusion covers certain contracts for investments which happen to include an interest of some kind in land. An example might be a unit trust or a debenture (a debenture is a type of charge (mortgage) used over the property of a company and it will usually include a charge over any land which the company has).

5.2.3.4 Certain trusts

Section 2(5) also expressly excludes 'the creation or operation of resulting, implied or constructive trusts'. This is in keeping with the terms of LPA 1925, s. 53(2), which excludes those trusts from the requirement in s. 53(1)(b) that declarations of trust must be in writing (see further Chapter 20).

This provision in s. 2(5) has proved to be far more important than might be expected at first sight. As we will see in 5.5, it is now playing a major part in the development of equitable relief for parties who mistakenly rely on invalid contracts.

5.2.4 Consequences of the 1989 Act

It is obvious that the changes introduced by the 1989 Act affect the way in which contracts are made for the sale of a fee simple or an existing lease. What we want to emphasise here is that the Act also has a considerable effect on the creation of equitable interests which arise from a contract to grant a legal estate or interest or from a failure to use the correct form of grant (see 2.5.3.1 and 2.5.4.2). In order to treat an agreement or a failed grant as giving rise to an equitable interest there now has to be a document which amounts to a written contract under the 1989 Act. This means that the help equity can give to informal transactions may well be more limited than in the past (see for example the effect which the Act has had on informally created mortgages—24.5.2.1).

5.3 Contracts made before 27 September 1989

5.3.1 LPA 1925, s. 40

Before 27 September 1989 any contract relating to land could be made orally or in writing, but if made orally was not enforceable unless there was some written evidence of it or some act of part performance.

These requirements were imposed by LPA 1925, s. 40, which provided:

> (1) No action may be brought upon any contract for the sale or other disposition of land or any interest in land, unless the agreement upon which such action is brought, or some memorandum or note thereof, is in writing, and signed by the party to be charged or by some other person thereunto by him lawfully authorised.
>
> (2) This section . . . does not affect the law relating to part performance . . .

You will note that these provisions refer to 'any contract for the sale or other disposition of land or an interest in land'. This is substantially the same wording as that used in s. 2 of the the 1989 Act, and thus the same range of transactions is covered by both statutory provisions.

We will now look in a little more detail at the s. 40 requirements, and will try to highlight the points of comparison between them and the new rules which we considered in the previous section.

5.3.2 Requirements of s. 40

5.3.2.1 Contracts could be made in writing or orally

(1) *Written contracts* Section 40 provided for the possibility of a written contract, which was normally made in the same way as it would be today (i.e. by both parties signing the same document, or by each signing a copy and exchanging it with the other).

However, it was also possible for a written contract to arise through correspondence between the parties, in a way which *Commission for the New Towns v Cooper (Great Britain) Ltd* [1995] Ch 259 suggests is no longer possible under the new rules (see 5.2.2.4).

(2) *Oral contracts* A *valid* contract could be created by oral agreement between the parties. Unlike s. 2 of the 1989 Act, s. 40 did not require writing for the formation of the contract and this is the most significant difference between the old and new rules. An oral contract, however, was not *enforceable* unless there was some written evidence of it, or some act of part performance.

5.3.2.2 **Oral contracts valid but unenforceable without writing or part performance**

The wording of s. 40 did not render an oral contract either void or voidable: it was merely unenforceable by action in the courts. This may seem like splitting hairs but the distinction could be important, as is illustrated by the case of *Low v Fry* (1935) 51 TLR 322. In that case the parties made an oral agreement for the sale of an estate in land and the purchaser gave the vendor a cheque for a portion of the purchase price. Later the purchaser decided not to proceed with the transaction and told his bank to stop payment of the cheque. The vendor was unable to enforce the contract to sell because of s. 40, but was able to recover on the cheque: this was not a case in which a cheque had been issued for a consideration which had totally failed, because the contract, though unenforceable, was valid.

5.3.2.3 **Written evidence of oral contract**

(1) *Form* Section 40 required a written 'memorandum or note' of the agreement. There was no prescribed form for this, and all that was needed was a written document which showed that an oral agreement had been made and set out its terms.

(2) *Content* In order to satisfy s. 40, the note or memorandum had to contain certain essential details: the names of the parties (or a description which identified them); a clear description of the property; and the consideration. If any of these was missing from the document, the courts would not enforce the contract. In addition, any other material terms of the contract had to be included; however, if any term was omitted, the party affected might choose either to waive it or to perform it (as appropriate). Having done so, he could then enforce the balance of the agreement (*Scott v Bradley* [1971] 1 Ch 850). There seems to be no scope for this approach under the 1989 Act (see 5.2.2.3 for the various ways in which the courts have dealt with omitted terms under the new rules).

(3) *Signature* The document had to be signed by the person against whom the contract was to be enforced. Thus if a purchaser alone had signed the document, he could not rely on it in suing the vendor—for fairly obvious reasons! There was no requirement that the document should be signed by the person seeking to enforce the contract, and this is another significant difference from the new rules, which require the written contract to be signed by both parties.

5.3.2.4 **An alternative to writing: part performance**

Even if there was no written evidence of an oral contract, it might still be enforceable if the plaintiff could show an act of part performance, that is that he had already performed some of his obligations under the contract.

Part performance was an equitable doctrine which arose fairly soon after the Statute of Frauds 1677 first introduced the requirement for written evidence of contracts relating to land.

The Statute of Frauds was intended to combat the numbers of cases of perjured evidence in cases relating to land by requiring written, rather than oral, evidence of contracts. However, the statute soon caused its own problems since it became possible for a vendor to agree orally to sell land, allow the purchaser to move in and improve the land, and then claim the land back (plus improvements) on the ground that there was no contract enforceable at law. Not surprisingly at this point, equity intervened. To prevent the statute being used as an instrument of fraud, the equitable doctrine of part performance was developed. This doctrine provided that if a party to a contract had acted on the contract in reliance on the promise of the other party, then the contract would be enforced in equity, despite the lack of a written memorandum.

Requirements for the operation of part performance

In order to use the doctrine of part performance, a plaintiff had to show that acts had been done which pointed clearly to the existence of a contract. In essence the plaintiff was claiming that he would not have acted as he did, had he not had a valid contract. In other words, his conduct was evidence of an agreement. At the same time, however, the courts emphasised their concern with general equitable principles: it would be unfair for a party to escape from his obligations when the other side had already acted in reliance on the contract. Both of these explanations of the doctrine run throughout the decided cases and, in *Steadman v Steadman* [1976] AC 536, Lord Simon commented on 'the uneasy oscillation between regarding the doctrine as a principle vindicating conscientious dealing and as a rule of evidence' (at p. 560).

It is probably easiest to explain part performance by giving an example of the operation of the doctrine. In *Rawlinson v Ames* [1925] Ch 96, the defendant had agreed to take a lease from the plaintiff but had asked the plaintiff to do some work on the land before the defendant moved in. The plaintiff did the necessary work under the defendant's supervision but the defendant then refused to take the lease, relying on s. 40 as there was no written contract. In this case the plaintiff was granted an order for specific performance of the oral contract. The court concluded that the plaintiff would not have carried out the improvements to the land at the defendant's direction had there not been a pre-existing contract.

More generally, in cases of a contract to grant a lease, the tenant's act of taking possession and the landlord's permission for this were regarded as acts of part performance by each party, so that either of them could enforce the contract.

Since part performance was a creation of equity, it was discretionary in its application (as are all equitable principles), and a court would decline to assist a party who relied on the doctrine if this would produce injustice, or if the party relying on the doctrine had 'dirty hands'.

The doctrine of part performance was specifically retained in 1925 by s. 40(2) which provided that the section 'does not affect the law relating to part performance'.

5.4 Part performance after the 1989 Act

5.4.1 Did the doctrine of part performance survive the 1989 Act?

The changes introduced by the 1989 Act to the rules governing contracts relating to land were based on the recommendations of the Law Commission Report on Formalities for Contracts of Sale etc. of Land 1987 (Law Com No. 164). The view of the Law Commission on part performance was that it should be abolished. It was suggested that the doctrine of estoppel might, in appropriate cases, be relied upon as an alternative (see para. 5.5), and the Law Commission concluded:

> We see no cause to fear that the recommended repeal and replacement of the present section as to the formalities for contracts for sale or other disposition of land will inhibit the courts in the exercise of the equitable discretion to do justice between parties in individual otherwise hard cases.

The 1989 Act makes no specific reference to the doctrine of part performance, neither continuing it nor abolishing it. The Act does, of course, repeal s. 40, but as we have seen s. 40(2) merely said:

> This section...does not affect the law relating to part performance...

Accordingly, to repeal s. 40 does not abolish the rule in itself and for some time after the Act came into force there was some judicial uncertainty about whether a party could still rely on part performance (see for example contrasting opinions in the Court of Appeal in *Firstpost Homes Ltd v Johnson* [1995] 1 WLR 1567 at 1571 and *Singh v Beggs* (1996) 71 P&CR 120 at 122). In time, however, the courts accepted that part performance had not survived the 1989 Act, and attention switched to the question of whether there was any other equitable concept which might be able to take its place.

5.4.2 What might replace part performance?

The Law Commission assumed that hard cases could be handled by the rules of estoppel, and there are certainly considerable similarities between these rules and the doctrine of part performance. A proprietary estoppel may arise where some representation has been made by one party and relied upon by another to his detriment (see 2.5.7). Where A allows B to act to his detriment in reliance on a belief that he will acquire an interest in A's property under an agreement which A knows is not a valid contract, it certainly could be argued that A's conduct amounts to such a representation, and that he should be estopped from denying that he is bound by the agreement.

There was some initial difference of opinion in the Court of Appeal as to whether estoppel could be used to assist parties who had failed to comply with the requirements of s. 2 (see *Godden v Merthyr Tydfil Housing Association* [1997] NPC 1, and *Bankers Trust Co. v Namdar* [1997] NPC 22). The matter was eventually considered more fully by the Court of Appeal in *Yaxley v Gotts* [2000] Ch 162, and since that time the courts have used the two equitable concepts of proprietary estoppel and the constructive trust to provide relief in hard cases arising under s. 2.

5.5 Estoppel and constructive trusts

5.5.1 *Yaxley v Gotts*

In this case the claimant and the first defendant ('Gotts Senior') had agreed that Gotts Senior would acquire the freehold of a large house, already divided into flats, and that the claimant, a self-employed builder, would carry out the necessary development work on the property and act as managing agent for the defendant. In return, the claimant was to be given the ground floor of the house, which he would divide into two flats and then let. No written contract was made, the claimant being content to rely on what he described as 'a gentleman's agreement'. Matters went ahead as agreed, save that the property was bought by the second defendant ('Gotts Junior'—son of the first defendant) and the property was registered in his name. No interest in the property was granted to the claimant. Some four years later, the parties fell out, and the claimant was excluded from the property. He then sought a declaration that he was entitled to ownership of part of the house.

At first instance, the judge held that on these facts a proprietary estoppel arose, and that it was to be satisfied by a grant to the claimant of a rent-free lease of the ground floor for 99 years. The defendants appealed against the first instance decision, raising for the first time the argument that the agreement in question was, in effect, a contract for the sale or disposition of an interest in land, and should have been made in writing. The defendant also relied upon what we will call the 'public policy' argument, namely the well-established principle (set out in *Halsbury's Laws of England*, 4th edn. Reissue, Vol. 16, pp. 849–50) that:

> the doctrine of estoppel may not be invoked to render valid a transaction which the legislature has, on grounds of general public policy, enacted is to be invalid.

The three members of the Court of Appeal agreed in dismissing the appeal and upheld the award to the claimant of the 99-year lease. However, they reached this conclusion by different routes, with the result that the decision as a whole is of some complexity.

Robert Walker LJ gave great weight to the argument based on public policy. He identified Parliament's requirement for written contracts as being based on the conclusion that the need for certainty in contracts relating to interests in land outweighed the disappointment of those who made informal bargains in ignorance of the statutory requirements, and concluded that:

> If an estoppel would have the effect of enforcing a void contract and subverting Parliament's purpose it may have to yield to the statutory law which confronts it (at p. 175).

In other words, Yaxley could not rely on estoppel to overcome the lack of a written contract.

Nevertheless, an alternative way of assisting those who act in reliance on an informal agreement was to be found in another equitable concept, the constructive trust. We consider such trusts in detail in Chapter 20, but, for the present, all you need to know is that a constructive trust arises by operation of law, when equity regards a property owner's behaviour as unconscionable and as a result requires him to hold all or part of his property in trust for some other person. One of the many situations in which a constructive trust may be imposed is that of 'common intention': that is, where the parties have agreed that one will have an interest in property belonging to the other, and the non-owning party has acted to his or her detriment in reliance on that common intention.

There are clear similarities between the concepts of proprietary estoppel and the common intention constructive trust, and the course of dealing between Yaxley and the Gotts family could equally well give rise to an estoppel or justify the imposition of a constructive trust. As we have already noted (5.2.3.4), s. 2(5) of the 1989 Act expressly excludes 'the creation of resulting, implied or constructive trusts' from the requirement of a written contract imposed by s. 2(1). In the judge's view, this section allowed:

> A limited exception...for those cases in which a supposed bargain has been so fully performed by one side...that it would be inequitable to disregard the claimant's expectations...(at p. 180).

Accordingly, Robert Walker LJ upheld the first instance decision, but on the basis of a constructive trust, rather than on the principles of proprietary estoppel.

The other two judges, Clarke and Beldam LJJ, agreed that the claimant could rely on a constructive trust, and that the appeal should be dismissed on that basis. However, in addition, they each expressed views on proprietary estoppel and its possible use in the context of the 1989 Act and both considered that in interpreting the Act greater weight could be given to the views of the Law Commission than was considered appropriate by Robert Walker LJ (see pp. 176, 182 and 190).

Beldam LJ considered that the Law Commission's report made it clear that its proposals were not intended to affect the court's power to give equitable relief through the principles of estoppel and constructive trusts. Moreover the general principle that a party could not rely on an estoppel in the face of a statute depended upon the nature and purpose of the enactment, and the social policy behind it. The 1989 Act was not:

> aimed at prohibiting or outlawing agreements of a specific kind, though it had the effect of making agreements which did not comply with the required formalities void. This by itself is insufficient to raise such a significant public interest that an estoppel would be excluded (at p. 191).

Thus, while agreeing that the facts in the present case justified the finding that the first defendant held the property subject to a constructive trust in favour of the claimant, Beldam LJ also considered that the trial judge was entitled to reach the same conclusion by finding a proprietary estoppel.

As we hope you can see from this rather lengthy account of the case, the various judgments provide a good deal of material for analysis and discussion. Some writers regret the extension of constructive trusts into the area of contracts for the sale of land (see Smith (2000) 116 LQR 11), and there is also concern about further erosion of the distinction between proprietary estoppel and constructive trusts, a matter to which we return in Chapter 21 (see 21.8).

5.5.2 Estoppel and public policy

Not long after *Yaxley v Gotts*, the operation of estoppel in relation to other statutes was considered in two further cases.

In *Shah v Shah* [2002] QB 35 the Court of Appeal held that, in the particular circumstances of the case before it, public policy did not prevent the use of estoppel to provide relief from the consequences of failing to comply with the attestation requirements (i.e., requirements for witnessing the signatures of parties to a deed imposed by s. 1 of the 1989 Act (see 2.5.4.1(b)).

The other decision, *Actionstrength Ltd v International Glass Engineering IN.GL.EN SpA* [2003] 2 AC 541, concerned s. 4 of the Statute of Frauds 1677, which renders an oral guarantee agreement unenforceable, unless supported by some written note or memorandum. *Obiter dicta* of the House of Lords in this case suggest that the statutory requirement could be circumvented by estoppel *if the guarantor had given an express assurance that he would not rely on the Statute*. On the facts of the case, however, there had been no such assurance, and in the words of Lord Walker (at p. 557):

> it would wholly frustrate the continued operation of section 4 in relation to contracts of guarantee if an oral promise [of guarantee] were to be treated, without more, as somehow carrying in itself a representation that the promise would be treated as enforceable.

A further statement of the principle that estoppel should not be used to circumvent statutory provisions (although without any specific reference to public policy) is to be found in *obiter dicta* in *Cobbe v Yeoman's Row Management Ltd* [2008] 1 WLR 1752 (for which, see below), in which Lord Scott expressed the view (at para. 29) that:

> Proprietary estoppel cannot be prayed in aid in order to render enforceable an agreement that statute has declared to be void. The proposition that an owner of land can be estopped from asserting that an agreement is void for want of compliance with the requirements of s.2 is, in my opinion, unacceptable. The assertion is no more than the statute provides. Equity can surely not contradict the statute.

5.5.3 Decisions after *Yaxley v Gotts*

Since *Yaxley v Gotts*, the courts have considered a number of agreements which, under the old law, would have taken effect as oral contracts enforceable on the basis of part performance but which, under the new law, fail to create contracts because they do not satisfy the requirements of s. 2. In dealing with these cases, the courts have in general followed Robert Walker LJ in relying on constructive trusts, rather than on estoppel, to mitigate the effects of s. 2. In doing this, however, they usually emphasise the similarities between the two concepts, and consider first whether an estoppel can be established. If satisfied that the circumstances do give rise to an estoppel, the court is able to move fairly swiftly to the finding of a constructive trust. This process can be illustrated by two decisions of the Court of Appeal: *Kinane v MacKie-Conteh* [2005] EWCA Civ 45 [2005] WTLR 345 and *Oates v Stimpson* [2006] EWCA Civ 548.

5.5.3.1 *Kinane v Mackie-Conteh*

This case concerned a loan by the claimant (Kinane) to a company of which the defendant (Mackie-Conteh) was managing director. The two men agreed that the loan, and interest on it, would be secured by a charge over the director's house, and Mackie-Conteh and his wife signed a letter ('the security agreement'), agreeing to create such a mortgage. Before the 1989 Act, this oral agreement, evidenced by the letter, would have created a contract which, if specifically enforceable, would have given rise to an equitable mortgage (see 2.5.4.2). However, under s. 2, of course, there was no contract and no equitable mortgage. Despite the agreement, no mortgage was executed.

In due course, Kinane sought to enforce the security agreement, claiming that he had acted to his detriment in reliance on the common intention of the parties that he would be granted a mortgage and was therefore entitled to relief under a constructive trust (para. 10). In order to follow *Yaxley v Gotts*, the Court of Appeal had to show that the case before it fell within some exception to the general principles applied by the House of Lords in *Actionstrength*. The court considered that, in order to do this, the claimant had to show that there had been some representation by the defendant that the unenforceable security agreement was valid and binding, and that this representation consisted of more than merely providing him with that agreement.

The court was satisfied that there had been such a representation in this case. The claimant made it clear that he would not lend the money without security; the defendant responded by providing the security agreement, and thus persuaded the claimant to make the loan. By this conduct, the defendant represented to Kinane that the agreement was valid and binding (para. 28). Further, the claimant had relied upon this representation and acted upon it to his detriment by making an unsecured loan (para. 31), thus, in the court's view, meeting the requirements for establishing an estoppel.

A finding of estoppel was, however, not enough by itself: in order to bring the case within s. 2(5) the court must also be satisfied that the estoppel 'overlapped' with a constructive trust (para. 25), or, per Neuberger LJ at para. 45, that it was:

> an estoppel which can also properly be said to amount to a constructive trust.

Lord Justice Neuberger noted that there could be circumstances which gave rise to an estoppel but not to a constructive trust (para. 47). In his view, the essential characteristic of a proprietary estoppel which *did* give rise to a constructive trust was:

> the element of agreement, or at least expression of common understanding, exchanged between the parties, as to the existence, or intended existence, of a proprietary interest.

In the present case there had been a common understanding that Kinane would acquire an interest in land by means of the mortgage. This gave rise to a constructive trust and accordingly this was a case in which the claimant could rely on s. 2(5).

It is not altogether clear from the various judgments what relief was to follow from this conclusion, but Arden LJ's statement that 'an interest in land... is the appropriate relief in this case' (para. 33) suggests that she intended Kinane to receive security for the loan as originally intended.

5.5.3.2 *Oates v Stimson*

The parties in this case were two friends who had joined together to buy a house.

Title was registered in their joint names and they agreed to pay the mortgage instalments in equal shares. In 1997 O, having been made redundant, failed to contribute to the mortgage payments. It was subsequently agreed that O would move out of the house, S would take on all responsibility for the mortgage, and at some time in the future O would transfer his interest in the property to S for a payment of £2,500.

O moved out as agreed. S continued to live in the house, paid the mortgage instalments and undertook various repairs and improvements at his own expense. In 2000, three years after the agreement, S offered to pay £2,500 to O for the promised transfer of O's interest in the property. However, the value of the house had increased considerably over this period and O claimed to be entitled to a share in the property, which he valued at over £50,000.

As a result, S sought a declaration that he was entitled to the net value of the property (i.e., after repayment of the mortgage debt), less the £2,500 due to O under their agreement. This, of course, amounted to seeking the enforcement of the informal agreement for the sale of an interest in land, which, before *Yaxley v Gotts*, would have appeared to fall squarely within the terms of s. 2 of the 1989 Act and accordingly would have had no legal effect.

The trial judge dismissed O's claim to share in the increased value of the property and granted S the declaration he sought. The judge considered that S had acted to his detriment in taking on the mortgage repayments and making repairs and improvements to the property, and had done this in reliance on his agreement with O.

This decision was confirmed by the Court of Appeal in remarkably brief judgments. Sir Christopher Staughton appears to have reached his decision on the basis of proprietary estoppel (para. 13) without any consideration of the public policy considerations discussed in *Yaxley v Gotts*. By contrast, Auld LJ described O's conduct 'in reliance upon which [S] acted to his detriment and/or changed his position' as giving rise to:

> a constructive trust in favour of [S] rendering it unconscionable not to permit him to enforce the oral agreement for sale... (para. 15).

Such a perfunctory approach is in marked contrast to the lengthy analysis in *Yaxley v Gotts*, and it is interesting to note how far the Court of Appeal has moved since that earlier decision.

5.5.4 Can estoppel or constructive trust arise during negotiations?

Under the old law, in which a contract could arise by oral agreement between the parties, it was customary to label all preliminary negotiations as being 'subject to contract', in order to avoid the parties inadvertently becoming bound. Following the 1989 Act, it appeared for a time that this precaution was no longer necessary, but the decision in *Yaxley v Gotts* raised concerns that parties to unsuccessful negotiations might claim to have acquired rights to property under an estoppel or a trust.

These concerns seemed to be justified by the Court of Appeal decision in *Yeoman's Row Management Ltd v Cobbe* [2006] 1 WLR 2964, and although this decision was reversed on appeal by the House of Lords in *Cobbe v Yeoman's Row Management Ltd* [2008] 1 WLR 1752 it is still not impossible that such rights could arise from statements made during negotiations (see 5.5.4.2).

5.5.4.1 *Cobbe v Yeoman's Row*

The case concerned a written agreement between the claimant, Cobbe, an experienced property developer, and the defendant company, which owned a property suitable for development. The parties agreed that Cobbe would undertake the work and expense of obtaining planning permission for this property and, if successful, would buy the property at an agreed price. Both parties knew that this agreement was informal and not legally enforceable, and they intended to finalise the details and enter into a contract for sale at a later stage if planning permission was obtained. The process of obtaining planning permission was lengthy and expensive, and Cobbe spent time and money on the process. He was led to believe that the company regarded itself as bound in honour by the agreement and would not withdraw from it, but the company later decided that it would not honour the agreement and would require a considerably higher price for the property from Cobbe. However, it allowed Cobbe to continue his efforts on its behalf and did not tell him of its change of mind until planning permission had been obtained. Cobbe refused to pay the higher price asked by the company, and claimed to have acquired rights in the property by estoppel and/or a constructive trust.

The trial court's decision in Cobbe's favour was upheld by the Court of Appeal ([2006] 1 WLR 2964), which considered that the circumstances of the case gave rise to an estoppel, despite the fact that both parties knew that the agreement was not binding and that they intended to enter into a contract at a later stage. Mummery LJ emphasised (at para. 67) that :

> The estoppel here did not rest merely on the existence of the...agreement. It was founded on the fact that Mr Cobbe was induced and encouraged to believe that [the company] regarded the agreement as binding in honour and would not withdraw from its terms if [he] obtained planning permission; that Mr Cobbe relied on that inducement and encouragement, and that it was unconscionable for [the company] to rely on its strict legal rights.

The Court of Appeal decision was reversed on appeal by the House of Lords in *Cobbe v Yeoman's Row Management Ltd* [2008] 1 WLR 1752. Reasons for this decision were given in lengthy speeches by Lord Scott (with whom Lords Hoffmann, Brown and Mance agreed) and by Lord Walker (with whom Lord Brown also agreed). We will consider the House of Lords' decision under three headings:

1. the proprietary estoppel claim;
2. the constructive trust claim;
3. was Cobbe entitled to any relief?

1. The proprietary estoppel claim

Their Lordships had a number of reasons for considering that Cobbe had no right arising from proprietary estoppel. These included:

(i) *The failure of the claimant, and the lower courts, to identify the content of the estoppel on which he relied.*

A party who relies on estoppel in claiming rights in another's property is asserting that the owner is prevented from raising as a defence some matter of fact and/or law, which would otherwise defeat the claim. In this case the estoppel relied upon had not been specified in the pleadings nor in the judgments of the lower courts, and their Lordships were unable to identify any elements of the company's response to the claim which it should be estopped from raising (paras. 14–29). Lord Scott emphasised (para.16) that unconscionable behaviour by itself is not sufficient to ground a claim in proprietary estoppel:

> Unconscionability of conduct may well lead to a remedy but...proprietary estoppel cannot be the route to it unless the ingredients for a proprietary estoppel are present.

(ii) *The interest which Cobbe expected to receive was not certain*

Lord Scott reviewed a number of earlier decisions which established that an essential element of proprietary estoppel is the claimant's belief that he has or will acquire a 'certain interest' in the property in question. Here Cobbe could not be said to have an expectation that he would acquire a certain interest. Such expectation as he had was of further negotiations which, if successful, would result in a formal written agreement for such an interest (paras. 18 and 20; and see further 21.5.2).

This requirement of certainty has recently been considered and applied by the Court of Appeal in *Herbert v Doyle* [2010] EWCA Civ 1095.

(iii) *Cobbe knew that the agreement was not enforceable and was not misled by statements that the company was 'bound in honour'*

Lord Walker noted (para. 81):

> [t]he general principle laid down by this House in *Ramsden v Dyson* [[1866] LR 1 HL 129], that conscious reliance on honour alone will not give rise to an estoppel.

His Lordship emphasised the commercial context in which these negotiations took place and the effect this had on Cobbe's expectations and his reliance on the company's representations:

> Mr Cobbe's case seems to me to fail on the simple but fundamental point that, as persons experienced in the property world, both parties knew that there was no legally binding contract, and that either was therefore free to discontinue the negotiations without legal liability—that is liability in equity as well as at law... (para. 91).

In his Lordship's view, Cobbe was running a risk (i.e., by spending time and money on obtaining planning permission without any certainty that the later negotiations would be successful), but he ran that risk 'with his eyes open'. He knew that he had no legally enforceable right arising from the agreement, and was not misled by the company. Although its behaviour in allowing him to continue his efforts to obtain planning permission when it had already decided not to honour the agreement were 'unattractive' they were 'in the eyes of equity... not unconscionable'(para. 92).

2. The constructive trust claim

Writers and judges identify many different types of constructive trusts, among them the 'common intention' trust (relied upon by the Court of Appeal in *Yaxley v Gotts* [2000] Ch 162 and *Kinane v Mackie-Conteh* [2005] EWCA Civ 45) and the 'joint venture' trust on which Cobbe's claim in this case was based. We will tell you more about common intention constructive trusts in Chapter 20, but all you need to know about the joint venture trust is that it may arise when a party acquires property in pursuance of an agreement with another that both of them will use it for their joint purposes, but then appropriates it to his own use. In this case, however, the property had not been acquired for a common purpose, since the company had owned it before making the agreement with Cobbe and, as a result, he could not be said to have an interest under such a trust (paras. 30–36 and 76–78).

3. Was Cobbe entitled to any relief?

Although Cobbe was not able to establish a proprietary interest arising by estoppel or under a constructive trust, it was agreed that the circumstances entitled him to some relief (see para. 2 and the review of possible remedies at paras. 3–4). The value of the company's property had been increased by the planning permission obtained by Cobbe and in those circumstances it could be said that the company should compensate him for its 'unjust enrichment'. However, this did not mean that he was entitled to receive a share of that increased value, although that had been the basis of the award at first instance as confirmed by the Court of Appeal. The property had always had the potential for development, and as Lord Scott put it (at para. 41):

> The planning permission did not create the development potential of the property: it unlocked it.

By analogy, a locksmith who succeeded in opening a cupboard for its owner would have no right to a share of treasure contained in it, although he would be entitled to payment for his services. In the same way, Cobbe could not share the 'treasure', but was entitled to be paid for his work in obtaining planning permission and to recover all related expenses (paras. 44 and 93). In technical terms, Cobbe was entitled to the common law quasi-contractual remedy of a *'quantum meruit'* ('as much as he deserves'), and an order for payment of this was substituted for the original award.

5.5.4.2 Can equitable rights still rise from negotiations?

Undoubtedly the House of Lords' decision in Cobbe has made it almost impossible for a businessman to claim that an estoppel or constructive trust has arisen during commercial negotiations. It is however possible to imagine a scenario (perhaps in an exam question?) in which a first-time buyer, who has no legal or business experience, acts to his detriment in reliance on a representation that the vendor will sell only to him. To guard against this danger, it would still be wise to ensure that negotiations continue to be labelled 'subject to contract' (for a decision which held that use of this phrase defeated an estoppel claim, see *James v Evans* [2003] 3 EGLR 1).

5.6 The next stage: electronic contracts

While courts and practitioners were still working out the implications of the 'new' rules about contracts relating to land, the next change appeared on the horizon. We noted in Chapter 4 that the Land Registry is currently developing systems for the electronic transfer and registration of estates in registered land, and this process will extend to the making of the preliminary contract. Under the developed scheme, the contract will be made electronically, without the need for paper documents, and at the moment of creation the equitable interest arising under the contract will be noted as an encumbrance on the vendor's register of title. (See further 7.15.)

5.7 Effect of the contract: passing of the equitable interest

5.7.1 Purchaser becomes owner in equity

We have already mentioned the equitable maxim that: 'Equity regards as done that which ought to be done' (2.5.3.1). In the case of a contract to sell an estate in land, 'that which ought to be done' is the completion of the sale by the execution of a deed which conveys the legal estate to the purchaser. Therefore, the application of the maxim means that, as soon as there is an enforceable contract, the purchaser is treated in equity as already having received the benefits of a conveyance, and as being the true owner of the property for all equitable purposes.

This gives rise to a position in which there are two 'owners' of the property. The vendor remains the legal owner until the legal estate has been transferred to the purchaser, but the purchaser becomes the equitable owner as soon as the contract is concluded (*Lysaght v Edwards* (1876) 2 ChD 499, 506–10). The result is to make the vendor a trustee of the legal estate and the purchaser a beneficiary owning the equitable interest. The vendor is, however, an unusual trustee because he has more rights than most trustees (e.g., the right to demand the purchase price), and in fact he usually retains personal use of the land until the sale is completed.

5.7.2 Risk passes to the purchaser

As the purchaser becomes the beneficial owner in equity from the date of the contract, the basic rule is that the risk passes to him at that point and he should protect himself by insuring his interest in the property. It is the equitable interest which is the valuable interest in the land and its owner should insure. Indeed, should the house on the property burn down after contract but before conveyance, the purchaser is still bound to complete the purchase and pay over the purchase price (*Paine v Meller* (1801) 6 Ves Jr 349). Again, if the land should become the subject of a compulsory purchase order after contract, the purchaser must still proceed (*Hillingdon Estates Co. v Stonefield Estates Ltd* [1952] Ch 627).

In practice, however, the contract will very probably provide specifically that the risk remains with the seller until the estate is conveyed or transferred, but if this term is not included the purchaser is at risk and should insure.

5.7.3 Notional conversion of property

If you refer back to the brief section on Classification of Property (2.8), you will realise that the process of buying and selling land brings about a significant change in the nature of the property owned by each party. The purchaser, who before completion owned personalty in the form of money, exchanges it for realty, the estate in land, and the vendor makes a corresponding change from realty to personalty. This change of classification is not so significant today, but under the old law it could have far-reaching consequences because, for example, the rules about inheriting realty and personalty were very different. If one of the parties died after the contract had been made but before the estate was conveyed, the question would arise of how his property should be classified and who should inherit it. Was it fair to treat it as being in its original form when it was really subject to a specifically enforceable obligation to convert it into the other kind of property?

Equity's answer to this conundrum was to treat the property as notionally converted from the date of the specifically enforceable contract, so that the purchaser's interest was regarded as realty and that of the vendor as personalty. This notional conversion still occurs today when the contract for sale is concluded, although as we shall see it no longer operates in the case of trusts for sale, the other situation to which it used to apply (see 15.5.1.2 and 17.1.2.5).

5.8 Remedies for breach of contract

Once a contract has been concluded both the parties are legally bound to carry out their parts of the contract. Should either party fail to do this, a number of possible remedies are available to the other. All we will do here is to draw your attention to the range of remedies which are available, emphasising those which are of most significance in the land law context.

5.8.1 Damages

The common law remedy for breach of contract is damages. The usual measure of damages is the loss which the claimant has sustained as a result of non-performance.

Accordingly it is usually possible for the wronged party to claim damages for the loss of the bargain. Liability in damages may arise in a number of ways, for example, through refusal by either party to perform the contract or due to misrepresentation by the vendor. The Law of Property (Miscellaneous Provisions) Act 1989, s. 3 has removed old rules which limited the measure of damages in certain cases and now ordinary contractual principles will be applied.

5.8.2 Specific performance

For many centuries equity has accepted that in cases concerning land the common law remedy of damages is likely to be inadequate. This is because each piece of land is unique in character, and a disappointed purchaser cannot take any damages that he might obtain and buy another identical property (as he might were the subject of the contract a car or a piece of furniture). Accordingly, equity provided the remedy of specific performance, which can be used to compel the defaulting party to carry out his promise. The remedy is available to either party, so a vendor may also use it to force a purchaser to complete (*Hope v Walter* [1900] 1 Ch 257). Being equitable this remedy is discretionary in nature and will be refused if the applicant has 'dirty hands', that is, if he is in some way at fault himself in relation to the obligations under the contract.

As we have already seen, the availability of this remedy underlies a number of equitable interests (see 2.5.3.1 and 2.5.4.2), and accordingly this remedy is of particular importance to your study of land law.

5.8.3 Rescission

Rescission is a remedy which either party may elect to use should the other party break a term of the contract which is a condition precedent. An example of this would be if the vendor were unable to prove that he had good title to the land; the purchaser would then normally choose to rescind the contract. Rescission is an optional remedy and the wronged party can choose to affirm the contract instead and to seek damages for breach. It is only available in cases in which *restitutio in integrum* is possible; that is, it must be possible to return the parties to their original position.

Rescission of a transaction on the grounds of fraud, misrepresentation or undue influence will be considered further in relation to mortgages in Chapter 24.

5.8.4 Rectification

This remedy is available to correct an inaccurate written record of an oral agreement. The remedy is difficult to obtain as the court will require very strong evidence that the document does not record the oral agreement (*Joscelyne v Nissen* [1970] 2 QB 86 at 98), but we have seen an example of its use in *Wright v Robert Leonard Developments Ltd* [1994] NPC 49 to rectify a written agreement from which certain terms had been omitted (see 5.2.2.3).

5.8.5 Injunction

This equitable remedy is available to restrain a threatened breach of contract.

5.8.6 Declaration

In certain cases a declaration of the court on an issue may be a useful remedy, and LPA 1925, s. 49(1) provides for an application to be made to the court by vendor or purchaser. This process might, for example, be used if there were a dispute over the exact meaning of a term in the contract, or over a matter of proof of title.

5.9 Application to 3 Trant Way

We saw in Chapter 4 that Barbara Bell is thinking of buying 3 Trant Way from Victoria Ventnor. We can illustrate the changes in the law produced by the Law of Property (Miscellaneous Provisions) Act 1989, s. 2, by imagining that the two women have discussed the matter, have agreed that Miss Bell should have the property and have settled the price. Miss Bell, thinking she should have the matter set out clearly before she goes to see her solicitor, has written to Miss Ventnor setting out the terms that have been decided upon.

If these facts occurred before 27 September 1989 the parties would have concluded a contract at the time at which they made their oral agreement. However, that agreement would not have been enforceable. When Miss Ventnor received Miss Bell's letter she would have come into possession of a document which satisfied LPA 1925, s. 40, provided that Miss Bell had signed her letter and that it was sufficiently detailed. Thereafter Miss Ventnor could enforce the contract against Miss Bell. Miss Bell could not enforce against Miss Ventnor because Miss Ventnor had not signed a s. 40 memorandum.

If these events occurred on or after 27 September 1989 they would not create a valid contract. The document that exists does not comply with s. 2 of the 1989 Act because it is not signed by both parties. In addition it may only purport to record an existing agreement, whereas s. 2 requires that the contract be made in writing, and accordingly neither party would be bound until this had been done.

FURTHER READING

Formalities for the Contract of Sale, etc. of Land 1987 (Law Com No. 164) Parts IV and V (pp. 12–22).

Howell, 'Informal Conveyances and Section 2 of the Law of Property (Miscellaneous Provisions) Act 1989' [1990] Conv 441.

Steadman v Steadman [1976] AC 536—for further information on part performance; in particular, see speech of Lord Simon at p. 556.

Contractual remedies

Hanbury and Martin, *Modern Equity*, 19th edn., Sweet & Maxwell, 2012, Chapter 24, paras. 24–001–24–015, and 24–035.

Replacing part performance

Dixon, 'The Reach of a Proprietary Estoppel: A Matter of Debate', [2009] 73 Conv 85.

Griffiths, 'Part Performance—Still Trying to Replace the Irreplaceable?' [2002] 66 Conv 216.

McFarlane, 'Proprietary Estoppel and Failed Contractual Negotiations' [2005] 69 Conv 501.

Moore, 'Proprietary Estoppel, Constructive Trusts and s. 2 of the Law of Property (Miscellaneous Provisions) Act 1989' [2000] MLR 912.

Tee, 'A Merry-Go-Round For the Millennium' [2000] CLJ 23.

Thompson, 'Oral Agreements for the Sale of Land' [2000] 64 Conv 245.

Smith, 'Oral Contracts for the Sale of Land: Estoppels and Constructive Trusts' (2000) 116 LQR 11.

Cobbe

Fetherstonhaugh, 'Proprietary estoppel and s. 2—where are we now?' [2009] EG 25 April (No 0916) 98.

Griffiths, 'Proprietary Estoppel—the Pendulum Swings Again?' [2009] 73 Conv 141.

6

Unregistered land

6.1 Introduction: 3 Trant Way

You will remember that Barbara Bell wants to buy 3 Trant Way, the title to which is unregistered (see 4.1.2 and 4.2.3.2). In this chapter, we will look at what Barbara (or, more likely, her professional adviser) will have to do, either before or after exchanging contracts, to ensure that it is safe for her to buy the property.

As we explained in Chapter 4 (4.2.1), Barbara will need to check two things about the property she is planning to buy. She needs to make sure that:

- Victoria Ventnor, the vendor, owns the property she is offering to sell; and
- the property is free from any encumbrances (third-party rights) other than those which have already been revealed.

We will now look at how these two aspects of proving title are dealt with in the unregistered system.

6.2 Ownership of the estate

An owner of an estate in unregistered land proves (or 'deduces') his title to the estate by producing the title deeds to the property. These deeds are the documents by which he and his predecessors have acquired the estate. Typically, they will include documents such as: conveyances on sale; transfers by the personal representatives of a deceased owner to the person entitled under his will or intestacy (technically known as 'assents'); mortgages affecting the property; and trust deeds. From this collection of deeds, it should be possible to show that the estate has been correctly conveyed from one owner to another over the years and that it was last conveyed to ('vested in') the current vendor.

Obviously one cannot hope to produce an unbroken chain of deeds stretching right back to the Middle Ages or beyond, and so the habit began of accepting a title which had been proved for a certain long period of years. The parties to a contract for the sale of an estate may agree specifically on the length of the period which is to apply, but if no special agreement is made a standard provision is implied into the contract. Originally at common law the term implied was that one had to prove the devolution of the title for a period of at least 60 years, but this was reduced progressively and the relevant period is now 15 years by virtue of LPA 1969, s. 23.

In order to deduce title one has to start with a *'good root of title'*. This is a document which records a dealing with the whole legal and equitable interest in the land and which contains nothing to cast any doubts on the validity of the title. Usually a conveyancer will insist on a document which evidences a dealing for value, such as a conveyance on sale or a mortgage. The reason for accepting such a document is that one presumes that the purchaser in that transaction had himself investigated the title for the necessary period and that his taking the conveyance or lending money on mortgage indicates that he found no defect. The document taken as a good root of title will be the first document which is as old or older than the title period, that is, now, the first such document which is at least 15 years old. Accordingly, the good root of title might be a document which is 16, 30 or even 100 years old, depending on the dealings that have occurred in relation to the estate.

Once a good root of title has been shown, the vendor must produce every deed after the root of title which has affected the property. Under the current procedure, the vendor usually proves his title by providing copies or summaries of the documents (an 'epitome of title' or an 'abstract of title') to the purchaser or his solicitor. At a later stage in the process the purchaser or his solicitor will check the copies or summaries provided against the originals.

6.3 Checking for encumbrances

Certain encumbrances may be revealed while the purchaser is checking the vendor's title, but he must in addition make a range of other enquiries and inspections. As we shall see, many third-party rights will bind the purchaser whether he knows of them or not, but there are still some other rights which will not bind him if he can show that he has not discovered them, despite making all the right enquiries (see 6.5.2.2–3). The purpose of making these inquiries is therefore twofold:

- to inform the purchaser about encumbrances; and
- to enable him to override (take free of) certain rights of which he is unaware.

Making such enquiries can be a complicated and time-consuming business, and to help the purchaser the 1925 legislation introduced a system of registering certain encumbrances as land charges. These are now to be discovered by searching the appropriate register. A number of third-party rights, however, did not become registrable land charges and the purchaser has to rely on the old methods for finding out about them.

In the next two sections we look first at land charges and their registration, and then at the legal and equitable interests which are not registrable as land charges.

6.4 Land charges

6.4.1 Nature of land charges

Land charges consist of those interests in land which are set out in LCA 1972 (which replaced LCA 1925). Only interests which are included on the list in the Act are land charges. Interests which appear on the list should be protected by registration on the Land Charges Register, which is one of the five different registers kept by the Land Charges Department (LCA 1972, s. 1) (the other four are described briefly at 6.4.7).

6.4.2 Classes of land charge

Land charges are divided by the 1972 Act into six classes (A to F) and certain of those classes are further subdivided.

6.4.2.1 Classes A and B

These are not particularly common. They consist of charges on land arising under statutory provisions.

6.4.2.2 Class C

This class is subdivided into four subclasses. Before considering these in detail it is important to note that rights of a type which fall within this class are registrable as land charges only if they were created on or after 1 January 1926 (the date upon which the 1925 legislation came into force) or, more unusually, if the right was created before that date but was itself transferred to some other holder at a later time (LCA 1972, s. 2(8)).

(1) *Class C(i), the puisne mortgage* The puisne mortgage is defined in LCA 1972, s. 2(4), as a legal mortgage which 'is not secured by a deposit of documents relating to the legal estate affected'.

When lending money on the security of a mortgage, a mortgagee will normally take the deeds to the property away from the estate owner in order to prevent him dealing further with the property. If a legal mortgagee does take the deeds in this way, his mortgage is *not* a registrable land charge. It is supposed not to require registration, because the absence of the deeds is sufficient to alert any prospective purchaser to the possible existence of the mortgage. (As noted at 4.2.3.2, the creation of this type of mortgage will normally lead to the compulsory registration of the title to the legal estate which is subject to that mortgage.)

If the mortgagee does not take the deeds, the mortgage is a puisne mortgage and should be registered as a land charge. The puisne mortgage is a slightly unusual land charge because it is a legal interest in land, whilst most land charges are equitable or statutory interests.

(2) *Class C(ii), limited owner's charge* This is a land charge which arises when a tenant for life or statutory owner under the SLA 1925 (someone who has only a limited interest in the property—see Chapter 18), or another person with a similar interest, has paid inheritance tax under the Inheritance Tax Act 1984. Such persons may have a right to charge the repayment of the tax against the land (i.e., to recover from the rents and profits of the land money which they have paid out of their own pockets) and that right is a land charge.

(3) *Class C(iii), general equitable charge* This class of land charge forms a kind of 'dustbin' category. Into this class fall all equitable charges on property which are not specifically excluded from Class C(iii) by the Act itself. Charges excluded in this way, and therefore *not registrable* as land charges include:

- any charge which is secured by a deposit of documents relating to the legal estate affected (this means that an equitable mortgagee who does not have the title deeds to the property can register a C(iii) land charge, but an equitable mortgagee who has the deeds cannot do so);
- interests arising under trusts (i.e., a beneficiary under a trust of land cannot register his interest as a land charge);
- any charge which falls into another class of land charge.

(4) *Class C(iv), estate contract* An estate contract is any contract to convey or create a legal estate in land, or any option to purchase a legal estate or any right of pre-emption in respect of a legal estate (a right of first refusal). Thus in addition to contracts for the conveyance of a fee simple, and contracts for the grant or assignment of a lease, this class of land charges includes options to purchase the fee simple, and options contained in leases (such as options for renewal (*Phillips v Mobil Oil Co. Ltd* [1989] 1 WLR 888) and for the purchase of the reversion by the tenant).

Various statutes have added to this category of land charges: for example, the Landlord and Tenant (Covenants) Act 1995, s. 20(6), provides that a request for an overriding lease (explained in 12.4.2.3) may be registered under the LCA 1972 as if it were an estate contract.

Even where an option has been registered as a Class C(iv) land charge, it has been suggested that there is a need for further registration of an estate contract after notice has been given to exercise the option. However, it was held in *Armstrong and Holmes Ltd* v *Holmes* [1993] 1 WLR 1482 that there is no need for further registration: the registration of the option gives sufficient warning to any other prospective purchaser of the estate, and any conveyance to such a purchaser will be subject to the estate contract which arises from the option.

6.4.2.3 Class D

Class D is divided into three subclasses.

(1) *Class D(i), Inland Revenue charge* This is a land charge which arises in favour of the Inland Revenue when a liability to pay inheritance tax in respect of land has not been discharged.

(2) *Class D(ii), restrictive covenants* This class comprises any covenants or agreements which are restrictive of the user of land (other than those between landlord and tenant) and which were created on or after 1 January 1926 (at which date the 1925 property legislation came into force). An example would be a covenant, entered into in 1940, not to keep pigs on a particular property. The same covenant would not be a registrable land charge had it been created in 1920.

(3) *Class D(iii), equitable easements* This class consists of any easements, rights or privileges affecting land which were created on or after 1 January 1926, and which are equitable only. Equitable profits à prendre fall within this definition. It should be noted that *legal* easements or profits are not registrable as land charges.

6.4.2.4 Class E

These are very rare and consist of annuities created before 1926 and which are not registered on the register of annuities (which is one of the five registers maintained under the LCA).

6.4.2.5 Class F

This class consists of 'home rights' which were first created by the Matrimonial Homes Act 1967 and are now contained in the Family Law Act 1996 (as amended by the Civil Partnership Act 2004). These rights exist only in relation to couples who are legally married and to civil partners, and give a spouse or civil partner, who is not a co-owner of the matrimonial home, the right to occupy the home owned by the other spouse or civil partner. This right is considered in more detail at 27.3.3.1.

While all these classes of charge are important to a purchaser, who may find that the property which he is purchasing is less attractive or perhaps totally valueless to him because it is subject to a land charge, the ones that you will meet most commonly in your study of land law are classes C(i), (iii) and (iv), D(ii) and (iii) and F, and you should pay particular attention to these.

6.4.3 Registration of land charges

The application to register a land charge is made by the person who claims that right.

Registration is not made against the address of the property, but against the name of the person who was the estate owner at the date that the charge was created. This choice of method for registration has caused a number of problems with the system.

6.4.3.1 Incorrect names

It is not uncommon for an estate owner to be known by a nickname or abbreviated name. If a registration is made against an incorrect version of a person's name, a search made against the true name may not reveal the entry. Or it may be that the registration has been made correctly but that the searcher searches an incorrect name. Once again such a search may well not reveal the relevant entry. These problems have produced a certain amount of litigation, and examples are to be found in such cases as *Diligent Finance Ltd v Alleyne* (1972) 23 P&CR 346 and *Oak Co-operative Building Society v Blackburn* [1968] Ch 730. Essentially, in order to be safe, the person making a search has to be certain of using full correct names.

6.4.3.2 Searching against the names of all past estate owners

When an estate changes hands, the existing registrations of land charges are not altered but remain against the name of the original estate owner. Accordingly it is not sufficient to make a search simply against the name of the current estate owner. To be certain of finding all registered charges one must search against the names of all the estate owners since 1925. This is, however, impractical in most cases (though some conveyancers will still ask for the full list of names), because in proving his title a vendor is only obliged to go back to a good root of title, which, as we have seen above, may be only 15 years old.

The difficulties which this might cause may be illustrated by referring back to the title to 3 Trant Way. The history of No. 3 since 1925 has been as follows:

1926 The estate owner at the date at which the 1925 legislation came into force was Bill Brie.
1928 Land charge class D(ii) registered against the name Bill Brie.

1956 Bill Brie sold legal estate to Cathy Camembert.
1963 Land charge class D(iii) registered against the name Cathy Camembert.
1989 Cathy Camembert sold legal estate to Victoria Ventnor.
1989 Land charge class C(i) registered against the name Victoria Ventnor.

You will remember that Barbara Bell is considering buying 3 Trant Way from Victoria Ventnor. If Miss Bell agrees to purchase the estate, Miss Ventnor will produce the conveyance made to her by Cathy Camembert in April 1989 as the good root of title, but will not be required to produce any of the earlier deeds. Miss Bell will already know the name of her vendor, Victoria Ventnor, and will learn of Cathy Camembert from the 1989 conveyance. If she makes land charges searches against these names, she will discover the charges registered in 1963 and 1989. However, she will have no means of knowing that the property was once owned by Bill Brie and so will not discover the class D(ii) land charge registered in 1928. This land charge is a restrictive covenant and it is quite likely that it will still be capable of enforcement by a neighbouring landowner (see Chapter 26). Unfortunately for Barbara Bell, she will be deemed to have notice of this charge and will therefore still be bound by it (LPA 1925, s. 198). This is so even though Barbara had no means of discovering the registration.

This difficulty in the system was not originally envisaged as being of importance, because in 1926 the statutory title period was 30 years and it was expected that the registered title system, which does not use the Land Charges Register, would be generally in force quite quickly. Delays in the introduction of the registered land system and the reduction of the title period to 15 years exacerbated the problem. As a result in 1969 the law was amended by s. 25 of the LPA 1969, which provides that, should a purchaser of an estate or interest in the land suffer loss due to the existence of a registered land charge prior to the root of title, he may obtain compensation from a central fund administered by the Chief Land Registrar.

Now that we are some years on from this development, it is interesting to note that there has been very little call for compensation (one claim in the first 21 years following the introduction of the scheme: Land Registry Annual Report 1989–90, p. 11). It seems that the supposed difficulties were more apparent than real. Many land charges (such as mortgages) have a relatively short life, and are unlikely to be effective outside the search period. In the case of interests which may last for longer (such as rights under restrictive covenants), there are several ways in which a prospective purchaser may learn of them from the title deeds or associated papers. Thus conveyances within the period the purchaser is searching may well 'recite' previous dealings with the land and give details of the earlier conveyances which created the encumbrance. There is also the possibility of the purchaser having access to earlier land charge search certificates, which may be kept with the title deeds. It seems that in practice the purchaser does not often find himself bound by an active land charge of which he was not aware.

6.4.4 Effect of registration

Registering a right as a land charge ensures that anyone taking a later estate or interest in the land (most importantly, any purchaser of the legal estate) will take it subject to that right. This result is brought about by s. 198(1) of the LPA 1925 which provides that:

> The registration of any instrument or matter under the provisions of the Land Charges Act,... shall be deemed to constitute actual notice of such instrument or matter.

This refers back to the old equitable doctrine of notice (see 2.6.3), and in effect introduces a form of 'statutory notice'.

It should be noticed, however, that the fact that a charge appears on the register does not in any way guarantee that it is an effective charge, for under the Land Charges Rules 1974, r. 22, the Registrar is not concerned to check the accuracy of an application to register a charge. It is also possible that a charge may have been effective originally but is no longer so. Thus it may be that a purchaser can be compelled to continue with a purchase even though his searches reveal registered charges. All that is necessary is that the vendor should show that the apparent encumbrance does not in fact affect his title (*Bull v Hutchens* (1863) 32 Beav 615).

6.4.4.1 Searches

The practical consequence of LPA 1925, s. 198, is to ensure that a careful purchaser makes a search of the Land Charges Register. Such searches may be made at any time and they do not require the prior consent of the current estate owner. The register is a public record, which is open to anyone who is prepared to pay the search fee (LCA 1972, s. 9). On receipt of a search requisition a search is made and the result is communicated to the searcher in the form of a search certificate.

6.4.5 Effect of non-registration of a land charge

In general terms, failure to register a land charge may mean that the person entitled to it is unable to enforce it against a later purchaser for value. For the purposes of the Act, the term 'purchaser' is widely defined (s. 17(1)), so that it includes not only a person who buys a freehold estate, but also mortgagees, lessees and the acquirers of other interests, both legal and equitable. The statutory rules on non-registration are very detailed (see below), but the general policy is that, in order to bind a purchaser, the land charge must be registered before completion (i.e. the point at which the purchaser pays the money and receives the estate or interest), and that it cannot be enforced against him if it is not so registered.

We will now look at the provisions in more detail, and you will see that basically there are two rules: one for land charges of classes A, B, C(i), (ii) and (iii) and F; and another for land charges of classes C(iv) and D(i), (ii) and (iii).

6.4.5.1 Classes A, B, C(i)–(iii) and F

The general rule with these land charges (with slight variations for class A) is that unless they are registered before completion they cannot be enforced against a purchaser for valuable consideration of an estate in the land or of any interest in the land (LCA 1972, ss. 4(2)(5) and (8) and 17(1)).

Thus even the purchaser of an equitable interest in the property can take an interest free from an unregistered charge. For example, if X has a puisne mortgage (C(i)) over Blackacre, which he has failed to register, and later the fee simple owner grants an equitable mortgage to Y, Y will take free of X's rights, or in other words, Y's rights will take priority over X's. If the estate has to be sold to pay back the sums due under the mortgages, the debt owed to Y will be paid first and X may find that there is not enough money to pay him in full (see Chapter 24).

6.4.5.2 Classes C(iv) and D(i)–(iii)

The rule to be applied to these land charges is that unless they are registered before completion they cannot be enforced against the purchaser of a legal estate for money or money's worth (LCA 1972, s. 4(6)). This is the only person who can take the land free of the charge and thus the purchaser of any lesser interest in the property will still be bound by the charge. Thus if an estate contract (C(iv)) has not been registered and later an equitable mortgage is created by the fee simple owner the estate contract can be enforced against the equitable mortgagee: the equitable mortgagee is not the purchaser of a legal estate.

For an example of an unregistered option being enforceable against a later purchaser of an equitable interest, see the facts of *Sainsbury's Supermarkets Ltd v Olympia Homes Ltd* [2006] 1 P&CR 17, which we describe in 7.4.1.3.

6.4.5.3 What is the difference between a 'purchaser for value' and a 'purchaser for money or money's worth'?

This question arises because s. 4(5) refers simply to a 'purchaser', who is defined in s. 17(1) as a 'purchaser for value', while s. 4(6) speaks of a 'purchaser for money or money's worth'.

'Purchaser for value' is the wider term, and includes not only purchasers who give money or money's worth but also those who give consideration of a sort which cannot be computed in financial terms. An example of non-financial consideration would be found in an agreement to convey land in consideration of marriage or the formation of a civil partnership. The purchaser would be regarded as giving valuable consideration (see LPA 1925, s. 205(1)(xxi), as amended by the Civil Partnership Act 2004) but not money or money's worth, since it is not possible to put a financial valuation on these relationships. Such non-pecuniary consideration is relatively rare today, and most purchases of the legal estate are likely to be for money or money's worth.

6.4.5.4 Judicial interpretation of rules about unregistered land charges

In considering the rules about non-registration of land charges, you need to be aware that:

- the courts will not enquire into the adequacy of the consideration given by the purchaser;
- the fact that a purchaser knew about an unregistered land charge does not make it enforceable against him.

Both these points are illustrated in the House of Lords' decision in *Midland Bank Trust Co. Ltd v Green* [1981] AC 513. Here a father had granted his son an option to purchase a farm for £22,500. This agreement came within the definition of estate contract given in LCA 1972, s. 2(4)(iv), and so was registrable as a land charge. The son failed to register his option. Later his father wished to avoid carrying through his promise and, acting on advice, he conveyed the legal estate in the property to his wife for £500. At the date of this conveyance the farm was actually worth £40,000. In the Court of Appeal, it was held that the sale at such a considerable undervalue was not a sale for 'money or money's worth'. However, the House of Lords reversed this decision, holding that the unregistered land charge was unenforceable against the purchaser, and relying on the contractual rule that the court will not enquire into the adequacy of consideration, as long as the consideration is real. It would therefore appear that a sale for 1p would satisfy s. 4(6), providing that it was not made fraudulently.

Midland Bank Trust Co. Ltd v Green also illustrates the second important point: that a purchaser can take an estate free of an unregistered land charge even if he knows that the land charge exists. It was clear that the mother had known about her son's interest, but she was still able to take the estate free of it because he had not registered it.

6.4.5.5 Comparison with registered land

When you read Chapter 7 on registered land you will see that the result in *Midland Bank Trust Co. Ltd v Green* would have been very different if the title to the farm had been registered. It appears that the son was in actual occupation of the property and that his interest was known to his mother at the time of her purchase. Consequently, in the registered system, he could have claimed that his option was an overriding interest under s. 70(1)(g) of LRA 1925 (the forerunner of LRA 2002, Sch. 3, para. 2) and therefore binding on the purchaser.

A similar illustration of the difference between the two systems is to be found in *Lloyds Bank plc v Carrick* [1996] 4 All ER 630. Here, the defendant had sold her house on her husband's death, paid the proceeds to her brother-in-law and moved into a maisonette owned by him, on the understanding that it would become hers. In 1982, when those events occurred, this agreement, supported by part performance, was sufficient to satisfy the requirements of LPA 1925, s. 40 (see 5.3.2.4), and accordingly there was an enforceable contract between the two parties. The defendant lived in the property for a number of years; the legal estate was never conveyed to her, and predictably she did not protect her position by registering a land charge. During this time her brother-in-law mortgaged the property, without her knowledge, as security for his own debts, and when he defaulted on the repayments, the bank sought possession of the property. The defendant argued that her brother-in-law, having received full payment for the maisonette, held the legal estate in it as a bare trustee for her, and that her interest under this trust was not a registrable land charge and depended on notice (see 2.6.3). The Court of Appeal, however, rejected this argument, as well as others based on constructive trusts and proprietary estoppel (see Chapters 20 and 21), holding that her rights arose from the contract with her brother-in-law. Failure to protect that contract by registration as a class C(iv) land charge meant that it was void against the bank, which accordingly was entitled to enforce its security and take possession.

In his judgment Morritt LJ drew attention to the fact that the result would have been very different if title to the maisonette had been registered: the defendant was in actual occupation of the property and, as a result, her right under the estate contract would have been an overriding interest under LRA 1925, s. 70(1(g). However, the judge took the view that it was for Parliament, not the courts, to decide whether this distinction between registered and unregistered land should continue.

6.4.5.6 Right still enforceable against original owner

Although the effect of non-registration is that the charge cannot be enforced against the new owner of the estate, the right does still remain enforceable against the original owner who granted it. This may not be so satisfactory for the person entitled; for instance, if he has failed to register an equitable right of way (D(iii)) he will no longer be able to use the right over the land, but he may well have a remedy in contract against the original owner and may be able to recover compensation. This is so even though it is he who is really at fault, through failing to register his land charge.

6.4.6 Importance of obtaining a search certificate

The certificate which shows the result of a search of the Land Charges Register serves a dual purpose for the prospective purchaser. He learns from it of the registered land charges which will bind him if he proceeds with the purchase, but, almost more important, he can rely on it where necessary to prove non-registration, since s. 10(4) provides that the certificate shall be conclusive in favour of the purchaser. For this reason, it is common for a purchaser to make two searches of the register, first during his investigation of title, to discover what encumbrances bind the property, and again just before completion to ensure that nothing new has been registered since his earlier search and to show the state of the register at completion.

For practical purposes, a system of priority notices operates, so that a purchaser can search the register up to 15 days before he completes the transaction, and will then take free of any land charges registered between that search and completion. (You are unlikely to need much knowledge of this procedure, which is more a matter of conveyancing than of land law, but if you want details you will find them in LCA 1972, s. 11(5) and (6).)

6.4.7 Other registers maintained by the Land Charges Department

The other four registers maintained under LCA 1972, s. 1 contain registrations of: petitions in bankruptcy and pending actions relating to land; certain annuities created before 1926; court orders relating to land, and writs issued for the purpose of enforcing them; and deeds of arrangement between bankrupts and their creditors which affect land.

6.5 Legal and equitable interests which are not land charges

6.5.1 Enforcement of legal interests

A purchaser will automatically be bound by all legal interests in the land which are not land charges (and, as we have seen, most legal interests are not on the land charges list). This rule is usually expressed by saying that 'Legal rights are good against the world'. The reason for this rule is that if common law recognised an interest in the land it was regarded as a right *in rem* ('in the thing') which therefore bound anyone who purchased an estate or interest in the burdened land.

Thus the purchaser will be bound, for example, by rights such as legal easements and legal leases. Similarly if an estate is subject to a legal mortgage which is protected by a deposit of the title deeds, then anyone who buys the estate will buy it subject to the mortgage. (In practice the purchaser would insist that the vendor repay the debt on completion of the sale so that the mortgage is discharged and the purchaser is not affected by it; but if the purchaser did not know about the mortgage, and so did not require that this be done, it would bind him.)

6.5.2 Enforcement of equitable interests against the purchaser of the legal estate

We have already explained in Chapter 2 that the Court of Chancery developed the rule that equitable interests in land bound everyone who took the land except the bona fide purchaser of the legal estate without notice (see 2.6.3). In practice, the doctrine of notice imposed a heavy burden on the purchaser, who had to make exhaustive enquiries in order to avoid being said to have constructive notice of equitable rights which he had failed to discover. A major aim of the 1925 legislation, and of the statutory reforms which preceded it, was to facilitate the sale of land and to make the whole process less onerous for the purchaser. For this purpose, two new statutory procedures were introduced, which had the effect of making considerable inroads into the doctrine of notice.

6.5.2.1 Reducing the dangers of the doctrine of notice

The first procedure was that of land charge registration, which we have already discussed. Registration was suitable for equitable rights such as restrictive covenants and easements, which must continue to bind the land if they are to benefit those entitled to them. Land charge registration provides a relatively straightforward method by which a prospective purchaser can discover the existence of rights on the register, while taking free of any which do not appear there, and questions of constructive notice are no longer relevant.

The second procedure is known as 'overreaching'. It was introduced to facilitate the sale of trust property, which previously could be sold only with the consent of all the beneficiaries and which, therefore, presented considerable dangers to a purchaser. The new procedure was based on the idea that the rights of beneficiaries under a trust could be satisfied by money payments (of income or capital), and that they did not need to retain their old rights against the land.

Overreaching

The process was introduced by a series of Acts, culminating in the 1925 legislation (see LPA 1925, s. 2(1)). Under the overreaching procedure, subject to certain safeguards, the interests of beneficiaries under a trust involving land can be lifted from the trust property on its sale, and attached instead to the money paid by the purchaser (i.e., to the capital sum arising from the sale). Depending on the terms of the trust, the trustees will then either distribute the capital money among the beneficiaries, or will invest it so as to provide income for them.

The beneficiaries' interests are safeguarded in this process (in theory although not always in practice) by the statutory provision that any capital money arising must be paid to two trustees, or to a trust corporation. In no circumstances should the money be paid to only one trustee or to the beneficiaries. Provided this requirement is satisfied, the purchaser takes the legal estate free of the beneficiaries' interests, even if he has actual notice of them. However, if the requirements relating to the payment of capital money are not satisfied, the beneficiaries' interests are not overreached, and the purchaser will take subject to them, unless he can prove that he did not have notice of them.

We will discuss this process and the statutory provisions relating to it in more detail at 17.9.2.

6.5.2.2 Doctrine of notice today

For purchasers of unregistered land the significance of the notice rules was reduced considerably by the 1925 reforms. However, the doctrine still applies to the following equitable rights:

- rights excluded from registration as land charges, such as pre-1926 restrictive covenants and equitable easements, and restrictive covenants made between landlord and tenant (see 6.4.2.2–3);
- beneficiaries' rights under a trust which have not been overreached because the proper procedures were not followed (see above); and
- equitable rights which had not been identified by the courts at the time of the 1925 legislation and so are not included in the scheme of land charge registration.

These rights include, for example, rights arising from estoppel (see *Ives (E.R.) Investment Ltd v High* [1967] 2 QB 379, which we will consider further at 23.3.4.1) and certain rights of entry (*Poster v Slough Estates Ltd* [1968] 1 WLR 1515 and *Shiloh Spinners Ltd v Harding* [1973] AC 691).

In consequence, it remains essential for a purchaser of unregistered land to make thorough searches and enquiries if he is to avoid being held to have constructive notice of any of these equitable rights.

6.5.2.3 What searches must a purchaser make to avoid constructive notice?

The searches required of the purchaser are of two types: first, he must investigate the vendor's title correctly by examining the title deeds, and secondly, he must inspect the land itself.

- *Constructive notice of matters revealed by examination of deeds.* A purchaser is bound by any right which he would have discovered had he inspected the vendor's title deeds for the statutory period (e.g., *Worthington v Morgan* (1849) 16 Sim 547, in which no investigation was made). As a result of this rule, it is common for the owners of equitable interests to insist that a note of their rights is made on the deeds (e.g., written on the back of a deed) so that future purchasers will have actual notice of their rights if they read the deeds and constructive notice if they omit to do so.
- *Constructive notice of matters revealed by inspection of land.* The rule that the purchaser must also inspect the land is commonly called the 'rule in *Hunt v Luck*'. In the case of *Hunt v Luck* [1902] 1 Ch 428, a purchaser was held to have notice of all the rights of a tenant who was in occupation of the land, but not of the rights of the landlord from whom the tenant derived his title. As a result, a purchaser runs the risk of having constructive notice of any rights belonging to anyone in occupation, and should ensure that enquiries are made of any such person.

Occupation by the owner's spouse

There used to be some uncertainty about the application of the rule in *Hunt v Luck* to property occupied by married couples. It has become increasingly common over the last 50 years for a wife to contribute to the cost of acquiring the matrimonial home. In consequence, she may have an equitable interest in the property under an implied trust, even though the legal estate is vested only in her husband (see 2.5.2). At first, however, purchasers did not always think it necessary to enquire whether wives had such an interest. This attitude was accepted in *Caunce v Caunce* [1969] 1 WLR 286, in which it was held that a purchaser was entitled to presume that a wife lived in the property because of her relationship with the estate owner, and that her presence did not put the purchaser of the estate upon notice. However, this approach was heavily criticised by the House of Lords in the registered land case of *Williams & Glyn's Bank Ltd v Boland* [1981] AC 487 at p. 508 (see 7.10.4.6), and in *Kingsnorth Finance Co. Ltd v Tizard* [1986] 1 WLR 783 a wife's occupation of unregistered land was regarded as being separate from that of her husband. Accordingly, the rule in *Caunce v Caunce* should today be regarded as of historical interest only, marking the enormous change in social attitudes which has taken place since 1969.

Kingsnorth Finance Co. Ltd v Tizard is a very interesting case and well worth noting in detail. The facts were that Mrs Tizard had contributed to the purchase price of the original matrimonial home. She therefore had a beneficial interest, under an implied trust, both in that property and in a later house which was bought with the proceeds of sale from the first home, and conveyed into the sole name of her husband. Accordingly

Mr Tizard held the property in trust for himself and his wife. After some years the marriage failed, and the wife left the matrimonial home, but lived nearby and came in each day to care for the children, leaving some clothes and other possessions at the house. Subsequently the husband mortgaged the property without his wife's knowledge, having arranged for the preliminary inspection by the mortgagee's agent to be carried out in her absence. When the mortgage repayments fell into arrears, the mortgagee sought to enforce its security and was opposed by Mrs Tizard, who claimed that the mortgagee had had constructive notice of her beneficial interest in the property and therefore took subject to her rights.

The court held that Mrs Tizard had been in occupation of the property at the date at which the agent made his inspection and later when the charge was granted. It was said that occupation need not be exclusive, continuous or uninterrupted. The court did, however, agree that someone inspecting property under the rule in *Hunt v Luck* was not obliged to go as far as opening drawers or hunting in cupboards (which, if done, would have revealed the wife's possessions). However, since the agent had been told of the recent separation and the fact that Mrs Tizard still lived in the area, the court considered that the mortgagee was put on notice and should have made further enquiries. The inspection of the property at a pre-arranged date did not amount to making sufficient enquiry.

As a result the mortgagee, having constructive notice, took its legal interest in the property subject to Mrs Tizard's equitable rights as a beneficiary under the trust. This meant that the mortgagee could enforce its rights only against the husband's share, rather than against the whole property. In these circumstances Mrs Tizard agreed that the house should be sold and the proceeds divided between herself and the mortgagee, in proportion to their respective interests in the property. (For similar cases in which the court has ordered sale against the wishes of the beneficiary, see 17.8.5.)

The *Tizard* case, though only a first-instance decision, is of considerable importance because it widens the concept of occupation beyond its previously presumed limits. The judgment is helpful in giving a detailed indication of the type of investigation which will be needed if a buyer or mortgagee is to be safe from hidden rights, and certainly suggests that in cases in which it is known that a vendor or mortgagor is married it is advisable to insist on obtaining written approval from his or her spouse.

6.5.2.4 Effect of purchase without notice

As we have already seen, the bona fide purchaser for value of the legal estate will take free of any equitable interests of which he does not have notice. An important consequence of this is that anyone who later acquires the legal estate from that purchaser also takes free of the equitable interest, even if he actually knows about it (*Wilkes v Spooner* [1911] 2 KB 473).

Although the equitable interest cannot be enforced against the purchaser without notice or against his successor, it does remain enforceable against the person who originally was subject to it (such as a trustee or a person who created the equitable right), but, as we have noted in the case of unregistered land charges (see 6.4.5.6), the only remedy available is likely to be damages for breach of contract or, where appropriate, an action for breach of trust.

6.5.3 Enforcement of equitable interests against later acquirers of equitable interests

Thus far we have only considered the position of those who intend to buy a legal estate and who, if they do so, will take the property free of those equitable interests (which are not land charges) of which they have no notice, or which are overreached on sale. However, it is possible for someone to acquire only an equitable interest in the property, for example, by entering into a contract to buy the legal estate but never taking a conveyance of the legal estate. In such a case the intending purchaser has an equitable right to the land under the contract (see 5.7.1) and the question then arises of the extent to which he is bound by pre-existing equitable interests.

Obviously the rule protecting the bona fide purchaser of the legal estate does not protect a purchaser who acquires only an equitable interest in the property. In this case the rule which applies to interests in unregistered land is:

Where the equities are equal the first in time prevails.

Thus a later acquirer of an equitable interest will take priority over an earlier equitable interest only where the 'equities' are not equal. This will only arise if the owner of the earlier equitable interest has been involved in a fraud on the later acquirer or possibly if the earlier equitable owner has been grossly negligent about protecting his interests (see further on this, in relation to mortgages of unregistered land, Chapter 24).

6.6 Summary of searches to be made in relation to unregistered land

To summarise what we have told you so far, Barbara Bell (or her adviser) must make the following enquiries in respect of 3 Trant Way, in order to protect herself:

- a local land charges search (see 4.3.2.1);
- a land charges search against the names of all the estate owners during the title period;
- a thorough examination of the title deeds from the root of title onwards;
- an investigation of the occupancy of the land including questioning any occupants as to their rights.

6.7 The conveyance

Once Barbara Bell is satisfied with her enquiries and both parties have made the necessary arrangements, the time will have arrived for the completion of the transaction. She will pay the balance of the purchase price, provided either from her own resources or with money borrowed from a lender, to whom she will mortgage her newly acquired property. Victoria Ventnor, the vendor, will execute the deed (required by s. 52(1) of the LPA 1925), which will convey the legal estate to Barbara. An example of a very simple conveyance of 3 Trant Way is given at p. 82. Usually these documents are far longer and decidedly more complex than this example.

At the time of the conveyance the vendor will hand to the purchaser the title deeds to the property (unless he is selling only part of the land covered by the deeds, in which case the vendor will give the purchaser an undertaking to produce the deeds should

THIS CONVEYANCE is made the day of

BETWEEN VICTORIA VENTNOR of 3 Trant Way Mousehole in the County of Stilton ("the vendor") of the one part and BARBARA BELL of Oak Tree Cottage Elmdale in the County of Stilton ("the purchaser") of the other part.

WHEREAS the vendor is seised of the property hereinafter described for an estate in fee simple in possession free from incumbrances and has agreed with the purchaser for the sale thereof to her at a price of three hundred and sixty thousand pounds (£360,000).

NOW THIS DEED WITNESSETH as follows:

In consideration of the sum of three hundred and sixty thousand pounds (£360,000) paid by the purchaser to the vendor (the receipt whereof the vendor hereby acknowledges) the vendor with full title guarantee hereby conveys unto the purchaser all that piece or parcel of land known as 3 Trant Way Mousehole in the County of Stilton which for the purposes of identification only is shown and delineated in red on the plan attached hereto **TO HOLD** the same unto the purchaser in fee simple.

IN WITNESS of which the vendor has executed this deed in the presence of the attesting witness the day and year first before written.

Signed and delivered }
as a deed by the said }
VICTORIA VENTNOR }
in the presence of }

Victoria Ventnor

Julia Possum

JULIA POSSUM
198 THE HIGH STREET,
MOUSEHOLE,
STILTON

I.T. CONSULTANT

the purchaser ever require them). The purchaser (or probably his legal adviser) should, of course, check the deeds to ensure that the copies that he has previously seen are true copies of the original documents.

6.8 Application for first registration

Although Barbara is now the legal owner of No. 3, there is still one more thing she must do. You will remember that the system of registered title was finally extended to all parts of the country (including Stilton) in 1990, and so all property, wherever situated, will now be in an area of compulsory registration. In consequence, any new owner who has taken an estate under the unregistered system of conveyancing must apply to the Land Registry for first registration as registered proprietor.

In order to compel purchasers to apply for first registration, LRA 2002, ss. 6 and 7 provide that if a registration is not made within two months of the date of the conveyance that conveyance shall become void, with the result that the legal estate that has been conveyed to the purchaser will revert to the vendor, who will hold it on a bare trust for the purchaser.

Thus it is essential that once Barbara Bell has taken the conveyance of the legal estate in 3 Trant Way, she applies for first registration of her title without delay and we will see what this involves in the next chapter.

FURTHER READING

Cheshire and Burn, *Cheshire and Burn's Law of Real Property*, 18th edn., pp. 83–91 (doctrine of notice).

Hanbury and Martin, *Modern Equity*, 19th edn., Sweet & Maxwell, 2012, paras. 1-039–1-046 (doctrine of notice).

Harpum, 'Purchasers With Notice of Unregistered Land Charges' [1981] CLJ 213.

Thompson, 'The Purchaser as Private Detective' [1986] Conv 283.

Thompson, 'The Widow's Plight' [1996] Conv 295.

Yates, 'The Protection of Equitable Interests Under the 1925 Legislation' (1974) 37 MLR 87.

7

Registered land

7.1 Introduction

You may remember from previous chapters that the LRA 1925, which governed the system of registered land, was repealed and replaced by the Land Registration Act 2002 ('LRA 2002'), which in the main came into force on 13 October 2003. In this chapter we will concentrate on the terms of the new Act and the rules made under it (Land Registration Rules 2003 (SI 2003/1417) as amended ('LRR 2003')), and unless otherwise stated references in this chapter are to sections of LRA 2002. For convenience we will refer to the 'old' and 'new' systems, but we want to emphasise at the outset that although the old Act is completely repealed and replaced, the new Act is careful to maintain the continuity of the registered title system. In other words, it is not a question of abolishing one system and replacing it with another, but rather of continuing and improving the existing system.

7.2 Need for reform

7.2.1 Aim of registration

When compulsory title registration was introduced by LRA 1925, the aim of its creators was to simplify conveyancing by placing all the essential information about an estate in land on a register. Thereafter an intending purchaser would only need to look at the register in order to discover all that he needed to know about the property, including proof of ownership of the estate in the land and details of any rights which third parties had in respect of it. Instead of producing a bundle of title deeds in order to prove his title to the land, a vendor would simply have to produce a copy of the details on the register which the purchaser would check against the register. In theory this is an excellent idea, and indeed is still the aim of modern title registration, but as we will see the original system was subject to various problems.

7.2.2 Proposals for reform

These were developed by a joint working party of the Law Commission and the Land Registry ('the working party'). It issued a consultative document in 1998, followed in 2001 by a report with a draft Bill which, with some amendments, was subsequently enacted as the LRA 2002. In the course of this chapter we occasionally refer to these documents (describing them as 'the Consultative Document' and 'the Report') and references for both of them are given in the Further Reading section at the end of this chapter. Although you might think that by now they would be only of historic interest, it can be helpful to refer to them for explanation of sections of the Act which may appear confusing (so long as you remember that a few of the provisions they describe did not survive the legislative process and so do not appear in the Act).

The working party identified a number of problems with the existing system. A major difficulty arose from a category of rights known as 'overriding interests'. As we mentioned above, the original notion of land registration was that the register would provide a complete record of title, so that the purchaser would be able to buy in reliance on it with the minimum of other enquiries or inspections. However, it was thought necessary to accept that certain third-party interests should continue to bind the estate and be enforceable against the purchaser without appearing on the register. These rights were described as 'overriding interests', and their existence made it impossible to rely solely on the register. As defined by LRA 1925, s. 70(1), certain categories of overriding interests constituted a real risk to purchasers and meant that they still had to undertake a range of enquiries and inspections, in addition to checking the register. The working party proposed a reduction and redefinition of overriding interests, although it accepted that retaining some of them was unavoidable.

There was also a need to deal with a long-standing difficulty, which stemmed from the original belief that registration of title was merely a matter of conveyancing machinery. As a result, it was thought that the substantive law relating to the ownership of land remained the same in both registered and unregistered systems. In fact it had become increasingly obvious during the 75 years since the introduction of the LRA 1925 that there are real differences between the law relating to registered and unregistered land; a good example is to be found in the rules relating to adverse possession, which we discuss in Chapter 8. Despite its very slow introduction, registered title is now the predominant system of landholding in this country, and the joint working party took the view that, where necessary, substantive law should reflect the realities of this system, rather than being tied to the practice of unregistered conveyancing, which is rapidly becoming obsolete.

However, it is clear that the real impetus for tackling all these defects and improving the registered title system came from the need to facilitate the development of conveyancing by electronic means.

7.2.3 Electronic conveyancing (e-conveyancing)

Information technology is now an accepted part of most people's lives and we take for granted the provision of on-line services and electronic dealings. Yet by contrast various stages of the conveyancing process still require the use of paper documents and their physical delivery by post (or other similar means).

In fact, much of the preliminary work in the process is already done electronically, with all those involved communicating by e-mail and conducting investigations of title on line. The Land Registry currently holds over 23 million computerised titles, which can be accessed electronically, and relevant information held by other bodies is increasingly being computerised. Yet despite progress in these areas, the two milestones in the conveyancing process for registered land—the contract and the transfer—still have to be made by written documents which require physical delivery to the other party and, in the case of the transfer, to the Land Registry. These requirements are time-consuming and increasingly appear outdated and too slow for modern life. More worryingly, the gap of time between the transfer and the registration of the new owner (the 'registration gap') can cause real problems for the purchaser, since despite paying the purchase money and taking the transfer he has only an equitable interest in the property until the transaction has been completed by registration.

Under an electronic system, it would be possible to make both the contract and the transfer electronically, without the creation of any written document, and to communicate them to the Land Registry at the moment of creation. The effect of such communication would be to enter a notice of the contract automatically on the vendor's register of title and, in the case of the transfer, to register the purchaser as the new owner. This would not only be quicker and more cost-effective but would also mean that the register was updated at the very moment that the transaction took effect, thus avoiding problems which currently arise from delay in noting the contract or in registering the purchaser as the new owner.

The same system would operate for the creation of new interests in land. For example, certain leases granted out of a registered freehold would no longer be granted by deed and then registered, but would be created and registered simultaneously by use of computer systems.

7.2.3.1 Informal creation of certain interests

Despite the advantages of the new proposed system, the working party accepted that there is a limited class of rights which at present arise without any formal creation and which must be left free to do so even after the introduction of electronic conveyancing. Rights which can arise in this way include:

- an equity arising from proprietary estoppel;
- rights under a constructive or resulting trust;
- easements arising by prescription or by implied grant or reservation; and
- certain equities, such as a right to set aside a transaction for undue influence.

We know that this list may not mean very much to you at the moment, but the various rights will be dealt with at later stages in this book. The common characteristic of these rights is that they all come into existence without any formal grant, and it would therefore be completely inappropriate to say that they could not exist unless created by electronic transfer.

Further, the working party accepted that these informally created rights are unlikely to be protected in any formal way by entry on the register, and would therefore have to continue to operate as overriding interests, since it would be unreasonable to expect rights which arise informally to be protected by formal methods.

7.2.3.2 Moving to electronic conveyancing

We will tell you more about e-conveyancing in 7.15. However, you may like to note now that although the Land Registry has made progress in implementing this new system, the current position (in early 2012) is that further developments are now 'on hold' until there is an upturn in the property market and an improvement in the general financial situation (see 7.15.5).

7.2.4 LRA 2002

The new Act makes major changes in the system of registered land. In particular, it reduces the number of overriding interests and authorises the use of electronic contracts and transfers. In 7.15 we will tell you more about the progress being made by the Land Registry in developing electronic conveyancing.

One of the principal aims in making these changes was to bring about what is described as 'total registration': that is, to bring all land in England and Wales on to the register as soon as possible. In 2007 40 per cent of the land area of England and Wales was still unregistered (Land Registry Annual Report and Accounts 2006/7). The new Act seeks to speed the process by encouraging voluntary registration and by requiring the compulsory registration of relatively short leases (that is, leases for more than seven years).

In summary, the Act has two main objectives:

(1) to ensure that as many interests in registered land as possible are shown on the register (or, if not on the register, are not binding on purchasers); and

(2) to make arrangements that will allow dispositions of registered land to be handled electronically.

7.3 What can be registered?

Sections 3 and 4 of LRA 2002 provide for the registration of ownership of the two legal estates and of certain legal interests.

7.3.1 Registration of freehold and leasehold estates

All freehold estates are capable of being registered, but only certain leasehold ones are registrable, and we need to tell you which these are.

7.3.1.1 Leases with more than seven years to run

Under the old system, a leasehold estate was registrable only if the term in question was for more than 21 years. One of the most significant changes made by LRA 2002 is to extend compulsory registration to shorter leases, by requiring registration of all leases which at the date of transfer or grant have more than seven years to run.

In the past, the registration of title to relatively short leases was regarded as undesirable, because of the amount of work involved for the registry in first registering them and then removing them from the register when they expired. The proposed move to electronic conveyancing means that the administrative work involved in dealing with short leases is no longer a significant consideration. It is possible that when the electronic system is in operation compulsory registration will be extended to even shorter leases, probably to all leases with more than three years to run.

7.3.1.2 Leases which are registrable irrespective of length ('short registrable leases')

The Act provides for registration of two types of leases under which the tenant may not always be in possession of the property. These are:

- leases which are to take effect in possession more than three months after the date of grant (for more information about leases which take effect in the future, see 10.1.3.4); and
- leases in which the right to possession is discontinuous, for example timeshare arrangements for holiday accommodation, by which tenants are given rights of possession for specified periods each year.

In leases of these types, the fact that the tenant is not necessarily in possession of the land means that there is a real risk that a purchaser might buy the landlord's estate without discovering that it is subject to a lease. In consequence, the Act provides for the registration of title to such leases (which will be accompanied by an entry on the landlord's title) even where the lease is for not more than seven years.

7.3.2 Registration of legal interests

The Act provides (in s. 2(a)) for the registration of title to the following legal interests:

- a rentcharge;
- a franchise;
- a profit à prendre; and
- any other interest or charge which benefits or burdens any registered estate or interest.

This means that the ownership of legal rights over another's land, such as easements, rentcharges and charges by way of legal mortgage, can be registered by their owners in the same way that ownership of freehold and leasehold estates is registered.

This is not a new development, for title to these legal interests was registrable under LRA 1925, although it seems that in practice only rentcharges were registered with their own titles. However, s. 2(a) does add two further rights, franchises and profits à prendre in gross, to the list of registrable interests, and we need to explain briefly the nature of these two rights.

(1) *A franchise* is a privilege which the Crown has allowed a subject to exercise. It gives the holder some particular right, as for example to collect tolls or to hold a fair or market. Although medieval in origin, these can still be valuable property rights, but until LRA 2002 came into force there was no way of registering title to them.

(2) *A profit à prendre* (see 25.3) is the right to take something (wood, gravel, fish etc.) from another's land. The right may be 'appurtenant', that is, attached to another piece of land and used for its benefit, or it can be 'in gross', which means that it exists for the personal benefit of its owner and is not attached to any land. Appurtenant profits may be included in the registration of title to the land which

they benefit, but until the new Act there was no provision for the registration of title to profits in gross, although they can be of considerable value.

Rules governing the registration of title to the various legal interests listed in s. 2(a) form an important part of the registration system, but in what follows we will concentrate on registration of title to freehold and leasehold estates.

7.4 First registration

First registration is the process by which estates currently outside the registered title system are brought within it. As we explained in Chapter 4, the phased introduction of registration has been very slow, with the result that a number of properties are still subject to the old system of unregistered conveyancing, which we described in Chapter 6. The aim now is to bring these properties into the new system as quickly as possible, and eventually to achieve total registration (that is, to have titles to all estates in land on the register). For this purpose, LRA 2002 makes provision for both compulsory and voluntary first registration, and we will now look at each of these in a little more detail.

7.4.1 Compulsory first registration

7.4.1.1 Events which trigger the requirement to register title to an estate

Section 4 continues the existing system under which first registration is required whenever certain dealings with an unregistered legal estate occur. The dealings (sometimes referred to as 'triggers') specified in s. 4 include:

- transfer of:
  - an unregistered freehold estate; or
  - an unregistered leasehold estate with more than seven years to run at date of transfer
- grant of a lease (out of an unregistered estate) which:
  - is for more than seven years; or
  - is to take effect more than three months from date of grant (7.3.1.2)
- creation of first legal mortgage protected by deposit of title deeds over:
  - an unregistered freehold estate; or
  - an unregistered leasehold estate with more than seven years to run at date when mortgage created.

In this case, the mortgaged estate becomes compulsorily registrable even though it is not being transferred.

Dealing need not be for value

When compulsory registration of title was first introduced, estates became registrable only on specified dealings for value. Over the years, the range of triggers has been greatly extended, so that the obligation to apply for first registration now arises where the transfer is made:

- for value;
- as a gift;

- on a court order;
- by assent i.e., a form of conveyance used by personal representatives to transfer an estate to those entitled under the deceased's will or intestacy; or to the person next entitled under a SLA settlement (for which, see Chapter 18);
- by trustees partitioning trust land between beneficiaries (see new s. 4(1)(a)(iii));
- to a newly appointed trustee (see new s. 4(1)(aa)).

When registration of title was first introduced, the requirement of dealings for value meant that land held within family settlements was likely to remain unregistered for a long time. The gradual extension of compulsory registration to transfers of land within a trust means that such land is now far more likely to come onto the register.

7.4.1.2 **Who has to apply for first registration?**

Where the obligation to register arises on *the transfer or grant of an estate*, it is the new owner (e.g., the purchaser of a freehold estate or the tenant of a new lease) who must make the application.

Where the triggering event is *the grant of a mortgage*, the application must be made by the mortgagor (the owner of the mortgaged estate), although the mortgagee is entitled to apply for registration if the mortgagor fails to do so (s. 6(6) and r. 21 of LRR 2003).

7.4.1.3 **What happens if application for first registration is not made?**

In order to compel estate owners to apply for registration, s. 7(1) provides that if registration is not made within the required time (i.e., within two months of the triggering event—s. 6(4)) the transfer or grant of an estate or the creation of a mortgage will become void. Where the event in question was a transfer, the estate will revert to the transferor, who will hold it on trust for the transferee. Where the triggering event was the grant of a lease or a mortgage, the disposition will take effect as an estate contract (i.e., as a contract to grant the lease or mortgage). In all these circumstances, the person who failed to apply for registration will have to bear the costs of repeating the transaction, and might also run into other problems.

Example of problems caused by failure to register

An example of the difficulties which can be caused by failing to register in time is provided by the facts of *Sainsbury's Supermarkets Ltd v Olympia Homes Ltd* [2006] 1 P&CR 17. Hughes, the first defendant, had bought an unregistered estate and failed to complete his application for first registration. As a result, the estate reverted to the vendor, and Hughes was left with only an equitable interest in the property. He subsequently granted an option to purchase the estate to Sainsbury's Supermarkets Ltd ('Sainsburys'), which should have protected its interest by registration as a C(iv) land charge (see 6.4.2.2 and 6.4.5.2), but failed to do so. Later Hughes found himself in financial difficulties and the property was sold by court order on an application from one of his creditors. The property was bought by Olympia Homes Ltd ('Olympia'), who believed that it was acquiring the legal title, although in fact it could take only the equitable interest held by Hughes. Olympia applied for and was granted first registration. As we shall see, first registration vests the estate in the registered owner (even if, as here, he did not previously own it), so at this stage in the story the legal estate passed from the original vendor to Olympia.

The question arose as to whether Sainsburys' option was enforceable against Olympia. If Olympia had acquired the legal estate when it bought the property, it would have taken free of the option as an unregistered land charge (see 6.4.5.2). However, the fact that at the time of the sale Olympia could not acquire more than the interest held by

Hughes meant that it had taken only an equitable interest in the property and was accordingly bound by the unregistered land charge. On Sainsburys' application for rectification of the register the court ordered the entry of a notice protecting the option.

7.4.1.4 3 Trant Way

You may remember that we left Barbara Bell at the end of Chapter 6, having just completed her purchase of the unregistered freehold estate in 3 Trant Way. This, of course, was an event which under s. 4 triggered the requirement to apply for first registration of her title, and she must seek registration within two months of the conveyance to her. If she does not do so in time, the conveyance will become void, and the estate will revert to Victoria Ventnor. She will hold it on trust for Barbara, who in due course will have to meet all the expenses involved in re-conveying it to her.

In the next section, we will see what happens when Barbara Bell applies for first registration, but first we must look briefly at voluntary registration.

7.4.2 Voluntary first registration

In seeking to achieve the goal of total registration, s. 3 continues the process of voluntary registration of registrable estates and interests, which has always been available for owners who wish to register their titles although they are not yet required to do so.

The Land Registry is certainly doing all it can to encourage voluntary registration. Registration fees are reduced for voluntary applications, and more publicity is being given to the advantages of having a registered title, which is not only easier to deal with, but also under the new Act protects the owner from losing his title to a squatter (as to which, see Chapter 8).

7.5 Registering title for the first time

In this section we will outline what happens when Barbara Bell applies for first registration of title to her freehold estate in 3 Trant Way.

7.5.1 Investigation of title by the registry

We have seen that one of the purposes of registration is to provide any prospective purchaser with reliable information about the estate he is proposing to buy. He will want to be sure that the registered owner owns the property he is offering to sell and that it is free from any encumbrances (third-party rights) other than those which have already been disclosed to him. In dealing with Barbara's application for registration therefore, the registry will need to satisfy itself that she does indeed own the estate she wants to register and that as many third-party rights as possible are recorded on the register. It will do this by repeating the process her solicitor undertook on the purchase of the property, scrutinising the title deeds and the results of searches and enquiries, all of which must be submitted with the application for registration. Indeed, the registry may be even more careful than a purchaser or a professional adviser would be, for the title once registered is guaranteed. Thus if the registry makes a mistake it may have to compensate anyone who suffers a loss as a result. If necessary, the registry will raise queries with Barbara, and may even require her to make additional searches and enquiries to clarify uncertain points.

7.5.1.1 Cautions against first registration

Where a person claims to have an interest against an estate in unregistered land, he may register a 'caution against first registration', which will ensure that his claim is considered by the registrar when dealing with such an application. This process was available under LRA 1925 and continues under LRA 2002 (ss. 15–22).

We will now go on to consider the form of the register, and the way in which the results of the registry's investigations are recorded on it.

7.5.2 Form of the register

The opening words of LRA 2002 are:

> There is to continue to be kept a register of title kept by the registrar (s. 1(1))

and no changes are made to the structure of the register by the Act or the rules made under it (LRR 2003).

Individual registers The 'register of title' consists of a number of individual registers, one for each estate registered (LRR 2003, r. 2). This means that, since there may be more than one estate in one piece of land (for example, a fee simple and a term of years), there may be several individual registers for the same piece of land.

Parts of the register The individual register for an estate consists of three parts:

- the property register;
- the proprietorship register; and
- the charges register.

We know that it can be difficult to visualise the individual register and its parts, and so we suggest that while reading this section you look at the copy of the fictional register for the freehold estate of 1 Trant Way, which is shown on p. 93. Each title is allocated a title number by the registry and you will see that ST1234 is the title number for 1 Trant Way.

7.5.2.1 Property register

This part of the register describes the property, including the type of estate ('freehold' or 'leasehold'), and invariably refers to a filed plan. The filed plan is prepared from the largest size of ordnance survey map and on the register entry the land concerned is shown edged in red. Usually the description of the property is simply its postal address but a different type of description may sometimes be necessary (for instance, if the registration is of a field with no address).

The property register may also contain details of easements, such as a right of way, which *benefit* the registered estate.

7.5.2.2 Proprietorship register

This part of the register shows the class of the title, here 'title absolute' (see 7.5.4), and gives the name of the registered owner of the estate and his address. The owner is described as the 'registered proprietor'. The proprietorship register will also record any restrictions on the power of the proprietor to deal with the land, for example if he is a trustee or a bankrupt (see 7.8.1.2).

Land Registry

Official copy of register of title

Title number ST1234 **Edition date 01.03.1992**

- This official copy shows the entries in the register of title on 20 June 2008 at 11:39:46.
- This date must be quoted as the "search from date" in any official search application based on this copy.
- date at the beginning of an entry is the date on which the entry was made in the register.
- Issued on 20 June 2008.
- Under s.67 of the Land Registration Act 2002, this copy is admissible in evidence to the same extent as the original.
- For information about the register of title see Land Registry website www.landregistry.gov.uk or Land Registry Public Guide 1 – A guide to the information we keep and how you can obtain it.
- This title is dealt with by Land Registry Stilton office.

A: Property register

The register describes the registered estate comprised in the title.

STILTON : MOUSEHOLE

1. (01.03.1992) The Freehold land shown edged with red on the plan of the above title filed at Land Registry and being 1 Trant Way, Mousehole (ST14 3JP)

B: Proprietorship register

This register specifies the class of title and identifies the owner. It contains any entries that affect the right of disposal.

Title absolute

1. (01.03.1992) PROPRIETOR: VICTOR VENN of 1 Trant Way, Mousehole, Stilton ST14 3JP.

C: Charges register

This register contains any charges and other matters that affect the registered estate.

2. (01.03.1992) A Conveyance of the land in this title dated 30 September 1934 made between (1) Mary Brown and (2) Harold Robins contains the following covenants:

   "The purchaser hereby covenants with the Vendor for the benefit of her adjoining land known as 15 Trant Avenue to observe and perform the following stipulations and conditions:

   1. No building erected on the land shall be used other than as a private dwellinghouse.
   2. Nothing shall be done or permitted on the premises which may be a nuisance or annoyance to the adjoining house or to the neighbourhood."

End of register

7.5.2.3 Charges register

The charges section carries the details of certain encumbrances (i.e., third-party rights) which bind the estate (see 7.8.1.1).

7.5.3 Classes of title

The property and proprietorship registers, when read together, will tell the purchaser the nature of the property registered and who owns it. The type of estate is clear, since it will be described as either freehold or leasehold land, and rights which benefit the estate (such as easements over adjoining property) are also described.

The register will also indicate how good the proprietor's title is, by recording a 'class' (or 'grade') of title, awarded on first registration and showing how reliable the title is considered to be.

The quality of the titles investigated may vary considerably: one title may prove to be entirely sound; another might be based only on the rights a squatter has established by possession of the land for some years (see Chapter 8 on title by adverse possession); and another may suffer from some technical defect. Accordingly the registration system provides for seven classes of title: three for freehold estates and four for leasehold estates.

Sections 9 and 10 of LRA 2002 specify the classes of title available for freehold and leasehold land respectively as follows:

- classes of freehold title:
  - absolute freehold
  - qualified freehold
  - possessory freehold
- classes of leasehold title:
  - absolute leasehold
  - good leasehold
  - qualified leasehold
  - possessory leasehold

Where an inferior class of title is awarded on first registration, the registrar may later upgrade it to a better class (s. 62), and we will note the circumstances in which this may be done as we consider each class of title.

Most applicants for first registration will be granted absolute freehold title and absolute or good leasehold title. We will consider these in some detail first and will deal more briefly with the inferior classes of title later in 7.5.6.

7.5.4 Absolute freehold title

Absolute freehold title is the best class of title known to the registered land system and it is very nearly indefeasible (though see 7.12 on alteration of the register).

Section 9(2) provides that absolute title to a freehold estate may be registered where the title to the estate is such:

> as a willing buyer could properly be advised by a competent professional adviser to accept.

However, this does not mean that the registrar has to demand a perfect title, for s. 9(3) provides that in deciding to register an applicant with absolute freehold title, the registrar may disregard a defect in title if he considers that it will not cause the title to be disturbed. The fact that the registrar may award an absolute title in these circumstances means that registration can have a curative effect and prevent future purchasers concerning themselves with technical, but unimportant, defects. This is one reason why owners sometimes choose to register their estates voluntarily.

7.5.4.1 Effect of registration with absolute freehold title

Under s. 11(2)–(3), the effect of registration of a freehold estate with absolute title is to vest that freehold estate in the registered proprietor, together with all interests which benefit the estate (e.g., an easement, such as a right of way or a right of drainage which the estate enjoys over neighbouring land).

In general, the applicant for first registration will already own the legal estate (the purpose of the registry's enquiries being to ensure that this is the case). However, if it happens that by mistake someone other than the legal owner is registered as proprietor, the registration will nevertheless be effective and will vest the estate in the registered proprietor in accordance with s. 11(3). A recent example of this is to be found in *Sainsbury's Supermarkets Ltd v Olympia Homes Ltd* [2006] 1 P&CR 17 (see 7.4.1.3).

7.5.4.2 Encumbrances binding the estate

As you know, an estate may be subject to a wide range of third-party rights, including leases, easements, mortgages and rights under trusts, restrictive covenants and estate contracts. Section 11(4)–(5) provides that a proprietor registered with absolute title takes the estate free from all such encumbrances, except for:

- interests noted on the register;
- overriding interests;
- squatters' rights of which the proprietor has notice; and
- rights of beneficiaries (where the registered proprietor holds the land as a trustee).

We will consider each of these categories in turn.

(1) *Interests noted on the register* On first registration, the registrar will aim to record on the estate's register of title as many as possible of the encumbrances which burden it. Depending on the nature of the right, this will be done either by entering a notice in the Charges Register or by putting a restriction in the Proprietorship Register (see 7.8.1 for an explanation of the nature of these two entries and the circumstances in which each is used).

(2) *Overriding interests* Schedule 1 lists certain interests that 'override' first registration or, in other words, will bind the estate although not entered on the register. The list includes:

- most leases for not more than seven years;
- interests of persons in actual occupation;
- legal easements and profits; and
- a range of legal and statutory rights.

The first of these, short leases, will not be entered on the register because they are of limited duration and, for the time being at least, the registry does not want to clutter the register with them. However, the other interests listed in Sch. 1 will be entered on the register if the registry is aware of them, and s. 71(a) and LRR 2003, r. 28 impose a duty on the applicant to inform the registry of any such interests of which he is aware. Thus Sch. 1 really acts as a safety-net, to preserve those interests which bind the unregistered estate but are not identified and recorded on first registration.

(3) *Squatters' rights of which the proprietor has notice* We will explain the rules about adverse possession and squatters' rights more fully in Chapter 8. All you need to know at this stage is that if the owner of unregistered land loses possession of it to another person, his right to recover the land from the dispossessor may be extinguished after 12 years by the Limitation Act 1980. Once this has happened, the dispossessor (usually called an 'adverse possessor' or 'squatter') is regarded as the legal owner. Once he has acquired ownership in this way, he can go out of possession and still retain ownership.

Under the old Act (LRA 1925, s. 70(1)(f)), the rights of the adverse possessor were overriding and bound the estate on first registration and on any subsequent disposition. This meant that if a purchaser had bought the land and secured first registration without being aware of the squatter's rights (as he might if the squatter was not in occupation), he could lose his title to the estate if the squatter subsequently claimed ownership. One of the changes made by LRA 2002, Sch.1 is to reduce the overriding effect of the squatter's rights, so that if he is not in actual occupation of the property his rights do not override first registration, unless, under s. 11(4)(c), the proprietor has notice of them.

Interestingly, this provision appears to produce the unusual result of first registration invalidating an interest which bound the estate immediately before it was registered, since in the unregistered system the dispossessed owner is subject to rights under the Limitation Act irrespective of notice.

(4) *Beneficiaries' rights* A trustee who is registered as first proprietor is bound by those rights of beneficiaries under the trust of which he has notice, even if they are not protected by entry on the register. The trustee cannot free himself of his obligations to the beneficiaries merely by securing a registration which does not mention their interests.

7.5.5 Absolute leasehold title and good leasehold title

As compared with the purchaser of a freehold estate, the purchaser of a leasehold estate has an extra dimension to consider when checking that the vendor can transfer the estate that he has contracted to give. Like the purchaser of the freehold estate, he will check the devolution of the title to the leasehold estate that he is buying, and will want to see that it has been correctly passed from one owner to another until it reached the vendor. However, in addition, the purchaser will often wish to be reassured that the landlord (lessor) who granted the lease was actually entitled to do so. Thus the purchaser really needs to investigate the landlord's title to the superior estate in order to check that he had a good title to that estate and therefore had the right to grant the lease which the purchaser intends to buy.

Under s. 10(2), absolute leasehold title is granted only if the registrar is satisfied with both the lease and the superior title from which it is derived. Thus if X, a freehold owner, grants a lease to Y, Y can be registered with absolute leasehold title only if the registrar is satisfied that the lease is good and that X's freehold title is good. This should cause no difficulty where X's estate is already registered or where Y has a contractual right to investigate the freehold title. If Y does not have this right, however, and the lease has been granted out of an unregistered estate, he may well be unable to satisfy the registrar as to his landlord's title, and in such a case the leasehold estate could be registered only with good leasehold title (for which, see below).

7.5.5.1 Effect of registration with absolute leasehold title

Registration with absolute leasehold title vests the leasehold estate in the owner subject to the encumbrances described in the case of absolute freehold title and, in addition, to all express and implied covenants, obligations and liabilities imposed by the lease or incidental to the land (s. 12(3)–(5)).

The result of the registration is that the registrar will guarantee that the lease was effectively granted and will also show on the leasehold title any covenants which bind the freehold estate and which therefore bind the lease as well as the superior title (see Chapter 26).

7.5.5.2 Effect of registration with good leasehold title

This class of title is granted when the registrar is satisfied that the lease itself is good but where there is no evidence of the quality of the superior title (s. 10(3)). In such cases the registry cannot be absolutely sure that the lease was validly granted by a person with power to grant such an estate. Apart from the fact that the superior title cannot be guaranteed, good leasehold title has the same effect as registration with absolute leasehold title (s. 12(6)).

Upgrading

Good leasehold title may be upgraded to absolute title if the registrar is satisfied as to the superior title (s. 62(2))—as, for example, he will be if title to that estate is registered at a later date.

7.5.6 Other classes of title

These other classes of freehold and leasehold title occur relatively seldom, so we will deal with them briefly.

7.5.6.1 Freehold titles

(1) *Qualified freehold title* Qualified freehold titles are extremely rare ('perhaps one in a hundred thousand registered titles is qualified'—Ruoff & Roper, *Registered Conveyancing*, 1991, para.5–08). Such a title is granted:

> if the registrar is of the opinion that the person's title to the estate has been established only for a limited period or subject to certain reservations which cannot be disregarded... (s. 9(4)).

The details of the defect will be entered on the register. Such a situation might arise if a purchaser of an estate in unregistered land had decided to take the risk of not investigating the title to the property as thoroughly as is usual. As we have seen (6.2), it is normal to search back to a deed which is at least 15 years old. If the purchaser had accepted a deed made only 10 years ago and later applied for first registration, it is likely that he would be registered only with qualified title.

Section 11(6) provides that registration with qualified title has the same effect as registration with absolute title:

> except that it does not affect the enforcement of any estate, right or interest which appears from the register to be excepted from the effect of registration.

Thus if an estate is registered with qualified title because the applicant did not investigate title for the full statutory period, any later purchaser will know that he runs the risk of finding that the estate is subject to some defect which was not discovered on the earlier investigation of title.

Upgrading Qualified title may be upgraded to absolute title at any time if the registrar 'is satisfied as to the title to the estate' (s. 62(1))—for example, where the defect which led to the original classification is no longer a matter of concern.

(5) *Possessory freehold title* Possessory titles are less good than absolute titles but fortunately are fairly rare, occurring in only about 1 per cent of cases. Such titles are registered in cases in which the ownership of the estate is evidenced purely by the fact that the estate owner is in occupation of the land, or that he is in receipt of the rents and profits from the occupant (s. 9(5)). This situation might arise if the deeds to the property had been lost, or if the estate owner had acquired his rights merely through long use of the land (title by adverse possession—see Chapter 8).

Registration with possessory title has the same effect as registration with an absolute title, save that it is subject to any adverse pre-registration estates, rights or interests (s. 11(7)). Thus the danger of having a title which is possessory only is that someone may appear who has a better claim to the estate (for example, the original owner who has been dispossessed by the squatter).

Upgrading In time, any competing claims to the estate would be extinguished by the Limitation Act 1980 (see Chapter 8) and so the possessory title would become quite safe from disruption. To take account of this, the system provides that, provided the registered proprietor is in possession of the land, the possessory title may be upgraded to absolute title after it has been registered for 12 years.

It is also possible for possessory title to be upgraded to absolute title at any time if the registrar is satisfied as to the title to the estate (s. 62(1))—for example, if missing title deeds are found.

7.5.6.2 Leasehold titles

The Act provides for qualified and possessory leasehold titles, and their upgrading to good or absolute leasehold titles, but in practice little use is made of these provisions.

7.5.7 First registration of title to the freehold estate in 3 Trant Way

If all goes well with the registry's investigation, Barbara Bell will be registered with absolute title which, as we have already seen, means that she will hold the freehold estate free of all encumbrances except for:

- registered charges (which will include any mortgage she has granted to secure money borrowed to pay the purchase price);
- interests which are protected by a notice or restriction on the register;
- any right which overrides first registration under Sch. 1; and
- any interest acquired under the Limitation Act 1980 of which she has notice.

7.5.7.1 Evidence of registration

On completion of the registration process, Barbara Bell will receive a 'title information document', which consists of a cover sheet around official copies of the individual register and title plan. The copy of her register will be similar in appearance to that shown on p. 93, although of course with different details about the property.

7.6 Dealings with a registered estate

7.6.1 No. 3 Trant Way

Once title to 3 Trant Way has been registered, it will become subject to statutory rules about how future dealings with the estate must be conducted if they are to have legal effect. If Barbara ever wishes to sell the house, to let it or to mortgage it, or to grant easements or certain other rights over her property, she must not only use a deed (to satisfy LPA 1925, s. 52(1)), but must also comply with other requirements which are set out in LRA 2002, s. 27.

7.6.2 Dispositions which must be completed by registration

Section 27(2) sets out a list of registrable dispositions, that is the dispositions or dealings with a registered estate which must be completed by registration. They include:

- a transfer of the registered estate;
- the grant of a lease for more than seven years;
- the grant of certain leases irrespective of length (including the future leases and leases providing for discontinuous possession which we described in 7.3.1.2);
- the express creation of interests under LPA 1925, s. 1(2)(a),(b) and (e), that is:
  - a legal easement or profit
  - a legal rentcharge
  - a right of entry in respect of a legal lease or a legal rentcharge;
- the grant of a legal charge (i.e., a mortgage).

7.6.3 What happens if a disposition is not completed by registration?

Section 27(1) provides that the dispositions listed above do not take effect at law until registration requirements are met (see 7.6.4). In other words, these dispositions will not create or transfer legal estates or interests until they are registered. This is a very important addition to the basic requirement for the use of a deed which we noted earlier (2.5.4.1), and it is essential to remember that, where title is registered, you need a deed plus registration to create or transfer a legal estate or interest.

For the time being, an unregistered disposition will take effect in equity i.e. it will give the transferee an equitable right to the estate or will create interests such as equitable easements or mortgages. However, when the electronic system of conveyancing is in operation, dispositions which are not completed by registration will have no effect at all, not even in equity (see 7.15.2.2).

7.6.4 Registration requirements

7.6.4.1 Transfer of registered estate

A transfer of an estate which is already registered requires the entry of the transferee as proprietor, and we will see this rule in operation later when the Armstrongs complete their purchase of 1 Trant Way (7.13).

7.6.4.2 Grant out of a registered estate

A grant of a new registrable estate or interest, such as a lease, mortgage, rentcharge, or easement, must meet two requirements:

(1) *The grantee must be registered as owner of the new estate or interest.* In some cases this involves opening a new individual register, and this is what will be done in the case of a lease or a rentcharge.

A new easement, however, is registered by adding it to the register of the estate which it *benefits* (where it will appear in the property register—see 7.5.2.1).

Similarly, a registered charge (i.e. a mortgage) does not require a separate register and is registered in the Charges Register of the estate which it binds (i.e., in the third section of the register of title for the property subject to the charge.

(2) *The estate or interest must be entered on the register of the estate which it burdens.* In general this is done by putting a notice in the Charges Register of the title to the burdened estate. Thus a notice of a lease will be put on the register of the land-lord's estate, and a notice of an easement will be put on the register of the estate over which it is to be exercised. However, no separate notice of a registered charge is needed, because the actual registration of the charge is made by entry on the register of the burdened property.

7.7 Buying a house with registered title

7.7.1 No. 1 Trant Way

Having followed Barbara Bell's progress in buying a house with unregistered title and applying for first registration, we now need to turn our attention to the other househunters, Mr and Mrs Armstrong, who are planning to buy 1 Trant Way (4.1.1). The title to this property is registered (4.2.3.2), and like any other home-buyer, the Armstrongs will want to check two things about the property. They need to make sure that the vendor, Victor Venn, owns the estate he is offering to sell, and that it is free from any encumbrances other than those which have already been disclosed to them.

7.7.2 Does the vendor own the estate?

As we can see from the specimen register on p. 93 Victor Venn is the registered proprietor of the freehold estate in 1 Trant Way, and is registered with absolute title. This is the best title available (see 7.5.4), and the Armstrongs can have reasonable confidence in buying the property, although they need to be aware that the system does provide for subsequent alteration of the register for various purposes, including the correction of mistakes.

The Armstrongs, or more likely their professional adviser, will need to obtain a copy of the register of title for 1 Trant Way. At some stage they will also need to make an official search of the register, but this is all that needs to be done to satisfy themselves that Victor does truly own the estate. There is no need to investigate title in the old way, described in Chapter 6 in respect to the purchase of unregistered land, which involved checking through past dealings with the property as shown by old title deeds. The register is conclusive of the fact that Victor owns the freehold estate in No. 1.

7.7.3 Are there any encumbrances which bind the property?

The effect of LRA 2002, s. 29(1) and (2) is that the buyer of a freehold estate registered with absolute title takes it free of all encumbrances except for:

- registered charges (i.e., legal mortgages, which will appear in the charges section of the register);
- interests protected by notice on the register;
- overriding interests.

If the title to the estate is less than absolute (i.e., qualified or possessory) the purchaser will be subject in addition to any exceptions appearing on the register (see 7.5.6.1), and where the estate is a leasehold one he will also be bound by obligations imposed by the lease but not noted on the register.

The specimen register for No. 1 (at p. 93) shows that Victor Venn is registered with absolute title to a freehold estate, so the encumbrances which could affect the Armstongs are limited to rights protected by entries on the register and overriding interests, and we will consider these separately in the next two sections.

The provisions of s. 29(1) and (2) apply not only to a person who buys the registered estate, but also to those who take under any other registrable disposition for valuable consideration. In what follows, we will explain the rules by reference to the buyer of the registered estate, but they apply equally to a range of other disponees, including legal mortgagees and tenants taking grants of registrable leases.

7.8 Interests protected by entries on the register

7.8.1 Entries under LRA 2002

Under the new system, there are two types of entry which can be used to protect third-party rights:

- notices; and
- restrictions.

7.8.1.1 Notices

Notices are entered in the third part of the register of title (the Charges Register).The Act defines a notice as 'an entry in the register in respect of the burden of an interest affecting a registered estate or charge' (s. 32(1)). The fact that an interest is the subject of a notice does not necessarily mean that the interest is valid. However, if the interest *is* valid, the notice ensures both that it binds any purchaser for valuable consideration (s. 32(3)), and that he knows about it before he takes the estate.

There are certain interests which cannot be protected by notice (s. 33). They include:

- interests under a trust of land or SLA settlement, which should be protected by a restriction;
- a lease for not more than three years the title to which is not required to be registered. The provision is phrased in this way so as to permit the automatic entry of notice on the registration of any of those short leases which, exceptionally, are registrable (7.3.1.2); and
- a restrictive covenant between lessor and lessee, so far as it relates to the demised premises.

Apart from these interests, all other interests *may* be protected by notice, and in a number of cases the Act provides that such an entry *must* be made.

*Circumstances in which a notice **must** be entered*
As we explained in 7.6, certain dealings with the registered estate must be completed by registration if they are to have legal effect. In most cases where the dealing creates a new estate or interest the registration process includes the compulsory entry of a notice of the new estate or interest on the register of the estate which it binds.

*Circumstances in which a notice **may** be entered*
All encumbrances which are not registrable interests, or excluded by s. 33, may be protected by notice. Interests in this category include: estate contracts; equitable leases, mortgages and easements; and restrictive covenants (but not interests under trusts, which as we have seen are excluded by s. 33). Section 29 provides in effect that a purchaser of the registered estate for valuable consideration takes free of any interests which are not overriding and not protected by notice on the register. This means that it is essential for anyone entitled to such an interest to ensure that it is protected in this way. At first registration, the registrar will enter notices protecting any such rights of which he is aware. Apart from that, notices are entered on the application of the registered proprietor or the person who claims the right which is to be protected.

In addition, the Act provides that rights which would otherwise take effect as overriding interests may instead be protected by notice (s. 37). This is in accordance with the general policy of reducing the number of interests which can bind a purchaser without appearing on the register. As we shall see, a number of overriding interests depend upon matters such as actual occupation or recent use by the person entitled, or the state of the purchaser's knowledge and the enquiries he has made. It is therefore much safer to protect such interests by notice. Once such an entry has been made, the interest in question loses its overriding status (s. 29(3)).

Agreed and unilateral notices
An *agreed notice* will be entered only with the agreement of the registered proprietor. Such a notice will be appropriate where he himself has created the interest, as for example in the case of a new restrictive covenant which burdens his land, or in an equitable mortgage created to secure a loan to him.

A *unilateral notice* may be entered without the consent of the registered proprietor, possibly in circumstances in which he denies the existence of the interest.

The proprietor must be informed of the entry of a unilateral notice and has the right to apply for its cancellation. If the person lodging the notice maintains the claim, there are procedures for determining its validity. If no objection is made, the notice protects the interest as adequately as an agreed notice.

7.8.1.2 **Restrictions**

LRA 2002, s. 41(1) defines a restriction as:

> an entry in the register regulating the circumstances in which a disposition of a registered estate... may be the subject of an entry in the register.

In other words, it is a restriction on dealings with the registered estate. Where a restriction is entered in the register, no entry in respect of a disposition to which the restriction applies may be made in the register otherwise than in accordance with its terms.

The restriction may impose a complete ban on any dealing (as for example in the case of bankruptcy) or may impose conditions that must be met before any dealing will be registered. Thus a restriction can be used to ensure that any necessary consent is obtained for a transaction, or to require that capital money from a dealing with trust property is paid to two trustees or a trust corporation (i.e., that requirements for overreaching the beneficiaries' interests are met). In the latter case, the entry of such a restriction will also have the effect of indicating to a prospective purchaser that the property is subject to a trust.

Circumstances in which a restriction must or may be entered

There are certain circumstances in which the registrar *must* enter a restriction. For example where two or more persons are registered as proprietor (with the result that a statutory trust arises—see 15.3), the registrar must enter a restriction designed to secure that interests capable of being overreached on the disposition of the estate are overreached (s. 44(1)). The registrar must also comply with any court order requiring him to enter a restriction.

Restrictions *may* also be entered on the application of the registered proprietor or of any person with a sufficient interest in the making of the entry, with or without the proprietor's consent. Where the application is without consent, the proprietor must be notified of it, and there is a process for dealing with any objections to the application.

A restriction is not an alternative to a notice

The Act provides that a restriction must not be used to protect an interest which is capable of protection by notice (s. 42(2) and s. 46(2)).

7.8.1.3 Resolving disputes

It is very possible that applications to enter unilateral notices or restrictions will give rise to disputes between registered proprietors and applicants. Some procedure is needed to resolve such disputes, and also to handle various other contentious issues which may arise from registry decisions on matters such as first registration, upgrading of an existing title and rectification of the register. Under the old system, issues of this sort were decided by the registrar, but there were concerns that it might appear that decisions were being taken about property rights without any opportunity for the aggrieved party to have his case heard by an 'independent and impartial' tribunal, (as required by Art. 6 of the Human Rights Convention).

As a result, LRA 2002 (ss. 107–113 and Sch. 9) created a new office, that of Adjudicator to the Land Registry. Despite its name, the office is completely independent of the registry and there is provision for appeal on specified grounds from the Adjudicator to the High Court. It is through reports of these appeals that you are likely to come across the work of the Adjudicator; see, for example, our account later in this chapter (7.12.4.2) of the Court of Appeal's decision in *Baxter v Mannion* [2011] 1 WLR 1594.

7.8.2 Entries under LRA 1925

Under the old system there were four types of entry which could be used to protect encumbrances and alert purchasers to them: notices, restrictions, cautions and inhibitions. In general terms, they performed the same functions as the present agreed and unilateral notices and restrictions. Entries made in these old forms retain their effect under the transitional provisions of LRA 2002 (s. 134 and Sch. 12 paras. 1 and 2).

7.8.3 The register of No. 1 Trant Way

If you look back at the specimen register for this property on p. 93, you will see that restrictive covenants contained in an earlier conveyance have been protected by the entry of a notice in the Charges Register. The effect of this notice has been continued by the transitional provisions mentioned earlier, and if the Armstrongs go ahead with their purchase of the house, they will take it subject to these covenants.

There are no other entries on the register, and the Armstrongs might think that this means there are no other third-party rights affecting the property. However, they need to remember that there may well be other encumbrances which will override the transfer to them and will bind the estate in their hands even though there are no entries referring to these rights on the register.

7.9 Interests that override a registered disposition

These interests bind anyone taking under a registered disposition, including a purchaser for valuable consideration, although they are not recorded on the register and so cannot be discovered by inspecting it. The existence of such interests has always been a flaw in the registered title system, preventing the register being the perfect reflection of title which it was originally intended to be (indeed, a standard examination question used to describe the existence of overriding interests under LRA 1925 as 'the crack in the mirror of title'!)

LRA 2002 reduced the number of potential overriding interests, by redefining some of them, and by providing that others would lose their overriding status, either immediately or after a period of time.

In addition, when dealing with first registration or the registration of a dealing with a registered estate, the registry makes every effort to note on the register any interests which would otherwise have overriding effect, and s. 71 requires applicants for registration to reveal any such interests of which they know. Once an interest has been noted on the register it is no longer capable of taking effect as an interest that overrides (s. 29(3)).

Nevertheless, although categories of overriding interests are reduced for the future, existing overriding interests retain their effect under the transitional provisions of the Act either for a limited period or indefinitely (see s. 134 and Sch. 12, paras. 7–13). This means that although for the purposes of your study of land law you will probably concentrate on the new categories of overriding interests, purchasers like the Armstrongs (and their professional advisers) will need to be aware for many years to come that estates may be subject to certain overriding interests as defined in the old scheme.

7.9.1 Why are there two lists of overriding interests in LRA 2002?

LRA 2002 provides two lists of overriding interests: Sch.1 lists interests which override first registration, and Sch. 3 lists interests which override a registered disposition (i.e., later dealings with the registered estate).

To understand why the Act provides two separate lists, you need to remember that an applicant for first registration already has the legal title to the estate and holds it subject to encumbrances which bind it under the rules relating to unregistered land. First registration does not transfer or alter the title to the estate (it is said to have 'no dispositive effect'); it merely records the state of the title already held by the applicant. By contrast, registering a disposition of a registered estate (either its transfer or the creation of a registrable interest granted out of it) does actually give the new owner a legal title which he did not have before. Questions, therefore, arise as to which encumbrances should bind the property in the hands of the new owner, and, under s. 29, registration can actually alter the encumbrances which bind the estate, by, for example, freeing it from those which are not protected in the prescribed way.

The earlier Act provided only one list of overriding interests (see LRA 1925, s. 70(1)), which did not distinguish between first registration and registration of a disposition, but there is a very real difference between them, and it is for this reason that separate statements about the relevant overriding interests are provided in the two schedules of the new Act. While there is a good deal of overlap between the two lists, there are also significant differences relating to:

- short leases;
- the rights of persons in actual occupation; and
- legal easements and profits.

However, we are concerned here with the interests which would bind the Armstrongs if they buy 1 Trant Way (i.e., become parties to a registered disposition), and so we must concentrate on the terms of Sch. 3.

7.9.2 Interests that override a registered disposition under LRA 2002 Sch. 3

As we describe the overriding interests listed in Sch. 3, we will also tell you how they compare with the previous list of overriding interests contained in LRA 1925 s. 70(1). For this purpose, we will divide overriding interests into four groups:

- interests which remain overriding;
- interests which remained overriding for a period of 10 years;
- interests which were redefined and substantially reduced;
- interests omitted from Sch. 3, which cease to be overriding.

7.9.2.1 Interests which remain overriding

Paragraphs 4 to 9 of Sch. 3 list various rights which were overriding under LRA 1925 s. 70(1) and which override registered dispositions under the new Act. They include: customary and public rights, local land charges and rights in connection with mines and minerals. You may remember from Chapter 4 that local land charges are recorded in their own register (see 4.3.2.1), and since these charges will override a registered disposition, that register should be checked by anyone buying registered land.

7.9.2.2 Interests which remained overriding for a period of 10 years

Paragraphs 10 to 14 of Sch. 3 list a range of interests described as 'miscellaneous', which include a franchise, a manorial right and rights in respect of embankments, sea walls and the repair of a church chancel. These were all overriding under the old Act, but gave rise to concern because they might be difficult to discover and could be burdensome. Their overriding status could not be abolished at once, because there were fears that this might contravene the Human Rights Act 1998 (by depriving the owner of a property right), but under s. 117 they cease to be overriding from 13 October 2013 (that is, 10 years after the Act came into force). Until this date, those entitled to such a right have been able to protect them, free of charge, by entering a notice or, where title to the burdened land is not yet registered, a caution against first registration (see 7.5.1.1).

It is important to realise that these rights will not cease to exist in 2013: they merely lose their overriding status but will continue to bind the estate if protected in the appropriate way.

7.9.2.3 Overriding interests which were redefined and substantially reduced

Paragraphs 1 to 3 of Sch. 3 cover three types of interests which were overriding under LRA 1925:

(1) short leases;

(2) rights of persons in actual occupation; and

(3) easements and profits.

The range of interests within each of these categories is, however, very much reduced.

1. *A leasehold estate granted for a term of not more than seven years*
Schedule 3, para. 1 shortens the length of a lease which can be overriding from 'not exceeding 21 years' to 'not exceeding seven years'. This change is a consequence of the reduction in the minimum length of a registrable lease. Under LRA 1925, the title to leases for more than 21 years was compulsorily registrable, whereas registration requirements now apply to leases for more than seven years. Thus, para. 1 provides that leases which are not independently registrable (and therefore noted on the landlord's title) may take effect as overriding interests binding the landlord's estate.

Short registrable leases (see 7.3.1.2) are specifically excluded by para. 1 from the category of short leases which override registered dispositions.

This category of overriding interests is not expressly limited to legal leases, but in interpreting the similar provision in LRA 1925 s. 70(1)(k) it was held in *City Permanent Building Society v Miller* [1952] Ch 840 that the use of the word 'granted' excluded equitable leases, because they are not the subject of a grant. It seems likely that this interpretation will apply equally to the terms of para. 1.

2. *Interests of persons in actual occupation (Sch. 3, para. 2)*
This is such an important and interesting category of overriding interests that it must be considered in some detail and so will be dealt with separately in 7.10.

3. *Certain legal easements and profits*
Under LRA 1925 s. 70(1)(a) all legal easements and profits were overriding. In addition it was held in *Celsteel Ltd v Alton House Holdings Ltd* [1985] 1 WLR 204 (based on a provision of the Land Registration Rules 1925), that certain equitable easements could be overriding.

This very wide category of overriding interests is considerably reduced by the provisions of LRA 2002, Sch. 3, para. 3. In order to be overriding, an easement or profit must satisfy a number of conditions, which we consider below.

(i) *The interest must be legal* Paragraph 3 states at the outset that it applies only to legal easements and profits, so equitable interests of this kind are no longer overriding.

(ii) *The interest must arise otherwise than by express creation* Before explaining this requirement, we need to say a brief word about the way in which legal easements and profits are created.

Creation of easements and profits These interests may be created expressly by granting another person a right over one's land, or by reserving a right over land which one is transferring to another person. In certain cases, where there is no express creation, the law may *imply* a grant or reservation, so that easements and profits can be created without any express words appearing in the documents relating to the burdened land.

In addition, these rights can be created by a long period of use (known as prescription), again without any documentary evidence of their existence.

The rule that expressly created easements and profits cannot be overriding is not expressly stated in LRA 2002, but results from a combination of the following provisions (most of which we have already noted in 7.6):

- in order to create a *legal* interest, an express grant or reservation of an easement must be completed by registration;
- when the grant or reservation is registered, a notice is automatically put on the register of the burdened land;
- rights protected by notice cannot operate as overriding interests (s. 29(3));
- if not completed by registration, an express grant or reservation creates only an *equitable* interest.

The effect of these provisions in respect of expressly created easements and profits is that:

- *those completed by registration* cannot be overriding because they are protected by notice; and
- *those not completed by registration* cannot be overriding because they are only *equitable* (and para. 3 is limited to *legal* easements).

This means that the only easements or profits which can be overriding under para. 3 are those which arise from implied grant or reservation, by prescription (or as a result of the operation of LPA 1925, s. 62—for which see LRA 2002, s. 27(7), and 25.8 in Chapter 25). Such interests represent a danger to the purchaser; as overriding interests, they will not be entered on the register and yet may be very difficult to discover from an inspection of the property (as for example in the case of underground drains). To guard against this, the range of easements and profits which can be overriding is reduced even further by additional conditions set out in para. 3(1)–(2).

(iii) *The interest must satisfy the conditions imposed by para. 3(1)–(2)* In substance, para. 3(1)–(2) provides that a legal easement or profit arising otherwise than by express grant or reservation will be overriding only if it satisfies one of the following conditions:

(a) it is registered under the Commons Act 2006 (or its forerunner, the Commons Registration Act 1965) as, for example, might be the case with a profit of grazing; or

(b) the purchaser actually knew of its existence; or

(c) the purchaser did not know of it but it would have been obvious on a reasonably careful inspection of the land over which it is exercised; or

(d) even if it does not fall within (a) to (c) above, it has been exercised within the period of one year ending with the date of the disposition in question.

We realise that the rules about overriding easements and profits are complicated, and hope the following summary will help.

An easement or profit will be overriding if:

- it is legal; and
- it has arisen by:
  - implied grant or reservation; or

- by prescription; or
- under LPA 1925, s. 62; and

- it satisfies one of the following requirements:
  - registration under the Commons Act; or
  - existence known by purchaser; or
  - obvious on reasonably careful inspection; or
  - used in previous year.

7.9.2.4 Interests omitted from Sch. 3 which cease to be overriding

Schedule 3 omits the following categories of interests which were overriding under LRA 1925, s. 70(1).

1. *Rights acquired or in the course of being acquired under the Limitation Acts (LRA 1925, s. 70(1)(f))*

Under the old law, the right of a registered proprietor to recover his land from someone who dispossessed him used to be extinguished by the Limitation Act 1980 after 12 years. Once this had happened, the adverse possessor was said to have 'acquired rights under the Limitation Act', and could require the registrar to register him in the place of the registered proprietor. Once the squatter had acquired a right to the land in this way, he could go out of possession and yet still retain his right to be registered as owner. This made the overriding nature of his rights under LRA 1925 very dangerous to a purchaser, who would be bound by those rights even although there was no way of discovering them.

Under LRA 2002 a squatter retains any right to registration acquired by completing the limitation period before the Act comes into force, but there is no specific provision that such a right should be overriding. A purchaser will be bound by it only if the squatter is in actual occupation at the relevant time and can satisfy the other requirements of Sch. 3 para. 2.

Where the squatter had not completed the limitation period before the Act came into force, he is governed by the new rules about adverse possession, for which see 8.6.

2. *Rights of a person in receipt of the rents and profits*

Under LRA 1925, s. 70(1)(g), the rights of a person who was not in actual occupation of the land but was in receipt of rents and profits from it were overriding. This protected, for example, the rights of a tenant under a head lease who was receiving rent from his subtenant. Provision for this is not included in Sch. 3, and as a result such rights are no longer overriding.

3. *Rights excepted from the effect of registration with possessory, qualified or good leasehold title (LRA 1925, s. 70(1))h))*

The definitions in LRA 2002, ss. 11 and 12 make it clear that the excepted rights are binding on the registered proprietor, and in consequence it is not necessary to provide separately for those rights to be overriding.

7.10 Interests of persons in actual occupation

This is a very important category of interests that override a registered disposition, and requires detailed consideration.

7.10.1 Statutory provisions

Under Sch. 3, para. 2 certain interests of persons in actual occupation at the time of a disposition override that disposition and will bind the purchaser, despite the fact that they are not recorded on the register of title. The earlier definition of this group of overriding interests was to be found in LRA 1925 s. 70(1)(g), which classified as overriding:

> The rights of every person in actual occupation of the land or in receipt of the rents and profits thereof, save where enquiry is made of such person and the rights are not disclosed.

As we shall see, the new Act makes a considerable reduction in this category of overriding interests, but there is still a good deal of common ground between the old and new provisions, and interpretation of the earlier law continues to be relevant (see *Thomson v Foy* [2010] 1 P&CR 16 and *Link Lending Ltd v Bustard* [2010] EWCA Civ 424—both of which are considered at 7.10.4). We will therefore continue to refer to earlier case law, where appropriate, to illustrate how the new law is likely to work.

The terms of Sch. 3, para. 2 are considerably longer and more complicated than those of s. 70(1)(g), and we think it would be helpful to set out the actual wording. Schedule 3, para. 2 provides that a registered disposition is subject to:

> An interest belonging at the time of the disposition to a person in actual occupation, so far as relating to land of which he is in actual occupation, except for—
>
> (a) an interest under a settlement under the Settled Land Act 1925;
>
> (b) an interest of a person of whom inquiry was made before the disposition and who failed to disclose the right when he could reasonably have been expected to do so;
>
> (c) an interest –
>
> (i) which belongs to a person whose occupation would not have been obvious on a reasonably careful inspection of the land at the time of the disposition, and
>
> (ii) of which the person to whom the disposition is made does not have actual knowledge at that time;
>
> (d) [a future lease which is compulsorily registrable (see 7.3.1.2)] which has not taken effect in possession at the time of the disposition.

7.10.2 What interests override under para. 2?

It should be noted that para. 2 does not create any new right to occupy the property, but rather gives overriding effect to any interest already belonging to the occupier, which has not been protected by an entry on the register.

Thus if the occupier is a tenant under a lease which gives him an option to purchase the reversion (i.e., the right to 'buy out' his landlord's interest) the option may well be held to be overriding and enforceable against a purchaser of the landlord's estate, although there is no mention of it on the register of that estate (*Webb v Pollmount* [1966] Ch 584).

Similarly, where a beneficiary under a trust is in actual occupation of the land her rights have been held to be overriding and binding on the purchaser (see, for example, *Hodgson v Marks* [1971] Ch 892, and *Williams & Glyn's Bank Ltd v Boland* [1981] AC 487, which we will tell you about in 7.10.4.6).

We must emphasise that the occupier's rights will be overriding only if they amount to a recognised interest in land. As a result, it is essential when dealing with a problem concerning this class of overriding interests that you should begin by identifying the recognised property interest which the occupier is seeking to enforce.

7.10.2.1 Exclusion of certain rights

You should also note that in some instances persons have rights and are in occupation but nonetheless their rights will not override because of a specific statutory exclusion. Thus the right of a spouse or civil partner to occupy the home (see 6.4.2.5 and 27.3.3.1) is not capable of overriding and must be protected by means of an entry on the register if it is to bind a purchaser (Family Law Act 1996, s. 31(10)). As a result it is necessary to check that there is no specific exclusion for the right that you are considering.

Two further exclusions are added by LRA 2002 Sch. 3, para. (2):

(a) *interests under a SLA settlement* (para. 2(a))

Under LRA 1925, s. 86(2), the rights of a beneficiary under such a settlement had to be protected by an entry on the register, even if he was in actual occupation, and this continues to be the position under the new Act.

(b) *future leases which are compulsorily registrable (unless they have already taken effect in possession at the time of the disposition) (para. 2(d))*

We have already seen that leases of this type cannot be overriding under Sch. 3, para. 1, and para. 2(d) ensures that they do not become overriding by virtue of actual occupation.

7.10.3 Comparison of LRA 2002 Sch. 3, para. 2 with LRA 1925 s. 70(1)(g)

The terms of s. 70(1)(g) were very wide and constituted a real risk for unwary purchasers. The provisions of para. 2 are much narrower. There is no reference to the rights of a person in receipt of rents and profits (see 7.9.2.4), and the range of interests which can bind as a result of actual occupation is considerably reduced. In order to do this, the paragraph sets out a list of requirements which must be satisfied if an interest belonging to a person in actual occupation is to be overriding. The wording of the provision is a little complicated, but in substance it prescribes the following conditions.

7.10.3.1 The interest must relate to land of which the person is in actual occupation (see proviso to para. 2)

This requirement is designed to deal with situations such as that in *Ferrishurst Ltd v Wallcite Ltd* [1999] Ch 355, in which an occupier's overriding interest under LRA 1925 s. 70(1)(g) was held to extend to a part of the land comprised in the registered title which he did not in fact occupy.

7.10.3.2 If asked about the interest, the person to whom it belongs must not have failed to disclose it 'when he could reasonably have been expected to do so' (para. 2(b))

This requirement is similar to that in LRA 1925 s. 70(1)(g) ('save where inquiry is made of such person and the rights are not revealed'), although the new version suggests that there could be some circumstances in which failure to disclose might be 'reasonable'. It is thus slightly less draconian than the earlier wording, under which non-disclosure automatically deprived the right of its overriding effect. The new wording seems to provide an opportunity for debate as to when non-disclosure would be reasonable. Would it be reasonable, for example, where a beneficiary under a resulting trust is unaware that contribution to the purchase price gives a share in the beneficial interest in the property?

7.10.3.3 The occupation must have been obvious on a reasonably careful inspection of the land OR the purchaser must have had actual knowledge of the interest (para. 2(c))

In fact, para. 2(c) states these two requirements in the negative (i.e., occupation must not be obvious and interest must not be known to the purchaser). Both conditions must be fulfilled if the interest is not to take effect as an overriding interest. We have rephrased the provision because we think it is easier for you to remember as positive conditions, and to see that satisfying either of them allows the interest to override the disposition. Do note, however, that it is the *occupation* which must be obvious, and the *interest* which must be known.

Thus to summarise: an interest which satisfies the other conditions of para. 2 will override a disposition if:

- the purchaser actually knew about the interest, even if the occupation was not obvious on a reasonably careful inspection of the land; or
- the occupation was obvious on such an inspection, even if the purchaser did not know about the interest.

This means that provided the occupation is discoverable, the purchaser may still be bound by an interest of which he does not know. To avoid this, it is essential that any persons seen to be in occupation should be asked whether they have any interests in the property, and in fact doing so has been standard practice since the decision in *Williams & Glyn's Bank Ltd v Boland* [1981] AC 487 (for which, see 7.10.4.6).

The two requirements derived from para.2(c) were considered by the High Court in *Thomas v Clydesdale Bank PLC* [2010] EWHC 2755.

Clydesdale Bank PLC ('the bank') had obtained a county court order for possession of the family home owned by B, the former partner of Ms Thomas ('T'). T had claimed that she had a beneficial interest in the property, arising from a common intention constructive trust (see 15.2.2.2), and that this interest bound the bank because she had been in actual occupation of the property at the date of the mortgage. For medical reasons, T had not been able to attend the trial, so that judgment was given against her in her absence. Her application to set aside the order had been refused, and she appealed against this decision to the High Court. In order to succeed, T had to satisfy the court that 'she had a reasonable prospect of success at the trial'.

The mortgage had been granted after B had completed the purchase of the property, but before the couple moved into the house. At this time, major reconstruction work was being carried out, and T's claim of actual occupation was based on the presence of workman on the site and her regular visits to the property. The court considered that on these facts T had reasonable prospects of establishing actual occupation (see further on this point 7.10.4.2).However, the bank claimed that even if there was actual occupation, T could not satisfy the requirements of para.2(c), which raised the question of what was required to establish:

- that occupation was obvious on a reasonable careful inspection of the land; or
- that the bank must have had actual knowledge of the interest.

On the first point (at paras. 38–40) Ramsey J did not consider that:

> the objective phrase 'reasonably careful inspection' imposed any requirement that the person inspecting had any particular knowledge or was required to make reasonable enquiries...it is the visible signs of occupation which have to be obvious on inspection.

He considered that T would have reasonable prospects of establishing that a person carrying out an inspection would have been aware of the work being done on the property and of T's visits to it (para. 38).

On the second point (at paras. 47–49), the judge rejected the bank's suggestion that it could be said to have 'actual knowledge of the interest' only if it had received formal evidence of it (for example, from the submission of a deed). He noted that interests belonging to a person who relies on 'actual occupation' will rarely be ascertainable from a legal document. It would be sufficient to show that the bank had actual knowledge of the facts which were said to give rise to the alleged interest. Here the bank had been aware that B had a new partner, that T was intending to contribute to the cost of buying the property and that it was to become the family home. The judge considered that T had reasonable prospects of showing that the bank had actual knowledge of her interest.

T's appeal against the refusal to set aside the order for possession was accordingly allowed.

7.10.4 Some questions about the operation of Sch. 3, para. 2

7.10.4.1 *Thompson v Foy*

Thompson v Foy [2010] 1 P&CR 16 is the first case in which the provisions of Sch.3 para. 2 have been considered, and is of particular interest for its summary of the case law arising from s. 70(1)(g), a summary which Mummery LJ has recently described as 'accurate and helpful' (see *Link Lending Ltd v Bustard* [2010] EWCA Civ 424, at para.13).

The facts

Mrs Thompson ('T'), the claimant, inherited the family home when her husband died. She transferred the title to the house to her daughter, Mrs Foy ('F'), so that F could raise a large loan, secured by a mortgage of the property. It was agreed that the money so borrowed would be shared between mother and daughter. The property was mortgaged to The Mortgage Business ('TMB'), but F did not pay any of the money she raised over to her mother. T then claimed that her daughter had exercised 'undue influence' over her in persuading her to transfer the title, and that therefore she had a right in equity to set the transfer aside (for more information about the equitable doctrine of undue influence, see Chapter 24).

How would this right affect the mortgagee?

There used to be some doubt as to whether such a right (described as 'a mere equity') had effect only between the parties to the transaction or whether it had the status of an interest in land which could bind a later purchaser of the property. However, this uncertainty is resolved by LRA 2002, s. 116, which declares for the avoidance of doubt that, in relation to registered land, a mere equity has effect from the time it arises as an interest capable of binding successors in title (see para. 134 of judgment, and text at 21.7.1). If T had such an equity, it would have arisen at the time when the transactions were made (para. 114) i.e., before the grant of the mortgage to TMB. This meant that, under LRA 2002, s. 29, T's interest would have priority over the mortgage, provided it was protected by an entry on the register or took effect as an overriding interest. Unsurprisingly, there was no entry on the register but T claimed that she had been in actual occupation of the property and consequently had an overriding interest under LRA 2002, Sch. 3 para. 2.

The decision
Lewison J found on the facts that F had not exercised undue influence over her mother. In consequence, T had no right to set the transactions aside and the issue concerning overriding interests did not arise. However, in case he was wrong in finding that there was no undue influence, the judge examined the arguments put forward in support of the claim to an overriding interest and indicated what his decision would have been on that issue (paras. 118–131). This section of his judgment does not, of course, form part of the ratio of the case, but it is extremely interesting as being the first judicial consideration of Sch. 3 para. 2, and the judge's observations, although *obiter dicta*, are well worth noting.

It is clear from the judge's references to decisions on the application of LRA 1925, s. 70(1)(g) that he regarded them as relevant to the interpretation of LRA 2002 Sch. 3 para. 2, and so we will now turn to the questions that arose on the earlier provisions and the view taken of them in the courts. As we go, we will note the observations of Lewison J and tell you how he would have decided T's claim to an overriding interest if he had been required to do so.

7.10.4.2 What is meant by 'actual occupation'?

In the words of Lord Wilberforce in *Williams & Glyn's Bank Ltd v Boland* [1981] AC 487 at pp. 504–5, 'it is the fact of occupation that matters' and what is required is 'physical presence on the land and not some entitlement in the law'. The courts have been reluctant to suggest any test for what is 'essentially a question of fact', pointing out in *Abbey National Building Society v Cann* [1991] 1 AC 56 at p. 93 that:

> ... 'occupation' is a concept which may have different connotations according to the nature and purpose of the property which is claimed to be occupied.

This is well illustrated by the decision of the Court of Appeal in *Lloyds Bank Plc v Rosset* [1989] 1 Ch 350. The Rossets had been allowed by their vendor to start work on renovating the property they wished to buy before contracts were exchanged. This involved the daily presence of builders on the site and regular visits to the property by the wife, who carried out a good deal of the work herself. At completion, the property was mortgaged to the bank by the husband (the sole transferee). Later, he defaulted on repayments and the bank sought possession of the property. The wife claimed that she had a beneficial interest in the house, arising from a common intention trust (see 15.2.2.2) and that this bound the bank as an overriding interest by virtue of her 'actual occupation' at the date of the mortgage. She succeeded in this claim at first instance, and the bank appealed against this decision.

In the Court of Appeal, Nicholls LJ said (at p. 377F) that he could see no reason:

> why a semi-derelict house...should not be capable of actual occupation whilst the works proceeded and before anyone has started to live in the building.

The court considered (Mustill LJ dissenting) that the physical presence of the wife when working on the property amounted to the necessary 'actual occupation' and in addition expressed the view that the presence of the builders as employees or agents of the Rossets was sufficient to establish the couple's occupation. Accordingly, the court rejected the bank's appeal and confirmed the lower court's decision.

As we explain in 20.5.4, this decision of the Court of Appeal was reversed by the House of Lords in *Lloyds Bank Plc v Rosset* [1991] 1 AC 107, on the grounds that the wife had not established her claim to a beneficial interest. As a result, their Lordships expressed no view on the question of her actual occupation, and the Court of Appeal's decision on this point has recently been relied upon by the High Court in considering very similar facts in *Thomas v Clydesdale Bank PLC* [2010] EWHC 2755 (see 7.10.3.3).

A more extreme example of occupation of an uninhabitable site is provided by the Court of Appeal decision in *Malory Enterprises Ltd v Cheshire Homes (UK) Ltd* [2002] Ch 216, in which the land in question was awaiting development by Malory Enterprises Ltd, which claimed an overriding interest in respect of it under s. 70(1)(g). In the words of Arden LJ (at para. 80):

> If a site is uninhabitable...residence is not required, but there must be some physical presence, with some degree of permanence and continuity.

Here the company had maintained fences around the land and taken other physical measures to exclude trespassers, and the court considered that this amounted to 'actual occupation'.

If occupation is established but the interest claimed was not known to the purchaser, the question will then arise of whether the occupation was 'obvious on a reasonably careful inspection of the land' (Sch. 3, para. 2(c)). It seems possible that in a situation similar to that in *Malory Enterprises Ltd v Cheshire Homes (UK) Ltd* the Court might hold that there was occupation but that it was not obvious, but this must of course be very much a decision on the facts.

7.10.4.3 When must the person be in actual occupation?

As we have seen (7.2.3), there is a gap in time between the transfer of the estate and the completion of that transfer by registration at the registry. In dealing with claims to overriding interests based on actual occupation, the courts have had to decide at which point in this process it is necessary for the claimant to be in occupation.

LRA 1925

Section 70(1)(g) did not specify when the claimant had to be in occupation, and so the matter had to be considered in some detail by the House of Lords in *Abbey National Building Society v Cann* [1991] 1 AC 56. Although the facts involve the purchase of a registered estate, it was the concurrent grant by the purchaser of a mortgage which was said to be subject to the overriding interest. The facts were as follows.

Cann bought a property with the aid of a mortgage from the Abbey National, representing to the Society that the house was for his sole occupation, although in fact he intended it to be occupied by his mother and uncle. On the day of the transfer and the creation of the charge, the Canns' furniture arrived at the property some 35 minutes before the charge to the Society took place and at that point there were also removal men on the premises moving in items on the mother's behalf. The charge was not completed by registration until a month later and by that time it was quite clear that Cann's mother and uncle were both in occupation of the premises. Both claimed that they had interests in the property by reason of contribution, and, when Cann defaulted on the mortgage payments, they asserted that their rights had priority to those of the Society (i.e., that their rights were overriding under s. 70(1)(g) and bound the mortgagee).

The House of Lords was of the opinion that the purchaser is bound by all overriding interests in existence at the date of registration. However, there were difficulties in holding that a person who went into occupation between transfer and registration could acquire an overriding interest under s. 70(1)(g), because that section clearly contemplated that the purchaser would make enquiries of any person in occupation, and the proper time for making such enquiries is before the transfer. As a result, the House of Lords took the view that in order to succeed under s. 70(1 (g),a claimant must show he was in actual occupation at the date of the transfer. Any rights he might have would then be capable of being overriding interests, and, if those rights were still in existence at the date of registration, they would bind the purchaser.

Applying this to the facts of the case, the House of Lords held that the preparatory work of moving in furniture did not constitute actual occupation, and that accordingly the Canns were not in occupation at the time of transfer, when the charge to the society was created.

LRA 2002

Schedule 3 para. 2 defines the overriding interest as '[a]n interest belonging *at the time of the disposition* to a person in actual occupation' (emphasis added), but gives no guide as to whether the disposition occurs at the time of the grant or of the subsequent completion by registration. The distinction was of significance in *Thompson v Foy* [2010] 1 P&CR 16, because the judge found as a fact that the claimant, T, had been in actual occupation of the property on the date at which the mortgage was granted but had given up occupation by the date of its registration.

The judge's conclusion on this question (at para. 121) was that:

> If actual occupation must exist at one date only, then in my judgment the date of disposition [i.e., the grant] is the relevant date.

His reasons for this view were:

> First, s.27(2)(f) identifies the disposition as the grant of a legal charge, not its completion by registration. Second, the language of s.29(1) contemplates that the time of the disposition and the time of registration may be different...Third, Sch.3 para.2(c) contemplates an inspection at the time of disposition. This must mean an inspection at the date when the legal documents are executed and the money is released.

However, the judge left open the question of whether there must be actual occupation at the date of registration as well as at the date of disposition. His own opinion was that the wording of Sch. 3 para. 2 indicated that occupation at both dates was required, but he noted that the leading texts of Ruoff & Roper and Gray & Gray took the contrary view, and left the matter for consideration in some later case (see paras. 122–6). As yet, there has been no further discussion of this point, but you may like to note that in summarising the facts in *Link Lending Ltd v Bustard* [2010] EWCA Civ 424, at para. 3, (see 7.10.4.4) Mummery LJ described the date on which the relevant mortgage was registered as being 'the key date'.

7.10.4.4 What happens if the occupier is absent temporarily from the property?

LRA 1925

There is little direct authority on the application of s. 70(1)(g) in these circumstances, although one would think it is quite likely that an occupier who is unaware of the vendor's intention to sell or mortgage the property may be away at the relevant time—on holiday, perhaps, or in hospital. An apparent decision in such a case is to be found in *Chhokar v Chhokar* [1984] FLR 313, in which a husband, who was seeking to deprive his wife of her equitable interest in the matrimonial home, completed the sale of the property to his accomplice while his wife was in hospital. The husband then absconded with the proceeds of sale, and on her return from hospital the wife was excluded from the house by the purchaser, so that she was not physically present on the property when he was registered as proprietor. Noting that the wife's furniture was in the house on the date of registration, the Court of Appeal said that it had no difficulty in holding that she was in occupation at that date, and went on to describe her right in the property as an overriding interest which bound the purchaser. This would appear to be a clear decision on the point, but unfortunately, although the court described the interest as 'overriding', there is no reference to the provisions of LRA 1925, and the language of the report suggests that the whole transaction may have taken place in the unregistered system of title, i.e., before first registration.

It may be helpful to note that similar questions arise under other statutory provisions requiring occupation (for example, under the Rent Acts), and that in such cases the courts take into account whether the occupier had a continuing intention to return, and whether his or her belongings remained in the property. As the Court of Appeal put it in *Hoggett v Hoggett* (1979) 39 P&CR 121 at p. 128:

> Going to hospital for a few days could not be regarded as going out of occupation, any more than if the [occupier] had gone on a weekend visit to a friend, or, indeed, gone out shopping for a few hours.

The decision in *Hoggett* was relied upon in *Thompson v Foy* [2010] 1 P & CR 16, para. 127, in which Lewison J summarised the position on temporary absence under the old Act as being that:

> If the person said to be in actual occupation at any particular time is not physically present on the land at that time, it will usually be necessary to show that his occupation was manifested and accompanied by a continuing intention to occupy.

LRA 2002

The effect of temporary, possibly involuntary, absence has now been considered by the Court of Appeal in *Link Lending Ltd v Bustard* [2010] EWCA Civ 424. Ms Bustard ('B'), who suffered from a serious psychiatric condition, had been tricked into transferring the registered title of her house to a Mrs Hussain ('H'). The transfer was stated to be by way of sale, but B received no payment for the property. She remained in the house but, unknown to her, H mortgaged the property to Link Lending ('Link'), and later defaulted on the repayments. On Link's application for a possession order, it was claimed on B's behalf that she had a right to set the transfer aside, due to her lack of legal capacity, and that her right to do so bound the bank, because she had been in actual occupation at the date of the mortgage.

At trial, Link conceded that B had a right against N to set aside the transfer, but denied that she had been in actual occupation at the relevant date. At the time the mortgage was granted, B had been absent from the property for over a year, having been taken into residential psychiatric care under the Mental Health Act 1983. Nevertheless the judge, guiding himself by *Thompson v Foy*, held that in the particular circumstances of the case B had 'a continuing intention to occupy' and so had remained in actual occupation of the property.

On Link's appeal to the Court of Appeal, Mummery LJ emphasised the fundamental point that the existence of actual occupation is essentially a question of fact, to be decided on the basis of evidence before the court. The factors to be weighed by a judge in a case such as this included (at para. 27):

> The degree of permanence and continuity of presence of the person concerned, the intentions and wishes of that person, the length of absence from the property and the reason for it and the nature of the property and personal circumstances of the person

In this case, the facts were not all one way. Some of them supported B's claim, while others were against her. On balance, however, the trial judge had found that she was in actual occupation. The matters on which he had relied included: the presence of B's furniture and belongings in the house; the fact that she continued to regard the house as her home and was determined to return to live there; her brief but regular accompanied visits to the property; the payment on her behalf of bills relating to the property; and the fact that there had been no final decision by the medical authorities that she would never be able to live there again.

The Court of Appeal considered that the judge's finding that B was in actual occupation was a conclusion which he could properly draw from these circumstances, and accordingly dismissed Link's appeal.

One question remains: at what point in a period of prolonged absence will actual occupation come to an end? In *Stockholm Finance Ltd v Garden Holdings Inc* [1995] LTL (26 October 1995), the court rejected a claim based on actual occupation in which the claimant had been absent from the property for a full year, Robert Walker J stating that:

> ...there must come a point at which a person's absence from his house is so prolonged that the notion of his continuing to be in actual occupation of it becomes insupportable

This decision was considered by the Court of Appeal in *Bustard*, but distinguished on its facts (see paras. 21 and 30).

7.10.4.5 Is the presence of possessions in the property enough to establish actual occupation?

LRA 1925

As noted above, it seems that in cases of temporary absence the presence of the occupier's belongings on the premises may help to establish actual occupation. However, it was held in *Strand Securities v Caswell* [1965] Ch 958 that the presence of belongings alone, without any previous occupation and intention to return, was not enough to establish occupation for the purposes of LRA 1925, s. 70(1)(g).

In this case, Caswell had a lease of a London flat. The lease, being for just over 39 years, fell into the category of leases which at that time could be registered, but did not have to be (a rule which was changed by LRA 1986). In fact, the title to the lease was not registered, nor was it protected by an entry on the landlord's title. Caswell kept some furniture and clothing at the flat but did not live there. The property was occupied by his stepdaughter who had moved in with his permission, because her marriage had broken down. She occupied the flat as a licensee (that is, as someone with permission—a licence—to do so). As we shall see in Chapter 23, the protection given by the law to licensees can vary considerably according to the individual's circumstances, but the general principle, which applied in this case, is that this type of agreement can be terminated at any time and gives the licensee no rights in the land.

The landlord sold its interest in the property, and the new owner claimed that the lease was void against it because the lease was neither registered nor protected by an entry against the landlord's estate. The Court of Appeal rejected the tenant's claim that he had an overriding interest under LRA 1925, s. 70(1)(g), because, although he had rights in the property (the lease), he was not in occupation. The presence of his belongings at the property did not amount to occupation for the purposes of the Act.

The stepdaughter was of course in occupation of the property, but unfortunately she did not have any recognised property interest in the flat and so had no rights which were capable of being overriding. The court did suggest that, had she occupied the flat at the request of her stepfather and in order to look after it for him, he might have been regarded as being in occupation through an agent. However, on the facts as they stood, she was clearly there because of her own needs and not as Mr Caswell's agent. The House of Lords has since confirmed, in *obiter dicta* in *Abbey National Building Society v Cann* [1991] 1 AC 56, that occupation through an agent is possible.

LRA 2002

The question of whether the presence of belongings in the property was sufficient to establish actual occupation under Sch. 3 para. 2 arose in *Thompson v Foy* [2010] 1 P&CR 16 because by the time the mortgage was registered, T was no longer living in the property. Although her possessions remained there, and she went back at intervals to collect them, she had formed the intention of never returning to live there. The judge accepted that the presence of possessions in a property could establish actual occupation during temporary absence if there was an intention to return (see his references to *Strand Securities Ltd v Caswell* and *Hoggett v Hoggett* at para. 127), but he considered that the presence of possessions without the intention to return was not enough. He found therefore that T was not in actual occupation at the date of registration (paras. 130–1), although as we noted above (7.10.4.3), he left open the question of whether actual occupation was required at this stage.

7.10.4.6 Can several people be in actual occupation of the property at the same time?

In the past, particular difficulties arose when the vendor and the person claiming under s. 70(1)(g) were both living in the property. This was the position in *Hodgson v Marks* [1971] Ch 892, in which it was held that Mrs Hodgson was to be regarded as being in actual occupation of premises even though she shared the property with the registered proprietor. Mrs Hodgson had been the original owner of the estate and had transferred it to her lodger under an arrangement by which it was clear that she was transferring only the legal title and not the beneficial rights to the property. As a result, he held the legal estate on trust for her. When the former lodger sold the property (in breach of his duties as trustee), the purchaser was held to be bound by Mrs Hodgson's rights to the property. Since she was the true beneficial owner of the property, the purchaser was in the position of a trustee and was compelled to convey the legal estate to her. This case illustrates very well the dangers of the s. 70(1)(g) overriding interest, since the purchaser had bought an estate which in reality was worthless.

Similar difficulties concerning shared occupation used to arise in the case of married women living in houses owned by their husbands. They might well have a beneficial interest arising from contribution, but, as we have already seen in the case of unregistered land (6.5.2.3), their presence in the property was attributed to their marital status, and they were not regarded as being in occupation for the purposes of s. 70(1)(g) (*Bird v Syme-Thomson* [1979] 1 WLR 440). However, a more modern approach to the role of the married woman was adopted by the House of Lords in *Williams & Glyn's Bank Ltd v Boland* [1981] AC 487. This case involved a wife who had acquired an interest in her husband's property by contributing to the purchase price, and so had become a beneficiary under a resulting trust of the land. She lived in the property with her husband, who was the sole registered proprietor. Mr Boland mortgaged the property to his bank and used the money raised in his business. Later, when he failed to make his mortgage repayments, the bank sought vacant possession of the premises, so that it could sell the estate in order to repay the loan. Mrs Boland then claimed that she had rights in the property and that, as she had been in occupation of the premises when the mortgage was granted, the bank's rights as mortgagee were subject to her prior beneficial interest. The House of Lords considered that the wife's occupation of the premises could be distinguished from that of her husband, and accordingly upheld Mrs Boland's claim that she had an overriding interest which bound the bank.

As a result of *Hodgson v Marks* and *Williams & Glyn's Bank Ltd v Boland*, it appeared that a purchaser or mortgagee could be bound by the rights of all those occupying the property with the vendor, including any of his relatives. It seemed possible that even children would be included in the category of those in actual occupation: they are certainly capable of having a beneficial interest in the property. However, the Court of Appeal held in *Hypo-Mortgage Services Ltd v Robinson* (1997), *The Times*, 2 January 1997, that a child cannot be a person in actual occupation for the purposes of s. 70(1)(g). The court made it clear that its ruling applied to all minors, not merely to those of 'tender years' (as in the case before it), explaining that children 'had no right of occupation of their own: they were only there as shadows of occupation of their parent'. No thought appears to have been given to minors over the age of 16, who could be married or cohabiting, and who could have acquired an interest in their homes through contribution. For a critical comment on this decision, see [1997] Conv 84.

7.10.4.7 How can a purchaser take free of the occupier's rights?

It has to be recognised that despite *Williams & Glyn's Bank Ltd v Boland*, there can be circumstances in which a purchaser can take his interest free of the rights of a person in actual occupation, and we consider three of these situations below.

1. *Overreaching*

As we explained in Chapter 6 (6.5.2.1) the process known as 'overreaching' enables land subject to certain trusts to be sold free of the beneficiaries' interests, provided that the purchase price is paid to at least two trustees, who hold the money upon trust for the beneficiaries in place of the land. In *Boland*, the mortgage was made and the money received by the sole registered proprietor so that overreaching could not operate. However, in *City of London Building Society v Flegg* [1988] AC 54 mortgage money, which arose when a second mortgage was made, was paid to two legal owners who held the estate upon trust for themselves and the Fleggs. In these circumstances the House of Lords held that the interests of the Fleggs, who were beneficiaries under the trust, were overreached by that payment, even though the beneficiaries had been in occupation of the premises at the date of the charge. The effect of that decision was to allow the mortgagee to get priority over the rights of the Fleggs and to be able to sell the property free of their interests. The beneficiaries were left only with the right to sue the legal owners, their trustees, for breach of trust, since the legal owners had used the mortgage money for their own purposes.

This decision is very hard for those placed in the position of the Fleggs, since the legal owners who have entered into this kind of transaction are often bankrupt or have fled the country and it is often a matter of pure chance whether the property has one or two legal owners. However, the decision of the House of Lords is in harmony with the overreaching rules which are fundamental to much of the 1925 property legislation.

2. *Express agreement*

The decisions in *Hodgson v Marks* and *Boland* constituted a considerable risk for intending purchasers, and *Boland* in particular caused great concern among professional mortgagees, such as building societies and banks. Conveyancers speedily developed procedures for guarding against the results of that decision, and the practice has evolved of requiring anyone in occupation of the property in addition to the mortgagor to sign documents agreeing that any rights they may have will be subordinated to those of the mortgagee (such consent, however, may sometimes be set aside on the grounds of 'undue influence' (24.17.2)).

3. *Implied agreement*

Even where there is no express agreement, it is possible that the occupier's rights will not prevail against a mortgagee. In *Paddington Building Society v Mendelsohn* (1985) 50 P&CR 244 the competition was between a beneficiary under a resulting trust, who was in occupation of the property and who had known that a mortgage advance would be needed in order to purchase the property, and the building society which had granted that mortgage. In such a case the Court of Appeal held that the occupier had impliedly consented to the creation of the mortgage since the possibility of acquiring an interest in the property was dependent upon that mortgage. Thus the occupier could not claim an interest having priority to the rights of the building society. As a result of this decision the *Boland* and *Flegg* issues will usually arise now only in cases of second mortgages or sales.

More recently this approach was adopted by Lewison J in *Thompson v Foy* [2010] 1 P&CR 16, as the last stage in the hypothetical decision which he was outlining i.e., *if* T had the right to set the transaction aside and *if* that right was overriding by virtue of her actual occupation, could the mortgagee take free of the right if it could show that she had agreed to the mortgage? The judge considered the decision in *Paddington Building Society v Mendelsohn* and held that on the evidence T knew about the mortgage and wanted it to happen. If he had been required to decide the point, he would have held therefore that T had agreed to the mortgage and could not enforce her right against the mortgagee.

7.11 Discovering encumbrances: searches and enquiries

Now that we have looked at the way in which encumbrances are classified and protected in the registered title system, we should mention briefly the searches and enquiries which will have to be made by the Armstrongs, the prospective purchasers of 1 Trant Way.

7.11.1 Searching the register

All we need to say here is that the Armstrongs will of course have to make a search of the register: to satisfy themselves that Victor Venn is the registered proprietor of the estate and to see whether any encumbrances have been noted on the register.

We cannot deal here with the mechanics of searching the register, save to mention that a purchaser who completes within a specified period after an official search (the 'priority period') is not affected by any amendments made to the register in the interval.

As noted at 7.9.2.1, a search should also be made of the local land charges register, because these charges are listed in Sch. 3 as overriding a registered disposition.

7.11.2 Inspecting the land

A physical inspection of the land should be made, from which the purchasers may discover overriding interests such as easements, and the existence of occupiers other than the vendor. Most important, in view of Sch. 3, para. 2, enquiries should be made of any such occupiers as to the nature of their rights and, as we have seen (7.10.4.7(2)), the usual practice would be to require them to agree to waive any rights which they might have against the purchaser.

This need to inspect the land and make enquiries of the occupiers may remind you of the rule in *Hunt v Luck* [1902] 1 Ch 428, which we have discussed in connection with unregistered land (6.5.2.3). We need therefore to consider briefly whether the doctrine of notice has any role to play in the registered title system.

7.11.3 Do notice rules apply to registered land?

At a quick reading of LRA 1925 s. 70(1)(g), there did appear to be considerable similarities between it and the rule in *Hunt v Luck*. Nevertheless, there were significant differences between the two. Under paragraph (g) it was not enough for the purchaser to show that he made all the reasonable enquiries which would protect him from constructive notice in the unregistered system: if the rights existed, he was bound by them, even if he could not reasonably be expected to have discovered them. The only occasion on which he could take free of such rights was if he made enquiries of the occupier and the rights were not disclosed. In this way there were clear differences between the operation of the statutory rule and the doctrine of notice.

This view was expressed by Lord Wilberforce in *Williams & Glyn's Bank Ltd v Boland* [1981] AC 487 at p. 504:

> In my opinion... the law as to notice as it may affect purchasers of unregistered land... has no application even by analogy to registered land.... In the case of registered land, it is the fact of occupation that matters. If there is actual occupation, and the occupier has rights, the purchaser takes subject to them. If not, he does not. No further element is material.

Surprisingly, however, there were two later decisions of the Court of Appeal (*Lloyds Bank plc v Rosset* [1989] Ch 350 and *Abbey National Building Society v Cann* [1989] 2 FLR 265) in which the court apparently considered that the question of whether a purchaser could discover the rights through reasonable enquiries was relevant to the application of s. 70(1)(g). Moreover, Purchas LJ in *Rosset* even went so far as to say that the words of the subsection:

> clearly were intended to import into the law relating to registered land the equitable doctrine of constructive notice (at p. 403).

On appeal in both these cases, the House of Lords made no reference to this aspect of the judgments in the Court of Appeal (*Abbey National Building Society v Cann* [1991] 1 AC 56; *Lloyds Bank plc v Rosset* [1991] 1 AC 107).

In the Consultative Document, the working party concluded that 'there should in general be no place for concepts of knowledge or notice in registered land' (para. 3.46), and recommended that the new Act should state that the doctrine of notice has no application in dealings with registered land except where the Act expressly provides to the contrary (para. 3.44). In fact, there is no express statement to this effect in LRA 2002, but the terms of s. 29 (and the basic rules about priorities set out in s. 28—see 7.14) certainly appear to leave no room for the operation of the equitable doctrine of notice. As the Report puts it (at paras. 5.16–17):

> As a general principle, the doctrine of notice...has no application whatever in determining the priority of interests in registered land. [Apart from a number of very limited situations] issues as to whether [a] disponee had knowledge or notice of a prior interest, or whether he or she acted in good faith, are irrelevant.

The specific situations in which knowledge, notice or good faith are relevant under the Act are noted below.

7.11.3.1 Situations in which knowledge etc is relevant

(1) On first registration, the registered proprietor takes subject to the rights of an adverse possessor of which he has notice (s. 11(4)(c)—see 7.5.4.2(3)).

(2) The provisions of Sch. 3, paras. 2 and 3 (interests of persons in actual occupation and easements and profits à prendre which override a registered disposition) involve requirements of actual knowledge or a reasonably careful inspection of the property, which may remind you of the rules about actual and constructive notice. However, the Report emphasises that these provisions are not drawn from notice-based principles, but are derived by analogy from the requirement of conveyancing law that a seller must disclose to the buyer certain incumbrances which are not obvious on a reasonably careful inspection of the land and of which the buyer does not have actual knowledge. (Report, para. 5.21.)

(3) There are two special cases, involving Inland Revenue charges under the Inheritance Tax Act 1984 and dispositions by a proprietor who has become bankrupt. In these cases, LRA 2002 follows the pattern of the legislation governing these matters, which does involve the concepts of notice and good faith (ss. 31 and 86).

7.12 Alteration of the register and indemnity

7.12.1 How safe is it to rely on the register?

We have seen how a prospective purchaser of registered land, like the Armstrongs, can ascertain who owns the estate and obtain information about the encumbrances binding upon it. We now need to consider how safe it is to rely upon the register. As we have said, there are different grades of title, and if one buys an estate with less than title absolute there will obviously be a degree of risk involved. The Armstrong's vendor is registered with title absolute (see p. 93), but they will want to know exactly how safe an absolute title is. Can they assume that the title is indefeasible and that they will not be disturbed at some date in the future by someone else claiming the estate? Unfortunately one would have to tell them that even an absolute title is not completely safe, for there are circumstances in which the register can be altered, even against a registered proprietor with absolute title.

In some cases a person who suffers loss due to an alteration of the register may apply for financial compensation from a central fund, and it is sometimes said therefore that in the case of registered land the State guarantees the title, because it provides a system of compensation for those who suffer from any deficiencies in the system. The 'State guarantee' concept is not altogether true however, because, as we shall see, compensation is not available to every individual who suffers a loss.

7.12.2 Background to the new provisions of LRA 2002

Under LRA 1925 the whole process of changing entries on the register was known as 'rectification'. While the joint working party had no major criticism of the substance of the Act's provisions about rectification, it commented adversely on the way in which they were drafted, saying that they tended to obscure the real nature of rectification and the manner in which it operated (Report, para. 10.4). It was thought that some of the difficulty was caused by the fact that the term 'rectification' was used to describe all alterations of the register, ranging from removing obsolete entries and remedying minor clerical slips to the correction of major errors which substantially affected existing property rights. In consequence, the provisions in the new Act about changes to the register (to be found in s. 65 and Sch. 4) use a different terminology.

7.12.3 Redefinition of terms

The overall process of making changes to the register is now described as 'alteration' of the register, and 'rectification' is defined in Sch. 4, para. 1 as a type of alteration which:

(a) involves the correction of a mistake; and

(b) prejudicially affects the title of the registered proprietor.

7.12.4 Power to alter the register

Schedule 4, para. 2 provides that the court may order alteration of the register for the purpose of:

(a) correcting a mistake,

(b) bringing the register up to date, or

(c) giving effect to any estate, right or interest excepted from the effect of registration.

Under Sch. 4, para. 5, the registrar is also empowered to alter the register without a court order on these three grounds and, in addition, is given power to remove superfluous entries.

7.12.4.1 Protection of the registered proprietor in possession

Read on their own, paras. 2 and 5 give extremely wide powers to alter the register, and one can imagine that the Armstrongs might feel that the title they propose to buy is somewhat insecure. However, these provisions are substantially curtailed by paras. 3(2) and 6(2), which provide that alterations which amount to rectification (i.e., which correct mistakes and prejudicially affect the title of the registered proprietor) may not be made:

> without the proprietor's consent in relation to land in his possession unless—
>
> (a) he has by fraud or lack of proper care caused or substantially contributed to the mistake, or
>
> (b) it would for any other reason be unjust for the alteration not to be made.

In the past there has been some difficulty about the circumstances in which a proprietor can be said to be in possession and this is clarified in s. 131.

Subject to the restriction on rectification against a proprietor in possession, an application to the court or registrar for alteration must be approved, provided that the relevant body has the power to do so, 'unless there are exceptional circumstances which justify not making the alteration' (Sch. 4, paras. 3(3) and 6(3)). There is thus an element of discretion in the process, but the new Act indicates that the usual practice must be to alter the register.

7.12.4.2 Example of rectification of register against proprietor in possession

The recent decision of the Court of Appeal in *Baxter v Mannion* [2011] 1 WLR 1594 resulted in the rectification of the register to correct a mistake, in circumstances in which the court held that it would be unjust not to do so despite the fact that the proprietor was in possession.

The case arose from an application by B to the Land Registry to be registered as owner of a field, of which M was already the registered proprietor. B based this application on a claim that he had been in adverse possession of the field for the last 10 years, making use of the new procedure introduced by ss. 96–98 and Sch. 6 of LRA 2002 by which a squatter can claim title to land after a 10 year period of adverse possession (see 8.6). The Registry gave the required notice of this application to M who, because of difficult family circumstances, failed to object to this application within the prescribed period. As a result, B was registered as owner of the land. M later applied to the registrar for rectification of the register, claiming that B had never been in been in adverse possession of the land. Accordingly his registration under Sch. 6 was a mistake, which should be corrected under the provisions of Sch. 4, para.5.

As the matter was contentious, it was referred to the Adjudicator (see 7.8.1.3), who found on the evidence about B's use of the field that he had not satisfied the requirements for establishing adverse possession. Based on this finding of fact, the registration of B was held to be a mistake, which the registrar should correct.

B appealed unsuccessfully to the High Court (*Baxter v Mannion* [2010] 1 WLR 1965) and then to the Court of Appeal.

On both appeals, two questions were considered:

(1) *Was the registration of B a 'mistake' within the meaning of Sch. 4, para. 2?*

There is no definition in the Act of what constitutes a mistake for the purposes of Sch. 4, para. 2. However, the court had no difficulty in rejecting B's argument that the provision for correcting a mistake referred only to procedural errors, such as failure by the registrar to give the registered owner notice of a squatter's application. Registering an applicant who had not been in adverse possession was a mistake, because he had not satisfied the precondition for making that application (see Jacob LJ at para. 24).

(2) *Was this a case in which the register should be rectified against a registered proprietor who was in possession?*

Although B had not been in adverse possession before his application, it was accepted by both parties that he was in possession after his registration as proprietor. As a result, the register could be rectified against him only in the circumstances set out in Sch. 4 para. 6. In the High Court, Henderson J noted (at para. 63) that there was no evidence before the court to support a finding of fraud, but he had no hesitation in holding that the second limb of para. 6(2) applied:

> it is clear that [B] was never entitled to be registered as proprietor of the field, and in my view simple justice requires that, in the absence of strong countervailing factors, [M] should now be able to regain title to his property. I can discern no countervailing factors which would make it unjust for [B] to be deprived of his adventitious title to the field, and on the contrary I see every reason why he should.

The Court of Appeal upheld the judge's decision on this point, agreeing that it was a matter of 'simple justice'. It had been argued that M's failure to respond to the Registry's notice in time had made it unjust to rectify the register against B, but Jacob LJ considered (at para. 42) that:

> Mere failure to operate the bureaucratic machinery is as thistledown to [M] losing his land and [B] getting it when he had never been in adverse possession.

B's appeal was accordingly dismissed, and the registrar was ordered to re-instate M as registered proprietor of the field.

7.12.4.3 **Alteration to give effect to an overriding interest**

Paragraphs 3 and 6 may well reassure the Armstrongs, but it is important for them to realise that the protection given to the proprietor in possession does not prevent the register being altered against him to give effect to overriding interests. This has always been the case, although the statutory reason for it has changed with the redrafting of the provisions.

Under LRA 1925 (s. 82(3)), altering the register to give effect to an overriding interest was specifically excepted from the protection given to the proprietor in possession. The danger to a purchaser who bought land subject to an overriding interest is well illustrated by the case of *Chowood Ltd v Lyall* [1930] 2 Ch 156 in which the registered proprietor of an estate was held to be bound by the rights of an adverse possessor, which were overriding under LRA 1925, s. 70(1)(f). In consequence, the register was rectified by removing the portion of the property occupied by the squatter from the registered title. The fact that the registered proprietor was in possession did not protect him, because the rectification was made for the purpose of giving effect to the overriding interest.

Under LRA 2002 (Sch. 4, paras. 3 and 6), the protection of a proprietor in possession applies only to a particular type of alteration—rectification—which as we have seen is limited to an alteration which 'involves the correction of a mistake'. Altering the register to give effect to an overriding interest is not regarded as correcting a mistake because, as we have seen, all registration of title is made subject to any overriding interest which may bind the estate. Thus amending the register to take account of an overriding interest is an 'alteration' but not a 'rectification' and so does not entitle the proprietor in possession to the benefits of paras. 3 and 6.

7.12.5 Indemnity

A person who suffers loss due either to a rectification of the register, or to a refusal to rectify, may be able to claim compensation (an 'indemnity') under LRA 2002, Sch. 8, paras. 1(a) and (b). Compensation may also be paid to the person in whose favour the register is rectified for any loss he has suffered in spite of the rectification.

No compensation is payable where the loss suffered by a claimant is caused wholly or partly by his own fraud, or wholly by his negligence. Where the loss is caused only partly by the claimant's negligence, compensation is reduced to take account of his share in the responsibility (Sch. 8, para. 5).

These new provisions continue the previous rules about indemnity. Both old and new schemes appear to provide fairly generously for compensation, but there has always been a hidden limitation which prevents the payment of compensation when the register is changed to give effect to an overriding interest.

Under the 1925 Act this limitation resulted from the requirement that before an indemnity could be paid it had to be shown that the loss which the applicant suffered was due to the rectification, or due to the refusal to rectify. As a result of this provision it was held in *Re Chowood's Registered Land* [1933] Ch 574, *Re Boyle's Claim* [1961] 1 WLR 339, and *Hodgson v Marks* [1971] Ch 892 that where the register was altered to give effect to an overriding interest no compensation would be payable. In such cases the loss was caused by the proprietor acquiring an estate which was subject to an overriding interest. When the register was rectified the alteration gave effect to an existing state of affairs and did not cause any fresh loss (i.e., the loss was not due to the rectification).

Under the new Act indemnity is payable only in respect of loss caused by rectification or refusal to rectify. As we saw above, alteration of the register to give effect to an overriding interest does not constitute 'rectification' in its new sense of correcting a mistake, and so it remains the case that compensation is not payable in these circumstances.

From this one can see just how dangerous overriding interests can prove to be for a purchaser of a registered estate, particularly where, as in *Hodgson v Marks*, the effect of the overriding interest is to deprive him of the whole estate. It is for this reason that LRA 2002 makes such efforts to reduce the range of overriding interests which can bind a purchaser and cause him loss in this way.

7.13 Transfer and completion by registration

Once the Armstrongs are satisfied with their enquiries and have made any necessary arrangements, the time will have come for the completion of the transaction. They will pay the balance of the purchase price, provided from their own funds or with money borrowed from a lender, to whom they will mortgage the property. Victor Venn will execute a transfer made by deed, using the appropriate Land Registry form. An example of such a transfer is given at pp. 128–30.

The transfer of a registered estate is one of the dispositions which must be completed by registration (see 7.6) and does not take effect at law until this is done. This means that a transfer of a registered estate, unlike a conveyance of unregistered land, does not have the effect of conveying the legal title to the purchaser. The vendor remains the legal owner until the transfer has been registered, and meanwhile the purchaser continues to own the property in equity, as he has done since the contract was concluded (see 5.7.1).

It is this period of time between transfer and registration, known as the 'registration gap', which can be so dangerous to purchasers. The risks which they run in not completing their transactions by registration are well illustrated by the decision in *Barclays Bank plc v Zaroovabli* [1997] Ch 321. Here the bank had been granted a mortgage by the registered proprietor in 1988, but did not register its charge until 1994. During the intervening six years the mortgage took effect in equity only, and was not protected by any entry on the mortgagor's title. Although the terms of the mortgage provided that the mortgagor should not grant any lease of the property without the bank's consent, the mortgagor did in fact grant such a lease some two months after the creation of the mortgage. In 1995, when the mortgagor was unable to repay the loan, the bank sought possession of the property as a preliminary to selling the house and realising its security. The court held that the restriction on the mortgagor's power to grant leases operated only in the case of a legal mortgage, so that the lease created while the bank had only an equitable mortgage was a valid one. Since that lease had been granted before the mortgage was completed by registration, the tenant's lease, and her rights under the Rent Acts, which she derived from the lease, were binding on the bank when it eventually acquired a legal mortgage on registration. As a result, the tenant was entitled to remain in the property, and the value of the bank's security was considerably reduced by the fact that there was a sitting tenant and the house could not be sold with vacant possession.

Although the decision in *Barclays Bank plc v Zaroovabli* concerns the grant of a mortgage, exactly the same principles will apply on the sale of any registered freehold or leasehold estate. If the Armstrongs go ahead with their purchase, it is essential that they complete the transaction by registration without delay, and do not risk leaving the legal estate in the hands of Victor Venn. Of course, when electronic conveyancing is in operation, transfer (or grant) and registration will occur simultaneously, and purchasers will no longer have to worry about the registration gap. In the last section in this chapter, we will look at that part of LRA 2002 which provides for the introduction of this new system, but before doing that we need to deal briefly with the rules which govern the priority of competing equitable interests in registered land.

7.14 Priority of competing equitable interests

In describing the Armstrongs' purchase of 1 Trant Way we have been concerned with the position of a purchaser who buys a legal estate. However, it is necessary to consider as well the position of someone who acquires an equitable interest in registered land. Examples of purchasers acquiring such interests can be found in the creditor who lends money on the security of an equitable mortgage or the tenant who has no formal lease but holds under an equitable one. In addition, we have already seen that purchasers like the Armstrongs will have only an equitable interest in the property if they do not complete the disposition by registration.

For purchasers of such equitable interests, questions may arise as to whether they are bound by interests created before their own, and whether in turn their interest will bind any later interest, or, possibly, be postponed to it. We have already considered these questions about the priorities of competing interests in relation to the purchase

Land Registry
Transfer of whole of registered title(s)

If you need more room than is provided for in a panel, and your software allows, you can expand any panel in the form. Alternatively use continuation sheet CS and attach it to this form.

Leave blank if not yet registered.	1 Title number(s) of the property: ST1234
Insert address including postcode (if any) or other description of the property, for example 'land adjoining 2 Acacia Avenue'.	2 Property: 1 TRANT WAY, MOUSEHOLE, STILTON, ST14 3JP
	3 Date:
Give full name(s). Complete as appropriate where the transferor is a company.	4 Transferor: VICTOR VENN For UK incorporated companies/LLPs Registered number of company or limited liability partnership including any prefix: For overseas companies (a) Territory of incorporation: (b) Registered number in the United Kingdom including any prefix:
Give full name(s). Complete as appropriate where the transferee is a company. Also, for an overseas company, unless an arrangement with Land Registry exists, lodge either a certificate in Form 7 in Schedule 3 to the Land Registration Rules 2003 or a certified copy of the constitution in English or Welsh, or other evidence permitted by rule 183 of the Land Registration Rules 2003.	5 Transferee for entry in the register: ARNOLD ARMSTRONG and ARRIETY ARMSTRONG For UK incorporated companies/LLPs Registered number of company or limited liability partnership including any prefix: For overseas companies (a) Territory of incorporation: (b) Registered number in the United Kingdom including any prefix:
Each transferee may give up to three addresses for service, one of which must be a postal address whether or not in the UK (including the postcode, if any). The others can be any combination of a postal address, a UK DX box number or an electronic address.	6 Transferee's intended address(es) for service for entry in the register: 1 TRANT WAY, MOUSEHOLE, STILTON, ST14 3JP
	7 The transferor transfers the property to the transferee

Place 'X' in the appropriate box. State the currency unit if other than sterling. If none of the boxes apply, insert an appropriate memorandum in panel 11.	8 Consideration [x] The transferor has received from the transferee for the property the following sum (in words and figures): three hundred and fifty thousand pounds (£350,000) [ ] The transfer is not for money or anything that has a monetary value [ ] Insert other receipt as appropriate:
Place 'X' in any box that applies. Add any modifications.	9 The transferor transfers with [x] full title guarantee [ ] limited title guarantee
Where the transferee is more than one person, place 'X' in the appropriate box. Complete as necessary.	10 Declaration of trust. The transferee is more than one person and [x] they are to hold the property on trust for themselves as joint tenants [ ] they are to hold the property on trust for themselves as tenants in common in equal shares [ ] they are to hold the property on trust:
Insert here any required or permitted statement, certificate or application and any agreed covenants, declarations and so on.	11 Additional provisions

The transferor must execute this transfer as a deed using the space opposite. If there is more than one transferor, all must execute. Forms of execution are given in Schedule 9 to the Land Registration Rules 2003. If the transfer contains transferee's covenants or declarations or contains an application by the transferee (such as for a restriction), it must also be executed by the transferee.	12 Execution Signed as a deed by Victor Venn in the presence of: Victor Venn Signature of witness: Michael Moggie Name MICHAEL MOGGIE Address 14 The Broadway, Mousehole, Stilton Signed as a deed by Arnold Armstrong in the presence of: Arnold Armstrong Signature of witness: Rita Ratty Name RITA RATTY Address 148 Downhole Way, Mousehole, Stilton Signed as a deed by Arriety Armstrong in the presence of: Arriety Armstrong Signature of witness: Rita Ratty Name RITA RATTY Address 148 Downhole Way, Mousehole, Stilton

WARNING
If you dishonestly enter information or make a statement that you know is, or might be, untrue or misleading, and intend by doing so to make a gain for yourself or another person, or to cause loss or the risk of loss to another person, you may commit the offence of fraud under section 1 of the Fraud Act 2006, the maximum penalty for which is 10 years' imprisonment or an unlimited fine, or both.

Failure to complete this form with proper care may result in a loss of protection under the Land Registration Act 2002 if, as a result, a mistake is made in the register.

Under section 66 of the Land Registration Act 2002 most documents (including this form) kept by the registrar relating to an application to the registrar or referred to in the register are open to public inspection and copying. If you believe a document contains prejudicial information, you may apply for that part of the document to be made exempt using Form EX1, under rule 136 of the Land Registration Rules 2003.

Form TR1 is Crown copyright and has been reproduced with the kind permission of Land Registry.

of a legal estate, but now need to think how they affect the purchaser of an equitable interest.

This is one area in which the LRA 2002 made a complete break with the past, so for once we need not tell you about the earlier rules, except to say that they were complicated and in some cases even uncertain. The new rule is that priority between equitable interests depends solely on the date at which they were created. This rule is set out in s. 28, and although the language of that section is far from transparent we assure you that that is what it means.

We saw in 6.5.3 that the rule which applies to competing equitable interests in unregistered land is that 'where the equities are equal, the first in time prevails' (i.e., interests rank in chronological order, unless the holder of an earlier interest has behaved in such a way that equity considers it would be fair to postpone his interest to that of a later purchaser). It is important to realise that s. 28 creates an entirely different rule in respect of registered land: the first in time prevails irrespective of its holder's behaviour.

This new rule has been applied recently by the High Court in *Halifax plc and Bank of Scotland v Curry Popeck* [2008] EWHC 1692 (Ch). The court was asked to determine the relative priorities of two equitable interests, one arising from a charging order imposed to enforce a judgment debt and the other an equity arising from proprietary estoppel (which, under LRA 2002, s. 116, is now recognised as capable of binding a purchaser—see 21.7.1). Both interests arose as a result of fraudulent mortgage transactions by a third party and the facts of the case are complicated. We suggest that you do not concern yourself with them, but simply note that the court applied s. 28, emphasising (at para. 25) that the new provision removed the qualification that priorities might be changed if the holder of the prior equity was at fault. As a result, the court held that the first interest to be created, the equity arising from estoppel, had priority over the later one.

Although questions about priority can arise in respect of any equitable interest, they are most commonly found in situations involving the grant of several mortgages over the same property, and we will consider them further in Chapter 24.

7.15 Electronic conveyancing

As we explained in 7.2.3, the underlying purpose of reforming the registered title system was to facilitate the development of electronic conveyancing. Part 8 of LRA 2002 contains the provisions which are needed to bring such a system into operation, although the details remain to be completed by rules made under the Act.

7.15.1 Communications network

An essential element in the new scheme is the development of a secure electronic communications network which all professionals engaged in the conveyancing process (such as conveyancers, surveyors, estate agents and lenders) can use for communications both between themselves and with the Land Registry. The provision of such a network is authorised by s. 92, and we explain how the Registry proposes to use it in 7.15.3.

7.15.2 Use of electronic contracts and transfers

Section 93 provides for the use of electronic contracts and transfers in a range of dealings with the registered estate which are to be specified by rules made under the Act. It also prescribes the formalities required for making such documents and their effect.

7.15.2.1 Formalities and effect

Electronic documents must make provision for the time and date when they take effect. They must have the electronic signature of each person by whom they purport to be authenticated, and these signatures must be certified. Further conditions may be prescribed by rules.

An electronic document which satisfies these conditions is to be regarded as being made in writing and signed (or in the case of a corporation, sealed) by the individual or corporation whose signature it bears. The document is to be regarded for the purpose of any enactment as a deed, and requirements of attestation (that is, the witnessing of its execution) will not apply to a document in this form (s. 91(4), (5) and (8)). This means that an electronic document will be capable of satisfying the requirements of s. 2 of the Law of Property (Miscellaneous Provisions) Act 1989 with regard to a written contract, as well as those of LPA 1925, s. 52(1) in respect of the deed needed to effect the grant or conveyance of a legal estate.

7.15.2.2 Compulsory use of electronic system

Section 93 authorises the making of rules which would require prescribed dispositions, and contracts to make those dispositions, to be made by electronic documents and simultaneously communicated electronically to the registry. This would mean, for example, that the disposition and its completion by registration would both happen at the same moment, thus removing the present gap between transfer and registration.

Section 93(2) provides that where electronic creation and communication is required, the disposition or contract would only have effect if those requirements are met. This provision for compelling parties and practitioners to use the electronic system is seen by the Land Registry as being very much a matter of last resort. The Registry plans to introduce the new arrangements on a voluntary basis, hoping that the benefits they offer will win over most users. Nevertheless the time may come when compulsion is required to complete the change to the new methods, and it is important to realise that in such a case dispositions and contracts which were not made and communicated electronically would have no effect at all: that is, they would be ineffective in both law and equity.

Inevitably there would be circumstances in which such a sanction would be thought to have a disproportionate effect or in which it would appear unconscionable for one party to rely on the other party's failure to observe the new requirements. We have seen in Chapter 5 that this happened with the Statute of Frauds in 1677, and that equity developed the doctrine of part performance to mitigate its rigours. More recently courts have been sympathetic to litigants who rely on proprietary estoppel or the constructive trust to avoid the effects of the Law of Property (Miscellaneous Provisions) Act 1989, s. 2 (see 5.5). Only time will tell whether the terms of s. 93(2) will be enforced strictly by the courts, but some commentators have already expressed concerns that they may be circumvented by the use of equitable principles (see Dixon [2003] 67 Conv. 136, at 153–5).

7.15.3 How the new system will work

The creation of the communications network will mean that the Registry can be involved at all stages of the conveyancing process. The draft contract will be developed in electronic form and will be available to the registry. This will enable it to check and correct any errors (e.g., in title number, name of party etc.) at an early stage, and will also enable it to begin to prepare a notional register. This will help to validate the conveyancing process, identifying any queries or problems (which at present may not be spotted until after transfer) and will thus speed the process of formal registration.

When the parties are ready to enter the formal contract, they will agree on the date and time at which it will become effective (i.e., the equivalent of agreeing when the exchange of contracts is to take place under the present system). The contract will be released electronically, and this will bring it into effect and simultaneously enter a notice of it as an encumbrance on the vendor's register of title.

Completion will take place in a similar way. The deed of transfer will be prepared and activated electronically, with simultaneous transmission to the registry. This will bring the notional register into operation, so that transfer and registration will take place at the same moment, thus closing the registration gap.

7.15.4 Importance of move to electronic conveyancing

The introduction of electronic conveyancing will have tremendous significance for the operation of the registered title system. It will not only remove the gap between transfer and registration which, as we have seen, can cause problems, but will also reduce very considerably the number of interests which can be created 'off the register'.

7.15.4.1 Interests created 'off the register'

At present, a grant or transfer made by a paper transaction creates a valid equitable interest, even though it is not legally effective until completed by registration. Similarly, as we have seen, equitable interests may arise under any contract for the grant or transfer of a legal estate or interest in land. Where the parties do not go ahead and complete the formalities, interests made 'off the register' in this way may last for many years, and have often been protected as overriding interests by virtue of actual occupation.

When the new system is in full operation, equitable interests will no longer arise from registrable but unregistered dispositions, and the creation of estate contracts by electronic means only will ensure that equitable interests arising from them are automatically noted on the register. This will gradually reduce the number of interests which can be created off the register and which either take effect as interests that override a registered disposition or require protection by subsequent entry on the register. This means that purchasers will be able to buy with even greater reliance on the register, although it must be remembered that certain interests (for example, those under resulting trusts) will continue to arise informally and could take effect as overriding interests (see 7.2.3.1).

7.15.5 Progress in introducing e-conveyancing

It was always clear that developing the appropriate systems and procedures was likely to be a long process. The registry has worked to introduce the new system in phases, testing elements through pilot schemes before making them more generally available. It has already developed a system for the electronic discharge of mortgages (i.e., the removal of the registered charge from the mortgagor's title when he has repaid the debt), and was moving towards the introduction of electronic mortgages and transfers. As part of this process during 2010, the registry undertook a consultation on draft rules relating to the creation and signature of e-mortgages and e-transfers. As a result of responses to this consultation, it has now decided:

> to put the development of an e-transfer system 'on hold' for the immediate future and to delay implementation of the planned new rules until the return of a healthier financial climate and a more active property and mortgage market.

The registry emphasises that this does not mean that it is abandoning its work on e-conveyancing, and it remains committed to implementing the scheme in the future (see *Report on responses to e-conveyancing secondary legislation part 3*, para. 5.2 available at www.landregistry.gov.uk.

FURTHER READING

Chamberlain, 'Sign up to complete the Register' (2005) EG No. 0548 215 (voluntary registration).

Cooke, 'The Land Registration Bill 2001' [2002] Conv 11.

Dixon, 'The Reform of Property Law and the Land Registration Act 2002: A Risk Assessment' [2003] 67 Conv 136.

Harpum, 'Property in an Electronic Age', *Modern Studies in Property Law, Vol.1: Property 2000*, Hart Publishing, 2001, p. 4.

Land Registration for the Twenty-First Century A Consultative Document, 1998, Law Com No. 254; in particular: Part I (need for reform); Part IV (overriding interests); and paras. 11.2–11.20 (electronic conveyancing).

Land Registration for the Twenty-First Century A Conveyancing Revolution, 2001, Law Com No. 271; in particular: Part I (objectives of Land Registration Bill); and Part II (summary of changes).

Ruoff and Roper, *Registered Conveyancing*, Sweet & Maxwell, looseleaf edn., Pt. 1 General Principles.

Tee, 'The Rights of Every Person in Actual Occupation: An Enquiry into Section 70 (1)(g) of the Land Registration Act 1925' [1998] CLJ 328.

Electronic conveyancing

Chamberlain, 'Early learning is key' (2005) EG No. 0548 218.

E-Conveyancing—A Land Registry Consultation May 2002 Parts 2, 4 and 6 (and in particular paras. 6.1–6.2.11).

The Strategy for the Implementation of E-Conveyancing in England and Wales, Land Registry 2005 (in particular, para. 4.2.8).

8

Acquisition of an estate by adverse possession

8.1 Introduction

So far we have been dealing only with estates in land which have been acquired in a formal manner. However, as we mentioned in the introduction to Part II, it is also possible to acquire an estate in land by adverse possession. The LRA 2002 makes major changes to the process of acquiring registered land by adverse possession, but the old rules continue to apply to unregistered land (and to registered land where the period of adverse possession was completed before the new Act came into force).

We will begin this chapter by considering the application of the old rules to another house in Trant Way.

8.1.1 No. 4 Trant Way

The title to 4 Trant Way is not registered. The current inhabitant is Sidney Sorrell. Mr Sorrell moved into the property 15 years ago as a squatter, and has occupied it ever since. Fifteen years ago the house was in a bad state of repair and seemed to have been abandoned by its previous owners. Mr Sorrell has never received any complaints about his occupation of the premises and has made considerable improvements and alterations. He has had the electricity and gas supplies restored and has paid rates in respect of the property.

The original owner of the fee simple in 4 Trant Way was Oscar Oregano, who died six months ago at the age of 98. His entire estate was inherited by his nephew Nicholas Oregano, who has just discovered that his uncle had neglected the property in Trant Way and that it has been taken over by Mr Sorrell.

8.1.2 Importance of possession in English land law

There is an old saying that 'Possession is nine-tenths of the law'. In the case of title to land this saying was particularly true. Since the earliest times, title to land has been based on a form of possession, technically called 'seisin'. If two people had a dispute concerning the ownership of an estate in land, the court would decide the case in favour of the person who could show that he had been seised of the land at the earlier date, or who could show that his predecessors in title had the earlier seisin. Thus prior seisin would decide the issue as between the two claimants.

Technically there is a difference between possession and seisin, but today this is of no real importance, because possession is always regarded as clear evidence of seisin and therefore the two concepts are normally coexistent. A dispute about ownership would therefore be decided in favour of the party who could show prior possession of the property.

8.1.3 Title was relative

The result of this emphasis on the fact of possession is that in the past in England title to land has been treated as relative rather than as absolute. Absolute title involves the idea that there can be only one owner, whose title is 'not merely better than other titles: it is good and they are non-existent or at the best bad' (Lawson and Rudden, *The Law of Property*, 2nd edn., p. 45).

By contrast, in proceedings in an English court where one person claimed land occupied by another, the court was concerned to determine only which of the two parties before it had the better claim: it was not seeking to identify the one 'true' owner. The system of registered title introduced the concept of absolute title into English land law, but by that time the rules of adverse possession were established on the basis of relative title. Thus in the following situation:

1994 A is the fee simple owner of property

1995 B takes possession of the land

2003 C takes possession of the land

if B sues C in order to recover the land, C cannot defend the claim by saying that A, and not B, is the true owner of the estate. A court will consider only the competing claims of B and C, and will therefore regard B as being the better claimant because he has the prior estate (*Nicholls v Ely Beet Sugar Factory* [1931] 2 Ch 84 and *Mount Carmel Investments Ltd v Peter Thurlow Ltd* [1988] 1 WLR 1078).

8.1.4 Application to 4 Trant Way

If we apply this approach to the position of 4 Trant Way we can see that both Sidney Sorrell and Nicholas Oregano have claims to the property.

Mr Sorrell is currently in possession of the property, and is accordingly presumed to be seised of an estate in fee simple. However, Nicholas Oregano also has a claim to the property because he can show that his uncle Oscar was once in possession of the property, and that therefore his uncle was also seised of an estate in the property. That estate is, of course, an inheritable interest, and Nicholas can show that he has inherited the estate under the terms of his uncle's will. Accordingly Nicholas Oregano has an older estate in the property (and no doubt could produce his uncle's deeds to prove this). As a result one would presume that, in any dispute between Nicholas and Mr Sorrell about the ownership of the property, Nicholas would be regarded as having the better right to the property.

Thus far all seems fairly straightforward, but in fact the dispute between Nicholas and Mr Sorrell is likely to be affected by the provisions of the Limitation Act 1980, so that Nicholas's apparent rights may prove to be worthless.

8.1.5 Effect of the Limitation Act 1980

Most legal systems provide that a claimant must commence court proceedings within a prescribed time (the 'limitation period') or lose his right to sue. Provisions of this sort are necessary to ensure that claimants bring their cases promptly, while the necessary evidence is available, and that defendants are not harassed by stale claims, which they may have difficulty in meeting when witnesses have disappeared and recollections have become blurred.

The current limitation provisions are contained in the Limitation Act 1980. Section 15, which now applies only to unregistered land (and to registered land where the period of adverse possession was completed before LRA 2002 came into force on 13 October 2003) provides that the limitation period in respect of claims to recover land is 12 years. Thus generally, if someone with a prior estate in land allows it to be occupied by a squatter for 12 years, he will lose his right to recover the property from the interloper. So in our example, although Nicholas Oregano can prove that his uncle was in prior possession of the land, he may not be able to bring a claim to recover the land from Mr Sorrell because the right to sue has been time-barred. At one time the original owner's title continued even after the limitation period had elapsed, so that although he could not sue to recover the land he could rely on his title as a defence if he took possession again without a court action. However, today the rule is that at the end of the limitation period the original owner loses both his right to sue and his title to the property (Limitation Act 1980, s. 17).

8.1.6 Justification for adverse possession

It may seem somewhat surprising that our legal system allows one person to take land belonging to another and to keep it as his own, and indeed this is sometimes described as 'land theft'. Cases of this sort always arouse public concern and comment when they hit the headlines and, as we shall see later (8.7), were thought to be vulnerable to attack under the Human Rights Act 1998. The example we have given you is of this type: Sidney Sorrell must have known that he had no right to the house when he moved in, and yet it seems that he may now be regarded as having the better title to it.

You should be aware, however, that many claims to title by adverse possession do not arise from a deliberate taking of another's property, but rather through some kind of mistake. Boundaries between neighbouring properties are often far from clear, and one owner may occupy a small strip of his neighbour's land in the genuine belief that it belongs to him. Other cases can arise from mistakes on the part of a vendor, who purports to sell the same piece of land to two different purchasers (as, for example, happened in *Bridges v Mees* [1957] Ch 475). In cases such as these, the rules of adverse possession can be beneficial in helping to bring the legal title into line with the position on the ground.

In fact, there are several good reasons for retaining a system which allows title to be acquired in this way (in addition, of course, to the general reasons underlying any form of limitation of claims, which we have noted above at 8.1.5). We cannot deal in any detail here with the justifications for adverse possession, but have included some references at the end of the chapter, if you want to know more.

In outline, there seem to be three main ways in which the system of adverse possession is beneficial, although, of course, they do not all apply in every case.

(1) *Mistake* Adverse possession may assist an innocent party who has spent money and time on land which he believes to be his own, but who cannot establish a

claim to proprietary estoppel (see Chapter 21), because there has been no encouragement or acquiescence by the owner.

(2) *Keeping land in use* The possibility of acquiring title in this way helps to ensure that land abandoned by its owner is not left to become derelict, or taken out of the property market because its occupier cannot prove title to it.

(3) *Facilitating investigation of title* Perhaps most importantly, it is said that the system of adverse possession facilitates and cheapens the investigation of title to unregistered land. This is because, in general terms, a purchaser is probably willing to assume that any claim to the land arising before the statutory period of title (currently a minimum of 15 years—see 6.2) has been barred under the 12-year limitation period, so that he will be safe in taking a title shown for the minimum period.

This last reason of course is not a consideration when dealing with registered land, but nevertheless, as we shall see (8.5), the Law Commission considered that title by adverse possession still had a useful role to play in the registered system, and provision for it is made in LRA 2002, although in an amended form.

Under LRA 2002 there is now a considerable difference between the new rules governing adverse possession of registered land, and the old rules which relate to unregistered land and to some outstanding claims to registered land. However, the requirements for establishing that a person has been in 'adverse possession' remain the same under both sets of rules, and we will deal with these first, before going on to see how the two systems now diverge once adverse possession has been established.

8.2 Establishing adverse possession

We need to begin by clarifying some of the terms we will use in talking about adverse possession:

(1) *Adverse possessor' and 'squatter'*

Either of these phrases can be used to describe the person who has dispossessed the owner, and we use them interchangeably.

(2) *'Paper owner' or 'documentary owner'*

Some writers and judges use one or other of these phrases to describe the dispossessed owner, thus indicating that he has acquired title by formal means. This distinguishes him from the squatter who, as we shall see (8.3), is also regarded as owning an estate in the land, albeit acquired informally. We shall simply talk about 'the dispossessed owner', but you need to understand the other terms in case you meet them elsewhere.

(3) *'Estate' and 'title'*

You will see that the squatter is sometimes said to acquire 'an estate' in the land, and on other occasions to acquire 'title' to it. In the context of adverse possession, these terms are used synonymously (*Central London Commercial Estates Ltd v Kato Kagaku Co. Ltd* [1998] 4 All ER 948 at p. 958), and you do not need to try to distinguish between them.

In order to claim title by adverse possession, the squatter must show that:

- he has been in possession of the land (8.2.1); and
- the possession has been 'adverse'(8.2.2); and
- the adverse possession has lasted for the prescribed time (8.2.3).

We will look at each of these requirements in turn.

8.2.1 Possession

The squatter must take possession of the land, either by dispossessing the owner or by entering at some time after the owner has discontinued his own possession. There are two essential elements of possession, both of which must be shown to exist:

- the fact of possession; and
- the intention to possess.

8.2.1.1 The fact of possession

What is required here is described by Slade J in *Powell v McFarlane* (1970) 38 P&CR 452 at p. 471:

> what must be shown as constituting factual possession is that the alleged possessor has been dealing with the land in question as an occupying owner might have been expected to deal with it and that no-one else has done so.

What the squatter actually does with the land depends on its nature. If it is a house, he may live in it; if it is a piece of land adjoining his garden, he may fence and cultivate it. In some circumstances more occasional use may be enough, as in *Red House Farms (Thornden) Ltd v Catchpole* [1977] 2 EGLR 125, where shooting wildfowl was held to be a sufficient act of possession, because that was the only purpose for which the land could be used. Whatever the nature of the land, the squatter must be able to show that he has exclusive possession of it; sharing possession with the owner is not enough.

8.2.1.2 The intention to possess ('animus possidendi')

As well as taking physical possession of the land, the squatter must have the intention to possess it, defined by Slade J in *Powell v McFarlane* (1979) 38 P&CR 452 at p. 471 as:

> the intention, in one's own name and on one's own behalf, to exclude the world at large, including the owner with the paper title...so far as is reasonably practicable and so far as the processes of the law will allow.

The squatter must not only have this intention; he must make it clear to the world, including the owner (if he is present) that he intends to possess the land. As the Court of Appeal put it in *Prudential Assurance Co. Ltd v Waterloo Real Estate Inc* [1999] 2 EGLR 85 at 87:

> the claimant must, of course, be shown to have the subjective intention to possess the land, but he must also show by his outward conduct that that was his intention.

Proving the necessary intention

In general, the courts are loath to rely on the claimant's own statement about his intentions, because it may so easily be self-serving, and accordingly, they will tend to look for conduct from which the necessary intention may be inferred.

An example of conduct sufficient to show such an intention is to be found in *Buckinghamshire County Council v Moran* [1990] Ch 623, in which the adverse possessor had cultivated a piece of the council's land which adjoined his garden, fencing it and installing a gate which he chained and padlocked. In the view of the Court of Appeal (at p. 642), the locking of the gate amounted to a 'final unequivocal demonstration of the defendant's intention to possess the land' and to exclude the owner.

You should note that all that is required here is an intention to possess; the squatter does not have to show that he intended to *acquire title* to the property. Thus in *Buckinghamshire County Council v Moran*, the squatter knew that the council had plans for the future use of the land, and made it clear that he intended to keep the land only until the council required it. The Court of Appeal was, however, satisfied that he intended to take possession of the land until that time, and this was sufficient, after completion of the limitation period, to enable him to claim title by adverse possession.

Conversely, it is not fatal to the squatter's claim if he took possession believing that he was entitled to the property, either as a tenant or as the freehold owner. Thus in *Lodge v Wakefield City Council* [1995] 38 EG 136 the appellant, a former tenant of the council, had not paid any rent under the tenancy since 1974, but did not become aware of this fact until the late 1980s, believing, in the meantime that he was in possession of the land as tenant. The Court of Appeal rejected the council's contention that time did not run against it until the possessor became aware of his true position, holding that the former tenant had had the necessary intention to possess the property and that his possession was adverse from the time he ceased to pay rent, even if he himself was not aware of this.

Similarly, it appears from the decision in *Hughes v Cook* (1994), *The Independent*, 21 March 1994 that title by adverse possession can be acquired where the possessor occupies the land under a mistaken belief that he is already the owner of the estate, and indeed, as we mentioned earlier, such mistakes often form the background to cases of adverse possession. At the same time, it must be remembered that other cases can involve the deliberate taking of property which the squatter knows is not his. The rules of adverse possession impose no requirement of good faith, and bad faith is relevant only in the exceptional case of the owner claiming that the squatter has acted fraudulently (see 8.2.3.1).

The owner's state of mind

Having considered what is required of the squatter by way of intention and knowledge, it may be helpful to deal here briefly with the owner's state of mind. There is no requirement that he should know about the adverse possession; use must be open, so that he has the opportunity of finding out about it, but the fact that he does not do so is no bar to the squatter's claim (*Powell v McFarlane* (1979) 38 P&CR 452), and the squatter is under no obligation to draw the owner's attention to what is happening (*Topplan Estates Ltd v Townley* [2005] 1 EGLR 90 at para. 85). Nor does the owner even have to be aware that he owns the land: adverse possession can operate against an owner who believes that the land already belongs to the squatter (see Gray and Gray, para 9.1.50).

8.2.1.3 *Pye v Graham*

The requirements for establishing adverse possession which we have outlined above were considered and affirmed by the House of Lords in *J. A. Pye (Oxford) Ltd v Graham* [2003] 1 AC 419. In this case Pye, who were property developers, were the registered owners of fields adjoining the Grahams' farm. Pye hoped to obtain planning permission to build on the fields, but meanwhile permitted the Grahams to make limited use of them, at first under a written grazing licence for a period in 1983 and then by permission to cut hay in 1984. Further licences were requested in 1984 and 1985; these requests were not answered but the Grahams continued to use the land from 1986 to 1999. In 1997 Michael Graham, the current owner of the farm, registered a caution against Pye's registered title (see 7.8.2.) on the basis that he had acquired title by adverse possession. Pye sought to 'warn off' this caution (i.e. have it removed from the register) and in 1999 commenced proceedings for possession.

Although Neuberger J at first instance ([2000] Ch 676) held that adverse possession had been established, the Court of Appeal ([2001] Ch 804) considered that Graham's evidence showed that he did not have the necessary intention to possess the property to the exclusion of the owner. His evidence made it clear that he intended to carry on using the land in the hope that Pye would subsequently renew the grazing licence, and that he would have been willing to pay for the use of the land if asked to do so. In these circumstances, the court held that the intention to possess had not been established; there was thus no dispossession of Pye and time had not started to run against them under the Limitation Act.

On appeal, the House of Lords reversed the Court of Appeal decision, holding that the Grahams had been in adverse possession of the property and that time had run in their favour ([2003] 1 AC 419). In explaining this decision, Lord Browne-Wilkinson, with whom the others concurred, considered and approved the principles stated by Slade J in *Powell v McFarlane* (1977) 38 P&CR 452. At para. 40, Lord Browne-Wilkinson emphasised the need for both:

- *the fact of possession*—defined as 'a sufficient degree of physical custody and control'; and
- *the intent to possess*—defined as 'an intention to exercise such custody and control on one's own behalf and for one's own benefit'.

This second element, the intention to possess, was an essential ingredient in establishing adverse possession. The fact that physical control by itself was not enough could be illustrated by the hypothetical situation in which a person in occupation of a house in the owner's absence might be, depending on his intention, a friend of the owner who was looking after it for him, a temporary trespasser seeking only a night's lodging, or a squatter who intended to remain in the property. In order to establish adverse possession the occupier must show an intention to use the property for his own benefit, but he did not have to intend to acquire ownership of it (*Buckinghamshire County Council v Moran* [1990] Ch 623 was approved on this point), and most significantly in the present case, a willingness to pay for the use of the land did not indicate an absence of intention to possess. As Lord Browne-Wilkinson put it (at para. 46):

> Once it is accepted that the necessary intent is an intent to possess not to own and an intention to exclude the paper owner only so far as is reasonably possible, there is no inconsistency between a squatter being willing to pay the paper owner if asked and his being in the meantime in possession. An admission of title by the squatter is not inconsistent with the squatter being in possession in the meantime.

Support for this view was to be found in the observations of Lord Diplock in the Privy Council decision in *Ocean Estates Ltd v Pinder* [1969] 2 AC 19, which it appeared had not been given sufficient weight by the Court of Appeal in the present case (para. 46).

In their Lordships' view, both the elements necessary for adverse possession were present in the Grahams' use of the land belonging to Pye. They had physical control of the property (the fields being surrounded by hedges and accessible only through gates which they controlled), and they had the necessary intention to use the land for their own purposes, maintaining and using it as though it was part of their farm. The Grahams were thus entitled to be registered as owners, but it should be noted that several of their Lordships expressed concerns about the apparent injustice of this result (see further 8.7).

8.2.2 Possession must be adverse

There is no statutory definition of 'adverse', but it may be understood as meaning possession which is inconsistent with the rights of the owner, (although it is clear that it does not have to be in any way hostile or aggressive). The adverse possessor is, in fact, in possession as a trespasser. In consequence, anyone taking possession with the consent of the owner, for example under a lease or a licence, will not be in adverse possession, and so cannot acquire rights under the Limitation Act. When a licence comes to an end or is withdrawn, time will, of course, start to run against the owner if the licensee remains on the land without acknowledging his title.

8.2.2.1 Possession by tenants under a lease

It is not possible for a tenant to lay claim to the freehold title because clearly he occupies the land with the permission of the estate owner and in accordance with the terms of his lease. In the case of a lease for a fixed term, or a periodic tenancy granted in writing (for which, see 10.1.2) time only starts to run against the former landlord if the tenant remains on the land at the end of the term or period, not paying rent or acknowledging the owner's title in some way.

Oral periodic tenancies

A tenant who holds the land under a periodic tenancy where there is no lease in writing is, however, in a special position. In the case of such oral tenancies the limitation period will run against the landlord as soon as the first period of the tenancy ends. However, should the tenant pay rent after this date the period will restart from the date that the rent was paid (Limitation Act 1980, Sch. 1, para. 5). Thus if a periodic tenant with an oral lease fails to pay rent he may be able to obtain title to the leased property (*Moses v Lovegrove* [1952] 2 QB 533), and should a landlord in such a position wish to excuse his tenant from paying rent, he should require that the tenant give a regular written acknowledgement of the landlord's title.

8.2.2.2 Possession by a licensee (i.e., with permission or consent of the owner)

Permission or consent may be given expressly, but it is also possible for the court to infer it from the circumstances of the case (an 'implied licence'). An example of this is to be found in *Colin Dawson Windows Ltd v King's Lynn, West Norfolk BC* [2005] 2 P&CR 19. The claimant ('Dawsons') had used land belonging to the defendant as a car park for some 16 years and claimed to have acquired title to it by adverse possession. The Court of Appeal, however, was satisfied that during this period there had been sporadic negotiations between the parties for the sale of the land to Dawsons, and held that as a result the claimant's continuing possession had been with the implied permission of the owner and was not adverse. In the words of Rix LJ (at para. 39):

> It is natural to draw an inference of permission where a person is in possession pending negotiations for the grant of an interest in that land.

The Court of Appeal adopted a similar approach in *Batsford Estates (1983) Company Ltd v Taylor* [2006] 2 P&CR 5. Here the owner of a farm, having made unsuccessful attempts to persuade a former tenant and his son (the defendant) to leave the property, decided to take no further action for the time being. The Court of Appeal considered that the continued possession by the defendant was with the implied permission of the owner, so that the defendant could not claim title by adverse possession.

8.2.2.3 **Land reserved by owner for specific purpose**

A question which has arisen in a number of cases is whether a squatter's possession can be said to be 'adverse' when the owner is deliberately not using the land because he is keeping it for some special use in the future.

In *Leigh v Jack* (1879) 5 Ex D 264 the owner of some land had intended to use it to build a highway but no action had been taken to start the construction of the road. From 1854 onwards a neighbouring landowner had used the property to store materials used in his factory and in 1865 and 1872 he had erected fences on the land. The court held that none of these actions amounted to adverse possession of the disputed property, because the prior owner of the property had no intention to build upon or cultivate the land and therefore the actions of the neighbouring owner were not inconsistent with the intentions of the prior owner. In the words of Bramwell LJ (at p. 273):

> in order to defeat a title by dispossessing the former owner, acts must be done which are inconsistent with his enjoyment of the soil for the purposes for which he intended to use it: that is not the case here, where the intention of the plaintiff... was not either to build upon or cultivate the land, but to devote it at some future time to public purposes.

In later cases, this statement was treated as giving rise to the rule that an owner who was keeping land dormant for some particular purpose in the future was not dispossessed by a squatter who made use of it in the meantime. In a further development, this approach came to be supported by the idea that a person who occupied land for which the owner had no immediate use did so under an implied licence from the owner (*Wallis's Caytown Bay Holiday Camp Ltd v Shell-Mex and BP Ltd* [1975] QB 94).

The theory of an implied licence was, however, regarded as doubtful, and Sch. 1, para. 8(4) of the Limitation Act 1980 now specifically provides that the existence of such a licence shall not be assumed merely because the squatter's occupation is not inconsistent with the owner's present or future enjoyment of the land. (This does not, of course, prevent a court from inferring an implied licence from the actual circumstances of the case—see 8.2.2.2.)

The effect of this statutory provision on the 'rule' in *Leigh v Jack* was considered by the Court of Appeal in *Buckinghamshire County Council v Moran* [1990] Ch 623. In this case the council had acquired a plot of land in 1955, for the purpose of constructing a road diversion. It was known that the roadworks would not be carried out for many years and so the council merely fenced the plot from the road (but not from the neighbouring properties) and initially sent council workmen to cut the grass and keep the plot in order. From the late 1960s the owners of one of the neighbouring properties, to the knowledge of the council, began to cut the grass on the council's plot and keep it tidy. From that time on the council ceased to send its workmen to the plot. The neighbouring property changed hands several times and was bought by Moran in 1971. Moran knew that the title to the empty plot was vested in the council, but the plot appeared to form part of the garden of the property which he had bought and was always maintained as such. As we have noted above (at 8.2.1.2), he erected a fence and a gate, which was secured with a lock and chain.

In 1976 the council wrote a letter disputing his rights to use the plot but thereafter took no action to recover it for at least nine years. Thus by the time that the action was brought Moran and his predecessors in title had been using the plot as a garden for well over 12 years. The council argued, however, that as it had not had any use for the plot, other than to let it lie fallow until the road scheme could go ahead, the possession of Moran and his predecessors had not been adverse to the council's rights. The Court of Appeal held, however, that Moran had established a good claim to title by adverse possession over the plot of land. The court doubted the existence of any special rule applicable to these circumstances, and distinguished *Leigh v Jack* on the ground that the squatter in that case had not satisfied the court of his intention to exclude the owner.

The Court of Appeal's decision in *Moran* was expressly approved by the House of Lords in *J. A. Pye (Oxford) Ltd v Graham* [2003] AC 419, in which Lord Browne-Wilkinson described the suggestion that the adverse nature of possession depended not on the intention of the squatter but on that of the owner as 'heretical and wrong' (para. 45).

8.2.3 Adverse possession must last for the prescribed time

It is important to realise that the rules we are going to tell you about in this section apply only to adverse possession claims in respect of:

- unregistered land; and
- registered land under LRA 1925 (i.e., land subject to a claim by a squatter who completed the limitation period before LRA 2002 came into force).

These rules have no place in the new system introduced by LRA 2002.

A squatter on unregistered land, who satisfies the requirements for adverse possession which we have noted above, must then remain in possession for the period prescribed by the Limitation Act, which is generally 12 years (s. 15). Possession must be continuous; if the squatter gives up possession and then retakes it at a later date, the owner will have a new claim. Time will start to run afresh, and the squatter will have to complete the full limitation period after his second entry.

Although the period generally required to bar the owner's claim is 12 years (Limitation Act 1980, s. 15), we need to look in a little more detail at the circumstances in which:

- time starts to run;
- an owner is given extra time in which to reclaim possession; and
- time may stop running.

8.2.3.1 When does time start to run?

Time will start to run against a prior owner only once he has been dispossessed or has discontinued possession (Limitation Act 1980, Sch. 1, para. 1) and when adverse possession has been taken by another person (para. 8).

In the case of 4 Trant Way it would appear that at some date more than 15 years ago Oscar Oregano abandoned the use of the property. However the limitation period did not start to run against Mr Oregano, or his successors, until a third party (Mr Sorrell) took possession of the property 15 years ago.

Postponement of limitation period

In the case of claims based on fraud or for relief from the consequences of a mistake, and in any case where a fact relevant to the claimant's claim has been deliberately concealed from him by the defendant, time does not start to run under the Act until the claimant has discovered the relevant matter, or could have done so with reasonable diligence (Limitation Act 1980, s. 32).

8.2.3.2 Extension of time within which owner may bring claim

The Limitation Act 1980 makes detailed provisions for extending the limitation period where the dispossessed owner is subject to a disability (i.e., is under age or lacks capacity to conduct legal proceedings under the Mental Health Act 1983) and therefore unable to bring an action to recover the land during the normal limitation period (ss. 28 and 38(2) as amended by the Mental Capacity Act 2005, s. 67 and Sch. 6 para. 25).

Similarly there are special rules relating to beneficiaries with future interests under settlements of land, enabling them to bring actions to recover the land when they become entitled to possession of it, even if this is outside the normal limitation period (s. 15(2)).

8.2.3.3 What will stop time running?

Provided the limitation period has not yet been completed, time will stop running in the following circumstances:

- *the owner starts proceedings to recover the land;*
- *the squatter provides written acknowledgement of the owner's title* The owner may require this if he is content for possession to continue but wants to avoid losing his right to the land. However, such an acknowledgement may also be given inadvertently by the squatter if, for example, he offers to buy the land from the owner (see *Edginton v Clark* [1964] 1 QB 367; and more recently *Ofulue v Bossert* [2009] 1 AC 990).
- *the squatter goes out of possession, leaving the property vacant* If, however, another person takes possession of the property, time will continue to run in his favour, and he can complete the limitation period by adding his time to that of his predecessor. This is the case irrespective of whether he acquires the property with the co-operation of the first squatter (for example, by sale, gift or on succession), or by dispossessing him. Such a dispossessor may bar the original owner simply by completing the limitation period, but he will have to hold for the full 12-year period in order to bar the first squatter's right to recover the land from him.

So far in this chapter we have been considering rules which, unless otherwise indicated, are relevant to all adverse possession claims. However, we have now reached the point at which the various systems diverge, and in the next few sections we will deal with the special rules relating to:

- adverse possession of unregistered land (8.3);
- adverse possession of registered land under LRA 1925 (8.4);
- need for reform of rules relating to registered land (8.5); and
- adverse possession of registered land under LRA 2002 (8.6).

8.3 Adverse possession of unregistered land

In this section we will look at the position of a squatter in adverse possession of unregistered land who has completed the limitation period of 12 years (Limitation Act 1980, s. 15).

You should be aware that in the case of unregistered land the adverse possessor is regarded as having an estate in fee simple from the moment when he first takes possession (*Leach v Jay* (1878) 9 ChD 42 at p. 45), although until the limitation period has been completed, his title is always liable to be defeated by the owner. Thus even before the period is completed, the squatter has the rights and powers of an owner, against everyone except the person he has dispossessed. This means that he can sue for torts against the land (such as trespass and nuisance), and can recover the land if he himself is dispossessed by a third party.

8.3.1 Completing the limitation period

When a squatter has completed the limitation period the dispossessed owner's right to recover the land is barred and his title to the estate is extinguished (Limitation Act 1980, s. 17). In other words, there is no longer anyone with a better title to the land.

It used to be thought that at the end of the limitation period the Limitation Acts vested the previous owner's estate in the squatter. This is what is meant by references you may see in reported cases to 'a parliamentary conveyance'. It was however held in *Tichbourne v Weir* (1892) 67 LT 735 that the Acts did not have this effect. Instead, the previous owner's title is extinguished (as provided now by the Limitation Act, 1980 s. 17), and the squatter holds his own estate in the land under a new title.

The estate held by the squatter is regarded as a fee simple, irrespective of whether his adverse possession has been against the fee simple owner or only against a tenant (see Megarry and Wade, para. 35–063).

8.3.2 Third-party rights over the land

The squatter takes the land subject to all the rights which affect it, such as, for example, easements or restrictive covenants benefiting neighbouring landowners. His title to the land is acquired by operation of law, not by any transfer or conveyance to him. Consequently, he is not a 'purchaser' in the technical sense (see 2.6.3.2), and so cannot take advantage of the rules which invalidate certain third-party rights against purchasers. As a result, he is bound by such rights despite the fact that he has no notice of them or that they have not been protected by registration on the Land Charges Register.

8.3.3 Completing the limitation period against a tenant

Completion of the limitation period against a tenant will bar that tenant's right to recover the land and extinguishes his title against the squatter. Despite the fact that the dispossessed owner held only a leasehold estate, the squatter is regarded as holding a freehold estate. He does not take over the leasehold estate which was held by the tenant, and so does not enter into any relationship with the landlord or become liable as a tenant on the covenants in the lease.

Although completing the limitation period bars the tenant's rights against the squatter, it does not affect the position of his landlord. The landlord has no right to physical possession of the land (and therefore no claim against the squatter) until the lease comes to an end. Thus, the squatter may complete the limitation period against the tenant and be able to stay on the land for the duration of the lease, but once it comes to an end, the landlord will be able to recover possession from him. It is only if the squatter remains on the land for a further limitation period after the lease has ended that he will be able to bar the landlord's rights and extinguish his estate.

8.3.4 No. 4 Trant Way

From what we have said so far, you will have realised that there are a number of factors to be taken into account when deciding whether a claim to recover unregistered land is time-barred. These include: the need for possession to be adverse; the possibility that the person who has been dispossessed is a tenant or is under a disability; and the chance that there are persons entitled to future interests in the land. It should not, therefore, be too readily assumed that occupation of another's land for a simple period of 12 years will necessarily allow one to obtain good title as against any prior owners.

However, unless Nicholas Oregano can show that his uncle lacked the capacity to bring legal proceedings when Sidney Sorrell moved into 4 Trant Way, it would seem that he has little chance of recovering the property. Mr Sorrell's actions seem to be clear evidence of adverse possession commencing 15 years ago. Moving into a house, renovating it and going to the lengths of paying the rates are all actions which are inconsistent with the title of the prior owner.

As a result, Mr Sorrell is well-placed to defend any action for possession brought against him by Nicholas Oregano. However, he would be in a very different position if Nicholas were to sell the property to a third party, who applied for first registration of title. Provided Sorrell was in actual occupation at the time of registration, his right to the property would be overriding (LRA 2002, Sch. 1, para. 2—see 7.5.4.2(2)), and the purchaser would be bound by it. If, however, Sorrell was not in occupation at that time, the purchaser would be bound only if he had notice of the right (LRA 2002, s. 11(4)(c)- and see further 7.5.4.2 (3)).

Mr Sorrel is, therefore, at risk of losing his rights to 4 Trant Way, and would be well advised to apply for first registration of his title to the property. If he can show that he has satisfied the requirements for acquisition of the estate by adverse possession, he will be registered with a possessory title, which in time could be improved into absolute title (see 7.5.6.1(2)). As well as protecting him from the consequences of any sale by Nicholas Oregano, registration will facilitate the conveyancing process if he should wish to sell the property, and will also reduce the chances of any future squatter being able to acquire title against him.

8.4 Adverse possession of registered land under LRA 1925

In this section we will look very briefly at the position of a squatter in adverse possession of registered land who completed the limitation period of 12 years before LRA 2002 came into force on 13 October 2003.

Under the old law relating to registered land time ran against the registered proprietor in exactly the same way as it did against the owner of unregistered land, and his right of action against the dispossessor was barred under the Limitation Act 1980 s. 15 at the end of 12 years. However, some variation of the existing rules was needed at the end of the limitation period, to take account of the fact that the registered proprietor remained owner of the estate until someone else was registered in his place. Accordingly, LRA 1925 s. 75(1) provided that the proprietor's title was not extinguished at the end of the limitation period (as it would be in unregistered land), but would be held by him in trust for the squatter, who could then apply for registration in his place (s. 75(2)).

The transitional arrangements in LRA 2002 provide that where the completion of the limitation period had given rise to a trust before the Act came into force, the squatter is entitled to be registered as proprietor of the estate (Sch. 12, para. 18(1)). Provided the squatter stays in actual occupation of the land, his rights under the trust will be overriding (under LRA 2002, Sch. 3, para. 2—see 7.10), and so will bind anyone who buys the land from the dispossessed owner. However, if the squatter goes out of occupation his rights will no longer be overriding, and the purchaser will take free of them. Therefore any adverse possessor who completed the limitation period before 13 October 2003 should be advised to make an immediate application for registration of his title to the estate.

8.5 Need for reform of rules relating to registered land

We have already seen in Chapter 7 that a Joint Working Party of the Law Commission and the Land Registry made major proposals for the reform of the registered title system, most of which have been enacted in LRA 2002. The Consultative Document (*Land Registration for the Twenty-First Century A Consultative Document*, 1998, Law Com No. 254) identified a number of problems in relation to adverse possession of registered land, and we will note these briefly.

(1) *Rules based on unregistered system of title* The adverse possession rules were developed by reference to unregistered land, where title is relative, and were inappropriate in a system where title is absolute and depends on registration. Adjustments had been made to the basic rules in their application to registered land (most notably in the imposition of the statutory trust by LRA 1925, s. 75(1)), but these were not thoroughly thought through, and appeared inadequate to deal with the sort of questions raised in recent litigation. (For further information on this point see Consultative Document paras. 10.27 10.42.)

(2) *Adverse possession undermines registered title* The registered proprietor ought to be able to rely on registration as safeguarding his title, but he could in fact lose it to a squatter in substantially the same way as if it were not registered. The fact of registration did nothing to preserve his title for him.

    The possibility of adverse possession also affected the purchaser from the registered proprietor. He should be able to buy relying on the state of the register and his own inspection of the land. However, the overriding interests of the squatter under LRA 1925, s. 70(1)(f) could constitute a trap for him, since once the squatter had completed the limitation period, he could leave the land while still retaining his title to it (see 7.5.4.2(3) and 7.9.2.4(1)).

(3) *Difficulty in justifying adverse possession of registered land* We have seen that adverse possession can be of benefit in simplifying the investigation of title of unregistered land (8.1.6), but this does not apply to registered land, where title depends on the register. Ability to justify the process as being in the public interest (rather than simply benefiting the squatter) would become even more important with the advent of the Human Rights Act 1998 (see 8.7).

Despite these problems with the existing law, the working party considered that there was still a role for adverse possession in respect of registered land, most notably to facilitate dealings with land which had been abandoned by its owner, and should not be allowed to become derelict and unmarketable. However, it proposed a number of changes to the system then in operation. It recognised that these would increase the differences between the rules for registered and unregistered land, but considered that this was inevitable and that it was time to accept that the two systems involve differences in substantive law as well as in conveyancing procedures. Accordingly the Consultative Document recommended the introduction of a completely new system of adverse possession for registered land, and this new system was introduced by LRA 2002.

8.6 Adverse possession of registered land under LRA 2002

The new scheme for dealing with adverse possession of registered land is set out in LRA 2002, ss. 96–98 and Sch. 6. The new arrangements apply to all claims based on adverse possession of registered land (except of course for those in which the limitation period was completed before the Act came into force—see 8.4). Thus the old rules governing adverse possession of registered land cease to apply: time does not run against the registered proprietor under the Limitation Act 1980, and the provisions for imposing a statutory trust are abolished with the repeal of LRA 1925.

Under the new arrangements, an adverse possessor who wishes to be registered as proprietor of an estate can obtain that registration:

- by applying for it (8.6.1); or
- on a court order following his successful defence of a court action (8.6.3).

8.6.1 Application by adverse possessor for registration

Schedule 6 prescribes the following process.

(1) Under Sch. 6, the squatter may apply to the registrar to be registered as proprietor of a registered estate if he has been in adverse possession of that estate for ten years (para. 1).

It is important to remember that the squatter will have to establish his adverse possession according to the rules we have already considered (8.2), which all continue to apply. In calculating the period of possession it is still possible for one person to complete a period begun by another (Sch. 6, para. 11(2)).

For a case in which the register was rectified against an applicant who had achieved registration, but without satisfying the requirements for establishing adverse possession, see *Baxter v Mannion* [2011] 1 WLR 1594 (noted at 7.12.4.2).

(2) On receiving the application, the registrar must give notice of it to the registered proprietor, and to a number of other people with interests in the property, including any legal mortgagees and, where the estate in question is leasehold, the freehold owner and any intervening landlords.

(3) Where such notice is given and the recipients either do not respond or do not oppose the application, the applicant may be registered as proprietor of the estate (para. 4). Thus in such cases, which will usually arise where the property has been abandoned, the period for acquiring title by adverse possession is reduced from 12 to 10 years.

(4) Where the proprietor or some other recipient of the notice does respond and opposes the application, it will in general be rejected.

However, the Act provides that in three special cases the application may be accepted despite opposition to it. These exceptional cases may be summarised as involving:

- estoppel;
- some other right to the land; and
- reasonable mistake as to boundaries.

We consider these exceptional cases in more detail in 8.6.2.

(5) If the application for registration has been opposed and consequently rejected, the registered proprietor (or other interested person) now has the opportunity to recover the property from the squatter. However, if this is not done and the applicant remains in possession for a further two years from the date of the rejection, he may then make a further application under para. 6 for registration. Paragraph 7 provides that in such a case he is entitled to be entered in the register as the new proprietor.

Thus a minimum period of 12 years adverse possession continues to give title to the property, by entitling the possessor to be registered as proprietor, but in circumstances in which the proprietor has been informed of the squatter's presence and given an opportunity to safeguard his title.

We must emphasise that the periods of 10 and 12 years involved in this process are *minimum* periods. A squatter may well be in adverse possession for a much longer time before applying for registration but, however long he possesses the land, he cannot acquire title to it save through the process of registration.

8.6.2 Three special cases in which squatter may be registered despite opposition to application

We will now consider in a little more detail the exceptional cases noted above in which an applicant may be registered after 10 years adverse possession despite opposition from the registered proprietor. Provision for this aspect of the new scheme is made by para. 5 of Sch. 6, and is based on the recommendations of the Joint Working Party, which considered that in these three cases 'the balance of fairness plainly lies with the squatter and he or she should prevail' (Consultative Document 14.3.6).

8.6.2.1 Estoppel

Under para. 5(2) the applicant is entitled to be registered:

> where it would be unconscionable because of an equity by estoppel for the registered proprietor to seek to dispossess the applicant and the circumstances are such that the applicant ought to be registered as proprietor.

As we explained in 2.5.7, an estoppel may arise where one person has made a representation to another (by words or conduct) and the other has acted in reliance on that representation to his detriment (for example, where an owner allows another to build on his land in the mistaken belief that it belongs to him). In such circumstances, the representor is estopped from going back on his representation and the situation is said to give rise to an equity in the claimant (i.e., the right to some relief). It is for the court to decide how that equity is to be satisfied.

In the case of applications under Sch. 6, the relief may take the form of registering the applicant as owner of the land in question, but s. 110(4) provides that if the circumstances are not such that he should be registered, the Adjudicator must decide how else the equity is to be satisfied (see 7.8.1.3) with, if necessary, an appeal to the High Court (s. 111).

It may seem strange to talk of adverse possession in this context, but the working party explained that if a person with such rights is in possession of the land, it will be easier and cheaper for him to apply for registration under Sch. 6 than it would be to seek to enforce his rights through the courts (*Land Registration for the Twenty-First Century A Conveyancing Revolution*, 2001, Law Com No. 271, para. 14.37—'the Report'). The same considerations apply to the next ground for registration (applicant has some other right to the property).

8.6.2.2 Some other right to the land

Paragraph 5(3) provides for registration:

> where the applicant is for some other reason entitled to be registered as the proprietor of the estate.

This category is intended to cover situations in which the adverse possessor does in fact have some right to the land. The examples given by the working party include situations where he is entitled to the land under the will or intestacy of the deceased proprietor or where a prospective purchaser of the estate is entitled to it under a bare trust, which has arisen because he has paid the full purchase price to the vendor but has not taken a transfer of the legal estate (the Report, para. 14.43).

8.6.2.3 Reasonable mistake as to boundaries

Paragraph 5(4) provides for registration of the applicant where the land in question is adjacent to his own, the exact line of the boundary between the two has not been determined and during at least 10 years of adverse possession he has reasonably believed that the land belongs to him.

Thus, under the new scheme, a squatter who has been in possession for just 10 years will be able to acquire title to the estate by registration if he can make out his claim under one of the three exceptions noted above. For critical comment on these provisions, see Dixon, 'Adverse Possession and the Land Registration Act 2002' [2009] 73 Conv 169 at 174.

8.6.3 Defence to proceedings for possession

So far we have been considering the situation in which the adverse possessor takes the initiative and applies for registration. However, the question of his entitlement to the estate may be raised in a very different way, by the registered proprietor bringing proceedings against him to recover possession. In general terms, s. 98 allows the adverse possessor to raise in his defence those matters on which he could rely in making an application for registration under Sch. 6, and s. 98(5) provides that if he is successful in establishing his defence, the court must order the registrar to register him as proprietor of the estate in question.

8.6.4 What does an adverse possessor obtain on registration?

Under Sch. 6, a successful applicant will be registered as proprietor of the estate of which he has been in adverse possession. This means that if he has dispossessed a leasehold owner, he will be registered as proprietor of that leasehold estate.

8.6.5 Adverse possessors and purchasers

We have already considered in Chapter 7 the extent to which the rights acquired or being acquired by adverse possessors can bind the purchaser of registered land under the new Act (see 7.9.2.4(1)). All we will do here is to remind you briefly that under the old system these rights were a separate category of overriding interests (LRA 1925, s. 70(1)(f)) and did not depend on actual occupation. Thus, if the squatter completed the limitation period and then went out of occupation, a purchaser would still be bound by his rights, although he might have no way of discovering them.

Under the new Act, a squatter's rights will have an overriding effect on the sale of the registered estate only if he is in actual occupation and can claim that his rights are overriding under Sch. 3, para. 2.

8.7 Adverse possession and HRA 1998

As we mentioned earlier, acquisition of title by adverse possession could appear to be incompatible with the provisions of the European Convention for the Protection of Human Rights and Fundamental Freedoms ('the Convention'), which is incorporated into national law by the Human Rights Act 1998 ('HRA 1998'—see further Chapter 3).

In the case of unregistered land, completion of the necessary period extinguishes the owner's title to the land, without any reference to a court (Limitation Act 1980, s. 17). The owner is deprived of his property without compensation, arguably in breach of both Art. 1 of the First Protocol (protection of property) and Art. 6 (right to a fair trial).

Similar considerations apply to adverse possession under the old rules relating to registered land where the registered proprietor loses first his beneficial interest in the land (under the statutory trust imposed by LRA 1925, s. 75(1)) and later his legal title, again without reference to any court and without compensation. Although there is scope under the Convention for justifying interference with certain rights as being in the public interest, it was thought that loss of title to registered land would be particularly difficult to justify. Adverse possession of unregistered land can be said to be of general benefit by simplifying and shortening the investigation of title (8.1.6.(3)), but this consideration would not apply in the case of registered land, where investigation of title has already been simplified by registration.

8.7.1 *Pye v Graham*

Human rights issues were raised in *J. A. Pye (Oxford) Ltd v Graham* [2003] 1 AC 119 (see 8.2.1.3). They were dealt with fairly briefly in the House of Lords, because HRA 1998, which came into effect on 2 October 2000, does not have retrospective effect and so did not apply to the case. Nevertheless, concerns about the human rights implications of this case were expressed both by the trial judge and in the House of Lords. At first instance ([2000] Ch 676 at 710) Neuberger J described the supposed justification for adverse possession in no uncertain terms:

> A frequent justification for limitation periods generally is that people should not be able to sit on their rights indefinitely...However, if as in the present case the owner of land has no immediate use for it and is content to let another person trespass on the land for the time being, it is hard to see what principle of justice entitles the trespasser to acquire the land for nothing from the owner simply because he has been permitted to remain there for 12 years. To say that in such circumstances the owner who has sat on his rights should therefore be deprived of his land appears to me to be illogical and disproportionate. Illogical because the only reason that the owner can be said to have sat on his rights is because of the existence of the 12-year limitation period in the first place; if no limitation period existed he would be entitled to claim possession whenever he actually wanted the land...disproportionate because, particularly in a climate of increasing awareness of human rights including the right to enjoy one's own property, it does seem draconian to the owner and a windfall to the squatter that, just because the owner has taken no steps to evict a squatter for 12 years, the owner should lose...land to the squatter with no compensation whatsoever.

These views were shared by at least some members of the House of Lords ([2003] 1 AC 419), Lord Bingham saying (para. 1) that he would echo the misgivings expressed by Neuberger J, and Lord Hope speaking of the 'apparent injustice of the result' (para. 67).

8.7.2 *Pye v United Kingdom*

In the event, the concerns expressed in *Pye v Graham* appeared to be well justified, since on losing the appeal to the House of Lords the former owners, Pye, began proceedings against the UK government in the European Court of Human Rights ('ECtHR'). In *J. A. Pye (Oxford) Ltd v United Kingdom* [2005] 3 EGLR 1, the ECtHR held that Pye's rights under the Convention had been violated and that they were entitled to compensation for the loss of their land.

However, this decision was later reversed by the Grand Chamber of the ECtHR on appeal by the United Kingdom government in *J. A. Pye (Oxford) Ltd v United Kingdom* [2007] ECHR 700, the Grand Chamber holding by a majority (10 out of the 17 judges) that there had been no violation of Pye's rights.

The judgments on both the application and the appeal follow the same pattern, and in effect consider three questions.

8.7.2.1 Did the statutory provisions on adverse possession amount to an interference by the state with the applicant's rights under the Convention?

The Grand Chamber held that there had been an interference with Pye's rights under the Convention, and that the Chamber had been correct in dealing with the case under Art. 1 of the First Protocol ('the Article'). It thus rejected the government's claim that the case should have been determined only by reference to Art. 6 of the Convention, which deals with the right to a fair trial. However, as we noted in Chapter 3 (see 3.2.4), the Article contains three distinct rules and the Grand Chamber did not agree with the original decision as to the part of the Article that was applicable in the case. The Article provides:

> Every...person is entitled to the peaceful enjoyment of his possessions. No one shall be deprived of his possessions except in the public interest and subject to the conditions provided for by law and by the general principles of international law.

> The preceding provisions shall not, however, in any way impair the right of a State to enforce such laws as it deems necessary to control the use of property in accordance with the general interest...

On hearing Pye's application, the Chamber had considered that their loss of property amounted to a 'deprivation of possessions', within the second sentence of the first paragraph. By contrast the Grand Chamber held that the case was one of 'control of use' by the state under the second paragraph. The Grand Chamber considered a number of its previous decisions on the circumstances which bring a case within one or other of these provisions, and concluded (at para. 66) that:

> The statutory provisions which resulted in [Pye's loss of ownership] were thus not intended to deprive paper owners of their ownership, but rather to regulate questions of title...

If you are not familiar with the case law on human rights you may find it difficult to understand the significance of the distinction that is being made here, but it is relevant to the question of liability to pay compensation (see below).

Under Art. 1, interference with property rights may be justified on the grounds of 'public interest' (in the case of deprivation of possessions) or of 'general interest' (in the case of control of use under the second paragraph), and this led to the second question of whether adverse possession could be justified.

8.7.2.2 Could the law of adverse possession be justified on the grounds of general interest?

In judging what is in the general interest the ECtHR accepts that national authorities are better placed than an international judge to appreciate what is required in a particular state. It therefore respects the judgment of the state legislature unless that judgment is manifestly without foundation. In stating this principle, the Grand Chamber commented (at para. 71) that:

> [t]his is particularly true in cases such as the present one where what is at stake is a longstanding and complex area of law which regulates private law matters between individuals.

The Grand Chamber noted that a large number of member states had systems for transferring title, without the payment of compensation, which were similar to the common law principles of adverse possession (para. 72). It also noted that adverse possession of registered land had been retained by the LRA 2002 (albeit with amendments) and accepted that the UK Parliament had thus confirmed that such a system continued to be in the general interest (para. 73). The Grand Chamber therefore reached the same conclusion as that of the original Chamber, namely that:

> [t]here existed...a general interest in both the limitation period itself and the extinguishment of title at the end of the period (at para. 74).

Thus the control of the use of property through the rules of adverse possession could be justified as being in the general interest. However, the method used for exercising such control must be proportionate: in other words, there must be a fair balance between the general interest, which was being protected, and the interests of the individual, whose rights were being curtailed. This brings us to the third question to be considered by the Grand Chamber.

8.7.2.3 Did the rules of adverse possession produce a proportionate result?

In considering this question, the ECtHR has to weight the interests of the individual against the general interest: in this case, to decide whether the outcome for Pye represented a fair balance between general and individual interests (i.e., whether it was proportionate).

It is on this third question that the judgment of the Grand Chamber differs completely from that of the original Chamber, although the arguments advanced by the UK government were very much the same on both occasions. We will look briefly at each of these judgments, although of course it is the decision of the Grand Chamber which prevails.

(1) *Judgment of the Chamber on application by Pye [2005] 3 EGLR 1*

In seeking to show that the rules of adverse possession were not unfair to the dispossessed owner, the government relied on the fact that there was a long limitation period, that the law on adverse possession was well established, so that Pye knew that they risked losing title, and that such loss could have been avoided reasonably easily by granting a licence for the use of the land or by taking proceedings to recover possession.

Despite these arguments the Chamber considered that the result for Pye was disproportionately harsh; and it also noted that the changes made by LRA 2002 showed that the UK Parliament was aware of the deficiencies in the earlier law, most notably in the lack of any warning for the dispossessed owner that time was running against him. The Chamber concluded (at para. 75) that the application of the rules of adverse possession:

> imposed upon [the applicants]...an excessive burden and upset the fair balance between the demands of the public interest, on the one hand, and the applicants' right to the peaceful enjoyment of their possessions, on the other.

The Chamber accordingly held that the applicants' right under Art. 1 of the First Protocol had been violated by the UK government. Article 41 of the Convention provides for the payment of compensation for the violation of Convention rights, and the Chamber would deal with this question at a later date if it was not previously settled by agreement between the parties.

(2) *Judgment of the Grand Chamber on appeal by UK government [2007] ECHR 700*

It has to be said that there was nothing new in the material considered on the appeal. The same arguments were put forward again by both parties and the same test was applied on both occasions (see para. 75), namely:

> whether a fair balance has been struck between the demands of the general interest and the interest of the individuals concerned.

It simply appears that the Grand Chamber found the arguments put forward by the government more compelling than those relied upon by Pye. Thus the Grand Chamber gave greater weight to the fact that the rules of adverse possession had been in force for many years, that the limitation period was a relatively long one, and that it would have taken very little action on the part of Pye to have stopped time running against it (paras. 77 and 78).

By contrast, the Grand Chamber was dismissive of the main points on which Pye relied (points which, interestingly, have been considered so significant by those who criticise the English system).

1. *Lack of compensation*

The fact that the interference with Pye's rights arose from control of use, rather than from the deprivation of possessions (see above), meant that the case law on compensation was not directly applicable (para. 79). Moreover, the Grand Chamber was persuaded by the government's argument that permitting claims for compensation would undermine the whole purpose of a limitation system, which is designed to promote certainty by preventing the bringing of stale claims (para. 79).

2. *Absence of procedural protection*

The court noted that Pye had not been without procedural protection, since they could have recovered possession by court action at any time during the limitation period. Even after time had run against them, they could argue in the courts (as they had done) that the squatter had not been in 'adverse possession'. The Grand Chamber noted that the Land Registration Act 2002 had provided additional procedures to protect the paper owner, but took the reassuringly robust view (at para. 81) that:

> Legislative changes in complex areas such as land law take time to bring about, and judicial criticism of legislation cannot of itself affect the conformity of the earlier provisions with the Convention.

3. *Size of Pye's loss and the squatter's gain*

The Grand Chamber commented, rather unsympathetically, that the acquisition of rights by an adverse possessor must go hand in hand with a corresponding loss of property rights for the former owner (para. 83), adding that limitation periods, if they are to fulfil their purpose, must apply regardless of the size of the claim. The value of the land could not therefore be of any consequence to the outcome of the present case (para. 84).

Taking all these matters into account, the Grand Chamber concluded that the fair balance required by the Article between the general interest and the interest of the individual involved 'was not upset in the present case' (para. 85), and as a result held that there had been no violation of Art. 1 of the First Protocol.

8.7.3 What is the status of *Pye v UK* in English law?

This question was considered by the Court of Appeal in *Ofulue v Bossert* [2009] Ch 1. There is no need to consider the facts of the case, save to note that it concerned adverse possession of registered land and that, as in *Pye v Graham*, the limitation period had been completed before the Human Rights Act 1998 came into force.

On appeal, the dispossessed owners, the Ofulues, argued that the court should make its own assessment of whether the English rules of adverse possession had a legitimate aim, and whether they maintained a fair balance between the general interest and the interests of the dispossessed owner. In other words, they claimed that the exercise already carried out by the ECtHR must be undertaken by the English courts every time they considered a case involving adverse possession. Adopting this approach, the appellants sought to show that the facts of their case could be distinguished from those in *Pye v UK*, and that it was therefore open to the Court of Appeal to find that the law of adverse possession violated their Convention rights, despite the ECtHR's holding to the contrary on the facts in Pye's case.

In dismissing the appeal, the court emphatically rejected this approach. English courts are required to take account of judgments of the ECtHR, and would have to have very good reasons for departing from the jurisprudence of that court (paras. 30–3). Accordingly the court considered that it should follow the decision in *Pye v UK* (para. 4). The Strasbourg court had held that in general it was for the national government to determine the rules for extinction of title by adverse possession, and it had also held that the English rules had a legitimate aim and were proportionate in balancing individual and general interests. The judgment of the court on these matters was of general effect and not simply in the context of the specific facts of *Pye v UK*, and it would not be appropriate for the present court to re-examine these matters from the perspective of individual cases (paras. 52 and 53).

In *Ofulue v Bossert* [2009] 1 AC 990, the Ofulues appealed unsuccessfully to the House of Lords against aspects of the Court of Appeal's decision which dealt with an alleged acknowledgement of title by the Bosserts. There was no appeal against the court's judgment on the human rights issue, and the position on that remains as described in the text above.

FURTHER READING

Dockray, 'Why Do We Need Adverse Possession?' [1985] Conv 273.

Gray and Gray, *Elements of Land Law*, 5th edn., Oxford University Press, 2009, paras. 9.1.6–9.1.13 (the rationale of acquisition by adverse possession).

Megarry and Wade, *The Law of Real Property*, 8th edn., Sweet & Maxwell, 2012, paras. 4-001–4-013 (ownership, possession and title).

Proposals for reform

Land Registration for the Twenty-First Century A Consultative Document, 1998, Law Com No. 254, Part X (in particular, 10.1–10.19, and 10.43–10.64).

Land Registration for the Twenty-First Century A Conveyancing Revolution, 2001, Law Com No. 271, Part XIV (in particular, 14.1–14.8—summary of changes).

LRA 2002

Dixon, 'Adverse Possession and the Land Registration Act 2002' [2009] 73 Conv 169.

J.A.Pye (Oxford) Ltd v United Kingdom (Grand Chamber)

Dixon, 'Adverse Possession, Human Rights and Land Registration: And They All Lived Happily Ever After?' [2007] 71 Conv 552.

Dixon, 'Human Rights and Adverse Possession: The Final Nail?' [2008] 72 Conv 160 (note on *Ofulue v Bossert*).

Radley-Gardner and Small, 'Shut out of Europe' [2007] EG—15 September 2007 (No. 0737) 228.

PART III

Legal estates

Introduction

Having considered the general background to the modern law relating to land, we will examine in this Part the nature of the two legal estates.

You will recall that, under the provisions of LPA 1925, s. 1(1), there are two legal estates in land:

(a) the fee simple absolute in possession—the freehold estate;

(b) the term of years absolute—the leasehold estate.

The fee simple estate, or freehold, is the larger of the two estates, being capable of lasting indefinitely, and it underpins everything else that we deal with in this book. Leasehold estates, for example, are created out of the freehold (or out of a superior lease which is itself derived directly or indirectly from the freehold) and thus derive their validity from the existence of the fee simple.

In view of the importance of the freehold estate, you may find it rather strange that our chapter on it (Chapter 9) is relatively short, but you should remember that other aspects of the estate are dealt with throughout the book—for example in relation to trusts and co-ownership. Further material on the nature of the estate will be found in Chapter 28, where we outline the rights which a freehold owner has over his land.

By contrast with the freehold estate, you will find that, because of the additional complexities involved in the landlord and tenant relationship, we have to explain rather more detailed rules in relation to the leasehold estate, and so are devoting four chapters to this topic. In Chapter 10 we consider the nature and characteristics of a lease, and the ways in which it is created and brought to an end. In Chapter 11 we deal with the rights and duties of the landlord and tenant who are the parties to the lease, in Chapter 12 we consider how leasehold covenants are enforced, and in Chapter 13 discuss the remedies available to one party when the other is in breach of duty.

In Chapter 14 we give you a very brief account of a new form of landholding, called 'commonhold', which was introduced by the Commonhold and Leasehold Reform Act 2002, but so far has failed to establish itself.

9

The freehold estate

9.1 Introduction

9.1.1 5 Trant Way

The estate in fee simple in 5 Trant Way (i.e., the freehold) is owned by David Derby. He has decided to give the estate to one of his three nephews and is considering the following three possible dispositions:

- giving the estate to his nephew Eric 'on condition that he does not marry';
- giving the estate to his nephew Frank 'until he finds full-time employment' (Frank is at present a student);
- giving the estate to his friend George for life and then to his nephew Hal for life, 'provided that Hal marries before George dies'.

It is necessary to consider whether each of these three possible gifts would vest in the nephew or friend concerned a legal fee simple absolute in possession, or whether the gift would create an interest in land which is less than a legal estate.

As we mentioned briefly in Chapter 1, the phrase 'fee simple absolute in possession' imposes a series of requirements, all of which must be satisfied if the estate is to qualify as a legal one. We will now look at these requirements in more detail, and consider whether David's proposed gifts would satisfy them.

9.2 Fee simple

We have already explained (at 1.5.1.2 and 1.7.1.1) that a fee simple used to be an estate in land which was inheritable by the heirs general of its owner. This distinguished the fee simple from the life estate (which was not inheritable) and the fee tail (which was inheritable only by a restricted class of heirs, e.g., 'heirs of the body male'). When the rules of intestate succession were changed in 1925, the concept of 'the heir' became in the main obsolete, and it was no longer correct to define the fee simple as being inherited by the general heirs. It is, however, still true that the fee simple is an estate which lasts indefinitely, so long as there is anyone entitled to take the property under the will or on the intestacy of the previous owner.

The other two freehold estates which used to exist (the life estate and the fee tail) do not come within the definition of legal estates in LPA 1925, s. 1(1), and, since they are not on the list of legal interests in s. 1(2), they therefore took effect after 1925 as equitable interests under s. 1(3). This meant that the legal fee simple had to be held on trust to give effect to such interests. We have already noted that, as a result of TOLATA 1996, it is no longer possible to create a new entailed interest (1.7.1.4).

9.3 Absolute

The word 'absolute' in s. 1(1) indicates that there must be no provision in the grant of the fee simple which might cause it to end prematurely while there is still someone qualified to take it. Fees which are subject to such provisions are known as 'modified' fees, and can arise in two forms:

- conditional interests; and
- determinable interests.

The disposition of 5 Trant Way to Eric Derby 'on condition that he does not marry' would be a conditional interest, whilst a disposition of the property to Frank Derby 'until he finds full-time employment' would be a determinable interest.

9.3.1 Conditional interests

A conditional interest arises where a fee simple is granted subject to a limitation which provides that the grantor will be able to re-enter the property at some date in the future on the occurrence (or non-occurrence) of specified events. In such a case the grantor appears initially to be giving a fee simple absolute, but then reserves the right to recover the land (right of re-entry). This type of arrangement is said to be an interest subject to a condition subsequent. Such interests did not comply with the requirements of LPA 1925, s. 1(1), and so, under the terms of that statute, could not amount to legal estates.

However, this rule gave rise to immediate problems when the 1925 legislation came into force, because many estates were subject to rentcharges, which usually provided that the owner of the rentcharge would be entitled to re-enter the land if the payments secured by the rentcharge were not made. In certain parts of the country (e.g., Bristol and Manchester) most of the fee simple estates were then subject to rentcharges, and the effect of s. 1(1) was to turn all these estates into equitable interests, since they were all subject to a right of re-entry on occurrence of a specified condition.

As a result, the Law of Property (Amendment) Act 1926 was passed, and the Schedule to that Act amended LPA 1925, s. 7(1), to read:

> [A] fee simple subject to a legal or equitable right of entry or re-entry is for the purposes of this Act a fee simple absolute.

This wording was, however, wider than was necessary to deal solely with the problem caused by rentcharges and produced the result that all fees simple subject to a right of re-entry became legal estates. Thus a conditional fee simple will be a legal estate within the meaning of LPA 1925, s. 1(1). Therefore, if 5 Trant Way is given to Eric Derby in fee simple on condition that 'he does not marry', Eric will receive a legal estate. The form of words used may, however, give rise to objections on the grounds of public policy, and in addition could possibly be said to infringe Eric's right to respect for private and family life under the Human Rights Act 1998 (see 9.5).

9.3.2 Determinable interests

A determinable fee is one which according to its terms will last only until a specified event occurs, or does not occur. Thus a grant of the fee simple in 5 Trant Way to Frank Derby 'until he finds full-time employment' is a determinable fee. The fee lasts only until Frank gets a job. The fee would still be determinable even if it is very unlikely that the specified event will ever occur, because from the outset the period of the interest has been cut down. Such interests are not within LPA 1925, s. 1(1), and are not saved by s. 7(1) as amended. Since they are not included in the list of legal interests in s. 1(2), they take effect as equitable interests under s. 1(3).

The grantor retains an interest in the land, known as the 'possibility of reverter', and when the determining event occurs the property reverts automatically to him.

9.3.3 Differences between conditional and determinable fees

Whether a grant creates a conditional fee or a determinable fee may well be an accident of wording, and the grantor may not intend to create one rather than the other. The same arrangement can often be expressed in either way. Thus a grant 'to A on condition that he does not become a lawyer' is a conditional fee and creates a legal estate, subject to a right of re-entry; whilst a grant 'to A until he becomes a lawyer' is a determinable fee, which can only be an equitable interest. Because of this many students (and even courts, see *Re Moore* (1888) 39 ChD 116) find it difficult to distinguish between the two classes of right. The following lists of expressions which have been categorised as creating either conditional or determinable fees may help in identifying the nature of a particular grant:

CONDITIONAL	DETERMINABLE
'on condition that...'	'until...'
'providing that...'	'as long as...'
'but if...'	'for the duration of...'
	'while'

However, although the distinction between the two types of fee appears to be a matter of form, rather than of substance, the difference can be of considerable importance to the grantee. We have already seen that a conditional fee takes effect as a legal estate, while a determinable fee can exist only as an equitable interest. A further difference will be experienced if the specified event occurs, for in the case of the determinable fee the interest will immediately come to an end and the grantee has no further right to the land. By contrast, the fee on condition subsequent will in fact continue until the grantor or his successor exercises his right of re-entry, and so the grantee could find himself entitled to remain on the land almost indefinitely.

Thus a distinction which might seem to the grantor to be little more than a matter of style can have far-reaching consequences for the grantee and, as Parker MR said in *Re King's Trusts* (1892) 29 LR Ir 401 at 410, the difference between the two produces a rule which is 'little short of disgraceful to our jurisprudence'.

9.3.4 Reverter to transferor on failure to apply for first registration

We saw in 7.4.1.3 that where a transfer triggers a requirement of first registration, the estate will revert to the transferor if the transferee fails to apply for registration within the prescribed period. Where the estate in question is a fee simple, the possibility that this might happen could give rise to doubts as to whether it is a fee simple absolute, and accordingly LRA 2002, s. 7 (4) provides that the possibility of such reverter is to be disregarded for the purposes of determining whether a fee simple is a fee simple absolute.

9.4 In possession

9.4.1 Future interests

Landowners may wish to create future interests in their property, that is, interests which will come into existence on the happening of some future event such as the performance of a condition precedent (i.e., a condition which has to be fulfilled before the grantee can enjoy the property). An illustration of such a condition is provided by the grant of 5 Trant Way to David Derby's friend George 'for life', and then to his nephew Hal for life, 'provided that Hal marries before George dies'.

If the gift was made in these terms, Hal would, at the outset, have no interest in the property, but merely a chance of acquiring one in the future. Rather confusingly, he is said to have a 'contingent', or 'conditional', interest, but in fact no interest in the land will arise until the condition is met. Should Hal marry before George's death, he will have satisfied the condition and will then have a future interest in the property; that is, an interest entitling him to possession of the house at some time in the future. For two reasons, this interest would not be capable of being a legal estate: not only is it for life, but it also takes effect in the future, and so does not satisfy the requirement of LPA 1925, s. 1(1), that to be legal a fee simple must take effect in possession. Thus, under the Act, a future interest, even in fee simple, cannot be legal and takes effect only in equity.

9.4.2 Remainders and reversions

We must now mention two technical terms used to describe future interests: 'remainders' and 'reversions'.

A 'reversion' arises where a grantor gives away an estate, or series of estates, which will last for a shorter time than his own estate. The gifts to George and Hal are an example of this, for David Derby has a fee simple, which is capable of lasting forever, and he would have given away, at the most, only two life interests. When they came to an end, the property would revert to Mr Derby, or, if he was dead, would form part of his estate and devolve according to the terms of his will, or by the rules of intestate succession. The grantor therefore has a future right to the property from the date of the gift, and that future right is called a 'reversion'.

If, however, the grantor were to give away his full estate to a series of people, he will have kept no reversion in the property and the future interests he has created will be called 'remainders'. Thus, if Mr Derby were to provide that, after George and Hal have died, the property should belong in fee simple to Ian, the grantor will have no reversion, and Hal and Ian would both be said to have remainders. George would have an interest in possession, and would be entitled to enjoy the property immediately the gift took effect.

We have seen that the full fee simple absolute in possession is the only freehold estate which can exist in law, and that, with the exception of the conditional interest for Eric Derby (see 9.3.1), all the other dispositions which David Derby wants to make can take effect only in equity. In order to give effect to his wishes, therefore, it would be necessary to make use of a trust, so that the legal fee simple would be held by trustees and Mr Derby's other nephews and his friend would be entitled to equitable interests for the period and on the conditions stated in the grant (see further Part IV).

9.5 Intervention of public policy

It should not be thought from what has gone before that an estate owner is entitled to grant estates or interests subject to any limitations that he wishes. It is clear that the courts will intervene in cases in which a limitation is considered to be contrary to public policy. Thus in general a grant of an estate 'on condition that A does not marry' will be regarded as being contrary to public policy and the grant will take effect absolutely and free of the objectionable condition (*Kelly v Monck* (1795) 3 Ridg Parl Rep 205). It is permissible, however, to make a provision the purpose of which is simply to provide for someone until he or she marries, rather than to prevent marriage (*Jones v Jones* (1876) 1 QBD 279). Thus normally an estate which is determinable on marriage is not so objectionable. David Derby, therefore, would be well-advised to reconsider the proposed grant to his nephew Eric, for the present wording could result in a fee simple absolute free from condition.

It should also be noted that there are other cases in which public policy will intervene, e.g., where a disposition might have the effect of discouraging the religious education of a child (*Re Borwick* [1933] Ch 657) or preventing an adult taking public office or being employed in the armed services (*Re Edgar* [1939] 1 All ER 635; *Re Beard* [1908] 1 Ch 383). Obviously, however, the views expressed by the courts on such clauses are likely to vary with the times.

9.5.1 Restrictions on alienation

One class of conditions or determining events to which the courts have always taken strong exception consists of provisions by which the grantor tries to restrict the power of the recipient to dispose of the property freely. Ever since the statute *Quia Emptores* in 1290 it has been a principle of the law that generally an estate owner should have a free and unfettered power to alienate his property. Across the centuries the courts have continued to enforce this principle. Thus in *Hood v Oglander* (1865) 34 Beav 513 at p. 522 it was said that a condition preventing alienation at any time would be void. The courts will, however, tolerate some restrictions on disposal of an estate which fall short of an absolute bar and indeed in some cases have been remarkably tolerant in dealing with restrictions which prevent disposal outside a particular family. Thus in *Re Macleay* (1875) LR 20 Eq 186 a disposition to someone 'on condition that he never sells it out of the family' was upheld. One cannot guarantee, however, that modern courts would be so generous and in any event this decision was rather more limited in its scope than may first appear: the recipient alone was bound by the condition, it did not bind anyone to whom he transferred the estate, and it only prevented a *sale* outside the family, the recipient could *give* the property to anyone. Despite this limited approval given to such a restriction upon disposal, it is best to avoid such arrangements for fear that they may be struck down, leaving the estate owner with a free power to alienate the property. However, as we shall see (17.5.1) it may be possible under TOLATA 1996 to create a trust for the specific purpose of retaining land, and it is certainly possible to provide that trust property cannot be alienated without the consent of specified persons.

9.5.2 Implications of Human Rights Act 1998

It is suggested in Gray and Gray at para. 3.1.33 that the Human Rights Act may be effective in striking down objectionable limitations:

> Although, like the determinable fee simple, the conditional fee has spawned a rich case law, some of the common law elaboration of this form of estate ownership may have been rendered redundant by the advent of the Human Rights Act 1998. The capacity for invidious discrimination so freely offered to the eccentric testator may in certain instances fall foul of Convention-based guarantees of individual freedom.

It is certainly possible to imagine limitations which might infringe the prohibition of any discrimination which might affect the enjoyment of Convention rights (Art. 14) or violate rights such as those to respect for private and family life (Art. 8) or to freedom of conscience and religion (Art. 9). It seems that, as yet, no limitation has been challenged on any of these grounds, but the point is worth bearing in mind if you find yourself advising an 'eccentric testator'.

FURTHER READING

Megarry and Wade, *The Law of Real Property*, 8th edn., Sweet & Maxwell, 2012, paras. 3-052–3-069 (types of fee simple).

Smith, *Property Law*, 7th edn., Pearson Longman, 2011, pp. 35–43 (freehold estates).

10

The leasehold estate

10.1 Introduction

10.1.1 2 Trant Way

A few weeks ago, the Stilton Recorder carried the following advertisement in its property section:

> 2 Trant Way, Mousehole, Stilton.
> Leasehold maisonette. 99-yr. lease
> Pleasant maisonette, being ground and first floor of this elegant Victorian property.
> 2 recep. 2 bedrm. Bathrm. Sep WC. Spacious kitchen/breakfast rm.
> £250,000.

The current freehold owner of No. 2 is Fingall Forest, who is a widower and who has no children. He has lived there for many years, and title to the property is still unregistered. Mr Forest has decided that the house is too large for his needs and he has had it divided into three sections:

- a flat, consisting of the second floor of the property, in which he lives;
- the ground and first-floor maisonette, which is now for sale 'leasehold' (a 99-year lease); and
- the basement, which Mr Forest has let on a weekly tenancy to an old friend, Gerald Gruyere, at a rent of £175 a week.

Mr Forest's estate agent has now found a prospective purchaser for the maisonette, James Harding.

These two transactions, the sale of the maisonette on a 99-year lease, and the letting of the basement on a weekly tenancy seem at first glance to have very little in common. However, we shall see that although these rights to use property appear very different from each other, they both fall into the category of leases (or tenancies); that is to say, both are 'terms of years absolute'. We should mention here that in modern use the terms 'lease' and 'tenancy' are interchangeable, although there is a tendency to use the word 'tenancies' when speaking of periodic (weekly or monthly) arrangements.

10.1.2 Fixed term and periodic tenancies

The lease of the maisonette for 99 years is an example of a lease for a *fixed term*, that is, for one period which can last for weeks, months or years, as the parties agree. At the end of the agreed period, the lease ends automatically, without either side having to give the other notice.

By contrast, the letting of the basement on a weekly tenancy is an example of a *periodic tenancy*. It is not granted for a fixed number of weeks, but runs on indefinitely, from week to week, until one of the parties does not want to continue the arrangement, and therefore gives notice to the other. In a similar way, tenancies can run on from month to month, quarter to quarter or year to year, being known as monthly, quarterly or yearly tenancies respectively.

Leases for a fixed term and periodic tenancies are the types of lease most frequently encountered. We will concentrate on these at first in this chapter, and will leave until later any consideration of other forms, such as tenancies at will and at sufferance, tenancies by estoppel and concurrent leases (for all of which, see 10.10).

10.1.3 Term of years absolute

In general, a legal lease creates a legal estate, which itself is called a 'lease' or, more technically, a 'term of years absolute'. It appears, however, from the House of Lords' decision in *Bruton v London & Quadrant Housing Association* [2001] 1 AC 406 that it is possible for a lease to create the contractual relationship of landlord and tenant between the parties, without giving an estate in land to the tenant. The House of Lords held that this had happened in the special circumstances of *Bruton*, and we will consider this decision and its consequences in more detail later (see 22.2.4.4). We must emphasise here though that the situation in *Bruton* was unusual, and that, in general, a tenant taking under a legal lease will hold a legal estate.

As we have already mentioned, the technical name for this estate is 'term of years absolute'. This may seem less strange at first sight than that used to describe the freehold estate (fee simple absolute in possession), but nonetheless it is necessary to consider carefully the terminology used.

10.1.3.1 The 'term'

The Law of Property Act 1925 requires that the leasehold estate should be for 'a term', that is, for a fixed period rather than for an indefinite one. Thus in *Lace v Chantler* [1944] KB 368, it was held that a lease 'for the duration of the war' was not a legal estate because it was not for a fixed term, since at the time that the lease was granted the exact period for which it would continue to exist could not be known until it had ended.

A lease 'for 99 years', or other specified period, is clearly 'a term' which satisfies the requirements of LPA 1925, s. 1(1); but is this true of a periodic tenancy? One would imagine that a periodic tenancy which runs on indefinitely from one period to another could not be an estate in land, because when it commences one does not know how long it will last. However, the law does regard such a tenancy as satisfying the requirement of a fixed term, because it is regarded as being a lease for a period (fixed term), followed by another lease for that period, and so on until the lease is correctly terminated. As Lord Templeman explained in *Prudential Assurance Co. Ltd v London Residuary Body* [1992] 2 AC 386 at p. 394:

> A tenancy from year to year is saved from being uncertain because each party has power by notice to determine at the end of any year. The term continues until determined as if both parties made a new agreement at the end of each year for a new term for the ensuing year.

Therefore, even the tenant with a periodic tenancy does have a lease for a fixed term, which is thus capable of being a legal estate.

10.1.3.2 'Of years'

It is clear also that a 99-year lease is a term *of years* but a periodic tenancy will be for a period of a year, or frequently less than a year. Nonetheless the periodic tenancy will still qualify as a legal estate, as would a lease for, say, a fixed period of three months, because LPA 1925, s. 205(1)(xxvii), provides that:

> the expression 'term of years' includes a term for less than a year, or for a year or years and a fraction of a year or from year to year.

Therefore, all that is necessary is a fixed period, and accordingly it is possible to grant a lease for a very short period (e.g., two days) even though this is not likely to be common.

In *Smallwood v Sheppards* [1895] 2 QB 627 it was held that a legal lease could be created for a period of three successive bank holidays, that is, for three separate days. More recently, it has been accepted that a time-sharing arrangement, giving the right to use a holiday cottage for one week a year over an 80-year period, can amount to a legal lease for 'a single discontinuous period' (*Cottage Holiday Associates Ltd v Customs and Excise Commissioners* [1983] 1 QB 735).

10.1.3.3 'Absolute'

The inclusion of this word in the definition of the leasehold estate causes some difficulty. When used to describe the fee simple it means, as we have seen in Chapter 9, that the estate is not liable to end prematurely, before the full period is up. However, leases often provide for determination before the term has run its full course; for example, as we shall see, it is common practice to provide that the landlord may forfeit the lease for any breach of covenant by the tenant. Indeed some long leases even contain provisions allowing either the landlord or tenant, or both, the right to terminate the lease early on notice. Such clauses are often called 'break clauses'. However, there has never been any suggestion that such a provision prevents the lease taking effect as a legal estate, even though that lease cannot be described as absolute in the same sense as the fee simple. It is in fact difficult to explain the use of the word 'absolute' in this context, and it may be helpful to note the view expressed by Megarry and Wade at para. 6–019 that, in this context, 'This word is not used ... in any intelligible sense ...'.

10.1.3.4 No requirement for the leasehold estate to be 'in possession'

One further difference between the statutory definitions of the two legal estates may be noted here. We have seen already in Chapter 9 that, in order to be legal, a fee simple absolute must take effect 'in possession', and that a future interest cannot be a legal estate. There is no similar provision in LPA 1925, s. 1(1) with regard to leases and accordingly leases may be granted to take effect in the future and still have the status of legal estates.

Leases to start in the future
A lease granting a term which does not start immediately but at some time in the future is called a *'reversionary lease'*. In order to prevent the creation of such interests very far into the future, LPA 1925, s. 149(3), provides that any lease expressed to commence more than 21 years from the date of the instrument which creates it is to be void.

Similarly, a contract to grant a lease, which, when granted, will take effect more than 21 years from the date of the grant, is also void. On this latter point, it is important to note that the time-limit specified in s. 149(3) still relates to the period between the grant of the lease and the commencement of the term; the section does not impose any restriction on the length of time which may elapse between entering into the contract to grant a lease and actually making the grant. Thus it is possible, and, indeed, standard practice, for a landlord to covenant that he will, if the tenant wishes, grant him a further term when the present lease ends (option for renewal). Any such option can be enforced at the end of the lease, however long the original term may be.

10.2 Basic requirements for a lease

10.2.1 Definition of a lease

The lease has been defined (see *Woodfall's Law of Landlord and Tenant*, Sweet & Maxwell, Release 48, May 2004, para. 1.003) as, 'the grant of a right to the exclusive possession of land for a determinate term less than that which the grantor has himself in the land'. This definition identifies three essential elements, which we consider in detail in the following sections:

- exclusive possession (10.2.2),
- determinate (i.e., certain) term (10.2.3),
- term less than that of the grantor (10.2.4).

10.2.2 Exclusive possession

Exclusive possession is an essential ingredient of a lease; without exclusive possession there can be no lease. Exclusive possession is the right to use premises to the exclusion of all others, including the landlord himself. In the words of Lord Templeman in *Street v Mountford* [1985] AC 809 at p. 816:

> The tenant possessing exclusive possession is able to exercise the rights of an owner of land, which is in the real sense his land albeit temporarily and subject to certain restrictions. A tenant armed with exclusive possession can keep out strangers and keep out the landlord.

If the occupier has no right to exclusive possession of the premises then his right to use the premises cannot amount to a lease, but may be some lesser right, such as a licence or possibly an easement (for example, to store goods on the premises). However, the fact that a person has been given exclusive possession is not conclusive proof that he has a lease, for it is also possible to have a licence, or certain other rights in land, with exclusive possession. This point is also emphasised by Lord Templeman in *Street v Mountford* (at p. 818):

> There can be no tenancy unless the occupier enjoys exclusive possession; but an occupier who enjoys exclusive possession is not necessarily a tenant. He may be owner in fee simple, a trespasser, a mortgagee in possession, an object of charity or a service occupier. To constitute a tenancy the occupier must be granted exclusive possession for a fixed or periodic term certain in consideration of a premium or periodical payments.

However, this case also emphasises that normally, where there is exclusive possession, the courts will regard the arrangement as a lease.

It should be noted that although exclusive possession normally gives the tenant the right to exclude everyone else, including the landlord, from the premises, the lease may reserve the right for the landlord to enter the premises on certain occasions (e.g., to inspect the state of repair of the property). Such a right must be exercised at reasonable hours and in a reasonable manner and does not prevent the tenant having exclusive possession, though a right for the landlord to come and go as he pleased without the tenant's permission would have this effect. Thus in *Appah v Parncliffe Investments Ltd* [1964] 1 WLR 1064, in which the 'landlord' had reserved the right to come into the premises as and when he chose in order to empty meters and change linen, the arrangement was held to be a licence, since the occupier did not have exclusive possession.

These points may be summarised by saying that, for a lease to exist, the tenant must have exclusive possession, but exclusive possession is not in itself conclusive evidence of the existence of a lease. There is extensive case law on the significance of exclusive possession in distinguishing between leases and licences, and we will tell you more about this in Chapter 22 (see especially 22.2.3).

10.2.3 Determinate term

We have already seen that a lease must be granted for a period which is certain, and that both fixed-term and periodic tenancies satisfy this test. In addition the commencement of the period must also be certain. Normally, if no mention is made in the agreement, it will be deemed to start immediately (*Furness v Bond* (1888) 4 TLR 457). If, however, one has only an agreement for a future lease, it will be void unless it is clear at what date the lease is to start, either from an express term in the contract or by inference (*Harvey v Pratt* [1965] 1 WLR 1025).

10.2.3.1 Lease for life or until marriage or civil partnership

You might think that a lease 'for T's life' or 'until T marries' would be void because the duration of such a lease is not certain. At common law, however, such grants, providing they were made by deed, had the effect of creating respectively a life estate and an estate determinable on marriage. These were freehold estates, which could last for an uncertain time; they were often created as family arrangements, but the life estate created by a lease for life could also be of a commercial nature, involving rent or other payment by the tenant.

Under the 1925 property legislation, life estates and determinable estates could no longer exist at law. Those created as part of family settlements would in future take effect as equitable interests under a trust (see 1.7.1.4 and 9.2), while commercial leases for life were dealt with by the provisions of LPA 1925, s.149(6).

LPA 1925, s. 149(6)

Under s. 149(6), (as amended by the Civil Partnership Act 2004, s. 81 and Sch. 8, para. 1), a lease for life, or until marriage or the formation of a civil partnership, which has been granted at a rent or in consideration of a fine (premium) will be converted automatically into a fixed term of 90 years determinable on the specified event. The term, it should be noted, does not terminate automatically on the event. It terminates if thereafter either party to the agreement (including the tenant's personal representatives in the case of death) serves on the other one month's notice, expiring on a quarter day.

A lease comes within s. 149(6) even if it is granted 'to T for the lifetime of X', so the life specified need not be that of the tenant but might be that of a third party, or of the landlord himself. The section applies to all cases of leases determinable on marriage, civil partnership or death (provided they are granted for value), so even if L, in an attempt to 'get it right', grants T a lease for '100 years determinable on T's earlier death' this will also be converted into a term of 90 years determinable on death.

The Supreme Court has recently made use of LPA 1925, s. 149(6) in an interesting but unexpected way in *Berrisford v Mexfield Housing Co-operative Ltd* [2011] UKSC 52 (see 10.2.3.3).

10.2.3.2 **Attempts to avoid requirement of a fixed period**

In some circumstances a landlord may want to permit the use of his property for an uncertain period. This was the position with wartime lettings, where leases were made 'for the duration of the war', but were held to be invalid because they did not create a term for a certain period (*Lace v Chantler* [1944] KB 368). More recent cases have involved owners who intend to redevelop their land at some future date, and so want to avoid creating leases for fixed periods which might delay them when they are ready to start work. For a time it was thought that this could be achieved by creating a periodic tenancy with a provision that the landlord would not give notice to quit until he was ready to redevelop the land. This gave the tenant some measure of security, but enabled the landlord to regain possession when needed.

An example of this practice can be found in *Re Midland Railway Co.'s Agreement* [1971] 1 Ch 725. Here the landlord claimed to have ended a periodic tenancy by giving notice, in breach of a term of the lease that it would do so only if the property was required for its own business. The Court of Appeal held that the restriction on the right to give notice was enforceable, and that the notice given by the landlord was therefore invalid. The court rejected the argument that the restriction made the term of the lease uncertain and therefore void under the rule in *Lace v Chantler*, holding that this rule did not apply to periodic tenancies.

Some 20 years later, however, a similar provision restricting the right of a landlord to give notice for an indefinite period was held to be void by the House of Lords in *Prudential Assurance Co. Ltd v London Residuary Body* [1972] 2 AC 386. The case arose from a transaction in 1930 in which a freehold owner of a shop with frontage to the street sold the front strip of his property to the local authority to enable it to widen the road. The authority then leased the strip back to its former owner, the lease providing that it was to continue until the property was required by the landlord for the road work. It was obviously intended that this arrangement would be for a relatively short period, but the land was never needed for this purpose, and the lease was still in existence some 40 years later. The current landlord had no road-widening powers and, if the restriction on giving notice was valid, it would never be able to end the lease.

The House of Lords reviewed earlier cases which had led to the decision in *Lace v Chantler* and held that the certainty rule applied to periodic tenancies just as much as to fixed-term leases (thus overruling the Court of Appeal's decision in *Re Midland Railway Co's Agreement*). The ability of either party to end a periodic tenancy by notice was an essential element in meeting the requirement of certainty. In Lord Templeman's words (at p. 394):

> A tenancy from year to year is saved from being uncertain because each party has power by notice to determine at the end of any year. The term continues until determined as if both parties made a new agreement at the end of each year for a new term the ensuing year. A power for nobody to determine or for one party only to be able to determine is inconsistent with the concept of a term from year to year...

In this case, the restriction on the landlord's right to give notice made the length of the lease uncertain, and accordingly the lease had been void from the outset. However, the fact that the tenant had gone into possession and paid an annual rent meant that he had an implied yearly periodic tenancy (for which, see 10.3.2), and this could be ended by six months' notice.

Although the decision in this case was unanimous, several of their Lordships expressed regret and dissatisfaction with the result, which left the shop owner with no frontage to the street. Lord Browne-Wilkinson in particular commented (at p. 396) that it was difficult to think of a more unsatisfactory outcome or one further away from what the parties to the 1930 agreement could ever have contemplated, and ended by expressing the hope that the Law Commission would consider:

> whether there is in fact any good reason for maintaining a rule which operates to defeat contractually agreed arrangements between the parties...and which is capable of producing such an extraordinary result.

Twenty years after *Prudential*, during which there has been no review of the certainty rule, the hope that the Law Commission will look into the matter has been expressed once again, this time by the Supreme Court in *Berrisford v Mexfield Housing Co-operative Ltd* [2011] 3 WLR 1091.

10.2.3.3 *Berrisford v Mexfield Housing Co-operative Ltd* [2011] 3 WLR 1091

Facts

Ms Berrisford ('B') was the tenant of a housing association, Mexfield Housing Co-operative Ltd ('Mexfield'). Mexfield, and many other housing associations of the same type, used a standard occupancy agreement, which purported to grant each tenant a periodic tenancy and set out the terms of the tenancy, including provisions for bringing it to an end. The tenant could end the tenancy by giving one month's notice, but the association could exercise its right of re-entry (thus ending the tenancy) only in specified circumstances, which included the tenant being in arrears of rent or in breach of other terms of the agreement.

These provisions, restricting the landlord's right to give notice, had been widely used by housing associations before *Prudential* and continued in use after it, apparently because the effect of that decision was not recognised. However, it seems that at some stage Mexfield became aware of the position and, wishing to end B's tenancy, purported to do so by giving a month's notice. B refused to vacate the property and Mexfield sought an order for possession.

Both the High Court and the Court of Appeal followed *Prudential* in holding that the restriction on the landlord's right to end the lease by notice resulted in uncertainty about the length of the term and therefore invalidated the purported grant of a periodic tenancy. Instead, B held under an implied periodic tenancy arising from her entry into possession and the payment of rent. That monthly tenancy could be ended by the landlord on one month's notice, and Mexfield was entitled to possession of the property.

Supreme Court decision

It seemed that B's appeal to the Supreme Court would provide an opportunity for a re-consideration of the certainty rule. However, B's counsel conceded that the lease *was* void for uncertainty, and successfully based the appeal on the submission that the agreement between the parties created a tenancy for life, which was converted into a 90-year term by LPA 1925, s. 149(6) (see 10.2.3.1).

This somewhat surprising argument was supported by authority, which was accepted by all members of the court and forms the basis for their individual judgments allowing B's appeal. The stages of the argument are set out clearly by Lord Neuberger and are as follows.

From the mid-thirteenth century onwards an attempt to grant a lease for an indefinite period was treated by common law as creating a freehold life estate (paras. 39–41). The estate created in this way would end on the death of the tenant, but also could be ended on any earlier event which had been specified as determining the purported lease (para. 50). Thus if the agreement between B and Mexfield had been made at any time before 1926, it would have created a life estate, determinable either on B's death or earlier in accordance with the provisions of the agreement. When the property legislation came into force (on 1 January 1926) the estate would have been converted into a 90-year term under LPA 1925, s. 149(6); although the statute refers to the term ending only on the death of the tenant, the Supreme Court was satisfied that the provisions of the agreement would also have been carried on into the new term (para. 50). The effect of s. 149(6) was not limited to leases in existence when the legislation took effect, and the purported grant made by Mexfield to B in 1993 had the effect of creating a 90-year lease determinable on B's death or as provided in the agreement.

Accordingly, the court allowed B's appeal, holding that Mexfield was not entitled to possession.

An alternative submission

The court's decision on the lease for life argument was sufficient to dispose of the appeal, but members of the court went on to express opinions on an alternative submission made on B's behalf, namely that the occupancy agreement created a contractual licence, enforceable between the parties.

The suggestion that the purported grant of an uncertain term might be enforced as a contractual licence had been rejected in *Lace v Chantler* [1944] KB 368, at 371–2, the court taking the view that if the parties had intended to create a lease and failed to do so, they could not say that they had really intended to create a contractual licence. Since then, however, the House of Lords in *Street v Mountford* [1985] AC 809 had made it clear that the nature of an interest in land is decided by legal criteria, not by the name which the parties attach to it or purport to create. *Street v Mountford* is a very important decision, and we deal with it in detail in Chapter 22 (see 22.2.3), but all you need to know here is that the House of Lords held that all the requirements for the creation of a lease were satisfied, and that therefore the parties had created a lease, despite labelling it as a licence. By contrast, in the case now before the Supreme Court, the parties described the agreement as a lease, but failed to satisfy the essential requirement of certainty, and had therefore in fact created only a licence. All the terms of such a contractual licence were enforceable between the contracting parties, and accordingly the licence would continue until determined in accordance with the agreement.

It is important to remember that the court's observations about contractual licences were not necessary to the decision between the parties and are therefore only *obiter dicta*. Nevertheless they may in future be helpful to companies and other 'artificial persons', who do not have a natural life and so would not be able to rely on the 'lease for life' argument available to a human tenant.

10.2.3.4 The problem of the certainty rule, and how to overcome it

In *Berrisford v Mexfield* members of the Supreme Court joined in deploring the effect of the certainty rule: there was no practical justification for the rule (para. 34), and its consequences were described as 'bizarre' and as 'having an Alice in Wonderland quality' (at paras. 95 and 88). In fact, the court's decision in the present appeal only added to the problem, Lord Clarke commenting (para. 105) that :

> It is a mystery to me why in 2011 the position of a tenant who is a human being and a tenant which is a company should in this respect be different.

The court echoed the words of Lord Browne-Wilkinson in *Prudential*: change was needed, and this would best be undertaken by Parliament, preferably following a full review by the Law Commission. We can only wait and see whether any action will follow this time!

Meanwhile it is worth noting the following ways in which prospective landlords and tenants can avoid being bound for fixed periods, without falling foul of the certainty rule:

- granting a lease for a fixed term with a provision for earlier determination on the occurrence of a certain event. For example, a lease for a fixed term could have been granted during the war with a provision for determination if the war ended earlier, and this would satisfy the certainty rule (see *Lace v Chantler* [1944] KB 368);
- granting a periodic tenancy that provides that during a prescribed period notice shall not be given by the landlord, unless for a specified purpose. Thus in *Breams Property Investment Co. v Stroulger* [1948] 2 KB 1 the landlords agreed not to give notice for three years, unless the property was needed for their own use;
- creating an express tenancy at will, as in *Manfield & Sons Ltd v Botchin* [1970] 2 QB 612 (see 10.10.3);
- creating a contractual licence (see Chapter 22).

10.2.4 Term less than that of the grantor

An owner in fee simple is able to grant a lease of his property for any term because the fee simple is itself effectively perpetual. Thus there is nothing to prevent a fee simple owner granting a lease to a tenant for 9,000, or even 90,000 years. In fact 99-year leases are common and 999-year leases, though hardly frequent, are to be found in practice.

10.2.4.1 Underleases and subleases

However, whilst there can only be one fee simple estate in one piece of land, there can be more than one term of years. A tenant may himself grant a lease of the premises (a *sublease*) to a subtenant, as long as this sublease will last for a shorter period than the original lease (the *head lease*). The subtenant may also grant a further lease of the same premises (an *underlease*) to an undertenant, as long as the underlease is for a shorter period than the sublease. Thus if L, the fee simple owner, grants T a 99-year lease of a property on 1 January 1980, T may grant a sublease to S for any shorter period (e.g., 25 years) and S may grant an underlease to U for any period shorter than the sublease (e.g., a monthly tenancy). This can be expressed diagrammatically as follows:

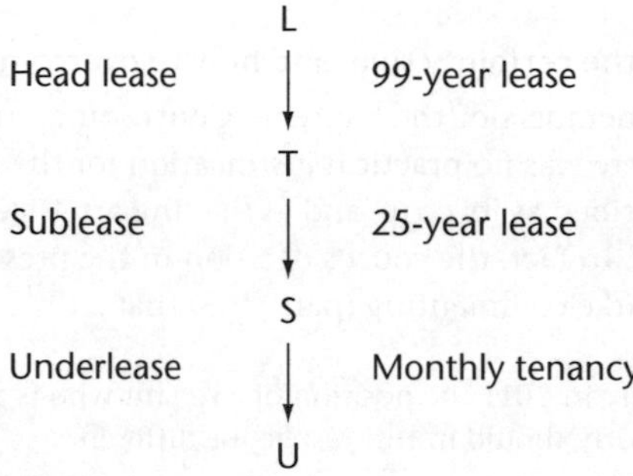

Alternatively, you may like to picture these transactions as shown in the diagram below, in which L, T and S is each pictured as 'carving' a lesser estate out of his own estate. (However, if you find this way of looking at things only more confusing, just ignore the diagram!)

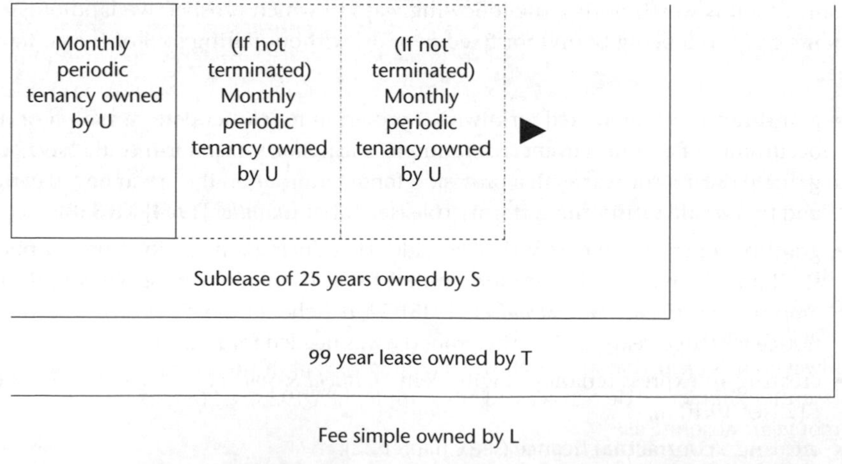

In both diagrams, L is a landlord, T and S are both tenants and landlords, and U is a tenant only. Each of these four people has a legal estate in the property concerned. S may recover the property by bringing U's periodic tenancy to an end (this can be done by serving notice, but today this right to terminate such a lease may be affected by statutory provisions which give security of tenure to certain tenants; see 10.5.1). T will recover the use of the property when S's 25-year term expires. Thus S and T both have a right that the property will revert to them on the expiration of the terms which they have carved out of their own. This right is called a *'reversion'*, and since S and T are owners of leasehold estates they are each said to have a *'leasehold reversion'*. Once T's 99-year lease expires, the fee simple owner L (or his successors) will recover the property and thus L has a *'freehold reversion'*. Finally, we should mention that although the terminology of 'sublease' and 'underlease' given above is in common usage, it is not used consistently by all lawyers and you may find cases of what we call 'underleases' being called 'subleases'.

The process of creating further terms out of a leasehold estate may continue almost indefinitely, so long as each subsequent lease will end before the end of the term belonging to the person who grants it. However, if the grantor attempts to create a lease as long or longer than his own term, no new lease will be created and instead the grant will operate as an *assignment* (i.e., a transfer) of the grantor's own lease (see 10.4.3.2).

10.2.5 Is payment of rent an essential requirement?

We have now discussed the three essential elements identified in Woodfall's definition of a lease (see 10.2.1). You may have noticed that that definition makes no mention of the payment of rent or premium as being an essential characteristic of a lease. It is true that leases are usually commercial arrangements, in which the tenant pays for his use of the land, either by regular instalments throughout the lease (rent, technically called *'rent-service'*) or by a lump sum at the start of the lease (called a *'premium'* or *'fine'*), or by a combination of both.

These different types of payment are illustrated by the arrangements which Fingall Forest is making with his new tenants (see 10.1.1). The basement is being let on a weekly tenancy at a rent of £175 a week; this is typical of periodic tenancies, in which rent is payable at regular intervals (e.g., weekly, monthly, quarterly or annually). With a long lease for a fixed period (e.g., a 99-year lease), it is more usual for the tenant to pay a premium or fine at the start of the lease, and then to pay a smaller, sometimes almost nominal rent, usually called *'ground rent'*, on a yearly or half-yearly basis. Alternatively, it is possible, although less usual, to have a lease in consideration of one initial payment of a lump sum, rather than in consideration of the periodical payment of rent (*Hill v Booth* [1930] 1 KB 381). In general, therefore, a tenant will pay some rent to his landlord, although in the case of ground rent it may be a trivial sum of money. We know from the newspaper advertisement for Fingall Forest's maisonette that the 99-year lease is to be granted at a premium of £250,000, but there is no mention of a ground rent, and this is something that the prospective purchaser will need to check before entering into a contract for the lease.

However, it is clear that although the payment of rent or premium is usual, it is not an essential characteristic of a lease. For example, LPA 1925, s. 205(1)(xxvii), defines a term of years absolute as:

> a term of years... whether or not at a rent.

The limitation of other provisions in that Act to leases *at a rent or premium* (for example, s. 149(3) and (6)) implies that a valid lease can exist where there is no provision for payment in either form. Such leases are likely to be found as a part of family settlements, or as conveyancing devices, for instance, in connection with mortgages.

There was, therefore, some surprise when Lord Templeman in *Street v Mountford* [1985] AC 809 appeared to suggest (in the passage quoted at 10.2.2) that the payment of a premium or rent was necessary to constitute a tenancy. However, in *Ashburn Anstalt v Arnold* [1989] 1 Ch 1 the Court of Appeal confirmed that rent is not an essential characteristic of a lease and said that the remarks in *Street v Mountford* were not to be read as introducing such a requirement. In *Ashburn Anstalt v Arnold* a vendor of a leasehold estate had been given by the purchaser the right to exclusive possession of the premises rent-free until a specified date, the agreement to continue thereafter until terminated by a quarter's notice. This arrangement was held to be a lease and Fox LJ said, at p. 10:

> ...the reservation of rent is not necessary for the creation of a tenancy.

Ashburn Anstalt v Arnold was overruled on other grounds by the House of Lords in *Prudential Assurance Co. Ltd v London Residuary Body* [1992] 2 AC 386. However, the long-established principle that it is possible to have a lease without payment of rent has been affirmed by the Court of Appeal in *Skipton Building Society v Clayton* (1993) 66 P&CR 223.

Finally, it should be noted that although rent and premiums usually take the form of money payments, it is possible for payment to be made in kind or through the performance of services.

10.3 Creation of leases

In this section, we will consider:

- express grant of a legal lease (10.3.1):
- implied grant of a legal lease (10.3.2);
- what happens in law and equity if the requirements for creating a legal lease are not observed (10.3.3);
- equitable leases (10.3.4);
- comparison of legal and equitable leases (10.3.5).

10.3.1 Express grant of a legal lease

There are three forms of express grant, each of which is appropriate for creating a specific type of lease:

- grant made orally or in writing—to create leases of three years or less which satisfy requirements of LPA 1925, s. 54(2)
- grant by deed—to create leases for longer than three years, but not more than seven years; and shorter leases which do not satisfy requirements of LPA 1925, s. 54(2)
- grant by deed plus registration of leasehold title—to create leases for more than seven years.

10.3.1.1 Grant made orally or in writing

As we noted in Chapter 2 (2.5.4.1), the general rule imposed by LPA 1925 s. 52(1) is that a deed must be used to create or transfer a legal estate. This rule is, however, inconvenient when one is dealing with a short lease or a periodic tenancy. Accordingly an exception to the requirement for a deed is provided by LPA 1925, s. 54(2) in respect of certain leases for not more than three years (which includes periodic tenancies—*Hammond v Farrow* [1904] 2 KB 332 at 335).

Section 52(4) provides that a lease of not more than three years may be made orally or in writing (the technical term is 'by parol'), provided that the lease:

- takes effect in possession; and
- is at the best rent reasonably obtainable; and
- does not require the payment of a premium ('fine').

The provision that no premium is payable is self-explanatory, but we need to look briefly at the other two requirements.

1. *The lease must take effect in possession* This means that the lease must begin at the date of the grant, not at some time in the future, and as a result a reversionary (future) lease, even one for not more than three years, must always be granted by deed. For an application of this rule, see *Long v Tower Hamlets LBC* [1998] Ch 197.

2. *The lease must be granted 'at the best rent'* The Court of Appeal has recently confirmed in *Fitzkriston LLP v Panayi* [2008] EWCA Civ 283 that 'best rent' means 'market rent'. In this case, it was argued for the tenant that the rent agreed between a landlord and tenant must be taken to be the best rent available at the time of grant (the unexpressed reason being, of course, that if anyone else was willing to pay a higher rent, the landlord would not have let the property to the current tenant). This argument was rejected by Rix LJ, who commented (at para. 27) that if it was correct:

> the statute calling for a best rent would be meaningless, because, in every case, the best rent in question would be the agreed rent.

In this particular case, a valuation of the property, prepared independently and before the grant of the lease, had regarded it as capable of fetching a much higher rent than was subsequently agreed. Thus there was clear evidence that the lease did not satisfy the requirements of LPA 1925, s. 54(2), and accordingly the tenant failed to establish his claim to a periodic tenancy.

In practice, most short leases do take effect in possession and satisfy the requirement for the best rent, and accordingly are granted without a deed, in simple written form or by word of mouth. It is most unlikely that Mr Gruyère, the weekly tenant of the basement flat at 2 Trant Way, has a deed setting out his lease. Indeed, as he is a friend of the landlord, Mr Forest, he may well have no written document at all. Nonetheless, Mr Gruyère will have a legal lease if his rent of £175 a week satisfies the 'best rent' test.

Where a periodic tenancy is expressly granted, the grant will usually indicate the type of tenancy being created (i.e., yearly, quarterly, monthly or weekly).

10.3.1.2 Grant by deed

Leases which are longer than three years but not more than seven years (and shorter leases which do not satisfy the requirements of LPA 1925, s. 54(2)), are subject to the general rule set out in s. 52(1) of that Act, which states that a grant is not effective to create a legal estate 'unless made by deed'. This means that such a lease should be signed, witnessed and delivered in accordance with the requirements of the Law of Property (Miscellaneous Provisions) Act 1989 s. 1.

10.3.1.3 Grant by deed plus registration of leasehold title

Leases for more than seven years must be granted by deed in accordance with LPA 1925 s. 52(1), and must be registered as required by LRA 2002 (see 7.3.1.1 and 7.6).

(a) *Registered land* Where the owner of a registered estate grants out of it a lease for more than seven years, the grant is a disposition which must be completed by registration, and does not operate at law until this has been done (LRA 2002 s. 27(1) and (2)). Until then, the grantee has only an equitable right to the lease. When the lease is registered, a notice of it will be entered on the landlord's registered title.

(b) *Unregistered land* Where a lease for more than seven years is granted by the owner of an estate which is itself not yet registered, the grant of the lease creates a legal estate and the new tenant must then apply for registration of his title to that estate. If he does not make the application in the prescribed time, his legal estate ceases to exist and the grant operates as a contract to grant the lease (LRA 2002 ss. 4(1)(c) and 7(2)(b)).

In accordance with these rules, the proposed grant of the 99-year lease of the maisonette at 2 Trant Way should be made by deed and followed by an application for registration.

10.3.1.4 Registrable short leases

In general, the procedure for an express grant of a lease is as we have described above. However, we need to remind you that grants of leases taking effect in possession more than three months after grant and leases giving discontinuous possession (e.g., under timeshare schemes) must be completed by registration whatever their length (see 7.3.1.2).

10.3.2 Implied grant of a legal lease

Because a lease for not more than three years may be created without any formalities, it is possible for certain leases to arise by implication, from the actions of the parties. Where it could be shown that a person was in possession of land with the owner's consent and that rent calculated on a periodic basis was paid and accepted, the common law would presume the existence of a periodic tenancy (*Martin v Smith* (1874) LR 9 Ex 50). This presumption could, of course, be rebutted by showing a contrary intention but, in the absence of any evidence about what the parties had intended, common law would fill the gap by inferring the creation of a periodic tenancy.

In more recent times, however, the introduction of various forms of statutory protection for tenants meant that it was no longer safe to presume the intention to create a tenancy, and the courts now emphasise the importance of discovering the real intentions of the parties (see *Cardiothoracic Institute v Shrewdcrest Ltd* [1986] 1 WLR 368). Thus, as stated by Nicholls LJ in *Javad v Mohammed Aqil* [1991] 1 WLR 1007, at p. 1012:

> the inference sensibly and reasonably to be drawn will depend upon a fair consideration of all the circumstances, of which payment of rent on a periodical basis is only one, albeit a very important one.

In this case, the occupier had gone into possession in the course of negotiations for a fixed-term lease, and had paid a quarterly sum described as 'rent'. When the negotiations broke down, and the owner sought to recover possession, the occupier claimed that a quarterly tenancy had arisen from the payment and receipt of rent. The Court of Appeal, having regard to all the circumstances, including the continuing negotiations, refused to infer an intention to create a periodic tenancy, and held the occupier to be a tenant at will only (see 10.10.3).

Other decisions in which the courts have refused to infer an implied grant include *Manfield & Sons Ltd v Botchin* [1970] 2 QB 612 (express grant of a tenancy at will), and *Tickner v Buzzacott* [1965] Ch 426 (landlord was unaware that the person paying rent was not the person he had in contemplation).

In many cases, however, it may well be found that the parties' intentions are consistent with the grant of a periodic tenancy. The occupier may have gone into possession under a contract to grant a fixed-term lease, which is never performed, or under a defective grant (e.g., a lease for more than three years not made by deed), or on the other hand may 'hold on' in the property after a previous lease has come to an end. In these circumstances, if rent is paid and accepted on a periodic basis, a periodic tenancy may arise by implied grant.

The type of periodic tenancy arising by implication will in general depend upon the period for which the rent is said to be due rather than upon that for which it is paid. Thus a yearly tenancy will arise by implication if the tenant is in possession of the land and is paying a rent which is stated as an annual sum, even if payments are actually made in monthly instalments (*Ladies' Hosiery and Underwear Ltd v Parker* [1930] 1 Ch 304). However, this is only the general rule, and it is possible for the period of the tenancy to be determined by other terms of the agreement which indicate a particular period (e.g., reference to provisions for notice), or by local or business custom.

It is important to realise that leases arising by implied grant come within the terms of LPA 1925, s. 54(2) (relating to informal creation of leases for not more than three years), and so are legal leases.

10.3.3 Non-compliance with requirements for legal grant: position in law and equity

We can identify two situations in which parties do not comply with the requirements for the grant of a legal term of years absolute:

- the parties make an agreement for a lease, but never proceed to the formal grant; or
- the parties attempt to make the formal grant but fail to do it properly e.g., the grantor purports to grant a lease for more than three years, but does not use a deed, or he does use a deed but the registration requirements are not observed.

In both situations, the parties have not created the legal lease they intended. It is true that a legal periodic tenancy may arise by implied grant if the tenant, relying on the contract or the defective grant, goes into possession, and rent is paid and accepted (10.3.2), but this will probably fall far short of the term which the parties originally intended to create.

Where there is an agreement to grant a lease, both law and equity may be able to assist one of the parties with remedies for breach of contract. Moreover both systems may treat a defective grant as a contract to grant a lease and give relief accordingly. Of course, these contractual remedies will be available only if the parties have complied with the statutory requirements for contracts relating to land in force at the time when the agreement or the defective grant was made. The rules for the form of such contracts are dealt with in detail in Chapter 5, but it may be helpful to summarise them here.

10.3.3.1 Formal requirements for contracts relating to land

1. *Contracts made before 27 September 1989*

Contracts could be made orally, but were not enforceable unless evidenced in writing, or, for the purposes of equity, by part performance (LPA 1925, s. 40).

- *Written evidence* There might be written evidence of the contract itself or, where the parties attempted to grant a lease but failed to do it properly, the defective grant might constitute sufficient written evidence for the transaction to be treated as such a contract.
- *Part performance* If the tenant had been allowed to enter into possession of the property and had paid rent, these actions amounted to sufficient acts of part performance by both parties and the contract would be enforceable in equity (see *Rawlinson v Ames* [1925] Ch 96).

2. *Contracts made on or after 27 September 1989*

Under the Law of Property (Miscellaneous Provisions) Act 1989 contracts must:

- be made in writing;
- contain all the terms agreed between the parties; and
- be signed by both parties.

Contracts for leases for not more than three years are exempted from these requirements.

As we have seen (5.4), it is generally accepted that the doctrine of part performance can no longer apply, although there may be cases in which equity will assist by means of proprietary estoppel or the constructive trust. There is also some doubt as to whether a defective grant of a lease is likely to meet the current statutory requirements for a written contract (see Howell [1990] Conv 441), but this would of course have to depend on the exact nature of the documents in any particular case.

10.3.3.2 Remedies for breach of contract

Assuming that a party to an agreement for a lease or a defective lease can satisfy the relevant statutory requirements, he can seek the common law remedy of damages for breach of contract. However, it is the relief available from equity, in the form of an order for specific performance of the contract, that may well prove of greater value to him, and we consider this in the next section.

10.3.4 Leases in equity: the doctrine in *Walsh v Lonsdale*

Provided the requirements as to the form of the contract are satisfied, either party may seek an order for specific performance of the contract which, if awarded, would result in the proper execution of a legal lease.

As we explained in Chapter 2, the equitable maxim that equity regards as done that which ought to be done will apply in this situation. In consequence, equity regards the relationship between the parties as being what it would be if the order for specific performance had been made and the lease executed. As a result, the parties are treated as having had a lease in equity from the date of the contract. Exactly the same approach is adopted where a defective grant is treated by equity as a contract for a lease (*Parker v Taswell* (1858) 2 De G & J 559).

The existence of an equitable lease depends, however, on the availability of specific performance, and it is important to remember that this is a discretionary remedy and subject to the usual equitable rules. Thus the party seeking to enforce the contract must not delay unduly and must 'come to equity with clean hands'. Accordingly, he must not himself be in breach of any of the terms of the agreement. Although the court in *Parker v Taswell* (1858) 2 De G & J 559 said that equity would not usually refuse its help unless the applicant's breaches are 'gross and wilful' (at p. 573), there are several cases where relief has been refused because of the applicant's behaviour. In *Coatsworth v Johnson* (1886) 55 LJ QB 220, in which the tenant of a farm was in continuing breach of an obligation to cultivate the land in a proper manner, the tenant was refused an order for specific performance. A similar position arose in *Cornish v Brook Green Laundry Ltd* [1959] 1 QB 394, in which the performance of certain works by the plaintiff was a condition precedent to the grant of lease and those works had not been performed. However, you may like to note the view expressed in Gray and Gray at para. 4.2.85 that 'the courts tend not to refuse equitable assistance in circumstances where relief against forfeiture would normally be granted under a legal lease' (as to which, see 13.4.5).

There may, of course, be reasons other than the applicant's behaviour which make the court unwilling to grant specific performance, as, for example, in *Warmington v Miller* [1973] QB 877, where the effect of granting the order would have been to procure the breach of a term in a superior lease.

In cases where, for one reason or another, specific performance is not available, the parties are not subject to an equitable lease, and the only remaining possibility for redress would be to seek damages at law for breach of contract.

10.3.4.1 Application of legal and equitable rules

The interaction of common law and equitable rules and of the provisions of the Supreme Court of Judicature Act 1873, s. 25(11), is clearly illustrated by the leading case of *Walsh v Lonsdale* (1882) 21 ChD 9. In this case, the landlord and tenant had entered into a written agreement (not under seal and so at that time not a deed) under which a mill was to be let to the tenant for seven years. The rent was to vary according to the productivity of the mill and it was agreed that the tenant would pay the rent annually, in advance, if the landlord so demanded. The tenant thereupon took possession of the mill and paid rent at six-monthly intervals, in arrears, for a year and a half. At this point the landlord demanded the next year's rent in advance, in accordance with the written agreement. The tenant refused to pay rent in advance and the landlord accordingly distrained for it (a 'self-help' remedy—see 13.3). The tenant thereupon sued, claiming that the distraint was unlawful, and applied for an interim injunction to restrain the landlord.

It is clear from the rules set out above that the relationship between the landlord and tenant in this case differs depending upon whether one applies the legal rules or the equitable rules.

At law, the tenant had an implied legal lease arising from his possession of the property and the payment of rent. Payment of rent at six-monthly intervals gives rise to an annual tenancy and, since rent had been paid and accepted in arrears, law would presume that it was a term of the legal lease that rent should be paid in this manner.

In equity, however, the act of entering the property and paying rent merely supports the written agreement, which is an agreement for a lease of seven years with rent payable annually in advance. Provided that the party seeking to enforce had done nothing wrong, this contract would be enforced by equity with an order for specific performance (finally producing the lease originally intended). In the meantime, since 'Equity regards as done that which ought to be done', the parties would be regarded by equity as already having a seven-year lease, under which rent was payable annually in advance.

Which lease then prevailed: the annual legal lease or the seven-year equitable lease? Only if the equitable lease prevailed would the landlord's action in distraining be proper. The Supreme Court of Judicature Acts 1873 and 1875 required that, where the rules of law and equity conflict, the equitable rule should prevail (a provision now contained in the Supreme Court Act 1981, s. 49(1)). The court applied this provision, and accordingly held that the equitable lease prevailed and that therefore the landlord's actions were lawful.

For a modern application of these principles, see *R v Tower Hamlets LBC, ex parte Von Goetz* [1999] QB 1019. Here the Court of Appeal held that a written lease for 10 years created an equitable estate which was a sufficient 'term of years' to entitle the applicant to a renovation grant under the Local Government and Housing Act 1989. The council had refused the grant because it regarded the equitable interest as too precarious, but in Mummery LJ's view:

> There may be circumstances in which an equitable lease is overridden, but in most cases a person with an equitable lease is in the same position as a person who has had a legal estate vested in him by deed.

10.3.5 Is an equitable lease as good as a legal lease?

Since normally an equitable lease can be converted into a legal lease by obtaining an order for specific performance, and since in the meantime equity will uphold the rights of the parties as though the legal lease had already been granted, it has often been said that, 'A contract for a lease is as good as a lease' (see *Re Maughan* (1885) 14 QBD 956). However, this is not necessarily true, for a variety of reasons, which we will consider in the following paragraphs.

10.3.5.1 Equitable remedies are discretionary

We have already seen that recognition of an equitable lease depends upon the availability of an order for specific performance. Whereas a legal remedy (e.g., damages) will be available without reference to the behaviour of the claimant, an equitable remedy is not available where the claimant has 'dirty hands'. Thus a contract for a lease is only 'as good as a lease' if the circumstances are such that an order for specific performance can be obtained.

10.3.5.2 Enforcement against third parties

There are difficulties with equitable leases when the position of third parties is involved. Let us assume that L, a freehold owner, agrees to give T a five-year lease of property and that this agreement is specifically enforceable. T will have an equitable lease of the property. If later L sells the fee simple of the property to P, P may not necessarily be bound by T's lease because it is only an equitable interest in the property.

In the case of *unregistered land* the contract for a lease will be an estate contract, a C(iv) land charge, under LCA 1972, s. 2(4) and will bind P only if it was registered as a land charge before the date of the conveyance to him (LCA 1972, s. 4(6)). If it is not registered, P will not be bound by it, even if he knew of the agreement, because notice is irrelevant in the case of registrable but unregistered land charges (see 6.4.5.4). By contrast, a legal lease will 'bind all the world'.

If title to the land is *registered*, P, as a person taking the estate for valuable consideration, will take free of T's equitable lease unless it has been protected by a notice on the register of title to that estate, or is capable of taking effect as an overriding interest (LRA

2002, s. 29 and Sch. 3). We have already mentioned that it is very unlikely that an equitable lease will be treated as an overriding interest under Sch. 3, para. 1, which is likely to be limited to *legal* leases (7.9.2.3(1)). However, if at the time of the transfer to P, T was occupying the property and could satisfy the other requirements of Sch. 3, para. 2, he could claim that his equitable lease was overriding as the interest of a person in actual occupation. Nevertheless, as *Strand Securities Ltd v Caswell* [1965] Ch 958 shows, there are circumstances in which a tenant may not be in actual occupation at the relevant time, and a tenant with an equitable lease would therefore be well advised to protect his position by making an entry on the register. By contrast, a legal lease for not more than seven years will override under Sch. 3, para. 1, and a longer lease will require completion by registration, with a notice automatically put on the landlord's title.

Thus, while a legal lease will bind any purchaser, an equitable lease will only be binding in certain circumstances. Since such equitable leases usually only arise in cases in which the parties are unaware of the legal formalities for the creation of a lease, it is most unlikely that the tenant will know that he has to take further steps to protect his interest.

Where an equitable lease is not protected in the appropriate way, and so cannot be enforced against the purchaser of the legal estate for value, it is worth remembering that the tenant may also have a legal periodic tenancy, arising from his going into possession and the payment and receipt of rent. *Walsh v Lonsdale* (1882) 21 ChD 9 shows that where both legal and equitable rights are available, the equitable right prevails, and indeed the tenant may often prefer to rely on an equitable lease which gives him a longer term. However, if for some reason the equitable right cannot be enforced, either party may fall back on the protection of the legal lease.

10.3.5.3 Do the covenants run?

A further defect of the contract for a lease arises in relation to the covenants in the lease. Each party to the lease will usually undertake certain duties, such as to pay rent or to keep the property in repair, by entering into covenants set out in the lease. Such covenants are not only enforceable between the original parties to the lease, but, provided the lease is legal, will normally run to bind and benefit both a purchaser from the landlord and a purchaser from the tenant. However, this has always depended on the purchaser acquiring an estate in the property; in the case of a purely equitable lease there is no legal estate in existence, and so the benefits and burdens of the covenants do not pass automatically if the tenant assigns his interest, although they probably do so on an assignment by the landlord.

As we shall see, the Landlord and Tenant (Covenants) Act 1995 substantially alters the rules governing this matter in respect of leases granted on or after 1 January 1996 (s. 1(3)) and we will look further at the old and new rules relating to equitable leases in Chapter 12 (12.5.3.2 and 12.6.3).

10.3.5.4 Contract is not a conveyance

A further disadvantage of an equitable lease is that, whilst a legal lease comes within the definition of a 'conveyance' for the purposes of LPA 1925, s. 62, and so carries with it automatically certain rights enjoyed in connection with the land, a contract for a lease does not fall within s. 62 and so does not carry with it such benefits. We will explain this more fully in Chapter 25 (see 25.8).

10.3.5.5 Other differences

There are other ways in which an equitable lease is not the equivalent of a legal lease. Thus whilst certain 'usual covenants' (a term of art explained at 11.3.3) are implied into a contract for a lease, they are not implied into a full legal lease and the parties are bound by the stated terms only. In this case, the contract for a lease seems to have an advantage over a poorly drafted legal lease.

A further difference, which is a disadvantage to the tenant, is that a purchaser of an equitable lease is not the purchaser of a legal estate and so will be bound by certain earlier equitable interests in the property. Where title to the land is unregistered, he cannot claim to be a 'bona fide purchaser of a legal estate for value' in respect of earlier rights to which the notice rules apply, nor can he claim the benefit of LCA 1972, s. 4(6), and so will be bound by unregistered class C(iv) and D land charges. He will of course be a purchaser within s. 4(5) and (8) of the Act and will take the property free of unregistered class C(i)–(iii) and F land charges (see 6.4.5).

Where title to the land is registered, he will be bound by earlier equitable interests (see 7.14).

From all this it can be seen that it is certainly not the case that a contract for a lease is as good as a lease. These rules provide a strong incentive for ensuring that leases are correctly granted but, unfortunately, are not understood by many landlords and tenants. Accordingly, it is fortunate that the most common types of informal leases (periodic tenancies) are saved from this unsatisfactory position under the provisions of LPA 1925, s. 54(2).

10.4 Disposition of leases and reversions

10.4.1 Power of disposition

Both landlord and tenant have legal estates which may pass to others on sale, by way of gift or under the rules of testate or intestate succession. In what follows, we are primarily concerned with disposition on sale, but it must be remembered that there are other occasions besides sale on which leases and reversions may pass to new owners.

10.4.2 Sale of the freehold reversion

It is always possible for the owner of the reversion in fee simple (the freehold landlord) to sell his estate in the land. This will be done in the normal manner by conveyance, in the case of unregistered land (see Chapter 6), and by transfer and registration, in the case of registered land (see Chapter 7).

10.4.2.1 Unregistered land

In the case of unregistered land, the purchaser will acquire the fee simple subject to any legal lease which exists, regardless of whether he knew of its existence, for 'Legal rights are good against the world' (6.5.1). Thus the purchaser of the fee simple becomes the tenant's new landlord and, as we shall see later, takes over most if not all of the original landlord's rights and duties under the lease.

10.4.2.2 Registered land

Where the title to the fee simple is registered the position varies according to the length of the lease.

If the lease is for not more than seven years it will be an overriding interest under LRA 2002 Sch. 3, para. 1, and so will bind the purchaser of the fee simple even if he did not know of it (see 7.9.2.3(1)).

If the lease is for more than seven years (or is one of the few leases requiring registration irrespective of length) it must have been registered in order for it to take effect as a legal lease. When this is done the lease will also be noted on the charges register of the landlord's title, and anyone who takes the landlord's estate for valuable consideration will take subject to the lease (LRA 2002 s. 29; see 7.6).

10.4.3 Sale of the lease by the tenant

A sale of his leasehold estate by the tenant is also possible (subject to any covenants in the lease restricting this right). The disposition (transfer) of a lease is usually called an *'assignment'*.

10.4.3.1 Express assignment

Since the assignment of a lease is the conveyance or transfer of a legal estate it should be made by deed (LPA 1925, s. 52(1)). This rule applies even to leases for not more than three years, because s. 54(2) provides an exception only for the original grant of such leases and does not apply to assignments (see *Crago v Julian* [1992] 1 WLR 372).

However, a defective assignment will be regarded in equity as a contract to assign, provided that it satisfies the formalities for a contract relating to land. Where such a contract arises, either party may then apply for an order for specific performance in order to effect a full legal assignment. Meanwhile of course, equity 'regards as done that which ought to be done', and will regard the transaction as an equitable assignment.

10.4.3.2 Assignment by operation of law

An exception to the requirement for a deed arises in cases in which the assignment takes effect due to operation of law. This can be important in cases in which a tenant purports to grant a sublease of the property but grants a term which is equivalent to, or greater than, the unexpired portion of his own lease. As we have already seen (10.2.4.1) such a disposition takes effect as an assignment of the lease rather than as the creation of a sublease. The reason for this is that a sublease can only be created if the tenant retains some interest in the property when he grants the sublease: he must be in such a position that he will recover the property at some point. In other words he must retain the leasehold reversion. If he parts with the property for the whole of the remainder of his head lease there is no leasehold reversion and the transaction can only take effect as an assignment of the head lease and not as a sublease (*Beardman v Wilson* (1868) LR 4 CP 57).

If the purported sublease is for not more than three years it will probably have been made orally or in writing (in reliance on s. 54(2)). If the effect of the agreement is to transfer the whole remaining term of the head lease to the 'sublessee' (in fact, the assignee) the result appears to be a valid legal assignment without the use of a deed. Lord Greene MR seems to have accepted this reasoning in the case of *Milmo v Carreras* [1946] KB 306 at p. 312, on the ground that such an assignment arose by operation of a rule of law and this approach has more recently been followed in *Parc (Battersea) Ltd v Hutchinson* [1999] 2 EGLR 33.

10.4.4 Sale of a leasehold reversion

We have already seen that the owner of a leasehold reversion performs two roles, being at the same time both the tenant of the head lease and the landlord of the sublease.

Thus the sale of his estate must involve a consideration of the rules relating to both a lease and a reversion; the assignment of his lease must take the form described above, while the question of whether his purchaser takes subject to the sublease depends on principles similar to those relevant to the sale of the freehold reversion.

10.5 Determining a lease

10.5.1 Statutory protection for tenants

Leases can be brought to an end in a number of ways. Some of these methods of determining a lease have a reduced effect today, however, due to the provisions of various statutory codes, relating respectively to residential accommodation, business premises and agricultural holdings. In a variety of ways these statutory provisions enable the tenant to remain on the property even after the tenancy has been terminated in accordance with contractual rules.

Additionally, individual tenants (or, in some cases, a group of tenants) of residential property may have a statutory right to buy the landlord's freehold reversion, so as to become the fee simple owners of their homes, instead of holding them merely as tenants.

For these various statutory provisions, which are in general outside the scope of this book, reference may be made to Megarry and Wade, or Cheshire and Burn, or to a suitable specialist text on the law relating to landlord and tenant.

10.5.1.1 Some general points about statutory protection

There are three general points which it may be helpful to mention here:

(i) In general, the introduction of new forms of statutory protection does not supersede the earlier rules, which continue to apply to tenancies already created under them. Thus, in respect of residential accommodation, the Rent Act 1977 continues to govern those tenancies within its terms which were granted before 15 January 1989, when the Housing Act 1988 came into operation.

(ii) The statutory codes employ a wide variety of technical terms, including, for example: 'protected tenancy', 'statutory tenancy', 'restricted contract', 'protected shorthold tenancy', 'assured tenancy' and 'assured shorthold tenancy'. We mention these terms here simply because you may come across references to some of them, either elsewhere in this book or in reports of cases. For the purposes of this book, you do not need to know anything more about these terms beyond the fact that they are created and defined by the relevant statutes, but if you should want further information it is to be found in the books referred to above.

(iii) The protection given to tenants by some of these codes is very considerable. For example, security of tenure under the Rent Act 1977 could pass on the tenant's death to any member of his family who was living with him at that time, and there could be a further similar transmission on the death of that second tenant. The landlord's inability to recover possession, and the fact that the rent he could charge was subject to statutory control, forms the background to many of the decisions about residential licences which we shall consider in Chapter 22, and explains why landlords were so anxious to avoid the statutory provisions by granting licences rather than leases.

10.5.2 Common law rules for determining leases

Despite the statutory provisions noted above, the older common law rules governing the determination of a lease are still of great importance, because in general the statutory rules which protect the tenant at the end of his lease do not come into effect until after the contractual tenancy has been terminated. Accordingly, a landlord who wishes to end a tenancy may first have to terminate the contractual tenancy and then take further action in order to bring to an end the tenant's statutory protection.

At common law a lease may be determined in any of the following ways:

- expiry;
- notice to quit;
- surrender;
- merger;
- enlargement;
- disclaimer;
- forfeiture.

In addition, there are modern decisions which suggest that the contractual doctrines of frustration and repudiation by fundamental breach may apply to leases, and we will discuss these after the other methods of determining a lease have been considered (see 10.6).

10.5.2.1 Expiry of term

A fixed-term lease gives rise to few problems, since it will expire automatically once the specified term comes to an end. In such cases it is not necessary for either party to the lease to take any action in order to terminate the lease.

In addition, if a lease is granted for a fixed term but is subject to earlier termination on the occurrence of a specified event, then the lease terminates automatically when the event occurs (see *Doe d Lockwood v Clarke* (1807) 8 East 185 and *Great Northern Railway Co. v Arnold* (1916) 33 TLR 114). As we have already seen, commercial leases determining on death, marriage or the formation of a civil partnership are affected by statutory provisions requiring notice and do not terminate automatically (see 10.2.3.1).

Break clauses

Some fixed-term leases contain clauses ('break clauses') allowing one party, or both, to determine the lease on notice before the term expires. The break clause may be exercisable on the occurrence of certain events (for example, if the landlord wants to redevelop the property), or at specified intervals throughout the term (e.g., at the end of the 7th or 14th year in a 21-year lease). Such a lease will usually provide for notice to be given before the break clause is exercised.

10.5.2.2 Notice to quit

Periodic tenancies run on indefinitely, from one period to the next, until one party gives notice to the other that he does not wish the arrangement to continue. In this context it is important to remember the basic principle underlying the periodic tenancy (as explained by the House of Lords in *Hammersmith LBC v Monk* [1992] 1 AC 478 at p. 490) that:

> continuation beyond the end of each [period] depends on the will of the parties that it should continue . . . and the tenancy continues no further than the parties have already impliedly agreed upon by their omission to serve notice to quit . . . it is by his omission to give notice of termination that each party signifies the necessary positive assent to the extension of the term for a further period.

It was always open to the parties to make any agreement they pleased about the form and period of notice required. In the absence of such agreement, however, the common law would apply standard rules, and more recently the statutory codes designed to protect tenants have created a number of requirements which cannot be varied by agreement.

(1) *Form of notice* In general there appears to be no requirement at common law that notice must be given in writing, at least in the case of tenancies created orally (*Timmins v Rowlinson* (1765) 3 Burr 1603). However, under s. 5(1) of the Protection from Eviction Act 1977, notice to quit in respect of premises let as a dwelling must be given in writing. In addition any such notice must be given in a statutory form which draws to the attention of the tenant the fact that he may be entitled to security of tenure under statutory provisions. The provisions of Part I of the Housing Act 1988 thereafter generally prevent the landlord from recovering possession of such premises without a court order. Most business tenancies must also be terminated by written notice, in the statutory form, under the provisions of the Landlord and Tenant Act 1954.

(2) *Period of notice* The correct period for notice will vary according to the type of lease or tenancy involved and these are considered separately below. However, there are certain statutory amendments to these rules which apply to leases of dwellings, business premises, and agricultural holdings, and to long residential tenancies at low rent. These rules are more appropriately dealt with in a detailed text on landlord and tenant law, but we must mention here that any notice to quit premises let as a dwelling must be given not less than four weeks before the date on which it is to take effect (Protection from Eviction Act 1977, s. 5(1)) unless the lease falls within one of the excluded categories set out in s. 3A. The exempt categories cover the sort of situation where the tenant has something more of the character of a 'lodger', rather than that of a normal tenant.

In the absence of any express agreement between the parties (which must not, of course, exclude the statutory provisions), common law will govern the length of notice required. Save in the case of a yearly tenancy, the correct period for notice is a full period under the lease. Thus, for a quarterly tenancy one gives a quarter's notice, for a monthly tenancy a month's notice, and for a weekly tenancy a week's notice. The notice should expire at the end of one period of the lease. A yearly tenancy can be terminated by half a year's notice, expiring at the end of a year (*Doe d Shore v Porter* (1789) 3 TR 13).

(3) Excluding the right to give notice It is clear from *Breams Property Investment Co. Ltd v Stroulger* [1948] 2 KB 1 that the landlord's right to give notice does not have to be identical with that of the tenant, and the decision also shows that one party's right to give notice may be restricted for a defined period.

As we have already seen (10.2.3.2), it is not possible to exclude the right to give notice for an indefinite period, because this has the effect of making the periodic tenancy uncertain, and therefore void under the rule in *Lace v Chantler* [1944] KB 368, as applied by the House of Lords in *Prudential Assurance Co. Ltd v London Residuary Body* [1992] 2 AC 386.

When a purported grant is invalidated in this way, the 'tenant' may be able to claim to have an implied periodic tenancy, arising from going into possession and paying rent on a periodic basis. Such a tenancy will then be determinable by the appropriate notice. Where the 'tenant' is an artificial person, such as a company or corporation, this outcome will be the best it can hope for (unless it chooses to claim to hold under a contractual licence). However, following the Supreme Court decision in *Berrisford v Mexfield Housing Co-operative Ltd* [2011] UKSC 52, a *human* tenant will be able to claim that the purported grant created a lease for life, which has been converted into a 90-year term under LPA 1925, s. 149(6). Such a lease will be determinable by notice on the death of the tenant, or during his lifetime in accordance with the termination provisions in the purported grant (see 10.2.3.3).

10.5.2.3 **Surrender**

A surrender is the means whereby a tenant relinquishes his estate to his landlord, the reversioner, with the agreement of the landlord. A surrender releases the tenant from any future liability under the lease but does not release him from liability for past actions (e.g., past breaches of covenant) (*Richmond v Savill* [1926] 2 KB 530). Accordingly, the landlord would still be able to seek compensation for any past losses arising from such breach. It should be noted, however, that the circumstances of the surrender may be such that the landlord will be taken to have waived his right to compensation for past breaches (*Dalton v Pickard* [1926] 2 KB 545).

(1) *Express surrender* Since a surrender is a dealing with a legal estate in land, it should be done expressly and by deed. This is true even where one wishes to surrender a short lease, for the exemption in LPA 1925, s. 54(2), applies only to the grant of such leases and not to their surrender. A defective surrender (e.g., a surrender which, due to mistake, is unwitnessed) may operate in equity as a contract to surrender the lease, under the usual principles.

(2) *Surrender by operation of law* No deed is required, however, in cases in which the lease is surrendered by operation of law (LPA 1925, s. 52(2)(c)). In practice this is quite common, since often the surrender is evidenced by the actions of the parties who would thereafter be estopped from denying the fact of the surrender (*Foster v Robinson* [1951] 1 KB 149). Such surrenders commonly arise when a landlord accepts back possession of the property and agrees that the tenant will be under no further liability. Thus in *Phené v Popplewell* (1862) 12 CB NS 334 a surrender was held to have been made without formalities when the landlord accepted back the premises, painted out the name of the former tenant on a signboard and put up a board advertising the property as being available to let. Since a surrender requires the agreement of both parties, no such surrender will arise from a purely unilateral act (e.g., the tenant returning the key without the landlord's assent, *Cannan v Grimley* (1850) 9 CB 634), and the other party to the lease may insist on the continued performance of the lease. A recent example of this is to be found in the Court of Appeal decision in *Bellcourt Estates Ltd v Adesina* [2005] 18 EG 150.

Surrender by operation of law may also occur in situations where landlord and tenant have agreed variations to the terms of the current lease, which are so significant that they can take effect only through the creation of a new lease. Such a new lease could not be granted except on the basis that the old one had been surrendered, and the law will achieve the result sought by the parties by implying both a surrender of the old lease and a grant of a new one.

10.5.2.4 Merger

A merger arises when the tenant acquires the immediate reversion to his lease or a third party acquires both the lease and the immediate reversion. In such an event the tenant would, in theory, become his own landlord, or the third party would become both landlord and tenant. This is ridiculous, unless there is some specific reason for wishing the lease and the reversion to remain separate, and so normally the lease will merge into the reversionary estate when they come into the hands of the same owner. However, this only occurs where it is the intention of the owner that the estates should merge, and LPA 1925, s. 185, preserves the equitable rule to this effect.

Since a merger involves the acquisition of the superior estate, the events which give rise to it can usually only be effected by deed (LPA 1925, s. 52(1)).

10.5.2.5 Enlargement

In practice, this is very rare, because under the provisions of LPA 1925, s. 153, it can only be done in the case of a lease originally granted for 300 years or more and upon which no rent of any money value is payable. Where the numerous conditions of s. 153 are satisfied, the tenant may execute a deed of enlargement, which has the effect of increasing his interest to that of an estate in fee simple, and thereby extinguishing the title of the previous fee simple owner.

10.5.2.6 Disclaimer

A right to disclaim a lease normally arises by statute. The most common examples are the rights of trustees in bankruptcy and liquidators of companies to disclaim certain property under the provisions of the Insolvency Act 1986. A disclaimer releases the tenant from future liabilities under the lease.

10.5.2.7 Forfeiture

In certain circumstances it is possible for a landlord to forfeit a lease for breach, by the tenant, of one of the terms of the agreement. This method of determining a lease is considered in detail in the section dealing with remedies for breach of leasehold covenants in Chapter 13.

10.6 Determination by discharge of contract

Historically, the relationship between a landlord and his tenant was viewed as no more than a contractual one, so that the tenant's rights under the arrangement were enforceable only against his landlord. At a later stage, the tenant was able to assert his rights to possession of the land against anyone who dispossessed him. He thus came to be regarded as having an estate in the land, which was enforceable against the whole world. In consequence, it is generally possible to view the lease as operating on two levels, being both a contract between the landlord and the tenant and a conveyance creating an estate in the land. In most of this chapter so far, we have been focusing on the lease-as-conveyance, and have been describing the special rules governing the estate which it creates. However, there are circumstances in which parties to the lease may wish to emphasise the contractual nature of the arrangements between them. We will look at this dual aspect of leases in a little more detail in 10.8, but need to note here the way in which two methods of discharging contracts have been applied to leases.

If you have already studied the law of contract, you may remember that there are a number of ways in which contracts may be discharged so that parties no longer have any obligations under them. Two forms of discharge, frustration and repudiatory breach, have been held by the courts to be applicable to leases, and therefore constitute two further ways in which a lease may be brought to an end.

10.6.1 Frustration

In general, the doctrine of frustration applies in cases in which external factors prevent the parties to an agreement performing their obligations under the contract. As explained by Lord Simon in *National Carriers Ltd v Panalpina (Northern) Ltd* [1981] AC 675, at p. 700:

> Frustration of a contract takes place when there supervenes an event (without default of either party and for which the contract makes no significant provision) which so significantly changes the nature (not merely the expense or onerousness) of the outstanding contractual rights and/or obligations from what the parties could reasonably have contemplated at the time of its execution that it would be unjust to hold them to the literal sense of its stipulations in the new circumstances; in such case the law declares both parties to be discharged from further performance.

It may well happen that property let to a tenant becomes unusable, through no fault of his own or the landlord's, and the tenant may claim that as a result his lease is frustrated. It used to be thought that he would not succeed, for he had an estate in the land and his duties under the lease would continue. Thus, if the house on the property was destroyed by fire, the tenant was still obliged to pay any rent due under the lease, for he still had an estate in the land (*Matthey v Curling* [1922] 2 AC 180). In the old case of *Paradine v Jane* (1647) Al 26, a tenant was evicted from the property by the King's army during the Civil War. The tenant was held to be liable to pay the rent on the property, for the risk of such interference was that of the current legal occupier of the land. This rule is generally in the best interests of others who have an interest in the land which is based on that of the tenant (e.g., a mortgagee who has taken a mortgage of the tenant's estate), who would otherwise be deprived of their interest or security.

At the date of *Paradine v Jane*, the doctrine of frustration of contract had not been developed. Even after it had emerged in the nineteenth century, there was for many years considerable uncertainty whether the doctrine could ever apply to a term of years. The issue appears to have been settled, at long last, by the House of Lords in *National Carriers Ltd v Panalpina* (Northern) Ltd [1981] AC 675. In that case the lease was of a warehouse. For some 20 months during the lease the street giving access to the premises was closed by the local authority, because a neighbouring derelict property was in a dangerous condition. The tenants were thus prevented from using the warehouse for that period. They failed to pay rent and defended an action for its recovery by claiming that the lease had been frustrated. The House of Lords considered that in the circumstances the lease had not been frustrated because the interruption of 20 months (in a 10-year lease) did not destroy the entire contract. Their Lordships did, however, accept the principle that in exceptional circumstances the doctrine of frustration could apply to a lease. Lord Wilberforce said (at p. 697):

> [T]hough such cases may be rare, the doctrine of frustration is capable of application to leases of land. It must be so applied with proper regard to the fact that a lease, that is, a grant of a legal estate, is involved. The court must consider whether any term is to be implied which would determine the lease in the event which has happened and/or ascertain the foundation of the agreement and decide whether this still exists in the light of the terms of the lease, the surrounding circumstances and any special rules which apply to leases or to the particular lease in question.

In reaching this conclusion, their Lordships considered in some detail the argument that a lease is more than a contract, because it creates an estate in land. They were not, however, persuaded that this was any reason for refusing to apply the doctrine of frustration, if justice required its use. Frustration would have the effect of ending the estate prematurely, but, as we have seen, a leasehold estate is already capable of ending prematurely, for example on the occurrence of some prescribed event, or on forfeiture for breach of covenant. The argument that termination of the estate could prejudicially affect third parties (such as mortgagees) who have taken an interest in it, was noted, but was not regarded as a sufficient reason for excluding the doctrine. In dealing with the questions raised by this case, several members of the House of Lords found support from developments in the United States and in Canada, in which the doctrine of frustration has been applied to leases. It was accepted that in reality the question is one of where the risk should fall: upon the tenant or upon the landlord.

The circumstances in which a lease may be frustrated remain to be seen, but would almost certainly include the destruction of the land itself (by cliff-fall, rising sea levels or other natural occurrence), and possibly the total destruction of buildings (by analogy with *Taylor v Caldwell* (1863) 3 B & S 826, in which a contract granting a licence for use of buildings was held to be frustrated when the premises were destroyed by fire). Views expressed in the House of Lords suggest that frustration may also apply where property is let for a specific use which then becomes illegal (as for example during the Prohibition era in the United States when tenants were discharged from their obligations to pay rent for premises which they had taken for the specific purpose of using as liquor saloons).

However, the House of Lords emphasised that frustration of a lease is likely to occur only very rarely, or, to paraphrase a Gilbert and Sullivan operetta: 'not "never" but "hardly ever" '!

10.6.2 Repudiatory breach

This method of discharging a contract involves a breach by one party of an obligation under the contract which is so fundamental that its breach is tantamount to his repudiating or rejecting the contract as a whole. In such a situation, the innocent party may accept the repudiation and treat it as terminating the contract, or may choose to ignore it and treat the agreement as continuing.

10.6.2.1 Repudiation by the landlord

In *Hussein v Mehlman* [1992] 2 EGLR 87 the question arose of whether repudiatory breach could apply to a three-year residential lease (described throughout by the court as 'a contract of letting'). Under covenants implied by the Landlord and Tenant Act 1985, s. 11, the landlord was under a duty to keep in repair the structure and exterior of the house, and the installations for the supply of water, gas and electricity and for space and water heating. He was in serious breach of these covenants, and the court found that he had no intention of performing them. In the view of the judge 'the tenants suffered real hardship as a result of the breach and were deprived of an essential part of what they had contracted for... the breach vitiated the central purpose of the contract of letting' (at p. 91). After 15 months, the tenants handed back the keys and vacated the property, claiming that the landlord's behaviour constituted repudiatory conduct which they accepted, thus ending the lease and their obligations under it.

In the County Court, Assistant Recorder Sedley QC considered whether a repudiatory breach of a contract of letting was legally possible, and held that it was. An earlier opinion that repudiation was not applicable to leases (*Total Oil Great Britain Ltd v Thompson Garages (Biggin Hill) Ltd* [1972] 1 QB 318 at p. 324) was based on the view that a lease is essentially different from other contracts, and derived support from the then-accepted principle that the doctrine of frustration did not apply to leases. However, as we have already seen, the House of Lords in *National Carriers Ltd v Panalpina (Northern) Ltd* [1981] AC 675 had more recently emphasised the contractual aspects of the lease and specifically accepted that in exceptional circumstances a lease can be frustrated. This enabled the court in *Hussein v Mehlman* to conclude that *Total Oil* had ceased to be an authority for the proposition that a lease cannot be repudiated. Support for the view that a lease could be repudiated was to be found in a number of nineteenth-century cases in which it was treated as 'axiomatic that a contract of letting could be terminated by an innocent party without notice if the other party failed to fulfil a fundamental term of the contract' (at p. 89). Thus the judge held that a lease can be ended on repudiation by the other party and that, on the facts before him, the landlord's behaviour constituted repudiatory conduct, which had been accepted by the tenants. The lease had come to an end, and both parties were released from their obligations under it.

Although the decision in *Hussein v Mehlman* was only at first instance and in the County Court, it has received considerable attention, and is recognised as a significant development. Its effect at present is to introduce into English land law another method of terminating a lease, which is already recognised in other jurisdictions.

Some five years after the decision in *Hussein v Mehlman*, repudiation of a lease was accepted by the Court of Appeal apparently without question in *Chartered Trust plc v Davies* (1997) 76 P&CR 396. In this case, the tenant of a unit in a shopping mall withheld rent because the business carried on in the premises was adversely affected by the landlord's failure to control the activities of other tenants in the mall. The tenant claimed that the landlord had broken his covenant not to derogate from his grant (see 11.2.1.2), and that this was so serious that it amounted to a repudiatory breach. This claim was accepted at first instance and the decision was upheld by the Court of Appeal. The judgment, given by Henry LJ, deals in some detail with derogation from grant, but does not discuss repudiation, merely saying at the end that the trial judge's finding of repudiation was one which he was entitled to make (at p. 409). Despite its brevity, and the fact that no mention is made of *Hussein v Mehlman*, this would seem to support the view that a lease can now be treated as repudiated. However, you may like to note the view expressed in Megarry and Wade at para. 18–106 that success in claiming repudiation may depend on the length of the lease:

> Clearly both the length and the terms of the lease will be relevant to whether there has been a breach that will justify treating it as terminated. The longer the lease, the more artificial it is to regard it as other than an estate in land. It is therefore only in relation to shorter lettings that an allegation of discharge by breach is normally likely to be successful.

10.6.2.2 Repudiation by the tenant

In *Hussein v Mehlman* [1992] 2 EGLR 87 at 90 the judge considered that the concept of repudiatory breach could be used against the tenant as well as against the landlord:

> If the obligation to pay rent is as fundamental as the obligation to keep the house habitable, it will follow that a default in rent payments is a repudiatory act on the tenant's part.

Such breaches of covenant by the tenant may at present be dealt with by the remedy of forfeiture which, as we shall see (at 13.4.2), is subject to statutory controls protecting the tenant and giving him opportunity to remedy the breach and avoid forfeiture. The Assistant Recorder suggested that the landlord's right to terminate on repudiatory breach by his tenant might in some way be modified by the provisions in the lease relating to forfeiture, so as to provide similar safeguards against repudiation. As yet, however, there has been no reported case in which a landlord has acted upon a repudiatory breach by his tenant, and so we do not know how such a claim would be dealt with by the court.

In 2006, the Law Commission proposed major changes to the law of forfeiture, some of which would increase the protection available to tenants (see 13.4.7). The report, *Termination of Tenancies for Tenant Default* (2006, Law Com No. 303 Cm 6946) mentions at para. 2.3 that its proposals would not affect the ability of the tenant to bring a tenancy to an end by accepting repudiatory breach by the landlord. By contrast, the proposed new termination procedure (see 13.4.7.2) would abolish the landlord's right to terminate the lease by any other means, such as forfeiture or acceptance of a repudiatory breach by the tenant (see draft Bill in App.1 of the report, and explanatory note on cl. 1).

10.7 Determination by joint tenants

As you will see in Chapter 16, it is possible for a legal estate (either freehold or leasehold) to be owned by several people together, in the form of co-ownership known as 'joint tenancy'. In general, the rules about leases which we have considered so far apply to joint tenants of the estate in exactly the same way as to a sole tenant, but we do need to mention briefly here the special principles governing the termination of a lease which is jointly owned.

As Lord Bridge explained in *Hammersmith LBC v Monk* [1992] 1 AC 478 at p. 490:

> ...all positive dealings with a joint tenancy require the concurrence of all joint tenants if they are to be effective. Thus a single joint tenant cannot exercise a break clause in a lease, surrender the term, make a disclaimer, exercise the option to renew the tenancy or apply for relief from forfeiture.

This requirement that all joint tenants should agree to all dealings with the estate has a somewhat unexpected result when applied to the ending of a periodic tenancy. As we explained in 10.5.2.2, the theory underlying periodic tenancies is that their running on from one period to another depends on the will of the landlord and tenant that they should continue in this way. The notice to quit is an indication by one side to the other that he does not want to continue, i.e., does not want the lease to be renewed for another period.

In the context of a jointly owned tenancy, this means that all the joint tenants must want the tenancy to continue by being renewed for another period. If one of the tenants does not want to continue, the necessary agreement for renewal is not present and accordingly the periodic tenancy will come to an end. This means that, as the House of Lords held in *Hammersmith LBC v Monk* [1992] 1 AC 478, a notice to quit given by one joint tenant, without the concurrence of the other(s), is effective to determine a periodic tenancy.

The facts of *Monk*'s case were that a cohabiting couple held a joint periodic tenancy of a council flat, which was terminable on four weeks' notice. After some time, the woman left her partner and moved out of the flat. The local authority agreed to rehouse her if she ended the periodic tenancy she already held from it, and she therefore gave the appropriate notice to quit without her co-tenant's knowledge or consent. The House of Lords held that this was a valid notice to quit which brought the periodic tenancy to an end, and the council was entitled to recover possession of the flat and evict the other joint tenant. Members of the House of Lords agreed that at first sight it seems amazing that one co-owner, acting unilaterally, can terminate the other owner's rights in his home. However, their decision was based both on the nature of periodic tenancies (as we have explained above), and also on general contractual principles:

> If A and B contract with C on terms that are to continue in operation for one year in the first place and thereafter from year to year unless determined by notice at the end of the first or any subsequent year, neither A nor B has bound himself contractually for longer than one year... the agreement is intended to continue beyond the initial term only if and so long as all parties to the agreement are willing that it should do so (at p. 483).

The fact that the decision in *Monk* is consistent with the basic principle, however, does not alter the fact that its effect is to deprive the other co-owner of his property and his home, and you might expect that by now this way of ending a lease would have been challenged on human rights grounds.

There have in fact been two major human rights decisions arising from the termination of a tenancy by a 'Monk-notice' (*Harrow LBC v Qazi* [2004] 1 AC 983 in the House of Lords and *McCann v UK* [2008] 47 EHRR 913 in the European Court of Human Rights). Each of these decisions, however, was concerned with the process by which a local authority landlord had regained possession of the property, rather than with the fact that the tenancy had been brought to an end by one joint tenant without the other's consent.

The statutory protection of tenants is in general beyond the scope of this book, so we can only tell you in very general terms that residential tenancies which have such protection may be terminated by the landlord only on prescribed grounds which must be established in order to obtain an order for possession. By contrast, where the tenancy has already been ended by one joint tenant giving a Monk-notice, the statutory protection no longer applies. If the other tenant remains in the property, he becomes a trespasser, and can be evicted by a summary process. In both *Qazi* and *McCann*, the local authority had recovered possession by this summary procedure, and both decisions are concerned only with the human rights implications of this process. Thus although both cases are of considerable procedural significance, they have no effect on *Monk* itself, which remains unchallenged.

10.8 'Contractualisation' of leases

In the previous two sections we have noted some recent developments which emphasise the contractual nature of the lease and play down its proprietary aspects. In *Panalpina* the House of Lords applied the contractual doctrine of frustration to leases, while in *Monk* it was guided by general contractual principles in considering the effect of notice given by one of two joint tenants. Again, the Court of Appeal in *Chartered Trust* has apparently accepted that leases can be determined by acceptance of repudiatory breach.

These examples all relate to the process of ending a lease. However, the trend is also apparent in other cases. For example, in *C. H. Bailey Ltd v Memorial Enterprises Ltd* [1974] 1 WLR 728 (on retrospective increases in rent following a rent review) Lord Denning rejected the suggestion that the matter was to be governed by considerations derived from feudal conceptions about the landlord–tenant relationship, saying:

> It is time to get away from the medieval concept of rent... in modern law, rent is not conceived of as a thing, but rather as a payment which a tenant is bound by his contract to make to his landlord for the use of the land.

The importance of the contractual relationship was also emphasised by Lord Browne-Wilkinson in *Prudential Assurance Co. Ltd v London Residuary Body* [1992] 2 AC 386 as he queried the justification for the ancient rule which requires leases to be certain, a rule which he described as operating to 'defeat contractually agreed arrangements between the parties'.

By contrast, Morritt LJ in his dissenting judgment in *Ingram v IRC* [1997] 4 All ER 395 at p. 422 considered that:

> It is easy to make too much of the contractual nature of the relationship. The feature of a tenancy which distinguishes it from a licence or merely contractual right of occupation is the lessee's right to exclusive possession. But this right is a consequence of the ownership of the legal estate; it is not merely a contractual right, or it could not be the feature which distinguishes a lease from a licence.

It seems that this approach was favoured by the House of Lords, which reversed the decision of the Court of Appeal ([2001] 1 AC 293), Lord Hoffmann saying that in the particular circumstances of the case 'the contractual nature of the lease seems to me a matter of conveyancing theory rather than substance' (at p. 304). A similar emphasis on the lease as a property interest is to be found in *PW & Co. v Milton Gate Investments Ltd* [2004] Ch 142 (for which, see 10.9.4).

Nevertheless, despite *Ingram*, it remains true that recent developments reveal a tendency by the courts to view the lease, at least initially, primarily as a contract. The development is summed up by one writer (see Bright [1993] Conv 71) as follows:

> when determining leasehold issues the courts will start from the premise that their foundation is in contract, instead of being reluctant to apply more general contractual principles to leases because of the fact that as property interests they are somehow special and sheltered from the rigours of contract.

The development we have noted in this section has been, so far, one of emphasis. As we explained in 10.6, the lease has been seen traditionally as operating on two levels, being both contractual and proprietary, and the shift in recent decisions has simply shown reliance on one aspect rather than another. *Bruton v London & Quadrant Housing Trust* [2000] 1 AC 406, however, introduced what seems to some commentators to be a new explanation of the nature of leases. It appears now that it is possible to have a contractual or non-proprietary lease, which gives rise to a landlord and tenant relationship but does not create an estate in the property. We will consider this analysis in more detail later (22.2.4.4), but it is worth noting here that some leases, albeit perhaps only a few, seem to have now come full circle, and returned to their purely contractual origins.

10.9 Effect on subtenant of determination of head lease

As we have seen (10.2.4.1), a tenant may himself grant a lease of the premises, giving his subtenant an estate for a shorter period, which he has carved out of his own estate. The resulting position can be portrayed diagrammatically:

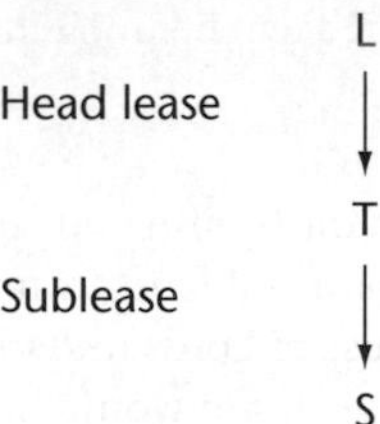

In this situation, S's term clearly depends upon the continuance of the head lease, and the general rule is that it comes to an end automatically if the head lease expires, or is determined by L's giving notice to quit or forfeiting the lease for breach of covenant.

10.9.1 Effect of surrender or merger

The general rule described above does not, however, apply in the cases of surrender or merger, which are recognised as exceptions to it.

Thus, in the situation illustrated above, a surrender of the head lease by T will not end the sublease which T has granted to S. In the words of Cockburn CJ in *Mellor v Watkins* (1874) LR 9 QB 400 at p. 404:

> ... when a person vountarily surrenders his lease, he cannot by so doing put an end to an undertenancy created by himself...

S will become a tenant of L, on the terms and conditions of the sublease. In other words, the surrender has no real effect on the subtenant; it merely alters the person to whom he is to pay his rent and to whom he owes a duty to observe the covenants in the sublease (LPA 1925, s. 150).

Similarly, if T's head lease and L's reversion merge, either in T or in some third party, the new owner of the combined estate will hold it subject to the sublease, and S's position will be in all respects the same as we have described in relation to surrender. In both cases, there is no hardship in the head landlord, or his successor, being bound by the sublease, because he has consented to the arrangement which has produced this situation.

10.9.2 Head lease ended on tenant's initiative

Although the effect on the subtenant of the determination of the head lease is in general well established, there was, until recently, some uncertainty about his position in cases where the head lease was brought to an end on the initiative of the tenant, through operating a break clause or by giving notice to quit to his landlord (sometimes called an 'upwards notice'). Despite various *obiter dicta* on this matter, and one unreported first-instance decision (*Brown v Wilson* (1949)), it emerged in *Pennell v Payne* [1995] QB 192 that there was no authority on this point binding on the Court of Appeal. The court was therefore required to decide as a matter of policy between the competing interests of a hypothetical subtenant and a head landlord ('hypothetical' because no sublease had been granted in this case). If the sublease were to survive the determination of the head lease, the tenant would impose his subtenant on the landlord against the landlord's will; if, on the other hand, the sublease were to end, the tenant, by ending his own lease, would destroy the interest he had created, thus derogating from his grant. Faced with this choice, the Court of Appeal took the view (at p. 270) that:

> the considerations against allowing a tenant unilaterally to foist his subtenant upon the landlord are in total compelling

and the court held that if the tenant terminated his lease by an upwards notice, the landlord would be entitled to regain the land from the subtenant. This decision was subsequently approved by the House of Lords in *Barrett v Morgan* [2000] 2 AC 264.

In such a case, it is likely that the tenant would be liable to his subtenant for breach of his covenant for quiet enjoyment (as to which, see 11.2.1.1) and Lord Millett, in *Barrett v Morgan*, suggests that a subtenant, if forewarned, could seek an injunction to restrain his landlord (the tenant under the head lease) from serving the upwards notice.

10.9.3 Head lease ended by landlord with tenant's consent

Finally, we should note that the fact that the landlord's notice to quit is served by pre-arrangement with the tenant who does not oppose it, because he wants to determine the sublease, does not prevent that sublease from ending along with the head lease. In *Barrett v Morgan* ([1999] 1 WLR 1109), the Court of Appeal had held that in such circumstances, where the landlord and tenant had agreed on a course of action, the notice was consensual rather than unilateral. The termination of the lease by notice in this way was indistinguishable from surrender, and accordingly the sublease survived the determination of the head lease and bound the landlord.

This decision was, however, reversed on appeal by the House of Lords (*Barrett v Morgan* [2000] 2 AC 264), Lord Millett (at p. 274) describing the lower court's decision as having

> the extraordinary result that the parties to a tenancy cannot achieve together by agreement what either can achieve alone without it.

To the House of Lords the essential distinction was not between consensual and unilateral acts, but between agreements made by the parties to the head lease before and after the grant of the sublease. A subtenant takes his interest subject to the terms of the head lease agreed *before* his tenancy was created, and his title cannot survive the termination of the head lease in accordance with those terms (e.g., by the head landlord giving notice). By contrast, his title cannot be prejudiced by any agreement (such as for surrender) between the parties to the head lease which is made *after* the creation of his sublease.

10.9.4 Can these rules be displaced by agreement?

This question arose for decision in *PW & Co. v Milton Gate Investments Ltd* [2004] Ch 142. The case concerned a head lease which included a break clause exercisable by the tenant, and also a provision that a penalty was payable by the tenant on premature determination of the lease, unless at that time at least 75 per cent of the building was sublet. The lease also provided that any subleases would survive the ending of the head lease and would bind the head landlord. However, by the time the tenant ended the head lease, the original landlord had assigned its reversion and the new landlord (Milton Gate Investments Ltd) demanded payment of the penalty despite the fact that the property was sublet. Accordingly, PW & Co. sought a declaration that it was not liable to pay the penalty because the subleases continued in existence and the property was therefore sublet.

The court refused the declaration, holding that the general rules applied and could not be varied by contrary provisions in the lease. As a result, the subleases came to an end with the ending of the head lease. In reaching this decision, the court emphasised that a lease is not merely a contract but also creates an estate in land, and that a sublease cannot last longer than the estate out of which it has been created. This emphasis on the lease as property makes the case of particular interest at a time when, as we saw in 10.8, other decisions are stressing the contractual aspect of leases.

10.10 Some more types of lease

10.10.1 Special forms of tenancy

So far in this chapter we have concentrated on leases for a fixed term and on periodic tenancies, but it is now time to mention three more types of lease: tenancies at sufferance, tenancies at will and tenancies by estoppel. We will also consider concurrent leases, which arise where a landlord grants two or more leases, taking effect at the same time, in respect of the same piece of land.

10.10.2 Tenancies at sufferance

Tenancies at sufferance are rather peculiar in that they arise purely by operation of law and entirely without any form of agreement between the landlord and the tenant. They arise in cases in which the tenant originally had a valid tenancy but continues to occupy the property after the expiration of that term. This occupation must be without the landlord's consent, for if the tenant remains with the landlord's assent he holds as a tenant at will rather than at sufferance, while if the landlord dissents the former tenant is in the position of a trespasser.

Thus, in *Remon v City of London Real Property Co. Ltd* [1921] 1 KB 49 in which a tenant remained in possession of the premises after a valid notice to quit had expired, the tenant was held not to be a tenant at sufferance since his landlords had taken action to endeavour to remove him from the premises. Scrutton LJ said (at p. 58):

> [T]enants by sufferance seem to have been confined to persons who held over without the assent or dissent of their landlords, and not to have included persons who held over wrongfully in spite of the active objection of their landlords.

In such a case there is no real tenancy, despite the name 'tenancy at sufferance' and no real relationship of landlord and tenant. The landlord cannot sue for rent (but may claim recompense for the use of the land—called 'mesne profits'). Should the landlord accept rent then this will normally give rise to a fresh periodic tenancy (*Mann v Lovejoy* (1826) Ry & M 355 and *Doe d Clarke v Smaridge* (1845) 7 QB 957). At common law the tenant at sufferance was in a very precarious position, because the landlord was able to recover possession of the premises, even by force. However, the landlord's rights are now subject to s. 6 of the Criminal Law Act 1977 and, in the case of residential accommodation, to s. 3 of the Protection from Eviction Act 1977.

10.10.3 Tenancies at will

The tenancy at will may arise in any case in which the tenant occupies the land with the permission of the landlord on the terms that the tenancy may be terminated by either party at any time. Parke B once described the tenancy at will as being the lowest estate known to the law (*Doe d Gray v Stanion* (1836) 1 M & W 700), although at an earlier date Littleton had said that a tenant at will 'hath no certain nor sure estate'. Unlike the tenancy at sufferance it does give rise to a real relationship of landlord and tenant and rent may be payable (*Anderson v Midland Railway Co.* (1861) 3 El & El 614), although this is unusual. However, it must be noted that a tenancy at will, being for an uncertain period, appears to fall outside the definition of 'term of years' provided by the 1925 legislation, and thus be incapable of amounting to a legal estate. As a result, it used to be suggested that the tenancy would take effect in equity, but this of course involves the notion of a trust, which seems remarkably cumbersome in the usual circumstances of a tenancy at will. Megarry and Wade (at para. 17–106) now suggests that:

> probably the best analysis of [the tenancy at will] is that it is a form of tenure but one that confers no estate. Although an estate cannot exist without tenure, there seems no reason why tenure should not exist without any estate. A may hold land of B, but for no fixed period and merely for so long as B may allow.

10.10.3.1 Creation

The tenancy at will may be *expressly granted* (as in *Manfield & Sons Ltd v Botchin* [1970] 2 QB 612), and, as we saw in 10.2.3.4, is useful in situations where the parties do not wish to commit themselves to a fixed period.

It may also arise by *implication* from the act of the parties. Thus a tenancy at will may be inferred where a former tenant continues to occupy the property with his landlord's consent after his lease has expired (as in *Dean and Chapter of the Cathedral and Metropolitan Church of Christ Canterbury v Whitbread* (1995) 72 P&CR 9). It may also arise where the purchaser of a freehold or leasehold estate is allowed into possession of the property before the conveyance or transfer, or grant of the lease, has been concluded, and we have already seen an example of this in *Javad v Mohammed Aqil* [1991] 1 WLR 1007 (10.3.2). Again, an owner may allow friends or members of his family to occupy his property for an indefinite period, and this arrangement may give rise to a tenancy at will. However, recent case law suggests that today the courts will be more inclined to regard some of these arrangements as licences, rather than as tenancies at will (*Heslop v Burns* [1974] 1 WLR 1241; *Street v Mountford* [1985] AC 809), and this is considered further in Chapter 22.

10.10.3.2 Determination

A tenancy at will may be brought to an end in a number of ways. On the one hand, it may be converted into an implied periodic tenancy, if rent is paid and accepted on a regular basis; while on the other hand, the whole arrangement may be determined at will by either side, without any period of notice. Moreover, the relationship is a personal one, so that it ends if either party dies, or assigns his interest to another.

10.10.4 Tenancies by estoppel

10.10.4.1 Circumstances in which tenancies by estoppel arise

So far, we have assumed that the leases we are considering have been created by a landlord who has a right to grant an estate or interest in the property, either by virtue of being a fee simple owner or having a valid, superior lease. It may be, however, that the person purporting to grant the lease proves to have a defective title himself. In earlier cases, he may be a mortgagor who under pre-1926 law has conveyed his full estate to the mortgagee as security for a loan. In more recent times, he may have only an equitable lease (as in *Industrial Properties (Barton Hill) Ltd v Associated Electrical Industries Ltd* [1977] 1 QB 580), or may be in the process of buying the property, but not yet have completed the purchase (*Church of England Building Society v Piskor* [1954] Ch 553). Yet again, as in *Bruton v London & Quadrant Housing Trust* [2000] 1 AC 406, he may be only a licensee.

Before the amendment of LPA 1925 s. 44 by LRA 2002, a prospective tenant had no right to investigate his landlord's title, unless provision for this was made in the preliminary contract. Thus a tenant might well take a lease in good faith and only later discover the truth. In such cases the tenant is not, however, able to repudiate his obligations under the lease, relying on the landlord's defective title, nor is the landlord able to deny the existence of the tenant's lease. In other words both parties are estopped from later denying one another's title (see *Industrial Properties (Barton Hill) Ltd v Associated Electrical Industries Ltd* [1977] QB 580). In this situation, there is said to be a tenancy 'by estoppel'.

We should mention briefly here that since the decision of the House of Lords in *Bruton v London & Quadrant Housing Trust* [2000] 1 AC 406 it appears that the parties are also bound by a contractual lease, which creates a landlord and tenant relationship between them, despite the fact that no leasehold estate has been created. A full account of this decision and its implications can be found in Chapter 22 (see 22.2.4.4).

10.10.4.2 Estoppel by representation and estoppel by grant

There are two ways in which a tenancy by estoppel may arise. The prospective landlord may make a specific representation about his title, for example reciting in the document granting the lease that he is the fee simple owner of the property. He is then estopped by this representation from denying the title. However, even if he does not make such a statement, the fact that he purported to grant the lease is considered sufficient to create an estoppel by virtue of the common law principle that a grantor is precluded from disputing the validity and effect of his grant (see *First National Bank v Thompson* [1996] Ch 231 at 237, a decision which, though dealing with a mortgage by estoppel, states the general principles which apply equally to tenancies). Although both forms of estoppel may prevent denial of the landlord's title, there are some differences between the way in which they operate.

Estoppel by grant arises only where the grantor has no legal estate at all in the land at the date at which the purported grant was made. If he had some legal estate, less in extent than that which he purported to grant, the whole estate would pass to the grantee and no tenancy by estoppel would arise. Thus, if the landlord had, for example, a leasehold estate for five years and attempted to grant a sublease for a longer period than his own lease (e.g., for 25 years) the purported grant of the sublease would not create a lease by estoppel but would operate as an assignment of the existing five-year term (see 10.2.4.1).

Estoppel by representation By contrast, where the estoppel arises from a specific representation by the grantor about his title, he is estopped from denying that he has the particular estate which he claimed to hold. The fact that he has some lesser estate does not prevent the estoppel operating, so that a tenancy by estoppel for the full period which he purported to give will come into existence.

Finally, we must emphasise that both these forms of estoppel are common law developments. We mention this in case you should be tempted to explain tenancy by estoppel by reference to the principles of equitable proprietary estoppel (i.e., representation, reliance and detriment), which are discussed at various other points in this book. It is important to realise that the forms of estoppel we are considering here are quite distinct, being derived from different authorities and operating on different principles.

10.10.4.3 Rights and duties under a tenancy by estoppel

As between themselves, the parties have all the rights and duties of a landlord and tenant. Moreover, such a tenancy can be assigned and in general binds the grantor's successors, although the rules on this vary depending on whether the estoppel arises by grant or by representation (see further Megarry and Wade, paras. 17-125–17-132). The tenancy is also regarded as a lease for the purpose of various statutory codes protecting the tenant (e.g., the Rent Acts).

Thus, unless an owner with superior title intervenes, a tenancy by estoppel is generally as effective and binding as any other lease (*Gouldsworth v Knights* (1843) 11 M & W 337). If, however, at any time the superior owner does assert his claim to the property, then the tenant may become liable to the superior owner, to compensate him for the use of the land. In such a case, or if evicted by a superior owner, the tenant may then dispute his landlord's title and resist successfully a claim for rent. In the *Industrial Properties* case [1977] 1 QB 580 Lord Denning MR said (at p. 596):

> Short of eviction by title paramount, or its equivalent, ... the tenant is estopped from denying the title of the landlord. It is no good his saying: 'The property does not belong to you but to a third person' unless that third person actually comes forward and successfully makes an adverse claim ... If the third person ... makes no adverse claim or is debarred from making it, the tenant remains estopped from denying the landlord's title.

10.10.4.4 Feeding the estoppel

If at any time during the continuance of the lease by estoppel the landlord obtains a full legal title to the land, this acquisition of title is said to 'feed' the lease by estoppel, which thereupon becomes a full legal lease (*Rawlin's Case* (1587) Jenk 254). Thus, if a purchaser, before taking a conveyance of the fee simple estate, should purport to grant a lease of the property, that lease will take effect only as a lease by estoppel, but will become a full legal lease as soon as the fee simple is conveyed to the purchaser.

This can cause problems when the purchaser obtains a mortgage in order to finance the purchase of the estate but later fails to keep up his mortgage repayments. Both the lease and mortgage must have been created after title to the estate vested in the purchaser but in which order? If the first thing that happened was the feeding of the estoppel, the property over which the mortgage was granted was the estate subject to the lease and thus the mortgagee (the lender) would be bound by the pre-existing legal lease. If, however, the mortgage was made before the legal lease was created, the result would be different: the mortgage would take priority and the mortgagee could sell the mortgaged estate free of the lease.

It used to be thought that, even if all the documents were prepared and signed in advance, there must be a moment ('a scintilla of time') between the vesting of the legal estate in the purchaser and the creation of the mortgage during which the estoppel could be fed (see *Church of England Building Society v Piskor* [1954] Ch 553). The defendants in *Abbey National Building Society v Cann* [1991] 1 AC 56 (see 7.10.4.3) relied upon this argument (although not in relation to tenancy by estoppel), claiming that there had been a scintilla of time between the transfer to Cann and his grant of the mortgage to the building society, and that in this brief moment their beneficial interests took effect and became overriding interests under LRA 1925, s. 70(1)(g). The House of Lords rejected this argument, holding that the transfer and the grant of the mortgage, both of which occurred on the same day, were to be regarded as happening together, and overruling *Church of England Building Society v Piskor*. Since this decision it seems, therefore, that although a tenancy by estoppel may be fed by the acquisition of the legal estate it cannot gain priority over a mortgage created at the same time.

10.10.5 Concurrent leases

Finally, a brief mention must be made of concurrent leases, or 'leases of the reversion' (not to be confused with reversionary or future leases, which we described earlier in 10.1.3.4). When L has granted a lease to T, it is possible for L to grant another lease to A in respect of the same piece of land. A cannot take physical possession of the property, because T is already entitled to that, so the lease to A is regarded as a lease of L's reversion on T's lease. If the lease to A is longer than that to T, A will eventually be able to take physical possession of the property, but if it is for the same period, or a shorter one, he will never be able to enter, and he acts simply as T's landlord, collecting any rent due and enforcing covenants in the lease. Thus in the diagram below, L, the fee simple owner, granted a lease for 25 years to T in 2000 and then in 2010 granted a 15 year lease of the same property to A. A became T's landlord and was able to collect and keep rent from T and to enforce T's covenants. As the leases of both T and A end on the same date in 2025, A will never be able to take physical possession of the property; if, however, his lease had been for longer than 15 years, he would be able to enter the property when T's lease ends.

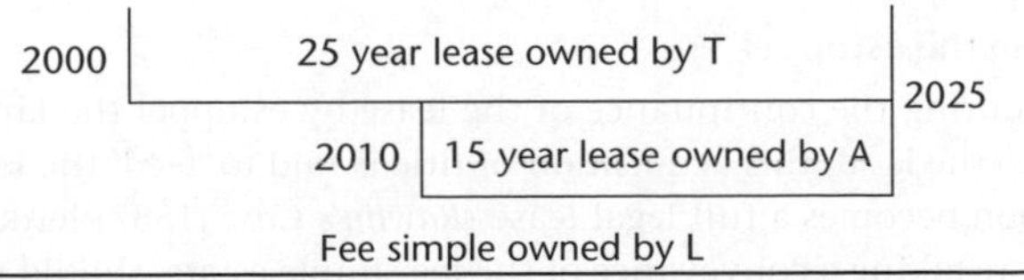

In the past, concurrent leases were not granted very often, except as the conveyancing device which permitted the creation of successive mortgages of the same estate (see Chapter 24). However, under the Landlord and Tenant (Covenants) Act 1995, a landlord may, in certain circumstances, be required to grant a lease of the reversion (described by the Act as 'an overriding lease'), and as a result concurrent leases may become more common. We shall explain in Chapter 12 how the 'overriding lease' works (see 12.4.2(3)), when describing the changes introduced by the Act.

FURTHER READING

Certainty of term

Bridge, 'Periodic tenancies and the problem of certainty of term' [2010] 74 Conv 492 at 496–7.

Bright, 'Uncertainty in Leases—Is it a Vice?' (1993) 13 LS 38.

Megarry and Wade, *The Law of Real Property*, 8th edn., Sweet and Maxwell, 2012, paras. 17-068–17-074 (*Mexfield Housing Co-operative Ltd v Berrisford*).

Smith, 'What is Wrong With Certainty in Leases?' [1993] Conv 461.

Smith, 'An Uncertain Shift' [1998] Conv 326.

Javad v *Aqil*

Bridge, 'Tenancies at Will in the Court of Appeal' [1991] CLJ 232.

Repudiation

Bright, 'Repudiating a Lease—Contract Rules' [1993] Conv 71.

Harpum, 'Leases as Contracts' [1993] CLJ 212.

Pawlowski and Brown, 'Repudiatory Breach in the Leasehold Context' [1999] 63 Conv 150.

11

Obligations of landlord and tenant

11.1 Introduction

11.1.1 Obligations of landlord and tenant

Every lease, even the most informal, contains provisions which define the obligations of the landlord and tenant under the lease. In a formally granted long lease it is likely that these obligations will be detailed and complex, and will be embodied in a long document. In the case of an informal periodic tenancy the obligations will be few, and will, in the main, be implied into the agreement by operation of law.

11.1.2 Covenants and conditions

Obligations in a lease may be imposed in one of two ways: by covenants or by conditions.

A *'covenant'* is a promise made by one party (the *'covenantor'*) for the benefit of another party (the *'covenantee'*) which is contained in a deed. As all leases for more than three years should be made by deed (LPA 1925, s. 52), normally the promises made in the lease will be covenants. However, there is a problem in the case of shorter leases, which can be created informally (s. 54(2)) and which therefore will not require a deed. It appears, however, that the promises in such leases are still to be regarded as enforceable covenants (see *Boyer v Warbey* [1953] 1 QB 234 which involved a written lease for three years, at 12.5.3.1, and *Weg Motors Ltd v Hales* [1962] Ch 49).

Covenants must be distinguished from *'conditions'*, which may also impose obligations on a tenant. A lease may contain a provision that the continuance of the term is conditional upon the fulfilment by the tenant of his obligations. If the tenant breaks that condition, the landlord will have an automatic right to bring the term to an end. By contrast, a landlord does not automatically have a right to end the lease for breach of a covenant, and must make express provision for this in the lease.

Covenant or condition? The question of whether a particular term in a lease is a covenant or a condition is a matter which is decided by reference to the intention of the parties. Generally, the courts presume that the terms of the lease are covenants, unless clear words are used to show that the obligation is intended to be a condition. Thus, in *Doe d Henniker v Watt* (1828) 8 B & C 308 it was held that a term in which the tenant 'stipulated and conditioned' that he would not assign or sublet the property, was a condition rather than a covenant. In fact most obligations, even the most fundamental (e.g., to pay rent) will be covenants rather than conditions.

11.1.3 Express, implied and usual covenants

Every lease, however simple, contains some covenants, because certain basic covenants by both landlord and tenant are *implied* into every lease. (It should always be remembered that a lease is a reciprocal arrangement which accordingly imposes obligations on the landlord, as well as upon the tenant.) Some leases, typically long leases, contain in addition to (or in substitution for) the *implied covenants* a very large number of *express covenants*. It is not possible to include here a list of all possible covenants because there are huge variations in such matters depending on the circumstances. We will accordingly deal only with the common express covenants and with implied covenants.

In addition there is a list of covenants, called the *usual covenants*, which are important in cases in which the grant of a lease is preceded by a contract to grant the lease (as is normal conveyancing procedure in the case of long leases). In such cases it is an implied term of the contract that the lease, once granted, will contain at least the 'usual covenants' and thus the parties can be obliged to include those covenants when the lease is granted. In the following sections we look first at express covenants, and then at implied and usual covenants, but before doing so will first consider some practical examples of the formats used for various leases.

11.1.4 Some examples of leases

11.1.4.1 2 Trant Way: basement flat

You will recall from the last chapter (10.1.1) that the basement flat at 2 Trant Way has been let by Fingall Forest, the fee simple owner, to his friend Gerald Gruyère at a rent of £175 per week. This agreement was made orally and no further terms were specified. Mr Gruyère has been in possession of the flat for some time and pays his rent regularly.

11.1.4.2 2 Trant Way: maisonette

The ground and first-floor maisonette of 2 Trant Way is to be let by Fingall Forest to James Harding. The lease term is to be 99 years and Mr Harding is to pay a premium of £250,000 and a ground rent of £100 per annum, for the first 10 years, with a provision for regular increases thereafter. The draft lease, which has been prepared by Mr Forest's solicitor for approval by Mr Harding's legal adviser, is a very detailed document, which is over 40 pages long. In this lease, which will be made by deed and must be completed by registration (see 10.3.1.3), the tenant will undertake a long list of obligations, ranging from a promise not to keep pets to covenants not to assign, sublet or part with possession without the landlord's consent and to contribute to the cost of maintaining the structure of the premises. The landlord will also enter into a number of covenants, including a covenant to keep the building insured (though the tenant will pay a share of the insurance premium).

11.1.4.3 6 Trant Way

The fee simple in 6 Trant Way was owned by Irene Ivy. On 25 March 1979 Mrs Ivy granted a 40-year lease of the property to John Jarlsberg. The lease was made by deed and is in the following form:

> THIS LEASE made the 25th day of March 1979 between IRENE IVY of 15 Proudie Street, Grantchester in Stilton (hereinafter called 'the landlord') of the one part and JOHN JARLSBERG of 63 Upper Terrace, Mousehole in Stilton (hereinafter called 'the tenant') of the other part WITNESSETH as follows:
>
> 1. The landlord hereby demises unto the tenant ALL THAT messuage or dwelling-house, together with the garden, offices and outbuilding thereto belonging, known as 6 Trant Way, Mousehole in the County of Stilton, which premises for the purposes of identification only are outlined in red on the plan attached hereto, TO HOLD the same unto the tenant from the 25th day of March 1979 for the term of 40 years YIELDING AND PAYING therefore the yearly rent agreed or determined in accordance with the provisions of clause 2 hereof by equal quarterly instalments in advance on the usual quarter-days (the first payment to be made on the date hereof).
>
> 2. (a) The rent shall be £3,000 per annum for the first five years of the said term.
>
> (b) [Rent review clause for later portion of term.]
>
> 3. The tenant hereby COVENANTS with the landlord as follows:
>
> (a) To pay the rent hereby reserved on the days and in the manner aforesaid without any deductions whatsoever.
>
> (b) To pay all rates, taxes and outgoings of an annual or recurring nature in respect of the demised premises.
>
> (c) Not to use or permit the use of the demised premises or any part thereof otherwise than as a private dwelling-house.
>
> (d) Not without the prior written consent of the landlord to assign, sublet or part with possession of the whole or part of the demised premises.
>
> [Further covenants by the tenant.]
>
> 4. The landlord hereby COVENANTS with the tenant as follows:
>
> (a) That the tenant paying the rent hereby reserved and observing and performing the covenants on his part herein contained shall peaceably and quietly hold and enjoy the premises hereby demised during the said term without any interruption or disturbance by the landlord or any person claiming under or in trust for the landlord.
>
> (b) That if at any time during the continuance of the term hereby created the tenant shall desire to purchase the fee simple reversion in the demised premises the landlord on receipt of six months' notice in writing from the tenant shall assure the demised premises unto the tenant in fee simple in consideration of a sum equal to 95 per cent of the market value of the premises, such value to be assessed as at the date upon which such notice shall expire.
>
> [Further covenants by the landlord, including one 'to keep in repair the structure and exterior of the premises'.]
>
> 5 PROVIDED ALWAYS and it is hereby expressly agreed and declared as follows:
>
> (a) That if at any time the rent hereby reserved or any part thereof is 21 days in arrears (whether formally demanded or not) or if the tenant has failed to observe or perform any of the tenant's covenants herein contained, the landlord may re-enter upon

the demised premises or any part thereof in the name of the whole and thereupon the term hereby granted shall absolutely determine but without prejudice to any claim by the landlord against the tenant for any antecedent breach of the covenants herein contained.

...

IN WITNESS whereof the hand and seal of the landlord and of the tenant have been hereunto set the day and year first above-written.

SIGNED SEALED AND DELIVERED
by the said landlord [Signature of Irene Ivy] SEAL
in the presence of:
[Signed by witness]

SIGNED SEALED AND DELIVERED
by the said tenant [Signature of John Jarlsberg] SEAL
in the presence of:
[Signed by witness]

[There follows a plan of the property.]

(Note that this lease was made before the Law of Property (Miscellaneous Provisions) Act 1989 came into force and thus it complies with the old formalities for a deed and was signed, sealed and delivered.)

11.2 Express covenants

There is a very wide range of express covenants which can be made by landlord or tenant, and, as we have already said, all we can do here is to mention the most important express covenants and discuss general matters of construction. One point which can be made about all express covenants is that usually they will be construed strictly against the landlord, since it is he who was responsible for the form of the lease.

11.2.1 Express covenants by the landlord

11.2.1.1 Landlord's covenant to allow tenant quiet enjoyment

The effect of this covenant is that the landlord must let the tenant into possession of the premises and that the landlord will be liable if the tenant's enjoyment of the property is substantially disturbed by any action of the landlord or by the action of someone deriving an interest in the property from the landlord. The landlord is not responsible for the actions of unrelated third parties.

It should be noted that the covenant for 'quiet enjoyment' is not about noise made by the landlord. It is a wider concept involving any acts which prevent the tenant from using the demised premises. The creation of considerable amounts of noise might, of course, have this effect (as was accepted by the House of Lords in *Southwark LBC v Tanner* [2001] 1 AC 1—see below), but the word 'quiet' in this context means 'uninterrupted', rather than 'noiseless', enjoyment of the property, and most of the cases involve something other than noise.

1. *Examples of breach*
An obvious example of the breach of this covenant is the case of *Perera v Vandiyar* [1953] 1 WLR 672 in which the landlord tried to force the tenant out of the premises by continual harassment of a serious nature, including having the gas and electricity supplies to the property cut off. Such severe breach of a landlord's basic obligations can also amount to a criminal offence under s. 1(3) or 1(3A) of the Protection from Eviction Act 1977 if the landlord's intention is to force the tenant to leave the premises (see 13.2.1).

It has also been held to be a breach of the covenant to erect scaffolding which prevents the tenant gaining access to the premises (*Owen v Gadd* [1956] 2 QB 99). Other examples of breach of this covenant include: removing the windows and doors (*Lavender v Betts* [1942] 2 All ER 72); persistently threatening the tenant in an attempt to force him to leave (*Kenny v Preen* [1963] 1 QB 499); and causing the land to subside by carrying out mining activities beneath the surface (*Markham v Paget* [1908] 1 Ch 697).

It should be noted, however, that acts which merely inconvenience the tenant do not amount to a breach of the covenant, particularly if the act complained of occurs outside the demised area. Thus, in *Browne v Flower* [1911] 1 Ch 219 a landlord who erected an external staircase, outside the demised premises, was held not to have broken the covenant even though persons using the new staircase were able to look in through the windows of the demised premises and the tenant was thereby deprived of his privacy.

2. *Condition of property*
It should also be noted that the covenant for quiet enjoyment does not impose on the landlord any liability in respect of the condition of the property at the start of the lease. In *Southwark LBC v Tanner* [2001] 1 AC 1 the tenants of a block of flats complained that noise from each other's flats seriously affected their quality of life, and claimed that their landlord was in breach of its covenant of quiet enjoyment. It was generally agreed that the neighbouring tenants were using their flats in a normal manner, and that the disturbance they caused to each other was attributable to the lack of soundproofing between the flats, which were old and not constructed to modern standards.

The House of Lords accepted in principle that excessive noise may constitute a substantial interference with the tenant's enjoyment of his property, and could amount to a breach of the covenant for quiet enjoyment. However, this covenant is prospective, that is to say, it is a covenant that the tenant's enjoyment will not be disturbed by any act of the landlord or those claiming under him *after* the tenancy has begun. It does not apply to things done *before* the grant of the tenancy, even though these may have continuing consequences for the tenant. Here, the cause of the problem was the lack of soundproofing, which existed before the premises were let and before the landlord had given its covenant for quiet enjoyment.

The House also drew attention to the fact that in general (with minor exceptions—see 11.3.1.2) there is no implied warranty by the landlord as to the condition or fitness of the premises; it is understood that the risk is on the tenant, who takes the property as he finds it ('caveat lessee'—'let the lessee beware'). In Lord Hoffmann's words (at p. 12):

> It would be entirely inconsistent with this common understanding if the covenant for quiet enjoyment were interpreted to create liability for disturbance or inconvenience or any other damage attributable to the condition of the premises.

Whether such a liability should be created, with its resulting financial burdens on private and public landlords, was a question for Parliament not for the judges.

3. *Acts of persons claiming under landlord*

A landlord may be liable under this covenant even if the act amounting to a breach is committed by a third party. He will only be liable, however, for the lawful actions of those deriving their title under him, or for the actions of his servants or agents within the scope of their authority. The landlord is not liable for actions committed by persons deriving their title from him who are acting in excess of their own legal rights. In *Sanderson v Berwick-upon-Tweed Corporation* (1884) 13 QBD 547, a tenant complained that he was unable to use the demised premises (a farm) in a normal way because of flooding caused by drains on two neighbouring farms which were also owned by the landlord. Both the neighbouring farms were also let to tenants. On one farm the drains were in good order but the flooding was caused by the excessive use of them by the tenant: here the tenant was acting in excess of his lawful rights. On the second farm the tenant was using the drains perfectly properly, but flooding was being caused by a defect in the drain: here the tenant was acting within his lawful rights. The landlord was held not to be liable for the damage caused by the actions of the first tenant, but was liable for damage caused by the actions of the second.

4. *Acts of persons with superior title*

The landlord is not responsible for acts committed by a person with a title which is superior to (rather than derived from) the landlord's title. Such a superior title is described as a 'title paramount'. This rule creates a substantial danger for the tenant, as is demonstrated by the case of *Jones v Lavington* [1903] 1 KB 253. In that case a tenant, who had only 8½ years left to run on his own lease, purported to grant a sublease of the property for 10½ years. (As we have already seen (10.2.4.1), this in fact operates as an assignment of the lease.) In due course the freehold owner recovered the property from the 'subtenant' two years before the 'sublease' should have ended. The 'subtenant' could not resist the claim of the freehold owner because the original tenant had no power to give more than he had got (*nemo dat quod non habet*) and could only give an 8½-year term. An action by the 'subtenant' against the tenant also failed because the tenant was not liable for actions by someone with title paramount (the freehold owner). However, we have already noted (at 10.9.2) the Court of Appeal's view that a subtenant would have a claim for breach of this covenant if his landlord determined the head lease by giving notice to quit to his own landlord (or possibly by operating the provisions of a break clause), thus automatically destroying the sublease (*Pennell v Payne* [1995] QB 192).

11.2.1.2 Covenant that landlord will not derogate from his grant

It is a general principle of law that you must not take away with one hand what you have given with the other, because to do so is to derogate from your grant (*Palmer v Fletcher* (1663) 1 Lev 122). To a certain extent this covenant overlaps with the covenant for quiet enjoyment but since this covenant not to derogate from the grant can be broken without there being a physical interference with the use of the premises, it is still worth considering it separately.

1. *Examples of breach*

A good illustration of the point is provided by *Aldin v Latimer Clark, Muirhead & Co.* [1894] 2 Ch 437, in which premises had been let to a tenant subject to a covenant that the tenant would use the property to run the business of a timber merchant. The demised premises included a wood-drying shed which depended on a natural flow of air passing on to the demised premises from neighbouring property, which also belonged to the landlord. Buildings were erected on the neighbouring property which prevented the free flow of air to the drying shed and thereby rendered it useless. This did not amount to a breach of the covenant for quiet enjoyment because there was no physical interference with the demised premises. These facts did, however, amount to a breach of the obligation placed on the landlord not to derogate from his grant, because the action complained of prevented the very use for which the demised premises had been let.

Another example is provided by *Harmer v Jumbil (Nigeria) Tin Areas Ltd* [1921] 1 Ch 200, in which land was let to store explosives. In order to store such items the tenant had to obtain a licence and it was a condition of the licence that there should be no other buildings within a specified distance. Accordingly the tenant was entitled to prevent the landlord from building on neighbouring land, which he also owned, because this would lead to the loss of the tenant's licence and prevent him from using the premises for the purpose for which they were let.

The tenant who relies on this principle must have made it clear to the landlord at the time of the grant what use he has in mind for the land (*Robinson v Kilvert* (1889) 41 ChD 88). Also the act complained of must actually interfere with the contemplated use and it is not sufficient to say that the landlord's actions have made the use more expensive or less profitable. Thus, permitting a competing business to be run from a neighbouring property has been held not to be derogation from grant (*Port v Griffith* [1938] 1 All ER 295—a decision considered and applied in *Romulus Trading Co. Ltd v Comet Properties Ltd* [1996] 2 EGLR 70).

2. *Acts of persons claiming under landlord*

Once again the landlord is liable also for the actions of persons deriving title from him (*Aldin v Latimer Clark, Muirhead & Co.* [1894] 2 Ch 437). An illustration is provided by *Chartered Trust plc v Davies* (1997) 76 P&CR 396. A tenant of a unit in a shopping mall complained that trade was adversely affected by the activities of neighbouring shopkeepers (such as blocking access to the shop), which were held at first instance to constitute nuisance. The common landlord had the power to stop the activities complained of, but did not do so. He was held by the Court of Appeal to have continued or adopted the nuisance committed by his other tenants, and thus to have derogated from his grant.

11.2.1.3 Landlord's covenant to grant a further term (option for renewal)

It is quite common to include a covenant giving the tenant a right to renew the lease for a further period on the expiration of the first term. The tenant is free to choose whether or not to exercise this option; if he does so, the landlord is bound to grant the further term. The option is enforceable against the landlord's successor or assignee but, perhaps rather surprisingly in the landlord–tenant context, such an option in a lease of unregistered land has to be registered as a class C(iv) land charge if it is to be enforced against a purchaser of the legal estate for money or money's worth (*Beesly v Hallwood Estates Ltd* [1960] 1 WLR 549).

Perpetually renewable leases

A covenant to grant a further term can give rise to problems if it is badly drafted. In *Northchurch Estates Ltd v Daniels* [1947] Ch 117, a lease for a year contained a clause which gave the tenant a right to renew the lease at the end of the year 'on identical terms and conditions'. Unfortunately this clause, if interpreted literally, means that the second term will include an identical provision allowing the tenant to call for a third term, the third term a clause providing for a fourth, and so on. As a result, the tenant would have a right to renew the lease perpetually. This caused considerable difficulties for the landlord, who would be able to terminate this perpetual lease only if the tenant broke a term of the agreement or forgot to give notice of his wish to renew.

Such perpetually renewable leases are subject to s. 145 and Sch. 15 of the Law of Property Act 1922 (which applies to all leases created after 1925). These provisions convert the affected lease into a fixed term of 2,000 years, subject to a right of the tenant to terminate the lease on 10 days' notice in writing on any occasion on which the original lease would have expired if it had not been renewed. The landlord has no similar right to terminate.

These rules produce a result in which a landlord is heavily penalised for the careless drafting of the original lease. Usually it is quite clear that the original intention of the parties was that the tenant should have the right to renew the lease for a second term, with a further right to a third and final term at his choice. In *Northchurch Estates Ltd v Daniels* the real intention of the parties was that the tenant should have a lease for one year with a right to renew the lease twice if he so chose. The unfairness of transforming such an agreement into a 2,000-year term, when three years were intended, is obvious. Accordingly, in more recent decisions the courts have reversed their earlier tendency to apply a literal interpretation of such leases and have adopted a more liberal approach, in order to prevent tenants obtaining an unjustified windfall through poor drafting (see, e.g., *Marjorie Burnett Ltd v Barclay* [1981] 1 EGLR 41).

11.2.1.4 Landlord's covenant to sell the reversion to the tenant (option to purchase)

In appropriate cases, a covenant of this sort may be included. We have given an example in the lease of 6 Trant Way (see pp. 209–10), and will consider questions about the enforcement of such an option later, at 12.8.1.3.

11.2.2 Express covenants by the tenant

11.2.2.1 Tenant's covenant to pay rent

Very few leases are concluded without there being an express agreement between the parties about the payment of rent. It is a general rule that the rent must be certain (a court cannot enforce an uncertain agreement) but this rule may be satisfied by providing a means whereby the rent is to be determined (e.g., rent to be set by a surveyor chosen by a named body). It is also common to include a clause whereby the rent is to be reviewed (usually with a view to increasing it) at intervals during the lease: see cl. 2(b) in the lease at pp. 209–10. A great deal of case law on the interpretation of such rent-review clauses exists, but this is beyond the scope of this book. For further information you should consult a specialist text on landlord and tenant law.

11.2.2.2 Tenant's covenants not to assign, sublet or part with possession

A tenant is the owner of a legal estate in land and it is a basic principle of English law that an estate in land is freely alienable. However, the right to sell, or otherwise dispose of, an estate can be limited if the estate owner enters into a covenant to that effect. Most landlords take great care when selecting tenants (e.g., to ensure that they are of good character and can pay the rent) and, quite reasonably, will wish to ensure that the premises do not come into the hands of some less desirable person through assignment or subletting. Accordingly it is common to include in a lease a covenant which restricts the tenant's right to assign, sublet or otherwise part with possession of the demised premises.

1. *Absolute and qualified covenants*

Covenants against assigning, subletting or parting with possession come in two forms:

- an absolute covenant, i.e., not to assign, etc.;
- a qualified covenant, i.e., not to assign, etc., without the landlord's consent.

In the case of the absolute covenant, it is open to the tenant to ask the landlord if he will allow a particular disposition, but the landlord is under no obligation to agree to this, even if he is acting quite unreasonably in refusing. By contrast, if the covenant is in the qualified form that the tenant may not assign etc. *without consent*, the position is affected by s. 19(1)(a) of the Landlord and Tenant Act 1927, which implies into such a covenant the proviso that 'consent is not to be unreasonably withheld'.

2. *When is refusal of consent unreasonable?*
Although the Landlord and Tenant Act 1927 implies the proviso that 'consent shall not be unreasonably withheld', it gives no guidance on what would constitute reasonable grounds for refusal.

The only statutory provisions on the matter are to be found in anti-discrimination legislation, which provides that it is unlawful to discriminate, on specified grounds, in any dealings with property, including refusal of consent (see Chapter 3).

Turning to case law, the nearest approach to a general principle is to be found in the statement of the Court of Appeal in *Houlder Bros v Gibbs* [1925] 1 Ch 575: to be an acceptable reason for refusal of consent, an objection must relate to the personality of the intended assignee or to the use which he is likely to make of the property. (As summarised more recently by Aldous LJ in *Jaison Property Development Co. Ltd v Roux Restaurants Ltd* (1996) 74 P&CR 357 at p. 359, the landlord is entitled to require 'acceptable use and acceptable assignees'.) This can be a helpful guide, but it does have the effect of excluding a number of reasons which, to the landlord at least, may well seem good. Thus, in *Houlder Bros v Gibbs* the assignment was opposed because the proposed assignee already occupied other property belonging to the landlord, who feared that if the assignment was permitted, the assignee would give up that other property, which would be difficult to relet. This quite understandable reason was rejected by the Court of Appeal, which took the view (at p. 583) that a refusal was not reasonable where

> the reason given is independent of the relationship between the lessor and the lessee, and on the grounds which are entirely personal to the lessor and wholly extraneous to the lessee

or, as the Court of Appeal put it in *International Drilling Fluids Ltd v Louisville Investments (Uxbridge) Ltd* [1986] Ch 513 (at p. 520),

> where the refusal was designed to achieve a collateral purpose unconnected with the terms of the lease.

The approach in *Houlder Bros v Gibbs* was criticised by the House of Lords in *Tredegar v Harwood* [1929] AC 72. However, although their Lordships were again considering what constitutes unreasonable refusal, they were not dealing with a proposed assignment or subletting, but with a request by the tenant for permission to insure the property with an insurer other than the one prescribed by the terms of his lease. The landlord refused consent on the grounds that it was more convenient for the management of his properties to have them all covered by the same insurer. The House of Lords regarded this as reasonable grounds for refusal, and their Lordships indicated that they considered the approach in *Houlder Bros v Gibbs* to be too narrow. Nevertheless, the views expressed by their Lordships, although always referred to with respect, were no more than *obiter dicta*, and the Court of Appeal continued to refer with approval to its earlier decision (see, for example, *Bickel v Duke of Westminster* [1977] QB 517). This approach has now been confirmed by the House of Lords in *Ashworth Frazer Ltd v Gloucester CC* [2001] 1 WLR 2180, which, perhaps surprisingly, makes only a brief reference to *Tredegar* v *Harwood*, and does not refer to the criticism voiced there of *Houlder Bros v Gibbs*.

3. *The 'Ashworth Frazer' principles*
In *Ashworth Frazer,* Lord Bingham identified three 'overriding principles' (see [2001] 1 WLR paras. 3–5), which should guide the courts in deciding whether a landlord's refusal of consent is unreasonable.

(i) *A landlord is not entitled to refuse his consent to an assignment on grounds which have nothing to do with the relationship of landlord and tenant in regard to the subject matter of the lease* In stating this first principle, his Lordship adopted the restatement of the *Houlder Bros v Gibbs* formula to be found in the *International Drilling* case ([1986] Ch 513 at 520). It is important to realise that satisfying the *Houlder Bros v Gibbs* test is only the first step in the process of deciding whether the landlord's refusal is reasonable. His reason for refusing may well relate to the nature of the assignee or his proposed use of the property, and yet still be regarded by the court as unreasonable.

(ii) *The question of whether the landlord's conduct is reasonable or unreasonable is a question of fact* The House of Lords in *Ashworth Frazer* emphasised that the question of whether the landlord's conduct is reasonable is always a question of fact, to be decided on the circumstances of each particular case. Previous decisions on similar reasons for refusal may be referred to for guidance, but they should not be regarded as laying down legal rules as to what is or is not reasonable.

The House of Lords was particularly concerned to emphasise this approach because, in the case before it, the Court of Appeal had held itself bound by an earlier decision that particular grounds for refusal were unreasonable. In *Ashworth Frazer,* the landlord, Gloucester CC, had refused consent to an assignment because it considered that the assignees' proposed use of the property would be in breach of a covenant in the lease. At first instance, the landlord's refusal had been held not to be unreasonable, but on appeal by the tenant the Court of Appeal considered itself bound by its earlier decision in *Killick v Second Covent Garden Property Co. Ltd* [1973] 1 WLR 658, in which the court had held that the landlord's belief that the assignee would use the premises in breach of the user covenant was not an acceptable ground for refusing consent to assign. If assignment took place, the landlord would still be able to enforce the covenant, and would be in no worse position than if the assignor himself had proposed to break it. In *Ashworth Frazer* the Court of Appeal treated the *Killick* decision as establishing a rule that consent could not reasonably be refused in such circumstances, and accordingly held that the landlord's refusal in the case before them was unreasonable.

In reversing the Court of Appeal's decision on this point, the House of Lords overruled *Killick*. In Lord Rodger's words (at para. 68):

> ... it cannot be said as a matter of law, that the belief of a landlord, however reasonable, that the proposed assignee intends to use the demised premises for a purpose which would give rise to a breach of a user covenant, cannot, of itself, be a reasonable ground for witholding consent to the assignment.

The correct approach would be to ask what the reasonable landlord would do when asked to consent in these circumstances. While it was true, as *Killick* had said, that the landlord would have the same ability to enforce the covenant against the assignee as he would have had against the assignor, a reasonable landlord might well consider that his position would be significantly altered by the assignment. After the assignment, he could find himself involved in the trouble and expense of enforcing the covenant, whereas he had previously had a tenant who was prepared to comply with it. The probability that the assignee might break the covenant could be enough to justify the withholding of consent.

Whether refusal on such grounds was reasonable must, however, be decided as a question of fact on the circumstances of each case. Lord Rodger was at pains to emphasise that, in overruling *Killick*, the House of Lords were not substituting a contrary rule of law that it would always be reasonable to refuse consent on these grounds; there could be circumstances where refusal of consent for such a reason would be unreasonable. Accordingly, the case was remitted to the Chancery Division, for consideration of whether in the particular circumstances of the case the landlord's refusal was reasonable.

(iii) *The landlord is required to show that his conduct was reasonable, not that it was right or justifiable* Not a lot is said in *Ashworth Frazer* about this third principle, but it has been considered and explained by the Court of Appeal in *NCR Ltd v Riverland Portfolio No. 1 Ltd* [2005] 22 EG 134. As Carnworth LJ put it (at para. 31):

> It is of course of the essence of a reasonable decision that there were reasons for it, which can be justified at some level, even if only by showing that they were genuine and not wholly fanciful...What is not required, however, is for those reasons to be justified by reference to some objective standard of correctness.

In other words, it is sufficient if the landlord's refusal was based on concerns about the proposed transaction which a reasonable man might have, even though others might take a different view (para. 33).

Examples of reasonable and unreasonable refusals

While bearing in mind the House of Lords' warning that previous decisions on refusal of consent must be regarded as illustrative only and not taken as laying down rules of law, it is still often helpful to consider previous decisions on specific grounds of refusal. For example, it has been held unreasonable to refuse consent on the ground that a proposed tenant has diplomatic immunity (*Parker v Boggon* [1947] KB 346) or because the landlord wants to recover possession for himself (*Bates v Donaldson* [1896] 2 QB 241).

Examples of acceptable reasons for refusal include: the unsatisfactory nature of the assignee's references (*Shanly v Ward* (1913) 29 TLR 714); the fact that the proposed assignment would interfere with the future development of the property (*Pimms Ltd v Tallow Chandlers Co.* [1964] 2 QB 547); and the fact that assignment back to the original tenant would enable him to operate a break clause and bring the lease to an end (*Olympia & York Canary Wharf Ltd v Oil Property Investments Ltd* [1994] 2 EGLR 48). For further examples of valid reasons for refusal of consent see Cheshire and Burn, pp. 265–6.

Finally, you may like to note that *International Drilling Fluids Ltd v Louisville Investments (Uxbridge) Ltd* [1986] Ch 513 provides an answer to a question on which there had been some divergence of authority: could the landlord be said to be acting unreasonably in refusing consent if he did not take into account the effect that this would have on the tenant? In the view of the court (at p. 521):

> there may be cases where there is such a disproportion between the benefit to the landlord and the detriment to the tenant if the landlord withholds his consent...that it is unreasonable for the landlord to refuse consent

The court considered that the case before it was of this type, and accordingly held that the landlord's refusal was unreasonable.

4. *Landlord and Tenant Act 1988 ('the 1988 Act')*

Before the 1988 Act, the landlord could cause the tenant inconvenience and even financial loss by delay in dealing with his request for permission to assign, or by unreasonably refusing such permission, and the tenant had no redress for any damage this caused him (see *Design Progression Ltd v Thurloe Properties Ltd* [2005] 1 WLR 1, paras. 1–3). To deal with this situation, the 1988 Act imposed several statutory duties on the landlord and provided remedies for breach of these duties.

Thus:

- The landlord must respond to the tenant's request for consent 'within a reasonable time' (s. 1 (3)).
- The landlord must reply to the request in writing, and if refusing consent, must give his reasons for refusal in that reply (s. 1(3)).
- In the past, there was uncertainty as to whether a landlord who has to justify his decision in subsequent court proceedings may rely on reasons for refusal which he did not give to the tenant at the time. In interpreting the new provisions of the Act, it has now been held that the landlord cannot subsequently rely on reasons which are not given in his written response (*Footwear Corp. Ltd v Amplight Properties Ltd* [1998] 3 All ER 52, approved by the Court of Appeal in *GoWest Ltd v Spigarola* [2003] QB 1140, at para. 18).
- If the landlord refuses consent, the burden of proof is on him to prove that refusal was reasonable (s. 1(6)).This is a change from the pre-Act rule, under which the tenant was required to prove that the landlord's refusal was unreasonable.
- The tenant is given the right to sue the landlord for breach of his statutory duties (s. 4).

5. *Agreement in advance of request*

While the provisions of the 1927 and 1988 Acts have the effect of improving the tenant's position, a more recent amendment to s. 19(1) of the 1927 Act, introduced by the Landlord and Tenant (Covenants) Act 1995, s. 22, is designed to assist the landlord. It applies only to 'new tenancies' as defined by the Act (in outline, those created on or after 1 January 1996—see further at 12.1.3), and, moreover, residential leases are specifically excluded. In the case of leases within the provisions, s. 22 provides that the landlord and tenant may enter into an agreement specifying the circumstances in which the landlord may in the future withhold his consent to any assignment etc. and the conditions subject to which any consent may be given. If the landlord subsequently withholds consent on the ground that such circumstances exist or attaches such conditions to the granting of consent, he shall not be regarded as acting unreasonably. The agreement need not be contained in the lease, and can be made at any time before the tenant seeks consent.

6. *What should tenant do if landlord refuses consent?*

Where a lease contains a covenant not to assign etc. without consent the tenant who wishes to assign should, of course, ensure that he does ask the landlord for permission. However, if the tenant asks for permission and it is refused there are three courses of action open to him:

- He may seek a declaration from the court that the landlord's refusal is unreasonable and that he is therefore entitled to assign, sublet or part with possession.
- He may seek a remedy (damages or an injunction) for the landlord's breach of statutory duty under the 1988 Act (s. 4). (For an exceptional award of exemplary or punitive damages where the landlord had been 'deliberately obstructive', see *Design Progression Ltd v Thurloe Properties Ltd* [2005] 1 WLR 1).
- He may take the risk and make the disposition, which will be effective even if it is in breach of covenant (*Parker v Jones* [1910] 2 KB 32: subletting; *Old Grovebury Manor Farm v W. Seymour Plant Sales* [1979] 3 All ER 504: assignment). It should be remembered, however, that the proposed assignee or subtenant may well refuse to proceed unless the landlord's consent has been obtained, as to do otherwise could

well cause him problems in the future. It the tenant does take this course of action, the landlord may sue for breach of covenant and possibly seek to forfeit the lease.

7. *Strict interpretation of covenant*
It should be noted that covenants of this type are strictly interpreted. Accordingly a covenant forbidding 'assigning' does not prevent the creation of a subtenancy or a licence; similarly a covenant against 'subletting' does not prevent an assignment or the creation of a licence.

11.2.2.3 Other covenants by the tenant

The covenants mentioned above are only examples of the more common covenants. There are many other covenants in use, e.g., covenants about noise levels, keeping animals, not erecting signs or other external additions (e.g., window-boxes). One common covenant is a covenant restricting the use of the premises, for example, to use as 'a private dwelling only' or for a particular type of business. In leases of premises such as public houses or petrol stations, there could be a tie or solus agreement, by which the tenant agrees to take all his supplies (beer or petrol, as the case may be) from the brewery or petrol company which is letting the premises to him (although note that in certain circumstances such a provision might now be void under Art. 85(1) (now Art. 81) of the EC Treaty; see *Passmore* v *Morland* [1999] 1 EGLR 51).

11.2.3 Express covenants by landlord or tenant

11.2.3.1 Covenants concerning repairs

Most leases for any period other than the shortest will contain detailed covenants obliging the landlord or the tenant to effect certain repairs. These covenants vary considerably with the circumstances, but in the case of a long lease (e.g., 99 years) it is quite normal for the tenant to be obliged to undertake all necessary repairs, including structural repairs to buildings. In shorter leases the burden may well be shared, with the tenant undertaking to decorate and to carry out internal repairs, whilst the landlord agrees to maintain the structure. The landlord will have an implied right to enter the premises in order to inspect, but this right must be exercised reasonably.

A covenant 'to repair' involves not only the maintenance of the existing property but will include replacement of parts which are irreparable (*Lurcott v Wakeley* [1911] 1 KB 905) and even complete rebuilding if the structure is destroyed, for example, by fire (*Bullock v Dommitt* (1796) 2 Chit 608). Obviously it is wise to insure against such risks.

11.2.3.2 Covenants to insure

In some cases the landlord will covenant to insure premises (though the tenant may have to agree to pay some, or all, of the premium), whilst in others the tenant will undertake this obligation. Such covenants will be broken if the property is uninsured for any period, however short, and even if no damage occurs during that time (*Penniall v Harborne* (1848) 11 QB 368).

11.3 Implied and usual covenants

In many leases, the parties will not need to rely on the implied covenants because they will have regulated all necessary matters by express covenants in the lease. If, however, a lease contains express covenants but is silent on certain issues (e.g., contains no covenant referring to quiet enjoyment), implied terms will be added to the express terms in the lease.

In the absence of express provision, the following covenants are regarded as being of such fundamental importance and so much part of the landlord and tenant relationship that they are implied into every lease. They will all be implied into the oral lease of the basement flat at 2 Trant Way, made between Fingall Forest and Gerald Gruyère (see 11.1.4.1).

11.3.1 Implied covenants by the landlord

11.3.1.1 Landlord's covenants for quiet enjoyment and non-derogation from grant

Covenants by the landlord for quiet enjoyment and non-derogation from grant will be implied into every lease which does not expressly provide for them. (For details of these covenants see 11.2.1.1 and 11.2.1.2.)

11.3.1.2 Landlord's covenants about the condition of the property

Subject to the obligations imposed by the covenants for quiet enjoyment and non-derogation from grant, there is in general no implied covenant that the premises will be fit for any particular purpose.

This is true even where the premises are domestic in character and yet prove to be unfit for human habitation (*Lane v Cox* [1897] 1 QB 415). This general rule arises because of the application of the principle of *caveat emptor* ('let the buyer beware'); it is for the prospective tenant to examine the property and decide whether it is fit for his purpose. However, the general rule is modified in the case of furnished houses and houses let at a low rent.

1. *Where a house is let furnished*

It is clear from a number of authorities that if a house is let furnished then it must be fit for human habitation at the start of the term (*Smith v Marrable* (1843) 11 M & W 5). It should be noted that this implied condition relates only to the state of the premises at the commencement of the term, and the landlord is not liable under this heading if the premises become unfit during the lease term (*Harrison v Malet* (1886) 3 TLR 58; *Sarson v Roberts* [1895] 2 QB 395).

2. *Where a house is let at a low rent*

A covenant by the landlord that the premises are fit for human habitation is implied into certain leases at a low rent by the Landlord and Tenant Act 1985, s. 8. The levels of rent prescribed are, however, so low (e.g., maximum of £80 a year in London) that today very few premises come within the provisions of the Act, and accordingly we will say no more about them.

11.3.1.3 Landlord's covenants to repair: short leases

In general there is no implied obligation on the landlord to maintain or repair the property, but under ss. 11–14 of the Landlord and Tenant Act 1985, certain covenants by the landlord are implied into all leases of dwellings for a term of 'less than seven years'. The covenants implied are:

(a) to keep the structure and exterior in repair; and
(b) to keep in repair and working order the facilities for the supply of water, gas, electricity, sanitation, space heating and water heating.

11.3.1.4 General duty of care

Where a landlord is under a duty to repair (either by reason of express covenant or under the statutory provisions noted above), s. 4 of the Defective Premises Act

1972 imposes on him a duty in tort, to see that all persons who might reasonably be expected to be affected by defects in the state of the premises are reasonably safe from injury or damage to their property caused by such defect. Under the Act the landlord will also be liable to any person who acquires an interest in a dwelling which was built by the landlord, or where the landlord has done any work in connection with its provision.

Originally there was some doubt as to whether this duty extended to the tenant himself. However, it was held by the Court of Appeal in *Sykes v Harry* [2001] QB 1014 that the tenant is included in the category of 'persons who might reasonably be expected to be affected', and the landlord in that case was held liable for physical injury caused to his tenant by a defective gas fire.

In the later decision of *Alker v Collingwood Housing Association* [2007] 1 WLR 2230 the Court of Appeal emphasised that the landlord's liability under s. 4 of the Defective Premises Act 1972 arises only if the defect that has caused injury or damage can be attributed to a failure to repair or maintain the property. The claimant in this case had been seriously injured when she put her hand through a pane of glass in her front door. The glass was of a type which is today regarded as a safety hazard (although probably acceptable when the property was built), but it had not been damaged in any way before the accident and was not in need of repair.

At first instance, Mrs Alker succeeded in her claim against the landlord for compensation for breach of its statutory duty, but this decision was reversed by the Court of Appeal. The court reviewed its earlier decisions on such claims, and at para. 10 quoted the words of Gibson LJ *in McNerny v Lambeth Borough Council* [1989] 19 EG 77 at 83:

> . .. statutory protection for those in occupation of defective premises is geared to the landlord's obligation to repair the premises. It goes no wider than the repair covenant.

The duty to repair or maintain could not be said to include an obligation to make the property safe by dealing with defects in it which did not arise from disrepair. To hold otherwise would be to transform the statutory obligation to protect against the effects of disrepair into a statutory warranty that the premises were reasonably safe (paras. 16 and 17). Such a warranty would impose a major liability on landlords:

> if it were to be desired to impose such a liability, it would be for Parliament to effect it.

11.3.2 Implied covenants by the tenant

11.3.2.1 Tenant's covenant to pay rent

As we have already explained (at 10.2.5), it is perfectly possible to have a lease without an obligation to pay rent. Accordingly a covenant to pay rent will not be implied automatically into every lease. However, the payment of rent is usual and it will normally be the intention of the parties that it should be paid.

11.3.2.2 Tenant's covenant to pay rates and other taxes on the premises

The tenant is under an implied obligation to pay all the rates and taxes for which the landlord is not made expressly liable, either by the terms of the lease or under a rule of law. Because tenants are impliedly liable for the rates and similar obligations, such as council tax, on a property, they should take care to ascertain whether their rent is inclusive or exclusive before they enter into the agreement, as fairly large sums can be involved.

11.3.2.3 Tenant's liability for damage or disrepair

A tenant's implied duties in respect of damage or disrepair are usually said to arise from his liability for 'waste'. Waste may be defined as an act or omission which alters the state of the land, and it can even include changes which *improve* the land (*'ameliorating waste'*). We are concerned here, however, with the sort of behaviour which may damage the property and it is usual to divide such waste into two categories:

- voluntary waste—which consists of doing something which should not be done, such as knocking down a wall; and
- permissive waste—which consists of leaving undone something which ought to be done, such as failing to prevent a wall falling down.

The distinction is therefore between causing damage and failing to prevent damage, and liability for permissive waste thus has the effect of imposing on the tenant a duty to repair. The extent of liability for waste depends on the type of lease involved and so we will consider the various leases separately.

1. *Weekly tenancies*

Generally the rule is that a weekly tenant is liable for voluntary waste but not for permissive waste: in other words he may not knock a wall down but he can let it fall down (*Mint v Good* [1951] 1 KB 517). The duty is increased beyond this point, however, by the further rule that he must use the premises in a 'tenant-like manner' (per Denning LJ, *Warren v Keen* [1954] 1 QB 15 at 20). This means that the tenant must clean the premises, mend the electric light if it is fused, unstop blocked sinks and generally 'do the little jobs about the place which a reasonable tenant would do'. The exact duties of the tenant under this heading are not entirely clear, however, and each case must be judged on its facts.

2. *Monthly and quarterly tenancies*

The rules here seem to be the same as for a weekly tenancy.

3. *Yearly tenancies*

The position here is similar to that of other periodic tenancies save that additionally a yearly tenant is deemed to be obliged to keep the premises wind and water-tight (*Wedd v Porter* [1916] 2 KB 91). This obligation is, however, rather watered down by the further rule that the tenant is not liable for 'fair wear and tear' (*Warren v Keen* [1954] 1 QB 15). This means that he is not responsible for the gradual deterioration caused by normal use or by the normal action of the elements (*Haskell v Marlow* [1928] 2 KB 45), so that he does not have to replace stone steps which are worn down by use or tiles which are blown off the roof by the wind.

4. *Fixed-term tenancies*

A tenant with a fixed term of years is certainly liable for voluntary waste. The position with regard to permissive waste was less clear, and an earlier edition of *Woodfall* expressed the view that there was 'considerable doubt whether a tenant for years would be found liable for permissive waste if the matter were thoroughly tested at the present day' (*Woodfall's Law of Landlord and Tenant*, Sweet & Maxwell, Release 41, para. 13.124). However, after a very thorough review of case law and juristic writing, the High Court in *Dayani v Bromley LBC* [1999] 3 EGLR 144 has now held that a tenant for years can be liable for permissive waste. Thus, if a lease for a fixed term makes no express provision about repairs, there will be an implied term that such a tenant should maintain the premises in the condition in which he received them at the start of the term.

11.3.2.4 Tenant's obligation to allow landlord entry

In general, as the tenant has exclusive possession, he may exclude the landlord from the premises. However, a term will be implied that the landlord is to be allowed to enter the premises if the landlord is under a duty to repair (*Saner v Bilton* (1876) 7 ChD 815). This will give the landlord a right, to be exercised reasonably, to enter and inspect and carry out necessary repairs. A similar implied term is also included where statutory provisions require a landlord to repair.

11.3.3 Usual covenants

We cannot end our general discussion of covenants in leases without mentioning the class of such agreements which is normally described as 'the usual covenants'. In any instance in which the grant of a lease is preceded by a contractual agreement, it is an implied term of that contract that the lease, when granted, will contain the usual covenants (*Propert v Parker* (1832) 3 My & K 280) and the lease may therefore be rectified if these are not included when it is granted. The class of usual covenants is not entirely fixed and will vary depending on the area in which the property stands or because of the nature of a trade run on the premises. In *Flexman v Corbett* [1930] 1 Ch 672, it was suggested that a covenant must be regarded as 'usual' if nine out of ten leases of the same kind would include the term. It was also pointed out that 'what is normal in Mayfair or Bayswater is not usual... in Whitechapel' (per Maugham J at p. 678). The following covenants are, however, always regarded as 'usual':

- the tenant will pay rent;
- the tenant will pay rates and taxes (other than those which must, by statutory provision, be borne by the landlord);
- the tenant will keep the premises in repair;
- if the landlord has expressly covenanted to repair, he will be allowed reasonable access to view and repair the premises;
- the landlord will allow the tenant quiet enjoyment and that he will not derogate from his grant; and
- the landlord will have a right to re-enter should the tenant fail to pay his rent (but not in the case of the breach of other covenants).

A more recent decision, *Chester v Buckingham Travel Ltd* [1981] 1 WLR 96, provides an example of the court accepting a wider range of covenants as being 'usual' in a modern commercial lease, including both restrictions on the use or alteration of the buildings, and a right of re-entry for the landlord for breach of any covenant in the lease.

FURTHER READING

Covenant not to assign

Fancourt, 'Licences to Assign: Another Turn of the Screw?' [2006] 70 Conv 37 (rather detailed, but worth reading selectively).

Covenant to repair

Cheshire and Burn's Modern Law of Real Property, 18th edn., pp. 227–37, and 246–50.

12

Enforcement of leasehold covenants

12.1 Introduction

Having identified various leasehold covenants in Chapter 11, we need now to consider the effect these covenants have on:

- the original parties to the lease;
- their successors in title (those who acquire the lease or the reversion from the original tenant or landlord); and
- subtenants (those who hold a sub-lease granted by the original tenant or his successor in title).

12.1.1 Enforcement between the original parties to the lease

There is little problem when one is dealing with either of the original parties to the lease, because between the original landlord and tenant there will be privity of contract, with the result that either party can enforce an obligation against the other, as is normal in the case of any contractual promise.

12.1.2 Enforcement after the lease or the reversion has passed to new owners

We have seen in Chapter 10 that both landlord and tenant have legal estates in the property which may pass to other owners by sale, as gifts or by succession on death (see 10.4). The position where L, the landlord, has granted a lease to T, the tenant, and subsequently both parties transfer their estates to other owners can be shown diagrammatically as follows:

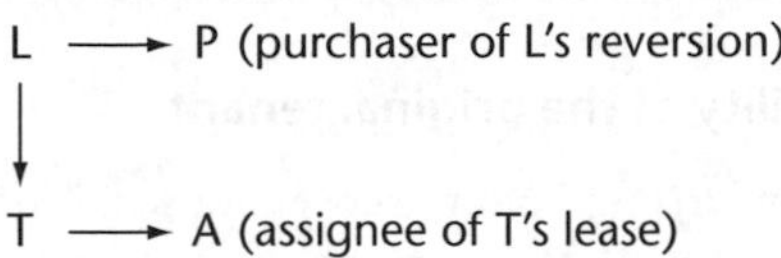

In such circumstances two questions arise:

- do the original parties to the lease (L and T) retain any rights or duties under the covenants once they have parted with their estates?
- are the covenants in the lease enforceable by or against the new owners of the lease and the reversion (A and P)?

The Landlord and Tenant (Covenants) Act 1995 (which we will refer to in future as 'the 1995 Act') makes major changes in this regard, but these changes are not retrospective, despite the Law Commission's recommendation that they should be (*Landlord and Tenant Law: Privity of Contract and Estate* (Law Com No. 174)). As a result, there are now two very different sets of rules in operation, the choice of which to apply depending, in general, on whether the lease was created on or after 1 January 1996 (the date on which the Act took effect), or before that date. Leases can, of course, be granted for very long periods, and in consequence the older law, relating to covenants in leases created before 1996, will continue in operation for many years to come—certainly for much of this century.

12.1.3 New and old leases

(a) *New leases* Most of the provisions of the 1995 Act apply only to *'new tenancies'*, which the Act defines in s. 1(3) as tenancies granted on or after the date on which the Act came into force (i.e., 1 January 1996).

(b) *Old leases* Leases which do not fall within the definition of 'new tenancies' are described by the Act as *'other tenancies'*, but we will refer to them in the rest of this chapter as 'old leases'.

As you would expect, this category of leases consists mainly of tenancies granted before 1 January 1996. However, it also includes leases granted after that date if they are made under an agreement (which includes an option or right of first refusal) or a court order which was in existence before the Act came into force (s. 1). In consequence of this, it is likely that the effect of the old law will be further prolonged by the exercise of options to renew contained in long leases.

Finally, we should mention that there are a few provisions in the 1995 Act which apply to both new and old leases, and we will note these briefly in 12.4.

The fact that there are now two completely different sets of rules in operation makes the material covered in this chapter quite complicated and it may make it easier to work your way through it if you note that in the next five sections (12.2–12.6) we will deal first with the position of the original landlord and tenant, after they have assigned their estates, and then with the position of the assignees who have taken those estates. In each case we will look at the rules for old leases first and then go on to describe the changes which affect new leases.

12.2 Old leases: position of original parties after transfer of lease and/or reversion

12.2.1 Continuing liability of the original tenant

The contractual obligation arising from the covenant will usually continue even if the covenantor has disposed of his interest in the property, for generally covenants are so phrased that they relate not only to the covenantor's acts and omissions but also to those of his successors in title and persons deriving title under him. Even if the covenantor does not covenant expressly in these terms, they will be implied into the covenant by LPA 1925, s. 79 which provides that:

> A covenant relating to any land of a covenantor... shall, unless a contrary intention is expressed, be deemed to be made by the covenantor on behalf of himself his successors in title and the persons deriving title under him...

Accordingly, in leases granted before 1996, an original tenant will usually have covenanted not only about his own conduct, but also about that of his assignees ('successors in title') and subtenants ('persons deriving title under him'). Thus, if a tenant has covenanted that he will not do a specified act, he can still be sued by the landlord even after he has disposed of his whole estate and despite the fact that the act complained of is that of his assignee, for he is in breach of his covenant that neither he nor his successors will do that act (*Thursby v Plant* (1690) 1 Saund 230).

In this way, the original tenant will remain liable throughout the whole term of the lease for any breach of covenant by his successors in title. As we shall see later, the burden of most covenants in a lease will pass on the assignment of the lease or the reversion, so that the new estate owner will become personally liable for any breach. This means that the covenantee often has a choice between suing the present estate owner, who has caused the breach, or proceeding against the original covenantor. It is usually more convenient to proceed against the present owner, if only because it is easier to find him, but if he should disappear, or be not worth suing, it may be better to try to recover from the original covenantor.

12.2.1.1 Hardship caused by continuing liability

The fact that the original tenant remained liable for any breach of covenant by his successors throughout the whole term of the lease had always been capable of producing apparently unfair results, largely because the original tenant was often unaware of the provisions of LPA 1925, s. 79, and did not appreciate fully the obligations he was assuming. However, economic difficulties during the 1980s intensified the hardship experienced by original tenants. Many found themselves being held liable for breaches of covenant committed by current tenants, who were in financial difficulties and could not afford to pay rent or perform other covenants. The lease had often passed through a series of assignments, and it might well be that the original tenant knew nothing of the current holder, and certainly had no control over him. It was these difficulties which led to pressure for change.

12.2.2 Continuing liability of original landlord

So far, we have concentrated on the position of the original tenant, but it is important to note that the same general principles apply to the landlord, who will be presumed to have covenanted for himself and his successors in title, in accordance with LPA 1925, s. 79. He will thus remain liable on his covenants after assigning the reversion, and so could find himself being sued by the tenant for breaches of covenant committed by the assignee (the tenant's current landlord).

12.2.3 Excluding continuing liability by agreement

From a legal point of view, it was always possible to avoid continuing liability by covenanting at the outset in terms that excluded the operation of s. 79 and provided that liability would cease on assignment. In reality, however, no landlord would accept a covenant in these terms from a prospective tenant, and a properly advised tenant would be unlikely to agree to such a limitation of his landlord's liability.

12.2.4 Possible indemnity for original covenantor held liable for breach

If the original covenantor (whether tenant or landlord) does have to compensate for breach of covenant, he will naturally want to recoup his losses and may do so in one of two ways. To illustrate this, we will assume a series of assignments of a lease, which may be shown diagrammatically as follows:

L
↓ Lease
T —Assignment→ A1 —Assignment→ A2 —Assignment→ A3

L has recovered damages from T in respect of a breach of covenant by A3, and two courses of action are now open to T.

1. *Proceeding against A3*

T may seek to recover directly from A3, relying on the rule in *Moule v Garrett* (1872) LR 7 Ex 101 that:

> where one person is compelled to pay damages by the legal default of another, he is entitled to recover from [that person] the sum so paid.

However, the fact that L preferred to sue T may suggest to T that it will not be worthwhile to proceed against A3 and so he may prefer the second course of action.

2. *Proceeding against A1*

T is able to do this because any assignment of a lease includes an implied covenant by the assignee to indemnify the assignor for any breach of covenant in the lease. (See for *registered land*, LRA 2002 s. 134 and Sch. 12 para. 20; and for *unregistered land*, LPA 1925, s. 77.)

Thus, T may sue A1, because A1 covenanted to indemnify T against such claims. Thereafter, A1 may sue A2 and A2 may sue A3, also on the basis of the indemnity covenant which is implied into every assignment.

It is, of course, important to realise that in the situations we have just been considering, where a claimant has a choice of whom to sue, he can recover only one set of damages, and there is no question of his gaining double compensation by proceeding against two different defendants in respect of the same breach of covenant.

12.3 New leases: position of original parties after transfer of lease and/or reversion

In contrast with the rule for old leases, under which the original covenantor remains liable on his covenants despite assigning his estate, the 1995 Act provides release from their covenants for both tenant and landlord (save for personal covenants—for which, see 12.3.3). For the tenant, release is automatic, subject to certain exceptions which we note below. For the landlord, release is obtained with the consent of the tenant or on a court order.

12.3.1 Release of the original tenant

Where a tenant assigns his lease, s. 5 of the 1995 Act provides that, from the assignment, he is released from the burden of his covenants and ceases to be entitled to the benefit of the landlord's covenants. The section relates to any assigning tenant, and therefore applies to an assignee who himself assigns, as well as to the original tenant under the lease. However, assignees have always been freed from future liability on the covenants in the lease when they in turn assign (*City of London Corporation v Fell* [1994] 1 AC 458 at p. 465), and the principal beneficiary from this provision will undoubtedly be the original tenant and covenantor, who is thus freed from the continuing liability on his covenants. To accord with this major change in the law, the Act includes two consequential provisions:

(a) It provides that LPA 1925, s. 79 (by which a covenantor is deemed to covenant on behalf of himself, his successors in title and the persons deriving title under him), shall not apply to new tenancies (s. 30(4)(a)).

(b) The statutory provisions which insert implied indemnity covenants into assignments of leases (see 12.2.4) are repealed in respect of new tenancies (s. 30(2)–(3)). Nevertheless, as we shall see, there may be occasions where the assigning tenant is not released from his liability under the covenants, and it might therefore be wise for the tenant to include an express covenant for indemnity in the assignment, since he can no longer rely on the implied one.

12.3.1.1 Circumstances in which the tenant remains liable

It is important to note that there are certain circumstances in which the tenant will not be freed from his continuing liability. He continues to be liable in the case of 'excluded assignments', which are defined in s. 11(1) as:

(a) assignments in breach of a covenant in the tenancy, i.e., assignments of the lease by a tenant in breach of an absolute or qualified covenant against assignment; and

(b) assignments by operation of law, for example, on death, where the estate vests in the deceased's personal representatives, or on bankruptcy, where the estate vests in the trustee in bankruptcy.

Where the tenant (or his estate) remains bound by his covenants after assignment, he will be freed by the next assignment of the lease which is not an excluded one (s. 11(2)(b)).

12.3.1.2 Authorised guarantee agreement

Although the tenant may be freed automatically from continuing liability on his covenants, it should be noted that the landlord may require him to enter into an 'authorised guarantee agreement', by which he guarantees the assignee's performance of the covenants in the lease (s. 16). The landlord is permitted to do this only when:

(1) his consent to the assignment is required under the lease; and
(2) he makes the giving of the guarantee a condition of his consenting to the assignment.

The guarantee is to last only while the assignee is liable under the covenants of the lease and must end when his liability ceases, i.e., the tenant giving the guarantee cannot be required to guarantee performance by successive assignees. Thus although it may look at first sight as though the Act is taking away with one hand what it has just given with the other, the tenant's position is in reality still considerably better than it would be under the old rules, where his liability as original covenantor would normally continue throughout the full period of the lease.

12.3.2 Release of the original landlord

The 1995 Act provides for the release of the landlord from his covenants on the assignment of the reversion (s. 6), but this release does not take place automatically on the assignment as it does for the tenant. Instead, the Act creates a procedure under which the landlord is required to give notice to the tenant, informing him of the proposed or actual assignment of the reversion, and requesting release from the covenants. The landlord will be released if the tenant consents, or does not respond within the prescribed period; if the tenant refuses consent the landlord may apply to the court, which may either uphold the tenant's objection or declare that it is reasonable for the covenant to be released. Details of the procedure (content of notice, time limits, etc.) are to be found in s. 8 of the Act.

The provisions of s. 11 relating to excluded assignments (which we have noted above in connection with the release of the tenant) apply also to assignments by the landlord, with the result that assignment by operation of law does not end the continuing liability of the original landlord.

Where a landlord has not been released from liability (for example, because the assignment is an excluded one, or because the tenant successfully opposes the landlord's application), he may apply for release on any future assignment of the reversion (ss. 7 and 11(3)(b)).

The provisions of the Act in relation to the landlord may appear to be less favourable than those applying to the tenant, but it must be remembered that the tenant has no say in the landlord's choice of an assignee (despite the fact that the assignee will become the tenant's new landlord), whereas very often the requirement of the landlord's consent to any assignment of the lease gives him an adequate opportunity to 'vet' any prospective new tenant (although the original tenant will still be released from continuing liability even where the landlord's consent to assignment is not required). The creditworthiness of a new landlord is very relevant to a tenant where, for example, the landlord has repairing obligations under the lease, and if there is any doubt about the financial standing of the assignee the tenant may well want the current landlord's liability to continue, and so oppose the application for release.

12.3.3 No release from personal covenants on assignment

As we shall see later when we consider the position after transfer of the lease and the reversion, most covenants in a lease will be enforceable between the new landlord and tenant (see 12.5 and 12.6). However, any covenant which normally would pass in this way may be worded so as to make it clear that it is intended to be a *personal covenant*, benefiting or binding only the original tenant or landlord. In *BHP Petroleum Ltd v Chesterfield Ltd* [2002] Ch 194 the question arose of whether a covenantor who assigns his estate is able to free himself from liability on his personal covenants.

In this case, the original landlord had undertaken to carry out certain remedial work to the property and it was clear from the agreement that this was to be a personal obligation which would not be enforceable against the landlord's successors (see para. 17). On assigning the reversion, the landlord served a notice on the tenant seeking release from its covenants and the tenant did not respond. Subsequently, the tenant sought to enforce the obligation to remedy certain defects against the original landlord, and the defendant claimed that it had been released from the obligation by its assignment of the reversion and the tenant's failure to serve a counter-notice. The Court of Appeal rejected this claim, holding that the provisions of the Act concerning release applied only to a 'landlord covenant' (see 12.6.1) which, relying on the definition of 'landlord' in s. 28(1) of the Act, the court defined (at para. 59) as:

> an obligation falling to be complied with by the person who may from time to time be entitled to the reversion on the tenancy.

By contrast, an obligation under a personal covenant by the landlord does not bind successors; it therefore falls outside the definition of a 'landlord covenant', and so does not come within the statutory provisions for release from 'landlord covenants'. Thus, the original landlord may secure release from burdens which will pass to his assignees, but cannot free himself from a personal covenant. The court considered that this interpretation accorded with the basic principle underlying the statutory provisions for release which was, in the words of Lightman J at first instance (quoted with approval by the Court of Appeal at para. 29):

> that the release of a landlord or tenant from a covenant was intended to be sequential upon, and only sequential upon, a parting by the landlord or tenant with his interest in the property let and the successor taking his predecessor's place as the party responsible for complying with that covenant.

Accordingly, the original landlord remained liable on his personal covenant and was obliged to remedy the defects which had become apparent.

12.3.4 Is it still possible to exclude continuing liability by agreement?

We noted in connection with old leases that it was always possible for a covenantor to avoid continuing liability by express provisions in the covenant, but that in practical terms this was not likely to be acceptable to the other party. However, such an exclusion, contained in new leases, did arise for consideration by the House of Lords in *London Diocesan Fund v Phithwa* [2005] 1 WLR 3956. (Rather confusingly, some reports refer to this decision, and proceedings in the lower courts, as *Avonridge Property Co. Ltd v Mashru*—see for example [2006] 01 EG 100—but we assure you both references are to the same case.)

In 2002 the defendant, Avonridge Property Co Ltd ('Avonridge'), acquired an existing lease of various small shops, which it sublet to individual tenants in exchange for large premiums and nominal rents. Each sublease contained a covenant by Avonridge that it would pay the rent due on the head lease to the head landlord, the London Diocesan Fund ('LDF'), but with the additional provision that it would not continue to be liable to its tenants on this covenant if it disposed of its interest in the property (i.e. if it assigned the head lease).

Very shortly after granting the subleases, Avonridge assigned the head lease to Phithwa, who failed to pay the rent due to the head landlord and subsequently disappeared. The head landlord began proceedings to forfeit the head lease (which would destroy the subleases); the subtenants applied for relief under the relevant statutory provisions (see 13.4.5.2); and were granted new leases to be held directly from LDF at a market rent. This meant that the subtenants were very much out of pocket: they had paid for the value of their leases by way of the premiums and were now required to pay rent as well.

Accordingly the subtenants sued Avonridge, their former landlord, for breach of its covenant to them that it would pay the rent due under the head lease, claiming that it still remained liable on this covenant despite the term in the covenant that liability should end on its assignment of the reversion. The effect of that term would be to free the landlord from its covenant without complying with the statutory procedure for release, and the claimants alleged that the term was designed to avoid that procedure and was therefore void under s. 25 (which invalidates any agreement restricting the operation of the Act).

The House of Lords rejected this claim (Lord Walker dissenting). Their Lordships explained that the provisions of the Act were designed to deal with situations in which the covenantor's liability continued after assignment. It had always been possible, before the Act, for the covenantor to provide expressly that his liability would end on assignment, and there was nothing in the Act which changed this. Avonridge had not sought to avoid the statutory provisions, but had simply continued to exercise a right which had always existed and was not affected by the Act.

12.3.5 Loss of benefit

We have concentrated so far on the release of the assignor from the *burden* of the covenants, but it must be noted that when this occurs under the statutory provisions he also ceases to be entitled to the *benefit* of the other party's covenants under the lease (ss. 5(2)(b) and 6(2)(b)). However, s. 24(4) specifically provides that this loss of benefit does not affect any rights arising from an earlier breach of covenant (see further 12.7).

12.4 Provisions of 1995 Act which apply to both old and new leases

12.4.1 Help for former tenants and their guarantors

Sections 17–20 of the Act provide further help for former tenants who may have continuing liabilities in respect of leases even after they have been assigned. These sections apply to 'both new and other tenancies' (s. 1(2)), and so will apply to leases granted before 1 January 1996, which in general continue to be governed by the older law, as we have already described. This part of the Act will be of particular relevance to original tenants under these pre-1996 leases, who remain liable on their covenants for the whole period of the lease, but they will also be of benefit to tenants under new leases who have been required by their landlords to enter into authorised guarantee agreements under s. 16 (see 12.3.1.2), or who for some reason have not been released from their covenants on assignment.

12.4.1.1 Guarantors

These provisions of the Act also apply to guarantors of the former tenant. So far, we have not referred to the practice of landlords requiring a tenant or assignee of a lease to provide guarantors or sureties for his performance of the covenants in the lease. In general, such matters are beyond the scope of this book, but the practice is a common one, and guarantors can be seriously affected in times of recession by the inability of tenants to meet their commitments. The protection given to the tenant by these sections is accordingly extended to his guarantor, and references to the former tenant in the following accounts of ss. 17–21 should be read as including any guarantors, even though we do not specifically mention them.

12.4.2 Three forms of help

The Act assists the tenant in three ways:

- by restricting the arrears that can be recovered;
- by ensuring that the tenant is not made subject to increased liability by variation of the terms of the lease; and
- by giving him an opportunity to acquire a landlord's rights over the current tenant.

12.4.2.1 Restriction of liability for rent or service charge

Section 17 provides that a landlord cannot recover from a former tenant arrears of rent or other fixed payments (such as service charges), unless within six months of the money becoming due the landlord has notified the former tenant of the amount due and of the fact that he intends to recover the money. The purpose of this provision is to put an end to a practice of some landlords, who allowed arrears to accumulate, sometimes over a period of years, before having recourse to the former tenant, who meanwhile had no knowledge that the current tenant was in breach of covenant.

12.4.2.2 Restriction of liability where tenancy is subsequently varied

It is always possible to vary the terms of a lease by agreement between the landlord and the tenant and such a variation may result in an increased liability for the tenant. Accordingly, the Act provides that the former tenant shall not be liable to pay any charge which arises from a variation of the tenant's covenants which was made after he had assigned the lease (s. 18(2) and (3)).

It is a different matter, however, if the original lease itself provided for some future variation of the tenant's obligations (for example, by a rent review clause), in which case the original tenant might well be bound by the enhanced obligation.

12.4.2.3 Right to an overriding lease

A former tenant who remains liable on his covenants may be described as having responsibility without power, since he is liable for breach of covenants committed by assignees of the lease, without having any control over them. It is true that he is responsible for the choice of his own assignee, but he has no say in the making of any subsequent assignment (unless he makes special contractual arrangements for this). He may very well be unaware of breaches of covenant by an assignee, and even if he knew of them has no way of compelling the landlord to take action.

A solution to these difficulties is offered by s. 19 which gives the former tenant the right to require the landlord to grant him an 'overriding lease'. This will take effect as a concurrent lease, or a lease of the reversion (see 10.10.5), and its effect is to make the former tenant the immediate landlord of the defaulting current tenant. This means that he has the landlord's power to enforce the covenants in the lease against the tenant and, if there are further breaches, can take action to remedy them, if necessary by forfeiting the lease and seeking to relet the property.

For a practical account of the ways in which this new device may assist the former tenant, see Williamson (2006) EG No. 0605 267.

12.5 Old leases: position of new landlord and/or tenant after transfer of lease and/or reversion

12.5.1 The problem

Although, as we have seen, the original covenantor in an old lease remains liable for breach of covenant, most covenantees would in general find it more convenient to proceed against the person who has actually caused the breach. Accordingly, it is often essential to know whether an assignee of a covenanting tenant, or a purchaser of a reversion from a covenanting landlord, can be made directly liable for breaches of covenant. Similarly such an assignee may well wish to know whether he has a right to enforce the original covenants in the lease. The problem here is that such an assignee is a later arrival on the scene, and is not a party to the contract between the original landlord and tenant. It is possible to assign *rights* under a contract, but it is a basic principle of contract law that *duties* under a contract cannot be passed to a person who was not a party to the original contract. However, as the leasehold estate developed, it was necessary to find ways of continuing to enforce the covenants despite successive changes in the ownership of the lease and the reversion. In the words of Lord Templeman in *City of London Corpn v Fell* [1994] 1 AC 458 at 464:

> . . . common law, and statute following common law, were faced with the problem of rendering effective the obligations under a lease which might endure for a period of 999 years or more beyond the control of any covenantor.

The rules which common law and statute developed to deal with this problem apply only to leases created by deed. We will consider these first, and will note the rules which apply to leases made without a deed later, at 12.5.3.

12.5.2 Leases made by deed

Two requirements must be satisfied before a leasehold covenant can be enforced by or against an assignee of the lease or the reversion:

- there must be privity of estate between the relevant parties (see 12.5.2.1); and
- the covenants in question must 'touch and concern the land' or 'have reference to the subject-matter of the lease' (see 12.5.2.2).

12.5.2.1 There must be privity of estate between the relevant parties

There is said to be privity of estate when two persons have a relationship of tenure with each other. In other words privity of estate arises when there is a relationship of landlord and tenant between the parties. If the following situation exists:

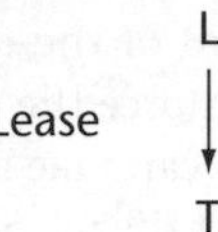

then there is both privity of contract and privity of estate between L and T. If T later assigns his lease to A, A becomes L's tenant and L becomes A's landlord. There will be privity of contract between L and T but privity of estate between L and A:

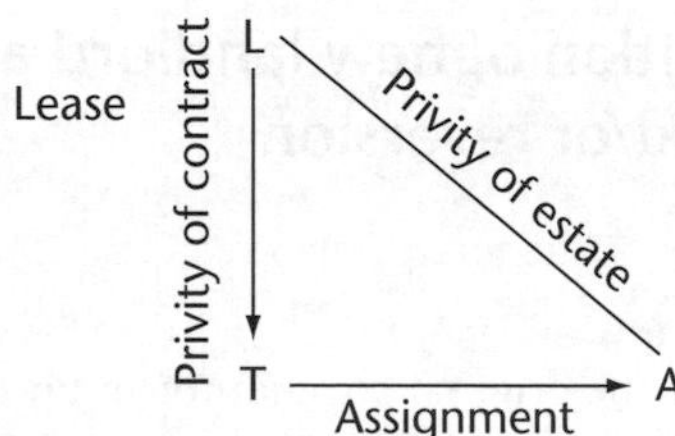

Similarly, if the landlord, L, sells the reversion to P, a purchaser, there will continue to be privity of contract between L and T but there will be privity of estate between T and P:

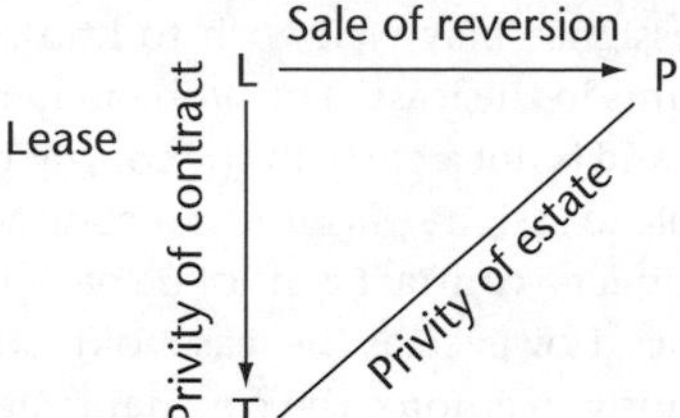

If the landlord sells the reversion and the tenant assigns the lease the situation illustrated below will arise:

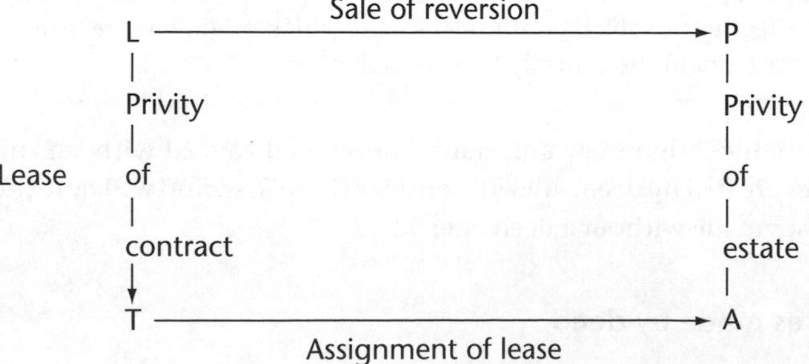

Thus, there will be privity of estate between the purchaser of the reversion, P, and the assignee of the lease, A; they are, respectively, the new landlord and the new tenant.

Where privity of estate exists, some leasehold covenants will be enforceable between the current landlord and tenant, even although there is no privity of contract between them.

In general, covenants cannot be enforced unless there is at least privity of estate between the parties, but there are certain exceptional cases in which enforcement is possible despite the fact that there is no relationship of either contract or estate (see 12.5.2.3 and 12.9.1.1).

12.5.2.2 **Covenants must 'touch and concern' the land or 'have reference to the subject-matter of the lease'**

There are only certain leasehold covenants which will run to benefit or bind assignees of the lease or the reversion.

1. *Assignment of a lease*

The rule which applies when a tenant assigns a lease is that the assignee will acquire the burden and benefit of all covenants in the lease which *'touch and concern'* the demised premises. This rule is derived from *Spencer's Case* (1583) 5 Co Rep 16a, in which it was held that a covenant made by a tenant to build a brick wall on the premises could be enforced against an assignee of the tenant. By contrast however, if the tenant had covenanted to build a wall on other property belonging to the landlord, that covenant would not bind an assignee of the tenant because it did not 'touch and concern' the demised premises.

Under the rule in *Spencer's Case*, the assignee acquires not only the burden of certain covenants in the lease, but may also receive the right to enforce such of the landlord's covenants as 'touch and concern' the land.

2. *Assignment of a reversion*

The rules which apply to the purchaser of the reversion from the landlord are similar to those which apply to the tenant's assignee, but are covered by statutory provisions under LPA 1925, ss. 141 and 142. The rule here is that covenants run to bind and benefit a purchaser where the covenant 'has reference to the subject-matter of the lease'.

3. *Meaning of 'touching and concerning' and 'having reference to the subject-matter of the lease'*

It is generally accepted that the two phrases, 'touching and concerning' and 'having reference to the subject-matter of the lease', have the same meaning, and any explanation of one of them can be taken as applying equally to the other. Unfortunately, it has proved very difficult to define either phrase in such a way as to provide a clear test for identifying those covenants which will run on assignment, and all we can do here is to note certain suggestions that have found favour with the courts.

In *Breams Property Investment Co. Ltd v Stroulger* [1948] 2 KB 1 at 7 the Court of Appeal approved a passage in Cheshire's *Modern Real Property* (still to be found in the current edition of Cheshire and Burn—see p. 304) which suggested that the appropriate test for identifying a covenant which 'touched and concerned' the land was:

> whether the covenant affects the landlord qua [as] landlord or the tenant qua tenant. A covenant may very well have reference to the land, but, unless it is reasonably incidental to the relation of landlord and tenant, it cannot be said to touch and concern the land....

It may be thought that this test only substitutes one formula for another, and is not particularly helpful in practice. It does, however, explain the decision in *Woodall v Clifton* [1905] 2 Ch 257, in which it was held that an agreement by the landlord giving the tenant an option to purchase the reversion did not come within the rule in *Spencer's Case*, because the covenant did not affect the parties as landlord and tenant but as vendor and purchaser.

A further statement of the process to be followed in deciding whether a covenant 'touches and concerns' is to be found in *P & A Swift Investments v Combined English Stores Group plc* [1989] AC 632 in which Lord Oliver drew together criteria from earlier decisions and (at p. 642) set out what he described as 'a satisfactory working test' for whether a covenant touches and concerns the land. The case under consideration concerned the assignment of the reversion and Lord Oliver formulated his test accordingly, but it can be expressed more generally by saying that a covenant touches and concerns the land if three conditions are met.

(i) The covenant is of benefit to the covenantee only while he holds an estate in the land: that is, while he remains a landlord or a tenant. Thus for example, a tenant's covenant to repair the property benefits the original landlord only while he retains his interest in the land: once he has assigned the reversion he is not affected by the state of the property and so is not benefited by the tenant's performance of his covenant. It would seem that this first condition is very similar to the *Breams Property* test of affecting the landlord qua landlord etc.

(ii) The covenant affects the nature, quality, mode of user or value of the covenantee's land (for an earlier statement of this condition see Russel LJ in *Horsey Estate Ltd v Steiger* [1899] 2 QB 79 at 89).

(iii) The covenant is not stated to be personal; that is, it is not worded so as to bind only a specific covenantor or to benefit only a specific covenantee.

Despite this guidance from the courts, it remains difficult in borderline cases to predict whether or not a covenant will run on assignment. As long ago as 1931 Romer LJ, in *Grant v Edmondson* [1931] 1 Ch 1 at 28, described the rules as being:

> purely arbitrary, and the decisions for the most part quite illogical.

This criticism has continued to the present day (see, for example, Gray and Gray paras. 4.5.42–54), and eventually resulted in major reform of the rules by the 1995 Act. The old rules, however, continue to apply to leases granted before the Act came into force, and so it is necessary to note briefly examples of covenants which do and do not 'touch and concern'.

Covenants which 'touch and concern' It would be impossible to compile a complete list of all covenants which satisfy the rule in *Spencer's Case*, and it is probably enough for your purposes to note that all the standard covenants discussed in Chapter 11 will do so.

Covenants which do not 'touch and concern' Covenants which do not 'touch and concern' and so do not run on assignment may be described as 'collateral' covenants. They include: non-competition clauses (*Thomas v Hayward* (1869) LR 4 Ex 311; covenants to keep other property in repair (*Dewar v Goodman* [1909] AC 72), and covenants to repair chattels which are not fixed to the land *(Williams v Earle* (1868) LR 3 QB 739).

Further examples of both categories may be found in Cheshire and Burn, pp. 304–7 and Megarry and Wade, paras. 20-038–20-040.

Personal covenants It is important to realise that any covenant that would normally be regarded as touching and concerning the land, and therefore running on assignment, may be worded so as to make it clear that it is intended to be a personal covenant, benefiting or binding only the original tenant or landlord, and in that case will not run on assignment. It is also possible to create a covenant which is personal to one party but not to the other. Thus, for example, a covenant could give a personal right to a tenant, which could not be passed on to his assignee but would run with the reversion and be enforceable against the landlord's assignees (see *System Floors Ltd v Ruralpride Ltd* [1995] 1 EGLR 48).

In case you are confused, we should mention that covenants which do not touch and concern the land may also be described as 'personal' covenants, because they do not run on assignment and so are enforceable only between the original parties. However, we think it is helpful to distinguish between covenants that *cannot run* ('collateral' covenants) and covenants that are of a type which *could run*, but are prevented from doing so by the agreement of the parties ('personal' covenants).

12.5.2.3 Enforcement by assignee against original covenantor

There is one final point we want to mention here, because students sometimes find it confusing. The continuing liability of the original tenant, even after he has assigned his lease, combined with the fact that the right to enforce certain covenants in the lease runs to the assignee of the reversion means that covenants can be enforced by the current landlord against the original tenant, even though there has never been any privity of estate between them. This does seems surprising, in view of the general rule that covenants can be enforced only where there is privity of contract or privity of estate. It is, however, clear from decided cases that the assignee of the reversion does have the right to enforce against the original covenantor in this way (see, for example, *Parker v Webb* (1693) 3 Salk 5 (91 ER 656) and *Milverton Group Ltd v Warner World Ltd* [1995] 2 EGLR 28). It seems that the right to enforce the contract passes to the new landlord automatically under the relevant statutory provisions (now LPA 1925, s. 141), without its having to be expressly assigned. It is suggested that in a similar way the assignee of the lease might enforce against the original landlord, again without any privity of estate between them, but there is no decision on this point. (See further, Megarry and Wade, para. 20–016.)

12.5.3 Leases not made by deed

As noted at the end of 12.5.1, the rules we have been discussing so far apply only to leases made by deed. We will now consider the different rules which apply to legal leases granted orally or in writing, and to equitable leases.

12.5.3.1 Legal parol leases

These are leases made orally or in writing. The old rule expressed in *Elliott v Johnson* (1866) LR 2 QB 120 was that covenants did not run on the assignment of a parol lease: the principles in *Spencer's Case* applied only to legal leases made by deed. However, it was held in *Boyer v Warbey* [1953] 1 QB 234 that the rule in *Spencer's Case* could also apply to a written lease for not more than three years which created a legal estate by virtue of LPA 1925, s. 54(2). Accordingly, a covenant made by the tenant to pay £40 towards repairs at the end of the term ran to bind an assignee of the written lease. It seems probable that the same approach would be adopted in the case of oral leases within the s. 54(2) exception, but no mention was made of this in *Boyer v Warbey*, so the position remains uncertain.

12.5.3.2 Equitable leases

The rule that covenants in a legal lease will run to benefit or burden an assignee of the lease or reversion depends upon the assignee's acquiring an estate in the property.

1. *Position of new tenant*

In the case of an equitable lease, the tenant has no estate, merely an equitable right to specific performance of the agreement for a lease, and therefore the benefits and burdens of the terms of the agreement do not pass automatically to the new tenant.

The right to enforce a contract may, however, be assigned, and so if the landlord were to make some promise in the original agreement (e.g., to repair the structure) the benefit of that promise could be assigned to a purchaser from the tenant. The new tenant would be able to sue the landlord to enforce the landlord's part of the contract.

By contrast, whilst the *benefit* of a contract may be assigned, the *burden* is not transferable. If the tenant under an equitable lease agrees to decorate the interior of the property, the burden of this agreement cannot be transferred to a person buying the lease from the tenant. The original tenant will remain contractually liable for any breach of the agreement, but the landlord will not be able to take action against the new tenant (*Purchase v Lichfield Brewery Co.* [1915] 1 KB 184).

In *Boyer v Warbey* [1953] 1 QB 234, Denning LJ suggested that the position we have just described had changed as a result of the Judicature Acts 1873–5:

> . . . since the fusion of law and equity, the position is different...There is no valid reason nowadays why the doctrine of covenants running with the land—or with the reversion—should not apply equally to agreements under hand as to covenants under seal; and I think we should so hold, not only in the case of agreements for more than three years which need the intervention of equity to perfect them, but also in the case of agreements for three years or less which do not.

As we have noted above, *Boyer v Warbey* was dealing with a written legal lease for three years. Remarks about equitable leases were therefore merely *obiter dicta*; and although they pointed the way to a solution of this problem, they have not been taken up in any later decision.

2. *Position of new landlord*

So far, we have been considering what happens if the *tenant* under an equitable lease assigns his interest. The passage quoted above from *Boyer v Warbey* implies that similar difficulties arise if the *landlord* transfers his interest in the land, i.e., assigns his reversion on the equitable lease.

In fact there are a number of earlier decisions which hold that equitable leases are covered by the statutory provision that the *benefit* of the lessee's covenants runs with the reversion (see, for example, *Rickett v Green* [1910] 1 KB 253, interpreting s. 10 of the Conveyancing Act 1881, the forerunner of LPA 1925, s. 141).

There has as yet been no decision on whether the *burden* of the landlord's covenants runs to the assignee under LPA 1925, s. 142, but the reasoning of the decisions on the running of the benefit would seem equally applicable to the running of the burden (see Megarry and Wade, para. 20–062).

The various difficulties and uncertainties about the running of covenants in equitable leases provide a further reason for saying that an equitable lease is not as 'good as' a legal lease (see 10.3.5.3). These problems are now resolved in the case of new tenancies by the provisions of the 1995 Act (see 12.6.3), but old leases, of course, are still subject to them.

12.6 New leases: position of new landlord and/or tenant after transfer of lease and/or reversion

The 1995 Act makes very considerable changes to the rules relating to the running of covenants on the assignment of the lease or the reversion. In doing so, it introduces two new technical terms: 'landlord covenants' and 'tenant covenants'.

12.6.1 Landlord covenants and tenant covenants

These covenants are defined in s. 28(1) as the covenants to be performed by the landlord and tenant respectively; in other words, the classification of the covenant is determined by considering who is to bear its burden. For an interpretation of the statutory definition of these terms, see *BHP Petroleum Ltd v Chesterfield Ltd* [2002] Ch 194, in which, as we noted in 12.3.3, the Court of Appeal held that 'landlord covenants' are those which fall to be complied with by the person who may from time to time be entitled to the reversion (i.e., the current landlord), and do not include personal covenants by the original landlord. Although the court in this case was concerned only with landlord covenants, it seems most likely that a similar approach would be adopted in defining 'tenant covenants'.

12.6.2 Transmission of benefit and burden of covenants and rights of re-entry

Section 3 of the Act provides that the benefit and burden of all landlord and tenant covenants in the tenancy shall be annexed to the whole and each and every part of the demised premises and of the reversion in them, and shall pass on the assignment of the whole or any part of the premises or of the reversion. Section 4 makes a similar provision in respect of the landlord's right of re-entry (i.e., to repossess the property for breach of covenant).

Thus, in general, all the covenants in the lease (with the exception of personal covenants, which are specifically excluded by s. 3(6)(a)) will run on the assignment of the lease or the reversion, and there will be no need to consider whether covenants 'touch and concern the land' or 'have reference to the subject matter of the lease' (*Spencer's Case* (1585) 5 Co Rep 16a and LPA 1925, ss. 141 and 142—see 12.5.2.2). The Act specifically states that its provisions apply to a landlord covenant or a tenant covenant 'whether or not the covenant has reference to the subject matter of the tenancy' (s. 2(1)(a)), and the Act further provides that nothing in LPA 1925, ss. 141 and 142 shall apply in relation to new tenancies (s. 30(4)(b)). Thus covenants which under the old law will be classified as 'collateral covenants', and accordingly will not pass on assignment, will under the Act run to benefit and burden assignees of new tenancies and their reversions.

12.6.3 Equitable leases

A further welcome change is that by virtue of s. 28(1), which defines 'tenancy' as including an 'agreement for a tenancy', the new rules about the running of covenants apply to equitable leases just as they do to legal ones, thus freeing the parties to new agreements from the problems we have noted above at 12.5.3.2.

12.6.4 Requirement for registration

The Act specifically provides that it shall not operate to make enforceable against any person any covenant which would otherwise be unenforceable against him by reason of its not having been registered under the LRA 2002 or the LCA 1925 (s. 3(6)(b), as amended by LRA 2002). Thus options to renew the lease, or to purchase the reversion will still continue to require protection by entry on the register of title or by registration as a class C(iv) land charge.

12.7 Breach of covenant before assignment

In considering whether the benefit and burden of leasehold covenants will run to the new owner when the lease or reversion is assigned, we have assumed that the covenants in the lease have been observed up to the time of the assignment. But what happens if there has in fact been a breach of covenant before the assignment? Who is liable, and who can take action in respect of the breach?

12.7.1 Who is liable?

The party who has committed the breach remains liable for it, even if he has subsequently assigned his estate. If the burden of the covenant is capable of running on assignment, the assignee is bound by it for the future, but he does not take on liability for pre-existing breaches. This seems almost self-evident, but if authority is needed it can be found in *Duncliffe v Caerfelin Properties Ltd* [1989] 2 EGLR 38, and in s. 23(1) of the 1995 Act, in respect of new leases.

12.7.2 Who can take action?

The answer to this question is surprisingly complicated, and depends upon whether it is the reversion or the lease which has been assigned.

12.7.2.1 Assignment of reversion

Here yet again there are different rules for old and new leases.

Old leases

The right to take action for any pre-existing breach of covenant passes to the new landlord with the assignment of the reversion (LPA 1925, s. 141, as interpreted in *Re King* [1963] Ch 459), and the former landlord loses his right to sue the tenant.

New leases

We noted earlier (12.3.5) that when an assignor is freed from the burden of his covenants he also loses the benefit of the other party's covenants. However, s. 24(4) specifically provides that this does not affect any rights he may have arising from a pre-existing breach of covenant, and as a result the right to sue for earlier breaches of covenant by the tenant now remains with the former landlord. Accordingly, s. 23(1) provides that the new landlord cannot sue for breaches which have occurred before the reversion was assigned to him, although under s. 23(3) he is entitled to re-enter and forfeit the lease for such a breach.

12.7.2.2 Assignment of lease

In this case, the position is the same for both old and new leases: the former tenant may sue the landlord in respect of breaches occurring during the currency of his lease even after he has assigned it. This right may be valuable if he has spent money remedying a breach for which the landlord was responsible, and which had to be remedied before the assignee would agree to take the lease: see for example *City and Metropolitan Properties Ltd v Greycroft Ltd* [1987] 1 WLR 1085.

12.8 Enforcement of covenants in the Trant Way tenancies

Now that we have outlined the rules relating to the enforcement of covenants in a lease between both the original parties and their successors, it may be helpful to consider how these apply to some of the inhabitants of Trant Way.

12.8.1 6 Trant Way—an old lease

As we have seen (at 11.1.4.3), 6 Trant Way was held by John Jarlsberg on a 40-year lease, granted in 1979, i.e., well before the operative date of the 1995 Act. Some time ago, Jarlsberg moved away to a different part of the country to take up a new job, and, with the consent of his landlord, Irene Ivy, he sold his lease to Keith Kale. Later, Irene Ivy sold the fee simple estate in 6 Trant Way to Liam Lyle, who was registered as proprietor of the estate, i.e., he bought using the unregistered conveyancing procedure and thereafter applied for first registration of title. Keith Kale has now decided that he would like to take advantage of the option to purchase which was given to the original tenant by the original lease made between Mrs Ivy and Mr Jarlsberg (cl. 4(b), see pp. 209–10). Mr Kale has served written notice on Mr Lyle of his intentions. He has also been having some problems lately with the tile cladding on part of the exterior wall of the house and wants Mr Lyle to sort this out, under the landlord's repairing covenant in the lease, before the purchase of the property goes ahead.

In this situation we must consider:

- which of the terms in the original lease bind or benefit Mr Kale, the tenant's assignee; and
- which of the terms bind or benefit Mr Lyle, the purchaser of the freehold reversion.

The situation may be expressed diagrammatically as follows:

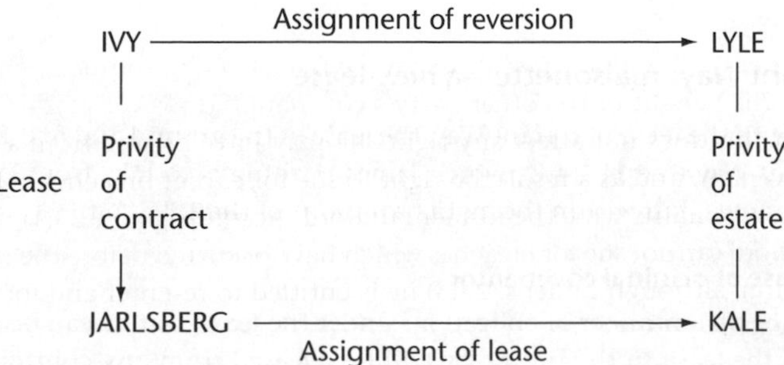

12.8.1.1 Enforcement of covenants between assignees of lease and reversion

As a result of the transactions which have occurred, Mr Lyle is now Mr Kale's landlord. There is privity of estate between them. Mr Lyle will be bound by any of the landlord's covenants (LPA 1925, s. 142) and will benefit from any of the tenant's covenants (s. 141) in the original lease which have 'reference to the subject-matter thereof'. Similarly, Mr Kale will automatically receive both the benefit and the burden of any covenants in the original lease which 'touch and concern' the land (*Spencer's Case* (1583) 5 Co Rep 16a).

This means that Mr Kale is bound by Mr Jarlsberg's covenants, and so is obliged to pay rent, to obtain the landlord's consent before assigning or subletting, and not to use the premises otherwise than as a dwelling. Mr Lyle has the right to enforce these covenants against him. In his turn, Mr Lyle is bound by Mrs Ivy's covenants for quiet enjoyment and for the repair of the exterior, and Mr Kale has the right to enforce these against him. It follows from this that Mr Kale should be able to require his landlord to remedy the problems he is experiencing with the exterior wall.

12.8.1.2 Continuing liability of original landlord and tenant

Although they probably do not realise it, both Mrs Ivy and Mr Jarlsberg remain liable on their covenants, even though both of them have given up all connection with the property. This means that if, for any reason, Mr Lyle fails to carry out the necessary repairs, Mr Kale could seek compensation from Mrs Ivy. In reality, though, this is only likely to happen if Mr Lyle is unable to meet his obligations for financial reasons.

12.8.1.3 Option to purchase the reversion

The question of whether Mr Kale has the right to enforce the option to purchase against his landlord is more complicated. It has been held that this covenant does not touch and concern the land: the option does not affect the parties qua landlord and tenant but qua vendor and purchaser (*Woodall v Clifton* [1905] 2 Ch 257). Accordingly, this right does not automatically benefit Mr Kale or burden Mr Lyle. The option did, however, give the original tenant, Mr Jarlsberg, an equitable interest in the fee simple estate. The benefit of that right could have been assigned to Mr Kale, as can the benefit of any chose in action, but a clear assignment of the right will be required if Mr Kale is to establish a claim to it.

Even if Mr Kale can prove that the benefit of the right has been assigned to him, he must still establish that the option is binding on Mr Lyle, who has bought the legal estate in fee simple. Mr Lyle will be bound by the equitable interest only if it had been protected as a C(iv) land charge before he purchased the fee simple (see *Phillips v Mobil Oil Co. Ltd* [1989] 1 WLR 888). If the option had not been registered it will not bind Mr Lyle and cannot be enforced against him.

12.8.2 2 Trant Way: maisonette—a new lease

By contrast with the lease of 6 Trant Way, the lease of the ground and first-floor maisonette at 2 Trant Way (see 11.1.4.2), which James Harding is to take from Fingall Forest, will, when granted, fall within the main provisions of the 1995 Act.

12.8.2.1 Release of original covenantor

James is taking on a number of obligations under the lease, but he can be assured that, if he assigns the lease in the future, he will be released from any continuing liability on the tenant covenants (provided he is not so foolish as to assign the lease without his landlord's consent, thus making an 'excluded assignment').

By contrast, assigning the reversion would not relieve Fingall Forest automatically from his liability on the landlord covenants, but he could seek release from his current tenant or, in case of refusal, from the court. If for any reason he was not released, he could make a further application on any occasion in the future when the reversion was assigned again.

12.8.2.2 Enforcement of covenants between assignees of lease and reversion

Assignees from the original landlord and tenant will take the reversion and the lease with the relevant benefits and burdens of the tenant and landlord covenants (with the exception of any which are expressed to be personal to the original parties). There will be no need to ask whether the covenants touch and concern the land (*Spencer's Case*) or have reference to the subject matter of the lease (LPA 1925, ss. 141 and 142); all that will be needed is a reference to the terms of s. 2 of the 1995 Act, which provides that the benefit and burden of all landlord covenants and tenant covenants are annexed to the premises and to the reversion, and pass on assignment.

12.9 Position of a subtenant

12.9.1 Covenants in head lease not enforceable against subtenant

We have seen that when a tenant assigns his lease, certain covenants in the lease are enforceable between the landlord and the assignee. If, however, the tenant, T, instead of assigning his lease, creates a sublease, we get a different situation. In such a case the subtenant, S, is the tenant of T and has no landlord and tenant relationship with L, the head landlord. Accordingly, there is neither privity of contract nor privity of estate between L and S, but there is both privity of contract and privity of estate between L and T and between T and S. This can be expressed in diagrammatic form as follows:

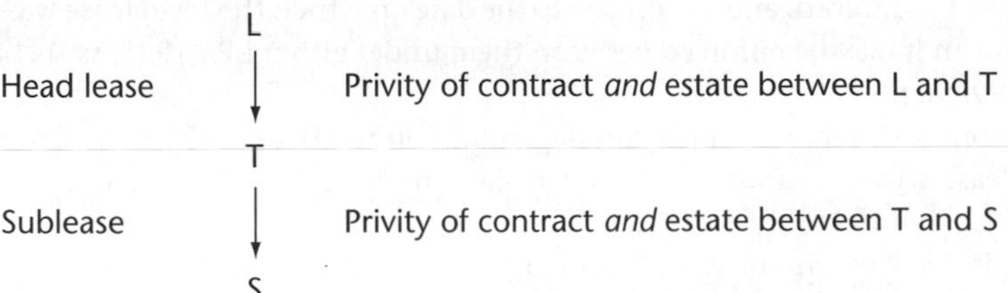

As a result, covenants in the head lease are not usually enforceable against a subtenant. However, since the tenant usually could be held liable for the actions of persons who derive their title from him he would normally take the precaution of including in the sublease the same set of covenants which he himself had entered into in the head lease. If T has done this, it would allow him to take action against S for breach of any covenant and thereby to protect himself against any liability to L.

12.9.1.1 Exceptions in respect of restrictive covenants

The only covenants in the head lease which could be enforced by L against S are those which restrict the use of the property. It has always been possible to enforce these against a subtenant if they satisfy the rules relating to restrictive covenants derived from *Tulk v Moxhay* (1848) 2 Ph 774 (which are dealt with in Chapter 26). A recent example is provided by *Hemingway Securities Ltd v Dunraven Ltd* [1995] 1 EGLR 61, in which it was held that a covenant not to assign or sublet without the landlord's consent was a restrictive covenant within the doctrine of *Tulk v Moxhay*, and could be enforced by the head landlord directly against the subtenant.

In addition, s. 3(5) of the 1995 Act now provides in respect of 'new tenancies' (in general, those granted on or after 1 January 1996) that:

> Any landlord or tenant covenant of a tenancy which is restrictive of the user of land shall, as well as being capable of enforcement against an assignee, be capable of being enforced against any other person who is the owner or occupier of any demised premises to which the covenant relates, even though there is no express provision in the tenancy to that effect.

The full effect of this provision remains to be seen, as does its relationship to the rule in *Tulk v Moxhay*, but it is certainly clear that it will enable the head landlord to enforce such covenants directly against the subtenant without reference to the equitable rules about restrictive covenants.

12.9.1.2 Assignment of sublease or reversion on head lease

The same principles will apply if S assigns his sublease to SA and if L assigns his reversion on the head lease to P:

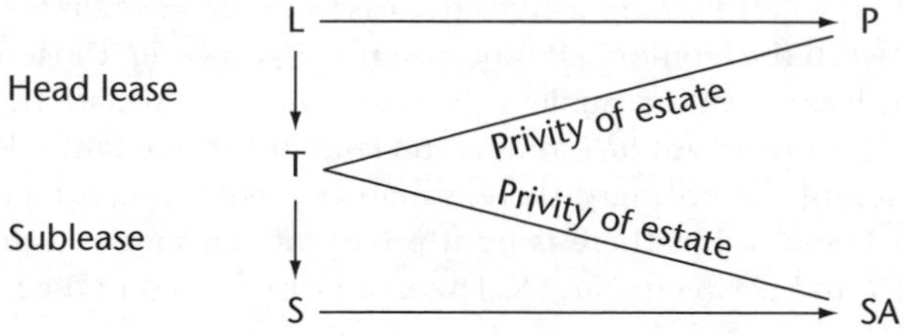

P becomes T's landlord, and, according to the date on which the head lease was granted, covenants in it may be enforced between them under either LPA 1925, ss. 141 and 142, or the 1995 Act.

SA becomes T's tenant, and, again depending on the date of the lease, covenants in the sublease will be enforceable between them under either the rule in *Spencer's Case* (1583) 5 Co Rep 16a or the 1995 Act.

There is, however, no relationship of any kind between P and SA, and no covenants (except those within either the *Tulk v Moxhay* rule or s. 3(5) of the 1995 Act) can be enforced between them.

12.9.2 Attempts by head landlord or subtenant to enforce covenants in leases to which they are not parties

So far, we have been considering the extent to which the head landlord might be able to enforce covenants in the *head lease* against the subtenant. However, the question also arises of whether he has any standing to enforce covenants in the *sublease* (to which he is not a party) against the subtenant. An example of an occasion on which a head landlord tried to do this is to be found in *Amsprop Trading Ltd v Harris Distribution Ltd*

[1997] 1 WLR 1025. In this case the subtenant had covenanted with *his* landlord that he would repair the property, and that if he did not do so the head landlord might enter and do the repairs, at the expense of the subtenant. The head landlord sought to enforce this covenant directly against the subtenant, relying on LPA 1925, s. 56, which provides that:

> a person may take . . . the benefit of any . . . covenant . . . respecting land, although he may not be named as a party to the conveyance [in which the covenant is made].

The landlord's claim was rejected because the covenant did not purport to be with him (i.e., did not name him as a covenantee), a requirement which has been developed by the courts in their interpretation of s. 56. Had this requirement been met, it seems that the head landlord could have relied on the section and enforced the covenant against the subtenant.

There may well be similar situations in which a subtenant wishes that he could enforce a covenant in the head lease against the head landlord. The head landlord may, for example, be in breach of his repairing obligations, and it would help the subtenant, who suffers the effects of disrepair, if he could proceed directly against him, instead of having to leave it to his own landlord to take action. It is possible that a tenant under an 'old' lease (i.e., one granted before 1 January 1996) could do this by relying on LPA 1925, s. 78, as interpreted in *Smith and Snipes Hall Farm Ltd v River Douglas Catchment Board* [1949] 2 KB 500 (see 26.4.1.4), but even if this were so it would not help a tenant under a new lease (granted after 1995), to which s. 78 no longer applies (s. 30(4) of the 1995 Act).

Where the lease in question is made on or after 11 May 2000, it seems likely that both head landlord and subtenant may be able to rely on the provisions of the Contracts (Rights of Third Parties) Act 1999, which came into force on that date. In outline, the Act provides that a person who is not a party to a contract (a 'third party') may enforce a term of the contract if either the contract expressly provides that he may do so, or if the term purports to confer a benefit on him, and the parties have not excluded the statutory provisions. As yet, there has not been any reported attempt to rely on the Act in this context, but it certainly seems that it could be used by head landlords and subtenants in the situations we have outlined above. (See further Law Commission Report, 1996, No. 242, para. 2.11).

12.9.3 7 Trant Way

An example of the working of these rules is to be found at 7 Trant Way which is owned in fee simple by Martin Mount. The property is divided into two parts: the ground floor (7A) being adapted for use as a shop, while the upstairs (7B) provides office accommodation. The entire property was let to Nigel Norman in 1982 for 99 years. The lease was made by deed and included a number of covenants on the part of Mr Norman, including covenants to pay rent, at present £2,000 per month, to keep the property in good repair and not to keep any animals on the property. Immediately after completion of the lease, Mr Norman sublet 7A to Olav Orion, who uses it as a showroom for his antiques business, and 7B to Paula Primrose, who carries on a small employment agency from the premises. The two subtenants both have monthly tenancies, which were granted in writing and which contain covenants identical in form to those in the headlease.

This situation can be expressed diagrammatically as follows:

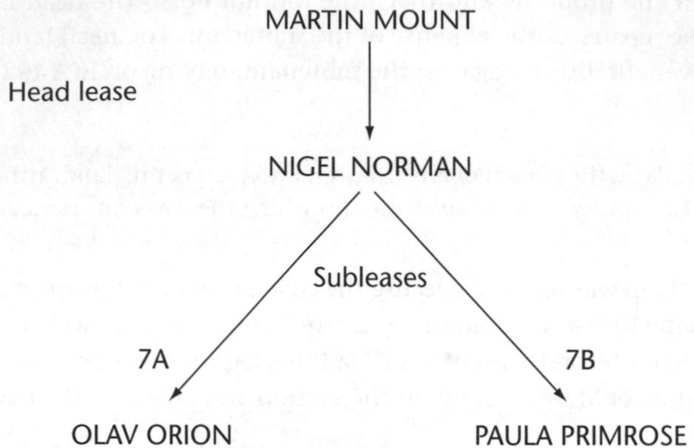

In this situation, Mr Mount can enforce the tenant's covenants in the head lease against Mr Norman, because there is privity of contract between them. There is, however, neither privity of contract nor privity of estate between Mr Mount and Mr Orion, or between Mr Mount and Miss Primrose, and so Mr Mount cannot take any action against either of the subtenants for breach of the covenants in the head lease (subject to the special rules in *Tulk v Moxhay* (1848) 2 Ph 774). Accordingly, should Mr Orion or Miss Primrose break a covenant, Mr Mount may sue only Mr Norman, who in the absence of any express provisions in his lease excluding the operation of LPA 1925, s. 79 is responsible for the actions of persons deriving title under him, and Mr Norman should then take action against Mr Orion or Miss Primrose.

FURTHER READING

'Touching and concerning'

Smith, *Property Law*, 7th edn., Pearson Longman, 2011, pp. 441–44.

1995 Act

Davey, 'Privity of Contract and Leases—Reform at Last' (1996) 59 MLR 78.

Walter, 'The Landlord and Tenant (Covenants) Act 1995: A Legislative Folly' [1996] Conv 432.

Williamson, 'The best way to deal with a nasty surprise' [2006] EG–4 February 2006 (No. 0605) (overriding leases).

Contracts (Rights of Third Parties) Act 1999

Elias, 'Third party benefits' [1999] EG (No. 9913) 117.

13

Remedies for breach of leasehold covenants

In the previous two chapters we considered the typical covenants which may be contained in a lease, and how the rights and duties arising from them may pass to assignees of the lease and the reversion. We must now go on to see what happens if some of these covenants are broken and what remedies are available to the other party. We will deal first with general contractual remedies which are, of course, available in respect of breach of covenant. We will then go on to consider in more detail some special remedies which are peculiar to leases, and in particular the landlord's power to forfeit the lease, i.e., to bring it to an end and to evict the tenant.

13.1 General contractual remedies

Where a party to a lease is in breach of covenant, the usual contractual remedies are available to the other party. Thus, for example, in appropriate cases either landlord or tenant may seek specific performance of a covenant by the other party to repair. Similarly, if a tenant uses the premises to run a business, contrary to a covenant to use the premises only as a dwelling, the landlord could seek an injunction to restrain the breach. Further, either party might decide to claim damages for breach of contract as an alternative or additional remedy. Finally, since *Hussein v Mehlman* [1992] 2 EGLR 87 (see 10.6.2), the possibility of acceptance of repudiatory breach as a discharge of the contract should also be borne in mind as a possible response to a breach of covenant by either landlord or tenant.

If you feel that you need it, further information on contractual remedies is available in any standard textbook on the law of contract. There are, however, a few important decisions on the specific enforcement of certain covenants in leases, which we need to consider here.

13.1.1 'Keep-open' covenants and specific performance

If you think of your local shopping precinct, you may see that one store, perhaps a grocery supermarket, is clearly a major attraction, bringing customers to the area and thus providing passing trade for other smaller shops in the precinct. In recognition of this fact, the landlords of such shopping areas may require the tenants of the major store to enter into a 'keep-open' covenant, i.e., to covenant that they will continue to trade in the premises leased to them for the period of their lease, or, if they no longer wish to carry on business there, until they have assigned or sublet the property with their landlord's consent.

It had always been thought that such covenants were not enforceable by an order for specific performance. This was because such an order, compelling the tenant to carry on business, would involve the court in supervising the way in which he did so, a role which the court is not willing to undertake. However, to everyone's surprise, an order of specific performance of such a covenant was granted by the Court of Appeal in *Co-operative Insurance Society Ltd v Argyll Stores (Holdings) Ltd* [1996] Ch 286. Thus Argyll Stores, who had closed its Safeways store in Hillsborough shopping centre in breach of its keep-open covenant, was required to continue to trade there until the end of the lease in 2014, or until it could assign or sublet the premises with its landlord's consent.

The Court of Appeal's decision was, however, reversed by the House of Lords in *Co-operative Insurance Society Ltd v Argyll Stores (Holdings) Ltd* [1998] AC 1. Lord Hoffmann, in a speech adopted by the other Law Lords, gave a number of reasons for holding that it was inappropriate to compel a defendant to carry on a business; while none of the reasons would necessarily be sufficient on its own, he said (at p. 16), that the cumulative effect seemed to show that the settled practice of refusing to order specific performance of such an obligation is based upon sound sense. Those reasons included: the difficulty of defining precisely what the defendant was required to do; the hardship caused to him by requiring him to carry on a loss-making business; the perpetuation of conflict between the parties who were required to continue in a hostile relationship; and the need for continuing supervision.

In terms of the principles governing the grant of specific performance, possibly the most significant of the reasons discussed by Lord Hoffmann relates to the need for continuing supervision. The suggestion that performance will require supervision by the court has often been given as a reason for refusing the order, because the court has no mechanisms by which it can ensure such supervision. Lord Hoffman's speech helpfully clarifies what is meant by 'continued supervision': not that the judge or some court official actually supervises ongoing performance, but that any failure to perform entitles the aggrieved party to return to court seeking the defendant's committal for contempt. An order to carry on an activity, such as a business, over an extended period of time, would give rise to the possibility of repeated applications to the court, alleging incidents of non-compliance. It would thus be expensive both to the parties and to the resources of the judicial system. A clean break, with the payment of damages for breach, would be a far better solution.

By contrast, an order to achieve a result, such as to repair property, does not involve the court in ongoing supervision. Provided the required outcome could be defined sufficiently precisely when the order was made, the court would, at most, have to decide on one further application whether the work had been done to a satisfactory standard, i.e., whether the desired result had been achieved. As we shall see (13.1.2.2), this distinction between carrying on an activity and achieving a required result has been relied upon in a later decision dealing with specific performance of repairing covenants, and the House of Lords decision in the *Argyll* case is not only relevant to keep-open covenants, but has a wider significance for the general principles underlying the award of specific performance.

13.1.2 Repairing covenants and specific performance

Although we have not dealt in any detail with repairing covenants, you should be aware that either party to the lease may be subject to an obligation to repair, either by express agreement or under certain covenants implied by common law or statute (see 11.3). In considering remedies for breach of such covenants, we need to note first some special statutory provisions which protect the tenant, and then recent case law developments which have made the remedy of specific performance available against both landlord and tenant.

13.1.2.1 Leasehold Property (Repairs) Act 1938

The background to this Act is to be found in the activities of property speculators, who would buy tenanted property in a poor state of repair at a low price, with a view to enforcing the tenants' repairing covenants and evicting them (by forfeiture proceedings) if they were unable to carry out the repairs. The Act applies to leases of not less than seven years, with at least three years left to run, and provides that proceedings to recover damages or to forfeit the lease for failure to repair may be brought only with leave of the court. Such leave is to be given only on specified grounds, which in general involve satisfying the court that the landlord has a valid reason for requiring repairs to be done immediately rather than at the end of the lease (e.g., that lack of repair is injurious to other occupiers of the property, or that leaving the repairs until later will substantially increase their cost).

13.1.2.2 Specific performance of repairing covenants

It used to be thought, on the supposed authority of *Hill v Barclay* (1810) 16 Ves Jun 402, that specific performance of a covenant to repair was not available against either a landlord or a tenant. Several reasons were suggested for this rule, including the problem of continued supervision by the court, discussed above in connection with the *Argyll* case.

Where the landlord was in breach of a repairing obligation, the tenant's only remedy therefore was to do the repairs himself, and then seek to recover the cost from the landlord, either by withholding rent (*Lee Parker v Izzet* [1971] 1 WLR 1688) or by suing for damages for breach of covenant. More recently, as we have seen (10.6.2), if the breach is sufficiently serious the tenant may regard it as repudiatory and treat the contract as discharged, freeing himself from further obligation but at the same time retaining the right to seek damages for breach.

Where it was the tenant who was in breach, the landlord could seek damages or forfeiture, subject of course to the provisions of the Leasehold Property (Repairs) Act 1938, noted above.

1. *Specific performance against a landlord*

The first change to the old approach is to be found in *Jeune v Queen's Cross Properties Ltd* [1974] Ch 97, where a landlord who had covenanted to maintain and repair the structure of a block of flats was ordered to reconstruct an exterior balcony which had collapsed. The balcony did not form part of the property leased to any of the plaintiff tenants, and since they did not have possession of it they would have had difficulty in following the usual route of doing the repairs and recovering the cost from the landlord. The court reviewed the supposed authority of *Hill v Barclay* (1810) 16 Ves Jun 402, and considered that it did not preclude the grant of an order of specific performance against a landlord. Statutory power to order specific performance of a landlord's repairing covenants is now to be found in the Landlord and Tenant Act 1985, s. 17, replacing the Housing Act 1974, s. 125.

2. *Specific performance against a tenant*

In *Jeune v Queen's Cross Properties Ltd, Hill v Barclay* was said in *obiter dicta* to be an authority for the proposition that specific performance of a repairing covenant could not be awarded against a tenant. However, some 25 years later such an award was made in a first-instance decision: *Rainbow Estates Ltd v Tokenhold Ltd* [1999] Ch 64. The facts of the case were unusual, in that the original landlord who granted the lease was a company controlled by the individuals to whom the lease was granted, and, possibly in consequence of this, there was no provision either for forfeiture for breach of covenant or for the landlord to enter and do repairs if the tenant failed to do so. The property was a listed building, in a serious state of disrepair; if the current landlords were not able to obtain specific performance of the tenants' repairing covenant there was no way in which they could effect repairs until the lease ended in some six years' time. In these circumstances the judge considered it appropriate to grant an order against the tenants for specific performance of their repairing obligations.

In doing so, he reviewed the reasons which used to be given for refusing specific performance to either landlord or tenant, and concluded that today 'there is little or no life in these reasons' (at p. 69). In particular, the supposed need for continued supervision by the court was no longer seen as a problem. An order to repair was an order to achieve a specified result, rather than to carry on an activity, and so, on the distinction drawn in the *Argyll* case (see 13.1.1), need not involve repeated applications to the court.

A further point which the judge had to consider was that the remedy of specific performance does not fall within the provisions of the Leasehold Property (Repairs) Act 1938. In consequence, a landlord would not need to obtain leave from the court before seeking this remedy (as he would have to do if seeking damages or forfeiture), and applications for specific performance could therefore be used to harass or oppress a tenant. In the judge's view, it would not be right to extend the Act by judicial interpretation to cover applications for specific performance, but the court would take care to ensure that such applications were not used to bring about the mischief which the Act was designed to remedy. An order for specific performance against a tenant was likely to be appropriate only in rare cases, but:

> subject to the overriding need to avoid injustice or oppression, the remedy should be available when damages are not an adequate remedy (at p. 73).

13.2 Tenant's remedies against a defaulting landlord

As we have seen above, the tenant has all the usual contractual remedies against his landlord in case of breach. In addition, there are various statutory provisions which may give the tenant additional protection against harassment or eviction, or may offer alternative ways of ensuring that the landlord complies with his repairing obligations.

13.2.1 Harassment or eviction

Treatment which is calculated to drive the tenant out of residential accommodation, whilst being a breach of the covenant of quiet enjoyment, may also amount to the criminal offence of harassment. This offence is committed where acts are done which are likely to interfere with the tenant's peace or comfort or where services, reasonably required for occupation of the premises as a residence, are withdrawn (Protection from Eviction Act 1977, s. 1(3) and (3A)). Only the local authority may institute proceedings for this offence, and the original provisions gave no real assistance to the tenant who wished to obtain a remedy in civil proceedings. However, the Housing Act 1988, s. 27, also provides a tenant who is a residential occupier with a statutory cause of action should he be evicted by his landlord. The ingredients of this tort are the same as those of the criminal offence under the Protection from Eviction Act 1977 but it is not necessary for a criminal conviction to have been obtained before the tenant brings his action. In addition to this statutory right, the tenant may also be able to found an action upon trespass, nuisance or even, if appropriate, assault, as well of course as on breach of contract.

13.2.2 Landlord's failure to repair

We have already considered the tenant's contractual remedies for the landlord's breach of his covenant to repair, but it may be that a tenant wants to avoid a direct confrontation in the courts with his landlord (possibly because the tenant cannot afford the legal costs) and yet wants to ensure that repairs to the property are made. You should therefore be aware that failure to repair can, in some circumstances, be dealt with by the local authority, under statutory powers contained in the Housing Act 1985, Pt VI, and thus in some cases a tenant may be able to seek the assistance of the local authority. It should, however, be noted that the statutory provisions concerning repair are only of assistance when the defects are serious in nature.

13.3 Landlord's remedy of distress

When the tenant fails to pay rent, the landlord may sue to recover it as a debt or may take the more extreme measure of bringing the lease to an end by forfeiture (13.4). At present, he also has the additional self-help remedy of distress. This allows him to enter the premises to seize goods belonging to the tenant (either personally or by using a bailiff) and then to sell them and keep the proceeds towards the unpaid rent.

13.3.1 The current law and the need for reform

Distress is a popular remedy with landlords, who regard it as a quick and inexpensive way of recovering rent arrears without court proceedings and as a deterrent to future non-payment of rent. But although certain goods are protected against seizure (such as clothing, basic household equipment and tools of the tenant's trade) the use of this remedy can cause considerable hardship to the tenant. The landlord's right to distrain arises the day after the rent becomes due and he is not required to warn the tenant of his intention to do so or give him any opportunity to avoid the process by paying the arrears. The goods may be sold soon after their seizure and a tenant who wishes to prevent sale by paying up may find that he is too late to do so. Moreover, enforced sales rarely produce a good price for the goods, and the tenant may find that he has been deprived of his property and yet is still in debt to his landlord.

The operation of this remedy has been reviewed and criticised, as being out of date and unfair to the tenant, on a number of occasions from the mid-1960's onwards. The enactment of the Human Rights Act in 1998 provided additional reasons for seeking reform. The law of distress allows the landlord to enter premises (very often the home of the tenant and his family) without permission or warning, and to deprive the tenant of his property without consideration of the matter by a court. There were concerns that distress, like other self-help remedies such as peaceful re-entry by a landlord without a court order or by a mortgagee (see 13.4.4.1 and 24.7.2) might prove to be a breach of rights guaranteed under the European Convention on Human Rights ('the Convention'), such as those to a fair trial (Art. 6), to respect for private and family life and the home (Art. 8) and to the peaceful enjoyment of possessions (Art.1 of the First Protocol).

In *Fuller v Happy Shopper Markets Ltd* [2001] 2 EGLR 32 at 36 Lightman J warned landlords of the dangers involved in levying distress:

> The ancient (and perhaps anachronistic) self-help remedy of distress involves a serious interference with the right of the tenant, under Article 8 of the European Convention on Human Rights, to respect for his privacy and home, and, under Article 1 of the First Protocol, to the peaceful enjoyment of his possessions. The human rights implications of levying distress must be in the forefront of the mind of the landlord before he takes this step, and he must fully satisfy himself that taking this action is in accordance with the law.

13.3.2 Proposed abolition of distress

Following a consultation by the Lord Chancellor's Department in May 2001 (*Enforcement Review Consultation Paper No. 5: Distress for Rent*), the Tribunals, Courts and Enforcement Act 2007, Part 3 and Sch. 12 made provision for the reform of the law of distress. However, this part of the Act has not yet been brought into force, and there is now some doubt as to when, if ever, the new scheme will come into operation (see Humphreys, 'Has CRAR been lost forever?' [2009] EG (No.0915) 96).

At this stage, therefore, we suggest that all you need to know about the new scheme is that:

- the common law remedy of distress would be abolished;
- landlords of *residential* property would no longer be able to seize tenants' goods for non-payment of rent;
- landlords of *commercial* property would be able to use a new statutory procedure known as 'commercial rent arrears recovery' (or 'CRAR').

13.3.2.1 CRAR

Under CRAR, landlords of commercial property would still be able to take and sell tenants' goods but the new procedure would include safeguards for tenants and be subject to supervision by the courts. If needed, a more detailed account of CRAR can be found in the supplementary material on the Online Resource Centre linked to this book at **www.oxfordtextbooks.co.uk/orc/landlaw14e/** (referenced as 'W13' i.e., 'W' plus chapter number).

13.3.2.2 Present position

Until the new statutory provisions are brought into force, it remains the case that landlords of both residential and commercial property can still seize their tenants' goods for non-payment of rent. The human rights concerns noted in *Fuller v Happy Shopper Markets Ltd* [2001] 2 EGLR 32 are still unresolved.

13.4 Landlord's remedy of forfeiture

This section is rather lengthy, and we hope that the following list of topics will help you to see where we are going:

- Does the landlord have a right to forfeit the lease? (13.4.1)
- What must the landlord do before forfeiture? (13.4.2)
- Is a breach of covenant capable of being remedied? (13.4.3)
- How does the landlord forfeit the lease? (13.4.4)
- Can there be any relief from forfeiture? (13.4.5)
- Application of forfeiture and relief rules to tenancies in Trant Way (13.4.6)
- Reform of law of forfeiture (13.4.7)

13.4.1 Does the landlord have a right to forfeit the lease?

In addition to the other remedies for breach of covenant which we have already noted, the landlord may have a right to forfeit the lease i.e., to bring the lease to a premature end and recover physical possession of the property, thus ridding himself of the tenant altogether. However, he has the right to forfeit the lease only if:

- there is a provision in the lease permitting re-entry; and
- he has not waived the breach of covenant.

13.4.1.1 Provision for re-entry

Where a tenant's obligation is phrased as a *condition*, the landlord has an automatic right to re-enter if the condition is broken (see 11.1.2). Where the obligation is imposed by *covenant*, the landlord has no such right, unless there is a specific provision in the lease authorising forfeiture for breach of covenant. An example of a typical clause is given in cl. 5(a) on pp. 209–10.

13.4.1.2 Waiver of breach

Even where the lease contains a provision which gives the landlord a right of re-entry for breach, the landlord will be prevented from forfeiting the lease if he can be shown to have waived the breach. Waiver may be express (e.g., if the landlord states that he will ignore a breach) or may be implied.

Implied waiver Implied waiver may cause difficulties to a landlord, since he may be taken to have waived a breach when he did not intend to do so. For an implied waiver to arise the landlord must first know that a breach has occurred and thereafter have acted in such a way that he has treated the lease as still continuing. The most common way of waiving a breach is found where the landlord claims or accepts rent from the tenant when he knows that a breach has occurred (*Segal Securities Ltd v Thoseby* [1963] 1 QB 887). However, any act which treats the lease as continuing will do (*Ward v Day* (1864) 5 B & S 359), although Slade LJ in *Expert Clothing Service and Sales Ltd v Hillgate House* [1986] 1 Ch 340 at p. 360 emphasised that where some act other than the acceptance of rent is in question:

> the court is...free to look at all the circumstances of the case to consider whether the act...relied on [as constituting waiver is] so unequivocal that, when considered

> objectively, it could only be regarded as having been done consistently with the continued operation of a tenancy...

Waiver by demand or acceptance of rent may cause problems for the landlord because he is bound by the actions or knowledge of his servants or agents. Thus, should the landlord's agent accept rent at a date at which the landlord knew of a breach, this would amount to waiver. Of course, where the breach of covenant in question is a failure to pay rent, making the formal demand which may be a necessary step in forfeiture proceedings (see 13.4.2.1 below) will not constitute waiver.

You may wonder what happens these days when so many payments are made automatically by standing order or direct debit, and come into the creditor's account without any action on his part. This point was noted briefly by the Court of Appeal in *Thomas v Ken Thomas Ltd* [2007] 1 EGLR 31, in which Neuberger LJ quoted with approval the statement in *Woodfall on Landlord and Tenant,* 2006, vol. 1 at para. 17.098 that:

> It is considered that where the rent is paid directly into the landlord's bank account (e.g., by banker's order) it is not accepted if the landlord rejects the payment or repays it as quickly as possible.

Is breach 'once and for all' or continuing? In considering whether a breach has been waived, it is helpful to distinguish between these two types of breach. For example, a covenant to develop property by a fixed date is broken 'once and for all' if development is not completed by that date, and waiver will deprive the landlord of his right to forfeit. By contrast, breach of a covenant to keep property in repair continues throughout the whole period of disrepair. If the property remains unrepaired after the waiver and beyond the time during which the landlord knew the breach would continue, a further right to forfeit will arise, unaffected by the previous waiver (*Segal Securities Ltd v Thoseby* [1963] 1 QB 887).

13.4.2 What must the landlord do before forfeiture?

There are formal requirements which a landlord must observe before forfeiting a lease, and these differ depending on whether the landlord seeks to forfeit for breach of the covenant to pay rent, or for breach of some other covenant.

13.4.2.1 Forfeiture for non-payment of rent

Theoretically, the first thing that the landlord must do, before he attempts to forfeit the lease for non-payment of rent, is to make a *formal demand* for the rent. The formal demand must be made by the landlord, or his agent, at the demised premises between the hours of sunrise and sunset on the day on which payment is due (see *Duppa v Mayo* (1669) Saund 282 at p. 287 n. 16). However, this performance is usually rendered unnecessary by a clause in the lease which specifies that the landlord may forfeit for non-payment of rent 'whether formally demanded or not' (see lease, cl. 5(a), pp. 209–10). In any event, s. 210 of the Common Law Procedure Act 1852 dispenses with the need for a formal demand in cases where the rent is at least half a year in arrears and there are insufficient goods on the premises to satisfy the debt should distress be levied.

13.4.2.2 Forfeiture for breach of other covenants: the s. 146 notice

Forfeiture of a lease for breach of covenants other than that to pay rent is governed by LPA 1925, s. 146. The aim of the procedure required by s. 146 is to allow the tenant a chance to remedy his fault before the ultimate sanction of forfeiture is imposed. Accordingly the section imposes a requirement upon the landlord to serve notice in the prescribed form. The s. 146 notice must:

(a) specify the breach;

(b) require that the breach be remedied, if it is remediable; and

(c) require the tenant to pay financial compensation for the breach.

Item (a) must be contained in all notices; item (c) need not be included if the landlord does not require financial compensation (*Lock v Pearce* [1893] 2 Ch 271). It is item (b), requiring the breach to be remedied, which has given rise to problems for both tenant and landlord.

For the tenant, there is the difficulty that the landlord is not required to give any information about the remedy he requires, and the tenant may therefore be unsure of exactly what he must do to avoid forfeiture. For the landlord, the difficulty is that he is required to ask for the breach to be remedied only if it is 'capable of remedy'. If the breach is irremediable, it is enough for the notice to specify the breach (and ask for compensation if required) and the landlord may then proceed to forfeit the lease. However, if the landlord adopts this approach and a court subsequently considers that the breach could have been remedied, the notice will be invalid and the landlord will not be able to proceed to forfeiture.

The question of which breaches of covenant are capable of being remedied has caused the courts considerable difficulty, and so much case law has developed on the point that we will consider it separately in the next section (see 13.4.3).

Meanwhile, we must note briefly what happens after the s. 146 notice has been served.

Giving the tenant time If the landlord is not asking for the breach to be remedied, he must still give the tenant a reasonable (albeit short) time in which to consider his position before taking any further steps to forfeit the lease (*Horsey Estate Ltd v Steiger* [1899] 2 QB 79 at 91).

Where the notice requires the tenant to remedy the breach, the landlord must give the tenant a reasonable time in which to do so. Obviously, some breaches may be swiftly remedied, whilst others may take some time. Where a reasonable time has elapsed without remedial action by the tenant, the landlord may proceed to forfeit the lease. For details of how he should do this, see 13.4.4.

If the tenant acts on the notice, remedying the breach and paying any compensation required, the matter is at an end and the landlord cannot take any further action. An unsatisfactory aspect of this, from the landlord's point of view, is that he is unable to rid himself of an unsatisfactory tenant, who commits repeated breaches of covenant but always remedies them at the last moment.

13.4.3 Is a breach of covenant capable of being remedied?

Since the mid-1980s there has been a very marked change in the courts' approach to the question of whether a breach of covenant is 'capable of remedy' within the terms of LPA 1925, s. 146(1).

13.4.3.1 The old approach: remedying the breach

In earlier decisions attention focused on the fact of a breach by the tenant, rather than on the harm which such breach might cause to the landlord. As Harman J commented in *Hoffmann v Fineberg* [1949] Ch 245 at p. 253:

> in one sense, no breach can ever be remedied because there must always... be a time in which there has not been compliance with the covenant.

However, s. 146 clearly contemplated that some breaches were remediable, and, in deciding which these were, the courts found it helpful to distinguish between:

- positive and negative covenants, and
- continuing breaches and once-and-for-all breaches.

Positive and negative covenants At first instance in *Rugby School (Governors) v Tannahill* [1934] 1 KB 695 at p. 701, MacKinnon J suggested that breach of a positive covenant could be remedied, but breach of a negative one could not:

> A promise to do a thing, if broken, can be remedied by the thing being done. But breach of a promise not to do a thing cannot in any true sense be remedied; that which was done cannot be undone.

However, *obiter dicta* in the Court of Appeal's judgment in this case ([1935] 1 KB 87 at pp. 90–1) cast some doubt on this proposition, and suggested that in some cases (although not in the one before the court) breaches of a negative covenant might be remedied by immediately ceasing the activity prohibited by the covenant and giving an undertaking against further breach. Thus, it appeared that some breaches of both positive and negative covenants might be remediable and attention turned to the nature of the breach.

Continuing and once-and-for-all breaches The courts considered that a continuing breach of a positive covenant, such as a continuing failure to repair, could be remedied by undertaking the repairs, for the performance of the covenant, even if later than it should be, would fulfil the obligation. Similarly, a continuing breach of a negative covenant, such as using the premises for the purposes of trade, could, as the Court of Appeal suggested in *Rugby School (Governors) v Tannahill*, be remedied by ceasing the use. By contrast, some covenants were broken once and for all on the occurrence of some event. A positive covenant to make alterations to a building by a prescribed date was broken once and for all when the work was not done by that date; a negative covenant against making alterations to the property without the landlord's consent was broken once and for all when the alterations were done without that consent. In the courts' view, such breaches could not be remedied; the breach had occurred on a given event in the past, and there was no way in which the tenant could re-write history to make it appear that it had not.

This rather literal approach to the question may have been logically correct, but must have been somewhat baffling to the tenant, who, for instance, might have been willing to undo the alterations he had made without consent, and could not see why this would not amount to 'remedying' the breach. It also led to a result which, although again logically correct, seemed somewhat strange: if the tenant had already ceased the activity complained of, the breach was, in the court's view, irremediable, because there was no longer any continuing breach which could be put right (a view taken by the Court of Appeal in *Scala House & District Property Co. Ltd v Forbes* [1974] QB 575, and subsequently described by O'Connor LJ in *Expert Clothing Service and Sales Ltd v Hillgate House Ltd* [1986] 1 Ch 340 at p. 364 as 'unsatisfactory').

The view that certain once-and-for-all breaches were irremediable may seem unduly harsh, but you should bear in mind that tenants in such a position were able to apply for relief from forfeiture (see 13.4.5), and that the courts did grant such relief even though the breach could not, technically, be remedied. An example is to be found in *Scala House & District Property Co. Ltd v Forbes*, where subletting without the landlord's consent was held to be an irremediable breach, but relief from forfeiture was granted. In deciding to give relief, the court took a number of reasons into account, including the fact that the sublease had been created through an error by the tenant's solicitor, and that the tenant had already procured the surrender of the sublease, so that the subtenant was no longer in possession.

Thus, tenants who had committed irremediable breaches could be saved from losing their leases, but nevertheless were involved in the uncertainty and expense of seeking relief from the court, while had the breach been treated by the landlord as remediable, it could have been remedied on a s. 146 notice without reference to the court.

13.4.3.2 The modern approach: remedying the harm caused

A major change in the courts' approach to the question of remediable breach is to be found in the Court of Appeal decision in *Expert Clothing Service & Sales Ltd v Hillgate House Ltd* [1986] 1 Ch 340. In this case both the covenants in question were *positive*: (a) to give notice to the landlord of any charge created over the property and (b) to reconstruct the premises for occupation by a stated date, or as soon as possible thereafter. The tenant charged the premises without giving notice, and allowed the specified date to pass without making the reconstruction. The landlord served a notice under LPA 1925, s. 146, which complained of the two breaches but did not require them to be remedied, and in subsequent court proceedings was granted an order for possession. On appeal, the Court of Appeal held that both of these breaches were remediable; accordingly the landlord's notice was invalid, and he was not entitled to possession.

In giving judgment, Slade LJ emphasised (at p. 358) that the principal object of s. 146 procedure is to give the tenant the opportunity to remedy the breach:

> An important purpose of the s. 146 procedure is to give even tenants who have hitherto lacked the will or the means to comply with their obligations one last chance... before the landlord re-enters.

In considering whether a breach was remediable, the court should focus on the harm which had been done to the landlord and on whether that harm could be remedied. The test was said (at p. 358) to be whether compliance with the covenant (albeit late) together with financial compensation would

> have effectively remedied the harm which the lessors had suffered or were likely to suffer from the breach.

In other words, emphasis shifts from attempting to remedy the breach (by 'undoing' it or trying to put the clock back) to remedying the harm which that breach has caused.

In certain cases compliance plus compensation would not be enough to remedy the harm caused by the breach, and in these cases the breach would be irremediable.

However, in the case before the court, any damage to the landlord by breach of the positive covenants was capable of being remedied by the late performance coupled if necessary with compensation. In *obiter dicta*, the court suggested that even negative covenants are very often capable of remedy by compliance, by ceasing to do the act complained of, so that if, for instance, a covenant has been broken by the erection of window-boxes, it may be remedied by removing the boxes and paying for the repair of any damage done.

Some 10 years later, this approach to the question of remediability was applied by the Court of Appeal to the once-and-for-all breach of negative covenants in *Savva v Hussein* (1997) 73 P&CR 150. Here the landlord had treated the breach of negative covenants (not to put up signs or alter the premises without the landlord's consent) as being irremediable. The court referred with approval to the approach adopted in *Expert Clothing Service & Sales Ltd v Hillgate House Ltd*, stating that the question posed there in relation to positive covenants was equally relevant in considering negative covenants. There was nothing in the statute or in logic that required the courts to differentiate between these two forms of covenant. The court accepted that it was established law that breach of a covenant not to assign without the landlord's consent could not be remedied (citing *Scala House and District Property Co. Ltd v Forbes* [1974] QB 575), but was of the opinion that failure to seek consent for other actions did not, by itself, make the breach irremediable. There was a remedy if the mischief caused by the breach could be removed. In the present case the breaches could have been remedied by removing the signs or restoring the property to its original condition, and the landlord's failure to require the tenant to remedy his breaches made the s. 146 notice invalid.

Following these two modern decisions of the Court of Appeal, it now appears that most breaches of covenant can be remedied, but there are still certain breaches which continue to be regarded as irremediable.

13.4.3.3 Breaches which cannot be remedied

Breaches causing irremediable harm

A breach of covenant cannot be remedied if it causes irremediable harm to the landlord. A number of earlier decisions regarded the use of premises for immoral purposes (*Rugby School (Governors) v Tannahill* [1935] 1 KB 87) or for gambling (*Hoffmann v Fineberg* [1949] Ch 245) as irremediable breaches of covenant, because the improper use would cast a stigma on the premises, which could not be removed by merely ceasing the use. (Note, however, that in *Glass v Kencakes Ltd* [1966] 1 QB 611 the tenant was held to have remedied his breach when he forfeited the sublease of his subtenant, who had used the premises for immoral purposes.) In more recent cases, breach has been held to be irremediable where the premises were used for the sale of pornographic material (*Dunraven Securities v Holloway* (1982) 264 EG 709), or for activities in breach of the Official Secrets Acts (*Van Haarlem v Kasner* (1992) 64 P&CR 214).

Although it is important to remember that changes in society's view of morality may make some activities less injurious to the property than they might have been formerly, it seems clear that breaches which in modern times would be seen as casting a stigma on the property would not satisfy the *Expert Clothing* test, and would therefore still be regarded as irremediable.

Other examples of breaches which cause irremediable harm to the landlord may be found in various hypothetical cases considered by the Court of Appeal in *Expert Clothing*. They include: breach of covenant to insure against fire, which would be irremediable after the property had burned down; and failure to alter or repair property where there is insufficient time to complete the work required before the end of the lease.

Breach of covenant against assigning, etc.

The examples of irremediable breach considered above are all consistent with the modern principle that a breach is remediable if the harm caused to the landlord can be remedied. However there is one further example that is not consistent with that principle: the breach of a covenant against assigning etc cannot be remedied even if the harm it caused to the landlord could be undone. On this point the Court of Appeal continues to regard itself as bound by its earlier decision in *Scala House & District Property Co Ltd v Forbes* [1974] QB 575 (see 13.4.3.1; *Expert Clothing Service and Sales v Hillgate House* (1986] 1 Ch 340 at p. 363; and *Savva v Hussein* (1997) 73 P&CR 150 at p. 154).

The matter was considered yet again by the Court of Appeal in *Akici v LR Butlin Ltd* [2006] 1 WLR 201. In this case the tenant was in breach of a covenant against sharing possession of the premises and at first instance the judge considered himself bound by *Scala* to hold that the breach was not capable of remedy. In the Court of Appeal, Neuberger LJ referred disparagingly to the *Scala* decision, describing it as 'demonstrably fallacious and inconsistent with common sense' (para. 74). If the matter had been free from authority, he would be attracted to the view that breaches of covenants against assigning and subletting could be remedied by re-assignment or surrender of the sublease. The judge accepted that the present court was bound by its earlier decision, but regarded it as applying only to transactions in breach of covenant which created or transferred a legal interest (i.e., to assignments and subleases; and, he suggested, also to mortgages granted in breach of covenants requiring the landlord's consent (para. 67)). There was, however, no need to extend the rule, and he considered that a breach of a covenant against sharing or parting with possession fell outside the terms of *Scala* and was capable of being remedied (para. 73). Observations to the contrary by Slade LJ in *Expert Clothing* were dismissed as being *obiter dicta* (para. 75).

You may like to note that these recent observations on the scope of *Scala* are themselves *obiter dicta*, since the decision of the Court of Appeal in favour of the tenant was based not on whether the breach could be remedied but on the invalidity of the landlord's s. 146 notice, which had failed to specify the breach accurately.

13.4.4 How does the landlord forfeit the lease?

Traditionally there were two ways in which the landlord could end the lease and regain possession of the property:

- by self-help; or
- by seeking a court order for possession.

Both methods were available irrespective of the reason for forfeiture.

13.4.4.1 Self-help by physical re-entry

It used to be open to the landlord to forfeit the lease by taking possession of the premises, and the lease came to an end with the landlord's entry on the property. Today this right is considerably restricted. Under the Protection from Eviction Act, 1977, s. 2, it cannot be used to forfeit leases of residential property. In cases where self-help is available, such as in leases of commercial property, the landlord must ensure that any such entry is peaceable and without force (Criminal Law Act, 1977, s. 6).

In *Billson v Residential Apartments Ltd* [1992] 1 AC 494 the House of Lords accepted that this method of forfeiture still existed for commercial property, but was very critical of it, referring to the actions of the landlord as 'a dawn raid' (p. 540) and describing physical re-entry as a 'dubious and dangerous method of determining the lease'

(p. 536). In addition, there are now concerns that this process may infringe rights under the Human Rights Act 1998 by depriving the tenant of his property (the estate in the land) without reference to a court.

13.4.4.2 Seeking an order for possession

The alternative and more acceptable method (and indeed the only method in respect of residential property today) is to obtain a court order for possession.

It is important to note that even where the landlord chooses to regain possession by court order, the lease is regarded as being forfeited at the outset, by the commencement of court proceedings. Although the former tenant may in fact remain on the land for some considerable time, pending the court action and enforcement of any resulting order, he is no longer a tenant and the landlord cannot enforce any of the obligations in the lease against him. A sum of money for use of the land during this period can be recovered, but technically this is not rent, but the 'mesne profits' payable by a trespasser on the land.

13.4.4.3 Statutory restrictions on forfeiture

Although the statutory protection of tenants is in general too detailed for this book (see 10.5.1), we must mention briefly that there are a number of provisions which regulate the operation of forfeiture procedures in relation to particular types of tenancies. An example, in respect of long leases of residential property, is to be found in ss. 168–169 of the Commonhold and Leasehold Reform Act 2002, which provides that a notice under s. 146 may not be served by the landlord, unless the tenant has admitted a breach of covenant or the fact that a breach has occurred has been determined by a leasehold valuation tribunal or in other court or arbitration proceedings. In addition, s. 168 of the Act prevents a landlord from forfeiting such a lease for failure to pay rent or other specified charges where the sum owed is less than a prescribed amount or has been due for less than a prescribed period.

13.4.5 Can there be any relief from forfeiture?

Even when the landlord has taken steps to forfeit the lease, the tenant may preserve his position by seeking relief.

In case of failure to pay rent, the tenant can generally obtain relief (i.e., be allowed to keep his lease) provided he pays the arrears of rent and any costs incurred by the landlord.

In the case of breach of covenants other than that to pay rent LPA 1925, s. 146(2), allows the tenant to apply to the court for relief. If the landlord has forfeited the lease by starting court proceedings, the tenant may seek relief at any time before the landlord actually re-enters the property. Rather surprisingly however, it was held in *Billson v Residential Apartments Ltd* [1992] 1 AC 494 that where the landlord uses the self-help method of retaking possession without reference to the court, the tenant may still seek relief after that re-entry. This seems to be another reason why the landlord would be well-advised to seek possession through the courts, although, if he does this, the tenant may of course seek relief in the course of the proceedings.

The tenant will usually obtain relief because he is at last willing, or able, to remedy the breach, but as we have already seen from the decision in *Scala House & District Property Co. Ltd v Forbes* [1974] QB 575 relief can also be available where the breach is technically irremediable. In such cases the court may need to weigh the harm caused to the landlord by the breach against the advantage which he will gain by recovering the property. Thus, in *Van Haarlam v Kasner* (1992) 64 P&CR 214 the court considered that the value to the landlord of forfeiting a lease with some 80 years left to run was out of all proportion to the damage caused by the tenant's irremediable breach, and indicated that it would have been willing to grant relief had the question arisen.

13.4.5.1 **Conceptual difficulties**

In describing the position of a tenant who obtains relief, it is usual to say that he is allowed to 'keep' his lease, or that the lease 'continues as though the landlord had never taken action to forfeit it'. It may occur to you that in saying this we appear to contradict our earlier statements that the lease is forfeited and comes to an end when the landlord re-enters the property or commences court proceedings. This apparent inconsistency draws attention to the conceptual difficulty about the status of the lease in what is sometimes described as a 'twilight' period. If the lease had really come to an end, you would expect the process of giving relief to be described as the granting of a new lease, but this is not the language that is used. Instead, it seems as though the lease is dormant and capable of being revived, rather than completely dead. We do not suggest that you concern yourself with this conundrum in any detail, but it is worth noting as one of the aspects of the current law that needs reform.

13.4.5.2 **Holders of derivative interests**

A number of people may hold interests derived from the lease, which will be lost if the lease itself is forfeited. Subtenants and mortgagees are both in this position and, as we note below, are entitled to seek relief from forfeiture. However, the landlord is not obliged to tell them that the tenant is in breach of covenant, and they may not find out about the impending forfeiture until a late stage of the proceedings.

There may also be others with an interest in the lease (for example, a person with an option to purchase the leasehold estate) who currently have no protection from forfeiture.

1. *Protection for subtenants when the head-lease is forfeited*

Under LPA 1925 s. 146(4), a subtenant may apply to the court for relief if the head lease from which he derives his title is forfeited. If relief is granted, the subtenant will become an immediate tenant of the head landlord, but for the period of the sublease, not for that of the head lease. The court may impose any conditions it sees fit upon the subtenant (e.g., compliance with covenants in the original head lease or payment of a higher rent—as in *London Diocesan Fund v Phithwa* [2005] 1 WLR 3956 (see 12.3.4)).

A similar provision in the County Courts Act 1984 (s. 138(9A)) enables the subtenant to seek relief where the forfeiture is for non-payment of rent.

2. *Protection for mortgagees where the lease is forfeited*

Relief from forfeiture may also be sought under the provisions relating to subtenants by a mortgagee who has lent money to a tenant on the security of his lease. If the lease is forfeited by the landlord for breach of covenant, the mortgagee will lose his security and could suffer considerable financial loss. As we shall see in Chapter 24, a mortgage of leasehold property is made by giving the mortgagee a sublease of the property, or a charge over the property which gives him the same rights as if the mortgage had been made by sublease. Accordingly, the mortgagee may seek relief from forfeiture in the same way as any other subtenant, and, if successful, will hold a lease directly from the landlord which will continue to provide security for the loan.

13.4.6 Application of the forfeiture and relief rules to tenancies at 7 Trant Way

You may recall from 12.9.3 that the current situation with regard to 7 Trant Way is as follows:

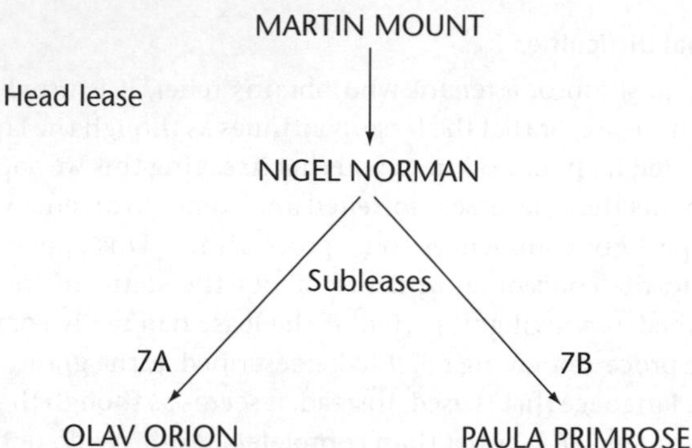

The head lease and both subleases contain covenants (a) against keeping animals on the property and (b) to keep the premises in good repair. Nigel Norman is also bound by a covenant to pay rent of £900 per month. For the last five months, Mr Norman has not paid his rent to Mr Mount, even though both the subtenants, Mr Orion and Miss Primrose, have been paying their rent regularly to Mr Norman. In addition, for the last three months Mr Orion has been stabling his daughter's pony in a shed at the back of the property. What can Mr Mount do to enforce the covenants which have been broken?

13.4.6.1 Enforcement of covenant against keeping animals

As we have seen already (12.9), there is no privity of contract or estate between a head landlord and a subtenant, and generally one of them cannot take action directly against the other. However, the covenant against keeping animals is a negative one, restricting the use of the property, and therefore Mr Mount could proceed directly against Mr Orion, seeking an injunction to restrain the breach, under the *Tulk v Moxhay* doctrine described in Chapter 26. Mr Mount could not rely on s. 3(5) of the Landlord and Tenant (Covenants) Act 1995 (12.9.1.1) because that Act, in general, applies only to leases granted on or after 1 January 1996, but this section could be used if a similar situation arose in respect of a lease which falls within the Act's provisions.

Alternatively, or additionally, Mr Mount may wish to take action against his tenant, Mr Norman. Provided the operation of LPA 1925, s. 79, was not expressly excluded in the lease, Mr Norman will have covenanted on behalf of 'persons deriving title under him', and so will be liable for the breach, even though it has been caused by his subtenant. Accordingly, Mr Mount should serve a s. 146 notice on Mr Norman. It is likely that this breach will be regarded as remediable (see *Savva v Hussein* (1997) 73 P&CR 150) and so the notice should ask that the situation be remedied. After service of the notice, Mr Mount must allow Mr Norman a reasonable period in which to remedy the breach. On receipt of the s. 146 notice Mr Norman would be advised to serve a similar notice on Mr Orion, who is himself in breach of a covenant in the sublease of 7A. The result will be either that Mr Orion ceases to keep the pony on the premises or that the sublease will be forfeited for the breach. Either result will have the effect of remedying the breach of the covenant in the head lease.

13.4.6.2 Forfeiture for non-payment of rent

The head lease contains the usual clause which exempts the landlord from making a formal demand for the rent and also contains a clause allowing him to re-enter the premises if any covenant is broken. Accordingly, unless Mr Mount has in some manner waived the breach complained of, he may start proceedings against Mr Norman to forfeit the lease for the non-payment of the rent. (Alternatively, as these are not residential premises, he could use the self-help remedy of physical re-entry, but for the reasons we noted earlier he would be better advised to seek an order for possession.) At or before the hearing Mr Norman may ask for relief from forfeiture, and this will normally be granted as long as he pays the back rent and the costs of the action. In practice any offer of payment, as long as it is reasonable (e.g., by instalments over a prescribed period) will be accepted by the court. If, however, Mr Norman cannot make a reasonable offer, the lease will be forfeited for breach of the covenant to pay rent.

13.4.6.3 Relief of subtenant

If, for any reason, the head lease is forfeited, Miss Primrose is placed in a difficult position. Although she has behaved perfectly properly, she is in danger of losing her own lease because it is dependent upon the head lease from which it is derived. Accordingly Miss Primrose should apply for relief under LPA 1925, s. 146(4). As she is wholly innocent, it is very likely that if the head lease is forfeited, Miss Primrose will be protected by the court. If this happens she will become a direct tenant of Mr Mount, for the period and upon the terms of her sublease but subject to any altered terms imposed by the court. If, however, Mr Norman manages to avoid the forfeiture of the head lease, Miss Primrose has nothing to fear. As long as the head lease is valid the sublease will be safe, provided, of course, that Miss Primrose continues to observe the covenants in her own sublease.

13.4.7 Reform of the law of forfeiture of leases

13.4.7.1 What is wrong with the current system?

It has long been accepted that the current rules about forfeiture of leases are in urgent need of reform. Defects identified in the present system include:

- the unnecessary complication of having different rules for covenants and conditions; and for failure to pay rent and for other breaches of covenant;
- the complexity of rules relating to failure to pay rent (we have not troubled you with any details of these rules, but they are very complicated);
- aspects of the process that are unsatisfactory for landlords:
  - dangers of inadvertent waiver;
  - inability to get rid of a tenant who persists in breaking covenants but always remedies the breach 'just in time';
  - fact that lease ends when landlord begins proceedings for forfeiture, so that he is no longer entitled to rent or the performance of other obligations;
- aspects of the process which are unsatisfactory for the tenant:
  - s. 146 notice not required to give any details of the remedy required by landlord;
  - forfeiture of a long lease may result in considerable loss of capital invested in its purchase;

- the lack of adequate protection for those with interests derived from the lease;
- the conceptual difficulties which arise from the termination of the lease by re-entry or the start of court proceedings, followed by a 'twilight' period during which the lease may be revived by relief; and
- the need to include clauses in leases providing for forfeiture and excluding the formal demand for rent.

13.4.7.2 **Law Commission proposals for reform**

For over 20 years now, the Law Commission has been putting forward proposals for change, most recently in the consultation paper *Termination of Tenancies for Tenant Default*, 2004, Law Com No. 284. Following the consultation, final proposals, together with a draft Bill, are contained in the report *Termination of Tenancies for Tenant Default*, 2006, Law Com No. 303 Cm 6946.

The 2006 report recommends the complete abolition of the current law of forfeiture and its replacement with a statutory scheme for the 'termination of tenancies for tenant default' (a useful overview of which is given in Part 2 of the report). The scheme would apply to all commercial leases and to residential leases for more than 21 years (shorter residential leases being in general protected by statutory provisions for security of tenure which are outside the scope of this book). Two methods of terminating a tenancy would be available to the landlord:

- making a 'termination claim' to the court; or
- using a 'summary termination process', which would not involve the court unless the tenant wished to do so.

An outline of these two procedures is available in the supplementary material on the Online Resource Centre linked to this book at **www.oxfordtextbooks.co.uk/orc/landlaw14e/** (referenced as 'W13' i.e., 'W' plus chapter number).

The new scheme is designed to deal with all the defects in the current law which are noted above (and, indeed, many others as well). Thus:

- it would apply to all breaches of a tenant's obligations under the lease, whether imposed by covenant or condition; and there would no longer be any difference between procedures for non-payment of rent and for other breaches;
- the position of the landlord would be improved: the concept of waiver of breach would have no place in the new scheme, and the lease would continue until the end of the termination proceedings, so that the landlord could continue to receive rent while he was taking steps to end the lease. Where a tenant repeatedly failed to observe his obligations under the lease, the fact that he had remedied the current default would not prevent the landlord from seeking termination;
- the position of the tenant would be improved. Where the landlord required him to remedy a default, he would be given details of what he was required to do. Where the landlord sought to terminate the lease, the court would have power to make a range of alternative orders, including an order for sale of the property, as a result of which the tenant might be able to recover some of the capital he had invested in buying the lease;
- the scheme would recognise a wide category of interests derived from the lease, including not only subleases and mortgages, but also equitable charges, options

and rights to acquire an overriding lease under the Landlord and Tenant (Covenants) Act 1995 (see 12.4.2.3). The report recommends that holders of these interests (to be known as 'qualifying interests') should have the same rights to information and protection as are given to the tenant himself under the proposed scheme;

- the new procedures would apply automatically to all leases created after the scheme came into operation, and to those existing leases which contained provisions for forfeiture for breach of covenant. In future, there would be no need to include a proviso for forfeiture in new leases, but the landlord would be required to give to the tenant an 'explanatory statement', in a prescribed form, setting out the landlord's right to take termination action in response to a tenant default;
- The lease would continue until ended on a date specified by a termination order from the court or at the end of the period prescribed for the summary process. Where the lease was ended without reference to the court, any interested party could make a late application for a 'post-termination order'. On such an application, the court could make a range of orders, including one for the grant of a new lease, but there would be no question of reviving the old lease.

13.4.7.3 What next?

There is, as yet, no indication of whether the recommendations of the Law Commission will be adopted. There was, however, very considerable support for the proposals during the consultation, and it is to be hoped that the report will not be left to gather dust on the shelf.

FURTHER READING

Specific performance

Tettenborn, 'Absolving the Undeserving: Shopping Centres, Specific Performance and the Law of Contract' [1998] 62 Conv 23.

Luxton, 'Are You being Served? Enforcing Keep-Open Covenants in Leases' [1998] 62 Conv 396.

Protection from harassment

Cowan, 'Harassment and Unlawful Eviction in the Private Rented Sector—A Study of Law In (-) Action' [2001] 65 Conv 249 (research findings on effectiveness of Protection from Eviction Act).

Distress

Walton, 'Landlord's Distress—Past Its Sell By Date?' [2000] 64 Conv 508.

Karas and Maurici, 'The human rights factor' [1999] EG—4 November 2006 (No.9917) 126 (the human rights implications for distress and other self-help remedies).

Dale, Rivers and Allen, 'Gently does it' [2007] EG—6 October 2007 (No. 0740) 264 (an account of the new CRAR procedure).

Humphreys, 'Has CRAR been lost forever?' [2009] EG—18 April 2009 (no. 0915) 96.

Forfeiture

Gravells, 'Forfeiture of Leases for Breach of Covenant: Pre-Action Notices and Remediability' [2006] JBL 830 (discusses *Akici v LR Butlin Ltd*, and some aspects of Law Commission Consultation Paper, 2004, No. 174).

Landlord and Tenant Law: Termination of Tenancies Bill, 1994, Law Com No. 221—Appendix C—defects in current law of forfeiture.

Termination of Tenancies for Tenant Default, 2006, Law Com No.303 Cm 6946—see in particular paras. 1.7–1.12 (problems of the current law) and Part 2 (overview of proposed scheme).

Bridge, 'A dinosaur close to extinction' [2006] EG—4 November 2006 (No. 0644) 187 (an account of the Law Commission's proposals by one of the commissioners).

14

Commonhold

Commonhold is a new system of land-holding introduced by Part 1 of the Commonhold and Leasehold Reform Act 2002, which came into force on 27 September 2004.

14.1 Why did we need commonhold?

Commonhold was designed to facilitate freehold ownership of 'interdependent properties'; that is, individual units such as flats in an apartment building, homes in a retirement village, and workshops or offices on an industrial estate. Although these sound like very different types of property—some residential and some commercial—they have several similarities.

For a start, there are likely to be 'common parts' in all these developments—such as stairs, lifts, and car parks—which do not belong to any individual unit but are used by all unit holders. Arrangements have to be made for ownership and upkeep of these areas.

The other similarity between all these developments is that, in the interests of all the owners, there need to be regulations controlling the use of individual units, and requiring each to be kept in a proper state of repair. If a flat in a block is allowed to deteriorate it can have an adverse effect on those above and below it, and obviously excessive noise or other anti-social behaviour will be of immediate concern to the neighbours. What is needed is a web of mutually enforceable covenants under which each unit holder takes on certain duties with the understanding that he also has the right to enforce the same obligations against other owners in the development.

This could easily be achieved at the outset by requiring each purchaser to enter into a mix of positive and negative covenants, the positive ones requiring him or her to keep the unit in repair and perhaps to contribute to the cost of maintaining the common parts, and the negative ones restraining certain activities, such as the keeping of pets. However, over the years the units are likely to change hands, and it is essential that the original covenants should run to bind and benefit the new owners. We have already seen that the burden of *restrictive* covenants made between freehold owners runs with the land (2.5.5; see further, Chapter 26); but unfortunately, the same is not true of *positive* covenants (26.4.2.2(1)), and as a result, there is no easy way to provide for the enforcement of positive obligations against successors of the original freehold owners.

Thus freehold ownership of flats and other interdependent units has always raised problems about ownership and management of the common parts, and enforcement of obligations between individual unit holders. For this reason, such properties are almost invariably sold on long leases. Common parts are retained and managed by the landlord and, when individual units change hands, covenants in the individual leases will run to benefit and bind the new owners (see Chapter 12).

14.2 Disadvantages of leasehold ownership

From the tenant's point of view, however, there are a number of disadvantages in leasehold ownership. Leases are of limited duration, and unlike freehold property a leasehold estate loses value as time goes by. Further, many tenants experience difficulty with their landlords, such as failure to do necessary repairs, and there is always the risk that a relatively minor breach of covenant may lead to forfeiture of the lease. As a result, it was thought that purchasers would prefer to have the freehold title to their property, and the commonhold system was developed to meet this need.

14.3 How commonhold works

Commonhold provides a system which can apply to both new and existing developments. Each unit holder owns the freehold estate in his property, and enters into a range of positive and negative covenants. These are enforceable between all unit holders in the property, and run to bind and benefit the new owner when a property changes hands. All unit holders are members of the 'commonhold association', a company limited by guarantee, which owns the common parts and is responsible for all aspects of managing the property. Unit holders take part in decisions affecting the commonhold through their membership of the association.

14.4 A disappointing start for commonhold

Despite the demand for freehold ownership of flats and similar property, there has so far been very little use of the commonhold system. Property developers seem to be wary of it, and it appears that by April 2011 only 17 commonhold registrations had been made (see Megarry and Wade, para. 33–001). Interestingly, the Law Commission continues to regard commonhold as a viable system, describing its provisions for the running of positive covenants as 'filling a major lacuna in the law' (see *Making Land Work: Easements, Covenants and Profits à Prendre*, Law Com No. 327, June 2011, at para. 1.10). It remains to be seen whether developers will share this opinion.

We know that commonhold in its present state is unlikely to merit much attention in your study of land law, but if it is of interest and you need to know more about it, you will find a full account in the supplementary material on the Online Resource Centre linked to this book at **www.oxfordtextbooks.co.uk/orc/landlaw14e.**

PART IV

Trusts and proprietary estoppel

Introduction

In this part of the book we move on to consider more complex forms of ownership, in which ownership at law and ownership in equity are separated. This is the area of trusts, with which you may have some general familiarity from your other reading. If, however, you have never previously had occasion to consider the law of trusts, you may find it helpful to read an introductory book on trusts and equity before going on to consider the special rules relating to trusts which have an estate or interest in land as the trust property.

We start in Chapter 15 with a brief outline of certain matters relating to trusts, and an explanation of the two forms of settlement which existed before the Trusts of Land and Appointment of Trustees Act 1996 (TOLATA 1996) introduced the new trust of land in 1997.

In Chapter 16 we consider the rules relating to co-ownership of land. As you will see, these are included in this part because all co-owned estates are subject to the statutory imposition of a trust (these days, the new trust of land). We then deal in detail with that new trust in Chapter 17.

In Chapter 18 you will find a short note about the SLA settlement, the other form of trust which still exists in relation to land, and in Chapter 19 we give a very brief account of the 'perpetuities and accumulations' rules. We understand that these topics are unlikely to be studied in detail these days, so we have reduced our coverage, but provide more detailed material on both of them on the Online Resource Centre: **www.oxfordtextbooks.co.uk/orc/landlaw14e/**.

Finally, we look in some detail at resulting and constructive trusts in Chapter 20 and in Chapter 21 consider the doctrine of proprietary estoppel.

15

Trusts: an introduction

In this introductory chapter we try to provide a brief outline of certain matters relating to trusts, but we would emphasise that what follows is a highly selective account, aimed simply at giving you the information we think you need for land law purposes.

15.1 Separation of title and enjoyment

We explained briefly in Chapter 2 (2.5.2) that the essential characteristic of the trust is the separation of title to property from the right to use and enjoy it. The trustee is the owner of the property (i.e. he has the 'title'), but he holds it not for himself but for the beneficiary, who has the right to use and enjoy the property. The beneficiary is protected by equity and accordingly has an equitable interest in that property. This equitable interest is sometimes described as 'the beneficial interest', and we use both terms interchangeably.

In general, the trustee will have the *legal* title (in a trust of land, he will usually hold the legal estate). However, it must be realised that it is also possible to create a trust of an equitable interest; for example, a beneficiary under a trust may transfer his equitable interest to some other person and direct him to hold it on trust for some third party. Thus, the interest of the beneficiary under a trust is always equitable, but that of the trustee may be legal or equitable, according to the nature of the property which is subject to the trust.

TITLE (usually legal, but could be equitable	**BENEFICIAL INTEREST** (always equitable)
Trustee/s	Beneficiary/ies

15.2 Express and implied trusts

In Chapter 2 we also noted that trusts may be created expressly or may arise without express creation through recognition by the courts. It is convenient to describe this second category of trusts, those which are not expressly created, as 'implied trusts'; this terminology was adopted by the court in *Cowcher v Cowcher* [1972] 1 WLR 425 at p. 430. This usage is convenient, as long as you are not confused by the fact that the phrase 'implied trust' is also used in LPA 1925, s. 53(2), to describe one type of non-express trust—see below.

15.2.1 Express trusts

While a trust may be *created* simply by the settlor manifesting an intention to do so, a trust relating to land will not be *enforceable* unless there is some written evidence of that intention. LPA 1925, s. 53(1)(b) provides:

> a declaration of trust respecting any land or any interest therein must be manifested and proved by some writing signed by some person who is able to declare such a trust or by his will.

Thus, while a trust of land may be created orally, a beneficiary will not be able to enforce his interest under it unless the trust is evidenced in writing. The trust will be valid, but unenforceable.

15.2.2 Implied (non-express) trusts

By contrast, writing is not required for the creation or enforcement of non-express trusts. LPA 1925, s. 53(2) provides that the earlier part of the section (which imposes the requirement for evidence in writing which we have noted above):

> does not affect the creation or operation of resulting, implied or constructive trusts.

15.2.2.1 Resulting trusts

Resulting trusts can be found in a variety of situations, but at present all you need to know is that such a trust may arise where one person contributes to the purchase price of property which is being bought by another. Unless the contribution was intended to be a gift, the new owner will hold the property on trust for himself and the contributor, each of them being entitled to a share in the beneficial interest proportionate to the amount which each has contributed.

15.2.2.2 Constructive trusts

Constructive trusts arise by operation of law rather than by the intention of the parties. They are imposed upon the owner of property, in general as a result of his conduct, so that instead of enjoying his property as beneficial owner, he is required to hold it, in whole or in part, for the benefit of some other person.

The form of constructive trust with which we are principally concerned in this book has come to be known as a 'common intention' constructive trust. It arises where two people, X and Y, have agreed (i.e., have shared or 'common' intentions) that Y shall have an interest in property owned by X. If Y acts to his/her detriment in reliance on this agreement, equity regards the property as subject to a constructive trust, under which X is obliged to give effect to the parties' common intentions. This type of constructive trust was developed in cases involving disputes about the family home (see Chapters 16 and 20), but the courts have also relied on it to enforce agreements for the 'sale or other disposition of interests in land' which do not satisfy the formal requirements of the Law of Property (Miscellaneous Provisions) Act 1989, s. 2 (see 5.5).

15.3 Statutory trusts

In certain circumstances statutes provide that property is to be held on trust. Thus, for example, statutory trusts operate in all cases of co-ownership of land, and similar trusts are applied to property where the owner has died without making a will (Administration of Estates Act 1925, s. 33(1)).

15.4 Circumstances in which land may be held on trust

It is always possible for a landowner to provide that his property should be held by trustees on trust for one adult beneficiary who is solely entitled to it (a 'bare' trust). More usually, however, land is held on trust for one of the following reasons:

- *The intended beneficiary is still a minor* i.e., under the age of 18 years (see 17.10.1).
- *The property is subject to co-ownership* i.e., two or more people are entitled to enjoy the property at the same time. As we mentioned above, a statutory trust is imposed in these circumstances (see further 15.5.3).
- *The property is to be enjoyed by several people* in succession as, for example, where land is given 'to A for life and then to B'. Where successive interests like these are created by a disposition, the arrangement is known as a 'settlement'.

15.4.1 Settlements

Before 1997 there were two forms of trust used to create settlements relating to land:

- the *strict settlement* (giving rise to what is usually called 'settled land'), the ancient form of settlement, governed largely after 1925 by the Settled Land Act 1925 (SLA 1925); and
- the *trust for sale*, which was slightly the more modern form and governed largely after 1925 by the LPA 1925.

In the main, these two forms of trust have now been replaced by a new type of trust, the trust of land introduced by the Trusts of Land and Appointment of Trustees Act 1996 (TOLATA 1996), which came into force on 1 January 1997. We deal in detail with this new trust in Chapter 17. Although we usually prefer to avoid excursions into historical matters, we feel that you need a very short explanation of the two older forms of settlement and how they developed, so that you can understand occasional references to them in later chapters.

15.5 A short historical background

15.5.1 The old ways of making settlements

15.5.1.1 Strict settlements (or 'Settled Land Act settlements')

We must begin by emphasising that we are describing a process which began in the Middle Ages, and that, as far as the history of the settlement is concerned, we are talking about people who owned large amounts of land. The landowner who made the sort of strict settlement we will describe probably owned at least several large country estates, and at a later period may also have had a London town house, a 'hunting-box' in the shires and a grouse moor in Scotland. The settlement in its developed form is designed to meet the needs of large landowners, like the Victorian Trollope's Duke of Omnium, rather than those of small modern owner-occupiers.

The purpose of making a strict settlement was in the main to ensure that the family estates (to which there might well be some sentimental attachment) remained in the family, passing intact to the heir, and that at the same time provision was made from the income of the estate for wives, widows and younger children. In a typical marriage settlement, made by a fee simple owner on his marriage, the settlor would deprive himself of his absolute title to the estate and create a mere life estate for himself, followed by a fee tail in favour of his eldest (probably yet unborn) son (see 1.5.1.3). He would also make provision for payments from the income of the estate: a personal allowance to his wife ('pin-money') during the marriage, with a larger sum to support her during her widowhood, if she survived him, and 'portions' for the daughters and younger sons to support them in later life. The settlor had thus split the legal fee simple into several smaller estates (a life estate, a fee tail and a reversion in favour of his general heirs—see 1.6 and 9.4.2), which was possible at law before 1926.

An alternative way of making the same provision was to give the full fee simple to trustees, directing them to hold on trust for the family on similar terms, so that the settlor and his heir took equitable interests under the trust equivalent to the life estate and the fee tail, and money payments were provided for the rest of the family.

Whichever form was adopted, the result was the same, for, although the land could be sold or mortgaged if all those entitled under the settlement were of full age and agreed to act together, there was no one person who by himself could dispose of the whole legal and beneficial interest. Thus the chances of the property being lost to the family were greatly reduced.

Settling property in this way certainly had the desired effect of keeping land in the family, but preventing alienation had its own disadvantages. Some settlements did permit limited sale and mortgaging, so that money could be raised to improve the rest of the estate, but if such powers were not expressly provided, the current owner of the estate might well find himself unable to raise money for much-needed repairs and improvements, and as a result the property would deteriorate. A series of nineteenth-century Acts, culminating in the Settled Land Act 1882, gave the current beneficiary (the 'tenant for life') powers to deal with settled land and even to sell it, despite the settlor's intentions.

15.5.1.2 Trusts for sale

As we have seen, the strict settlement was designed for landowners with a sentimental attachment to land which had probably been owned by their families for hundreds of years. It was not, however, particularly appropriate in the case of land which had been bought relatively recently, and as an investment rather than for occupation. Land on which housing estates or factories were built was of no sentimental value to its owners, and they usually intended to hold it as long as the yield was satisfactory but to sell and reinvest the proceeds when better bargains were available. Yet, all the same, such landowners might want to make settlements, in order to keep their capital intact for later generations and to provide for the present members of their families. Their needs were met by the use of the trust for sale.

Title would be vested in trustees, who would be under a duty to sell the property and reinvest the proceeds, but who could postpone sale until the time was right. The income until sale, and the resulting capital, could be held in trust for a series of beneficiaries, as defined in the trust instrument, and so the settlor could provide an income for family members without dividing his capital between them. The major defining factor in these trusts was that they imposed upon the trustees a *duty* to sell the trust property but usually also included a *power* to postpone the sale, so that the trustees could choose the best moment at which to realise the trust investment in the property.

However, the fact that the trustees were under a *duty* to sell brought into operation an equitable doctrine known as 'conversion'.

Doctrine of conversion

In any case where there is a specifically enforceable obligation to convert land into money, or money into land, the maxim that 'equity regards as done that which ought to be done' leads equity to treat the property as notionally converted from the moment the obligation arises. This notional conversion operates when any contract to buy or sell land is made (see 5.7.3), and also applied to all trusts for sale. The trustees for sale could be compelled to perform their duty to sell the trust property and so such property was treated by equity as though it had been sold already, and the beneficiaries were regarded as having interests in money rather than in the land. This may appear somewhat strange today, but seemed appropriate when the trust for sale was first developed as a commercial alternative to the strict settlement.

15.5.2 Disadvantages of having two forms of settlement

In origin, as we have seen, each type of settlement had its own specific purpose, the strict settlement being used where particular land was to remain in the family, and the trust for sale being employed where the land was an investment which changed from time to time. Both forms were retained in the 1925 property legislation, but in more recent years a number of problems became apparent.

The machinery for dealing with a settlement under the Settled Land Act 1925, although intended to facilitate the sale of the land, often appeared cumbersome and expensive. Moreover, the fact that the tenant for life now had the statutory power to sell the land meant that a settlement made in this form could no longer be relied upon to keep the land in the family.

Over the years, clever draftsmen managed to construct trusts for sale which gave most of the benefits of the SLA settlement, while retaining the advantages provided by the greater flexibility of the trust for sale. Although the trust for sale imposed a duty on the trustees to sell the property, it was possible to provide that the land should not be sold without the consent of certain named individuals. Paradoxically, it became easier to prevent the sale of family land by means of a trust for sale with provision for consents, rather than by relying on a SLA settlement. An example of this is to be found in the facts of *Re Inns* [1947] Ch 576 (for which see 17.5.2).

Gradually most property owners who wanted to create a settlement came to use a trust for sale and relatively few settlors would intentionally create a SLA settlement. Yet avoiding the creation of such a settlement required careful drafting and the fact that it could be created unintentionally constituted a trap for the unwary, particularly for those who made 'home-made' wills without legal advice. As a result, the availability of two methods of settling land came to be seen as a disadvantage to settlors rather than as a benefit.

15.5.3 Co-ownership and statutory trusts

The 1925 property legislation imposed statutory trusts for sale on most forms of co-ownership (LPA 1925 ss. 34(2), 35 and 36(1)). This meant that from then on most co-owners held the legal estate in their land on trust for themselves as beneficiaries. Up to this point in the book, we have spoken about trustees and beneficiaries as though they were different people, but it is possible for the same people to fulfil both roles, and this is what happens in cases of co-ownership.

The provision that co-owned property was subject to a trust for sale must be related to the overall policy of the 1925 legislation: to simplify conveyancing and to make it easier for a purchaser to buy land. The fact that co-owned property was subject to a trust enabled the purchaser to take advantage of the overreaching machinery (explained in 6.5.2.1). Provided the purchase money was paid to two trustees, the purchaser would take free of the beneficial interests and need not worry about questions of who was entitled in equity and whether they agreed to the sale. (In case you have any doubts at this point, we assure you that the overreaching process operates where co-owners receive the purchase money as trustees, even though they are also the beneficiaries of the trust.) Moreover, the fact that the statutory trust was a trust for sale meant that the doctrine of conversion applied. As a result, the beneficiaries were regarded as having interests in money rather than in the land itself, and this provided further reassurance for the purchaser.

The imposition of the statutory trust for sale does not seem to have caused any particular problems at the outset. This may well be because co-ownership was relatively uncommon at that time and was most likely to arise through inheritance. In such cases, where several people were entitled under a will or on intestacy, the usual course of action, even before the statutory trust, would be to sell the land and divide the proceeds between the beneficiaries.

In the course of the twentieth century, however, a rise in home ownership, combined with the change in the status of women, meant that co-ownership of residential property became increasingly common. Couples who bought a house or flat generally regarded it as their future family home and, if they thought about the matter at all, assumed that they had an interest in the land and the right to occupy it. The idea that they were under a duty to sell the property that they had just acquired and had no interest in the land and no right to occupy it, would have seemed completely unbelievable (or, as Lord Wilberforce put it in *Williams & Glyn's Bank v Boland*, 'just a little unreal'—[1981] AC 487 at 507). Indeed, some solicitors have said that they never even tried to explain these facts to their clients.

While relations between the co-owners remained happy, the nature of their rights and duties under the trust for sale would not be significant, but if disagreement arose between the owners the trust could cause real difficulties. In particular, problems were experienced on the breakdown of family relationships, where one partner might move out of the property and demand that it should be sold, leaving the remaining partner and any children without a home. It would be difficult for the remaining partner to oppose sale in these circumstances. The co-owners, as trustees of a trust for sale, were under a *duty* to sell and had only a *power* to postpone sale. Following the decision in *Re Mayo* [1943] Ch 302, the power to postpone sale had to be exercised unanimously. If the trustees were not unanimous in agreeing to postpone sale, they must perform their duty and sell the property. Thus one co-owner who wished to sell could compel the other to do so against his or her wishes.

Further, the trust for sale coupled with the doctrine of conversion meant that the co-owners' equitable interests under the trust were viewed as interests in money and not in the land. This meant that it could be difficult for one co-owner to claim a right to occupy the land against the wishes of the other.

As it became apparent that the statutory trust was having unintended consequences for modern home-owners, the courts tried to mitigate its effects by recognising limited rights of occupation (despite the doctrine of conversion), and by developing a concept known as 'the doctrine of continuing purpose'.

15.5.3.1 Doctrine of continuing purpose

This doctrine was developed by the courts in dealing with applications by one co-owner for an order for sale (under LPA 1925, s. 30) against the wishes of the other co-owner.

An early illustration of its use is to be found in *Re Buchanan-Wollaston's Conveyance* [1939] Ch 738. In this case a group of neighbours had jointly bought a piece of land adjoining their properties with the intention of keeping it as an open space and thereby preventing further building. Later one neighbour sold his house and wished also to realise the money he had tied up in the open land. His application for an order for sale of the co-owned property was rejected on the ground that the land had been bought for a particular purpose and that purpose was continuing to be satisfied by the retention of the property.

Other examples of the idea of the continuing purpose are to be found in cases about the matrimonial home. In *Jones v Challenger* [1961] 1 QB 176, a husband and wife jointly acquired property as a matrimonial home. After divorce proceedings the wife sought an order for sale. The court granted the order because the purpose for which the property was bought had ended on the divorce. However, it indicated that despite the statutory trust for sale an order might be refused in a case where there were children of the marriage and a home was still being provided for them and the other partner (in other words, where the purpose of providing a family home was still continuing, even though one partner had left it). In *Rawlings v Rawlings* [1964] P 398 Salmon LJ considered that in such a case an order for sale should be delayed until the children were grown up.

In these ways, the courts did their best to deal with the unforeseen consequences of imposing a trust for sale on co-owners, but by the end of the twentieth century it seemed desirable to make some statutory change to the rule.

15.6 Proposals for reform

The problems we have been discussing in relation to settlements and co-ownership, as well as many others, were identified by the Law Commission in 1989 in *Transfer of Land: Trusts of Land* (Law Com No. 181). This report provided a useful summary of the difficulties caused by the old system and set out proposals for major changes, which paved the way for the reforms introduced by the Trusts of Land and Appointment of Trustees Act 1996.

15.7 Trusts of Land and Appointment of Trustees Act 1996 (TOLATA 1996)

TOLATA 1996 came into force on 1 January 1997. The changes made by the Act are described in detail in Chapter 17, but in outline the difficulties we have been considering in this chapter were dealt with by the Act as follows:

- A new 'trust of land' was introduced, which
  - applies to all trusts which include land
  - becomes the only way of creating new settlements
- Trusts for sale were abolished:
  - existing trusts for sale were converted into trusts of land
  - attempts to create new trusts for sale take effect as trusts of land
- No new SLA settlements may be created:
  - existing SLA settlements continue and are governed by SLA 1925
  - attempts to create new SLA settlements take effect as trusts of land
- The statutory trust imposed on co-ownership became a trust of land not a trust for sale.

FURTHER READING

Clements, 'The Changing Face of Trusts' [1998] MLR 56.

Transfer of Land: Trusts of Land, 1989, Law Com No. 181 (in particular, Part I on problems of existing law and Part II on proposals for reform).

16

Co-ownership

16.1 Introduction

16.1.1 Background

At one time the normal pattern of land ownership in Britain was that the estate in land, unless it was a large property subject to a complex settlement, was vested in one person as sole beneficial owner. The family home, whether leasehold or freehold, tended to be held by the man, who was regarded as head of the household. Changes in social conditions and in particular the alteration in the status of women, have meant that today sole ownership has become far more rare and that it is normal for domestic property to be the subject of co-ownership.

Co-ownership may be created deliberately because the property is conveyed to two or more persons as co-owners, or may arise by operation of law, as for example where one person contributes to the purchase price of property bought by another and thus acquires an equitable interest in the property under an implied trust (15.2.2 and Chapter 20).

In studying co-ownership, you need a clear understanding of the distinction we explained in Chapter 15 between the legal title to the property and the equitable or beneficial interest (see 15.1). There can be co-ownership of the legal title or of the equitable interest or of both. For example, a husband and wife may be co-owners in law and equity (i.e., both of them own the legal estate and both are entitled to the equitable interest).

LAW Legal estate	EQUITY Beneficial interest
H and W	H and W

Alternatively, one of them (in this example, the husband) owns the legal estate, but holds it on trust for himself and his wife, either because of a specific provision for this in the conveyance to him, or because there is some agreement between them, express or inferred, which gives her an equitable interest under an implied trust (see 15.2.2).

LAW Legal estate	EQUITY Beneficial interest
H	H and W

In this chapter, we concentrate on the rules which apply where there is co-ownership of the legal estate, and in Chapter 20 we will tell you about the second possibility, in which the legal estate is held by a single owner, in trust for himself and others as co-owners of the beneficial interest.

16.1.2 Co-ownership in Trant Way

Mr and Mrs Armstrong have completed the purchase of the fee simple estate in **1 Trant Way** (see 7.7.1 and 7.13). The property was transferred 'to Arnold Armstrong and Arriety Armstrong' and they have now been registered as proprietors by the Land Registry.

12 Trant Way was bought last year by six friends who are all studying Outer Mongolian history on a four-year course at Mousehole University. The friends each contributed one-sixth of the purchase price and, because they were short of money, one of their number did the conveyancing himself. The property was transferred to all six: i.e., to Alice, Brian, Colin, David, Eric and Fanny. At the date of the conveyance Alice was 17 and all the others were 18. The intention was that the house was to be kept until all six graduated and that it should then be sold.

Unfortunately, this 'do-it'yourself' conveyancing was not entirely successful: there are a couple of errors in the transfer, and we will tell you about them in 16.2.5.

13 Trant Way belongs to a firm of chartered surveyors. The partners in the firm are Sidney Search and Frederick Find and the legal estate, a 99-year lease, has been registered in the names of the two partners.

16.1.3 Two forms of co-ownership

In modern law, there are two forms of co-ownership:

- joint tenancy (see 16.2); and
- tenancy in common (see 16.3).

16.2. Joint tenancy

16.2.1 The 'four unities'

The joint tenancy is, in a way, the more perfect of the two types of co-ownership. It is a method of ownership in which the co-owners are *not* regarded as having 'shares' in the land but as together owning the whole estate. It is as though the co-owners are not really treated as separate owners but as an inseparable group owner. Thus, if Arnold and Arriety Armstrong are joint tenants in respect of 1 Trant Way, we cannot say that Arnold owns half and that Arriety owns half. We must say that Arnold and Arriety together own the whole estate. In the notation used in this chapter we will place joint tenants inside brackets:

(Arnold and Arriety)

to indicate this relationship.

A joint tenancy cannot exist unless four requirements, known as the four unities, are satisfied. The unities are:

(a) time;
(b) title;
(c) interest; and
(d) possession.

(a) *Time* This unity requires that the interests of all the co-owners should vest (be acquired) at the same time. Thus in a disposition, 'to J for life and then to K and L', K and L have the unity of time because the interest of each vests on the death of J. In the case of Mr and Mrs Armstrong this unity exists because the interest of each vested when 1 Trant Way was transferred to them as co-owners.

(b) *Title* This requires that the co-owners should all have acquired their title by the same means, e.g., all from the same document. In the case of Mr and Mrs Armstrong they both derive their title from the transfer that, on registration, vested the legal estate in them.

(c) *Interest* For a joint tenancy to exist, the interests of all the co-owners must also be identical. Each interest must be of the same duration and of the same nature and extent. Thus, if one co-owner has a life interest and the other an interest in fee simple, they cannot be joint tenants because this unity is not present.

(d) *Possession* Finally, the co-owners must be equally entitled to the possession of the whole land. If one of them could point to a portion of the land and say, 'That portion is mine alone', then there would be no co-ownership. In such a case each would be a sole owner of a smaller part of the land. This would arise, for example, if two people were to divide one parcel of land between themselves and each took a different portion.

16.2.2 Right of survivorship

One crucial aspect of joint tenancy is the 'right of survivorship' or *jus accrescendi*. Since a joint tenant is not regarded as having a distinct share in the co-owned land, he or she is not able to dispose of his or her interest by will on death, nor will it pass on intestacy if no will is made. Instead, on the death of one joint tenant, the remaining joint tenants obtain the interest of the deceased. This is the natural result of regarding joint tenants as a kind of unified and indivisible group. The last survivor of the group will of course become a sole beneficial owner and will be able to dispose of the property as he or she pleases on death. With the joint tenancy it pays to be long-lived!

16.2.3 Joint tenancy now the only form of legal co-ownership

Before 1926, co-owners were able to hold the legal estate as either joint tenants or tenants in common. However, the 1925 legislation provided that tenancies in common of the legal estate could no longer be created (LPA 1925, s. 34(1)). This change was designed to facilitate the transfer of land: as we noted above, the right of survivorship attached to a joint tenancy has the effect of reducing the number of co-owners and eventually results in the sole ownership of the last survivor. This makes it easier for a purchaser to check the vendor's title, and so has the effect of simplifying the process of sale.

Thus today any conveyance of the legal estate to two or more persons will create a joint tenancy.

16.2.4 Statutory trusts imposed on co-ownership

The 1925 legislation also provided that in most forms of co-ownership the joint owners of the legal estate would hold it on trust for themselves, at first on a trust for sale (LPA 1925, ss. 34(2) and 36(1)) and, since 1997, on a trust of land. This had various advantages. It meant that anyone who bought the legal estate from joint tenants could take advantage of the overreaching machinery: provided the money was paid to two trustees, the purchaser would take free of the beneficial interests under the trust. It also meant that tenancies in common could still be created *in equity*, with the legal joint tenants holding in trust for themselves as tenants in common of the beneficial interest.

16.2.5 Number and age of joint tenants

In order to prevent a trust having an inordinate number of trustees, the Trustee Act 1925, s. 34(2) limits the number of trustees to a maximum of four, and provides that where more than four are named, the property vests in the first four listed. Thus the imposition of the statutory trust in cases of co-ownership means that there cannot be more than four owners of the legal estate, who will hold it on trust for themselves and any additional co-owners.

Trant Way

We have seen that the transfer of 12 Trant Way purported to vest the legal estate in the six students, one of whom, Alice, was at that time only 17 years old. Section 1(6) of LPA 1925 provides that a legal estate in land cannot be held by an 'infant' (i.e., a person under the age of 18 and today known as a 'minor'. See further 17.10.1).

As a result of these statutory rules, the title to the legal estate in No. 12 will be registered in the name of the first four named in the transfer who are over 18 (Brian, Colin, David and Eric), while Alice and Fanny will be owners in equity only.

16.2.6 Severing a joint tenancy

A relationship which begins as a joint tenancy need not continue as one, for it is possible for one or more of the joint tenants to sever the tenancy and convert the relationship with the other co-owners into a tenancy in common. Since 1926, a joint tenancy of the *legal estate* can no longer be severed (because the resulting tenancies in common may no longer be created at law), but severance of a joint tenancy of the *beneficial interest* remains possible. We will explain later the ways in which a joint tenancy may be severed (see 16.6), but we need to mention here that that the result of doing so is that each of the co-owners becomes entitled to an equal share under the resulting tenancy in common (*Goodman v Gallant* [1986] Fam 106, approved by the House of Lords in *Stack v Dowden* [2007] 2 AC 432, at para. 49). Thus if two co-owners sever their joint tenancy, each will be entitled to a half share in the beneficial interest.

16.3 Tenancy in common

Although it is no longer possible to create a tenancy in common of the *legal estate*, this form of co-ownership continues to exist *in equity* and provides an alternative way in which co-owners can hold the beneficial interest in their property.

16.3.1 Differences between joint tenancy and tenancy in common

Tenancies in common differ from joint tenancies in two important ways.

16.3.1.1 The 'four unities' are not required

The tenancy in common is not such a 'perfect' relationship of co-ownership. For such a tenancy to exist, only one unity is required, that of possession. This unity is essential for, if it did not exist, there would be no co-ownership but merely individual ownership of separate portions of land. Provided all the co-owners have the right to possession of the whole, there will be unity of possession and a tenancy in common will arise. The arrangement cannot give rise to a joint tenancy if the unities of time, title and interest are not satisfied.

16.3.1.2 Notional shares and no rights of survivorship

The tenant in common, unlike the joint tenant, is entitled to a notional share of the property (e.g., a half or a quarter), which he or she can dispose of during life or at death. Thus when one tenant in common dies, the remaining co-owners have no right of survivorship. The deceased's share in the property forms part of his or her estate and passes by will or under the rules of intestacy.

Although tenants in common have notional shares in the property, it is important to realise that these are undivided shares and that until the property is sold or partitioned all the tenants in common are entitled to possession of the whole of it.

16.3.2 Tenancy in common cannot exist at law

As noted in 16.2.3, it is no longer possible to create a tenancy in common of the legal estate, but this form of co-ownership continues to exist in equity. In the unlikely event that a modern conveyance purported to convey the legal estate to the new owners as 'tenants in common', they would still take that estate as joint tenants, but equity would give effect to their intentions by treating them as tenants in common of the beneficial interest in the property.

16.4 Creating a tenancy in common of the beneficial interest under a trust

Although it is no longer possible to create a tenancy in common of the legal estate, legal joint tenants may hold the legal estate in trust for themselves as tenants in common of the beneficial interest. The resulting position is shown in the following diagram.

LAW Legal estate	EQUITY Beneficial interest
(M and N)	M and N
Joint tenancy	Tenancy in common

A tenancy in common of the beneficial interest may be created by express declaration and may also arise under certain equitable presumptions.

16.4.1 Express declaration

The conveyance or transfer to the co-owners may make express provision as to the way in which they are to hold the beneficial interest.

16.4.1.1 Unregistered land

Where the title to the property is still unregistered, the conveyance could provide that the legal estate is conveyed to them as joint tenants, to hold to themselves as tenants in common in equity.

It is also possible to make an express declaration of an equitable tenancy in common by providing that the beneficial interest is to be held in 'undivided shares', the technical term sometimes used as a synonym for 'tenancy in common'. In fact, any words suggesting that the owners are to be regarded as owners of shares in the property, rather than as a kind of group sole owner, would prevent the creation of an equitable joint tenancy and would create a tenancy in common instead. Such phrases, known as 'words of severance', include:

- 'in equal shares'—*Payne v Webb* (1874) LR 19 Eq 26
- 'equally'—*Lewen v Dodd* (1595) Cro Eliz 443
- 'share and share alike'—*Heathe v Heathe* (1740) 2 Atk 121
- 'to be divided between'—*Peat v Chapman* (1750) 1 Ves Sen 542
- 'between'—*Lashbrook v Cock* (1816) 2 Mer 70.

16.4.1.2 Registered land

In the case of registered land, the transfer form now in use gives the transferees the opportunity to indicate whether they are to hold the property in trust for themselves as joint tenants or as tenants in common. If you look at Box 10 of the specimen transfer form at pp. 128–30, you will see that the Armstrongs have chosen to hold their beneficial interest as joint tenants. The transfer form also gives transferees the opportunity to say that they wish to hold as tenants in common in equal shares, while those who wish to hold as tenants in common of *unequal* shares could provide for this by completing the third option in Box 10. Unfortunately, some transferees fail to complete this part of the form in any way, with the result that there is no express declaration about the nature of their beneficial interests (see *Stack v Dowden* [2007] 2 AC 432, para. 52).

An express declaration of the nature of the beneficial interest is conclusive, unless it is varied by subsequent agreement or affected by proprietary estoppel (*Goodman v*

Gallant [1986] Fam 106, approved by the House of Lords in *Stack v Dowden* [2007] 2 AC 432 at para. 49).

16.4.2 Position where there is no express declaration

It may be that a conveyance or transfer to co-owners says nothing about how they intend to hold the beneficial interest. Historically, equity preferred the tenancy in common, because it considered that the notional entitlement to a share in the property and the owner's ability to dispose of this share at his death was a fairer form of co-ownership. Despite this preference, however, equity would in general follow the law: in other words, if the legal estate was held on a joint tenancy, the equitable or beneficial interest would follow the legal estate and would also be held on a joint tenancy.

There were, however, certain situations in which equity regarded the right of survivorship as being so unfair or inappropriate that it considered it unlikely that the parties had really intended it to apply. In such circumstances equity would presume that the parties held as tenants in common despite the fact that all the requirements for a legal joint tenancy were satisfied. With one major exception (relating to the family home—see 16.5), this presumption still operates today. It is, of course, always open to a party to rebut the presumption by showing that the co-owners had in truth intended to hold the beneficial interest as joint tenants, despite the apparent disadvantages.

16.4.3 The equitable presumption of a tenancy in common

In the following situations, equity will presume that joint tenants of the legal estate hold the beneficial interest as tenants in common.

16.4.3.1 Unequal contributions

If the co-owners have contributed unequal amounts to the purchase price, equity considers it unfair to impose upon them the equality of the joint tenancy and the effects of the right of survivorship, for it might be that the tenant who has contributed least may prove to be the longest lived, and thus become the sole owner of the whole property. Accordingly, in such cases equity has always presumed that unequal contributors hold the property as tenants in common, each co-owner having a share in the property proportional to his contribution to the purchase price (*Lake* v *Gibson* (1729) 1 Eq Rep 290; and, in modern law, *Bull v Bull* [1955] 1 QB 234). Another way of expressing this, using the language of trusts rather than of co-ownership, is to say that the property was held on a resulting trust (see 16.5.1.1). The presumption could, of course, be rebutted by clear evidence of an intention to the contrary: either that the parties should, after all, hold as joint tenants, or that the size of their shares under a tenancy in common should not correspond to the amount of their respective contributions.

This presumption has always been applied irrespective of the nature of the property or its owners, but in *Stack v Dowden* [2007] 2 AC 432 the House of Lords held that it was no longer appropriate in certain cases involving 'domestic property' (i.e., the family home). We will tell you more about this decision in 16.5.

16.4.3.2 Property belonging to business partners

Where the co-ownership is of a commercial character, the right of survivorship appears to equity to be inappropriate even in the case of equal contributions to the purchase price. Thus, in the case of partnership property, equity favours the tenancy in common, and so would presume that the beneficial interest in 13 Trant Way (owned by the chartered surveyors—see 16.1.2) is held on a tenancy in common (*Re Fuller's Contract* [1933] Ch 652).

16.4.3.3 Estate or interest granted to secure a loan

As we explain in Chapter 24, a mortgage is created by a borrower ('the mortgagor') who grants an interest in land to the lender ('the mortgagee') as security for the loan. Where two or more people lend money secured by the same mortgage, equity presumes that the beneficial interest in the land granted to them as security is held on a tenancy in common (*Morley v Bird* (1798) 3 Ves Jr 628). Thus the money owed to each creditor is secured on an identifiable share in the beneficial interest and that share would pass with the lender's estate if he died before the loan was repaid.

16.4.3.4 Other circumstances

It had been suggested that the three situations we describe above were the only ones in which joint tenants of the legal estate would be regarded by equity as tenants in common of the beneficial interest in the property. However, this view was rejected by the Privy Council in *Malaysian Credit Ltd v Jack Chia-MPH Ltd* [1986] 1 AC 549.

This case concerned joint tenants of leasehold business premises. As joint tenants, each was entitled to possession of the whole of the property (see 16.2.1(d)), but in practice they occupied separate and unequal areas of it, and rent and other outgoings were divided between them in proportion to the area that each occupied. When a dispute arose between them, the plaintiff, who occupied the smallest area, claimed that they were joint tenants in both law and equity, and sought an order for sale and the equal division of the proceeds between them. The two owners were not in partnership with each other, so did not come within the equitable presumption relating to partnership property, and there were no words in the grant of the lease that indicated an intention to hold as tenants in common. Despite this, the Privy Council considered that the beneficial interest in the property was held on a tenancy in common. In reaching this conclusion their Lordships were clearly influenced by the unequal contributions to outgoings, which they regarded as analogous to those unequal contributions to the purchase price of a property that would support a presumption of tenancy in common. Nevertheless, they rejected the plaintiff's suggestion that the circumstances in which such a presumption could operate were strictly limited. In Lord Brightman's words (at p. 560):

> Such cases are not necessarily limited to purchasers who contribute unequally, to co-mortgagees and to partners. There are other circumstances in which equity may infer that the beneficial interest is intended to be held by the grantees as tenants in common...one such case is where the grantees hold the premises for their several [i.e., separate] individual business purposes.

The circumstances in which equity may infer an intention to hold as tenants in common received further consideration from the House of Lords in *Stack v Dowden* [2007] 2 AC 432, and more recently from the Supreme Court in *Jones v Kernott* [2011] UKSC 53.

16.5 *Stack v Dowden* and *Jones v Kernott*

In order to understand the decisions in these cases you need to know something about resulting and constructive trusts, which we explained briefly in 15.2.2.

16.5.1 Relevance of resulting and constructive trusts

Before *Stack v Dowden*, these two types of implied or non-express trusts were generally discussed in the context of *'sole name'* cases i.e., where one person (X) owned the legal estate but was required by equity to hold it on trust wholly or partly for the benefit of another (Y).

16.5.1.1 Resulting trusts

Where Y has contributed to the purchase price of property acquired by X, X may be regarded by equity as holding the legal estate on a *resulting trust* for himself and Y, the shares in the beneficial interest being proportionate to their respective contributions. This of course is very similar to the position in co-ownership (or *'joint names'*) cases, where equity would presume that joint tenants of the legal estate who had made unequal contributions to the purchase price would hold in trust for themselves as tenants in common of the beneficial interest, in shares proportionate to the amount which each had contributed.

16.5.1.2 Common intention constructive trusts

By contrast, where X and Y have agreed that Y will have an interest in property belonging to X and Y has acted to his/her detriment in reliance on this shared understanding, X may be regarded by equity as holding the legal estate on a *constructive trust* for himself and Y, and obliged to give effect to their shared or common intentions about the nature of their beneficial interests (hence the name 'common intention constructive trust'). This type of constructive trust has been developed during the last 40 years in disputes about entitlement to a share in the family home. Where one partner (spouse or cohabitant) is the sole legal owner of the property (a *'sole name'* case) but agrees that the other partner will have an interest in it, and as a result that partner acts in some way to his or her detriment, equity may treat the owner as holding the property on a constructive trust for himself and his partner. In the case of a dispute about ownership of the property, the court will, of course, need to be satisfied that the legal owner did indeed make this agreement. It may be possible for the claimant to produce evidence of an express discussion and agreement between the partners, but more usually the court has to infer (i.e., deduce) the parties' intentions from their behaviour. We will consider some of the case law about inferring intention later in this chapter, and add more detail in Chapter 20.

16.5.1.3 Implied trusts in *Stack v Dowden*

In *Stack v Dowden* the House of Lords considered the rights of the parties in terms of resulting and constructive trusts, drawing on principles established in sole name cases and applying them in a joint names dispute. As a result, their Lordships sometimes use the language of implied trusts, rather than that of co-ownership: for example, they focus on whether the parties intended their shares under the trust to be equal or unequal, but do not relate this specifically to an intention to create a tenancy in common. As a result you may find at first that it is not always easy to relate what is said in this case to the rules we are describing.

We should also warn you that some statements in these decisions appear to suggest that joint tenants are entitled to individual shares in the property. We hope that these are really references to the shares that would be acquired if a joint tenancy was severed, but for the avoidance of doubt we must emphasise now that *joint tenants own the whole property between them and are not to be regarded as owning individual shares in it.* The question of 'shares' arises only if the parties intended at the outset to hold the beneficial interest as tenants in common, or if an existing beneficial joint tenancy has been converted into a tenancy in common by severance.

16.5.2 *Stack v Dowden*: the facts

In this case the parties were an unmarried couple who had lived together for some years. In the course of their relationship, they bought a house as a home for themselves and their children, and were registered as joint tenants of the legal estate. Unfortunately, the Land Registry transfer form in use at that time did not give transferees any opportunity to state that they were holding the property in trust for themselves or to describe the way in which they wished to hold the beneficial interest. When the parties' relationship came to an end, Ms Dowden ('D') apparently considered (or, more probably, was advised) that the beneficial interest in the property was held on a joint tenancy. Accordingly she served a notice of severance on her former partner which, if they were joint tenants in equity, would convert them into tenants in common.

Mr Stack ('S') then obtained a court order that the house should be sold and the proceeds divided equally between himself and his former partner. However, D had provided more than 50 per cent of the cost of acquiring the property and she appealed against this decision, claiming that she was entitled to a greater share. The Court of Appeal held that she was entitled to a 65 per cent share, and S appealed from this decision to the House of Lords. He claimed that the parties had been joint tenants of both the legal estate and the beneficial interest, and relied on the rule in *Goodman v Gallant* [1986] Fam 106 that severance of a beneficial joint tenancy produces a tenancy in common in equal shares.

16.5.3 *Stack v Dowden*: the House of Lords' decision

Lady Hale, delivering a speech with which Lord Hoffmann, Lord Hope and Lord Walker all concurred, described the issue in the case (at para. 40) as being:

> The effect of a conveyance into the joint names of a cohabiting couple, but without an explicit declaration of their respective beneficial interests, of a dwelling house which was to become their home.

In considering this issue, Lady Hale (at para. 54) started from the basic principle that where there is no express provision about how the beneficial interest should be held:

> it should be assumed that equity follows the law, and that the beneficial interests reflect the legal interests in the property.

In other words, the fact that S and D held the legal estate together as joint tenants raised a presumption that they were also joint tenants of the beneficial interest. However, the parties had made unequal contributions to the cost of acquiring the property, and you might expect that this would give rise to the equitable presumption of a tenancy in common or, to use the language of trusts, to a resulting trust.

This was the approach favoured by Lord Neuberger (see 20.6.5.1), but the majority of their Lordships considered that questions about entitlement to shares in the family home should not depend solely on the size of financial contribution (unless, of course that was what the parties had intended—see Lord Walker at para. 31). In Lady Hale's words (at paras. 60 and 69):

> These days the importance to be attached to who paid for what in a domestic context may be very different from its importance in other contexts or long ago... In law, context is everything, and the domestic context is very different from the commercial world. Each case will turn on its own facts, many more factors than financial contributions may be relevant to divining the parties' true intentions.

Accordingly, the House of Lords rejected the presumption of a resulting trust in cases involving the family home, and by implication also rejected the presumption of a tenancy in common arising from unequal contributions to the purchase price of such property.

The view that the presumption of a resulting trust is not appropriate in a domestic setting has been emphasised recently by Lord Walker and Lady Hale in *Jones v Kernott* [2011] 3 WLR 1121 (at para. 25):

> The time has come to make it clear, in line with *Stack v Dowden*, that in the case of a purchase of a house or flat in joint names for joint occupation by a married or unmarried couple, where both are responsible for any mortgage, there is no presumption of a resulting trust arising from their having contributed to the deposit (or indeed the rest of the purchase) in unequal shares.

Thus the basic presumption that equity follows the law and that a conveyance into joint names indicates both legal and beneficial joint tenancy is not displaced by the fact of unequal contributions and remains the starting point in joint names cases. To quote again from *Jones v Kernott* (at para. 15):

> ...the principle in *Stack v Dowden* is that a 'common intention ' trust, for the cohabitants' home to belong to them jointly in equity as well as on the proprietorship register, is the default option in joint names cases.

Stack v Dowden made it clear (see Lady Hale at para. 68) that it is possible to displace this presumption of beneficial joint tenancy by proving that at the time of acquisition (or, in some cases, at a later stage):

> the parties did intend their beneficial interests to be different from their legal interests, and in what way.

Although Lady Hale does not say so, this statement must refer to an intention to hold as tenants in common, in equal or unequal shares. The existence of such an intention has to be proved by the party who seeks to displace the presumption of a beneficial joint tenancy. However, their Lordships warned that this would be very difficult, Lord Walker describing it as 'a heavy burden' (para. 14) and Lady Hale saying that 'it is not a task to be lightly embarked upon' (para. 68).

Where a claimant (in this case, D) seeks to displace the presumption of beneficial joint tenancy, the court is being asked to infer the parties' intentions about two questions:

(1) Did they intend to have unequal shares in the beneficial interest (i.e., to create a tenancy in common)?; and if they did so intend

(2) What size did they intend those shares to be?

Lady Hale listed a number of factors that the court could take into account when seeking to discover the parties' intentions on these questions (see para. 69; and further consideration of this point at 20.6.4.2). Her Ladyship emphasised, however, that it is only in very unusual cases that taking such matters into account will result in a finding that the parties intended that their holding of the beneficial interest should not follow that of the legal title (para. 69).

It appeared, however, that the appeal under consideration was one of these 'very unusual cases' and Lady Hale found several factors that indicated that the parties did not intend to hold the beneficial interest as joint tenants. These factors included not only the greater financial contribution made to the cost of the house by D, but also the fact that her partner took responsibility only for certain clearly-defined areas of expenditure in relation to the house, and that both parties kept all their property, apart from the house, completely separate—there were no joint savings or investments. To her Ladyship, this conduct strongly indicated that the parties did not intend their shares in the house to be equal, and certainly did not intend the beneficial interest to be held on a joint tenancy with rights of survivorship. It follows from this that, from the outset, the beneficial interest must have been held on a tenancy in common in unequal shares although, rather confusingly, her Ladyship does not specifically say so. She simply states that there was no intention to hold as beneficial joint tenants and in the next sentence says that D has made good her claim to a 65 per cent share (para. 92).

16.5.4 Changing intention: *Jones v Kernott*

In *Stack v Dowden*, their Lordships accepted that the parties' intentions about ownership of the family home might change during the course of their relationship, Lady Hale noting (at para. 70) that in some cases there might be reason to conclude that:

> whatever the parties' intentions at the outset, these have now changed. An example might be where one party has financed (or constructed himself) an extension or substantial improvement to the property, so that what they have now is significantly different from what they had then.

The question of changed intentions, arising not from improvements to the property but from events occurring after the parties had separated, has now been considered by the Supreme Court in *Jones v Kernott* [2011] 3 WLR 1121.

16.5.4.1 The facts

Mr Kernott ('K') and Ms Jones ('J') were an unmarried couple who lived together for some nine years, originally in a caravan which belonged to J. In 1985, after the birth of their first child, J sold the caravan and used the proceeds to provide a deposit for a house, which the couple bought as a family home. The property and the necessary mortgage were in joint names, with the result that the parties held the legal estate in trust for themselves, but (as in *Stack v Dowden*) there was no statement of whether they intended to hold the beneficial interest as joint tenants or tenants in common.

The couple and their children lived together as a family, sharing household expenses, for over eight years, but their relationship broke down and K moved out of the property in 1993. J remained in the house with the children, paying the mortgage instalments and all other outgoings, while K made no further contributions to the cost of acquiring the property and provided little towards the maintenance and support of the children.

In 1995, the house was put on the market but did not sell, and about this time J and K agreed to cash their joint life insurance policy and divide the proceeds between them. K used his share as a deposit on another property, which became his home. For the next 11 years he took no interest in the house, while J continued to maintain the property and pay interest on the mortgage debt. In 2006, K asked for payment for his share of the property and in 2008 purported to sever the beneficial joint tenancy. Meanwhile J had started proceedings in which she claimed to own the entire beneficial interest in the property and sought a declaration to this effect under TOLATA 1996, s. 14 (see text at 17.8.3). She conceded that there had originally been a joint tenancy of the beneficial interest and that, if it had been severed in 1993 when the relationship ended, each would have been entitled to a 50% share (para. 43). However, she claimed that the parties' intentions had changed during the period following their separation.

J's claim raised two questions:

(1) Had the parties' original common intention to hold the beneficial interest as joint tenants changed?

(2) If that intention had changed, what was their new intention about the size of each share in the beneficial interest?

16.5.4.2 Decision at first instance

The county court judge discussed and applied the principles of *Stack v Dowden*, noting that their Lordships had recognised the possibility that intentions might change. In the case before him, there had been no discussion or agreement about the house when the parties separated, but from the evidence before the court he was able to infer that their intentions about their beneficial interests in the property had changed. Matters relied on in drawing this inference included:

- the length of time since the separation, during which K had shown no interest in the house;
- the very substantial financial contributions made by J, particularly in the 14 years since the separation; and
- the division of the proceeds of the insurance policy between the parties which, combined with J's assumption of financial responsibility for the house, had enabled K to buy a new home for himself.

In the absence of any indication of the parties' new intentions about the size of their shares, the judge held himself bound by the Court of Appeal decision in *Oxley v Hiscock* [2005] Fam 211 (see 20.6.3.2) to consider what was fair and just between the parties, bearing in mind what he had found with regard to the whole course of dealing between them. Having done so, he held that J was entitled to 90 per cent of the value of the house and K to 10 per cent.

This decision was reversed on K's appeal to the Court of Appeal (*Kernott v Jones* [2010] 1 WLR 2401), and J appealed to the Supreme Court.

16.5.4.3 Decision of the Supreme Court

The court was satisfied that a change of intention about the parties' beneficial interests could be inferred from the factors identified by the trial judge and that his decision as to the size of each share was correct. The court accordingly allowed J's appeal, reversing the Court of Appeal decision and holding that J and K were respectively entitled to 90 per cent and 10 per cent of the property.

The court's decision confirms the view expressed in *Stack v Dowden* that the intentions of parties to a common intention trust can change during the life of the trust, and establishes that such a change of intention:

- can rebut the *Stack v Dowden* presumption that a conveyance of a family home into joint names indicates both a legal and beneficial joint tenancy; and
- can result in a change in the size of the share in the property to which each party is entitled.

Although all five members of the court agreed on these points and on the outcome of the appeal, there was some variation between them on the reasons for that decision, most notably on the question of whether the parties' new intentions about the size of their respective shares were to be *inferred* (that is, deduced by the court from the parties' conduct) or *imputed* (that is, attributed to the parties by the court). This question is of significance in all cases involving common intention constructive trusts, and so we will postpone consideration of it until Chapter 20 (see 20.7).

A puzzle
The decision of the Supreme Court appears to raise an unanswered question about what happened to the parties' beneficial joint tenancy. The decision that they were entitled to unequal shares must surely mean that, at some stage in their relationship, that tenancy turned into a tenancy in common. This could have been done by severing the joint tenancy and, as we shall (16.6.2.2), severance can be effected by mutual agreement, inferred from the conduct of the parties. However, severance of a joint tenancy entitles each party to an equal share under the resulting tenancy in common, and there seems to be an unbridged gap between inferring severance (if that is what the court did) and holding that the parties were entitled to unequal shares. This reminds us, irresistibly, of Cinderella's godmother and the pumpkin: if some less fanciful solution appears in any academic literature, we will update you through the Online Resource Centre for this book (at **www.oxfordtextbooks.co.uk/orc/landlaw14e/**).

16.5.5 Questions about the application of *Stack v Dowden*

The House of Lords' decision in *Stack v Dowden* left a number of questions unanswered. We will consider those which relate to co-ownership here and postpone the more general question about the effect of the decision on common intention trusts until Chapter 20.

16.5.5.1 Which home-sharing relationships will give rise to the *Stack v Dowden* presumption?

Following *Stack v Dowden*, it was not clear how widely the 'domestic context' would extend and which home-sharing arrangements would come within it. The constructive trust cases which formed the background to the decision had all concerned property occupied by cohabitants or married couples, and commentators wondered whether the new approach would apply to property acquired for occupation in other family relationships or even by friends.

The question was first considered in *Adekunle v Ritchie* [2007] BPIR 1177. Some years before, Ritchie's mother had had the opportunity to buy the house in which she lived under the Right to Buy scheme (which entitled local authority tenants to buy their homes at substantial discounts). She was not able to obtain the necessary loan by herself and Ritchie, who lived with her, agreed to be a party to the mortgage and transfer. They were accordingly registered as joint tenants of the legal estate but, as in *Stack v Dowden*, the transfer contained no declaration about how they would hold the beneficial interest. Mrs Ritchie later died without making a will, and her administrators (Adekunle and another) applied for an order for sale of the house, so that the proceeds could be divided between the 10 children entitled under their mother's intestacy. Ritchie opposed the application. Relying on the *Stack v Dowden* presumption, he claimed that he and his mother had held the beneficial interest as joint tenants and that he was therefore solely entitled to the house by right of survivorship.

HHJ Behrens rejected the administrators' submission that *Stack v Dowden* applied only to home-sharing arrangements which involved a sexual relationship (para. 65). The present case related to a domestic relationship between mother and son, and in his view should be decided in accordance with the new approach. (For the decision in this case, see 16.5.5.3 below.)

The judge's view in Adekunle was approved by Lord Neuberger, sitting in the Court of Appeal in *Laskar v Laskar* [2008] 1 WLR 2695 (a case involving the joint tenancy of a mother and daughter—see 16.5.5.2 below). His Lordship noted (para. 16) that although the problem in *Stack v Dowden* related to a cohabiting couple, a number of remarks in Lady Hale's speech indicated that her reasoning was intended to apply to other personal relationships.

16.5.5.2 Is the *Stack v Dowden* presumption limited to property acquired as a family home?

This question arose for consideration in *Laskar v Laskar* [2008] 1 WLR 2695.

The case concerned a house bought as an investment by a mother and daughter and registered in their joint names. The property was let to tenants and was never used by the owners as a family home. The daughter had contributed just over 4 per cent to the cost of the property, but subsequently claimed to be entitled to a 50 per cent share, relying on the *Stack v Dowden* presumption that the beneficial interest was held on a joint tenancy. This claim was rejected by the Court of Appeal, Lord Neuberger saying that, despite the family relationship, it was not right to apply *Stack v Dowden* where the main purpose of the purchase was as an investment.

16.5.5.3 How difficult is it to rebut the *Stack v Dowden* presumption?

In *Stack v Dowden*, both Lord Walker and Lady Hale warned that it would be difficult to displace the presumption of a beneficial joint tenancy (paras. 14 and 68), and predicted that attempts to do so would succeed only in 'very unusual cases'. Interestingly, two of the three decisions we will consider here proved to be 'very unusual' (i.e., *Adekunle* and *Laskar*) and it is only in the third case (*Fowler v Barron*) that the presumption was upheld.

Adekunle v Ritchie [2007] BPIR 1177

We have already explained the facts of this case, and noted that HHJ Behrens considered that the mother–son relationship fell within the *Stack v Dowden* principle. He did however add (at para. 65) that:

> It may well be...that where one is not dealing with the situation of a couple living together, it will be easier to find that the facts are unusual in the sense that they are not to be taken to have intended a beneficial joint tenancy.

The judge then went on to identify a number of factors which led him to regard the case as very unusual. These included:

- the purchase and registration in joint names was undertaken to enable the mother to borrow money secured by a mortgage;
- the principal purpose of buying the house was to provide a home for the mother;
- the financial affairs of mother and son were kept separate; and
- the mother had nine other children and would not have intended the whole of her property to pass to Ritchie.

The judge accepted that there was a common intention that Ritchie should have some share in the beneficial interest, but these factors were a strong indication that the parties did not intend their shares to be equal (still less that the right of survivorship should operate on death). Ritchie had made some contribution to the mortgage repayments, but his overall contribution was considerably less than that of his mother, and the judge held that the parties 'are to be taken to have intended' that Ritchie should have a one-third share in the beneficial interest.

Laskar v Laskar [2008] 1 WLR 2695

As noted above, the Court of Appeal held that the *Stack v Dowden* presumption of equality did not apply in this case because the property had been bought as an investment, not as a family home. Accordingly, the court held that the parties' respective shares should reflect their contributions to the purchase price, and on this basis awarded a one-third share to the daughter.

However, Lord Neuberger considered that, even if the presumption had applied, it would have been rebutted (paras. 18–19). His reasons for this include:

- the parties' financial affairs were kept separate;
- the mother had several other children and there was no reason to think that she intended her daughter to receive a significant gift not shared with the other children;
- the parties' contributions to the purchase price were significantly different; and
- the daughter became a co-purchaser primarily because the mother could not afford the purchase on her own.

It is interesting to see how very similar these factors are to those identified in *Adekunle*.

Fowler v Barron [2008] 2 FLR 831

In this decision the *Stack v Dowden* presumption was applied and attempts to rebut it were unsuccessful.

The parties were former cohabitants who had lived together for some 23 years and, early in the relationship, had bought a house as a home for themselves and their baby son. Both the mortgage and the transfer were in joint names, but there was no declaration in the transfer about the nature of their beneficial interests. Throughout their relationship all payments relating to the acquisition of the property were made by Mr Barron (B), who also paid council tax and utility bills and other housekeeping expenses.

When the parties separated, Miss Fowler (F) claimed a half-share in the value of the family home. In opposing this claim, B asserted that his intention in buying the property in both names was to enable F to inherit the house if she was still living with him at his death. He had not understood that doing this would give F an immediate beneficial interest in the property.

At first instance, the trial judge held that there was no evidence of a common intention that each party should have an equal share in the property. In the absence of such an intention, the presumption of a resulting trust applied (in fairness to the judge, we must say that this judgment was given before the House of Lords' decision in *Stack v Dowden*). F had made no direct or indirect contribution to the cost of acquisition, and the judge held that she had no beneficial interest in the property.

In the Court of Appeal, Arden LJ referred to Lady Hale's statement in *Stack v Dowden* that the parties' whole course of conduct in relation to the property must be taken into account in ascertaining the parties' shared intentions about it, and held that the trial judge's concentration on financial contributions was an error of principle (paras. 29–31). Both parties had been registered as joint tenants of the legal estate and this gave rise to the presumption of joint beneficial ownership. A party seeking to rebut that presumption must satisfy the court that there was a common intention that the beneficial interest would be held in some other way. Both parties must have this intention, and the presumption could not be displaced by the intention of one party which had not been communicated to the other (para. 37).

In considering the parties' course of conduct in relation to the property, Arden LJ identified several matters which could assist the court to infer their common intentions. Although F made no direct contribution to the cost of acquisition, she spent most of her income on family expenses, such as clothes for the children, outings and family holidays. From this Arden LJ inferred (see paras. 41 and 46) that:

> The parties intended that it should make no difference to their interests in the property which party paid for what expense...There was no prior agreement as to who would pay for what...the parties simply did not care about the respective size of each other's contributions...the parties largely treated their incomes and assets as one pool from which household expenses [would] be paid.

A further significant point was that the parties had made mutual wills in favour of each other (para. 42). To Arden LJ this was evidence that they thought that they each had a beneficial interest in the property (although we have to say that in our view this does not necessarily suggest that they intended to hold as beneficial joint tenants). Further relevant matters were added by Toulson LJ (paras. 53 and 56), who noted that F was a party to the mortgage and therefore jointly liable on it, and that during the 17 years of home ownership she had 'contributed to the life and wellbeing of the family in financial and other ways'.

Taking all these matters into account the court concluded that there was no evidence of a common intention to hold the beneficial interest in any way other than as joint tenants. The presumption of equal beneficial interests had not been rebutted and F was held to be entitled to a half share in the property.

16.5.6 Significance of *Stack v Dowden* in context of co-ownership

The decision breaks new ground in the distinction it makes between 'domestic' and 'commercial' property, and in the majority opinion that the equitable presumption arising from unequal contributions should not be applied in cases involving a family home.

In the absence of any express declaration of a tenancy in common, it will now be presumed that where the legal estate in domestic property (the family home) is held by both partners, the beneficial interest will be held on a joint tenancy (despite unequal contributions to acquisition costs), unless the party who alleges that it is held on a tenancy in common can rebut the presumption by satisfying the court that this is what both partners intended.

By contrast, unequal contributions to the cost of commercial property will continue to give rise to a presumption of a beneficial tenancy in common, and the burden of proving a contrary intention so as to rebut that presumption will lie on the party who alleges a joint tenancy (although note the hint of a future reconsideration in *Jones v Kernott* [2011] 3 WLR 1121).

16.6 Severance of a joint tenancy

A relationship which begins as a joint tenancy need not remain so, for in certain circumstances it is possible for a joint tenant to sever his or her interest and thereby to convert it into a tenancy in common. A primary reason for severance may be to avoid the effects of the right of survivorship i.e., to create separate shares in the property, which can then be passed by will or intestacy on the death of a co-owner. It is never possible these days to sever a joint tenancy of the legal estate, for to do this would be to create a legal tenancy in common, which is prohibited by LPA 1925, s. 34(1). Accordingly LPA 1925, s. 36(2) provides that:

> No severance of a joint tenancy of a legal estate, so as to create a tenancy in common in land, shall be permissible.

Severance of an equitable joint tenancy is, however, still possible (and frequent in practice) and may be effected in a number of ways, which are set out in the proviso to s. 36(2) (as amended by TOLATA 1996, Sch. 2, para. 4(3)):

> Provided that, where a legal estate (not being settled land) is vested in joint tenants beneficially, and any tenant desires to sever the joint tenancy in equity, he shall give to the other joint tenants a notice in writing of such desire or do such other acts or things as would, in the case of personal estate, have been effectual to sever the tenancy in equity, and thereupon the land shall be held in trust on terms which would have been requisite for giving effect to the beneficial interest if there had been an actual severance.

When the equitable joint tenancy is severed, the joint tenant severing will take an equal portion of the interest as a tenant in common. Thus, if the property was expressly conveyed to two persons as joint tenants, on severance each will acquire a half share as tenants in common (*Goodman v Gallant* [1986] Fam 106 approved by the House of Lords in *Stack v Dowden* [2007] 2 AC 432 at para. 49).

We will now look in detail at these methods of severing.

16.6.1 Notice in writing

This is probably the simplest way today of severing a joint tenancy. There is no prescribed form for the notice, but it is essential that it contains a clear expression of the intention to sever the joint tenancy.

The notice must be served on all the joint tenants, by leaving it at their last known address or by posting it to that address by registered or recorded delivery (LPA 1925, s. 196(3) and (4); Recorded Delivery Service Act 1962, s. 1 and Sch. 1 para. 1).

Once the notice has been served in one of these ways it will be effective and will sever the joint tenancy, even if the co-owner does not in fact receive it (*Re 88 Berkeley Road*

NW9 [1971] Ch 648; and see *Kinch v Bullard* [1999] 1 WLR 423, in which a wife's notice was held to have severed the joint tenancy she held with her husband, despite the fact that she had changed her mind and prevented the notice from reaching him).

An interesting case on severance is *Grindal v Hooper* [1999] EGCS 150 (and see the article on the case at [2000] Conv 461). Here, in the conveyance to themselves, joint tenants had agreed that any notice purporting to sever their joint tenancy would not be effective unless it had been annexed to the conveyance to them. (This term takes one step further a usual conveyancing practice, under which notice of severance is noted on the title deeds as a warning to later acquirers.) One joint tenant served a notice that complied with s. 36(2) but was not annexed to the conveyance. On his death the survivor claimed that there had been no valid severance in this instance. The court held that the agreement between the joint tenants could not displace the effect of the statutory rule that a notice complying with s. 36(2) did effect severance. The parties had been tenants in common in equity from the point at which notice was validly given.

16.6.2 'Such other acts or things as would, in the case of personal estate, sever the tenancy in equity'

It may seem strange that methods of severing appropriate to personal property are prescribed here but it must be remembered that the old statutory trust for sale had the effect of notionally converting the beneficiaries' interest into an interest in money (i.e., personal property (see 2.8 and 15.5.1.2)). Although this conversion no longer occurs, due to TOLATA 1996, s. 3, the statutory provision has not been altered.

What 'acts or things' bring about severance in equity? The classic statement, to which later decisions usually refer with approval, is that of Sir William Page Wood V-C in *Williams v Hensman* (1861) 1 John & H 546 at p. 557:

> A joint tenancy may be severed in three ways: in the first place, an act of any one of the persons interested operating upon his own share may create a severance as to that share... Each one is at liberty to dispose of his own interest in such manner as to sever it from the joint fund losing, of course, at the same time, his own right of survivorship. Secondly, a joint tenancy may be severed by mutual agreement. And, in the third place, there may be a severance by any course of dealing sufficient to intimate that the interests of all were mutually treated as constituting a tenancy in common.

We will look at each of these three methods in turn.

16.6.2.1 'An act... operating upon his own share'

The example of this method given in *Williams v Hensman* is that of disposing of one's own interest in such a way as to sever it from the joint property—for example, on sale. This creates severance because it has the effect of destroying one of the unities essential to the joint tenancy: that of title. The purchaser does not share the unity of title with the other co-owners, for he takes under a different document and so cannot be a joint tenant with them.

In law, severance would occur when the estate was conveyed to the purchaser, but in equity, it takes place as soon as there is a specifically enforceable contract to sell. It will be remembered that equity recognises the purchaser as owner from the date of the contract (see 5.7) and the change of equitable ownership is enough to destroy the unities.

Where severance is effected by sale of the beneficial interest, the joint tenant cannot transfer his interest in the legal estate to the purchaser, for to do so would amount to severance of the legal joint tenancy, which is forbidden (LPA 1925, s. 36(2)). So, even after he has disposed of his beneficial interest, he continues to hold the legal estate as a trustee, and can only cease to be a trustee by releasing his interest to his fellow joint tenants or by retiring from the trust (Trustee Act 1925, s. 39).

Another example of alienation arises when one joint tenant charges (mortgages) his interest in the property. Acting alone, the joint tenant can only affect his or her own interest (the equitable interest) and can only charge it if it constitutes a share separate from that of the other co-owner. Thus, charging your own interest severs the joint tenancy (the legal owners would have to act together as trustees to charge the legal estate). In *First National Securities v Hegarty* [1984] 1 All ER 139, Bingham J held that the same effect occurred where a husband purported to mortgage the legal estate by resorting to the forgery of his wife's signature. The result was a charge operating only on the husband's interest, which severed the joint tenancy in equity.

An example which falls within this category (although this may at first seem odd) arises if one of the joint tenants is declared bankrupt. This is an involuntary effect of the law relating to bankruptcy which transfers the bankrupt's interest to his trustee in bankruptcy when a bankruptcy order is made. Thus, while not really an act of the bankrupt co-owner, it nonetheless does create a separate share in the property by means of a transferring disposition of the beneficial interest in the property.

16.6.2.2 Mutual agreement

Severance can be effected by the agreement of all the joint tenants. The agreement may, of course, be express, but can also be inferred from the conduct of the parties. The leading modern case which illustrates this method of severance is *Burgess v Rawnsley* [1975] 1 Ch 429. Here it was held that an oral agreement by one joint tenant to purchase the share of the other had effected a severance (because the parties were thinking in terms of 'shares'), even though such an agreement would not be legally enforceable because there was no written memorandum or part performance to satisfy LPA 1925, s. 40 (the predecessor to the Law of Property (Miscellaneous) Provisions Act 1989, s. 2). We noted in 16.6.2.1 that a contract must be specifically enforceable if it is to constitute severance under the first rule in *Williams v Hensman*; but in *Burgess v Rawnsley* [1975] Ch 429 at 444, Browne LJ emphasised that this requirement

> only applies where the suggestion is that the joint tenancy has been severed by an alienation by one joint tenant to a third party and does not apply to severance by agreement between the joint tenants.

The principle that an unenforceable agreement can serve as evidence of a common intention to sever was confirmed in *Hunter v Babbage* [1994] EGCS 8, in which a divorcing couple's unenforceable agreement was held to sever the joint tenancy, although the husband had died before the agreement could be formalised.

Another example of severance by agreement is to be found in *Re Woolnough* [2002] WTLR 595. Here, the joint tenants were brother and sister. They went to their solicitor together and both made wills, each leaving his or her interest in the property to the other but with a remainder to their niece. After the sister's death the brother changed his will and it became essential to know whether the joint tenancy had been severed by the making of the earlier wills. The court held that it had. This is because for each to make a will leaving a share to the other there must have been an intention on the part of both to treat themselves as each having a share. If they agreed that each had a share they must both have regarded themselves as having interests in common (rather than joint) because joint interests do not give rise to shares that can be disposed of by a will.

No severance by will

In considering the decision in *Re Woolnough* it is important to realise that the will-making was treated as evidence of a mutual agreement to sever, and that it was the agreement which effected severance. A joint tenancy cannot be severed by one tenant making a will which purports to dispose of his interest in the property. The will does not take effect until the death of the joint tenant. At the moment of death the right of survivorship operates, with the result that the deceased has no interest in the property to pass under the will.

16.6.2.3 'Any course of dealing [which shows] that the interests of all were mutually treated as constituting a tenancy in common'

In *Burgess v Rawnsley*, members of the Court of Appeal expressed views on this third category, although they emphasised that as the decision was based on the second ground (mutual agreement), these views were necessarily *obiter dicta*. Thus, Sir John Pennycuick explained that it includes 'negotiations which, although not otherwise resulting in any agreement, indicate a common intention that the joint tenancy should be regarded as severed' (at p. 447). It should be noted that Lord Denning MR gave a slightly wider interpretation (at p. 439), which seems to cover a unilateral declaration by the party wishing to sever:

> It is sufficient if there is a course of dealing in which one party makes clear to the other that he desires that their shares should no longer be held jointly but be held in common.

This does not seem to fit too well with the requirement of mutual behaviour stated in *Williams v Hensman*, and it should be noted that Sir John Pennycuick expressly states that in his view 'a mere verbal notice' (i.e., an oral notice) by one party to the other cannot operate as severance (p. 448). Written notice, of course, is validated by the statutory rules in LPA 1925, s. 36(3) and (4).

16.6.3 Forfeiture

One final method of severance, not covered by LPA 1925, s. 36(2) or *Williams v Hensman* (1861) 1 John & H 546 must be noted briefly. Should one joint tenant kill the other, it seems that the right of survivorship cannot operate because this would allow the killer to benefit from his or her criminal act. The general principle that this is not permitted is to be found in *In the Estate of Hall* [1914] P 1, and some recent decisions in Australia and New Zealand have applied this to cases of joint tenancy, although it seems there is as yet no English decision directly on the point. However, you should see the Forfeiture Act 1982 and the judgments in the Court of Appeal in *Dunbar v Plant* [1998] FLR 157, which suggest that the same result would apply in English law. On the impact of the forfeiture rule, see also *T.W.G.S. v J.M.G.* [2001] Ch 568.

For a detailed analysis of the overseas authorities on this point and the jurisprudence, see Gray and Gray, at paras. 7.4.99–7.4.107.

16.6.4 12 Trant Way: example of the operation of the severance rules

We saw in 16.2.5 that despite the fact that the transfer of this property purported to convey the legal estate to all six students, rules about the age and number of legal owners resulted in the estate vesting in the first four students named in the transfer who were over 18 (Brian, Colin, David and Eric), who hold the estate in trust for themselves, Alice and Fanny.

We have also seen in the course of this chapter that the way in which the students hold the beneficial interest depends on the presence of the four unities and the absence of any words of severance (that is, any words in the transfer indicating an intention to hold as tenants in common in equity). The four unities appear to be satisfied by the transfer, and we assume that there were no words of severance. All six contributed equally to the purchase price, so there is no question of equity presuming a tenancy in common. Even if the home-sharing arrangement fell within the rule in *Stack v Dowden*, we are not aware of any express or inferred agreement between the students to hold as tenants in common. It seems therefore that there are joint tenancies of both the legal estate and the beneficial interest, as shown in the following diagram.

LAW Legal estate	EQUITY Beneficial interest
(B, C, D and E)	(A, B, C, D, E and F)

The effect of the severance rules can be illustrated by assuming that the following events occur:

(a) Alice serves notice of severance on Brian, Colin, David, Eric and Fanny

(b) Brian sells his interest to Wilfred

(c) Colin dies.

This produces the devolution of title to the legal estate and the equitable interest shown below.

EVENT	LAW	EQUITY	EXPLANATION
	(B, C, D and E)	(A, B, C, D, E and F)	At start all are joint tenants in law and equity.
(a)	(B, C, D and E)	A (B, C, D, E and F)	Position at law not affected. A becomes tenant in common in equity with a one-sixth share, but others remain joint tenants *inter se* ('between themselves').
(b)	(B, C, D and E)	A, W (C, D, E and F)	Position at law not affected. In equity, severance by destruction of unities. W becomes tenant in common with a one-sixth share. C, D, E and F remain joint tenants *inter se* of four-sixths.
(c)	(B, D and E)	A, W (D, E and F)	Right of survivorship operates in law and equity. B, D and E hold the legal estate as joint tenants. A and W each own a one-sixth share of the equitable interest. D, E and F jointly own four-sixths of the equitable interest.

16.7 Relationship between co-owners

It is not uncommon for co-owners to have differences of opinion about the management of their property. In the case of family homes, in particular, disputes often arise when relationships break down and one owner may want to exclude the other from the property or even to sell it against the other's wishes. In considering how to deal with such problems, it is important to remember that co-owned land is always subject to a trust of land and accordingly is governed by the provisions of TOLATA 1996, which we consider in detail in the next chapter.

16.7.1 Is one co-owner able to sell the property against the wishes of the other(s)?

Where one co-owner wishes to sell the property (i.e., the legal estate) and cannot secure the agreement of the other(s), he will have to seek an order for sale from the court under TOLATA 1996, s. 14. There is no other way of proceeding. If the other co-owners hold the legal estate with him, he is unable to make a conveyance or transfer without their co-operation. If he is the sole owner of the legal estate, holding in trust for the other co-owners in equity, the decision of the Court of Appeal in *Bull v Bull* [1955] 1 QB 234 (see below) makes it clear that he cannot evict them in order to sell with vacant possession and must instead seek an order for sale.

For details of the court's powers under s. 14, and an account of decisions under the Act in co-ownership cases, see 17.8.

16.7.2 Does one co-owner have the right to exclude the other from the property?

We saw in Chapter 15 that the imposition of the statutory trust for sale, coupled with the doctrine of conversion, made it difficult for some co-owners to claim that they had a right to occupy the land. Where the legal estate was vested in all the co-owners, each one had a legal right to possession of the property and one could not lawfully be evicted by another. It was different, however, when the legal estate was held by one person in trust for himself and another, who consequently had only an equitable interest under the trust. Under the doctrine of conversion, the equitable interest was regarded as being in money and not in the land itself, and it was difficult to see how such an interest could give a right to occupy the land.

This problem was considered by the Court of Appeal in *Bull v Bull* [1955] 1 QB 234. Here a financial contribution by the mother to the purchase price of a house conveyed to her son created a resulting trust, in which the son held the legal estate in trust for himself and his mother as tenants in common. The house was bought to provide a home for both of them but after his marriage the son wanted his mother to move out, and finally sought a possession order against her. The court held that, while the trust for sale imposed a duty to sell, each beneficiary was entitled to occupy the property until it was sold. The son could not evict his mother by obtaining an order for possession. If he wished to bring the co-ownership to an end and could not do so by agreement, he should seek an order for sale from the court (under LPA 1925, s. 30), and on sale should divide the proceeds between himself and his mother. In effect, the court in this case 'glossed over' the effect of the notional conversion of the property, and after this decision the courts appeared willing to protect the occupation of equitable co-owners and did not press the statutory trust for sale to its logical conclusion.

With TOLATA 1996 the old difficulties have disappeared. The trust imposed on co-owners is now a trust of land, not a trust for sale, and the doctrine of conversion no longer applies. Under the trust, co-owners have interests in the land itself, and in certain cases have a statutory right to occupy the property under s. 12. Where several beneficiaries have this right and all wish to occupy the property, the trustees have the power to balance their interests under the provisions of s. 13, and may permit some to occupy while excluding others. Of course, in the case of the statutory trust imposed on co-owners, where the same people may be both trustees and beneficiaries, this may simply lead to further conflict, which will have to be resolved by the court under TOLATA 1996, s. 14. For details of the statutory right of occupation and the court's power to deal with disputes between co-owners, see 17.7.

16.7.3 Can one co-owner be required to pay rent to the other(s)?

Although each joint tenant of the legal estate is entitled to possession of the property, it often happens in practice, particularly where relationships break down, that one owner will move out of the property while the other continues to live there. If, at a later stage, the property is sold, each owner may claim that expenditure incurred between separation and sale should be taken into account in dividing the proceeds of sale between them. For example, the owner who moved out may have had to rent alternative accommodation, and may claim that the one who remained in the property ought to pay an 'occupation rent' which could be deducted from his or her share of the proceeds. Equally, however, the party in occupation may have spent money by paying mortgage instalments or on improving the property before sale, and wants to claim credit for these payments.

In the past, questions of this sort were decided by the courts under a process known as 'equitable accounting'. It was the practice of the courts to require a co-owner in sole occupation to give credit for an occupation rent only if the other owner had been turned out of the property (rather than leaving voluntarily), but the more recent approach has been that an occupation rent may be payable where it is necessary to do justice or equity between the parties (see per Lightman J in *Murphy v Gooch* [2007] EWCA Civ 603 at para. 10).

A claim to an occupation rent was one of the issues considered by the House of Lords in *Stack v Dowden* [2007] 2 AC 432. Stack had moved out of the family home and sought to recover the cost of alternative accommodation from his former partner, Dowden, who had remained with their children in the family home. As we explained above (16.7.2), TOLATA 1996, s. 13 gives trustees the power to permit some beneficiaries to occupy the trust property while excluding others, and s. 13(6) provides that in such circumstances the trustees may require the occupying beneficiaries to make 'compensation payments' to those who are excluded. In *Stack v Dowden* the House of Lords considered this provision, which it described as having replaced the old doctrines of equitable accounting. In Lady Hale's words (para. 94):

> The criteria laid down in the statute should be applied, rather than in the cases decided under the old law, although the results may often be the same.

Thus claims by co-owners for an occupation rent must now be made under the statutory provisions, and we will tell you more about this in the next chapter (see 17.7.4).

16.8 Ending co-ownership

There are three ways in which co-ownership may come to an end.

16.8.1 Partition

Where the land is sufficiently extensive it may prove convenient for the co-owners to decide to partition the premises between themselves. In this way each becomes a sole beneficial owner of a portion of the land. Such partition can always be effected by agreement between all the co-owners. Under TOLATA 1996, s. 7(1), trustees may partition the land and convey the portions thus created to the co-owners. Before exercising this power the trustees are required to obtain the consent of each beneficiary to whom a conveyance of a portion of the land is to be made (s. 7(3)).

We should perhaps remind you that, where title to land is still unregistered, partitioning it in this way is one of the new triggers inducing first registration (see 7.4.1.1), so each beneficiary who acquires land in this way will need to apply for first registration of the title to his plot.

16.8.2 Sale of the property and division of the proceeds

Again, this may be done by agreement or, where necessary, on the order of the court following an application under TOLATA 1996, s. 14.

16.8.3 Union of interests in one of the co-owners

16.8.3.1 On death

Where the beneficial interests are held by several co-owners as joint tenants, the survivor will become solely entitled to the property by right of survivorship.

This could create difficulties if the survivor wanted to sell the property, because it was almost impossible to prove to a prospective purchaser that the beneficial joint tenancy had not been severed at some time in the past. If there had been severance, the tenants would have been holding shares in the beneficial interest under a tenancy in common, and these shares would have passed on death to those entitled to take. If this had happened, the sole survivor, who appeared to be absolutely entitled, would in fact be holding the legal estate as trustee for himself and others. To guard against this, a purchaser might well insist on paying the purchase money to two trustees (to take advantage of the overreaching procedure), and this would involve the seller in the delay and expense of appointing another trustee. This problem has been resolved by the Law of Property (Joint Tenants) Act 1964, for which see 17.9.3.2.

16.8.3.2 By agreement

It is also possible in any co-ownership situation for one owner to acquire the interests of the others by agreement, and thus become solely entitled.

16.9 Some practical advice

We have chosen to keep this chapter relatively short, and to give you more information about co-ownership in the following chapter on trusts of land. This is because all co-owners are subject to the statutory trusts of land and therefore their rights and obligations are governed by the rules about those trusts which are contained in TOLATA 1996.

However, we know quite well that as examinations approach, students tend to revise some topics and leave out others. If you are thinking of doing this, do realise that co-ownership and trusts of land are very closely linked: it could be a mistake to revise one and leave out the other. In particular, you could have difficulty in dealing with a problem about co-owners unless you know something of the TOLATA 1996 provisions about:

- consultation of beneficiaries (17.5.3);
- beneficiaries' right of occupation (17.7); and
- the powers of the court under s. 14 of TOLATA 1996 (17.8).

You should also note that our account of *Stack v Dowden* [2007] 2 AC 432 is divided between this chapter and Chapter 20 (on resulting and constructive trusts).

FURTHER READING

Stack v Dowden

Cloherty and Fox, 'Proving a Trust of a Shared Home' [2007] CLJ 317.

Dixon, 'Case Note on *Stack v Dowden*' [2007] 71 Conv 352.

Neuberger, Chancery Bar Association Annual Lecture, 2008, paras. 8–22—available at www.chba.org.uk.

Pawlowski, 'Beneficial Entitlement—No Longer Doing Justice?' [2007] 71 Conv 354.

Piska, 'Distinctions without a Difference? Explaining *Stack v Dowden*' [2008] 72 Conv 451 (451–460)—case note on *Fowler v Barron*.

Swadling, 'The Common Intention Trust in the House of Lords: An Opportunity Missed' (2007) 123 LQR 511.

Severing a joint tenancy

Crown, 'Severance of Joint Tenancy of Land by Partial Alienation' (2001) 117 LQR 477.

Hayton, 'Joint Tenancies—Severance' (note on *Burgess v Rawnsley* and *Nielson-Jones v Fedden*) [1976] CLJ 20.

Percival, 'Severance By Written Notice—A Matter of Delivery?' (note on *Kinch v Bullard*) [1999] Conv 61.

Tee, 'Severance Revisited' [1995] Conv 105.

Jones v Kernott

Briggs, Co-ownership—An Equitable Non-Sequitur' (2012) 128 LQR 183.

Dixon, 'The Still Not Ended, Never-Ending Story' [2012] 76 Conv 83.

Gardner and Davidson, 'The Supreme Court On Family Homes' (2012) 128 LQR 178.

Hanbury and Martin, *Modern Equity*, 19th edn., 2012, para. 11–006.

Mee, '*Jones v Kernott*: inferring and imputing in Essex' [2012] 76 Conv 167.

Pawlowski, 'Imputed intention and joint ownership— A return to common sense' [2012] 76 Conv 149.

Yip, 'The rules applying to unmarried cohabitants' family home' [2012] 76 Conv 159.

17

Trusts of land

Unless otherwise stated, references to statutory provisions in this chapter are to the Trusts of Land and Appointment of Trustees Act 1996 ('TOLATA 1996').

17.1. Introduction

17.1.1 Trusts relating to land before 1997

In Chapter 15 we explained the ways in which trusts relating to land may arise, and outlined some of the reasons for which a property owner may create such a trust. In particular, we noted that an owner who wanted to give several people successive interests in his land (i.e. to 'create a settlement') had to choose between two forms: a Settled Land Act (SLA) settlement and a trust for sale. Both these types of settlement involved the use of a trust, but were governed by very different rules and procedures, which could be confusing for settlors.

A further difficulty arose where a settlor wished to give the benefit of his property to one person absolutely but preferred to leave the title to the estate, and its management, in the hands of trustees. The 1925 property legislation made no specific provision for such an arrangement, which is known as a 'bare trust', and consequently there could be uncertainty about the application of statutory rules to such a trust.

We also noted that most, but not all, forms of co-ownership were subject to a trust for sale imposed by the LPA 1925 and that the rules governing these statutory trusts were not always appropriate to the needs of the co-owners.

17.1.2 The Trusts of Land and Appointment of Trustees Act 1996

17.1.2.1 The new 'trust of land'

The Trusts of Land and Appointment of Trustees Act 1996 (TOLATA 1996) came into force on 1 January 1997. The Act introduced a completely new trust, the 'trust of land', which is defined by s. 1(1)(a):

> 'trust of land' means any trust of property which consists of or includes land.

Section 1(2)(a) expressly provides that the reference in s. 1(1) includes all descriptions of trust, including express, implied and resulting trusts, trusts for sale and bare trusts.

17.1.2.2 A new way of making settlements

From 1 January 1997 the new trust of land is the only way in which a new settlement may be created.

TOLATA 1996 provides that no new SLA settlements may be created (s. 2(1)); any attempt to create such a settlement will take effect as a trust of land. Section 2(6) and Sch. 1 deal with certain specific circumstances which formerly would have given rise to SLA settlements, and we will deal with these later (see 17.10).

An attempt to create a trust for sale will simply take effect as a trust of land under the statutory definition in s. 1(2)(a) (see further 17.1.2.5).

Thus in the future the problems associated with having two different ways of creating settlements will no longer trouble property owners who wish to make settlements.

17.1.2.3 Statutory trust imposed on co-ownership

The Act provides that the statutory trust imposed on co-owners becomes a trust of land rather than a trust for sale. It does this by amending the relevant provisions in LPA 1925: see s. 25(1) and Sch. 3 paras. 3 and 4. This means that co-owners are no longer under a duty to sell their land and are not subject to the doctrine of conversion, so that their interests in the property can be regarded as interests in land rather than in money.

17.1.2.4 What happened to existing SLA settlements and trusts for sale?

SLA settlements which were in existence at 1 January 1997 continue to exist in their original form and are not converted into trusts of land. You will find a brief note about these settlements in Chapter 18.

Trusts for sale which were in existence at 1 January 1997 were converted overnight into trusts of land, as a consequence of s. 1(2)(b), which makes it quite clear that the statute catches trusts created or arising before the commencement of the Act. This change affected both expressly created trusts for sale and also those imposed by statute, as for example in cases of co-ownership. As a result of the change in the nature of the trust, the trust property ceased to be subject to the doctrine of conversion so that the beneficiaries could in future be regarded as having interests in land rather than in money.

In general, the existing trusts for sale which were converted into trusts of land are subject to the new statutory rules about the trust of land which we describe in this chapter. There are, however, a few exceptional cases of existing trusts for sale to which some of the new rules do not apply (if you need to know about these, see s. 3(2) and s. 11(2)(b)).

17.1.2.5 What happens if a settlor tries to create a new trust for sale?

Section 1(2)(a) specifically provides that trusts for sale are included within the statutory definition of the new trusts of land. Thus although a settlor may still create a trust for sale (either by describing it as such or by imposing upon the trustees a duty to sell the trust property), the trust will be categorised as 'a trust of land' and will operate within the framework of rules provided by the Act.

The Act contains two important provisions which prevent trusts for sale operating as they used to do.

(1) The trustees have an *implied power to postpone sale* (s. 4(1)), which cannot be excluded by the settlor (see 17.4.2.6); and

(2) The doctrine of conversion no longer operates on property held under a trust for sale (see below)

No conversion under a trust for sale Section 3(1) provides that:

> Where land is held by trustees subject to a trust for sale, the land is not to be regarded as personal property...

In other words, the land is not to be regarded as converted into money (a type of personal property—see 2.8), and this means that the doctrine of conversion is no longer brought into operation by the trustees' duty to sell the trust property. You should note, however, that despite the marginal note to s. 3 ('Abolition of doctrine of conversion') notional conversion continues to apply in other circumstances where there is a specifically enforceable obligation to convert land into money, or vice versa—as for example under a contract to buy or sell land.

Summary The changes introduced by TOLATA which we have discussed in this section may be summarised as follows:

- With the exception of SLA settlements created before 1 January 1997, all trusts relating to land now operate as trusts of land.
- The new trust of land includes:
  - all expressly created trusts, whether they be for one beneficiary (a bare trust) or for several beneficiaries in succession (creating a settlement) or concurrently, and whether or not they impose a duty to sell on the trustees;
  - all implied trusts, whether resulting or constructive; and
  - all trusts imposed by statute—as in cases of co-ownership.
- Even where an express trust imposes a duty to sell upon the trustees, they have a power to postpone sale, which cannot be excluded, and the doctrine of conversion no longer applies to such a trust.

17.1.3 Contents of this chapter

The operation of the new trust of land is regulated by Part 1 of TOLATA 1996, and the rest of this chapter deals with these provisions. We will illustrate them by reference to

- John Brown, the owner of 20 Trant Way, who needs advice about creating a settlement in his will (see 17.2); and
- the six students who hold 12 Trant Way as co-owners (see 16.1.2), and are therefore subject to a statutory trust of land.

- At the end of the chapter we will note three special dispositions which would formerly have created SLA settlements but now give rise to trusts of land (17.10).

17.2. Creating a settlement of 20 Trant Way

The fee simple estate of 20 Trant Way is owned by John Brown, who lives there with his wife, Janet. John has not yet made a will, although his wife keeps urging him to do so. John has no doubt about what he wants to happen to the house and his investments when he dies: he wants them all to go to his wife, if she survives him, and then at her death to pass on to his two married daughters.

In legal terms, what John wants to do is to create a settlement, giving successive interests to members of his family: a life estate to his widow and a remainder in fee simple to his daughters. He is, however, very uncertain about how to achieve this. He remembers reading a newspaper article years ago, which said that all this could be done with a trust, but warned that there were several different types of trust and that it was important to choose the right one. Apparently, it was possible to make the wrong one by mistake, and this worries John, and has deterred him from doing anything. However, as we have already explained, settlors no longer have to choose between two forms of settlement and any trust of No. 20 which John might make would take effect as a trust of land under TOLATA 1996.

If John's will is professionally drafted, it will almost certainly contain an express provision that at his death his property is to pass to trustees to hold on trust for his wife during her lifetime and then for his daughters. The trust will be a trust of land and will be governed by the provisions of TOLATA 1996.

If, however, John prefers to make his own will, he may simply provide that his property is to go to his wife and then to his daughters, without referring to any trust. Before 1997, this sort of provision in a home-made will would have created a SLA settlement, with resulting expense and inconvenience, but we know from s. 2(1) of TOLATA 1996 that it is no longer possible to create such a settlement. Rather confusingly, the Act does not make any express provision for treating such a disposition as giving rise to a trust of land, and the fact that it does so has to be worked out from general principles. You may remember from Chapter 9 that after 1925 life estates and future interests can no longer exist as legal estates. Thus dispositions creating such interests can take effect only in equity, with the result that the legal fee simple must be held on trust to give effect to such interests. Under s. 1(1), such a trust will now take effect as a trust of land and thus, if John makes such a disposition, he will in fact create a trust of land, even though he does not say so in so many words.

17.2.1 Mixed trusts

We must remember that John owns some investments, which he also wants to leave successively to his wife and daughters. In order to constitute a trust of land, it is sufficient that the trust property 'includes land' (s. 1(1)(a)). Thus, mixed trusts, containing both land and personalty, will also be subject to the rules in TOLATA 1996. This is a useful rule because it allows a house and its contents, or, indeed, all the settlor's property, to be held under a single trust. As a result, John Brown will be able to create one trust which will apply to both his house and his investments.

17.2.2 What a settlor will want to know

If John is advised to create a trust of land, he will probably have a number of questions about it, such as:

- How many trustees are needed and who appoints them?
- What do trustees do?
- Are there any controls over what the trustees do?
- Will his wife be involved in looking after the property?
- Can he be sure that his wife will be able to live in the house as long as she wishes, but also be free to sell it if she wants to move to something smaller?
- What will happen if his wife and the trustees disagree about what is to be done with the house?
- Will the fact that the house is subject to a trust make it more difficult to sell if his wife wants to move?

The answers to all these questions are to be found in TOLATA 1996, and we will look at them in the following sections.

17.3. How many trustees are needed and who appoints them?

The rules about the number and appointment of trustees are to be found partly in the Trustee Act 1925 and partly in TOLATA 1996.

17.3.1 Number of trustees

It is usual to have a minimum of two trustees because the 'overreaching' provisions, which are designed to protect purchasers, will lead anyone dealing with the trust to demand signatures from at least two trustees on any receipt for capital money.

A trust can, however, function with only one trustee, as for example where the owner of the legal estate holds it in trust for himself and a friend who has contributed to the cost of buying the property (a 'resulting' trust). In such a case there is no need to appoint an additional trustee until the question of receiving capital money arises.

It is not possible to have more than four trustees of a legal estate: where there is an attempt to appoint more than four, the Trustee Act (TA 1925), s. 34(2) will vest the legal estate in the first four of full age (that is the first four listed but omitting anyone who is named but who is under 18 when the disposition takes effect). We have already seen an example of this happening in the case of the six students who bought No. 12 Trant Way (see 16.1.2 and 16.2.5).

17.3.2 Who appoints trustees?

In the case of an express trust, it is normal for the disposition creating the trust to specify who are to be the trustees. Thus, if John Brown decides to create a trust in his will, he will most probably name the trustees, who could be family members or friends, but could also be drawn from his professional advisers, such as his solicitors or bank.

The settlor may also nominate a person or persons to appoint trustees, including any additional or replacement trustees who may be needed in the future. If no appointor is named in the document creating the trust, any new appointments will be made by the existing trustees or, if they have all died, by the personal representatives of the last surviving trustee. If there is no one able or willing to appoint, the appointment may be made by the court, which can also make an order vesting the trust property in the new trustee(s). (For further details, see TA 1925, ss. 36, 41 and 44.)

Appointments of trustees must be made in writing and should be made by deed because a deed is needed in order to ensure that the legal estate in the land which is the trust property vests in the new trustee (TA 1925, s. 40).

17.3.3 Replacement and retirement of trustees

Section 36 of TA 1925 specifies the following circumstances which permit the replacement of a trustee: where a trustee dies; is out of the United Kingdom for more than 12 months; wishes to retire from the trust; refuses or is unfit to act (this would cover dishonesty or bankruptcy amongst other things); is incapable of acting (illness or mental incapacity); or is an infant (under 18).

A trustee may also retire, without a fresh appointment being made to replace him, under TA 1925, s. 39, but only if there remain at least two trustees or the remaining trustee is a trust corporation. Trust corporations are defined in s. 68(18) and include the Public Trustee and certain other corporations.

17.3.4 Control by beneficiaries of appointment and retirement

The impact of TA 1925 s. 36, is now modified by TOLATA 1996, ss. 19–21, which give powers to the beneficiaries to direct the person with the right to appoint under TA 1925, s. 36, so that the choice of new trustee is in fact no longer always controlled by the person who actually appoints. In addition s. 19 allows beneficiaries to require trustees to resign from the trust. The combination of these powers means that in many cases beneficiaries will be in a position to replace the trustees entirely should they disagree with them or replace particular trustees to whom they object. You should note, however, that the beneficiaries are not given the actual power to make the appointment but just the power to select the person(s) to be appointed.

You should also note that the beneficiaries' new powers do not apply to every trust. They do not apply if the settlor has in the trust instrument specified a person to appoint new trustees: in such a case the express wishes of the settlor take precedence and the beneficiaries have no power to direct the appointment of trustees of their choice (s. 19(1)(a)).

The new powers also only apply where the beneficiaries are all of full age and capacity and (taken together) are absolutely entitled to the trust property (TOLATA 1996, s. 19(1)(b)). Those are the conditions which would have to be satisfied in order to allow the beneficiaries to elect to end the trust under the rule in *Saunders v Vautier* (1841) 4 Beav 115 and to vest the trust property in themselves absolutely or to re-settle on new trusts with fresh trustees (which was the only way that, in the past, the beneficiaries could control the choice of trustee). Thus, TOLATA 1996 simply allows the beneficiaries to control the appointment of new trustees without the expense and possible adverse tax consequences of ending the old trust and creating a new one.

In order to exercise their powers under s. 19, the beneficiaries must be unanimous; they must all agree on the new appointment (or retirement) and must give a direction in writing (s. 19(2)). If the beneficiaries cannot agree, they cannot exercise the new power to give directions and as far as appointments are concerned the choice of the new trustee(s) remains with the person who has power to appoint under TA 1925, s. 36.

Finally, we should note that powers in TOLATA 1996, ss. 19–21, apply to all trusts and not just to the new trusts of land. Thus they apply also to existing SLA settlements and to trusts of pure personalty. It would be a mistake to think that TOLATA 1996 relates solely to trusts of land: the provisions of Part II of the Act are general in their application.

17.4. What do trustees do?

Whatever the nature of the trust property, trustees will own that property and be responsible for managing and maintaining it in the interests of the beneficiaries. The general topic of trustees' powers and duties is well beyond the scope of this book, and all we will tell you about here are the specific provisions relating to trusts of land which are to be found in TOLATA 1996.

17.4.1 Trustees hold the legal estate

If John Brown's will does create a trust of land in respect of No. 20 Trant Way, the legal estate in the property would be transferred after his death to the trustees, who would hold it for the duration of the trust.

17.4.2 Trustees' powers under TOLATA 1996

17.4.2.1 Powers of an absolute owner

Section 6(1) provides that:

> For the purpose of exercising their functions as trustees, the trustees of land have in relation to the land subject to the trust all the powers of an absolute owner.

This means that John's trustees would be able to manage the property as they thought fit, since the 'powers of an absolute owner' include the ability to sell the land, to mortgage it, to grant leases and to create other rights over it, such as easements or options.

In addition to these very general powers given by s. 6(1), the Act makes specific provision for five particular powers:

- to acquire land;
- to delegate functions to beneficiaries;
- to partition the trust land between the beneficiaries;
- to compel the beneficiaries to accept a conveyance of the trust land to themselves; and
- to postpone sale under a trust for sale.

17.4.2.2 Power to acquire land

Section 6(3) (as amended by the Trustee Act 2000, so as to include a reference to s. 8 of that Act) gives the trustees the power to acquire:

> freehold or leasehold land in the United Kingdom.

The trustees' power under s. 6(3) may be used to acquire land as an investment, or for occupation by a beneficiary 'or for any other reason' (TA 2000, s. 8(1), replacing an identical provision in s. 6(4) of TOLATA 1996). The provision in TOLATA 1996 resolved an earlier uncertainty as to whether it was permissible to use trust funds to buy a home for a beneficiary. John can therefore be assured that if he leaves the house in Trant Way in trust for his widow, his trustees will be able to sell the property and buy another home for her, if she ever wants to move.

17.4.2.3 Power to delegate functions to beneficiaries

Section 9(1) gives the trustees the power to delegate any of their functions to one or more of the beneficiaries. We consider this power in more detail in 17.6.

17.4.2.4 Power to partition

Section 7 gives the trustees power to partition the land between the beneficiaries, where the beneficiaries are all of full age and absolutely entitled. While of little use in the majority of cases, this power may assist where it is intended to divide a large estate between beneficiaries or even where a large house can effectively be partitioned into smaller lots. Partition requires the consent of the beneficiaries (s. 7(3)) and, where title to the land is still unregistered, also requires each of them to apply for first registration of title to his plot (see 7.4.1.1).

17.4.2.5 Power to compel beneficiaries to take conveyance

A new power for the trustees is contained in s. 6(2), which only applies where all the beneficiaries are of full age and absolutely entitled. This is a power which is designed to permit the trustees to force the beneficiaries to take a conveyance of the trust land, effectively making the beneficiaries themselves the trustees. This will enable the trustees, if they wish, to discharge themselves from the obligations under a settlement where it is no longer necessary for them to be involved.

It appears from the wording of this section that this power applies only where there are two or more beneficiaries. Where there is one beneficiary solely entitled to the trust property, the trustees may bring the trust to an end by conveying the property to him or her, and do not need specific statutory authority to do so (see further Megarry and Wade, para. 12–017).

17.4.2.6 Power to postpone sale under a trust for sale

Section 4(1) gives trustees of a trust for sale an implied power to postpone sale, even where they are under a duty to sell the property. This power cannot be excluded by the settlor; it is implied by s. 4(1):

> in the case of every trust for sale created by a disposition... despite any provision to the contrary made by the disposition.

This marks a change from the old law, since the power to postpone which was formerly implied under LPA 1925, s. 25(1) could be excluded by the settlor's expressing 'a contrary intention'. Section 4(1) applies to all trusts for sale of land, even those which were already in existence before the Act came into force, and which, therefore, might have contained an express exclusion of the power implied by LPA 1925, s. 25(1).

Situation where trustees disagree about postponing sale Although TOLATA 1996 makes it impossible for the settlor to exclude the power to postpone, there is no provision in the Act which prevents a minority of trustees refusing to postpone and insisting on sale, in reliance on the rule in *Re Mayo* [1943] Ch 302 (see above, 15.5.3). There must be unanimous agreement among the trustees to exercise their implied power to postpone sale; even if only one of them disagrees, they must perform their duty of selling the property.

Thus if the trust contains an obligation to sell and one trustee does not wish to postpone sale, the property will have to be sold even against the wishes of the majority of the trustees. In such a case, if the beneficiaries disagree with the one trustee, they may be able to prevent the sale by exercising their power under s. 19, to require that trustee to retire (if that power applies on the facts of the case). This may require fast action on the part of the beneficiaries, however, and they will have to agree about requiring the trustee's retirement. If this is not possible, another way of seeking to stop the sale could be an application to the court under s. 14 (which we consider later in 17.8.3).

17.5. Are there any controls over the exercise of trustees' powers?

As we have seen in the previous section, trustees have very wide powers under TOLATA 1996. Settlors like John Brown may be worried by the extent of those powers, fearing that they may be used to override the wishes of the beneficiaries or perhaps even be misused in the trustees' own interests. It may reassure John to know that there are a number of provisions in the Act which can have the effect of considerably limiting the trustees' powers and that in addition trustees are subject to strict duties in equity.

In outline, the conduct of trustees of a trust of land may be controlled as follows:

- by the settlor excluding or restricting their powers under TOLATA 1996;
- by the settlor requiring trustees to obtain prescribed consents before exercising powers;
- by the statutory requirement that trustees consult the beneficiaries and give effect to their wishes;
- by trustees' duties, breach of which amounts to breach of trust.

We will now consider each of these methods of control.

17.5.1 Exclusion and restriction of powers by settlor

The Act recognises that the wide powers it confers on trustees may not always be appropriate. Accordingly, s. 8(1) allows the settlor to exclude the powers contained in ss. 6 and 7 by making express provision in the disposition which creates the trust. This will still give the settlor who is creating an elaborately drafted express trust the chance to select the precise powers which the trustees should have in order to carry out the settlor's intentions, but means that in badly prepared, accidentally created or statutorily imposed trusts the trustees will have the wide powers which will allow them the best chance to produce a good result for the trust.

The wide terms of s. 8(1) mean that there is nothing to stop the settlor excluding the trustees' power to sell the property, and thus ensuring that the land would remain unsold for the duration of the trust. This possibility could be seen as an undesirable return to control by the 'dead hand' of the settlor; for possible ways of escaping its grip, see Watt [1997] 61 Conv 263.

17.5.1.1 Two powers which cannot be restricted or excluded

As we have already noted above, the implied power to postpone sale, given to trustees for sale by s. 4(1) of TOLATA 1996, cannot be restricted or excluded by the settlor. There is also no provision for the settlor to exclude or limit the trustees' powers to delegate functions to beneficiaries under s. 9(1) (see further 17.6).

17.5.2 Requirements for consents imposed by settlor

If the settlor wishes, he can require the trustees to obtain the consent of named individuals before exercising some or all of their powers. Section 8(2) says that where the settlor has done this:

> ...the power may not be exercised without the consent.

This means that if the trustees act without all the prescribed consents their act will constitute a breach of trust, and the beneficiaries could seek an injunction to restrain the breach, or could claim compensation from the trustees if it had already occurred.

The persons chosen by the settlor as persons whose consent should be obtained do not have to be beneficiaries or even persons who are in any way connected with the trust, but usually there will be some form of connection. Thus, John Brown, for example, could provide that his trustees must not exercise their power to sell 20 Trant Way without the consent of his widow and his two daughters.

Should it prove impossible to obtain the consent of a person specified in the trust instrument, it will be necessary for the trustees to protect themselves by making an application to the court under s. 14, which expressly mentions the possibility of the court making an order relieving the trustees of an obligation to obtain any consent before exercising a power.

Section 10(3) also contains provisions to deal with cases in which the person whose consent is required is a minor (under 18) at the time at which the need for consent arises. In this case the trustees should obtain the consent of a person who has parental responsibility for the minor.

The consents rules will permit settlors to tie the hands of their trustees by requiring that they obtain consent from someone who will be guaranteed to refuse. Although the trust of land no longer carries with it the obligation to sell which was a feature of the trust for sale, the power to sell is always available to the trustees under s. 6(1) which, as we have seen, provides that the trustees are to have 'all the powers of an absolute owner'. It is true that the power of sale could be excluded by the settlor under s. 8(1) of the Act, but if he does not want to do this he could instead use the requirement of consent to prevent the sale.

An old case that illustrates what can be done in this regard is *Re Inns* [1947] Ch 576, in which the settlor had left a large house by his will to his widow during her lifetime and thereafter to the district council, for use as a hospital. The trust instrument also provided that should the council use the property as a hospital, it would receive an additional gift of £10,000 to pay for equipment. It was provided that the property could not be sold without the consent of both the widow and the council. The widow wished to sell the property because it was too large and expensive for her to maintain but the council was forced to refuse its consent because if it gave consent it would lose its interest in remainder in the trust property and the additional £10,000 (because there would be no house to use as a hospital). The court held that these provisions in the trust instrument were valid and both consents were required in order to sell, even though the effect of enforcing them was to ensure that the property would never be sold.

17.5.3 Statutory requirement for consultation

You will realise that provision for consents will only be capable of being used in an express (and properly drafted) trust, because it is necessary to insert consent provisions into the trust instrument if they are to work. Accordingly, there has long been provision in trusts legislation requiring some degree of consultation of beneficiaries by trustees before the trustees exercised their powers. In the case of the trust for sale this requirement for consultation appeared in LPA 1925, s. 26(3). The advantage of these rules was that they applied automatically to a trust which arose by operation of law where the settlor might not really have been aware that a trust was being created and so would not, or could not, have provided for consents. The old requirements did not, however, work in an entirely satisfactory manner because they did not apply to expressly created trusts unless specifically included by the settlor.

Accordingly, the old requirements are adapted and extended in TOLATA 1996, s. 11(1), which provides:

> The trustees of land shall in the exercise of any function relating to land subject to the trust—
>
> (a) so far as practicable, consult the beneficiaries of full age and beneficially entitled to an interest in possession in the land, and
>
> (b) so far as consistent with the general interest of the trust, give effect to the wishes of those beneficiaries, or (in the case of dispute) of the majority (according to the value of their combined interests).

The mandatory requirement to consult and to 'give effect to the wishes' of the majority means that the wishes of the beneficiaries take priority over even an obligation to sell (where the settlor has imposed this); but you should note generally that the requirement to follow the wishes of the beneficiaries applies only 'so far as consistent with the general interest of the trust'.

If the trustees do not consult as required by s. 11(1), or ignore the results of consultation, the beneficiaries may seek an injunction to restrain any intended breach of trust by the trustees, or may claim compensation should the transaction to which they object have been completed.

17.5.3.1 Cases where there is no duty to consult

(1) *Duty to consult excluded* The duty to consult can be expressly excluded by the settlor in the disposition by which the trust was created (s. 11(2)(a)). The wording of the statutory provision suggests that the exclusion could be either total or in part (for example, excluding the need to consult a particular beneficiary). This rule reverses the old position under which trustees of an express trust were under a duty to consult only if this was expressly provided; a requirement to consult is now implied unless expressly excluded.

(2) *Beneficiaries compelled to take trust property* Another case in which the duty to consult will not apply is where the trustees are using the power under s. 6(2), to force the beneficiaries to take a conveyance of the trust property. In that case consultation is obviously pointless because this power would not be used unless there were

disagreement and the aim of s. 6(2) is to allow the trustees to free themselves of their trust obligations without the agreement of the beneficiaries.

17.5.4 Trustees' duties

Even if the settlor does not exclude or restrict the trustees' very wide powers or impose requirements for consent, the trustees are not free to do exactly what they want with the trust property. They are, of course, subject to all the general equitable rules about how trustees must conduct themselves. Thus, in all their dealings, the trustees must act in the interests of the trust as a whole and not, for example, for any personal advantage, for that would constitute a breach of trust.

The Act seeks to reinforce the general duties of trustees by a number of statutory provisions:

- *Section 6(1)* gives the trustees all the powers of an absolute owner 'for the purpose of exercising their functions as trustees', which could be interpreted as meaning that they could not exercise these powers for an improper purpose.
- *Section 6(6)* requires that the powers 'shall not be exercised in contravention of... any other enactment or any rule of law or equity'. Thus, for example, powers of investment must still be exercised in accordance with the requirements of the Trustee Act 2000.
- *Section 6(5)* provides that in exercising their powers the trustees shall have regard to the rights of the beneficiaries.

These provisions have given rise to some critical comment, which suggests that these duties are inherent in the role of trustee and do not need express statutory provision, but their inclusion may at least help to reassure settlors worried by the extent of the trustees' powers.

17.6. Can beneficiaries be involved in the management of the trust property?

17.6.1 Power to delegate

Section 9 allows trustees in appropriate cases to delegate any of their functions as trustees which relate to the land.

The functions which may be delegated are those 'which relate to the land' (s. 9(1)) and in consequence the trustees cannot for example delegate their power of choosing investments for any capital money which may arise from dealing with the land. Moreover, the Act specifically provides (s. 9(7)) that beneficiaries to whom trustee functions have been delegated shall not be regarded as trustees for other purposes—in particular, for the receipt of capital money.

It appears that the trustees' power of delegation cannot be excluded by the settlor. There is no provision in s. 9 for the expression of 'a contrary intent' and the power is not included in the general provisions for exclusion or restriction contained in s. 8(1).

17.6.2 To whom may trustees delegate?

Section 9(1) authorises delegation to:

> any beneficiary or beneficiaries of full age and beneficially entitled to an interest in possession in land subject to the trust.

It is important to emphasise that in order to be eligible under this provision, the beneficiary or beneficiaries must be 'entitled to an interest in possession'. Where a trust is designed to benefit several individuals in succession (as, for example, it would be if John Brown leaves his property to his wife for life and then after her death to his two daughters), the beneficiary entitled to actual enjoyment of the property (in this example, Mrs Brown) is said to have an interest 'in possession', while the later beneficiaries merely have 'future interests'—although in due course they too will have 'interests in possession'. Thus under s. 9(1) the trustees may delegate only to the beneficiary or beneficiaries who are currently entitled to enjoy the property. This means that the trustees could delegate some or all of their functions to Mrs Brown (which answers John's question about whether she could be involved in looking after the property), but they could not delegate to her daughters during her lifetime.

Where more than one beneficiary is entitled 'in possession' the trustees may delegate to one or more of them. A delegation to several beneficiaries can be expressed to be 'joint', in which case all the delegates must agree to any exercise of power, or 'separate', in which case decisions could be taken by one delegate alone. It is also possible to delegate on terms that the power may be exercised 'jointly or separately'.

17.6.3 Form of delegation, and its duration and revocation

Section 9 regulates various matters relating to the delegation. It must be made by all the trustees jointly, by power of attorney, that is by an authority given by deed to act as agent. The delegation may be for any period or indefinitely, and may be expressly revoked by one or more of the trustees. Further, it is automatically revoked by the appointment of a new trustee (so that the new trustee can consider whether he wishes to delegate his functions), and also by the delegate ceasing to be a beneficiary under the trust.

17.6.4 Liability of delegates and trustees

As we have seen, the trustees have the powers of an absolute owner for the purpose of exercising their functions (s. 6(1)), and it is, therefore, possible for a delegate of those functions to enter into major transactions affecting the property. If the delegate acted unwisely and in some way caused loss to the other beneficiaries, who would be liable?

Section 9(7) of the Act provides that beneficiaries to whom functions have been delegated:

> are, in relation to the exercise of the functions, in the same position as trustees (with the same duties and liabilities)....

This means that they would be liable for any behaviour which would constitute a breach of trust, and this potential liability may help to ensure that they act responsibly. If they fail to do so, however, and do not have the means to compensate the other beneficiaries for resulting loss, questions may well arise about the liability of the trustees, who made the delegation and thus enabled the beneficiaries to engage in these transactions.

In such a situation, the liability of the trustees was, under the original terms of the Act, surprisingly limited. Under s. 9(8) the trustees were required to exercise 'reasonable care' when deciding to delegate, but were not required to monitor the performance of the delegate thereafter, and so were not responsible for any loss which might be caused.

Section 9(8) was repealed and replaced by the TA 2000, which inserted a new s. 9A, dealing with both the decision to delegate and supervision after delegation. Under s. 9A(1), trustees considering delegation are subject to a duty of care, defined by the TA 2000, s. 1, as the duty of each trustee 'to exercise such care and skill as is reasonable in the circumstances', having regard to any special knowledge or experience that the trustee has (or, if a professional trustee, might be expected to have). Section 9A(2) imposes a duty on trustees who make a revocable delegation to keep that delegation under review, and if necessary to intervene by, for example, giving directions to the delegate or revoking the delegation. A trustee is not liable for any act or default of the delegate, unless the trustee has failed to comply with the duty of care in making or reviewing the delegation (s. 9A(6)).

17.7. Do beneficiaries have a right to occupy the trust property?

This is obviously an important question for a settlor like John Brown, whose main purpose in making a trust is to enable his widow to continue to live in the family home.

17.7.1 Before 1997

The question of whether a beneficiary had a right to occupy trust land caused real difficulty under the old law. It was clear that the current beneficiary of a SLA settlement (the 'tenant for life') was entitled to occupy the property (see Chapter 18). By contrast, in the case of trusts for sale the doctrine of conversion meant that the beneficiaries' interests were notionally in money and not in land, and in such circumstances it was difficult to maintain that a beneficiary had a right to occupy the land itself. As a result, settlors who wanted their beneficiaries to have this right had to make express provision for it when creating the trust. Unless this was done, a beneficiary had no *right* to occupy but might be permitted to do so at the discretion of the trustees.

We have already seen (16.7.2) that the statutory trust for sale imposed in cases of co-ownership caused particular difficulty, because equitable interests under such a trust were notionally in money and not in land and therefore could not give a beneficiary the right to occupy. This conclusion, however, was so inappropriate in the case of family homes that the courts did not apply the concept of conversion too strictly. Thus in *Bull v Bull* [1955] 1 QB 234 the Court of Appeal held that an equitable tenant in common had a right to occupy the property until sale and could not be evicted by the legal owner, and a similar approach was adopted by the House of Lords some years later in *City of London Building Society v Flegg* [1988] AC 54.

17.7.2 Under TOLATA 1996

Under the new Act all trusts relating to land (including those imposed on co-owners) take effect as trusts of land, and the doctrine of conversion no longer operates, even where there is an express duty to sell. As a result, beneficiaries under all trusts of land, however created, could be said to have interests in the land. However, the fact that a beneficiary now has an interest in land is not the end of the story. The interest is not in itself sufficient to give the beneficiary the right to occupy the property, since usually trust property should be regarded as an investment for the trust as a whole and not as something for the personal use of one or more beneficiaries. Accordingly s. 12 makes specific provision for the right to occupy.

17.7.3 Statutory right to occupy

TOLATA 1996, s. 12(1) provides:

> A beneficiary who is beneficially entitled to an interest in possession in land subject to a trust of land is entitled by reason of his interest to occupy the land at any time if at the time—
>
> (a) the purposes of the trust include making the land available for his occupation (or for the occupation of beneficiaries of a class of which he is a member or of beneficiaries in general), or
>
> (b) the land is held by the trustees so as to be so available.

Section 12(2) adds that the beneficiary has no right to occupy the land if it is 'either unavailable or unsuitable' for occupation by him.

You will note that by using the phrase 'entitled to an interest in possession' the Act limits this right to those beneficiaries who are entitled to actual enjoyment of the property and excludes those who currently have only a future interest (see 17.6.2). Thus, under the proposed trust of No. 20, only Mrs Brown would have the right to occupy the property during her lifetime, although at her death her daughters would acquire 'interests in possession' and consequently have a right to occupation.

Under the terms of s. 12(1), it seems that in an express trust it will be best to state expressly whether occupation is, or is not, one of the purposes of the trust. However, even in the absence of such a provision s. 12(1)(b) will allow a claim to exercise the right where the property is in fact available and suitable for occupation. Thus land held as an investment (for example, factories or office buildings) would not be suitable for residential occupation, while a house might be suitable for occupation but unavailable because it was let to a tenant or in the process of being sold by the trustees.

17.7.3.1 Exclusion or restriction of right to occupy

Where several beneficiaries are 'entitled in possession' and therefore have a right to occupy, s. 13 authorises the trustees to choose between them:

> Where two or more beneficiaries are...entitled under section 12 to occupy the land, the trustees of land may exclude or restrict the entitlement of any one or more (but not all) of them.

In addition, the trustees may impose reasonable restrictions on occupying beneficiaries (s. 13(3)). This will tend to mean that a set of terms for occupation will have to be drawn up and these may well draw on the sort of terms usually included in leases as a pattern. In a domestic case, one might expect conditions as to keeping the premises clean and in reasonable order, requirements to decorate from time to time, obligations not to use the premises for certain purposes, obligations to pay outgoings (see s. 13(5)) and other such terms.

17.7.3.2 Occupation by co-owners

Although ss. 12 and 13 speak of separate trustees and beneficiaries, their provisions apply also to cases of co-ownership where both roles are likely to be held by the same people. If there are disputes about occupation between the co-owners, the trustees' power under s. 13 to choose who shall occupy is unlikely to resolve the conflict, and it will probably be necessary for the court to deal with the matter on an application under s. 14 (see 17.8.2).

17.7.4 Compensation payments

Section 13(6) also permits the trustees to require any occupying beneficiary to make compensation payments to other beneficiaries who are not allowed to occupy, or to forgo other payments under the trust to which they would be entitled. This allows the imposition of something resembling a partial rent for the property, in order to ensure that other parties are not disadvantaged. Of course, this provision applies only where several beneficiaries are simultaneously 'entitled in possession' and, therefore, have a right to occupy the property. John Brown can be assured that it does not mean that his widow will have to pay rent to her daughters in order to be allowed to occupy the family home!

A claim to a compensation payment under s. 13(6) may arise between co-owners, for example at the end of a relationship when one of the partners moves out of the family home and has to pay for alternative accommodation. The court has always had the power, under a process known as 'equitable accounting', to require a beneficiary who remained in occupation to pay an 'occupation rent' to a beneficiary who was excluded from the property. In *Stack v Dowden* [2007] 2 AC 432, at paras. 93–4 and 150–1, the House of Lords noted that claims to such payments were now governed by the provisions of TOLATA 1996. Where the parties cannot settle the matter by agreement, this will involve an application to the court under s. 14 of the Act, and the consideration by the court of certain matters which it is required by s. 15 to take into account under any such application (see 17.8.3–4). In *Stack* v *Dowden* it was thought that the change to the statutory process would not make a great deal of difference to the outcome between the parties, Lord Neuberger expressing the opinion (at para. 150) that:

> it would be a rare case where the statutory principles would produce a different result from that which would have resulted from the equitable principles.

Nevertheless you may like to note that in the later case of *Murphy v Gooch* [2007] EWCA Civ 603, the Court of Appeal took a slightly different view of the significance of the change, Lightman J commenting (at para. 14) that under the previous equitable doctrine the court was concerned simply with achieving a just result between the parties, whereas:

> The wider ambit of relevant considerations means that the task of the court must now be...to do justice between the parties with due regard to the relevant statutory considerations and in particular (where applicable) the welfare of the minor, the interests of secured creditors and the circumstances and wishes of the beneficiaries specified. It remains to be seen whether taking these further considerations into account results in any significantly different outcome between the parties.

Do we still need equitable accounting?

This question was considered by the High Court in *French v Barcham* [2009] 1 WLR 1124.

The case concerned a house owned jointly by the Barchams, who held the property as beneficial tenants in equal shares. In 1994 a bankruptcy order had been made against Mr Barcham, and his half-share in the beneficial interest had vested in his trustee in bankruptcy. The Barchams continued to live in the house, and it was not until 2006 that the trustee (French) applied to the county court for an order for the sale of the property and a declaration as to how the proceeds of sale should be divided between himself as trustee and Mrs Barcham. In quantifying the amount which Mrs Barcham should receive in respect of her beneficial half-share in the property, the trustee sought to deduct a sum as notional rent due for the Barchams' occupation of the property since the bankruptcy.

The trustee's claim for an occupation rent was rejected by the district judge. He considered that, following the House of Lords' observations in *Stack v Dowden*, the old rules of equitable accounting no longer applied. Any claim for rent must be made under TOLATA 1996, and the relevant provision (s. 13(6)) made it clear that compensation payments were payable only where a beneficiary who was entitled to occupy the property had been excluded. A trustee in bankruptcy had no right to occupy the bankrupt's property, so was not in the position of an excluded beneficiary and therefore could not claim under s. 13(6).

On appeal by the trustee, the High Court took a different view of the effect of *Stack v Dowden* (see paras. 18–20). Blackburne J quoted Lady Hale's statement that:

> these statutory powers [i.e., the provisions of ss. 12–15] replace the old doctrine of equitable accounting under which a beneficiary who remained in occupation might be required to pay an occupation rent to a beneficiary who was excluded from the property.

The judge stressed that:

> it is important to note that [Lady Hale] referred to both parties having a right of occupation. . . . I do not understand her to have been suggesting that in cases where one of the parties has no statutory right of occupation, the statutory provisions have the effect that that party can no longer claim an occupation rent in any circumstances whatever . . . Where the scheme [under s.13(6)] applies, it must be applied. But where it plainly does not I do not see why the party who is not in occupation of the land . . . should be denied any compensation at all if recourse to the court's equitable jurisdiction would justly compensate him.

Accordingly Blackburne J, having reviewed a number of decisions made under the 'old' rules, allowed the trustee's appeal and ordered that Mrs Barcham's share of the proceeds of sale should be reduced by an amount equivalent to half of the rent which could have been obtained if the property had been let during her period of occupation.

17.8. How are disputes about the trust property resolved?

17.8.1 Opportunities for dispute

In considering the provisions of TOLATA 1996 we have already seen that a number of people may be involved in decisions about managing or disposing of the trust property. These include:

- beneficiaries entitled in possession, who:
  - must be consulted by the trustees

  - may be permitted to occupy the property
  - may have trustees' functions delegated to them
- persons whose consent is expressly required by the settlor for the exercise of some or all of the trustees' functions.

Each of these people may have very different views about what ought to be done with the trust property. In particular, where a family home is involved, there may be real difficulty in securing agreement about whether or not to sell it. In addition, the trustees themselves may disagree, or be uncertain, about how to exercise their powers. In an express trust, of the sort which John Brown may make, consultation and decision-making may be relatively straightforward for the trustees, since during Mrs Brown's lifetime she would be the only beneficiary 'beneficially entitled in possession' and therefore the only person whose wishes would be considered.

The situation is more complicated where two or more beneficiaries are entitled in possession. This could happen under an express trust (for example, where a settlor gives a life interest to two brothers), and is always found in the case of the statutory trust imposed on co-owners.

17.8.2 Disputes between co-owners

The statutory trust imposed on co-owners is subject to all the provisions of TOLATA 1996, including the requirement for consultation. When you read s. 11(1) (see 17.5.3), it sounds as though deciding on a course of action, such as selling the property, is relatively simple, the decision being taken by a majority of the beneficiaries who will direct the trustees what to do. In real life, however, it is likely to be a much more complicated matter, especially in cases of co-ownership. The same people are acting as both trustees and beneficiaries, they are very often connected by marriage or some other close relationship, and the property in question is their only home. The majority decision to sell may deprive the minority of a home and the proposal to sell may be only part of a larger dispute about the parties' future together. It therefore must not be assumed that having 'consulted the beneficiaries', the trustees can always readily give effect to the wishes of the majority, and a particular problem arises where the minority refuses to move out so that the property can be offered for sale with vacant possession. In fact, it seems that exactly this problem has arisen in respect of the co-owners of 12 Trant Way, whom we met in Chapter 16.

17.8.2.1 12 Trant Way

Following the events described in 16.6.4, the legal estate in the property is held by Brian, David and Eric, who hold it in trust for Alice and Wilfred as tenants in common, each entitled to a one-sixth share and for David, Eric and Fanny who as joint tenants own four-sixths of the beneficial interest:

LAW	EQUITY
(B, D and E)	A, W (D, E and F)

Recently, Eric and Fanny got engaged to each other and want to move out of No. 12 and find a separate flat, while David has lost interest in the history of Outer Mongolia and plans to withdraw from his course and go travelling. All three of them want to sell the house and take a share of the proceeds. However, Alice, who is in the second year of her course, wants to continue to live in the house until she finishes her course. Wilfred also wants the house to remain unsold.

If trustees Brian, David and Eric apply s. 11(1), those who want to sell will be in the majority, since between them they hold four-sixths of the beneficial interest. However, the trustees cannot simply go ahead and sell the property. In order to sell, they will need vacant possession, and *Bull v Bull* [1955] 1 QB 234 makes it clear that the minority cannot simply be evicted. The solution in this case, and indeed in any situation involving disputes about the trust property, is to apply to the court for an order under s. 14. We will look in detail now at the powers of the court under this section, and will consider later on how these might be applied in the case of the dispute at No. 12.

17.8.3 TOLATA 1996, s. 14

Section 14(1) provides:

> Any person who is a trustee of land or has an interest in property subject to a trust of land may make an application to the court for an order under this section.

17.8.3.1 Who may apply to the court?

Applications under this section may be made not only by trustees and beneficiaries, but also by anyone else with an interest in the property, such as a mortgagee or a trustee in bankruptcy.

In case you have not studied mortgages yet, we need to remind you that a mortgagee is a creditor who has lent money and been granted an interest in the borrower's land as security for the loan. If the loan is not repaid, the mortgagee has a right to sell the land and take the proceeds of sale to satisfy the debt (for details, see Chapter 24). Thus if the trustees have mortgaged the legal estate or a beneficiary has mortgaged his or her beneficial interest, the mortgagee may want the property to be sold, against the wishes of the beneficiaries.

Similarly, if one of the beneficiaries becomes bankrupt, his beneficial interest under the trust will vest in his trustee in bankruptcy, who may want the trust property to be sold so that the bankrupt's share of the proceeds can be used to pay his debtors.

17.8.3.2 What orders may be made by the court?

Under s. 14(2) the court is authorised to make any such order as it thinks fit relating to:

- the exercise of the trustees' functions; or
- the nature and extent of a person's interest in the trust property.

1. *Exercise of the trustees' functions*

Under s. 14, the trustees may apply for directions about the exercise of their functions, and in particular may seek orders releasing them from requirements to obtain consent or to consult the beneficiaries (s. 14(2)(a)). Beneficiaries who are dissatisfied with the way in which trustees have exercised their powers may want to raise questions about such matters as lack of consultation, delegation of powers or occupation of the property.

The court can restrain any proposed exercise of the trustees' powers or conversely can order them to act where they are failing to do so.

As we have seen, one of the questions which is most likely to raise problems, particularly among co-owners, relates to the sale of the trust property, and the court can order sale on the application of the trustees or of any person with an interest in the property.

2. *Nature and extent of a person's interest in the trust property*

Questions about the nature and size of an interest under a trust are particularly likely to arise in cases of implied trusts, where there may be real doubt about the existence or value of a beneficiary's interest under such a trust. We have already met this problem in 'joint names' cases in Chapter 16 (see 16.5), and will encounter it again in 'sole name' cases in Chapter 20 (see 20.6). The court can resolve such questions on an application under s. 14.

17.8.4 TOLATA 1996, s. 15

Section 15 provides guidance for the court on matters it must consider when determining an application. Section 15(1) reads:

> The matters to which the court is to have regard in determining an application for an order under section 14 include—
>
> (a) the intention of the person or persons (if any) who created the trust,
>
> (b) the purposes for which the property subject to the trust is held,
>
> (c) the welfare of any minor who occupies or might reasonably be expected to occupy any land subject to the trust as his home, and
>
> (d) the interests of any secured creditor of any beneficiary.

The matters which the court is required to consider are said to 'include' those listed in s. 15(1). This means that the court may also take other relevant matters into account (for example, the health of one of the parties—*Bank of Ireland Home Mortgages Ltd v Bell* [2001] 2 FLR 809).

Another point to note is that s. 15(1) gives no guidance on the relative importance of each of the factors mentioned, although in practice the court will have to weigh one against the other. For example, there may well be conflict between the interest of a mortgagee in recovering his money through the sale of the property and the welfare of a child who needs the property as a home. It is for the court to decide how much weight should be attached to each consideration and we will see how this works in practice in 17.8.5.

As well as considering the matters mentioned in s. 15(1), the court is required to consider the circumstances and wishes of the beneficiaries (s. 15(2) and (3)).

17.8.4.1 Application by a trustee in bankruptcy

Where a trustee in bankruptcy applies for an order for sale under s. 14, s. 15 does not apply. Instead, the matters which the court should consider are to be found in s. 335A of the Insolvency Act 1986, a new section inserted by TOLATA 1996 (Sch. 3, para. 23).

This new section provides that where the property in question includes the home of the bankrupt, or of his spouse or civil partner, the court considering the application for sale shall take into account:

- the interests of the bankrupt's creditors;
- the conduct of the spouse or civil partner in relation to the bankruptcy (essentially, whether he or she was a party to any fault);

- the needs and financial resources of the spouse or civil partner; and
- the needs of any children.

This accords with other provisions of the Insolvency Act 1986, which are designed to provide some short-term protection for the spouse or civil partner and children of a bankrupt, but at the same time to ensure that creditors are able to realise the bankrupt's assets within a reasonable period. Accordingly, the section goes on to provide that where the application for sale is made more than a year after bankruptcy, the court shall assume that the interests of the creditors outweigh all other considerations 'unless the circumstances of the case are exceptional' (s. 335A(3)).

17.8.5 How are these new provisions working in practice?

The brief explanation of the rules in ss. 14 and 15 given above cannot really indicate the likely approach of the courts to applying their new wider powers. A further unanswered question relates to the extent to which the courts are likely to be guided by decisions interpreting earlier similar provisions contained in LPA 1925, s. 30. We will now look at some of the decisions on applications under s. 14, and will then return to the hypothetical dispute between the owners of 12 Trant Way.

17.8.5.1 *Mortgage Corporation v Shaire* [2001] Ch 743

Taken as a whole, the facts in this case are complicated, but the particular point with which we are concerned can be dealt with separately and the facts which it involves are relatively simple. Mrs Shaire and her unmarried partner were the legal owners of their house, which they held on the statutory trusts imposed in cases of co-ownership (originally a trust for sale, converted into a trust of land by TOLATA 1996 on 1 January 1997). For reasons we need not explain, Mrs Shaire was held to be entitled to 75 per cent of the value of the property, while her partner was entitled to the remaining 25 per cent. After his death, it was discovered that he had mortgaged the property to secure a large loan, having forged Mrs Shaire's signature on documents which created a charge by way of legal mortgage. The mortgage repayments were in arrears and in order to enforce its security the chargee (i.e., mortgagee) sought an order for sale under TOLATA 1996, s. 14.

The court accepted that Mrs Shaire was not responsible for what had happened, and in consequence her share in the property was held not to be subject to the mortgage. The chargee was, however, entitled to the 25 per cent share in the property which had belonged to the deceased, and it could recover this only if the property was sold. However, Mrs Shaire wanted to remain in the property, in which she had lived since 1976, and so opposed the application for an order for sale.

In dealing with the question of whether to order sale, Neuberger J began by considering the position on the old law before the Act. There was clear authority (*Re Citro* [1991] Ch 142) that, save in exceptional cases, sale would be ordered on any application by a trustee in bankruptcy and that a similar approach was adopted in dealing with applications by mortgagees or chargees (*Lloyds Bank plc v Byrne & Byrne* [1993] 1 FLR 369). As we have seen, this approach in cases of *bankruptcy* is now given statutory force by the new s. 335A added to the Insolvency Act 1986 by TOLATA 1996. Should applications by *mortgagees and chargees* continue to be treated in the same way, or has the 1996 Act changed the law?

In the view of Neuberger J, the law on this point has been changed by s. 15 and it was no longer necessary to apply the same approach to applications by chargees as one would to those by trustees in bankruptcy. Among the reasons given for this view was the fact that 'the interests of the secured creditor' is just one of four factors to be taken into account under s. 15(1) and there is no suggestion that it is to be given any more importance than the interests of the children living in the house (p. 758). Further (at p. 760) the judge thought it not unlikely that:

> the legislature intended to relax the fetters on the way in which the court exercised its discretion...so as to tip the balance somewhat more in favour of families and against banks and other chargees. Although the law under [LPA 1925,] s. 30 was clear following *Citro* and *Byrne*, there were indications of judicial dissatisfaction with the state of the law at that time.

In the judge's opinion, s. 15 had changed the law and the court now had greater flexibility in dealing with applications of this sort. In doing so it must take account of the factors set out in s. 15(1) and the circumstances and wishes of the beneficiaries under s. 15(3). In addition, there might be other factors in a particular case which the court could or should take into account. Once the relevant factors to be taken into account had been identified, it was a matter for the court as to what weight to give to each factor in a particular case.

The decision in *Shaire* can be seen as an authority on the very specific point of the relative positions of a chargee and a trustee on bankruptcy on applications for sale under s. 14. There were, however, a number of more general observations in the judgment which we ought to note. In particular, the judge commented (at p. 758) on the change of emphasis resulting from the replacement of the statutory trust for sale by the trust of land:

> ...the very name 'trust for sale' and the law as it has been developed by the courts suggests that under the old law, in the absence of a strong reason to the contrary, the court should order sale. Nothing in the language of the new code as found in the 1996 Act supports that approach.

The judge also considered the extent to which the case law which grew up around s. 30, LPA 1925, may be relevant in interpreting ss. 14 and 15 of the new Act. An earlier County Court decision, *TSB Bank plc v Marshall* [1998] 3 EGLR 100 considered that the old case law remained relevant in interpreting the new provisions (thus confirming the view advanced by the Law Commission when the legislation was prepared). However, this led the judge, on facts very similar to those in *Shaire*, to apply the old rules in *Citro* and *Byrne*—which as we have just seen, were thought in the later case to be no longer applicable to chargees. Neuberger J accordingly disagreed with the conclusions reached in *TSB Bank v Marshall*, and (at p. 761) explained his own view on the extent to which old authorities would be of assistance in interpreting the new Act:

> On the one hand, to throw over all the wealth of learning and thought given by so many eminent judges to the problem....seems somewhat arrogant and possibly rash. On the other hand, where one has concluded that the law has changed in a significant respect so that the court's discretion is significantly less fettered than it was, there are obvious dangers in relying on authorities which proceeded on the basis that the court's discretion was more fettered than it now is. I think it would be wrong to throw over all the earlier cases without paying them any regard. However, they have to be treated with

> caution, in light of the change in the law, and in many cases they are unlikely to be of great, let alone decisive, assistance.

In case you are wondering what happened to Mrs Shaire, we will mention the outcome of the case briefly, although the way in which the judge exercised his discretion on the particular facts is of less general interest than the earlier part of his judgment. Having taken into account the various factors noted above, he concluded that the interest of the chargee in realising his security outweighed Mrs Shaire's wish to remain in her home, particularly given her ability to buy another house with her share of the proceeds. He indicated, therefore, that he was minded to order sale, unless Mrs Shaire found herself able to take on the amount owed to the chargee as an additional loan on which she would pay interest. He, therefore, postponed making an order so as to give the parties time to consider their positions—and we know no more.

While the decision between the parties in *Shaire* gave adequate protection to the mortgagee's interest, Neuberger J's view of the radical changes introduced by ss. 14 and 15 were seen by some commentators as likely to cause anxiety and concern among professional lenders. As Pascoe put it ([2000] 64 Conv 315 at 327):

> Neuberger J's approach is not one of consolidation and rationalisation; rather he is wiping the slate clean and starting afresh with secured creditors the likely casualties of the new approach. It will be a welcome change in the law for spouses, partners and children living in the property, but an inexpedient, prejudicial and financially detrimental development if one is a secured creditor.

However, a somewhat more conservative approach was subsequently adopted by the Court of Appeal in *Bank of Ireland Home Mortgages Ltd v Bell* [2001] 2 FLR 809.

17.8.5.2 *Bank of Ireland Home Mortgages Ltd v Bell* [2001] 2 FLR 809

In outline, the facts of this case were similar to those in *Shaire*. Mr and Mrs Bell were the legal owners of a house bought with a loan secured by a mortgage of the property, on which repayments were in arrears, the marriage having broken down. On an application by the mortgagees for an order for sale under s. 14, the trial judge accepted the wife's claim that her husband had forged her signature on the relevant mortgage documents, and in consequence held that the mortgage operated only as an equitable charge over his beneficial interest in the property. Although the wife's interest in the property was relatively small (10 per cent at most), the judge refused to order sale. In doing so, he took into account the fact that the property was purchased as a family home and was currently occupied by Mrs Bell and her son, who at that stage was still under age. He also took into account the fact that Mrs Bell was in poor health.

On appeal by the mortgagee, the Court of Appeal reversed the decision below and ordered sale, holding that the trial judge had erred in exercising his discretion under s. 15. The matters to which he had given weight in reaching his decision should either not have been regarded or deserved only slight consideration. The acquisition of the property as a family home and its continued occupation by the wife, on which the trial judge had relied, had ceased to be relevant considerations under s. 15(1)(a) and (b) with the departure of the husband on the break-down of the marriage. The occupation by the son might be relevant under s. 15(1)(c), but at the time of the trial he was not far from the age of majority, and his welfare 'should only have been a very slight consideration' (per Peter Gibson LJ at para. 28). The court agreed that the judge could properly have regard to the wife's poor health, but considered that this would be a reason for postponing sale rather than for refusing to order it.

By contrast, the trial judge had not mentioned the matter which the Court of Appeal regarded as most significant: that, with the addition of interest, the debt had now grown to more than £300,000. This was more than the value of the house, and was increasing daily. Peter Gibson LJ commented (at para. 31) that before 1996 the creditors' interest would prevail over that of the spouse and family of the debtor save in exceptional circumstances, and went on to say:

> The 1996 Act, by requiring the court to have regard to the particular matters specified in s. 15, appears to me to have given scope for some change in the court's practice. Nevertheless, a powerful consideration is and ought to be whether the creditor is receiving proper recompense for being kept out of his money, repayment of which is overdue.

By refusing to order sale the judge had condemned the bank to go on waiting for its money with no prospect of recovery from the Bells, and that seemed to the judge to be very unfair to the bank. The other two members of the Court of Appeal agreed with this approach, and sale of the property was ordered.

As far as the actual outcome for the parties is concerned, there is no significant difference between the decisions in *Shaire* and in *Bell*, the respective courts being willing to order sale in both cases. However, as we have seen, there is a considerable difference in the views expressed about the overall effect of s. 15, Neuberger J treating it as producing a significant change in the law, and Peter Gibson LJ seeing it as giving 'some scope for change in the court's practice'. The Court of Appeal made only a brief reference to *Shaire* (see para. 31), citing it as an example of the importance of giving due weight to the interests of the creditor, but it certainly appears from the judgments that Neuberger J's radical approach was not shared by the higher court.

17.8.6 12 Trant Way

In 17.8.2.1 we saw that there is a dispute between the owners of No. 12. David, Eric and Fanny, who are jointly entitled to four-sixths of the beneficial interest, want the house to be sold, while Alice and Wilfred, who are each entitled to a one-sixth share as tenants in common, are opposed to this. The problem could be solved by Alice and Wilfred buying out the interest of the other three, but if they cannot afford to do this those who want to sell will probably seek a court order under s. 14.

The relevant matters for consideration by the court on such an application would include the purpose for which the property is held (s. 15(1)(b)) and the wishes of the majority of the beneficiaries (s. 15(3)). In opposing the application, Alice will undoubtedly argue that the house was bought to provide accommodation for the students while at the university, and that she still wants to use the property for that purpose. In interpreting the reference to 'purpose' in s. 15(1)(b) the court may consider the 'continuing purpose' decisions on earlier applications under LPA 1925, s. 30 (see 15.5.3.1), in which one co-owner was not allowed to disrupt the continued use of the property for the purpose for which it had been acquired. However, Alice must realise that the court may well consider that the original purpose in this case has come to an end, since she is now the only one of the original owners who wants to live in the house. Unless Wilfred is able to produce some compelling argument for retaining the house, it seems more likely here that the court will give effect to the wishes of the majority and order sale.

17.9. Are purchasers willing to buy trust property?

When John Brown is thinking about creating a trust of his property, he may wonder whether doing so might make it more difficult to sell the house if Mrs Brown needed to move. The trustees would have the power to sell, but would any purchaser want to buy?

It is certainly true that many years ago, there were considerable dangers in buying trust property. We explained earlier (2.6.2) the general principle that if trustees sold property which was subject to a trust the purchaser would take the property subject to the rights of the beneficiaries if he knew (or ought to have known) of them. The purchaser in such a case, on acquiring the property, became no more than a trustee and held the property for the beneficiaries. However, during the nineteenth century, it became necessary to change this approach in some way. Economic reasons made it desirable to facilitate the sale of land held within family settlements and accordingly a series of statutes, culminating in the 1925 property legislation, established the process of 'overreaching' the rights of beneficiaries, and in addition introduced other measures designed to protect the purchaser.

17.9.1 Protection of the purchaser

17.9.1.1 Overreaching

We have already explained how overreaching works (6.5.2.1) and you will remember that it is a process by which, provided the proper procedures are followed, the beneficiaries' interests are lifted from the existing trust property and attached instead to the money paid by the purchaser, and in due course to any property in which the trustees may invest that money. Where overreaching operates, the purchaser will acquire the property free of the interests of the beneficiaries, even if he knows of those interests. The overreaching process is very important and we consider it in more detail in 17.9.2.

17.9.1.2 Protecting the purchaser from the consequences of breach of trust by trustees

We have seen that TOLATA 1996 imposes a number of duties upon trustees which are designed to protect the beneficiaries. These include duties:

- to obtain any consents required by the settlor (s. 8(2));
- to consult the beneficiaries (s. 11(1)), and to have regard to the beneficiaries' rights when exercising trustee powers (s. 6(5));
- to take care in making and reviewing the delegation of functions to beneficiaries (s. 9A); and
- to observe all statutory, legal and equitable rules in exercising trustee powers (s. 6(6)).

If trustees do not observe the relevant statutory requirements on these matters, they will be in breach of trust. Would this have any adverse effect on a purchaser from the trustees, and does he have to check that the trustees are behaving correctly in their dealings with him? If he did have to do this (for example, checking that four or five consents required by the settlor had been obtained), buying trust property could be very onerous and this would deter prospective purchasers.

There is also the possibility that the trustees' statutory powers have been limited in some way by the settlor under s. 8. What would be the purchaser's position if the trustees ignored the limitation and entered into some transaction with him which was outside their powers? Does he have to check whether there are any such restrictions?

The LPA 1925 contained several measures designed to protect the purchaser and reduce the enquiries he might have to make. These are re-enacted, with a number of additional provisions, in TOLATA 1996, as described below.

(1) *Consents* Where trustees are required to obtain more than two consents, the purchaser need only check that at least two consents have been obtained (s. 10(1)).

(2) *Consultation* A purchaser is not required to check that the trustees have complied with the statutory requirements for consulting the beneficiaries or having regard to their rights (s. 16(1)).

(3) *Delegation* Where trustees have purported to delegate their functions, a purchaser is entitled to presume that the delegate is a person to whom the delegation can be made, unless he knows that this is not so (s. 9(2)).

(4) *Duty to exercise powers in accordance with statutory, legal and equitable rules* Where trustees act in breach of this duty, any conveyance to a purchaser will not be invalidated by the breach if he has no actual notice of it (s. 16(2)).

(5) *Limitation of trustees' powers* The trustees should inform a purchaser of any such limitation, but it will not invalidate any conveyance to him if he does not have actual notice of it (s. 16 (3)).

When considering these provisions it is important to realise that they operate only in favour of the *purchaser.* If the *trustees* fail to observe the full statutory requirements they will be in breach of trust, but this will not invalidate the sale to the purchaser or make him liable to the beneficiaries in any way.

17.9.2 Details of overreaching procedure

17.9.2.1 Statutory rules

The statutory provisions which govern overreaching in relation to a trust of land are contained in LPA 1925, s. 2(1)(ii) and s. 27, as amended by TOLATA 1996, Sch. 3, para. 4(1). The provisions apply to both registered and unregistered land. In order to be protected, the purchaser must ensure that the capital money (purchase price or other capital sum arising on the transaction, such as a mortgage advance or the premium paid on the grant of a lease) is paid to no fewer than two trustees or to a trust corporation. The money must not be paid to the beneficiaries (unless they also happen to be the trustees and even then it will be usual to require a receipt from them in their capacity as trustees). It is for this reason that TA 1925, s. 39 seeks to ensure that there are never fewer than two trustees unless the trustee is a trust corporation. If a trust has, for some reason, only one trustee for the time being, a purchaser should insist on the appointment of a second trustee before he pays over any purchase money.

The importance of the second trustee is well illustrated by the two cases of *Williams & Glyn's Bank Ltd v Boland* [1981] AC 487 and *City of London Building Society v Flegg* [1988] AC 54, which we have already discussed in the context of registered land (see 7.10.4.6 and 7.10.4.7(1)).

In the *Boland* case, capital money (in the form of a secured loan from the bank) was paid to the sole registered proprietor, with the result that Mrs Boland's equitable rights were not overreached, so that the mortgagee took subject to her interest in the property. By contrast, in *Flegg* the mortgage advance was made to the two registered proprietors, who held as trustees for themselves and the Fleggs, and in consequence the Fleggs' interest was overreached. As a result, they no longer had an interest in the land which could be asserted against the mortgagee, but only an interest in the money in the hands of the trustees. Theoretically, beneficiaries in this situation are protected by their rights against the capital money, but in practice, of course, this may be illusory. In *Flegg*, the money had been applied for the trustees' own purposes, and although they might be liable to the beneficiaries for breach of trust, any judgment against them would be worthless if they did not have the financial means to meet it.

We must emphasise that the position would have been different if the trustees had actually exceeded their powers, for it appears that ultra vires transactions (i.e., transactions 'outside the powers' of the trustees) do not overreach the beneficiaries' interests (*State Bank of India v Sood* 1997 Ch 276 at p. 281). However, in *Flegg* the House of Lords took the view that the transaction in question was within the powers of the trustees, even if it was in breach of trust.

Is there any protection for a purchaser under an ultra vires transaction?

The fact that ultra vires transactions do not overreach the beneficiaries' interests might appear to create a dangerous situation for a purchaser.

In the case of *unregistered land*, however, purchasers under such a transaction would be protected by the provisions of s. 16(2), which provides in effect that contravention by the trustees of 'any rule of law or equity' shall not invalidate the conveyance to a purchaser who has no actual notice of the contravention. That subsection does not apply to registered land (s. 16(7)), because it is assumed that the purchaser will discover from the register any restrictions in relation to dispositions of the land and thus be warned of the need to comply with them.

Danger for purchaser of registered land?

It has been suggested that excluding registered land from the protection of s. 16 could put a purchaser at risk (see Ferris and Battersby [1998] 62 Conv 168). This view is not shared by other writers (see for example Dixon [2000] 64 Conv 267, and a further article by Ferris and Battersby [2001] 65 Conv. 221). Any danger there may have been appears to have been met by the terms of LRA 2002, s. 26, which relate to the protection of disponees (i.e., those who take under a disposition of registered land). Section 26 provides that subject to an exception for limitations protected by an entry on the register or imposed by the Act:

> a person's right to exercise owner's powers in relation to a registered estate or charge is to be taken to be free from any limitation affecting the validity of a disposition.

Section 26(3) adds that this provision has effect:

> only for the purpose of preventing the title of a disponee being questioned (and so does not affect the lawfulness of a disposition).

The effect of this provision appears to be that a purchaser who takes registered land under an ultra vires transaction will be protected, while the beneficiaries will retain their rights against the trustees for any breach of trust.

17.9.2.2 What happens if the capital money is not paid to two trustees?

The Law of Property Act 1925 does not say what the position would be if a purchaser does not comply with s. 27. Accordingly, one must in such a case consider the ordinary rules which determine whether a purchaser is bound by an equitable interest in land.

Unregistered land

The purchaser will take free of such interests in unregistered land where he is a bona fide purchaser for value without notice. Therefore it is possible to obtain a legal estate free of the beneficial interests, even where capital money is not paid to two trustees (*Caunce v Caunce* [1969] 1 WLR 286) although only if the purchaser can avoid the rigours of actual, constructive and imputed notice (see 2.6.3.4).

Registered land

Normally the purchaser will be aware of the trust and the rights of the beneficiaries because a restriction will have been entered on the register. Accordingly, the purchaser would be warned to insist on the appointment of a second trustee for his own protection.

However, you will remember from Chapter 7 that a purchaser is always at risk from overriding interests (which will bind him without any entry on the register). In the case of trust property, the interests of beneficiaries who are in actual occupation of the land could bind the purchaser under LRA 2002, Sch. 3 para. 2, just as Mrs Boland's interest bound the mortgagee under the earlier provisions of LRA 1925, s. 70(1)(g) in *Williams & Glyn's Bank v Boland* [1981] AC 487. Nevertheless, if the capital money is paid to two trustees, the overreaching provisions operate to overreach even an overriding interest as happened in *City of London Building Society v Flegg* [1988] AC 54, and in *Birmingham Midshires Mortgage Services Ltd v Sabherwal* (2000) 80 P&CR 256.

17.9.2.3 Overreaching outside the Act?

Interestingly, a slightly different problem arose in *State Bank of India v Sood* [1997] Ch 276, in which the issue was whether overreaching can only take place under s. 27 or whether there are other occasions upon which beneficial interests can be overreached. The issue arose in this case because there had been no payment of capital moneys at the time of the disposition in question.

The case involved a house that was registered in the names of the first and second defendants but which was held on trust by them for themselves and for the third to seventh defendants. All seven defendants occupied the premises and thus the beneficial interests under the trust were overriding interests under LRA 1925, s. 70(1)(g) in relation to later dispositions. The disposition in question was a mortgage of the premises to the bank. Normally, a mortgage will give rise to a mortgage advance and that advance would constitute capital money (that was the case in *Flegg*) but in this instance the trustees mortgaged the property as security for the discharge of their existing debts and for any future indebtedness. No actual moneys were advanced at the time the mortgage was granted.

Later, one of the trustees was made bankrupt and the bank tried to enforce its security, relying on the principle set out in *Flegg* that where overreaching occurred it was irrelevant that the beneficial interests were overriding interests under the LRA 1925, s. 70. The problem was that the bank could not rely on LPA 1925, s. 27 because no capital money had been paid. Nonetheless, the Court of Appeal held that in this case the interests of the beneficiaries had been overreached, saying that s. 27(2) was relevant only where capital money actually arose and that it did not mean that there could be no overreaching without capital money. In reaching this conclusion Peter Gibson LJ adopted the analysis of the position set out in Harpum's article 'Overreaching trustees' powers and the reform of the 1925 legislation' [1990] CLJ 277 that

> the exercise intra vires of a power of disposition which does not give rise to any capital money, such as an exchange of land, overreaches just as much as a transaction which does.

The case clearly establishes that the courts will consider whether other overreaching events have arisen. You may like to note that Peter Gibson LJ's judgment also provides a useful analysis of the overreaching provisions in the LPA 1925. (Also see Oldham, 'Overreaching where no capital monies arise' [1997] CLJ 494.)

17.9.2.4 What happens to capital money paid to trustees?

You may be wondering what happens to the proceeds of sale when they have been paid to the trustees and the rights of the beneficiaries have been overreached. This depends on the terms of the trust. It may be that the capital money is to be paid over to a sole beneficiary or divided between several beneficiaries. On the other hand, if the trust is to continue, the trustees could invest in any authorised investments, and their power to do so would include the purchase of any estate in land for any purpose (s. 6(3), TOLATA 1996). Of course, where this power is exercised the trustees will again hold land and this will give rise to a fresh trust of land.

17.9.3 Protecting a purchaser who buys land which has been subject to a trust

A trust of land comes to an end:

- when the trustees transfer the legal estate to beneficiaries who are absolutely entitled; or
- when a joint tenant becomes solely entitled to both the legal estate and the equitable interest by right of survivorship.

17.9.3.1 Beneficiaries absolutely entitled

A trust may come to an end when the beneficiaries are of full age and are absolutely entitled to the property (i.e., the interest of any earlier beneficiary has come to an end and there are no other conditions to be fulfilled before the beneficiaries may enjoy the property). This is the situation which might arise under a settlement created by John Brown, if he provides that the property is to go unconditionally to his daughters after the death of his wife. When Mrs Brown dies, the daughters will be absolutely entitled and the trustees may convey the legal estate in the house to them. The conveyance to the beneficiaries will bring the trust to an end, and the trustees should execute a 'deed of discharge', declaring that they are discharged from the trust (s. 16 (4) and (5)).

Anyone who wishes to buy property after it has been transferred to the beneficiaries in this way should insist on seeing the deed of discharge, which will show that the property is no longer subject to a trust. If such a deed cannot be produced, the purchaser should insist on paying the money to two trustees.

17.9.3.2 Surviving joint tenant becomes solely entitled in law and equity

We explained in Chapter 16 that where the legal estate and the equitable (beneficial) interest are both held on a joint tenancy, the right of survivorship will eventually vest the title and beneficial interest in the last surviving tenant. When this happens, the statutory trust imposed on cases of co-ownership comes to an end, and the survivor is entitled to sell the property and receive the proceeds of sale as absolute owner.

However, in the case of *unregistered land*, this situation could cause problems for a prospective purchaser.

The documents showing title would inform him that the land had been held by joint tenants, and accordingly he would know that the property had been subject to a trust. Was it safe for him to accept a conveyance from the sole survivor or should he demand the appointment of a second trustee? On the face of it, the survivor, through the right of survivorship, was solely entitled in law and equity and could dispose of the whole legal and beneficial interest. However, there was the danger that one of the deceased tenants might have severed his joint tenancy during his lifetime, creating a tenancy in common. He would thus have a share in the property which at his death would vest in someone other than the remaining original co-owner.

Usually, when severance is made, a note (a 'memorandum of severance') is endorsed on the original conveyance to the joint tenants, so that any later purchaser will know that a tenancy in common has been created. Nevertheless, the severance is valid even if this is not done, and so its absence is no guarantee to the purchaser that severance has not occurred. Thus, the apparent 'sole survivor in law and equity' might really be holding in trust for himself and another, and if the purchaser did not pay the purchase money to two trustees the overreaching provisions would not operate and he would take the land subject to the right of any beneficiary of whom he could be said to have notice. To guard against this danger, purchasers would insist on the appointment of a second trustee, even when in fact this was not necessary.

Statutory resolution of problem

The matter was finally resolved by the Law of Property (Joint Tenants) Act 1964. This statute ensures that where a sole surviving joint tenant sells, the purchaser will obtain good title free of any equitable interests and need not concern himself about the possibility of an earlier severance unless a memorandum of severance has been endorsed on or annexed to the conveyance which vested the property in the joint tenants. Accordingly, if a joint tenant does sever and wishes to avoid the possibility of the 1964 Act being used by a sole survivor of the original co-owners he should ensure that a memorandum of severance is so endorsed.

It should be noted that the 1964 Act does not apply to registered land (s. 3). Where co-owners who are joint tenants in law and equity are registered as proprietors of the legal estate, there will be no restriction on the register requiring payment to two trustees. When one of the joint tenants dies, the survivor should apply to the registry with evidence of the death (usually a death certificate) and the register will be amended to show the surviving joint tenant as sole proprietor. A purchaser from the survivor can then buy from him in reliance on the register.

The rest of this chapter

We have now dealt with all the questions that John might want to ask about trusts of land (17.2.2). However, there is still one matter that probably would not concern John, but that those who are studying land law may need to know about. Accordingly, in the next section of this chapter we will note certain dispositions that under the old law would have given rise to a SLA settlement and now take effect as trusts of land.

17.10. Trusts of land replace new Settled Land Act settlements

We have already noted that no more SLA settlements can be created after 1997, and have seen that any new arrangements which create successive interests in land will take effect as trusts of land (17.1.2.2). There are, however, three particular dispositions that under the old law would have taken effect as SLA settlements (or in one case as a trust for sale) and for which TOLATA 1996 makes specific provision in s. 2(6) and Sch. 1.

17.10.1 Conveyance to a minor or minors (that is, to a person or persons aged under 18)

The 1925 legislation introduced the rule that a minor cannot hold a legal estate in land (LPA 1925, s. 1(6)).

17.10.1.1 Before 1997

Attempts to convey such an estate to a minor operated as a contract to create a SLA settlement, and until this was done the person making the conveyance held the estate on trust for the minor. Where a conveyance was made to an adult and a minor, the adult held the legal estate on a trust for sale for himself and the minor.

17.10.1.2 After 1996

Under TOLATA 1996, a purported conveyance (and this will include LRA transfers) to a minor or a group of minors operates instead as a declaration of trust (Sch. 1 para. 1(1). Thus, in such a case, a minor can only become a beneficial (equitable) owner. The legal estate will have to be vested in an adult or adults as trustee(s).

Where a legal estate is conveyed to a minor or minors *and* an adult or adults, Sch. 1 para. 1(2) provides that that estate will vest in the adult(s) upon trust for the minor(s) and the adult(s) in question. We have seen an example of this in the transfer of 12 Trant Way (16.2.5).

17.10.2 Charges 'by way of family arrangement'

When explaining some of the background history in Chapter 15 (15.5.1.1), we noted that a typical settlement would ensure that the property would pass to a single heir (usually the settlor's eldest son), but would also provide for the maintenance of the settlor's widow and younger children. For this purpose, the settlement would create charges over the property, which gave these members of the family the right to receive payments from the income of the estate. Although less common today, this practice does still continue in some cases and this sort of arrangement is now governed by para. 3 of Sch. 1 to TOLATA 1996, which provides that in such a case the land becomes subject to a trust of land and is held on trust for the purpose of giving effect to the charge. Thus, were F to vest his legal estate in S (F's eldest son) but subject to periodic payments by S to his mother and younger brothers and sisters, this arrangement would create a trust of land, which would be subject to the provisions of TOLATA 1996.

17.10.3 Attempt to create an entailed interest

As we saw in 1.5.1.3, an entailed interest (formerly known as a fee tail) was created by a disposition in favour of 'the heirs of the body' of a specified person. If the holder of such an interest had no lineal descendants, the interest came to an end at his death and the property reverted to the donor or his successors, who were said to have a 'reversion' in it. In modern times, this succession of interests took effect as a SLA settlement (see further 15.5.1.1).

This form of settlement was regarded as inappropriate in modern law and under TOLATA 1996 it is no longer possible to create an entailed interest. Schedule 1, para. 5(1) provides that a purported grant of an entailed interest does not create that interest but instead takes effect as a declaration that the property is held in trust absolutely for the intended grantee. If a settlor purports to create an entailed interest in himself, the whole disposition is ineffective (para. 5(2)). Thus, no new entailed interests can be created. They were already quite rare and in time most existing interests of this sort will die out.

FURTHER READING

Barnsley, 'Co-owners Rights to Occupy Trust Land' [1998] CLJ 123.

Clements, 'The Changing Face of Trusts' [1998] MLR 56.

Hopkins, 'The Trusts of Land and Appointment of Trustees Act 1996' [1996] Conv 411 (and see Sydenham [1997] Conv 242).

Martyn, 'Co-Owners and Their Entitlement to Occupy Their Land Before and After the Trusts of Land and Appointment of Trustees Act 1996: Theoretical Doubts Are Replaced by Practical Difficulties' [1997] Conv 254.

Oldham, 'Overreaching where No Capital Monies Arise' [1997] CLJ 494.

Smith, 'Trusts of Land Reform' [1990] Conv 12.

Watt, 'Escaping s. 8(1) Provisions in "New Style" Trusts of Land' [1997] 61 Conv 263.

TOLATA 1996, s. 12

Bright, 'Occupation Rents and [TOLATA] 1996: From Property to Welfare?' [2009] 73 Conv 378.

Pascoe, 'Right to Occupy Under a Trust of Land: Muddled Legislative Logic' [2006] 70 Conv 54 (in general, too detailed; but see pp. 58–62 on questions arising from s. 12(1)).

TOLATA 1996, s. 15

Pascoe, 'Section 15 of the Trusts of Land and Appointment of Trustees Act 1996—A Change in the Law?' [2000] 64 Conv 315.

Probert, 'Creditors and Section 15 of the Trusts of Land and Appointment of Trustees Act 1996: first among equals?' [2002] 66 Conv 61 (case note on *Bank of Ireland Homes Mortgages Ltd v Bell*).

18

Settled Land Act settlements

Now that it is no longer possible to make new Settled Land Act settlements, we know that they are unlikely to feature in land law courses. However, it is important to remember that settlements created before TOLATA 1996 continue to exist and, unlike trusts for sale, were not converted into the new trusts of land (which is why you will still find references to them in LRA 2002). Just in case you come across one of these continuing settlements, we will deal very briefly in this chapter with the following three questions:

- who holds the legal estate in settled land?
- are there trustees?
- what sort of property may be subject to a SLA settlement?

18.1 Who holds the legal estate in settled land?

Although there are 'trustees of the settlement', the legal title to the settled land is held by the beneficiary currently entitled to the enjoyment of the property, who is known as the 'tenant for life'. In addition to being the legal owner and having the right to occupy the property, the tenant for life has wide powers to deal with the property, being able to sell all or part of the settled land, to grant leases over it and to raise money by mortgage for specified purposes. We noted in Chapter 15 that land tied up in family settlements often deteriorated because the beneficiaries could not raise money for repair and development (see 15.5.1.1) and these statutory powers were designed to remedy this problem. Consequently the SLA 1925 provides that the powers of the tenant for life under the Act may not be excluded by the settlor and attempts to restrict them in any way are void. This is why it is slightly surprising to find that under TOLATA 1996 the settlor can limit or exclude the wide powers given by the Act to the trustees, with the result that even the power to sell the property could be excluded (see 17.5.1).

It is important to realise that, although the tenant for life has these wide and unrestricted powers, he holds the estate on trust for himself and the other beneficiaries, and when exercising his powers he must have regard to the interests of all parties entitled under the settlement (SLA 1925, s. 107).

If there is no tenant for life (because for example, the current beneficiary is a minor), the powers of the tenant for life will be exercised by the 'statutory owner' (see Glossary).

18.2 Are there trustees?

Although the tenant for life holds the legal estate and has the power to deal with it, the Act requires the appointment of 'trustees of the settlement'. Their most important function is to receive any capital money arising from dealings with the property, in order to ensure that the beneficial interests under the settlement are overreached and the purchaser is not bound by them. Apart from this, the trustees' powers and duties are fairly limited. Their *consent* is required for certain major dealings by the tenant for life (such as the sale of the 'principal mansion house'), but in general the tenant for life is required only to give *notice* to the trustees of his intention to exercise certain powers, and normally the trustees have no right to prevent him entering into the proposed transaction.

18.3 What sort of property may be subject to a SLA settlement?

You may well think that SLA settlements are relevant only to the rather grand country estates we describe in Chapter 15. However, it must be remembered that these settlements could also be created 'by mistake' in home-made wills, with the result that a small semi-detached house could become subject to all the machinery of the SLA 1925. It was also possible for a settlement to arise in the most unexpected circumstances, as it did in *Binions v Evans* [1972] Ch 359 (see 20.3.2.2), in which a landowner allowed the widow of his former employee to remain in their cottage for the rest of her life, and thus inadvertently created a SLA settlement.

So in conclusion we just want to remind you that these settlements are not just for the rich and powerful—you may still come across them in the most unlikely places!

If you should want any more information about SLA settlements, you will find a full account of them in the Online Resource Centre: **www.oxfordtextbooks.co.uk/orc/landlaw14e/**. (referenced as 'W18').

19

Perpetuities and accumulations

19.1. Future interests

Before we leave the subject of trusts, we must give a brief account of the rules which govern the kind of future interests which can be created under them, and so this chapter will be concerned with the 'rule against perpetuities'.

Common law has always disliked uncertainty in relation to future interests in land. Uncertainty tends to make the property inalienable for some time, and common law has always opposed any arrangement which restricts free alienation. For example, should a settlor, who as yet has no children, wish to settle land upon 'the first of my great-grandchildren to obtain a law degree', it could easily be 70 or 80 years before the great-grandchild who is to take the gift can be ascertained. For that period of time there would be no one absolutely entitled to the property and, under the older trusts rules, there would have been no one with a power to dispose of it. As a result, the courts developed rules ('against perpetuities') which invalidated certain objectionable future interests. Unfortunately, the rigid application of these rules frequently led to ridiculous results, and eventually statutory amendments were made by the Law of Property Act 1925 (to a limited extent) and the Perpetuities and Accumulations Act 1964. Unfortunately this legislation did not replace the older rules and, by simply modifying them, made the law more (rather than less) complicated. Now the older rules have been considerably simplified by the Perpetuities and Accumulations Act 2009, which came into force on 6 April 2010. Here we deal with the rules in a very outline fashion, simply in order to indicate their complexity. A more detailed explanation of the rules can be found in the supplementary material on the Online Resource Centre linked to this book (at **www.oxfordtextbooks.co.uk/orc/landlaw14e/** referenced as 'W.19'.

You should first note that the rule against perpetuities is about grants or gifts that are to vest at some point in the future because at the time the grant takes effect the eventual beneficiary is not identified. Thus, a grant to:

> A for life and then to B

is not caught if A and B are both living and named people at the date of the grant. In this case, both A and B have an existing vested interest. A's interest is an immediate benefit, whereas B's will confer benefit in future. However, B already has rights that are vested in him—he already owns a future vested interest. The perpetuities rules relate to cases in which the recipient of the future interest cannot be definitely identified at the point of grant. Thus they relate to cases in which the future recipient is not an identifiable person at the point of the grant, such as a grant to 'A's first child to reach the age of 21'. In such a case, unless A already has a child aged 21 at the date of the grant, the actual beneficiary will only be identified and the future interest vest in him or her when one of A's children reaches 21.

19.2. The old rules

The basic perpetuities rule was that a contingent (conditional) future interest had to take effect, if it was to be valid, within the period of a 'life in being plus 21 years (plus any period of gestation)'. The rule is therefore sometimes described as a rule against remoteness of vesting. Any interest that offended the rule was, until legislative changes were made in the twentieth century, invalid from the start.

A simple example will serve to illustrate some of the problems that may result. If a settlor made a gift to:

> the first child of X to become an accountant

under the basic perpetuities rule the gift was invalid. This is because, unless X already has a child who is a qualified accountant, it is possible that X will have a child born later and who qualifies as an accountant more than 21 years after the death of X. Even if X already had an adult child who has nearly qualified, it is theoretically possible that that child might never qualify and that X may have another child born later, who qualifies more than 21 years after X's death. Because of this, even if this possibility is highly unlikely, the whole gift was void. X is the only 'life in being' and the possibility that the gift will result in the contingent gift to the child vesting more than 21 years after his or her death makes the whole gift invalid (though it might have been rescued by some of the legislative reforms made in the last century).

To make matters even more difficult, over time rules were developed about presumptions as to who could or could not have children and as to which lives did or did not count as 'lives in being'.

19.3. Legislative modifications before 2010

In 1925 some limited reforms were made to the rules, to deal with cases in which the only problem with the grant was that a disposition vested in someone at an age greater than 21. Thus this addressed the following type of grant:

> to A for life and then to the first of A's children to reach the age of 25.

This was void under the basic rules (unless A already had a 25-year-old grandchild) because even if A already had a 24-year-old child, that child might die and a child born after the date of the gift might reach 25 more than 21 years after A's death. Section 163(2), LPA 1925, allowed the age specified to be reduced to 21 in order to save the grant. This worked because A's child must reach 21 no longer than 21 years after A's death (plus any period of gestation—which was already permitted under the older rules).

Far more extensive reforms were made by the Perpetuities and Accumulations Act 1964. Of these, the most important were the introduction of

- a 'wait and see' rule;
- statutory provisions as to who is a 'life in being' in any case;
- further age reduction rules (and repeal of the 1925 provision);
- presumptions concerning fertility; and
- the possibility of choosing a fixed period of 80 years for the perpetuity period.

The most important in practice was 'wait and see', which instead of making the grant void from the start because it might break the rules, allowed you to wait through the perpetuity period to see whether in fact the grant will vest before the end of the period. Therefore, in the case of the grant to:

the first child of X to become an accountant

you could now wait to see whether a child of X qualifies in time, rather than having an entirely ineffective grant right from the start.

19.4. Breadth of application of old rules

The old perpetuities rules applied not only to settlements but also to options and rights of pre-emption (rights of first refusal). They also apply in relation to options to acquire interests and to future easements and restrictive covenants that are to take effect in the future and in relation to some areas of law outside the scope of this book (notably in relation to pensions). To discover more about these wider implications see the material on our related website (W.19) and see the article by Wilson, 'Grave consequences' [2007] EG 134.

19.5. Accumulations

Related to the perpetuities rules was another set of rules about the period for which income can accumulate in a trust. These rules are entirely statutory and were first created in 1880, due to fears that someone might set up a trust with power to retain all income in the trust for the whole perpetuity period (producing a very large pay-out when the trust ended, since all income was re-invested). The reason for creating the rules was that it was feared that permitting such long-term re-investment of all income could give greater financial power to the eventual beneficiaries than the State itself had.

The old rules are to be found in s. 164 of the LPA 1925 and s. 13 of the Perpetuities and Accumulations Act 1964. In essence, they permit accumulation only for the life of the settlor, or 21 years, or for the minority of any relevant persons (that is, until they reach 18), with some rules for extensions in special cases.

19.6. The Perpetuities and Accumulations Act 2009

The perpetuities and accumulations rules had, over the years, attracted a great deal of criticism because of their complexity and the fact that they applied to a wider range of arrangements than just trusts (for which they were designed) and thus had implications (for example) for commercial arrangements like pensions, options to purchase, some rights of pre-emption and future easements. In its report on *The Rules Against Perpetuities and Excessive Accumulations*, 1998, Law Com No. 251, the Law Commission recommended a radical overhaul of the rules and their confinement to trusts and settlements.

The Perpetuities and Accumulations Act 2009 (PAA 2009) was the outcome of these recommendations. The Act came into force in full on 6 April 2010. This Act replaces all the old rules as far as new trusts are concerned. The new system will apply to trusts that take effect after the commencement of the Act and to will trusts where the will is made after the coming into force of the Act: PAA 2009, s. 15. Pre-existing will trusts, even where the testator is still alive, were preserved, so that it was not necessary for everyone to reconsider any wills they had already made.

19.6.1 Trusts affected

Section 1 of the PAA 2009 specifies those arrangements to which the new rules apply and specifies that the rules will apply only to the arrangements specified. The effect is to remove from the ambit of the rules everything except successive interests under trusts.

19.6.2 Perpetuity period is 125 years

The main change made by the 2009 Act is that now the perpetuity period is 125 years in all cases: s. 5. This period applies even if the deed or will creating the trust purports to specify another perpetuity period: s. 5(2). This imposition of a universal statutory period renders the old common law rules about lives in being irrelevant for trusts created on or after 6 April 2010.

19.6.3 Adoption of fixed period in old 'royal lives' trusts

The PAA 2009 does also have some implications for pre-existing trusts because it allows the trustees of such trusts to elect to adopt a perpetuity period of 100 years if the trust period was to be determined by a 'royal lives' clause: s. 12. The trustees will have to execute a deed in order to apply the 100-year period. They will not be obliged to change but may wish to do so if it has become difficult or inconvenient to determine which royal descendants are still lives in being (the Royal College of Arms keeps a list to assist with the determination of such issues). For example, if the trust was subject to a period which depended on the lives of the descendants of Queen Elizabeth II, the trustees could in future elect to impose a fixed perpetuity period of 100 years from the commencement of the trust.

19.6.4 Rules on duration preserved

Do not forget that the perpetuity rule is not a rule about how long a trust can endure. It is simply a rule about remoteness of vesting. The rules about the duration of non-charitable purpose trusts (which is a matter of trusts law rather than land law and thus we do not deal with it here) is preserved by s. 18 of the PAA 2009.

19.6.5 Changes to accumulations rules

The PAA 2009 also makes important changes to the rules against accumulation of income. It abolishes the accumulations rules altogether, except in the case of charitable trusts: ss. 13 and 14. Charitable trusts are excepted because they are likely to continue for a much longer period than other trusts. Charitable trusts will be subject to an accumulation period, which must be either the life of the settlor or a period of 21 years: PAA 2009, s. 14.

19.6.6 Old rules are still important

The new perpetuity and accumulations rules should make life much easier for all those called upon to advise on trusts but it should be noted that the old rules will continue to apply to trusts that existed before 6 April 2010 and to pre-existing will trusts and thus are likely to have a lifespan of at least the next 100 years. The application of the 1964 Act is restricted to the older arrangements, which will continue to be subject to the old rules: s. 16 of the PAA 2009.

Therefore, it will be essential in each case to check exactly when the deed giving effect to the trust was created or the testator of a will trust died, in order to apply the correct set of rules.

FURTHER READING

Cheshire & Burn's Modern Law of Real Property, 18th edn., Oxford University Press, 2011, Chapter 15 (Future Interests).

Gallanis, 'The Rule Against Perpetuities and the Law Commission's Flawed Philosophy' (2000) 59 CLJ 284.

Lawson and Rudden, *The Law of Property*, 3rd edn., Oxford University Press, 2002, Chapter 13 (The Control of Endowment).

Megarry and Wade, *The Law of Real Property*, 8th edn., Sweet & Maxwell, 2012, Chapter 9 (Perpetuities and Accumulations).

Maudsley, *The Modern Law of Perpetuities*, Butterworths, 1979.

Wilson, 'Grave consequences' [2007] EG 134.

The longer version of the material relating to the old rules on the website related to this book (W.19).

20

Resulting and constructive trusts

20.1 Introduction

As we explained in Chapter 15, trusts may be created expressly or may arise without express creation through recognition by the courts. Under LPA 1925, s. 53(1)(b), an express trust is unenforceable unless evidenced in writing, but s. 53(2) provides that this requirement does not affect the creation or operation of resulting, implied or constructive trusts.

You will notice that s. 53(2) contemplates the existence of three types of trust for which writing is not required: resulting, implied and constructive. As you will see from the rest of this chapter, there is no shortage of material about resulting and constructive trusts, but it is not easy to say exactly what is meant by the term 'implied trust' in this context. Hanbury and Martin, *Modern Equity*, 19th edn., at para. 2–028, briefly outlines some suggestions as to what this category may include, but concludes that the classification of implied trusts

> serves little purpose, and the examples commonly given might preferably be regarded as express, resulting or constructive trusts, as the case may be

None of the possible types of implied trust, in the narrower sense, has any immediate relevance to your study of land law, and so we will say no more about them, but will go on to deal in more detail with resulting and constructive trusts.

20.2 Resulting trusts

There are several recognised situations in which a resulting trust arises, i.e., in which the court finds that a particular transaction has given rise to a trust, although there has been no express declaration.

20.2.1 Examples of resulting trusts

In some of these situations, the existing owner of property has transferred it to another person, in circumstances in which the beneficial interest returns or 'results' to the transferor. One example is to be found in the creation of an express trust, where the settlor directs the trustees to hold on trusts which do not dispose fully of the beneficial interest in the property. In these circumstances, the trustees will hold the property on a resulting trust for the settlor in respect of that remaining part of the beneficial interest.

Similarly, where an owner conveys property to a 'volunteer' (someone who does not give value for it), the new owner will hold on a resulting trust for the transferor—provided of course that he is not able to show that the property was given to him as a gift. A good example of a trust arising in these circumstances is to be found in *Hodgson v Marks* [1971] Ch 892.

Another typical situation in which a resulting trust may arise (and, for our purposes, one of the most important) is to be found where property is bought with money belonging wholly or in part to another. In these circumstances, the purchaser, who becomes the legal owner, holds the property on a resulting trust. Where he has made some contribution to the purchase price, he will have a share in the beneficial interest and will hold the property in trust for himself and the other person (*Dewar v Dewar* [1975] 1 WLR 1532); where he has made no contribution, he will hold the whole property for the other's benefit (*Dyer v Dyer* (1788) 2 Cox 92). We have already seen an example of such a trust arising in the case of the matrimonial home in *Kingsnorth Finance Co. Ltd v Tizard* [1986] 1 WLR 783 (see 6.5.2.3).

20.2.2 Presumption of intention, and ways of rebutting that presumption

In the various situations we have mentioned, the courts' recognition of the resulting trust appears to be based on the presumed intention of the person who has conveyed the property or provided the purchase money. This presumption is, however, rebuttable, and can be displaced by evidence of a contrary intention, for example to make a gift or a loan.

20.2.2.1 Rebuttal of presumption by evidence of 'common intention'

It appears from recent Court of Appeal decisions, now approved by the House of Lords in *Stack v Dowden* [2007] 2 AC 432, that the presumed intention that gives rise to a resulting trust may be rebutted by evidence that the parties had intended that the nature and size of their respective interests in the property should not depend solely on the contribution which each had made to the cost of acquisition. If this common intention can be established, it leaves the court free to recognise a constructive trust, under which the size of the shares is determined by the parties' intentions. This development is of particular significance in cases involving the family home and we will consider it in detail at a later stage (see 20.6).

20.3 Constructive trusts

20.3.1 Nature of constructive trusts

Constructive trusts arise by operation of law rather than by the intention of the parties. The court recognises such a trust as being imposed upon the owner of property, in general as a result of his conduct, so that instead of enjoying his property as beneficial owner, he is required to hold it, in whole or in part, for the benefit of some other person. Unfortunately it is almost impossible to give a simple explanation of what constitutes a constructive trust or to explain when it will arise. In *Carl-Zeiss Stiftung v Herbert Smith & Co. (No. 2)* [1969] 2 Ch 276, Edmund Davies LJ said, at p. 300:

> English law provides no clear and all-embracing definition of a constructive trust. Its boundaries have been left perhaps deliberately vague, so as not to restrict the court by technicalities in deciding what the justice of a particular case may demand.

The best approach, possibly, to understanding the cases is to concentrate upon certain circumstances in which a constructive trust has been imposed by the courts. These are summarised by Oakley in *Constructive Trusts*, 3rd edn., at pp. 30–1 as follows:

(a) where a person has obtained an advantage by acting fraudulently or unconscionably or (perhaps) inequitably;

(b) where a fiduciary has obtained an advantage as a result of a breach of his duty or loyalty; and

(c) where there has been a disposition of trust property in breach of trust.

If you are able to do so, you might find it helpful to spend a little time looking at Oakley (at the contents pages if nothing more!), to give yourself some idea of the very wide range of circumstances in which constructive trusts have been recognised. All we can do here is to deal with a few examples, in circumstances which are particularly relevant to land law. The examples we have chosen may all be described in Oakley's terms as having arisen as a result of fraudulent, unconscionable or, possibly, inequitable conduct. It is important, however, to remember that these are not the only circumstances which could lead the court to recognise a constructive trust.

20.3.2 Trusts arising from fraudulent or unconscionable behaviour

We have already noted in this book a number of statutory provisions requiring some form of writing for transactions involving land (e.g., LPA 1925, ss. 40, 52(1) and 53(1)(b); Law of Property (Miscellaneous Provisons) Act 1989, s. 2). Many of these provisions are derived from earlier statutory rules, in some cases dating back to the Statute of Frauds in 1677. At a fairly early stage, the courts of equity became concerned at the use which was being made of the statutory provisions. Estate owners who had acquired property subject to some oral understanding or agreement (perhaps to hold it on trust for the transferor) were using the lack of writing to avoid their undertakings and to claim absolute ownership of the property. In equity's eyes, such conduct was fraudulent, and in these circumstances the transferee would be compelled by the court to hold the property on trust (see, for example, *Rochefoucauld v Boustead* [1897] 1 Ch 196).

20.3.2.1 *Bannister v Bannister*

The approach in *Rochefoucauld v Boustead* [1897] 1 Ch 196 was applied by the Court of Appeal in the modern decision of *Bannister v Bannister* [1948] 2 All ER 133. In this case a purchaser had bought a cottage from his sister-in-law, on the understanding that she would be allowed to live in it rent-free for the rest of her life. The understanding between the parties was not recorded in any document. When the purchaser went back on his agreement and tried to obtain possession of the cottage, the defendant claimed that the oral agreement amounted to an informal declaration of trust, i.e., that the purchaser would hold the property upon trust for her for her lifetime. As we have seen, such a declaration of trust would normally require writing under LPA 1925, s. 53(1)(b), but the court held that the unconscionable conduct of the purchaser in seeking to avoid his undertaking gave rise to a constructive trust. He had promised his sister-in-law that she would have a life interest in the property and, consequently, held the property on trust to give effect to that interest.

A further point to note is that the agreement was held to have created a SLA settlement, under which the woman became the tenant for life, and had the power to call for the estate to be conveyed to her and the power to sell it (see Chapter 18).

20.3.2.2 *Binions v Evans*

The approach adopted in *Bannister v Bannister* was followed by the Court of Appeal in *Binions v Evans* [1972] Ch 359. Here a widow had been given the right to live in a cottage for her lifetime. According to the express terms of the agreement, she was to be a tenant at will, and she agreed to take care of the premises while she had the use of them. The property was then sold to purchasers, who agreed with the vendor that they would allow the widow to remain, and accordingly paid a reduced price for the cottage. Later, they sought to eject her, and the court had to consider the nature of her rights and whether they bound the purchasers for value. The Court of Appeal held unanimously that, although the agreement described the widow as a tenant at will, its terms were inconsistent with such a tenancy. The majority of the court (Megaw and Stephenson LJJ), applied *Bannister v Bannister*, holding that the agreement had given the widow a life interest, and accordingly had made her a tenant for life under a SLA settlement. In their view, the purchasers took with express notice 'of the agreement which constitutes or gives rise to, the trust' (at p. 370), and were accordingly bound by it.

By contrast, Lord Denning MR considered that the agreement gave rise to a contractual licence. We shall see in Chapter 23 that there are considerable difficulties in seeking to enforce such a licence against a purchaser from the original licensor. Here, however, Lord Denning considered that the circumstances justified the imposition of a constructive trust on the purchasers. The contract of sale had stipulated that the purchasers were to take subject to the widow's rights, and they paid a reduced price because of this. In Lord Denning's view (at p. 368):

> In these circumstances this court will impose on the [purchasers] a constructive trust for [the widow's] benefit: for the simple reason that it would be utterly inequitable for [them] to turn [her] out contrary to the stipulation subject to which they took the premises.

20.3.2.3 *Yaxley v Gotts*

We have already discussed *Yaxley v Gotts* [2000] Ch 162, together with some later Court of Appeal decisions on the same lines, in Chapter 5. Here we simply want to remind you that a constructive trust may exist where a vendor leads a purchaser to believe that their informal agreement is binding (despite failing to comply with the Law of Property (Miscellaneous Provisions) Act 1989, s. 2) and the purchaser acts on this belief to his detriment.

20.3.3 Trusts imposed as a result of inequitable conduct

The examples of constructive trusts which we have considered so far were imposed because of the fraudulent or unconscionable conduct of the estate owner. In the 1970s, the Court of Appeal, under the influence of Lord Denning MR, began to impose constructive trusts more widely, in cases where the conduct of the estate owner was regarded as 'inequitable', although not sufficiently blameworthy to be described as 'fraudulent or unconscionable'. Some of these decisions relate to contractual licences, and we will look at them in Chapter 23, although they are in general now discredited. Others form the background to the current law on common-intention constructive trusts, and are considered below in 20.5.2.

20.4 Resulting and constructive trusts of the family home

20.4.1 Introduction

It is always open to partners in a family relationship (whether they be spouses, civil partners or cohabitants) to make express arrangements about their respective property interests in the family home. In so-called *'joint names'* cases, in which the property is conveyed to family partners as *co-owners*, there is an opportunity for them not only to state that they are holding the legal estate on trust for themselves but also to indicate the nature of their beneficial interests (i.e., whether they hold the beneficial interest as joint tenants or tenants in common, and, if the latter, what is to be the size of their respective shares). In *'sole name'* cases, in which the conveyance is to one of the parties only, it could still include a declaration that the property is held in trust for both partners, and if the property had in fact been acquired by one partner before the relationship began, he/she could always make a separate declaration of trust.

For a variety of reasons, however, many couples do not regulate their interests in the family home in this way. We have already noted the difficulties which arise in joint names cases if the parties hold the legal estate as co-owners in trust for themselves but fail to specify the nature of their beneficial interests (see 16.4.5 and 16.5). Moreover, although co-ownership of the family home has become more common during the past 50 years, there are still many cases in which the more traditional approach is adopted, thus vesting the title in only one of the partners (usually but not inevitably the man) without any declaration of trust. Where one partner holds the legal title in this way, he or she is presumed to be entitled to sole beneficial ownership, and this presumption is rebutted only if the other partner can prove entitlement to a share in the property under some form of implied trust. Further, even where such a trust is established (either expressly or by implication) the size of the partners' interests under it may be uncertain and require determination by the court.

In general, questions about entitlement to a share in the family home come before the courts in two situations. They may arise from disputes between former partners who are separating at the end of their relationship, or may arise between the mortgagee of the property and one of the partners, who claims to have rights in the property which take priority over the mortgage.

20.4.2 11 Trant Way

The fee simple in 11 Trant Way is vested in Mark Mould, who bought the property in 1999. The house is also occupied by Sally Mould, Mark's wife, and their two children. Mrs Mould has not worked outside the home during the marriage, and has been fully occupied in bringing up the children and looking after the house and garden.

The Moulds' marriage appears to be a happy and successful one and they have no money worries, but if things did go wrong, either with their relationship or their finances, the considerations we are going to discuss could be very relevant.

20.4.2.1 Property adjustment orders on divorce or dissolution of civil partnership

If the Moulds' marriage were to end in divorce, they would find that the court has wide powers, under Part II of the Matrimonial Causes Act 1973 to make property adjustment orders, which require the transfer of property from one party to the other. Similar provisions apply on the dissolution of a civil partnership under the Civil Partnership Act 2004, s. 72 and Sch. 5 Part 2 and para. 21.

In exercising its statutory powers, the court is authorised to take into account a range of matters, which include: the financial resources and commitments of each party; their age; the duration of the marriage; and the contribution which each has made or is likely to make to the welfare of the family by looking after the home or caring for the family (Matrimonial Causes Act 1973 s. 25(2)). These provisions were not introduced, however, until 1970 (under the Matrimonial Proceedings and Property Act 1970) and before then the only way of obtaining a share in the former matrimonial home was by establishing entitlement under a trust.

20.4.2.2 Claims involving cohabitants

The provisions relating to property adjustment orders do not apply when a relationship between cohabitants comes to an end, and any claim to a share in the family home has to be decided according to the rules of property law, rather than by any consideration of what each party needs or deserves. As Millet J put it in *Windeler v Whitehall* [1990] 1 FLR 505 at p. 506, when considering a claim by a woman to a share in her former partner's property:

> It is not enough for her to persuade me that she deserves to have such a share. She must satisfy me that she already has it.

20.4.2.3 Claims involving mortgagees

As we noted above, a number of cases in this area arise when couples, whether married or not, find themselves in financial difficulties and their mortgagees seek possession of the property. When this happens, one partner may claim to have a share in the house, which takes priority over the mortgage, so that the mortgagee cannot enforce his rights against that share. This is, of course, the background to *Kingsnorth Finance Co. Ltd v Tizard* [1986] 1 WLR 783 (see 6.5.2.3). Thus, if the Moulds were to find themselves in financial difficulties, Sally Mould might want to claim that she was entitled to a share in the family home, despite the fact that the legal title is in her husband's name.

In such a case, where the dispute is not between the family partners themselves but between one of the partners and the mortgagee, the existence and size of any share in the beneficial interest will have to be decided in accordance with basic trust principles.

In dealing with these family home cases, the courts have developed a new type of constructive trust, which has come to be known as a '*common-intention*' trust. We are going to look in some detail at this development, but before considering the major decisions, we need to note some confusion in the language used by the courts when talking about resulting and constructive trusts.

20.4.3 Distinguishing between resulting and constructive trusts

20.4.3.1 Failure to distinguish

In our account of implied trusts so far, we have tried to draw a clear distinction between resulting trusts and constructive trusts. Unfortunately, the courts have not always been so careful to make this distinction. Lord Diplock in *Gissing v Gissing* [1971] AC 886 at p. 905, in referring to resulting, implied and constructive trusts, said:

> It is unnecessary for present purposes to distinguish between these three classes of trust.

This statement may be acceptable when taken in context, but it led other judges to use the phrases almost interchangeably. Thus, Lord Denning MR in *Hussey v Palmer* [1972] 1 WLR 1286 at p. 1289 said that although the plaintiff alleged that there was a resulting trust:

> I should have thought that the trust in this case . . . was more in the nature of a constructive trust: but this is more a matter of words than anything else. The two run together.

As a result of this approach being adopted over a number of years, it is often unclear which type of trust is involved in a particular decision, and as a result it is difficult to give a clear account of the circumstances in which each of these trusts operates.

This somewhat cavalier approach by the courts might suggest to you that the distinction is unimportant, and that you too could say: 'It doesn't matter which it is!'. However, a very different approach has been taken in recent cases, beginning with the Court of Appeal decision in *Drake v Whipp* (1995) 28 HLR 531.

20.4.3.2 Importance of distinction

In *Drake v Whipp* Peter Gibson LJ described the earlier judicial statements as 'a potent source of confusion' (at p. 533). It is now clear that the distinction between resulting and constructive trusts is of crucial importance in determining:

- the nature of the contributions that can give rise to the trust; and
- the approach to be adopted by the court in determining the size of each party's share in the property.

1. *Contributions*

The only contributions which can be relied upon to establish a resulting trust are those made at the time the property was acquired (i.e., contributions to the purchase price paid to the vendor before transfer). Later contributions, such as paying instalments due under the mortgage, do not create a resulting trust in favour of the party making the payments (*Curley v Parks* [2005] 1 P& CR DG 15).

By contrast, the payment of mortgage instalments, and a range of other contributions, can be relevant in establishing a constructive trust (see 20.5). Moreover, following the House of Lords' decision in *Stack v Dowden* [2007] 2 AC 432 it may even be that, in the future, a constructive trust could arise in a family setting without any financial contribution by one of the partners, although there is no decision as yet on this point.

2. *Size of share in property*

Under a *resulting trust*, the beneficiary's share is strictly proportionate to the amount he or she has contributed at the time of acquisition and later payments cannot be taken into account.

Under a *constructive trust*, the court has a much greater freedom to decide on the respective shares of the parties, which are not necessarily proportionate to their financial contributions (see 20.6).

Today, therefore, it is very important to distinguish between these two types of trust, but if you find the topic confusing it may help to remember that there is a genuine lack of clarity in many of the earlier cases.

20.4.4 Two questions for the court

Until *Stack v Dowden* [2007] 2 AC 432 (in which the parties were co-owners of the legal estate), the decisions which establish the principle of the common intention constructive trust had all arisen from claims by one partner (spouse or cohabitant) to a share in the family home, which was owned by the other partner.

In these cases of single legal ownership, the court is required to consider two questions:

- is the claimant entitled to a share in the beneficial interest i.e., does the legal owner hold the property on trust for himself and the claimant? And if so
- what is the size of the claimant's share in the beneficial interest?

In the next two sections we will look in detail at how the court goes about finding answers to these questions.

20.5 Establishing the claim to a share in the beneficial interest

20.5.1 *Gissing v Gissing*

We have already seen that a contribution to the purchase price is presumed to give rise to a resulting trust, and it has always been possible for a spouse or cohabitant to claim an interest in the property on the basis of such a contribution. However in the early 1970s, just before property adjustment orders were introduced, the House of Lords had to consider two cases in which the claim of a divorced spouse to a share in the family home was based not on direct financial contribution but on, in the one case, work done on the house and in the other, on relatively minor contributions to household expenses. In *Pettit v Pettit* [1970] AC 777, the house was owned by the wife. Her divorced husband's claim to a share in the proceeds of sale was based on redecorations and improvements to the property which he had carried out, and which he claimed had increased its value. In *Gissing v Gissing* [1971] AC 886 a wife, whose marriage had ended in divorce after some 30 years, sought to establish a claim to a share in the family home which was owned by her husband, relying on financial contributions she had made over the years in buying items of furniture and equipment, and paying for some improvements to the garden.

In each of these cases, the Court of Appeal had considered that the applicant was entitled to a share in the property, but the House of Lords did not share this view, and in both cases held that the claimants had no share in the beneficial interest. While the speeches in both decisions are of interest, it is Lord Diplock's speech in *Gissing v Gissing* which has received the most attention, as setting out the requirements for the modern common-intention constructive trust. The relevant passage runs as follows:

> A resulting, implied or constructive trust—and it is unnecessary for present purposes to distinguish between these three classes of trust—is created by a transaction between the trustee and the [beneficiary] in connection with the acquisition by the trustee of a legal estate in land, whenever the trustee has so conducted himself that it would be inequitable to allow him to deny to the [beneficiary] a beneficial interest in the land acquired. And he will be held so to have conducted himself if by his words or conduct he has induced the [beneficiary] to act to his own detriment in the reasonable belief that by so acting he was acquiring a beneficial interest in the land.
>
> This is why it has been repeatedly said in the context of disputes between spouses as to their respective beneficial interests in the matrimonial home that if at the time of its acquisition...an express agreement has been made between them as to the way in which the beneficial interest shall be held, the court will give effect to it—notwithstanding the absence of any written declaration of trust. Strictly speaking this states the principle too widely for if the agreement did not provide for anything to be done by the spouse in whom the legal estate was not to be vested, it would be a merely voluntary declaration of trust and unenforceable for want of writing. But in the express oral agreements contemplated by these dicta it has been assumed...that they provide for the spouse in whom the legal estate...is not vested to do something to facilitate its acquisition....What the court gives effect to is the trust resulting or implied from the common intention expressed in the oral agreement between the spouses that if each acts in the manner provided for in the agreement the beneficial interest in the matrimonial home shall be held as they have agreed.
>
> But parties to a transaction in connection with the acquisition of land may well have formed a common intention that the beneficial interest in the land shall be vested in them jointly without having used express words to communicate this intention to one another....In such a case...it may be possible to infer their common intention from their conduct.

Thus, it appears that there are two stages in establishing a common intention trust of this sort:

- an agreement; and
- some detrimental act in reliance on it.

20.5.1.1 The agreement

There must be an agreement between the parties at the time the property is acquired or, exceptionally, at a later stage, that the partner without the legal estate is to have a beneficial interest in the land. This agreement may be:

- express; or
- inferred from conduct.

1. *Express agreement*

Lord Diplock's requirement of an express agreement suggests that the parties must have agreed in so many words that one should have a share in the other's property. However, as applied in later cases and subsequently reworded by Lord Bridge in *Lloyds Bank v Rosset* ([1991] 1 AC 107 at 132–3), the requirement appears to be slightly less precise and becomes

> any agreement, arrangement or understanding reached between [the parties] that the property is to be shared beneficially.

In order to find such an agreement or arrangement, the court requires 'evidence of express discussions between the parties'. However, provided there is evidence of such discussion, the courts have been willing to accept that there was an agreement and common intention, although in at least two cases the discussions might equally well suggest that there was no such intention on the part of the owner. Thus in both *Eves v Eves* [1975] 1 WLR 1338 and *Grant v Edwards* [1986] Ch 638, there was evidence that one partner had made excuses to the other for having the property conveyed to him alone, rather than to both of them. A bystander hearing the conversation might suspect that the owner did not want his partner to have a share in the property, but on both occasions the court accepted that discussions of this nature about title to the property were sufficient to establish an intention to share. Lord Bridge in *Lloyds Bank v Rosset* treats these decisions as examples of express agreement under Lord Dipock's first category (see [1991] 1 AC 107, at 132–2), although you might be forgiven for thinking that the agreements were really inferred by the court.

2. *Agreement inferred from conduct*

Even if there is no express agreement, the court may be able to infer (i.e., deduce) one from the conduct of the parties. After the passage we have quoted, Lord Diplock went on to outline the type of conduct from which such an intention could be inferred. All the examples he gave involved reasonably direct contributions to the cost of acquiring the property; i.e., contributions to the outright payment of the price, or to the deposit and legal charges, or to the mortgage instalments. Indirect contributions to the mortgage repayments would also be acceptable if, for example, the claimant paid other outgoings so as to enable the estate owner to use his funds to pay off the mortgage debt. Such contributions, however, must be clearly referable to the acquisition of the property (i.e., it must appear that the contributor was meeting those expenses in order to facilitate mortgage repayments). In the absence of such evidence, mere contributions to household expenses by itself would not be enough.

20.5.1.2 Action by claimant to his detriment in reliance on agreement

Under LPA 1925 s. 53(1)(b) a declaration of a trust of land must be evidenced in writing. Thus simply establishing the agreement between the parties would not be enough to give the non-owner an enforceable share in the beneficial interest, unless the court could find an implied, resulting or constructive trust (for which writing is not required—s. 53(2)).

This explains Lord Diplock's second requirement: that the claimant has been induced to act to his detriment in the belief that he is acquiring an interest. For the owner to go back on the agreement after this has happened would be inequitable, and it is this that justifies the recognition of some sort of implied trust.

Lord Diplock's speech in *Gissing v Gissing* suggests that the sort of acts required to establish detriment are very much the same as those noted above from which an agreement may be inferred: contributions direct or indirect to the cost of acquisition. However, he did not exclude the possibility that other acts might be sufficient and for a time, under the influence of Lord Denning, the courts accepted a wider range of activities which do not involve financial contribution (see 20.5.2).

20.5.1.3 How were these principles applied to the facts of *Gissing v Gissing*?

The House of Lords considered that there was no evidence of any express agreement between the parties at the time the house was bought. Nor were the contributions by the wife sufficient to support the inference of a common intention. The contributions she made were not sufficiently referable to the acquisition of the property and, in consequence, the wife's claim to a share in the house belonging to her husband was rejected.

20.5.2 Lord Denning's interpretation of *Gissing v Gissing*

The immediate result of the decision *in Gissing v Gissing*, at least at Court of Appeal level, was an increased use of non-express trusts to achieve a fair result between the parties when a strict application of legal rules would appear inequitable. This development was very much associated with Lord Denning MR who read Lord Diplock's words as authorising the use of what he described as 'a constructive trust of a new model' wherever it was equitable to do so.

It was Lord Denning's view (expressed in *Hussey v Palmer* [1972] 1 WLR 1286 at 1290) that a non-express trust was imposed by law 'whenever justice and good conscience require it' and that it was to be applied:

> in cases where the legal owner cannot conscientiously keep the property for himself alone, but ought to allow another to have the property or the benefit of it or a share in it...

The Court of Appeal's approach during this period can be illustrated by two decisions, both of which involved cohabitants.

In *Eves v Eves* [1975] 1 WLR 1338 the woman had made no financial contribution (direct or indirect), but had done a good deal of manual work in restoring the house and garden, and had looked after her partner and cared for their children. In Lord Denning's view, it would in these circumstances have been inequitable for her partner to deny her a share in the house; equity would impose a constructive trust under which she would receive a quarter share.

In *Hall v Hall* [1982] 3 FLR 379 the parties had lived together for seven years. The woman had made no direct payments towards the cost of acquisition, but had paid for furnishings, bought a car and contributed to housekeeping expenses. The Court of Appeal considered that these contributions gave rise to a trust in her favour, Lord Denning saying (at p. 381):

> It depends on the circumstances and how much she had contributed—not merely in money—but also in keeping up the house; and if there are children, in looking after them.

20.5.3 A change of approach: *Burns v Burns*

The mid-1980s saw a change in the Court of Appeal's approach, and a more careful application of the principles in *Gissing v Gissing*. The new approach can be seen most clearly in *Burns v Burns* [1984] 1 Ch 317, which concerned an unmarried couple who had been living together for 19 years. The man was the legal owner of the house in which they lived and had provided the initial deposit and paid the mortgage instalments. For some time the woman stayed at home and cared for the children of the relationship. Later she undertook paid work and used her salary to pay some domestic bills and to buy furniture and equipment for the house and clothes for the children. She also redecorated the interior of the house.

On the approach adopted by Lord Denning, one would have expected these facts to support the recognition of some form of implied trust. On this occasion, however, the Court of Appeal followed very closely the principles laid down by Lord Diplock in *Gissing*, emphasising the need for some agreement, express or inferred from conduct. The conduct from which an agreement could be inferred was summarised in *Gissing* terms, as essentially involving some money payment referable to the acquisition of the property. A substantial contribution to housekeeping expenses would be sufficient if its intended effect was to enable the other partner to pay the mortgage instalments but such contributions by themselves without such an intention were not enough.

Mrs Burns' financial contributions were small and could not be said to be referable to the acquisition of the house and were no evidence of a common intention that she was to have a share. The decorating work she had carried out did not help her, the court following the view expressed on this by the House of Lords in *Pettit v Pettit* [1970] AC 777. Finally, the court had to consider the claim that the performance of domestic duties (running the household and looking after her partner and the children) was a sufficient contribution to entitle Mrs Burns to a share. We have seen that in *Hall v Hall* Lord Denning considered that such a contribution could be taken into account. The court in *Burns v Burns* was of the opinion that his view was not supported by precedent, nor was it consistent with principle; or, as May LJ put it more bluntly (at p. 342), Lord Denning's *dictum* 'was wrong'.

A useful summary of the court's position is to be found towards the end of the judgment of May LJ, and you may in particular like to note his concluding words:

> When the house is taken in the man's name alone, if the woman makes no 'real' or 'substantial' financial contribution towards either the purchase price, deposit or mortgage instalments by the means of which the family home was acquired, then she is not entitled to any share in the beneficial interest in that home even though over a very substantial number of years she may have worked just as hard as the man in maintaining the family in the sense of keeping the house, giving birth to and looking after and helping to bring up the children of the union.

20.5.4 *Lloyds Bank v Rosset*

Twenty years after its decision in *Gissing v Gissing*, the House of Lords attempted to restate the law on common intention constructive trusts in *Lloyds Bank v Rosset* [1991] 1 AC 107. Here property was purchased with money provided by the husband's family trust. On the insistence of the trustees the property was registered in the sole name of the husband. The house required a great deal of alteration and the necessary building work was paid for by the husband, with money obtained on an overdraft from his bank, secured by a charge on the property. Mrs Rosset made no financial contribution to the cost of the property, but was heavily involved in its renovation, giving instructions to the builders and later doing much of the decoration of the premises herself. The marriage broke down, with the husband moving out and failing to repay the loan, and the bank sought possession of the house. The wife claimed that she had a beneficial interest in the property under a constructive trust and that this took effect as an overriding interest binding on the bank under LRA 1925, s. 70(1)(g). Thus, this case came to the courts as a dispute between the claimant and her spouse's mortgagees and her claim, therefore, had to be decided on basic trust principles, rather than on the statutory provisions which would have applied if she had been asserting it against her husband in divorce proceedings.

Mrs Rosset's interest was said to derive from an express agreement reached in conversations with her husband, in reliance on which she had made a significant contribution to the acquisition of the property by the work she had done on its renovation. The judge at first instance rejected the claim of an express agreement but was prepared to infer a common intention from the wife's conduct in undertaking the work of renovation. This finding was, however, rejected by the House of Lords. The monetary value of the work done was trifling when compared with the cost of the property as a whole, and their Lordships doubted whether it would even have been enough to constitute detrimental reliance in the case of an express intention, let alone sufficient to support an inferred agreement. In Lord Bridge's view, the work done by Mrs Rosset was the sort of work which any wife might do to prepare a new home for occupation; it could not be said to be the sort of work which she would not have undertaken if she had not been expecting to acquire an interest in the house.

Lord Bridge, in a speech adopted by his brethren, decided against Mrs Rosset's claim on the simple basis that she had not established any agreement with her husband, express or inferred, that she was to have a share in his property. This was, in essence, a decision on the facts, and Lord Bridge doubted whether any further analysis of the relevant law would be helpful. Unfortunately, he went on to draw attention to what he described as 'one critical distinction', and in doing so created further confusion in this already complicated and difficult area.

The passage in question (at p. 132) reads:

> The first and fundamental question which must always be resolved is whether, independently of any inference to be drawn from the conduct of the parties in the course of sharing the house as their home and managing their joint affairs, there has at any time prior to acquisition, or exceptionally at some later date, been any agreement, arrangement or understanding reached between them that the property is to be shared beneficially. The finding of an agreement or arrangement to share in this sense can only, I think, be based on evidence of express discussions between the partners, however imperfectly remembered and however imprecise their terms may have been. Once a finding to this effect is made it will only be necessary for the partner asserting a claim... to show that he or she has acted to his or her detriment or significantly altered his or her position in reliance on the agreement in order to give rise to a constructive trust or a proprietary estoppel.
>
> In sharp contrast with this situation is the very different one where there is no evidence to support a finding of an agreement or arrangement to share, however reasonable it might have been for the parties to reach such an arrangement if they had applied their minds to the question, and where the court must rely entirely on the conduct of the parties both as the basis from which to infer a common intention to share the property beneficially and as the conduct relied on to give rise to a constructive trust. In this situation direct contributions to the purchase price by the partner who is not the legal owner, whether initially or by payment of mortgage instalments, will readily justify the inference necessary to the creation of a constructive trust. But, as I read the authorities, it is at least extremly doubtful whether anything less will do.

This passage may well have been intended as a restatement or summary of the rules in *Gissing v Gissing*, but the reference in the second paragraph to the need for direct contribution to establish an inferred agreement seems to limit the scope of the principles as so far understood, and to rule out the indirect contribution to mortgage repayments by meeting household expenses which was accepted as sufficient in both *Gissing v Gissing* and *Burns v Burns*.

In addition, some writers take the view that what is described in the second paragraph is really a resulting trust (see Thompson [1990] Conv 314), although the Court of Appeal in *Oxley v Hiscock* [2005] Fam 211 at para. 40 continued to regard Lord Bridge's second category as consisting of inferred common intention constructive trusts.

20.5.5 *Stack v Dowden*

Lord Bridge's statement in *Lloyds Bank v Rosset* was criticised by the House of Lords in *Stack v Dowden* [2007] 2 AC 432, Lord Walker (at para. 26) doubting if it took full account of the views expressed in *Gissing v Gissing*, and adding:

> Whet her or not Lord Bridge's observation was justified in 1990, in my opinion the law has moved on, and your Lordships should move it a little more in the same direction...

Lady Hale also commented that the law had moved on 'in response to changing social and economic conditions' (para. 60), and suggested that Lord Bridge may have 'set the hurdle' rather too high in describing the contributions needed to establish a common intention constructive trust (para. 63). Similar criticism is to be found in the Privy Council decision in *Abbott v Abbott* [2007] UKPC 53, in which Lady Hale quoted with approval from her own and other speeches in *Stack v Dowden*.

Interesting as these observations are, it is difficult to be sure of their precise effect. In *Stack v Dowden*, the House of Lords was concerned with the quantification of shares under an existing trust of jointly owned property. Their Lordships were not required to consider the process of establishing the existence of such a trust in a sole name case, which is what Lord Bridge was discussing. The comments in *Stack v Dowden* cannot, therefore, be more than *obiter dicta*, although they are of course highly significant as showing the House of Lords' current thinking on the matter. As we shall see in the next section, their Lordships adopted a 'broad brush' approach to quantifying shares, which involves considering the 'whole course of dealing in relation to the property' between the parties in order to infer their intentions about the size of their respective shares. Following *Jones v Kernott* [2011] 3 WLR 1121 (see 20.7), it seems very likely that the Supreme Court would favour a similar approach in seeking the intention necessary to give the non-owner a share in the beneficial interest, but as yet there is no authority on this point (see further, 20.8).

20.6 Quantifying the share

If the claimant can establish entitlement to a share in the beneficial interest—whether under a resulting or constructive trust—the court will then have to quantify the share, i.e., decide the proportion of the beneficial interest to which the claimant is entitled. This is an area in which there has been considerable development during the last few years, most notably in three Court of Appeal decisions:

Midland Bank v Cooke [1995] 4 All ER 562;
Drake v Whipp (1995) 28 HLR 531; and
Oxley v Hiscock [2005] Fam 211.

The approach taken in these three decisions was approved and adopted by the House of Lords in *Stack v Dowden* [2007] 2 AC 432. We have already told you something about this decision in dealing with co-ownership (see 16.5) but, in case you have not studied that topic yet, we will give a brief explanation here of the two forms of co-ownership (joint tenancy and tenancy in common), so that you can understand what was at issue in *Stack v Dowden*.

20.6.1 Co-ownership and *Stack v Dowden*

Unlike the cases considered so far in this chapter, in which the legal estate was owned by one of the partners, the parties in *Stack v Dowden* held the legal estate in their family home together as joint tenants. Co-owners hold the legal estate in trust for themselves, and may choose to own the beneficial interest under the trust in one of two ways:

- *as joint tenants* i.e., in the same way in which they hold the legal estate. Joint tenants are together regarded as owning the whole interest: the individual tenant is not entitled to a specific share, and when he dies, ownership remains with the survivor(s);
- *as tenants in common* Tenants in common are entitled to individual shares in the property, which they can transfer during their life and which pass with their estate on death.

A joint tenancy of the beneficial interest can be turned into a tenancy in common by a process called 'severance' (see 16.6), and when severance occurs each of the former joint tenants obtains an equal share in the property.

In *Stack v Dowden*, the relationship between the parties came to an end and Mr Stack ('S') obtained an order that the property should be sold and the proceeds divided equally between the two of them. This would have been the correct way of dividing the proceeds if the parties had been joint tenants of the beneficial interest in their home, as well as being joint tenants of the legal estate. Ms Dowden ('D'), however, claimed on appeal that she had provided the greater part of the acquisition costs and was therefore entitled to a greater share of the property. In co-ownership terms, this means that she claimed that the beneficial interest was held on a tenancy in common, under which she and her former partner were entitled to unequal shares.

In quantifying the respective shares of these co-owners, the Court of Appeal adopted the approach it had developed in cases involving single ownership of the legal estate, and the subsequent appeal by S to the House of Lords gave their Lordships an opportunity to consider that approach (for the result of the appeal, see 20.6.5).

Instead of giving you a chronological account of these decisions on quantification, we think it will be more helpful to note the main principles which emerge from them, but we will of course tell you about the facts and outcomes of the individual cases as we go.

20.6.2 Preference for constructive trust in cases involving the family home

We have already noted that the share taken by a beneficiary under a *resulting trust* is strictly proportionate to the amount of the original contribution (see 20.4.3.2). Where a *constructive trust* is involved, the size of each share depends upon the intentions of the parties, and the courts now consider that this is a more appropriate way of dealing with quantification in both sole and joint name cases involving the family home.

20.6.2.1 Court of Appeal decisions

The significance of the distinction between the two forms of implied trust was emphasised by the Court of Appeal in *Drake v Whipp* [1995] 28 HLR 531. In this case an unmarried couple bought a barn for conversion into a house, the property being conveyed to the man alone. The woman made a substantial contribution to the purchase price, but the costs of conversion, which were considerably greater than the purchase price, were largely borne by her partner. When the couple separated, the woman claimed a share in the beneficial interest proportionate to her contribution to the purchase price (40 per cent), while her former partner claimed that her share should be determined by reference to her contribution to the overall cost of purchase and conversion (which amounted to just under 20 per cent).

If the property was held on a resulting trust, the size of the share would depend simply on the contribution to the cost of acquisition, and the cost of subsequent enhancement would be irrelevant. However, if the property was subject to a constructive trust the court could adopt 'a broad brush' approach to determining the parties' respective shares (p. 536), and thus could take into account their individual contributions to the overall cost of the property.

On the facts before it, the Court of Appeal considered that the requirements for a constructive trust were satisfied (i.e., common intention plus detriment—p. 536), and the court was therefore able:

> [to] approach the matter more broadly, looking at the parties' entire course of conduct together (at p. 537).

Accordingly the court took into account a wide range of matters (for which, see 20.6.4 below), and in the light of these circumstances, considered that the woman was entitled to a one-third share.

A similar approach, based on the recognition of a constructive trust, is to be found in *Midland Bank v Cooke* [1995] 4 All ER 562 and *Oxley v Hiscock* [2005] Fam 211 (see 20.6.3.1–2). Thus it appeared from all three decisions of the Court of Appeal that once the necessary common intention to share the beneficial interest was established, the presumption of a resulting trust arising from contribution to the purchase price would be rebutted, and the parties would move into the greater freedom of the constructive trust, in which size of share does not depend solely on contributions to the purchase price. This approach has now been confirmed by the House of Lords in *Stack v Dowden* [2007] 2 AC 432.

20.6.2.2 *Stack v Dowden*

In this case their Lordships (with the exception of Lord Neuberger, whose views we consider in 20.6.5.1) showed a very clear preference for the use of the constructive trust in cases involving the family home. What one might describe as the 'bookkeeping' approach to quantification under a resulting trust was, in their view, inappropriate when dealing with cases involving the family home. In the words of Lady Hale (at para. 60):

> These days the importance to be attached to who paid for what in a domestic context may be very different from its importance in other contexts or long ago.

Similarly, in Lord Walker's view (para. 31):

> In a case about beneficial ownership of a [family] home...the resulting trust should not in my opinion operate as a legal presumption, although it may (in an updated form which takes account of all significant contributions, direct or indirect, in cash or in kind) happen to be reflected in the parties' common intention.

This view is emphasised again in the decision of the Supreme Court in *Jones v Kernott* [2011] 3 WLR 1121 at para. 25 (see 16.5.3).

Once the court is satisfied that the claim does arise under a constructive, rather than a resulting, trust, it must then seek to discover the parties' intentions about the relative size of their shares and give effect to them.

20.6.3 The court must discover and give effect to the intentions of the parties as to the size of their respective shares

In recognising the existence of a common intention trust, the court has already been satisfied that the parties intended the claimant to have a share in the beneficial interest (see 20.5). The court now has to look again at the parties' intentions in order to discover the size of their shares.

This is the approach originally adopted in *Gissing v Gissing* [1971] AC 886, in which Lord Diplock gave the following guidance on quantifying shares under a common intention constructive trust (see pp. 908–9):

- an express agreement between the parties as to the size of their shares would be conclusive;
- if there was no express agreement, the court might infer an intention from the conduct of the parties. In doing so, it might take into account any contributions made by the claimant, not only at the outset but during the course of the relationship as well;
- if no intention as to size of share could be inferred, the court might infer that the parties had intended the non-owner to have a share but had left the size of that share to be determined later:

  > when the mortgage was repaid or the property disposed of, on the basis of what would be fair having regard to the total contributions, direct or indirect, which each spouse had made by that date. Where this was the most likely inference from their conduct it would be for the court to give effect to that common intention of the parties by determining what in all the circumstances was a fair share.

  As the context of this quotation will show (if you look at the report), the contributions on which Lord Diplock would rely in inferring the parties' intentions are all of a financial nature;
- in the last resort, if no intention could be inferred the court would apply the maxim 'equality is equity' and regard each party as being entitled to a half-share.

This process of inferring an intention as to the size of the share has always seemed a somewhat artificial process, especially in cases such as *Midland Bank v Cooke* [1995] 4 All ER 562.

20.6.3.1 *Midland Bank v Cooke*

This case arose out of possession proceedings by a mortgagee, in which a wife claimed that she had a share in the family home which was binding on the mortgagee.

The Court of Appeal was satisfied that the wife had made a direct contribution, albeit a small one, to the purchase price of the matrimonial home owned by her husband, and apparently accepted that there had been sufficient agreement between husband and wife to give rise to a constructive trust. At first instance, the size of the wife's interest had been quantified by reference to the size of her contribution to the purchase price, and in consequence she was held to have a 6.47 per cent share in the house. On the wife's appeal, it was argued against her that this mathematical approach must be adopted in the absence of any express agreement between the parties as to their relative shares. Moreover, the parties had actually stated that they had not considered the matter at all when acquiring the property.

Surprisingly, Waite LJ considered (at p. 575) that:

> positive evidence that the parties neither discussed nor intended any agreement as to the proportions of their beneficial interest does not preclude the court, on general equitable principles, from inferring one.

In such a case the court should:

> undertake a survey of *the whole course of dealing between the parties relevant to their ownership and occupation of the property* and their sharing of its burdens and advantages [and should] take into consideration all conduct which throws light on the question of what shares were intended (our emphasis).

Accordingly, the Court of Appeal held that it was not bound to deal with the matter on the strict basis of the trust resulting from the cash contribution to the purchase price, and was free to attribute to the parties an intention to share the beneficial interest in some different proportion—in this case, in equal shares.

The methods used by the courts in quantifying shares by reference to the original intentions of the parties were reviewed at length by the Court of Appeal in *Oxley v Hiscock* [2005] Fam 211.

20.6.3.2 *Oxley v Hiscock*

This was yet another constructive trust case involving an unmarried couple and their family home. The woman had made financial contributions to the purchase price, but had been persuaded by her partner that the conveyance should be to him alone, to avoid any problems with her former husband. After the relationship ended, the woman applied under TOLATA 1996, s. 14 for a declaration that her former partner held the property on trust for both of them in equal shares.

The trial judge, following *Midland Bank v Cooke*, looked at 'the whole course of dealing' between the parties and from this inferred an intention that they would share the property equally. The defendant appealed from this decision, claiming that the property was held on a resulting trust with the shares proportionate to each party's contribution to the purchase price. This argument was rejected by the Court of Appeal, which confirmed the trial judge's finding of a constructive trust but varied her award to a 60:40 split in favour of the appellant.

The real interest of the case, however, lies in the observations of Chadwick LJ about the methods used in previous decisions to infer intention from the conduct of the parties. This process has always seemed rather artificial, especially in a case such as *Midland Bank v Cooke*, and the judge clearly regarded this approach as being unsatisfactory, describing it (at para. 71) as 'an unnecessary fiction' to attribute a common intention to the parties when the evidence showed that they had given no thought to the matter. By contrast the judge favoured an entirely different approach, saying that in his opinion what really happened in these cases was that the court itself decided on a fair division of the property between the parties. When dealing with questions about the size of shares:

> It must now be accepted that (at least in this Court and below) the answer is that each is entitled to that share which the court considers fair having regard to the whole course of dealing between [the parties] in relation to the property.

In our opinion the judgment in *Oxley v Hiscock* was to be welcomed for its more open approach to the role the court plays in quantifying shares and its recognition that the court is seeking to fashion a just solution between the parties, rather than to discover their non-existent intentions.

In *Stack v Dowden*, Lady Hale appeared to reject this approach, saying:

> The search is still for the result which reflects what the parties must, in the light of their conduct, be taken to have intended....it does not enable the court to abandon that search in favour of the result which the court itself considers fair.

However, in the case of *Jones v Kernott* [2011] 3 WLR 1121, at para. 53, Lady Hale described *Stack v Dowden* as giving 'qualified approval' to the statement in *Oxley v Hiscock*, and it has been adopted by the Supreme Court as a guide to courts required to 'impute' (rather than 'infer') the parties' intentions. We tell you more about *Jones v Kernott* and 'imputing' intention at 20.7, but first we will consider how a court 'infers' intentions from the parties' conduct.

20.6.4 What should the court consider when seeking to infer intentions from the conduct of the parties?

20.6.4.1 Court of Appeal decisions

In the three Court of Appeal decisions to which we have referred, the court took the view that in seeking to discover the parties' intentions, it should consider 'the whole course of dealing between them elevant to their ownership and occupation of the property...and take into consideration all conduct which throws light on the question of what shares were intended'. We have already noted this statement in our account of *Midland Bank v Cooke* (see 20.6.3.1), and a similar approach was adopted in both *Oxley v Hiscock* and *Drake v Whipp*. In the latter case the Court of Appeal said that it was appropriate to consider the parties' 'entire course of conduct together' ((1995) 28 HLR 531 at 537) and accordingly took into account a range of matters that included: direct financial contributions, the work each party did to improve the property, the joint bank account fed mainly by the man's earnings, and the fact that the woman paid for food and some other household expenses and took care of the housekeeping for them both.

20.6.4.2 *Stack v Dowden*

The approach developed by the Court of Appeal in recent years was approved and adopted by the House of Lords in *Stack v Dowden*. Lady Hale noted that, since *Gissing v*

Gissing, 'the law has indeed moved on in response to changing social and economic considerations', and went on to summarise the new approach to quantifying shares under a common intention trust in the following words (at para. 60):

> The search is to ascertain the parties' shared intentions, actual, inferred or imputed, with respect to the property in the light of their whole course of conduct in relation to it.

Later (at para. 69) her Ladyship indicated a range of matters which could throw light on the parties' true intentions in respect to their family home. She emphasised that in the domestic context there are many factors other than financial contributions which may be relevant, and a lengthy list of examples includes:

- advice or discussions at the time of the transfer;
- the purpose for which the house was acquired;
- the nature of the parties' relationship;
- whether they had children for whom they both had responsibility to provide a home;
- how the purchase was financed, both initially and subsequently;
- how the parties arranged their finances, whether separately or together or a bit of both;
- how they discharged the outgoings on the property and their other household expenses.

Finally, even the parties' individual characters and personalities 'may also be a factor in deciding where their true intentions lay'.

Reading through such a list makes one uneasily aware of the time and expense that could be involved in such an approach. Lady Hale herself appeared to be conscious of the dangers of opening the floodgates, for she noted that '[a] full examination of the facts is likely to involve disproportionate costs' (para. 68) and tried to discourage applications in cases similar to that before the court, by emphasising that it would be very unusual for a claimant holding under a legal joint tenancy to be able to convince the court that the parties had not intended the beneficial interest to be held in the same way. Unfortunately, this discouraging statement would have no effect in cases in which the legal title is held by only one of the partners, and one can imagine weighty files of evidence building up as legal advisers work their way through Lady Hale's 'checklist'.

One limitation of the matters which the court has to consider is the fact that the purpose of considering them is to discover the parties' intentions about the *property*. It does not have the wider purpose of drawing any conclusions about the nature of their *relationship*. (For Lady Hale's criticism of the trial judge for concerning himself with the relationship rather than with matters relevant to intentions about property, see para. 86.)

20.6.5 Outcome of *Stack v Dowden*

Despite several warnings (at paras. 14 and 69) of the difficulty that a claimant would face in attempting to show that legal joint tenants did not intend to hold the beneficial interest on a joint tenancy, Lady Hale was in fact able to find several factors in the case under consideration that showed just such an intention (see paras. 87–92). These factors included not only the greater financial contribution made to the cost of the property by D, but also the fact that her partner took responsibility only for certain clearly-defined areas of expenditure in relation to the house, and that, apart from the house, both parties kept all their property completely separate—there were no joint savings or investments. To her Ladyship, this conduct was a strong indication that the parties did not intend to hold the beneficial interest on a joint tenancy, which would have involved the right of survivorship and an entitlement to equal shares on severance. Accordingly, although Lady Hale does not say this in so many words, the parties must have intended to hold the beneficial interest as tenants in common and their Lordships held that D had made good her claim to a 65 per cent share in the property.

20.6.5.1 Lord Neuberger's speech

In conclusion, we must draw your attention to the views expressed by Lord Neuberger. His Lordship agreed on the outcome between the parties, but made it clear that his reasons for doing so differed from those expressed in other speeches.

Same basic principles should apply in all cases

A surprising feature of the other speeches is their emphasis on the need for a special approach to cases involving domestic partners and their family home. This is well illustrated by the words of Lord Hope (at para. 3):

> Where the parties have dealt with each other at arms length it makes sense to start from the position that there is a resulting trust according to how much each party contributed... But cohabiting couples are in a different kind of relationship. The place where they live together is their home. Living together is an exercise in give and take, mutual co-operation and compromise. Who pays for what in regard to the home has to be seen in the wider context of their overall relationship. A more practical, down-to-earth, fact-based approach is called for in their case.

We have already noted similar statements by Lady Hale and Lord Walker (see 20.6.2.2), and further references to the distinction between 'domestic' and 'commercial' property and relationships can be found throughout all three speeches (see paras. 14, 33, 42, 58 and 69).

By contrast, Lord Neuberger emphasised that the basic principles of law and equity must be applied in the same way in all cases, whether they be commercial or domestic (paras. 101 and 107). He favoured the resulting trust solution in all cases of unequal contributions, whatever the relationship between the parties (para. 112). He accepted that there may be evidence of the parties' common intention which is sufficient to rebut the presumption of a resulting trust and justify the use of the more flexible constructive trust, but he drew attention to the care which must be taken in deducing intentions about property ownership from evidence relating to family relationships (paras. 131–136).

Imputing and inferring intention.

In her speech, Lady Hale had referred to the search:

> to ascertain the parties' shared intentions, actual inferred or imputed.

The suggestion that intentions could be 'imputed' as well as 'inferred' concerned Lord Neuberger (see paras. 125–7) , who explained the difference between the two processes as follows:

> An inferred intention is one which is objectively deduced to be the subjective actual intention of the parties in the light of their actions and statements. An imputed intention

> is one which is attributed to the parties, even though no such actual intention can be deduced from their actions and statements, and even though they had no such intention. Imputation involves concluding what the parties would have intended, whereas inference involves concluding what they did intend.

Lord Neuberger considered that 'imputing an intention' was wrong in principle and conflicted with the earlier House of Lords' decisions in *Pettit v Pettit* [1970] AC 777 and *Gissing v Gissing* [1971] AC 886. However, the Supreme Court has recently made it clear in *Jones v Kernott* [2011] 3 WLR 1121 that intentions may be imputed when there is no evidence from which to infer them, and we will tell you about this in the next section.

20.7 *Jones v Kernott*

Jones v Kernott [2011] 3 WLR 1121 was a joint name case, in which Ms Jones claimed that the parties' original intentions about the size of their respective shares in the family home had changed when their relationship came to an end. This raised two questions:

(1) Had the parties' original common intention to hold the beneficial interest as joint tenants changed?

(2) If that intention had changed, what was their new intention about the size of each share in the beneficial interest?

At trial, the judge held that evidence before him about the parties' conduct after their separation enabled him to infer both their change of intention and also their new intentions about the size of their respective shares. You will find information about the facts of the case and the circumstances from which the judge drew these inferences in our fuller account of this decision at 16.5.4.

The Supreme Court upheld the trial judge's decision (following its reversal by the Court of Appeal). In doing so it confirmed the view expressed in *Stack v Dowden* that the intentions of parties to a common intention trust can change during the life of the trust, and established that such changed intentions can result in changes in the amount to which each party is entitled**.** The court's decision on this point is likely to be regarded in future as authoritative in both single name and joint names cases.

20.7.1 Imputing an intention

All five members of the court agreed that in cases where a court was required to quantify shares under a common intention trust, it would be permissible for the court to *impute* intentions about size of shares if there was no evidence from which such intentions could be *inferred*. In a joint judgment, Lord Walker and Lady Hale stated (at para. 31):

> ...we accept that the search is primarily to ascertain the parties' actual shared intentions whether expressed or to be inferred from their conduct. However...where it is clear that the beneficial interests are to be shared, but it is impossible to divine a common intention as to the proportions in which they are to be shared...the court is driven to impute an intention to the parties which they may never have had.

It is clear from this passage that the two judges regard the process of imputing intention as very much a 'last resort'. By contrast, Lord Kerr suggested (at para. 72) that courts should be willing to adopt the process of imputation at an earlier stage. He appreciated that:

> [t]here is a natural inclination to prefer inferring an intention to imputing one. If the parties' intention can be inferred, the court is not imposing a solution. It is, instead, deciding what the parties must be taken to have intended and where that is possible it is obviously preferable to the court's enforcing a resolution. But the conscientious quest to discover the parties' actual intention should cease when it becomes clear that this is simply not deducible from the evidence or that no common intention exists.... [t]he court...should not be reluctant to recognise, when it is appropriate to do so, that inference of an intention is not possible and that imputation of an intention is the only course to follow.

Lord Kerr and Lord Wilson were in no doubt that intentions could be imputed, and although Lord Collins did not refer specifically to the point, he was in general agreement with the joint judgment. Thus, following *Jones v Kernott*, it now appears to be established that in certain circumstances the court may impute an intention to the parties about the size of their shares. The question then arises of how the court is to set about the task of doing this.

20.7.1.1 How does a court decide what to impute?

In the words of the joint judgment (para. 47):

> If [the court] cannot deduce exactly what share was intended, it may have no alternative but to ask what their intentions as reasonable and just people would have been had they thought about it at the time.

At a later stage in the joint judgment (para. 69), a further answer, approved by other members of the court (paras. 74 and 87), is provided by quoting the words of Chadwick LJ in *Oxley v Hiscock* [2005] Fam 211, at para. 69:

> The answer is that each is entitled to that share which the court considers fair having regard to the whole course of dealing between them in relation to the property.

The link between these two formulations is provided by Lord Wilson (para. 83) who observes that reasonable people would intend only what is fair.

20.7.1.2 Were intentions inferred or imputed in this case?

At this point, there is some divergence in the reasons given by individual judges for their decisions. Three members of the court (Lord Walker, Lady Hale, and Lord Collins) accepted that the evidence before the trial judge was sufficient to enable him to infer both the change of intention and the size of the adjusted shares. By contrast, Lord Kerr and Lord Wilson held that, while the change in the parties' intentions could be inferred, it was not possible to infer any intention about the size of the shares. As a result, both judges imputed an intention to the parties to share the property between them in the proportions fixed by the trial judge, a division which Lord Kerr described as 'eminently fair'.

It is important to note that the Supreme Court's discussion of the possibility of imputing intentions to the parties relates only to the question about the size of shares, and that the first question (about the change of the original intention) was answered by drawing an inference from the evidence. It seems reasonably clear that at least three members of the court (Lord Walker, Lady Hale and Lord Collins) considered that any change in the original common intentions of the parties must be deduced from their conduct and cannot be imputed to them on the basis of what the court considers fair (paras. 51(3) and 52). However, you may like to note a passage in Lord Wilson's judgment (para. 84), in which his Lordship observes:

> [this] case does not require us to consider whether modern equity allows the intention required by the first question also to be imputed if it is not otherwise identifiable. That question will merit careful thought.

20.7.1.3 Significance?

It is too early to assess the significance of this aspect of the decision. The joint judgment, supported by Lord Collins, expresses the view (para. 32) that although the conceptual difference between 'inferring' and 'imputing' is clear, the difference in practice is not so great. By contrast, Lord Kerr (para. 67) considers that although the distinction may not in practice make a great difference to the outcome between the parties, it must result in the court reaching that decision by a very different process. He notes (at para. 74) that the exercise would be:

> wholly unrelated to ascertainment of the parties' views. It involves the court in deciding what is fair in light of the whole course of dealing with the property. As soon as it is clear that inferring an intention is not possible, the focus of the court's attention should be squarely on what is fair...

20.8 Significance of *Stack v Dowden* and *Jones v Kernott*

We have already considered the significance of *Stack v Dowden* at both stages of a joint names case i.e., rebutting the presumption of joint tenancy of the beneficial interest and quantifying each party's share in the property (see 16.5.6). We also know from *Jones v Kernott* that the parties' original intentions may change over time, thus displacing the original beneficial joint tenancy or altering the size of shares under a tenancy in common.

Questions remain, however, about the effect that the two decisions may have on sole name cases, and in considering them we need to look at the two stages of the process described in 20.4.4.

20.8.1 Establishing the claim to a share in another's property

In *Stack v Dowden*, Lady Hale noted (at para. 56) that:

> The starting point where there is sole legal ownership is sole beneficial ownership...and it is upon the non-owner to show that he has any interest at all.

This has always been the position, and it is for the claimant to establish rights in the beneficial interest under a resulting or constructive trust. Well before *Stack v Dowden* the Court of Appeal showed a preference for the constructive trust when it came to the second stage of quantifying shares (see 20.6.2), and it seems likely that the House of Lords' view that resulting trusts are generally inappropriate in domestic situations means that the constructive trust will become the courts' preferred choice at the first stage of the process as well.

What is less clear is whether the lower courts will still feel obliged to follow the Court of Appeal's decision in *Burns v Burns* [1984] 1 Ch 317, holding that the necessary agreement to share the beneficial interest cannot be inferred from anything less than 'real or substantial financial contributions to the cost of acquisition' (see 20.5.3). We have already noted the *Stack v Dowden* criticism of Lord Bridge's *dicta* on this point in *Lloyds Bank v Rosset* (20.5.5), but it remains to be seen whether this by itself will be enough to encourage the lower courts to adopt the 'whole course of conduct in relation to the property' approach of the House of Lords and the Supreme Court. It is, however, difficult to imagine that a Court of Appeal that was so ready to recognise the contributions made by Miss Fowler (in the joint names case of *Fowler v Barron* [2008] 2 FLR 831—see 16.5.5.3) would maintain the hard-line approach of the earlier Court of Appeal in *Burns v Burns*. In reality, it seems to be only a matter of time before the courts come to apply the *Stack v Dowden* approach when seeking to infer the intentions necessary to give rise to a constructive trust of solely-owned property. (On this, see further the note by Piska at [2008] 72 Conv 451 at 460–3.)

Looking ahead, we wonder whether the Supreme Court, moving on from *Jones v Kernott*, will ever go so far as to hold that the intentions required to establish a constructive trust might be imputed if there was no evidence from which they could be inferred. As always, we can only 'wait and see'.

20.8.2 Quantifying the share

As we have seen, the practice of quantifying the claimant's share by reference to the parties' whole course of conduct in relation to the property had been developed by the Court of Appeal before the decision in *Stack v Dowden*. The effect of the House of Lords decision, coupled with that of the Supreme Court in *Jones v Kernott*, is to adopt and confirm this approach, with the additional possibility of imputing intentions about the size of shares when there is no evidence from which they can be inferred.

FURTHER READING

Andrews, 'The Presumption of Advancement: Equity, Equality and Human Rights' [2007] 71 Conv 340.

Clarke, 'The Family Home: Intention and Agreement' (1992) 22 Fam Law 72.

Dunn, 'Whipping up Resulting and Constructive Trusts' [1997] Conv 467.

Eekelaar, 'A Woman's Place—A Conflict between Law and Social Values' [1987] Conv 93.

Gardner, 'Fin de siècle chez *Gissing v Gissing*' (1996) 112 LQR 378.

Oxley v Hiscock

Gardner, 'Quantum in *Gissing v Gissing* Constructive Trusts' [2004] LQR p. 541.

Thompson, 'Constructive Trusts. Estoppel and the Family Home' [2004] Conv 496.

Stack v Dowden

Cloherty and Fox, 'Proving a Trust of a Shared Home' [2007] CLJ 317.

Dixon, 'Case Note on *Stack v Dowden*' [2007] 71 Conv 352.

Dixon, 'The Never-Ending Story' [2007] 71 Conv 456—casenote on *Abbott v Abbott*.

Etherton, 'Constructive Trusts and Proprietary Estoppel: The Search for Clarity and Principle' [2009] 73 Conv 104 (104–115).

Neuberger, Chancery Bar Association Annual Lecture, 2008, paras. 8–22—available on www.chba.org.uk.

Pawlowski, 'Beneficial Entitlement—No Longer Doing Justice?' [2007] 71 Conv 354.

Piska, 'Distinctions without a Difference? Explaining *Stack v Dowden*' [2008] 72 Conv 451 (451–460)—casenote on *Fowler v Barron*.

Jones v Kernott

Briggs, Co-ownership—An Equitable Non-Sequitur' (2012) 128 LQR 183.

Dixon, 'The Still Not Ended, Never-Ending Story' [2012] 76 Conv 83.

Gardner and Davidson, 'The Supreme Court On Family Homes' (2012) 128 LQR 178.

Hanbury and Martin, *Modern Equity*, 19th edn., 2012, para. 11–006.

Mee, '*Jones v Kernott*: inferring and imputing in Essex' [2012] 76 Conv 167.

Pawlowski, 'Imputed intention and joint ownership—A return to common sense' [2012] 76 Conv 149.

Yip, 'The rules applying to unmarried cohabitants' family home' [2012] 76 Conv 159.

21

Proprietary estoppel

21.1 Introduction

In this chapter we want to tell you some more about proprietary estoppel, which we have already discussed in Chapter 5 as a possible substitute for the doctrine of part performance. We preface this account, however, by saying that estoppel as a whole is an area of law which is still very much in the developmental stage. Judges and academic writers are by no means sure yet how the various bits of the jigsaw fit together, and there is a good deal of debate on issues which in the main relate to classification. We mention this only in order to warn you not to be too confused by variations in the labels attached to apparently similar forms of estoppel. The only classification point we want to draw to your attention is that proprietary estoppel differs from other forms of estoppel in that it can be used to ground a legal claim, rather than simply being relied on as a defence against another's claim. It is usual to say that estoppel can be used as a shield but not as a sword; proprietary estoppel, as you will see from cases such as *Crabb v Arun DC* [1976] 1 Ch 179 can very definitely be used as a sword. (See also the observations of Cumming-Bruce LJ in *Pascoe v Turner* [1979] 1 WLR 431 at p. 436.)

21.1.1 Recent House of Lords' decisions

In the course of this chapter we will be referring to the decisions of the House of Lords in *Cobbe v Yeoman's Row Management Ltd* [2008] 1 WLR 1752 and *Thorner v Major* [2009] 1 WLR 776. We have already looked at *Cobbe* in some detail in Chapter 5 and will assume in this chapter that you are familiar with the facts and the decision. If in fact you do not know this case (perhaps because contracts relating to land do not feature in your course) we suggest that you refer back to our account of it at 5.5.4.

21.2 Nature of proprietary estoppel

Proprietary estoppel is usually said to be one of the two forms of equitable estoppel, the other being promissory estoppel.

The basis of equitable estoppel is explained by Lord Denning MR in *Crabb v Arun DC* [1976] 1 Ch 179 at p. 187 as follows:

> Equity comes in...to mitigate the rigours of strict law...it will prevent a person insisting on his strict legal rights...when it would be inequitable for him to do so having regard to the dealings which have taken place between the parties.

Thus, if one party promised not to enforce his legal rights and the other party acted upon this, equity would not allow the promisor to go back on his promise, even though it might not be enforceable against him on a contractual basis. This aspect of equitable estoppel, promissory estoppel, may be familiar to you from the law of contract, and you probably remember the decision *in Central London Property Trust Ltd v High Trees House Ltd* [1947] KB 130.

By contrast, proprietary estoppel arises from a representation by a property owner ('the representor') that another person ('the representee') has or will have some right in the representor's property. If the representee relies on this and acts to his detriment in some way (for example by spending money on the property), it would be inequitable or unconscionable for the owner to insist on his strict legal rights. In such a case, equity would regard him as being estopped from asserting his own rights to ownership of the land. A simple example is to be found in the hypothetical case discussed by Lord Cranworth in *Ramsden v Dyson* [1866] LR 1 HL 129 at pp. 140–1:

> If a stranger begins to build on my land, supposing it to be his own and I, perceiving his mistake, abstain from setting him right and leave him to persevere in his error, a court of equity will not allow me afterwards to assert my title to the land on which he had expended money on the supposition that the land was his own.

This sort of situation, in which the estoppel arises from the true owner's acquiescing in another's mistaken belief as to his own legal rights, led to the suggestion that the estoppel arises only where the person seeking to rely on it believes that he has an existing right in the property. However, in modern decisions, the doctrine has been extended to cover situations in which the claimant is led to believe, possibly by a promise, that he will have some right to the property in the future (see 21.3).

21.2.1 Relationship between promissory and proprietary estoppel

Promissory and proprietary estoppel are generally treated as two distinct forms of equitable estoppel. Rather surprisingly, however, in *Cobbe v Yeoman's Row Management Ltd* [2008] 1 WLR 1752 Lord Scott referred to proprietary estoppel as a 'subspecies of a promissory estoppel' and described Cobbe's claim as being to a 'promissory estoppel' (see paras. 14 and 23). In the House of Lords' second recent decision on proprietary estoppel, *Thorner v Major* [2009] 1 WLR 776, Lord Walker commented that he had some difficulty with Lord Scott's observation in the earlier case, but acknowledged that 'the terminology and taxonomy of this part of the law are...far from uniform' (para. 67). This reinforces our earlier comment that there is a good deal of uncertainty about the whole matter and we repeat our warning not to allow it to confuse you.

21.3 Expectations of future rights

A good example of an estoppel arising from expectations about future rights is to be found in *Crabbe v Arun District Council* [1976] Ch 179. In this case, the plaintiff had a right of access to his land through a gate leading from a road owned by the Council over which he had a right of way. He wanted to sell the part of his land which adjoined the gate, but intended to retain the rest of it, which lay further along the road. The Council agreed informally to grant him a right of way along the further stretch of road and to permit him to gain access to his property by a new gate. Relying on this understanding, the plaintiff completed the sale without reserving any right of way to the existing gate, but the Council did not grant the extended right of way, and indeed fenced the road so that the plot retained by the plaintiff became landlocked.

The Court of Appeal held that the Council had led the plaintiff to believe that he would be granted the right of way, and thus had encouraged him to act to his detriment in selling part of his land without reserving an easement over it. This gave rise to an equity in the plaintiff's favour which the court would satisfy by requiring the Council to grant the necessary right of way and right of access.

In a number of decisions since *Crabb v Arun DC* the courts have recognised that the encouragement of expectations relating to future rights (including an expectation of inheriting property) may give rise to an estoppel, with the result that the representor (or, after his death, his personal representatives) may be required to give effect to this expectation. This aspect of proprietary estoppel may be of particular interest in cases involving family arrangements. It provides an alternative route for spouses or partners who believed that they were to receive a share in the family home but cannot show the common intention necessary for a constructive trust. It may also be helpful when a person has been led to believe that he can continue to live in the house, but later has this permission withdrawn. We consider this second situation in more detail in Chapter 23, in connection with licences.

21.3.1 Expectations as to future inheritance

A number of influential decisions on proprietary estoppel arise from representations or assurances by a property owner about what will happen to his property at his death. Three of these cases are described briefly in this section, and we will tell you more about them at relevant points throughout the rest of the chapter.

21.3.1.1 *Re Basham* [1986] 1 WLR 1498

Re Basham was the first modern decision to recognise a proprietary estoppel arising from expectations of inheritance. The plaintiff had spent time and money caring for her stepfather after her mother's death and, instead of moving away from the area, had continued to live near him in order to help him. He led her to believe that she would inherit his house, but at his death she discovered that he had not made a will. As a result, the house would pass to members of his own family. The court was satisfied that these assurances had been given and that the plaintiff had acted to her detriment in reliance on them. This gave rise to an equity in the plaintiff's favour, which would be satisfied by declaring that the deceased's personal representatives held his estate in trust for her.

In the course of his judgment, Mr Edward Nugee QC stated the principles of proprietary estoppel in the following terms:

> where one person [A] has acted to his detriment on the faith of a belief which was known to and encouraged by another person [B] that he either has or is going to be given a right in or over B's property, B cannot insist on his strict legal rights if to do so would be inconsistent with A's belief.

21.3.1.2 *Gillett v Holt* [2001] Ch 210

In this case the claimant, Gillett, had been persuaded by Holt, a wealthy local landowner, to give up his plans for further education and leave school at an early age in order to work for Holt on his farm. Over the years Gillett was treated almost as a member of his employer's family, took on increasing responsibilities for the management of the property and was led to believe that, in due course, he and his family would inherit the whole property and the farming business carried on upon it. There was evidence that on several occasions when Gillett expressed concerns about his position, he received assurances that his future was secure and that the whole property would be left to him in Holt's will. Unfortunately, after some 40 years of a close working relationship, the two men fell out, the claimant was summarily dismissed and Holt made a new will, leaving his property elsewhere. In the resulting action, Gillett claimed that Holt was under an obligation founded on proprietary estoppel to bequeath to him substantially the whole of his estate.

At first instance, this claim was rejected, Carnwath J holding that the claimant had failed to establish that there was an irrevocable promise that Gillett would inherit. The judge also found against Gillett on the further ground that he failed to establish that he had suffered detriment as a result of relying on Holt's assurance.

The Court of Appeal reversed this decision, holding that there was no need for an express assurance that the promise would not be revoked ('it is the other party's reliance on the promise which makes it irrevocable' (p. 229). The court was also of the opinion that there was clear evidence that Gillett had suffered detriment through relying on the assurances about Holt's testamentary intentions which he had received over a prolonged period of time. As a result, Gillett had a right to relief arising from proprietary estoppel. The position was different from that in other inheritance expectation cases, because Holt was still alive and would continue to use his property. Nevertheless, the court ordered that the farm and farmhouse currently occupied by Gillett and his family should be transferred to him, together with a sum of £100,000.

21.3.1.3 *Thorner v Major* [2009] 1 WLR 776

In this case the claimant, David Thorner ('David'), had worked without payment for nearly 30 years on the farm of his older cousin, Peter Thorner ('Peter'), who had no children of his own. Peter was a man of few words and there was never any direct conversation between him and David about what would happen to the farm after his death. Nevertheless over the years David gained the impression from Peter's 'oblique remarks' (para. 24) that Peter intended him to inherit the farm. On one occasion some 15 years before his death, Peter gave David a document relating to his life assurance policies with the comment 'That's for my death duties' (para. 40). Peter did indeed make a will in which he left the farm to David (para. 44), but later revoked it in order to amend another disposition contained in it (not concerning David) and subsequently failed to make a new will. At his death, therefore, the farm with the rest of his property vested in his personal representatives who intended to deal with the property in accordance with the rules of intestate succession. David, however, claimed that he had a right to ownership of the farm and related property, arising from proprietary estoppel. He had relied on the representations or assurances of Peter that he would inherit the farm, with the result that he had not pursued other available opportunities to acquire employment or property and so had suffered detriment. This claim succeeded at first instance, the trial judge finding that the three ingredients of assurance, reliance and detriment were all established. He therefore ordered that David should receive the farm and other assets of the farming business (para. 48).

This decision was reversed by the Court of Appeal, on the grounds that the assurances relied upon by David were not sufficiently 'clear and unequivocal' and that there was no finding by the judge that Peter had intended David to rely on his statements.

On David's appeal, the House of Lords held that the assurances received by David were sufficiently clear, that they were intended to be taken seriously and to be relied on, and that the property David expected to receive was sufficiently certain. The House of Lords therefore allowed David's appeal and restored the order made by the trial judge. We will tell you more about the reasons for this decision later in the chapter (see 21.5.1–2 and 21.8.3).

21.4 Criteria for proprietary estoppel

The nineteenth century case of *Willmott v Barber* (1880) 15 Ch D 96 set out criteria for establishing proprietary estoppel and you may well see references to these in later cases. However, these criteria were applicable only to situations in which the representee believed that he had an *existing* right over another's land, and even in such cases could be unduly restrictive. Just over 100 years later, a very different approach was proposed in *Taylors Fashions Ltd v Liverpool Victoria Trustees Co. Ltd* [1982] 1QB 133 at pp.151–2, in which Oliver J suggested that, rather than trying to fit claims of proprietary estoppel into 'some preconceived formula', it would be better to adopt:

> a very much broader approach which is directed at ascertaining whether, in particular individual circumstances, it would be unconscionable for a party to be permitted to deny that which, knowingly or unknowingly, he has allowed or encouraged another to assume to his detriment...

This more flexible approach has been adopted with enthusiasm in a number of later cases. Most recently Lord Walker, in *Cobbe v Yeoman's Row Management Ltd* [2008] 1 WLR 1752 (at paras. 56–8) described *Willmott v Barber* as having proved to be 'something of a stumbling block in the development of equitable estoppel' and referred with approval to *Taylors Fashions* as 'having put this part of the law back on the right track'.

Nevertheless, their Lordships emphasised in *Cobbe* that, although unconscionable behaviour is an essential element, it is not enough in itself to give rise to an estoppel, Lord Walker saying (para. 46):

> Equitable estoppel is a flexible doctrine which the Court can use, in appropriate circumstances, to prevent injustice caused by the vagaries and inconstancy of human nature. But it is not a sort of joker or wild card to be used whenever the Court disapproves of the conduct of a litigant who seems to have the law on his side. Flexible though it is, the doctrine must be formulated and applied in a disciplined and principled way.

Similarly, Lord Scott (para.16) emphasised that:

> Unconscionability of conduct may well lead to a remedy but...proprietary estoppel cannot be the route to it unless the ingredients for a proprietary estoppel are present.

We have already mentioned three of these 'ingredients' for proprietary estoppel, namely representation, reliance and detriment. The decision in *Cobbe* highlights two other requirements which are essential in establishing a claim to rights arising from proprietary estoppel. To quote Lord Scott again (at para. 16):

> These ingredients should include... a proprietary claim made by a claimant and an answer to that claim based on some fact, or some point of mixed fact and law, that the person against whom the claim is made can be estopped from asserting.

In other words, the claimant (the representee) must specify:

- the right in the representor's property which he believed he had or would have (described by Lord Scott, using a term derived from earlier decisions, as 'a certain interest' (paras. 18–21); and
- the facts or law which would defeat the claim to that right and which the representor must therefore be estopped from raising.

This second point seems self-evident, and amounts to little more than saying that the claimant must give details of the estoppel which he seeks to establish, although, perhaps surprisingly, Cobbe had failed to do so.

The need to specify the estoppel on which the claimant relies requires no further consideration, but in the next section we will look in more detail at the other elements of proprietary estoppel:

- representation;
- a certain interest;
- reliance;
- detriment;
- unconscionability.

21.5 Essential elements

21.5.1 The representation

This may well, of course, be made in express terms, as it was in *Re Basham* [1986] 1 WLR 1498, and in some of the other cases which we will consider in Chapter 23. It may however be made more indirectly, as for example by encouraging a course of action which it would not be sensible for the claimant to undertake unless he was to be granted some interest in the property—thus raising the expectation that such a grant is to be made.

An old example of this approach, though not expressed to be decided on this basis, is *Dillwyn v Llewellyn* (1862) 4 De G F & J 517 in which a son was 'given' land by his father and thereafter built a house upon the land. No formal conveyance of the estate was ever made. Despite the usual rule that equity will not assist a volunteer (one who acquires property without giving value) and accordingly will not perfect an imperfect gift, the court held that the son was entitled to a conveyance of the fee simple because he had expended his own money on building, in reliance on his father's representation.

A modern example of the same principle, and one which was expressly decided on the basis of estoppel, is *Inwards v Baker* [1965] 2 QB 29. Here a son, acting on a suggestion of his father, built a bungalow on his father's land (partly at his own expense). Thereafter, the son occupied the bungalow in the belief that he would be able to remain there for his lifetime. However, when his father later died, the son discovered that the estate in the land had been left to other people. The Court of Appeal held that the son had a licence (i.e., permission) entitling him to remain in the property as long as he wished, because he had altered his position to his detriment in reliance on a belief induced by his father's conduct. In this case Lord Denning MR suggested that the operation of the rules of estoppel gave rise to 'an equity' in favour of the son, and that this equity should be satisfied by the grant of a suitable remedy, in this case a licence for life. (For a contemporary comment on this decision, see Maudsley [1965] 81 LQR 183.)

Finally, as we have seen in the quotation from Lord Carnworth in *Ramsden v Dyson* [1866] LR 1 HL 129, representations can be made by conduct, including complete silence, as where an owner stands by and watches another mistakenly building on his land and does nothing to correct the mistake (sometimes described as 'estoppel by acquiescence').

21.5.1.1 *Thorner v Major* [2009] 1 WLR 776.

Two further points about the nature of the representation (or assurance) were considered by the House of Lords in *Thorner.* We have already outlined the facts and decision in this case (21.3.1.3), and saw that the House of Lords reversed the Court of Appeal decision, holding that Peter's assurances to his cousin David were sufficiently clear and that there was evidence that he intended David to rely upon them.

1. *How clear must the representation be?*

The House of Lords' answer to this question is delightfully simple, although it remains to be seen how helpful it will be to parties trying to reach a settlement without litigation. In Lord Walker's words (at para. 56):

> I would . . . say (while conscious that it is a thoroughly question-begging formulation) that to establish a proprietary estoppel the relevant assurance must be clear enough. What amounts to sufficient clarity, in a case of this sort, is hugely dependent on context.

In this case the context was quite unusual: that of two hardworking country men ('taciturn and undemonstrative men committed to a life of hard and unrelenting physical work'—see para. 59). The judge had heard detailed evidence about the nature and circumstances of the two men, was sensitive to the unusual circumstances and was satisfied that Peter's oblique remarks were sufficient assurance.

Lord Walker's test of 'clear enough' was adopted and amplified by Lord Rodger (para. 26):

> . . . it is sufficient if what Peter said was 'clear enough'. To whom? Perhaps not to an outsider. What matters, however, is that what Peter said should have been clear enough for David, whom he was addressing and who had years of experience in interpreting what he said and did, to form a reasonable view that Peter was giving him an assurance that he was to inherit the farm and that he could rely on it.

2. *Must the representor intend the representee to rely on his assurances?*

The Court of Appeal had concluded that there was no evidence that Peter had intended David to rely on his representations. The House of Lords noted that, in reaching this conclusion, the Court of Appeal had been concerned with what Peter himself had actually known and intended. As a result, it had been influenced by the fact that there was no evidence to show that Peter was either aware of other opportunities open to David or had intended him to rely on the assurances so as to encourage him to continue his unpaid work on the farm. In other words, it had adopted a subjective test of intention ('what did this particular man actually intend') rather than applying the objective test adopted by Denning MR (in *Sidney Bolsom Investment Trust Ltd v E Karmios & Co (London) Ltd* [1956] 1 QB 529, at 540–1): a man must be taken to intend what a reasonable person would understand him to intend.

Thus, in Lord Hoffmann's words (para. 5):

> ...the Court of Appeal departed from their previously objective examination of the meaning which Peter's words and acts would reasonably have conveyed and required proof of his subjective understanding of the effect which those words would have upon David. In my opinion it did not matter whether Peter knew of any specific alternatives which David might be contemplating. It was enough that the meaning he conveyed would reasonably have been understood as intended to be taken seriously as an assurance which could be relied upon.

A similar view was expressed by Lord Scott (paras. 15–7), and Lord Walker noted (at para. 60) that the trial judge had found on the evidence that Peter's assurances, objectively assessed, were intended to be taken seriously and relied on. In his Lordship's opinion, there was no sufficient reason for the Court of Appeal to reverse the trial judge's findings and conclusion.

21.5.2 A certain interest

The essence of proprietary estoppel is that the representee is led to believe that he has or will acquire rights in the representor's property. In *Cobbe*, one of the reasons for the failure of Cobbe's claim was that he did not have any expectation of receiving an interest in the company's property: merely an expectation of further negotiations which might result in a contract for such an interest. The requirement that the claimant should expect to acquire an 'interest' and that that interest should be certain or specific could suggest that in the case of land the claimant requires some legal knowledge which enables him to identify the right in question at the time his expectation arises. However, in both *Cobbe* and *Thorner* their Lordships stressed the importance of considering whether the relationship between the parties was 'entirely at arms' length and commercial' (as in *Cobbe*), or 'familial and personal', with neither party having much commercial experience (as in *Thorner*). Such differences in context might be particularly relevant to the question of whether the interest which the claimant expected to receive was sufficiently defined. In 'domestic' cases, the claimant's expectations might well not be defined in legal terms, because both parties thought in terms of the tangible property rather than of intangible legal rights. By contrast, where the relationship was a commercial one, the parties could be expected to understand the legal position and to know, for example, that 'a gentlemen's agreement' or 'being bound in honour' had no legal weight and so could not raise expectations of receiving a certain legal interest. For discussions of this point, see Lord Walker in *Cobbe* at paras. 65–68 and Lord Neuberger in *Thorner* at paras. 96–98. This emphasis on the importance of distinguishing between commercial and family relationships would seem to go a long way towards modifying the apparent strictness of some of the statements in *Cobbe*.

Is the physical property sufficiently defined?
In *Thorner*, the extent of the farm had fluctuated over the years (parts being sold off and new areas being acquired). On David's appeal to the House of Lords (which was heard after the decision in *Cobbe*) the respondents claimed that, as a result of these changes to the area of the farm, the property which David expected to receive was not sufficiently certain. Their Lordships dealt with this issue fairly briefly, holding that there was no real uncertainty here. There was no reason to doubt that the common understanding was that Peter's assurances related to what the farm would consist of at his death (para. 62). Further, in considering the respondent's reliance on *Cobbe*, Lord Neuberger emphasised that that case was very different from the present one (paras. 94–5). In *Cobbe* there was no doubt about the physical identity of the property. However, there was total uncertainty as to the nature of the interest in the property, or other lesser benefit, which Cobbe expected to receive. By contrast, in the present case, the extent of the farm might change, but there was no doubt about the nature of the interest in it which David believed he would be given.

21.5.3 **Reliance**

It is an essential element in establishing estoppel that the claimant has relied on the represention, in the sense of being influenced or induced by it to act in a particular way. There are statements in earlier decisions which suggest that it is for the claimant to prove reliance, and this approach appears to have been adopted by Oliver J in *Taylors Fashions Ltd v Liverpool Trustees Co.* [1982] 1 QB 133 at p. 156. However, the contrary view finds strong expression in *Greasely v Cooke* [1980] 1 WLR 1306 at p. 1311 (the facts of which are outlined in 23.3.4), in which Lord Denning MR repeated a statement he had made in an earlier judgment (*Brikom Investments Ltd v Carr* [1979] QB 467 at pp. 482–3):

> Once it is shown that a representation was calculated to influence the judgement of a reasonable man, the presumption is that he was so influenced.

In *Gillett v Holt* [2001] Ch 210 the Court of Appeal accepted without question that reliance would be presumed, citing *Greaseley v Cooke* as authority for this.

The burden is thus on the person who made the representation and is now contesting the estoppel, to show that the claimant did not rely upon it.

Mixed motives
In seeking to show non-reliance, it may well be suggested that the claimant acted as he did for a variety of reasons, and was not influenced solely by the representation made to him. This problem of mixed motives was considered by the Court of Appeal in *Campbell v Griffin* [2001] EWCA Civ 990 [2001] W&TLR 981, the facts of which were as follows.

The claimant, Mr Campbell, had lived for many years as a lodger in a house jointly owned by an elderly couple, Mr and Mrs Ascough. As the Ascoughs became increasingly frail, they depended upon Campbell for practical help, and as time went by he gradually took on the role of an unpaid carer, preparing meals for them and helping them to wash and get to bed. At various times over the years he received assurances from them that he had a home for life. An attempt was in fact made by Mr Ascough to give effect to this assurance in his will, but by the time he did this his wife was suffering from senile dementia and was no longer capable of altering her own will to the same effect. Mr Ascough died before his wife, who took the whole property by right of survivorship (see 16.2.2), with the result that at her death the whole house passed to those entitled under her will. In these circumstances, the executors of the couple's wills were obliged to oppose Mr Campbell's subsequent claim of estoppel.

In the course of the trial, the claimant admitted that he had been influenced by feelings of affection and responsibility towards the elderly couple, who had treated him as one of the family, and that he would have acted as he did even without an expectation of receiving an interest in the property. In the light of this, the trial judge held that Mr Campbell had not acted in reliance on the assurances, and that in consequence no estoppel was established.

On appeal, the court considered the position of a claimant who realises that he had several reasons for incurring the detriment on which he relies. In the words of Robert Walker LJ (at para. 29):

> It would do no credit to the law if an honest witness who admitted that he had mixed motives were to fail in a claim which might have succeeded if supported by less candid evidence.

His Lordship quoted with approval the words of Balcombe LJ in *Wayling v Jones* (1993) 69 P&CR 170 at 173:

> The promises relied upon do not have to be the sole inducement for the conduct: it is sufficient if they are an inducement.

The Court of Appeal accepted that the assurances given by the Ascoughs were among the inducements which led Mr Campbell to act as he did, and in consequence found that he was entitled to equitable relief.

21.5.4 Detriment

While reliance on the representation may be presumed, the detriment resulting from that reliance must be proved by the claimant (*Gillett v Holt* [2001] Ch 210 at p. 232, rejecting the suggestion that the detriment could be presumed).

The detriment relied upon may often involve the expenditure of money (for example on property in which one believes one has or will have an interest—see, for example, *Pascoe v Turner* [1979] 1 WLR 431), but it does not necessarily have to do so. In *Crabb v Arun DC* [1976] 1 Ch 179 the detriment consisted of the plaintiff's selling off part of his land without reserving a right of way over it. In *Greasely v Cooke* [1980] 1 WLR 1306 a former maid had continued to live in the house and look after the family 'when otherwise she might have left and got a job elsewhere' (at p. 1312). In *Re Basham* [1986] 1 WLR 1498 the plaintiff and her husband had looked after her stepfather, providing meals for him and working in his house and garden, and had continued to live in the neighbourhood so that they could continue to care for him, rather than moving away.

In *Gillett v Holt* [2001] Ch 210, the Court of Appeal identified a wide range of matters which in its view constituted detriment: the claimant had left school without academic qualifications at the request of the defendant; he and his wife had subordinated their wishes to those of his employer in a number of ways, most notably in connection with their sons' education; they had sold their own house (and so had 'stepped off' the property ladder) and had lived as rent-paying tenants in a farmhouse owned by Holt, on which they had spent a good deal of their own money. In addition, by remaining in Holt's employment, Gillett had deprived himself of the chance to try to better himself in some way—although the court also accepted that he might have done less well with a different employer.

A difficulty sometimes experienced in seeking to establish detriment is that the claimant may appear to have derived considerable benefit from the arrangements to which he was a party. Thus, in situations such as those in *Dillwyn v Llewellyn* and *Inwards v Baker*, the claimants had had the advantage of occupying land without paying rent, while Gillett had found Holt to be a generous employer, and had benefited from gifts to the family and substantial help with the school fees. While things were going well between the two men, it would not have appeared that Gillett was acting to his detriment, and it was this that apparently led the trial judge to consider that the necessary element of detriment had not been established. However, the Court of Appeal (p. 232) was at pains to point out that:

> The issue of detriment must be judged at the moment when the person who has given the assurance seeks to go back on it.

In elaborating this point, the court quoted with approval (at pp. 232–3) a passage from the judgment of Dixon J in the Australian case of *Grundt v Great Boulder Pty Gold Mines Ltd* (1937) 59 CLR 641 at 674–5):

> The real detriment or harm from which the law seeks to give protection is that which would flow from the change of position if the assumption were deserted that led to it. So long as the assumption is adhered to the party who altered his situation upon the faith of it cannot complain. His complaint is that when afterwards the other party makes a different state of affairs the basis of an assertion of right against him then, if it is allowed, his own original change of position will operate as a detriment.

21.5.5 Unconscionability

Although unconscionability is not sufficient by itself to give rise to an estoppel (*Cobbe*, paras. 16 and 46), it is essential that the behaviour of the representor, in 'going back' on his representation, is serious enough to appear unconscionable or inequitable. In *Cobbe*, Lord Walker described unconscionability as 'unifying and confirming' the other elements of proprietary estoppel and suggested (para. 92) that:

> If the other elements appear to be present but the result does not shock the conscience of the court, the analysis needs to be looked at again.

21.6 Satisfying the equity

You may have noted from our account of various decisions, that the estoppel, when established, is said to give rise to an 'equity', by which we understand the courts to mean that the claimant has a right to some form of remedy in equity. Once the equity is established, the courts have to consider how to 'satisfy' it, i.e., to decide what relief should be given.

Over the years the courts have drawn on a range of remedies, including restraining the owner from exercising his rights, or requiring him to pay compensation or grant the claimant some interest in the land. In deciding what remedy to give, the courts seek to achieve 'the minimum equity to do justice to the plaintiff' (per Scarman LJ in *Crabb v Arun DC* [1976] 1 Ch 179 at p. 198), a statement repeated with approval in a range of judgments over the years.

In some cases the court has decided that the equity can be satisfied only by giving effect to the expectations which the representation has encouraged. Thus in *Re Basham* [1986] 1 WLR 1498 the plaintiff received the estate she had expected to inherit, and in *Crabb v Arun DC* [1976] 1 Ch 179 the landowner was granted the rights of access and way on which he had relied. In *Greasely v Cooke* [1980] 1 WLR 1306 the former maid was allowed to remain in the house as long as she wished, and similarly in *Inwards v Baker* [1965] 2 QB 29 the son was in effect given a licence for life. The most generous way of satisfying the equity is perhaps that to be found in *Pascoe v Turner* [1979] 1 WLR 431, in which, in rather exceptional circumstances, the fee simple owner was required to transfer the estate in the house to his former mistress (see further 23.2.4).

In other cases, however, it has been either impossible or, in the view of the court, inappropriate to satisfy the expectations of the claimant in full. In *Gillett v Holt* [2001] Ch 210 there could be no question of giving effect to the full expectations encouraged by Holt, since they were to take effect on his death and he was still very much alive! The court described its task of satisfying the equity in this case as presenting unusually difficult problems, but having regard to the extent of the property involved ordered that the farmhouse and farm currently occupied by the Gilletts should be transferred to them, together with a payment of £100,000.

In *Campbell v Griffin* [2001] EWCA Civ 990, Robert Walker LJ commented (at para. 34) that:

> Mr Campbell has a moral (and, as I see it, a legal) claim on the property, but it is not so compelling as to demand total satisfaction, regardless of the effect on other persons with claims on the Ascoughs' estate.

The court also took into account that the life interest which Mr Campbell had expected to receive would necessarily take effect under a trust of land, with resulting legal expenses and that there could well be disputes about the maintenance of the house. It accordingly favoured the 'clean break' approach, which would enable those with other interests in the property to benefit from them without delay, and therefore ordered the sale of the house and the payment to Mr Campbell of £35,000. It accepted that this would not be sufficient to buy him a home, but considered that it would be a reasonable contribution to the cost of doing so.

Another similar question, and on similar facts, arose in *Jennings v Rice* [2003] 1 P&CR 8, p. 100. For many years, Mr Jennings had worked, originally as a gardener, for an elderly and wealthy widow, who gradually came to depend upon him as her carer. After a time she no longer paid him for his work, but assured him that he had no need to worry and that 'this will all be yours one day'. Despite this, she died without making a will, leaving an estate which was valued at over £1 million. At first instance the trial judge accepted that Mr Jennings had acted to his detriment in reliance on the assurances and that it was unconscionable for the deceased to go back on her word. In deciding how to satisfy the equity that had arisen, he rejected Mr Jennings's claim that he was entitled to the whole estate, holding that the claimant was unaware of the true extent of the deceased's wealth and therefore could not have expected to receive her whole estate. He also rejected the alternative claim to the house and furniture (valued at £435,000), considering that the house was not suitable for Mr Jennings to live in on his own and also that a reward of such value would be excessive. He took into account the fact that the cost of full-time nursing care would have been in the region of £200,000 and that Mr Jennings could probably buy a suitable house for £150,000, and accordingly awarded the claimant the sum of £200,000. On appeal by Mr Jennings, who sought a greater award, the Court of Appeal upheld the lower court's decision.

The interest of the Court of Appeal's judgment in this case lies in its review of the various approaches which may guide a court in its search for an appropriate remedy, and we will look in more detail at this in 21.6.1. First, however, we must note a slightly earlier decision, *Sledmore v Dalby* (1996) 72 P&CR 196, in which the court refused to give any relief at all to the applicant.

In *Sledmore v Dalby* the plaintiff sought possession of a house which she owned, and which the defendant, her son-in-law, had occupied for over 30 years, initially in exchange for rent but subsequently on a rent-free basis. The defendant relied on proprietary estoppel, claiming that during his wife's lifetime he had been led to believe that the house would be left to her on her parents' death, and that at that period he had made various improvements to the house at his own expense. He had remained in the house for some 12 years after his wife's death, and assumed that he would be allowed to live there rent-free for the rest of his life. At first instance, the court gave effect to this expectation, refusing the plaintiff's application for possession and declaring that the defendant had a personal licence to occupy the house during his life, so long as he wished.

The Court of Appeal, however, took into account the relative circumstances of the two parties. The defendant's children were grown up, and had either left home or were capable of doing so; he was in employment; and he had the use of alternative accommodation, spending much of his time away from the house and using it on only one or two nights each week. By contrast, the plaintiff was an elderly woman who could no longer afford to remain in her present home, and accordingly needed the house to live in. The court emphasised (at p. 207) that in applying the equitable doctrine of proprietary estoppel

> . . . it is necessary to consider the extent of the equity created and what is, in the circumstances, the equitable way in which to give effect to it.

The court referred to a discussion of the law of estoppel to be found in a decision of the High Court of Australia (*Commonwealth of Australia v Verwayen* (1990) 170 CLR 394), and (at p. 208) quoted with approval the statement of Mason CJ that:

> A central element of [the doctrine of estoppel] is that there must be a proportionality between the remedy and the detriment which [it] is its purpose to avoid.

Having regard to these principles, and to all the circumstances of the case, the English Court of Appeal considered that it was no longer inequitable to allow the expectation raised some 18 years earlier to be defeated, and accordingly made an order for possession against the defendant. For a critical consideration of this decision, see Adams [1997] Conv 458.

21.6.1 How does the court decide on appropriate relief?

The decisions considered above illustrate the range of approaches which the court may be asked to adopt in giving relief. While the claimant hopes that the court will give full effect to his expectations, those opposing the claim may suggest that it would be enough to compensate him for the detriment he has suffered through his reliance on the representation. Thus, if a situation similar to *Pascoe v Turner* were to arise again, the claimant would hope for ownership of the house, while the other side might argue that it would be sufficient to repay the money spent on improvements to the property. Yet again, where the detriment in question consists of the performance of personal services it might be thought that the equity would be satisfied by payment for those services, plus if necessary reimbursement of out-of-pocket expenses.

In *Jennings v Rice* [2003] 1 P&CR 8 at p. 100, the Court of Appeal discussed these various approaches, emphasising that while each might be appropriate in some situations, there was no one approach which would apply to all circumstances. The court stressed that the guiding principle must be the need to do justice, or, as Robert Walker LJ put it (at p. 116):

> The essence of the doctrine of proprietary estoppel is to do what is necessary to avoid an unconscionable result.

The court drew attention to the flexibility of this form of relief and the importance of considering all the circumstances of each individual case. Further the judges emphasised the long-established principle that the relief given must be 'the minimum equity to do justice'. In some cases, such as *Pascoe v Turner*, the minimum required may be to give full effect to the claimant's expectations, but that is because this is what in needed in the circumstances of the case—not because there is any rule that the award must satisfy the expectation (see pp. 107–8). In each case, the court must go no further than is necessary to prevent unconscionable conduct and, as was said in *Sledmore v Dalby* (1996) 72 P&CR 196, must ensure that there is proportionality between the benefit and the detriment. As Hobhouse LJ explained in that case (at p. 209):

> This is to say little more than that the end result must be a just one having regard to the assumption made by the party asserting the estoppel and the detriment which he has experienced.

Thus again and again in *Jennings v Rice* the Court of Appeal returned to the point that there is no one correct formula by which a court can identify the relief to be given: it is a matter for the court's discretion, and the relief must be tailored to the specific facts of each case. In dealing with such applications the court will undertake a detailed consideration of all the circumstances, and you may like to note the following passage (at p. 115) in which Robert Walker LJ outlines some of the matters which a court might take into account:

> It would be unwise to attempt any comprehensive enumeration of the factors relevant to the exercise of the court's discretion, or to suggest any hierarchy of factors. In my view they include... factors [such as the] misconduct of the claimant... or particularly oppressive conduct on the part of the defendant. To these can safely be added the court's recognition that it cannot compel people who have fallen out to live peaceably together, so that there may be a need for a clean break; alterations in the benefactor's assets and circumstances...; and (to a limited degree) the other claims (legal or moral) on the benefactor or his or her estate. No doubt there are many other factors which it may be right for the court to take into account in particular factual situations.

This 'individually hand-crafted' approach may at first sight seem attractive, but it makes it very difficult to predict the outcome of any case involving proprietary estoppel, and thus must have a tendency to encourage litigants to try their luck in court rather then seeking to settle by some out-of-court process. The difficulties are described by Mummery LJ at the start of his judgment in *Yeoman's Row Management Ltd v Cobbe* [2006] 1 WLR 2964 at para. 2:

> It would be unwise, on the one hand, to cramp the court's competence to achieve just outcomes in as many cases as possible. On the other hand, simply doing what the court thinks is just and equitable on the facts of each individual case is liable to increase uncertainty in matters affecting property, in which certainty is important. Unpredictability and inconsistency also make it difficult for parties in actual or prospective litigation to obtain the sufficiently solid advice for negotiating sensible settlements.

A further difficulty arises from the fact that in some cases there is little explanation of the reasons underlying the judge's choice of relief. This seems to be particularly so when the relief takes the form of a money payment; in some cases (see for example *Powell v Benney* [2007] EWCA Civ 1283 at para. 18) the figure awarded seems to have been 'plucked out of the air' with no explanation of how the judge arrived at it. Such awards may well seem arbitrary to the parties themselves and provide little help in predicting the outcome of future cases. On this point, you may like to note a short passage from a recent article by Simon Gardner ((2006) 122 LQR 492 at 501):

> Discretionary justice, above all, cannot be seen to be done unless the judge gives an account of how he or she arrived at the response in question. By definition, in a discretionary jurisdiction, there is more than one possible response. What is needed is an explanation by the judge of why, to him or her, the particular outcome selected was the best one. That explanation can then be the subject of reflection and discussion, again helping to assure that judges do not reach their responses idiosyncratically (as 'men'), but do so as representatives of the law.

21.7 Nature of the equity arising from estoppel

As we have seen, the equity which arises from proprietary estoppel entitles the claimant to some form of equitable relief. What happens if the landowner who made the representation and so is subject to the equity transfers his property to another person after the equity arose, but before the claimant seeks relief in the courts? Is the equity a purely personal right, enforceable only against the original owner or does it have the character of a proprietary right, binding those who take the land from him?

21.7.1 Registered land

Until recently, there was little authority on the status of the equity in relation to registered land, although it appeared that it was the practice of the registrar to allow the protection of such an equity by means of a notice or caution on the register (see Megarry and Wade, para. 16–032 n. 279). There were also suggestions that the equity was capable of taking effect as an overriding interest under LRA 1925, s. 70(1)(g) (rights of persons in actual occupation), and this was supported by two decisions: *Habermann v Koehler* (No. 2) [2000] TLR 825 (see 23.3.4.1) and *Lloyd v Dugdale* [2002] 2 P&CR 13 167.

Shortly before the two decisions noted above, the position of the equity in relation to registered land was considered by the Joint Working Party of the Law Commission and the Land Registry, which developed the proposals for reform of registered title discussed in Chapter 7. The Working Party emphasised the increasing importance of the doctrine of proprietary estoppel, which in its view had become 'one of the principal vehicles for accommodating the informal creation of proprietary rights' (Consultative Document, 1998, Law Com No. 254, para. 3.33).

The status of the equity arising from estoppel was uncertain, but such authority as there was indicated that the equity was of a proprietary nature capable of binding successors, rather than a personal right against the original owner. It was desirable to clarify the status of the equity in relation to registered land, and during the consultation process it emerged that similar clarification was needed in respect of 'mere equities' (for which, see 2.5.6 and Report, Law Com No. 271, paras. 5.32–36).

Accordingly LRA 2002, s. 116 provides:

> It is hereby declared for the avoidance of doubt that, in relation to registered land, each of the following—
>
> (a) an equity by estoppel, and
>
> (b) a mere equity
>
> has effect from the time the equity arises as an interest capable of binding successors in title (subject to the rules about the effect of dispositions on priority).

Thus the equity arising from estoppel is now capable of binding a purchaser for valuable consideration of registered land if it is protected by an entry on the register or, alternatively, can take effect as an overriding interest if the person entitled is in actual occupation of the land (LRA 2002, Sch. 3, para. 2).

Section 116 of LRA 2002 has recently been applied by the High Court in *Halifax PLC and Bank of Scotland v Curry Popeck* [2008] EWHC 1692, in which an equity arising from estoppel was recognised as an interest in land capable of binding the holder of a later equitable interest (see 7.14—but note the warning there that the facts of this case are complicated).

21.7.2 Unregistered land

There are a number of decisions relating to licences of unregistered land in which the equity arising from estoppel has been held to bind third parties, and we will tell you about these in Chapter 23 (see 23.3.4).

21.8 Relationship between proprietary estoppel and constructive trusts

While reading this account of proprietary estoppel you have probably been reminded of the rules about common intention constructive trusts, derived from *Gissing v Gissing* [1971] AC 886, which we considered in Chapter 20. The need for detrimental reliance in establishing an estoppel is reminiscent of the requirement that the party claiming a share under a common intention constructive trust must show that he acted to his detriment in reliance upon the agreement between the parties. Over the years, judges have expressed a wide range of views about the relationship between the two concepts, and we will note some of them in this section.

21.8.1 Assimilation?

As case law on the common intention constructive trust developed, several judges commented on the apparent similarities between that type of trust and proprietary estoppel. Thus in *Grant v Edwards* [1986] 1 Ch 638 at pp. 656–7, Browne-Wilkinson VC based his decision on the existence of a constructive trust (at p. 657), but at p. 656 he suggested that:

> in other cases of this kind, useful guidance may in the future be obtained from the principles underlying the law of proprietary estoppel which...are closely akin to those laid down in *Gissing v Gissing* [1971] AC 886. In both, the claimant must to the knowledge of the legal owner have acted in the belief that the claimant has or will obtain an interest in the property. In both, the claimant must have acted to his or her detriment in reliance on such belief. In both, equity acts on the conscience of the legal owner to prevent him from acting in an unconscionable manner by defeating the common intention. The two principles have been developed separately without cross-fertilisation between them: but they rest on the same foundation and have on all other matters reached the same conclusions.

Similarly Nourse LJ in *Stokes v Anderson* [1991] 1 FLR 391 at 398–9, suggested that:

> It is possible that the House of Lords will one day decide to solve the problem [presented by earlier decisions] either by assimilating the principles of *Gissing v Gissing* and those of proprietary estoppel, or even by following the recent trend in other commonwealth jurisdictions towards more generalised principles of unconscionability and unjust enrichment.

We have also seen a similar approach in the Court of Appeal when dealing with cases arising from informal agreements for the sale or other disposition of an interest in land which do not satisfy the requirements of the Law of Property (Miscellaneous Provisions) Act 1989, s. 2 (see 5.5). In such cases concerns about public policy may prevent the court from basing its decision on proprietary estoppel which it was originally thought would take the place of part performance in helping deserving parties. Following *Yaxley v Gotts* [2000] Ch 162, the courts have been ready to find that the circumstances which give rise to proprietary estoppel will also support a finding of constructive trust, thus bringing the case within the s. 2(5) exception to the formal requirements.

The relationship between the two concepts when used in this context has been described in a variety of ways. In *Yaxley v Gotts* [2000] Ch 162 at 176 and 180 it was said that they 'coincide' and 'are clearly akin to each other', while in *Kinane v Mackie-Conteh* [2005] EWCA Civ 45 (at paras 31 and 48) estoppel was said to 'overlap' or 'amount to' a constructive trust. In *Kinane*, however, Neuberger LJ (at para. 47) provided some clarity by noting that not all estoppels give rise to a constructive trust:

> The essential difference between a proprietary estoppel which does not also give rise to a constructive trust, and one that does, is the element of agreement, or at least expression of common understanding, exchanged between the parties, as to the existence or intended existence, of a proprietary interest in the latter type of case.

We suggest that an illustration of an estoppel situation which does not give rise to a constructive trust can be found in the hypothetical case discussed in *Ramsden v Dyson* [1866] LR 1 HL 129 (see 21.2) in which a claimant builds on another's land, having formed the mistaken belief, without any discussion with the owner, that he himself owns the land. This makes it reasonably clear that although the two concepts may overlap, like intersecting circles, they are not identical, and more recent judicial utterances have begun to focus on the differences between the two concepts, rather than on their similarities.

21.8.2 Emphasising the differences

Obiter dicta in several cases suggest that the tide may be beginning to turn a little against the idea of assimilation. Sir Andrew Park, sitting as a judge in the Chancery Division of the High Court, is reported as having said in *Lalani v Crump Holdings Ltd* [2007] EWHC 47 (Ch), [2007] 08 EG 136 (CS) that:

> While there was an affinity between the two types of claim for a beneficial interest, a common intention trust tended to focus upon the current state of affairs, whereas proprietary estoppel was concerned with promises to do something in the future that would change the pre-existing situation. Moreover, the remedies available to the court were different.

Even more significant, perhaps, is the comment of Lord Walker in *Stack v Dowden* [2007] AC 432 at para. 37 that in *Yaxley v Gotts* he had given some encouragement to the approach which emphasises the similarities between the two concepts, but:

> I have to say that I am now rather less enthusiastic about the notion that proprietary estoppel and 'common intention' constructive trusts can or should be completely assimilated. Proprietary estoppel typically consists of asserting an equitable claim against the conscience of the 'true' owner. The claim is a 'mere equity'. It is to be satisfied by the minimum award necessary to do justice... which may sometimes lead to no more than a monetary award. A 'common intention' constructive trust, by contrast, is identifying the true beneficial owner or owners, and the size of their beneficial interests.

21.8.3 *Thorner v Major* [2009] 1 WLR 776

The most recent contribution to the debate about the relationship between proprietary estoppel and constructive trusts is to be found in *Thorner*, in which Lord Scott suggested that each concept had a distinct role to play in cases arising from expectations of future rights. In his view (at para. 19):

> ...a problem inherent in every case in which a representation about inheritance prospects is the basis of a proprietary estoppel claim is that the expected fruits of the representation lie in the future, on the death of the representor, and, in the meantime, the circumstances of the representor or of his or her relationship with the representee, or both, may change and bring about a change of intentions on the part of the representor.

The possibility of change of intention or circumstances had been recognised by other members of the Appellate Committee, who briefly considered various hypothetical situations (breakdown of relationship between Peter and David; need for farm to be sold to provide support for Peter in old age, etc.), but the general view was that it was unprofitable to speculate on what might have been. To Lord Neuberger, for example (paras. 87–9), the short answer here was that Peter's intentions and circumstances had not changed; if they had, David might still have been entitled to some relief and the court would have assessed this by reference to all the facts as it did in *Gillett v Holt* [2001] Ch 210 (see 21.3.1.2).

Lord Scott, however, taking a more theoretical approach (paras. 19–21), noted that proprietary estoppel was the obvious remedy where the representations relied on related to the acquisition of a more or less immediate interest in the property. However, representations about interests to be acquired in the future were, in a sense, conditional and did not fit comfortably into the concept of estoppel. He suggested that they were better explained as giving rise to a constructive trust, created by the common intention or understanding of the parties on the basis of which the claimant has acted to his detriment.

Consequently, he would prefer (para. 20):

> to keep proprietary estoppel and constructive trust as distinct and separate remedies, to confine proprietary estoppel to cases where the representation... on which the claimant has acted is unconditional and to address the cases where the representations are of future benefits, and subject to qualification on account of unforeseen future events, via the principle of remedial constructive trust.

21.8.4 Still a matter of debate

As you may imagine, the relationship between the common intention constructive trust and proprietary estoppel forms the subject matter of lively academic discussion, and we must leave you to pursue the details of this for yourself, if you wish to do so. A fuller consideration of the whole question, together with details of the relevant literature, will be found in Pawlowski, *The Doctrine of Proprietary Estoppel*, 1996, pp. 10–16; see also Megarry and Wade, paras 11-032 and 16–036; and journal articles listed at the end of this chapter.

FURTHER READING

Land Registration for the Twenty-First Century: A Consultative Document, 1998, Law Com No. 254, paras. 3.33–3.36.

Land Registration for the Twenty-First Century: A Conveyancing Revolution, 2001, Law Com No. 271, paras. 5.29–5.36.

Gardner, 'The Remedial Discretion in Proprietary Estoppel' (1999) 115 LQR 438.

Gardner, 'The Remedial Discretion in Proprietary Estoppel—Again' (2006) 122 LQR 492.

Megarry and Wade, *The Law of Real Property*, 8th edn., Sweet & Maxwell, 2012, Chapter 16 (Proprietary Estoppel).

Gillett v Holt

Thompson, 'Estoppel: A Return to Principle' [2001] 65 Conv 78.

Wells, 'The Element of Detriment in Proprietary Estoppel' [2001] 65 Conv 13.

Campbell v Griffin

Thompson, 'Estoppel, Reliance, Remedy and Priority' [2003] 67 Conv 157.

Jennings v Rice

Thompson, 'The Flexibility of Estoppel' [2003] 67 Conv 225.

Cobbe* and *Thorner

Dixon, 'Proprietary Estoppel: A Return to Principle?' [2009] 73 Conv 260.

Fetherstonhaugh, 'Proprietary estoppel and s.2—where are we now?' [2009] EG 25 April (No. 0916) 98.

Getzler, 'Quantum Meruit, Estoppel and the Primacy of Contract' (2009) LQR 196 (at 196–203).

Griffiths, 'Proprietary Estoppel—The Pendulum Swings Again?' [2009] 73 Conv 141.

Relationship between constructive trusts and proprietary estoppel

Etherton, 'Constructive Trusts and Proprietary Estoppel: The Search for Clarity and Principle' [2009] 73 Conv 104.

Ferguson, 'Constructive Trusts—A Note of Caution' [1993] Conv 114.

Hayton, 'Equitable Rights of Cohabitees' [1990] Conv 370.

Hayton, 'Constructive Trusts of Homes—A Bold Approach' (1993) 109 LQR 485.

Smith, 'Oral Contracts for the Sale of Land: Estoppels and Constructive Trusts' [2000] 116 LQR 11.

Thompson, 'Constructive Trusts, Estoppel and the Family Home' [2004] Conv 496 (at 505).

PART V

Licences

Introduction

We have now considered the two legal estates in land and the way in which they may be put in trust. Before we turn to consider the legal and equitable interests in land, we must look at the law relating to licences. Licences to use land are unusual in the sense that, although they are rights which concern the use of land, theoretically they create neither an estate nor an interest in land. Indeed the term 'licence' covers a diversity of rights to use land. Some of the problems which arise in this area are better illustrated if we look at some practical examples, before attempting to examine the law in detail.

Trant Way

Number 1 Trant Way has a small front garden with a short path leading to the front door, on which there is a door-knocker. Every day the postman, milkman and the paper-boy walk up to the front door in order to make deliveries.

Barbara Bell has completed the purchase of **3 Trant Way** (see Chapter 6) and has moved into the property. Her father, Bob Bell, has come to live in the 'granny flat' on the top floor. Mr Bell has his own separate front door and Barbara has given her father the only set of keys to the flat. She never enters her father's flat unless he invites her in. When Mr Bell moved in Barbara told him, 'You need never worry again, you will have a home here with me for as long as you live'. Since moving in, Mr Bell has used some of his savings to make improvements to the flat.

The fee simple estate of **8 Trant Way** belongs to Mildred Mumps, who bought it in 1984. The basement is a self-contained flat **(8A Trant Way**) which has been occupied by Laura Lymeswold since 1985. Miss Lymeswold pays Mrs Mumps £120 a week for the use of the flat. However, Mrs Mumps was keen to ensure that Laura did not obtain any statutory protection, and has always refused to give her a written lease. She has always told Laura, 'You only have a licence, dear. You must go if I say so.' Mildred has kept a key to the front door of the flat and lets herself in once a month to empty the gas and electricity meters and to check that the flat is clean and in good order.

Mrs Mumps occupies the rest of 8 Trant Way herself, together with Henry Mumps. Mildred and Henry are not married, but have lived together as husband and wife ever since Mildred first bought the property. They have two children, now grown up. Mildred has a very highly paid job and so, whilst she has always worked (apart from brief maternity leave when the children were born), Henry stayed at home to look after the children and still does all the cooking and cleaning. Henry is very clever at 'do-it-yourself' and, whilst he has never contributed financially to the purchase of the property or to the family living expenses, he has made considerable improvements to the property. Recently Mildred and Henry's personal relationship has been under some strain and now Mildred appears to be having an affair with another man. Henry is very worried that soon Mildred may tell him that she wants to end their relationship.

These four situations are very different in nature, but each may well be regarded by a court as giving rise to a licence. One, the 'licence' of Laura Lymeswold, may cause considerable problems if considered by the courts, since it is likely that Laura will allege that the arrangement is not a licence at all but a lease which gives her extensive rights under the Rent Acts. Two of the situations, those concerning the positions of Bob Bell and Henry Mumps, look like family arrangements which would only come before a court should the family relationships break down. The other situation, the front path, is one with which we are all familiar. Yet normally, when we walk on to someone else's land, we do not consider the nature of our right to do so.

In addition to these examples, there are many other types of rights which can amount to a licence to use land, for example, a licence to walk across another's property (which may look very like an easement) or a licence to run the sweet counter in a cinema foyer. These assorted rights give rise to three main problems.

- What is the nature of a licence, and how can it be distinguished from other rights?
- Are these licences enforceable against the original grantors, or may they be revoked at will?
- Are these licences enforceable against successors in title of the original grantors?

We will deal with the first of those questions in Chapter 22, and will then consider both aspects of enforceability in Chapter 23.

22

Nature of a licence

22.1 Introduction

The starting point for any consideration of the nature of a licence is the classic statement made by Vaughan CJ in *Thomas v Sorrell* (1673) Vaugh 330 at p. 351, that:

> A dispensation or licence properly passeth no interest, nor alters or transfers property in any thing, but only makes an action lawful, which without it had been unlawful.

(Oddly enough this case concerned the granting of alcohol licences and had nothing to do with land law, yet ever since it has been regarded as crucial to any discussion of licences to use land.) Put more simply, this means that a licence does not give the licensee an estate or interest in the land but does make his presence on the property authorised, so that he is not a trespasser.

If we look at our four examples (pp. 391–2) it is clear that Bob Bell, Laura Lymeswold and Henry Mumps could not possibly be regarded as trespassers; obviously they have permission to be on the properties concerned. What about the postman, and others, who use the footpath leading to the front door of 1 Trant Way? In this case the owners of 1 Trant Way have not expressly given permission to each caller to walk up to the front door, but they have impliedly done so by providing the path and by putting a knocker on the door. Thus someone who walks up to the front door and knocks would not be a trespasser, though a visitor who went further and prowled about the rest of the garden would have gone beyond the limits of the implied licence and would be trespassing. It is also open to the estate owner to limit the implied licence, e.g., by putting up a sign saying 'No salesmen' at the garden gate, and then any person who is a salesman and who fails to observe the restriction would also be a trespasser.

Once one has established that a person who is on the land is not a trespasser, one then has to establish whether that person has an estate or interest in the land. If the person has no property ('proprietary') interest giving him *the right* to be on the land, then it is usually true to say that he is there by *permission* and is a licensee of some kind. (Since the decision of the House of Lords in *Bruton v London & Quadrant HT* [2000] 1 AC 406 there is the further possibility that he may be a tenant under a non-proprietary lease, but this is a new and unfamiliar concept, which we will explain later when we consider the decision in *Bruton*—see 22.2.4.4).

The rights which are most commonly confused with licences are leases and easements and we will now consider these separately.

22.2 Distinguishing a lease from a licence

22.2.1 Nature of the problem

Sometimes it can be very difficult indeed to distinguish a lease from a licence. The agreement relating to 8A Trant Way is a good example of the type of arrangement which may give a considerable amount of difficulty to the lawyer who is asked to classify it. As we have already explained (at 10.5.1), the tenant's right to security of tenure under, for example, the Rent Acts was very considerable and landlords/licensors, like Mrs Mumps, sought to avoid the application of these rules by trying to grant licences, which have little protection, rather than leases, which were fully protected under the Acts.

Another source of difficulty is the fact that families such as the Bells often make informal arrangements without taking advice or considering the legal consequences of what they are doing. It is not until things go wrong between them, or one of them dies, that any thought is given to the nature of the interest which has been created (see for example *Errington v Errington* [1952] 1 KB 290, or *Nunn v Dalrymple* (1989) 59 P&CR 231).

22.2.2 Significance of distinction between a lease and a licence

The nature of a lease is essentially very different from that of a licence. In general, with the rare exception of the non-proprietary lease (see 22.2.4.4), a lease, if made in the proper form, creates a legal estate in the land, binding on both the landlord and his successors. The tenant has a property interest in the land, with which he can deal. He is able to sell or mortgage his estate, dispose of it on his death, and create lesser interests out of it, by granting subleases (see 10.2.4.1 and 10.4).

By contrast, the licensee has a mere permission to be on the land; he does not own a property interest in it, and therefore has nothing which he can sell or give to others. In general his rights, if any, are against the licensor, and are unenforceable against the licensor's successors, although there are exceptions to this, which we consider in Chapter 23.

In addition to these essential differences, resulting from the nature of the lease and the licence, there are many situations in which the distinction between the two is of considerable significance. As we have already indicated, one of the most important consequences of the distinction relates to the provisions for tenants' security of tenure under the Rent Acts, which did not apply to licensees. The statutory protection afforded to tenants of residential accommodation under leases granted on or after 15 January 1989 is by no means as great as it was under the Rent Acts, but the distinction between leases and licences is still important in determining the process by which the landlord may recover possession (see, for example, *Gray v Taylor* [1998] 1 WLR 1093). It is also highly relevant to the protection of business tenants under the Landlord and Tenant Act 1954, and to the imposition of the landlord's statutory duty to repair under the Landlord and Tenant Act 1985.

There are, however, many other areas in which the distinction is important. In a land law context, the question of whether a tenant has granted a sublease or a licence would be relevant in considering whether he had broken a covenant against subletting (see 11.2.2.2; *Brent LBC v Cronin* (1997) 30 HLR 43). Similarly the need for a written contract under the Law of Property (Miscellaneous Provisions) Act 1989, s. 2 (see Chapter 5) would apply in the case of a lease, but not to a licence. (See *Wright v Stavert* (1860) 2 E & E 721 on the earlier requirements as to form contained in the Statute of Frauds 1677.) Under the relevant statutory provisions, compensation for compulsory acquisition of land is payable to an occupier with a legal or equitable interest in the land, but not to a licensee (*Rochester Poster Services v Dartford BC* (1991) 63 P&CR 88); and accelerated procedures for recovering possession of land are available against licensees but not against tenants (*Crancour Ltd v Da Silvaesa* [1986] 1 EGLR 80; and *Esso Petroleum Co. Ltd v Fumegrange Ltd* [1994] 2 EGLR 90).

The distinction between leases and licences can also be of importance in branches of law which you might think were well removed from your study of land law. Thus, in the field of tort, the traditional view is that claims in respect of torts to land, such as trespass and nuisance, can be brought only by an occupier with a property interest in the land (such as a lease), and not by a mere licensee. Recent decisions show signs of relaxing this requirement (see, for example, *Manchester Airport plc v Dutton* [2000] 1 QB 133 with reference to trespass; and the speeches of some members of the House of Lords in *Hunter v Canary Wharf Ltd* [1997] AC 655, when considering a claim in nuisance), but the distinction remains relevant to an understanding of the older case law.

A particularly interesting example of the distinction in a tort-based claim is to be found in *Appah v Parncliffe Investments Ltd* [1964] 1 WLR 1064. The plaintiff occupied a room in a rooming-house. The lock on her door was defective, and as a result property was stolen from her room. She sued the proprietors, claiming damages for negligence, and the outcome of the action depended on the nature of her occupation. If she was a tenant, the defendant owed her no duty of care; but if she was a licensee, the defendant was under an obligation to take reasonable care of her property. After a detailed consideration of the nature of her occupation (for which see 22.2.3.1(1)), the Court of Appeal held that she was a licensee and accordingly entitled to recover damages for negligence.

Thus, although many of the cases which we consider in this chapter arose under the Rent Acts, it is important to remember that there are many other settings in which the distinction between a lease and a licence may be of crucial importance.

22.2.3 How to distinguish between a lease and a licence

The first step is to consider whether the arrangement between the parties satisfies the essential requirements for the existence of a lease.

22.2.3.1 Requirements for a lease: certainty and exclusive possession

We have already considered this topic in Chapter 10, and in particular have noted that a lease must be for a certain period, and give the tenant exclusive possession. If the grant is not for a certain period (and, since *Berrisford v Mexfield Housing Co-operative Ltd* [2011] 3 WLR 1091, cannot be 'rescued' under LPA 1925, s. 149(6)—see 10.2.3.3) it cannot create a lease, even if the occupier has exclusive possession. Conversely, a term which satisfies the certainty rule, but does not give the occupier exclusive possession, cannot be a lease and must be a licence. It can be difficult to decide whether or not an occupier has exclusive possession, and so we need to consider this matter in a little more detail.

1. *Exclusive possession*

Exclusive possession involves the right to use the premises to the exclusion of all others, including the landlord himself. As Lord Templeman explained in *Street v Mountford* [1985] AC 809 at p. 816:

> The tenant possessing exclusive possession is able to exercise the rights of an owner of land, which is in the real sense his land albeit temporarily and subject to certain restrictions. A tenant armed with exclusive possession can keep out strangers and keep out the landlord.

Clearly someone who occupies a hotel room or lives in someone else's house as a lodger or paying guest cannot be said to have exclusive possession in this way, and so cannot have a tenancy. To quote Lord Templeman again (at p. 818):

> The occupier is a lodger if the landlord provides attendance or services which require the landlord or his servants to exercise unrestricted access to and use of the premises. A lodger is entitled to live in the premises but cannot call the place his own.

The difficulty of applying this test for exclusive possession arises of course in borderline cases, such as *Appah v Parncliffe Investments Ltd* [1964] 1 WLR 1064, where only a minimum level of service was provided, and the judgment in that case is a useful example of the level of detail which a court may have to consider in deciding whether an occupier has exclusive possession.

In *Appah* the plaintiff had an agreement under which she occupied a room in a house in which 17 such rooms were separately occupied. Each room had some cooking facilities but the bathroom was shared. The agreement provided that (a) no notice was required if an occupant wished to leave; (b) the fee simple owner retained the right to enter the room to empty gas and electricity meters and to clean; and (c) rules were made specifying that guests had to leave by 10.30 p.m. and otherwise regulating the use of the premises. The court held that this agreement must amount to a licence, since the licensee did not have exclusive possession of the room: she had no right to exclude the landlord, and the making of rules concerning her use of the premises also indicated that she did not have a proprietary right amounting to a lease.

2. *Exclusive occupation*

Before leaving the topic of exclusive possession, we should draw your attention to the apparently similar phrase, 'exclusive occupation', which may cause you some confusion.

We suggest that the two phrases are best used to describe two different situations. A hotel guest will expect to have exclusive occupation of his room, in the sense that he will not be required to share it with another guest; he will not, however, have exclusive possession, in the sense of being able to exclude the proprietor and his agents, since they will have access to the room for cleaning and the provision of other services.

The same distinction can be made in the case of longer-term residential accommodation. Clearly an occupier who did not have exclusive occupation (because, for instance, he was required to share with other occupiers selected by the owner) could not claim to have exclusive possession; but the fact of sole or exclusive occupation would not mean that the occupier automatically had exclusive possession in the sense of controlling the property and being able to exclude the owner.

We are emphasising this point because some confusion between the two phrases has arisen from their use by Lord Templeman. In *Street v Mountford* he referred throughout to 'exclusive possession', save for one occasion when he substituted the phrase 'exclusive occupation' (at p. 822). In a later decision, however (*AG Securities v Vaughan* [1990] 1 AC 417 at p. 455), he explained that:

> Exclusive possession means either exclusive occupation or receipt of rents and profits.

He then used the phrase 'exclusive occupation' throughout the rest of his speech in apparently the same sense in which he had spoken of 'exclusive possession' in *Street v Mountford*. Although other members of the House of Lords in *AG Securities v Vaughan* continued to speak of 'exclusive possession', Lord Templeman's usage has sometimes been adopted in later cases, for example in *Family Housing Association v Jones* [1990] 1 WLR 779, where Balcombe LJ (at p. 788) emphasised the fact of sole occupancy as bringing the agreement within the terms of *Street v Mountford*. Despite this, however, we suggest that you should follow the language of *Street v Mountford* and in general use the phrase 'exclusive possession'.

22.2.3.2 Certainty and exclusive possession are not conclusive signs of a lease

Although a lease cannot exist unless there is a certain term and exclusive possession, it does not follow that an arrangement which satisfies these requirements necessarily creates a lease: the occupier may have exclusive possession for a fixed period and still be only a licensee:

> There can be no tenancy unless the occupier enjoys exclusive possession; but an occupier who enjoys exclusive possession is not necessarily a tenant (*Street v Mountford* [1985] AC 809 at p. 818).

At one time it was true to say that if an agreement did give exclusive possession then it was necessarily a lease (see *Lynes v Snaith* [1899] 1 QB 486) but this is no longer true for, from the 1950s onward, there has been a number of decisions in which it has been held that, despite exclusive possession, the occupant is only a licensee. Early examples are to be found in *Foster v Robinson* [1951] 1 KB 149, in which a former farm worker was allowed to remain rent-free in his cottage after retirement, and *Errington v Errington* [1952] 1 KB 290, in which a young married couple occupied a house belonging to the husband's father (see further 23.3.3). An arrangement whereby a homeless family was given exclusive possession of a house rent-free has also been held to create only a licence (*Heslop v Burns* [1974] 1 WLR 1241), and the same result is to be found in respect of exclusive possession of a room in an old people's home (*Abbeyfield (Harpenden) Society Ltd v Woods* [1968] 1 WLR 374).

The common theme in most of these cases of licences with exclusive possession was summarised as follows by Denning LJ in the case of *Facchini v Bryson* [1952] 1 TLR 1386 at p. 1389:

> In all the cases where an occupier has been held to be a licensee there has been something in the circumstances, such as a family arrangement, an act of friendship or generosity, or such like, to negative any intention to create a tenancy.

This statement draws attention to two issues: first, some act of generosity and, second, the intention of the parties to the arrangement. The importance of the intention of the landlord and tenant, or licensor and licensee, has been emphasised in other cases, such as *Marcroft Wagons Ltd v Smith* [1951] 2 KB 496, where the landlord, as an act of kindness, had allowed the daughter of the former tenant to remain in the property after her mother's death, but had refused to grant her a tenancy. In that case the court took notice of the fact that it was clearly not the intention of the owner to create a tenancy and that accordingly the agreement was a licence and not a lease.

22.2.3.3 **Grantor's expressed intention not conclusive**

This emphasis on the grantor's intention could give rise to difficulties, especially where property owners wanted to avoid the Rent Acts by granting licences rather than leases. Thus in nearly every case the intention of the grantor would be to create a licence, whilst the recipient would probably wish to receive a lease. As a result there are a number of cases in which the courts have held an agreement to be a lease, even where it is expressly described as a licence. An early example is to be found in *Facchini v Bryson* [1952] 1 TLR 1386, in which the Court of Appeal held that an agreement created a tenancy, although it expressly provided that it was not to do so. The court emphasised that it would look at the nature of the relationship created between the parties, and at their respective rights, not merely at the words they used. In the words of Denning LJ, to do otherwise 'would drive an articulated vehicle through the Rent Acts' (at p. 1390). In the same way, an arrangement for the use of a tennis court has been held to amount to a business tenancy even though it purported to be a licence (*Addiscombe Garden Estates Ltd v Crabbe* [1958] 1 QB 513).

Similarly, in *Street v Mountford* [1985] AC 809 the House of Lords held that a written agreement which stated that it was a licence and which referred to the payment of a licence fee rather than rent, was nonetheless a lease. It was agreed by all concerned that the agreement gave exclusive possession to Mrs Mountford (the occupier) but that, when it was signed, both parties expressed the intention to create a licence (Mrs Mountford signed a declaration to this effect). Lord Templeman said, however (at p. 819):

> If the agreement satisfied all the requirements of a tenancy, then the agreement produced a tenancy and the parties cannot alter the effect of the agreement by insisting that they only created a licence.

To put it another way:

> The manufacture of a five-pronged implement for manual digging results in a fork even if the manufacturer, unfamiliar with the English language, insists that he...has made a spade (at p. 819).

In other words, if the agreement satisfies the criteria for the creation of a particular interest in land, the parties cannot avoid this result by labelling it as something else.

A recent application of this principle, but in a reverse direction, is provided by *obiter dicta* in *Berrisford v Mexfield Housing Co-operative Ltd* [2011] 3 WLR 1091. Having decided the case on other grounds, the Supreme Court expressed the view that where a purported grant of a lease failed for lack of certainty, the fact that the parties described the agreement between them as creating a lease would not prevent the court from regarding it as creating a contractual licence.

Exceptional circumstances

Although giving exclusive possession prima facie indicates an intention to create a tenancy, there might on occasion be exceptional circumstances which would negative that intention. For example, it might be that the parties did not intend to enter into legal relations at all; or the owner might have no power to grant a tenancy; or again exclusive possession might be explicable by reference to some other legal relationship, such as vendor and purchaser (p. 821).

A recent example of this last exception is to be found in *Cameron Ltd v Rolls-Royce plc* [2008] L&TR 22. The claimant sought specific performance of an agreement for a lease that it had entered into with the defendant. At the time of the agreement, the defendant was already in possession of the premises, holding on at the end of a previous lease and, once the agreement was concluded, it was granted a licence to remain on the property pending the grant of the new lease. The defendant subsequently claimed that this 'licence' was in fact a lease within the rule in *Street v Mountford*. In outline, its reason for doing this was that the lease it claimed to have acquired in this way would be more favourable to it than the lease that the claimant had agreed to grant.

Mann J held that the case fell clearly within the vendor and purchaser exception recognised by Lord Templeman. The licence had been granted in the context of the acquisition of a larger interest and the grant was not in any way a 'stand-alone transaction' that could give rise to a lease under the *Street v Mountford* rule (paras. 22 and 26).

22.2.3.4 Summary of approach in Street v Mountford

Lord Templeman's speech in *Street v Mountford* provides a useful guide to the approach adopted by the courts in considering whether an agreement creates a lease or a licence. His account of earlier decisions is very full and can perhaps be slightly confusing. It may therefore be helpful to note the summary to be found towards the end of his speech (at p. 826):

> Sometimes it may be difficult to discover whether, on the true construction of an agreement, exclusive possession is conferred. Sometimes it may appear from the surrounding circumstances that there was no intention to create legal relationships. Sometimes it may appear from the surrounding circumstances that the right to exclusive possession is referable to a legal relationship other than a tenancy. [A further possibility, omitted from this summary but included at p. 821 of the report is that it may appear that the owner had no power to grant a tenancy]...But where...the only circumstances are that residential accommodation is offered and accepted with exclusive possession for a term at a rent, the result is a tenancy.

This summary gives rise to the following questions which you could ask yourself when considering whether an arrangement, which satisfies all other requirements for a lease, does in fact create a lease or merely a licence.

1. *Does the occupier have exclusive possession?*

As we have seen, this must be the starting point for any enquiry; if exclusive possession does not exist, there cannot be a lease, and the enquiry is at an end.

2. *If the occupier has exclusive possession, was there an intention to create legal relations?*

The existence of exclusive possession does not automatically indicate the existence of a tenancy, because it may have been given for some family or charitable motive, with no intention to create legal relations. The earlier decisions, summarised by Lord Denning in *Facchini v Bryson,* remain alive and well after the decision in *Street v Mountford,* and it is necessary to consider whether the parties intended to give rise to a legal relationship. Further, even if they did, the relationship need not be that of landlord and tenant: there are a number of other circumstances in which an occupier may have exclusive possession.

3. *What are the circumstances giving rise to the occupier's exclusive possession?*
Lord Templeman suggests a wide range of situations in which an occupier could have exclusive possession but not be a tenant. He might be:

- an owner in fee simple;
- a trespasser;
- a mortgagee in possession (see Chapter 24);
- a purchaser allowed into possession of the property before completion; or
- a service occupier i.e., an employee, such as a housekeeper or gardener who occupies residential accommodation belonging to his employer for the better performance of his duties.

As recognised by Pill LJ in *P. Dunwell v Hunt* (1996) 72 P&CR D6, this list is not exhaustive, and the Court of Appeal has recently added to it the relationship between a beneficiary and the trustees who allow him to occupy trust property (see *Gray v Taylor* [1998] 1 WLR 1093).

4. *Does the grantor have the power to grant a tenancy?*
There is only a brief reference to this point in *Street v Mountford* (at p. 821), supported by the example of a requisitioning authority. The matter was explored further by the Court of Appeal in *Bruton v London & Quadrant Housing Trust* [1998] QB 834 at p. 843, in which Millett LJ considered whether this exception is limited to cases where the grantor has no capacity to grant a tenancy (because for example such a grant is outside its statutory powers), or whether it extends as well to cases where the grantor has no estate or interest in the land. The House of Lords' decision in this case ([2000] 1 AC 406) adopts the more limited interpretation and confines the exception to lack of capacity (see further at 22.2.4.4).

A recent example of a situation in which the grant may be outside the grantor's powers is to be found in *Gray v Taylor* [1998] 1 WLR 1093. Here the Court of Appeal accepted the view of the trial judge that granting a tenancy of accommodation in an almshouse would be outside the powers of the trustees, because it might infringe the objects of the charity by permitting the grantee to remain in occupation although he had ceased to satisfy the conditions for residence.

5. *Are there any other exceptional circumstances in the case which might negative the intention to create a tenancy?*
The situations described by Lord Templeman are only examples, and there may well be other circumstances which would displace the intention. For attempts to establish these in some later cases concerned with housing for the homeless, see 22.2.4.2.

Asking the five questions we have considered above should enable you to see whether the arrangement you are considering could be said to fall outside the rule in *Street v Mountford*. Unless it does so, however, the position is clear: the grant of exclusive possession for a term at a rent creates a tenancy. In such circumstances, neither the parties' intentions, nor the label they attach to the transaction, will persuade the court to regard the arrangement as creating only a licence.

Thus, unless Mrs Mumps (see p. 391) could persuade a court that her retention of a key and her monthly visits to the flat have prevented Miss Lymeswold acquiring exclusive possession, it seems very likely that she would be found to have granted a tenancy of the basement flat, despite her insistence that she has given Laura only a licence.

22.2.4 Leases and licences since *Street v Mountford*

In the years since *Street v Mountford*, many cases on the lease/licence distinction have come before the courts. In general they involve no more than an application of the *Street v Mountford* principles to the facts of a particular arrangement, although even this can be difficult when it involves deciding whether or not the occupier has exclusive possession (a problem which did not arise in *Street v Mountford* where this point was conceded by the landlord). In the aftermath of *Street v Mountford* landlords wishing to avoid the security of tenure provisions went to great lengths to make it appear that the occupier did not have exclusive possession, and many cases involve the courts in deciding whether the written agreement represents the true state of affairs between the parties. Even where there was no intention to avoid the Rent Acts, the question of whether an occupier has exclusive possession can present difficulties, for example in relation to housing for the homeless and to shared accommodation.

22.2.4.1 Attempts to avoid the Rent Acts

Following *Street v Mountford*, the courts were required to consider a number of agreements designed to prevent the occupier acquiring exclusive possession and being able to claim a lease. Typical devices included: the retention of a key by the landlady, coupled with the reservation of her right to enter the premises at any time (*Aslan v Murphy* (Nos. 1 and 2) and *Duke v Wynne*, both reported at [1990] 1 WLR 766); the limitation of the hours at which the occupier might use the property (use excluded between 10.30 a.m. and noon each day—*Crancour Ltd v Da Silvaesa* [1986] 1 EGLR 80 and *Aslan v Murphy* (Nos. 1 and 2) [1990] 1 WLR 766); and provisions that the landlord himself might share the premises with the occupier, or permit others to do so (*Hadjiloucas v Crean* [1988] 1 WLR 1006; *Antoniades v Villiers* [1990] 1 AC 417). In considering these various provisions, the courts followed *Street v Mountford* in seeking to identify the true nature of the agreement between the parties and to disregard terms which the landlord had no real intention of enforcing but had inserted as a pretence to avoid statutory protection.

This approach is well illustrated by the comments of Lord Donaldson MR in *Aslan v Murphy* [1990] 1 WLR 766 at p: 773, on the retention of keys by the landlord/licensor. The fact that the owner retains a key does not by itself prevent the occupier having exclusive possession and holding a tenancy. The court must consider the purpose for which the key is retained. If it is to allow the owner to enter in an emergency, or to read the meters, or to do repairs, this would not by itself prevent the occupier from holding a tenancy; conversely if the purpose of having keys is to provide genuine services such as frequent cleaning and daily bed-making it could be inferred that the occupier was a lodger rather than a tenant. Having considered the circumstances in *Aslan v Murphy*, the Court of Appeal found that although the keys were retained so that the owner could provide services, no services were in fact provided, and in consequence the court held that the occupier was a tenant, not a mere licensee.

22.2.4.2 Housing for the homeless

The status of occupiers in hostels or other accommodation provided for the homeless has been considered by the courts in a number of cases.

In *Family Housing Association v Jones* [1990] 1 WLR 779, the appellant, who was homeless, was given a flat in premises operated by a housing association. The association itself held the premises as a licensee of the local authority, which owned the property, and the association's agreement with the appellant was described as being for the use of temporary accommodation and was expressed to be a licence. The housing association kept a set of keys in order to enter the premises to offer help to the occupier, to give her advice and to inspect the condition of the premises. The Court of Appeal found that the occupier had the right of 'sole occupation' (as to which, see 22.2.3.1(2)) for a term on payment of an accommodation charge, and applying *Street v Mountford* held that this arrangement created a lease and not a licence. Following its earlier decision in *Aslan v Murphy* the court considered that the retention of a key by the housing association was not decisive; in this case it had been done to assist the occupier, and did not prevent a tenancy from arising. In holding that the occupier was a tenant, the Court of Appeal rejected the suggestion that the housing association's role in providing temporary accommodation for the homeless should be considered as 'exceptional circumstances' which took the case outside the rule in *Street v Mountford*.

In *Westminster City Council v Clarke* [1992] 2 AC 288, the House of Lords adopted a similar approach, but reached a different conclusion on the facts. The council provided hostel accommodation for homeless single men under a licence agreement, which included the provision that an occupier could be required to change rooms or to share his room with another occupant. The House of Lords accepted that these provisions were genuine, being necessary for the proper management of the hostel, and were not included for the purpose of avoiding the Rent Acts. Accordingly, the occupier did not have exclusive possession of his room, and was a licensee and not a tenant. If you read the report of this case, you may note that the headnote describes the decision as overruling *Family Housing Association v Jones*; however, this does not appear to be entirely accurate, since the House of Lords considered only one aspect of the decision in *Jones*. Moreover, the decision in *Jones* was approved by the House of Lords in *Bruton v London & Quadrant Housing Trust* [2000] 1 AC 406, a case in which the court again refused to accept that the provision of housing for the homeless involved special circumstances which could negative the intention to create a tenancy (see further at 22.2.4.4).

22.2.4.3 **Shared accommodation**

A number of cases since *Street v Mountford* have involved the shared occupation of accommodation. As we have seen in Chapter 16, it is possible for a legal estate to be held by several people in a form of co-ownership known as 'joint tenancy', and it is open to a couple, or a group of friends, to take jointly a lease of property which they plan to occupy together. However, joint tenancy of a legal estate can exist only if certain requirements, known as the 'four unities', are satisfied (see 16.2.1). In general terms, this means that all the co-owners must be entitled to possession of the whole property (unity of possession), rather than having it divided up between them, and their interests in the property must start at the same time (unity of time), be derived from the same document (unity of title), and be identical as to nature and duration (unity of interest). This last requirement, of unity of interest, 'imports the existence of joint rights and obligations' (*Mikeover Ltd v Brady* [1989] 3 All ER 618 at p. 627), and means that each co-owner is both jointly and severally (i.e., individually) liable for any duties imposed by the estate. Thus, in a joint tenancy of a lease, each tenant is liable for the full rent due for the property, even though in practice he pays only his share of it.

It was against this background that the House of Lords considered two flat-sharing agreements, which came before it in 1988. In *AG Securities v Vaughan* [1990] 1 AC 417 the landlord/licensor owned a flat which had four bedrooms together with other normal living accommodation, such as a kitchen and bathroom. The flat was occupied by four people who were selected by the owner and who did not know one another. Each had arrived at a different time and each paid a different amount for the use of the flat.

Each had the use of one bedroom and the use of the other rooms in common with the other three. The owner did not dictate which room each occupier should have: that was agreed between the current occupiers. If an occupier left, the owner replaced him with a new occupier of the owner's choice but then left it to the four occupiers to settle between them the new room allocation. It was held that this arrangement constituted a licence because the occupiers did not (even jointly between themselves) have exclusive possession of the property. Lord Oliver of Aylmerton (at p. 471) said:

> The landlord is not excluded for he continues to enjoy the premises through his invitees, even though he may for the time being have precluded himself by contract with each from withdrawing the invitation.

In *Antoniades v Villiers*, also reported at [1990] 1 AC 417, a couple took a one-bedroom flat under written agreements which were described as 'licence agreements'. Each signed a separate agreement and each agreement provided that the 'licensor' might also occupy the premises or might license others to occupy jointly with the 'licensees'. The House of Lords held that this arrangement was clearly a lease and that the terms allowing for occupation by the landlord or others were simply pretences. It would be ridiculous to contemplate that the landlord intended to share the young couple's bed or that he genuinely intended to send others to do this.

It is clear that in *AG Securities v Vaughan* the unities required for a joint tenancy were in no way satisfied. The interests of the individual occupants arose at different times, and under different agreements; their individual obligations varied, and there was no sense in which each was jointly and severally liable, for example, for the payment of a rent due on the whole property. On the other hand, in *Antoniades v Villiers* both occupiers entered into identical agreements at the same time. The couple was originally quoted a single rent for the flat, but, on entering the agreements, each person was required to assume liability for half of that rent. In these circumstances the House of Lords considered that the written agreements did not give effect to the true intentions of the parties, and was able to hold that the occupiers were joint tenants of a lease, despite the apparent absence of the necessary joint obligations.

By contrast, in *Mikeover Ltd v Brady* [1989] 3 All ER 618, on facts very similar to *Antoniades v Villiers*, the Court of Appeal was satisfied that terms providing for the payment of separate rents were genuine agreements, representing the true intention of the parties that the monetary obligations of each occupier were to be entirely independent. Accordingly, the agreements were incapable of creating a joint tenancy, because there was no unity of interest, and the parties held only as licensees.

The factors to be taken into account when applying the decisions in *Vaughan* and *Villiers* were also considered by the Court of Appeal in *Stribling v Wickham* [1989] 2 EGLR 35. The court said that agreements for flat sharing of this type had to be construed in the light of all the surrounding circumstances, which would include the relationship between the sharers, the course of negotiations, the nature and the extent of the accommodation provided and the intended and actual mode of occupation. It was emphasised once again that it was the function of the courts to determine the true nature of 'the substance and reality' of the transaction.

22.2.4.4 ***Bruton v London & Quadrant Housing Trust* [2000] 1 AC 406**

This is the most recent consideration by the House of Lords of the lease/licence distinction. It deals with the interesting question of the relationship between *Street v Mountford* and the principles of tenancy by estoppel (see 10.10.4), but, as you will see, the House of

Lords' decision also has far-reaching consequences for our understanding of the nature of a lease.

The facts of the case were as follows. The trust held various properties (which were awaiting redevelopment) as a licensee of Lambeth Borough Council. (Subsequently the trust was granted a lease by the Council, but at the relevant time it held only a licence.) The trust used the properties to provide short-term housing for the homeless, entering into licence agreements with the individual occupiers. One of the occupiers, Mr Bruton, subsequently claimed that he had exclusive possession of his self-contained flat and that, despite the wording of the agreement, he was therefore a tenant under the principles of *Street v Mountford*. His purpose in doing this was to bring himself within s. 11 of the Landlord and Tenant Act 1985, which imposes a repairing obligation on landlords in respect of certain tenancies, but does not apply to licences. The trust itself had no estate in the land, and so could not grant a tenancy, but it was alleged that it was estopped from denying that it had done so. In other words, the occupier sought to combine the principles of *Street v Mountford* and the doctrine of tenancy by estoppel.

The occupier's claim was rejected by the Court of Appeal (see [1998] QB 834). At this stage, it seems to have been accepted by both parties that the trust could not have granted a tenancy because it had no estate in the property. In other words, it could not give what it had not got. It is in such circumstances that a tenancy by estoppel may arise, and it was a tenancy of this nature that the occupier claimed.

The Court of Appeal, however, considered that the situation in this case did not give rise to a tenancy by estoppel. In the words of Millett LJ (at pp. 842–3) such a tenancy is based on the principle that:

> A man who purports to grant a tenancy is not permitted to deny that he has done so by asserting his own want of title. If he has none, the grant creates a tenancy by estoppel.

In this case, the trust did not purport to grant a tenancy, because it was aware of its lack of title and specifically granted a licence. There was thus no purported grant which the trust could be estopped from denying, and accordingly no tenancy by estoppel arose.

The decision of the Court of Appeal was reversed by the House of Lords ([2000] 1 AC 406), which held that a tenancy had been created between the parties. On the facts of the case, the occupier had exclusive possession for a term at a rent; this raised a prima facie conclusion that he was a tenant, and the House of Lords did not agree that the special nature of the trust (as a charitable body providing short-term accommodation) was sufficient to take it out of the rule in *Street v Mountford*.

In holding that the occupier held a lease and was not just a tenant by estoppel, the House of Lords rejected the argument that the trust could not create a lease because it had no estate in the land. Lord Hoffmann explained that the creation of an estate is the usual but not essential consequence of a lease, and that an agreement which creates a landlord and tenant relationship is a lease, even though the landlord is unable to grant an estate to the tenant. In the words of Lord Hoffmann (at p. 415):

> ...the term 'lease' or 'tenancy' describes a relationship between two parties who are designated landlord and tenant. It is not concerned with the question of whether the agreement creates an estate or other proprietary interest which may be binding on third parties. A lease may, and usually does, create a proprietary interest called a leasehold estate or, technically, a 'term of years absolute'. This will depend upon whether the landlord had an interest out of which he could grant it. *Nemo dat quod non habet* [no-one can give what he has not got]. But it is the fact that the agreement is a lease which creates

> the proprietary interest. It is putting the cart before the horse to say that whether the agreement is a lease depends upon whether it creates an proprietary interest.

A similar view was expressed by Lord Hobhouse (at p. 418):

> The present case does not depend upon the establishing of an estoppel nor does any problem arise from the fact that the housing trust did not have a legal estate. The [appellant's] case depends upon his establishing that his agreement with the housing trust has the legal effect of creating a relationship of tenant and landlord between them. That is all. It does not depend upon his establishing a proprietary title good against all the world.

Thus, although the trust could not create a proprietary interest, the agreement between the parties satisfied the requirements of *Street v Mountford* and created a lease within the meaning of s. 11 of the Landlord and Tenant Act 1985.

We should note at this point that the House of Lords also took the opportunity to explain the operation of tenancy by estoppel. In what follows, their Lordships were presumably referring to the form of tenancy by estoppel which arises from the purported grant of a lease, rather than from the landlord's representation as to title (see 10.10.4.2), since it is clear from the facts that the trust had made no such representation. To quote Lord Hoffmann once more (at p. 415):

> I think Millett LJ [in the court below] may have been misled by the ancient phrase 'tenancy by estoppel' into thinking that it described an agreement which would not otherwise be a lease or tenancy but which was treated as being one by virtue of an estoppel. In fact...it is not the estoppel which created the tenancy, but the tenancy which created the estoppel. The estoppel arises when one or other of the parties want to deny one of the ordinary incidents or obligations of the tenancy on the ground that the landlord had no legal estate. The basis of the estoppel is that having entered into an agreement which constitutes a lease or tenancy, he cannot repudiate that incident or obligation.

And again (p. 416):

> ...it is the fact that the agreement between the parties constitutes a tenancy that gives rise to an estoppel and not the other way round. It therefore seems to me that the question of tenancy by estoppel does not arise in this case. The issue is simply whether the agreement is a tenancy.

22.2.4.5 **Implications of the decision in Bruton**

Although Lord Hoffmann speaks as though his analysis of the nature of a lease is well established and, indeed, obvious, it came as a considerable surprise to many lawyers. When considering tenancies at will (10.10.3), we have seen that it is possible to have the relationship of landlord and tenant without the creation of an estate, but this appeared to be an unusual but useful way of explaining an anomalous situation. Historically, of course, the lease did begin as a purely contractual relationship between the parties which gave no interest in the land, but once the notion of the leasehold estate had developed, it was generally thought that a lease inevitably created such an estate or interest. As Millett LJ put it in the Court of Appeal in *Bruton* ([1998] QB 834 at 845): 'A tenancy is a legal estate'.

In the light of the House of Lords' decision, however, it seems that we now have to divide leases into two categories; the proprietary lease, which creates an estate or interest in the land, and the contractual or personal lease—which does not. Lord Hoffmann makes it clear that leases will usually create a proprietary interest, but the possibility of a non-proprietary lease, even if rare, raises a number of questions. These include:

When may a non-proprietary lease be created?

Does it arise only where the grantor has no title, or may it be created in other circumstances?

How is a non-proprietary lease to be created?

The requirement of a deed in the case of leases for more than three years is imposed by the general rule in LPA 1925, s. 52(1) that a deed must be used for the conveyance or creation of a legal estate. Since no estate is created by a non-proprietary lease, it presumably can be created orally or in writing, whatever its length, and a contract for such a lease would not need to be made in writing.

In what circumstances will a court find a tenancy by estoppel?

If the agreement between the parties creates a non-proprietary lease, their rights and obligations must surely arise from that lease, and not from any estoppel. It is at first sight difficult to envisage the future use of tenancy by estoppel or, indeed, to understand why the concept has been used in the past if the non-proprietary lease has always been available to the courts.

What is the effect of a non-proprietary lease on third parties?

While the non-proprietary lease may be sufficient to determine the parties' rights and duties between themselves, its effect on third parties is far from clear. As we have seen (10.10.4), tenancies by estoppel bind and benefit not only the parties, but their successors. Will the non-proprietary lease by itself have the same effect, and will the benefit and burden of obligations under it run to the parties' successors? Presumably, rights under the tenancy could be assigned, but the transfer of burdens would be ruled out by the privity of contract rules. We have already noted (12.5.3.2) the considerable difficulties the courts have had in dealing with the running of covenants in equitable leases, where at least the landlord has an estate in the land and the agreement is capable of specific performance. Non-proprietary leases seem likely to pose even greater problems. Such problems might be resolved, however, if the parties to the contractual lease were estopped from denying the existence of a proprietary lease and the estoppel bound and benefited successors in the established way. This does not, however, explain why courts in the past have needed to rely on the concept of estoppel in dealing with the rights and duties of the original parties to the agreement.

As far as we know, there has as yet been no decision on this point, but you may like to note an observation of Lord Neuberger in *Berrisford v Mexfield Housing Corporation Ltd* [2011] UKSC 52. In *obiter dicta* the Supreme Court considered whether a purported grant of a lease which was void for uncertainty could instead be regarded as creating a contractual licence. It was suggested that such a notion might be inconsistent with the reasoning in *Bruton*. Lord Neuberger briefly explained (at para. 65) that there was no inconsistency, and in summarising the *Bruton* decision stated that the tenancy which had been created between Bruton and the trust:

> ... would thus have been binding as such not only on Mr Bruton and the trust, but also on any assignee of Mr Bruton or the trust.

Tantalisingly, nothing more was said on this point—and as it stands, it simply adds to the uncertainty arising from *Bruton*.

These questions, and a number of others, were posed in various case notes and articles in the legal journals, and we give references to some of them in the section on further reading at the end of this chapter. Although writers speculated on the nature and characteristics of what one author describes as 'a beast long thought extinct' (Dixon [2000] CLJ 25 at p. 27), it had to be accepted that questions would remain unanswered until *Bruton* was interpreted in later decisions.

22.2.4.6 Decisions after *Bruton*

So far, the only later decision that we need to note is that of the Court of Appeal in *Kay v Lambeth Borough Council* [2005] QB 352 (note that the appeal in this case to the House of Lords, reported at [2006] 2 AC 465, related to human rights issues and does not affect the aspect of the decision with which we are concerned here).

Following the House of Lords' decision in *Bruton*, Lambeth Borough Council terminated the trust's lease of the property (which had replaced the original licence) and sought to recover possession from the individual occupiers. Kay, and others, resisted the possession proceedings on a number of grounds, all of which were rejected by both the trial judge and the Court of Appeal. As far as most of the defendants' arguments are concerned, the fact that they held non-proprietary leases made no difference to the outcome, which would still have been the same if they had held proprietary leases giving them estates in the property.

Only one of the arguments put to the court is of interest in considering the effect of the non-proprietary lease. It arises from the replacement of the trust's original licence by a lease. We saw in Chapter 10 that in general a sublease ends with the ending of the head lease, but that exceptionally, where the head lease is surrendered, the head landlord is bound by any subleases (10.9.1). In *Kay*, the occupiers argued that this rule about surrender of a lease applied equally to the trust's surrender of its original licence (in exchange for the grant of the lease): at that point, the Council became bound by the occupiers' non-proprietary leases, remained subject to them thereafter, and so was not entitled now to recover possession of the property.

The Court of Appeal rejected this argument, apparently on the ground that the rule about surrender was limited to the surrender of a lease, and should not be extended to the surrender of a licence. However, it appears to have accepted the Council's argument that the occupiers could not take advantage of the surrender rule if they had no estate in the land (see generally paras. 74–86).

This case does not add a great deal to our understanding of the non-proprietary lease, and most of the questions noted above still remain unanswered.

For an article which discusses the Court of Appeal decision in *Kay*, notes further questions raised by *Bruton* and contains useful references for further reading, see Lower [2010] 74 Conv. 38.

22.2.5 Tenancies at will and licences

The distinction between a licence and this particular type of tenancy may cause you some difficulty. We have already described the characteristics of the tenancy at will (10.10.3), and you may remember that although it gives rise to a landlord–tenant relationship, it is thought that it does not create a legal estate, thus, at least before *Bruton v London & Quadrant Housing Trust* [2001] 1 AC 406, increasing its apparent similarity to a licence. Gray describes the tenancy at will as occupying 'an obscurely defined no-man's land between the periodic tenancy and the mere licence' (Gray and Gray, at para. 4.2.68), and it is certainly not easy to explain the distinction between this form of lease and a licence.

A significant difference between the two used to be found in the Limitation Act 1939; under s. 9, a tenancy at will was deemed to end after one year, so that time would start to run against the landlord (see Chapter 8), whereas a licensee's occupation remained permissive, so that he could never rely on the rules of adverse possession. It was this distinction between the two which provided the setting for *Heslop v Burns* [1974] 1 WLR 1241, and is essential to an understanding of that case; but it did not survive the Limitation Act 1980, which repealed s. 9 of the 1939 Act and did not replace it. Thus the present position is that time does not start to run in favour of a tenant at will until his tenancy has been brought to an end, and on this point therefore the distinction between tenancies at will and licences is no longer of great significance.

Gray and Gray note what used to be described as a vital difference between the two: the tenant at will is regarded as being in possession of the land, and is therefore able to sue a third party for trespass to the land (para. 4.2.70); but even this distinction seems to be eroded by the decision in *Manchester Airport plc v Dutton* [2000] 1 QB 133, allowing a licensee to maintain a claim in trespass.

For a further consideration of tenancies at will and licences, see the note by Bridge in [1991] CLJ 232.

22.3 Distinguishing an easement or profit from a licence

If A walks across B's land and it is clear from the circumstances that A is not a trespasser, then one must establish whether A has an easement (a right to walk across the land—a right of way) or a licence (he has permission to walk across the land). A similar question arises when C fishes in D's lake: does C have a profit or a licence? Once again one has to distinguish between the ownership of a proprietary right and the existence of a permission which merely prevents A from being a trespasser. The distinction may well be very important, because the grant of an easement or profit creates a right which cannot be revoked, whereas often the permission given in a licence can be withdrawn. Moreover, if a third party interferes with the enjoyment of an easement or profit, the person entitled has a right of action for this infringement, whereas a licence would at best be enforceable against the licensor.

Unfortunately, there is no simple method of distinguishing between an easement or profit and a licence. The only method of approach that can be adopted is to establish first whether the right claimed is capable of being an easement or profit (see Chapter 25), for if not, it can be only a licence. An illustration of this is to be found in *Hill v Tupper* (1863) 2 Hurl & C 121, in which it was held that the right to put pleasure boats on a canal could only be a licence and not an easement, because it did not benefit the claimant's land and thus failed to meet one of the criteria for establishing an easement (see further 25.2.1.3). Second, even if the arrangement is capable of giving rise to an easement or profit, it will amount to no more than a licence if the intention to create an interest in land is missing (see *Fitzgerald v Firbank* [1897] 2 Ch 96). An example of the operation of this second principle is to be found in *IDC Group Ltd v Clark* [1992] EGLR 187, in which an agreement for a fire escape route through a neighbouring flat was held to create only a personal licence and not an easement binding on successors in title.

FURTHER READING

Hill, 'Shared Accomodation and Exclusive Possession' (1989) 52 MLR 408.

Landlord and Tenant: Reform of the Law, 1987, Law Com No. 162, paras. 4.4–11.

Street, 'Coach and Horses Trip Cancelled? Rent Act Avoidance after *Street v Mountford*' [1985] Conv 328.

Bruton v London & Quadrant HT

Bright, 'Leases, Exclusive Possession, and Estates' (2000) 116 LQR 7.

Dixon, 'The Non-Proprietary Lease: The Rise of the Feudal Phoenix' [2000] CLJ 25.

Hinojosa, 'On Property, Leases, Licences, Horses and Carts: Revisiting *Bruton v London & Quadrant HT*' [2005] Conv 114.

Lower, 'The Bruton Tenancy' [2010] 74 Conv 38.

Pawlowski, 'Occupational Rights in Leasehold Law: Time for Rationalisation?' [2002] Conv 550.

Routley, 'Tenancies and Estoppel—After *Bruton v London & Quadrant HT*' [2000] MLR 424.

Tenancies at will and licences

Bridge, 'Tenancies At Will in the Court of Appeal' [1991] CLJ 232.

23

Enforcement of a licence

23.1 Introduction

Originally, since a licence gave no right in law and was a mere permission, it could be revoked at any time at the will of the licensor (with one exception, see 23.2.1). However, over the years a number of different types of licence have been recognised by the courts and it appears now that not all licences are so easily withdrawn by the licensor. There are also some decisions which suggest that licences may sometimes be enforceable against the licensor's successors, and this raises the question of whether it is really still true to say that a licence creates no interest in land.

Before considering these issues, however, we must give a brief description of the various types of licence.

23.1.1 Types of licence

23.1.1.1 Licences coupled with an interest

Sometimes licences do not stand alone but are coupled to some other right. An example would be the grant of a profit allowing A to cut wood on B's land. Obviously a licence must be implied into this agreement because A cannot exercise his right to cut wood unless he is permitted to go on B's land to do so. Another example of the operation of the rule is given in *Doe d Hanley v Wood* (1819) 2 B & Ald 724, at p. 738, in which it was said that if a man sells hay standing on his land he cannot later prevent the purchaser from entering the land to collect it (see also *Wood v Manley* (1839) 11 Ad & El 34 and *James Jones & Sons Ltd v Earl of Tankerville* [1909] 2 Ch 440).

23.1.1.2 Contractual licences

As the name suggests, a licence is a contractual one if it is conferred by contract, and this is so even if the right to enter land is only a secondary part of the contract (*Hounslow LBC v Twickenham Garden Developments Ltd* [1971] Ch 233). In most of the cases we will be considering, however, the primary purpose of the contract is to grant the licence in return for consideration; everyday examples are to be found in the purchase of tickets for rail travel or for cinema and theatre visits. Longer term contractual licences are to found in the licences to occupy premises, which we considered in the previous chapter. These are most usually commercial arrangements, granted in exchange for what is described as 'rent' or a licence charge, and are an important type of contractual licence.

Contracts giving rise to contractual licences will usually be expressly created, but you should notice that there have been occasions on which the courts were prepared to infer a contractual agreement giving rise to the licence. Thus, in *Tanner v Tanner* [1975] 1 WLR 1346 a contractual licence was inferred in favour of a woman who had given up a protected tenancy in order to move into a home provided by her lover and there to care for the children of the relationship. Lord Denning MR said that the court should infer a contract that the woman should remain in the property for so long as the children were of school age and accommodation was reasonably required.

A contractual licence was similarly found in *Chandler v Kerley* [1978] 1 WLR 693 in which a man had bought a house from his mistress and her husband at less than the market price on the understanding that he and the woman would live there together and that eventually they would marry. When the relationship ended soon after the purchase, the Court of Appeal held that the woman had a contractual licence to remain, which could be terminated only on reasonable notice (a year in this instance). A contractual licence was also inferred between a mother and daughter-in-law in *Hardwick v Johnson* [1978] 1 WLR 683.

Other cases, however, show that the courts will not always be willing to accept the existence of a contract in such cases. Indeed it seems unusual to construe arrangements of this nature as demonstrating the intention to create legal relations which is necessary in the law of contract. Thus, in *Horrocks v Forray* [1976] 1 WLR 230 a woman failed to establish that a contractual licence existed on the basis of a claim that she had subordinated her choice of residence and mode of life to the will of her former lover in return for a promise that she should have a permanent home. The Court of Appeal rejected her case on two grounds: first, the parties had no intention to enter into a legally binding agreement and, second, she had provided no consideration. (It should be recalled that the courts will not recognise consideration which they regard as being 'immoral' in character.) The situation in *Tanner v Tanner* was distinguished on the ground that in that case, '[T]he man and the woman were making arrangements for the future at arm's length' (at p. 745).

23.1.1.3 Bare licences

Bare licences may be seen as a sort of residuary category: permission to enter another's land may be described as a bare licence if it does not fall into any other category. These licences are essentially gratuitous, since if any charge was made for them, they would be regarded as contractual. A good example of a bare licence is the implied licence to walk up the garden path to the front door of 1 Trant Way (see p. 391). Most of us spend a large part of our lives as bare licencees, for every time we visit a friend's house, for example, or enter a shop we are acting as licencees (see *Davis v Lisle* [1936] 2 KB 434 at p. 440).

23.1.1.4 Licences by estoppel

In certain situations, which we consider later, an owner may be estopped (precluded) by his own representations from denying that another person has a licence to be on his land or from revoking a licence already given. These situations are sometimes described as creating a distinct type of licence (licences by estoppel or estoppel licences), but they may equally well be seen as operating on the existing categories of bare and, possibly, contractual licences, which we have already mentioned. To some extent this is no more than a question of presentation: what is important is that you are familiar with the relevant decisions and can recognise the occasions on which an estoppel is likely to arise. We have already dealt with some of the relevant decisions in Chapter 21, and will look at the application of estoppel to licence situations in 23.2.4 and 23.3.4 below.

23.2 Enforcement against the licensor

The question we have to consider here is whether the licensee can continue to enjoy his licence over another's land, even if the owner changes his mind and purports to revoke or withdraw that licence. As we shall see, the answer to this question depends very much on the type of licence which has been granted.

23.2.1 Licences coupled with an interest

This type of licence is not revocable as long as the proprietary interest (for example, the profit) continues.

23.2.2 Bare licences

A bare licence may be revoked at any time. Once the licence is revoked the former licensee must be given a reasonable period in which to leave and once that period has elapsed will become a trespasser if he remains on the property. In *Robson v Hallet* [1967] 2 QB 939 some police officers went up to the door of a house and knocked. In doing this they were licensees and within their rights. However, in the absence of a search warrant or other authority permitting the officers to insist on remaining, their licence could be revoked, although the householder had to give them reasonable time to leave the property.

23.2.3 Contractual licences

Originally, when considering revocation by the licensor the courts do not appear to have distinguished between bare licences and those which were granted for consideration. Thus, in *R v Inhabitants of Horndon-on-the-Hill* (1816) 4 M & S 562 a licence to build a cottage on a piece of land, the licensee making an annual payment for the right, was held nonetheless to be revocable at the will of the licensor.

The same view was taken in the famous case of *Wood v Leadbitter* (1845) 13 M & W 838, in which a race-goer was ejected by force from a racecourse even though he had paid one guinea (£1.05) for the right to enter the premises and view the racing. The race-goer was unsuccessful when he sued the race steward for damages for battery and false imprisonment, because the court said that his licence was revocable at the will of the licensor, despite the fact that this was in breach of contract. Since he had refused to leave when told to go, the race-goer had become a trespasser and reasonable force could be used to remove him. The licensor might be acting in breach of contract, but while common law would award damages against him for breach it would not compel him to perform his contract. This rigid view of the inherent revocability of any type of licence continued at least until the passing of the Supreme Court of Judicature Acts 1873 and

1875, after which time the availability of equitable remedies in all courts appears to have produced a considerable change in attitudes to the licence.

In *Hurst v Picture Theatres Ltd* [1915] 1 KB 1 a situation arose which was very similar to that in *Wood v Leadbitter*. In this case a cinema-goer was asked by the management to leave the premises because it was believed, incorrectly, that he had not paid for his ticket. When he refused to leave, the cinema-goer was ejected with the use of force and later sued for assault and false imprisonment. In this case the court found for the licensee cinema-goer. It was explained that since the licensee had a contract with the cinema to watch the film, the equitable remedy of an injunction to restrain breach or an order for specific performance of the contract would have been available to prevent the breach of contract, had it been possible to obtain the remedy in the short time before the breach actually occurred. Accordingly in equity the licensee did have a right to remain for the whole contractual period. In consequence he was not a trespasser and his removal was unjustified; and he was entitled to damages for assault and false imprisonment. Buckley LJ distinguished *Wood v Leadbitter* on the ground that the case had been heard in a court of law before the Supreme Court of Judicature Acts 1873 and 1875.

A rather surprising aspect of the majority judgment in *Hurst v Picture Theatres Ltd* (Phillimore LJ dissented) is that it treated the licensee's contractual right to view a spectacle (such as a film show or a race) as amounting to an 'interest'. The licence to enter the premises for this purpose was regarded as coupled to this interest, thus producing an irrevocable licence under the rules relating to licences coupled with a grant, which we considered above. Understandably, this approach has been much criticised; see for example the observations of Latham LJ in *Cowell v Rosehill Racecourse Co. Ltd* (1937) 56 CLR 605. However, although this approach forms the major part of the judgment in *Hurst v Picture Theatres*, Buckley LJ did offer another reason for the decision: the licence to view the spectacle contained an implied term that the permission would not be withdrawn before the end of the show, and equity would restrain revocation in breach of this term. It is this approach which has been developed in later cases, so that a contractual licence is now regarded as enforceable against the original grantor according to its terms. Thus, a contractual licence for a specified period cannot be revoked by the grantor until the contractual period has expired (*Hounslow London Borough Council v Twickenham Garden Developments Ltd* [1971] Ch 233). Should the licence be for an unspecified period, a term will be implied that the licence can be terminated upon reasonable notice (*Winter Garden Theatre (London) Ltd v Millennium Productions Ltd* [1948] AC 173).

If the licensor should purport to revoke the licence in breach of contract, the licensee may seek an injunction to restrain the breach or, in appropriate cases, an order for specific performance of the contract (as in *Verrall v Great Yarmouth BC* [1981] 1 QB 202).

23.2.3.1 **Limited statutory protection**

Where a licence constitutes a 'periodic licence' of a dwelling, s. 5(1A) of the Protection from Eviction Act 1977 (inserted by the Housing Act 1988) requires that the licence may not be terminated otherwise than after four weeks' notice in writing, such notice to be in the prescribed form. In addition s. 3(2A) and (2B) now provide that in the case of such licences the licensor may only recover possession of the property by court order. By these amendments the Housing Act 1988 has conferred a limited protection upon certain licensees and given them some of the rights enjoyed by tenants. The term 'periodic licence' is not defined but is likely to be construed as covering those licences which resemble periodic leases. It is not clear whether the term extends to cover bare licences or only relates to contractual licences. However, the provisions are likely to be used largely in relation to those contractual licences that closely resemble tenancies, save perhaps that the licensee does not have exclusive possession. Sections 3 and 5 do not apply to 'excluded licences', the largest category of these being licences under which the licensee shares facilities with the licensor.

23.2.4 Licences by estoppel

In Chapter 21 we explained how the principles of proprietary estoppel may prevent an owner relying on his strict legal rights when he has encouraged another in the mistaken belief that he has or will have rights in the property. This principle has been used in a number of cases to prevent a licensor revoking a licence (usually a gratuitous or bare one) and recovering possession from a licensee who has been led to believe that he will be allowed to remain in the property.

An early example of estoppel preventing the revocation of a licence is provided by *Plimmer v Wellington Corporation* (1884) 9 App Cas 699. Plimmer occupied part of the foreshore of Wellington Harbour as a 'licensee at will' of the Crown. With the encouragement of the government, and indeed at its request, he incurred expenditure in first erecting and later extending a jetty on the land. At a later stage, when questions as to the nature of his interest arose, he was held by the Privy Council to have acquired an irrevocable licence, because his dealings with the government:

> were sufficient to create in his mind a reasonable expectation that his occupation would not be disturbed (at p. 714).

Nearly a hundred years later, *Pascoe v Turner* [1979] 1 WLR 431 shows the Court of Appeal applying a very similar approach. The plaintiff and defendant had lived together as man and wife, in houses owned by the plaintiff, for almost ten years. When the relationship ended, the plaintiff moved out of their current house, telling the defendant that she had nothing to worry about: the house and its contents were hers. In reliance on this, she stayed in the house thinking that it belonged to her, and expended a considerable proportion of her small savings on repairs and improvements. In fact, the plaintiff did nothing to convey the property to her, so that she remained in occupation as a licensee; a couple of years later he gave her notice to terminate the licence and sought possession of the property.

At first instance, the judge considered that these events gave rise to a constructive trust, but the Court of Appeal did not agree. Instead, it identified the case as one of proprietary estoppel, holding (at p. 436) that the estoppel arose:

> from the encouragement and acquiesence of the plaintiff, when, in reliance upon his declaration that he was giving and, later, that he had given the house to her, she spent a substantial part of her small capital upon repairs and improvements to the house.

The court then had to decide how the equity, arising from the estoppel, was to be satisfied (see 21.6). The choice lay between granting the plaintiff a licence for life, and requiring the transfer to her of the fee simple. Having regard to the plaintiff's apparent determination to evict the defendant, and to the precarious nature of the licence ('she may find herself ousted by a purchaser for value without notice'—at p. 439), the court considered that it must compel the plaintiff to give effect to the defendant's expectations, and convey the fee simple to her.

A more recent example of the licensee being restrained from revoking a bare licence is to be found in *Matharu v Matharu* (1994) 68 P&CR 93, in which a licensor was estopped from recovering possession of a house from his daughter-in-law. The facts of the case were that the plaintiff owned a house which had been occupied by his son and daughter-in-law as their matrimonial home. He sought to recover possession from the daughter-in-law after the breakdown of the marriage and the death of his son. The Court of Appeal held that the defendant could establish an estoppel, arising from her mistaken belief, known to her father-in-law, that the house belonged to her husband, on which she had acted to her detriment in a number of ways. However, the court rejected the woman's claim that this entitled her to a beneficial interest in the property and held that she had no more than a licence to remain in the house 'for her life or such shorter period as she may decide' (at p. 103). Moreover, this limited right was subject to a requirement that she take on responsibility for some repairs to the property and for financial outgoings on it (including the mortgage repayments). Although there have been other decisions in which the equity recognised by the court has been satisfied by giving the licensee a mere right to remain in the property, this has not usually been coupled with such requirements, and it seems somewhat strange that the licensee here was required to pay off the mortgage debt without having any chance to acquire some share in the beneficial interest in the property.

There are a number of other decisions which make use of estoppel in the context of licences, but they involve enforcement against the licensor's successors, and so we will postpone consideration of them until 23.3.4.

23.3 Enforcement against successors of the licensor

As we have already seen in *Binions v Evans* [1972] Ch 359 (20.3.2.2), it may well happen that a licensor will sell his estate to a third party, leaving the licensee with the problem of whether his licence can be enforced against the new owner, or whether he is likely to face eviction from the property. Similar questions arise when the licensor becomes bankrupt or dies, and his trustee in bankruptcy or those entitled under his will or on intestacy seek possession of the property. In the case of some of the various types of licence that we have described above, these questions can be answered quite briefly. In the case of others, the law does not provide such clear answers. Again we will consider each type of licence separately.

23.3.1 Bare licences

With the bare licence there is no problem: since these licences can be revoked at will by the grantor they can certainly be revoked at any time by a successor in title of the licensor.

23.3.2 Licences coupled with an interest

These licences will bind a successor in title of the licensor if he is bound by the interest to which the licence is coupled. As long as the licensee can enforce that interest, he can insist on the continuance of his licence. Accordingly, the enforceability of these licences depends on issues outside the scope of this chapter, and the rules applicable will vary with the nature of the coupled interest.

23.3.3 Contractual licences

Hurst v Picture Theatres Ltd [1915] 1 KB 1 established that a contractual licence was enforceable just as any other contract is enforceable. This suggests that a contractual licence would not bind a successor to the original licensor, because such a person would not be a party to the original contract. It is part of standard contractual principles that whilst the benefit of a contract can be assigned to a third party the burden, or obligation, under the contract cannot be transferred. Indeed in two cases this rule has been applied to contractual licences. In *King v David Allen & Sons (Billposting) Ltd* [1916] 2 AC 54 the licensee had a contractual agreement under which it could display posters on the wall of a cinema. The House of Lords held that this contract could not bind a tenant who took a lease of the cinema from the licensor. In reaching this conclusion the court applied the normal rule that a contract creates a personal obligation enforceable only against the original parties. The Court of Appeal accepted the same principle in *Clore v Theatrical Properties Ltd* [1936] 3 All ER 483 and thus, whilst agreeing that the benefit of a licence could be assigned to a third party, said that the burden of the contract would not pass. Unfortunately for the licensee, this means that any contractual obligation to allow the licence to continue cannot bind a successor in title to the licensor.

This at least was the accepted position until the case of *Errington v Errington* [1952] 1 KB 290. A father bought a house in order to provide a home for his son and daughter-in-law. The property was conveyed to the father, but it was agreed that if the son and his wife paid all the mortgage instalments he would then convey the property to them. In due course the father died and the property vested in his widow as executrix (she was also beneficiary under the will). Thereafter the son went to live with his mother whilst the daughter-in-law remained in the property and continued to pay the mortgage instalments. At this point the mother attempted to revoke her daughter-in-law's licence. The Court of Appeal held that this licence was not revocable by the new owner, even though she was a third party to the original agreement. Denning LJ said that the original contractual arrangement gave rise to an 'equity' in favour of the daughter-in-law which was enforceable against a third party according to the notice rules. Since the new owner was a volunteer, having acquired the property as a gift, she was bound by the contract.

This decision can be criticised on the grounds that it flies in the face of normal contractual rules and is contrary to the decisions in two earlier, and binding, authorities. Furthermore, since at the date of the action the mother was still acting as executrix of her husband's estate and held the land in that capacity, she was not a third party at all but was bound as executrix by obligations which bound her husband's estate. The case, however, came to be regarded as authority for the proposition that in certain circumstances a contractual licence would bind a third party who acquired as a volunteer, or even one who bought the property with notice. In the view of Denning LJ (at p. 299):

> neither the licensor nor anyone who claims through him can disregard the contract except a purchaser for value without notice.

Errington v Errington was followed by a number of decisions in which a contractual licence was held to bind the licensor's successors. In *Binions v Evans* [1972] Ch 359 (see 20.3.2.2), the majority of the Court of Appeal based its decision on the existence of a Settled Land Act settlement, but Lord Denning MR regarded the arrangement as giving rise to a contractual licence, which would bind the purchaser with notice in accordance with the principle he had articulated in *Errington v Errington* (at p. 367).

In addition, the fact that the plaintiff had expressly taken subject to the defendant's licence and accordingly paid a reduced price would justify the imposition of a constructive trust.

The use of a constructive trust in the particular circumstances of *Binions v Evans* would appear to be fully justified, but relying upon that decision Lord Denning MR then developed the idea that constructive trusts arose in all cases involving contractual licences (see *DHN Food Distributors v Tower Hamlets LBC* [1976] 1 WLR 852).

The consequences of imposing a constructive trust were considered in some detail by Browne-Wilkinson J in *In re Sharpe* [1980] 1 WLR 219. The facts here were that a nephew bought a house, the bulk of the purchase money being lent to him by his elderly aunt, who was to live with him and his wife and be cared for by them. Unfortunately, the nephew was subsequently declared bankrupt, and the property vested in his trustee in bankruptcy, who sought possession of the house. The aunt claimed a right to remain in the house, at least until the loan was repaid.

In giving judgment, Browne-Wilkinson J confessed to feeling some uncertainty about the Court of Appeal decisions which spelt out irrevocable licences from informal family arrangements. He referred to decisions on both proprietary estoppel and contractual licences; in his view, the aunt had the right, as against her nephew, to remain in the property:

> whether it be called a contractual licence or an equitable licence or an interest under a constructive trust (p. 224).

The more difficult question, however, was whether that right was enforceable against the nephew's trustee in bankruptcy. In general, the trustee steps into the debtor's shoes, and takes his property subject to all rights and equities affecting it; he is, however, free to break any merely contractual obligations of the debtor. On which side of this line did the rights of the aunt fall: were they merely contractual obligations or did she have some interest over the property? In considering this question, the judge found guidance in *DHN Food Distributors Ltd v Tower Hamlets LBC* [1976] 1 WLR 852. If the licence was to be regarded as creating an interest in land, the use of a constructive trust was essential, since by virtue of LPA 1925, s. 40 (see 5.3.1), an enforceable interest in relation to land could not arise simply under an oral contract. Here the aunt's contractual or equitable licence did confer an interest under a constructive trust, which accordingly bound the trustee in bankruptcy.

In reaching this conclusion, Browne-Wilkinson J made it clear that he had considerable reservations about the current state of the law, describing it (at p. 226) as:

> very confused and difficult to fit in with established equitable principles.

Similar doubts about the decision in *Errington v Errington* and subsequent developments were expressed by a number of judges and academics, as for example by Russell LJ in *National Provincial Bank Ltd v Hastings Car Mart Ltd* [1964] Ch 665 at pp. 696–7. However, the House of Lords when considering the appeal in that case (under the name of *National Provincial Bank v Ainsworth* [1965] AC 1175) declined to express any final view on the matter, which accordingly remained unresolved for some considerable time.

The matter was, however, considered at some length by the Court of Appeal in *Ashburn Anstalt v Arnold* [1989] 1 Ch 1. Unfortunately all the remarks of the court upon this subject constitute *obiter dicta* because in the case the agreement under consideration was held to be a lease and not a licence. Nonetheless, having heard lengthy argument upon the *Errington* problem, the court felt it proper to express its views upon this subject. After a detailed consideration of the authorities, Fox LJ concluded (at p. 22):

> Before *Errington* the law appears to have been clear and well understood. It rested on an important and intelligible distinction between contractual obligations which gave rise to no estate or interest in the land and proprietary rights which, by definition, did. The far-reaching statement of principle in *Errington* was not supported by authority, not necessary for the decision of the case and *per incuriam* in the sense that it was made without reference to authorities which, if they would not have compelled, would surely have persuaded the court to adopt a different *ratio*. Of course, the law must be free to develop. But as a response to problems which had arisen, the *Errington* rule (without more) was neither practically necessary nor theoretically convincing.

As a result it seems most unlikely that in future it will be possible to argue that a contractual licence is binding on a third party to the contract and the contractual licence has been returned to its true place, which appears simply to be as part of the law of contract. The Court of Appeal did, however, accept that there might be cases in which the facts justified the imposition by the court of a constructive trust. It was emphasised that the courts will not take this step where the evidence is 'slender' and that the issue for the court in such cases is (at p. 27)

> whether the [third party] has acted in such a way that, as a matter of justice, a trust must be imposed...

The court agreed that the imposition of a constructive trust was justified by the facts of *Binions v Evans* [1972] Ch 359, where the purchaser had acted in breach of the term in his contract that he would take the property subject to the occupier's rights.

The remarks of the Court of Appeal in *Ashburn Anstalt v Arnold*, although theoretically only of persuasive authority, are helpful in clarifying the law on this issue, and were welcomed by Browne-Wilkinson V-C in *IDC Group Ltd v Clark* [1992] EGLR 187 at p. 189 as:

> [putting] what I hope is the quietus to the heresy that a mere licence creates an interest in land... [and] to the heresy that parties to a contractual licence necessarily become constructive trustees.

The decision in *Ashburn Anstalt v Arnold* was criticised (although not in relation to its comments on contractual licences) and overruled by the House of Lords in *Prudential Assurance Co. Ltd v London Residuary Body* [1992] 2 AC 386. However, this does not seem to have affected the persuasive force of its views on *Errington v Errington*.

In *Habermann v Koehler* (1996) 73 P&CR 515 at 523, the Court of Appeal referred to the case as being the decision which governs contractual licences, and more recently in *Lloyd v Dugdale* [2002] 2 P&CR 13 p.167 at 183 Sir Christopher Slade cited *Ashburn Anstalt v Arnold* as authority for the principle that:

> Notwithstanding some previous authority suggesting the contrary, a contractual licence is not to be treated as creating a proprietary interest in land so as to bind third parties who acquire the land with notice of it, on this account alone.

23.3.4 Licences by estoppel

In a number of cases in which the licensor would be estopped from revoking the licence, the courts have had to deal with the additional question of whether his successors in title are subject to that estoppel.

Two cases we have already noted, *Dillwyn v Llewellyn* (1862) 4 De G F & J 517 and *Inwards v Baker* [1965] 2 QB 29 (see 21.5.1), arose after the death of the licensor and involved questions about the extent to which those inheriting the deceased's property took subject to the licence. In both cases they were held to be bound by the rights which the licensee could have asserted against the licensor.

Similarly, in *Greasely v Cooke* [1980] 1 WLR 1306 the action to recover the property from the licensee was brought by family members who had inherited the property from the original licensor. The licensee, Miss Cooke, had lived in the house for nearly 40 years, having started work as a maid with the family when she was just 16. Over the years she came to be regarded as one of the family, living as the wife of one of the brothers, and caring for other members, including an invalid daughter. After the first 10 years she was no longer paid for her services, but was assured that she could regard the property as her home for the rest of her life. When her partner died, the younger generation, who inherited the house, sought to recover possession from her.

The Court of Appeal held that the various elements of proprietary estoppel were established in this case, and that the claimant had an equity arising from that estoppel, which, as in *Inwards v Baker* should be satisfied by allowing her to remain in the house for as long as she wished. This was enforced against the new owners, taking by inheritance, who were not able to evict her.

We have already considered the decision in *In re Sharpe* [1980] 1 WLR 219 in connection with contractual licences, but think it is worth mentioning here as well. Parts of the judgment suggest that the circumstances could give rise to an estoppel, and so the case could be seen as illustrating the enforcement of such an equity against the owner's trustee in bankruptcy.

23.3.4.1 Enforcement against purchaser for value

So far the decisions we have considered involve enforcing the estoppel licence against successors who are volunteers or who for some other reason are regarded as stepping into the shoes of the licensor. The really interesting question about the enforcement of these licences arises when the licensor's successor is a purchaser for value: can the equity be enforced against him?

It happened that the first cases in which this question was considered all involved unregistered land, and we will deal with these now and then go on to look at the position with regard to registered title.

Unregistered land

In *Inwards v Baker* [1965] 2 QB 29 at p. 37 Lord Denning MR stated that:

> any purchaser who took with notice would clearly be bound by the equity

but this must be considered as merely *obiter dicta*, since no purchaser was involved in the case.

In *Hopgood v Brown* [1955] 1 WLR 213, the Court of Appeal held that a purchaser for value was bound by an estoppel which had been binding on his vendor. However there was little discussion of this point, and in part at least the court seemed to argue by analogy from the legal doctrine of tenancy by estoppel rather than relying on the equitable concept of proprietary estoppel.

There is, however, one major decision, *E. R. Ives Investment Ltd v High* [1967] 2 QB 379, in which an equity arising from estoppel was enforced against a purchaser for value. The facts of this case were as follows. A building company, whilst erecting a block of flats, mistakenly allowed the foundations of the new building to encroach on to land belonging to a neighbour. When the neighbour objected, he was persuaded to accept a right of way across the courtyard of the new block (allowing access to his back garden from the road) in compensation for the continuing trespass. Thereafter, he built himself a garage, access to which was only possible via the courtyard. Later the owner of the block of flats sold the property and it was eventually resold to the plaintiffs. They bought it subject to the neighbour's right of way but subsequently claimed that since this right amounted to an unregistered D(iii) land charge (an equitable easement) it was not binding on them. The Court of Appeal held that the neighbour's right to cross the courtyard did bind the plaintiffs.

This decision appears to be reached on two separate grounds. The first ground is that it is a basic rule of law that one cannot take the benefit of an agreement without accepting a related burden. (This principle is discussed further in Chapter 26 in relation to covenants relating to freehold land and the decisions in *Halsall v Brizell* [1957] Ch 169—see 26.5.1.) Thus, as long as the plaintiffs wished to maintain their foundations on the neighbouring land they could not revoke the neighbour's right of way. This analysis causes few problems. It is the second reason given for the decision in this case which causes concern: that the actions of the original owner in allowing the neighbour to build his garage gave rise to an estoppel or, as Lord Denning MR put it, 'an equity arising out of acquiescence'. It was held that this 'equity', which is not a land charge and therefore was not void for non-registration, would bind a purchaser who bought with notice, as had the plaintiffs in this case. The decision is thus a rare example of the enforcement of an estoppel licence against a purchaser for value, and seems to elevate the licence by estoppel into some kind of quasi-interest in land.

This departure from traditional ideas about licences led to criticism (see Crane (1967) 31 Conv NS 332) and it must be said that since the dispute in *E. R. Ives Investment Ltd v High* could have been resolved on the point of the related benefit and burden alone, the discussion of the 'equity' arising from estoppel was quite unnecessary. The case, however, stands as authority for the proposition that licences in respect of unregistered land can bind third parties, including a purchaser for value, and the decision as a whole was referred to with approval by the Court of Appeal in *Thatcher v Douglas* (1995) 146 NLJ 282. It is also worth noting *obiter dicta* in *Lloyds Bank plc v Carrick* [1996] 4 All ER 630, in which Morritt LJ, referring to counsel's argument that proprietary estoppel cannot give rise to an interest in land capable of binding successors in title, observed that it was hard to see how that argument 'can surmount the hurdle created by the decision of this court in *E. R. Ives Investments Ltd v High*' (at p. 642).

Registered land

As we saw in 21.7.1, there was, until recently, little authority on whether an equity arising from estoppel would bind a purchaser of registered land, and none at all in the context of licences.

At last, however, in 1996, the question of the overriding effect of this equity was raised before the Court of Appeal in the case of *Habermann v Koehler* (1996) 73 P&CR 515. The facts were as follows. The defendants' employer was the registered proprietor of a house which he made available to the defendants, giving them an oral promise that they could live there rent-free for the rest of his life, and could buy the property from him at a reduced price. The defendants moved into the house on the strength of the arrangement, and for some time worked without payment for their employer. The property was then mortgaged, and some 10 years later was sold to the mortgagee to meet the mortgage debt. The purchaser sought possession of the property from the defendants, who in their defence relied on proprietary estoppel. It seemed that at last all the unanswered questions about estoppel licences, on which, as the Court of Appeal observed, 'there is much controversy', would arise in an appellate court for decision. Tantalisingly, however, the Court of Appeal considered that too many relevant factual questions had not been dealt with at first instance and, accordingly, remitted the case for a new trial.

At that further trial, the judge held that the option to buy the property could not be enforced against the purchaser under LRA 1925, s. 70(1)(g) because the occupier had not disclosed it on enquiry. However, it appears that the licensee's right to remain in the property was held to bind the purchaser. The court ordered the execution of a declaration of trust giving effect to the occupiers' right to remain in occupation of the property for the lifetime of the previous owner (that is, the occupiers' previous employer, who had created the licence). This first instance decision is recorded in the report of *Habermann v Koehler (No. 2)* [2000] TLR 825, in which the occupiers appealed, unsuccessfully, against the decision that their option was unenforceable. The purchaser did not appeal against the decision on the right to occupy, and accordingly there is no reference to that part of the first instance decision in the Court of Appeal's judgment. Nevertheless, it does appear that an equity arising from proprietary estoppel in a licence situation was held binding on a purchaser for value of registered land, albeit at first instance only (see further 23.4.3).

23.3.5 Could a contractual licensee rely on estoppel?

This is a question to which there is no clear answer and it has generated a certain amount of academic debate. As Pawlowski puts it in *The Doctrine of Proprietary Estoppel*, 1996, at p. 8:

> There are conflicting views as to whether a contractual licence and proprietary estoppel can overlap.

The question of whether there could be such an overlap seems to be of particular importance in the context of enforcing a licence against the licensor's successor. Following *Ashburn Anstalt v Arnold* [1989] 1 Ch 1 it is generally accepted that a contractual licence will not bind a third party (unless, of course, there are special circumstances which lead the court to impose a constructive trust). By contrast, as we have seen, the equity arising from proprietary estoppel now appears to be enforceable against successors in title and, as in *Habermann v Koehler (No. 2)* [2000] TLR 825, can result in a licence being enforced against a purchaser for value. If a contractual licensee could establish that he has acted to his detriment in reliance on a representation by the licensor—for example that the licence would not be revoked—could any resulting equity make that licence enforceable against a third party?

It seems that as yet there is no direct authority on this point. Megarry and Wade, para. 16–034, is of the opinion that:

> there is no reason why both a claim in contract and to an equity by proprietary estoppel should not normally arise from the same factual mix

and the same view is put forward by Thompson [1983] Conv 50. For the contrary view, see Briggs [1981] Conv 212 and [1983] Conv 285.

23.4 Are licences becoming interests in land?

At the start of this chapter we referred to the traditional idea that licences are mere permissions and do not constitute interests in land. Having looked at the modern case law, it is worth considering whether this is still true, or whether modern decisions mean that the licence has become, or is becoming, an interest in land.

23.4.1 What is an interest in land?

The authorities seem to suggest that the crucial factor, in deciding whether a right amounts to an interest in land, is whether the right is enforceable against third parties. A right which cannot be enforced against a successor in title is clearly not an interest in land. However, since the answer to the question, 'What rights bind successors in title?' appears to be, 'Those which are interests in land', this definition seems to be distinctly circular in nature (see Gray and Gray paras. 1.5.27–1.5.30). It is nevertheless the best that can be offered, and so, in considering whether a right creates an interest in land, attention centres on whether it binds third parties, and in particular the purchaser for value.

The other essential characteristic of an interest in land is that it is capable of being transferred to another person, passing either by itself, or on the transfer of the land to which it is attached. Thus, in considering whether licences can be regarded as interests in land, we need to ask not only whether they bind the licensors' successors but also whether they are transferable.

23.4.2 Is a licence transferable?

There is not a great deal of authority on this in English law, although it would seem that rights arising under a contract are usually assignable, subject, of course, to the specific terms of the contract. The question of whether the benefit of an estoppel could be assigned was considered and answered affirmatively in the Australian case of *Hamilton v Geraghty* (1901)1 SRNSW Eq 81 (see Cheshire and Burn, p. 941). In *E. R. Ives Investment Ltd v High* [1967] 2 QB 379, Lord Denning described such an equity as being available also to the claimant's successors in title (at p. 395). See further, Gray and Gray, para. 9.2.90.

23.4.3 Does a licence bind the licensor's successor?

As we have seen, it did appear at one time that contractual licences were to be regarded as binding everyone except the purchaser for value without notice (*Errington v Errington* [1952] 1 KB 290). The 1984 edition of Megarry and Wade, *The Law of Real Property*, 5th edn., at p. 808 stated that 'all the indications now are that contractual licences are capable of binding successors in title as equitable interests', adding that 'the courts appear to be well on their way to create a new and highly versatile interest in land'. This was, of course, written before *Ashburn Anstalt v Arnold* [1989] 1 Ch 1, and since the Court of Appeal's disapproval of *Errington v Errington* it seems unlikely that contractual licences will any longer be regarded as binding on the licensor's successor. There is still the possibility that in situations similar to that in *Binions v Evans* [1972] Ch 359 a constructive trust might be imposed, but the purchaser would then be bound by the beneficial interest under the trust, a recognised property interest, rather than by any right arising directly from the contractual licence.

As far as estoppel licences go, we have noted both the decisions in which the equity has been enforced against the licensor's successors and the new more general statutory provision relating to registered land that an equity by estoppel has effect 'as an interest capable of binding successors in title' (LRA 2002, s. 116—see 21.7). It would seem now that licences by estoppel are being accorded the status of interests in land, but you may like to note the contrary view expressed in Megarry and Wade (para. 16–06) that:

> although an equity arising by estoppel is probably best regarded as a species of equitable proprietary right, it is questionable whether an estoppel licence can be so regarded.

The correctness of describing an estoppel licence as an equitable proprietary right is described as 'open to doubt', mainly because LPA 1925 appears to prohibit the creation of new equitable interests (s. 4(1) proviso), and there is no decision pre-dating the Act in which an estoppel licence had been held to bind a third party. Moreover (para. 16–06):

> it is not obvious that a licence declared to be irrevocable by reason of estoppel should create an equitable interest in land when a contractual licence does not.

On this point, see also Megarry and Wade, para. 34–020, and Pawlowski, *The Doctrine of Proprietary Estoppel*, 1996, p. 9. It remains to be seen whether the courts will regard these views as persuasive.

23.5 Trant Way

The matters we have been discussing in this chapter could be relevant to two of the licensees described on pp. 391–2. Henry Mumps and Bob Bell are each living as licensees in property owned by another member of their family.

23.5.1 8 Trant Way

Henry is already worried about his position, fearing that Mildred wants to end their relationship, and possibly to turn him out of the house. If he could establish that he is entitled to a share of the beneficial interest under a common-intention constructive trust, he would have the right to remain in occupation, as well as a right to a share in the capital value of the house.

If he cannot establish such a trust, he will be left trying to show that he has an irrevocable licence to remain in the house. Decisions on implied contractual licences (such as *Tanner v Tanner* [1975] 1 WLR 1346) might be thought to give him some comfort, but as we have seen the courts have not always been willing to adopt this approach (see 23.1.1.2). Even if Henry could establish such a contract, since *Ashburn Anstalt v Arnold* [1989] 1 Ch 1 he would be at risk from anyone to whom Mildred might sell or mortgage the house.

The other possibility for Henry would be to seek to establish an estoppel, but for this he would need to show that Mildred led him to believe that he would be allowed to remain in the house, and that he had acted in reliance on this to his detriment.

Failing all else, Henry does have a limited statutory right to occupation under the Family Law Act 1996, and we will deal with this and consider Henry's position more generally in Chapter 27.

23.5.2 3 Trant Way

Although relations between Bob Bell and his daughter Barbara seem happy at the moment, it is worth noting that he might have a licence by estoppel which could be enforced against his daughter. Bob has spent money on his flat in reliance on her statement that he has a home for life. It is possible that if a dispute arose a court could hold that Bob had an irrevocable licence for life although the court would be free to satisfy the equity arising from estoppel in whatever way it thought best, and might choose to make only a money award, to compensate Bob for his expenditure.

FURTHER READING

Battersby, 'Contractual and Estoppel Licences as Proprietary Interests in Land' [1991] Conv 36.

Crane, 'Estoppel Interests in Land' (1967) 31 Conv 332.

Everton, '"Equitable Interests" and "Equities"—In Search of a Pattern' (1976) 40 Conv 209.

Moriarty, 'Licences and Land Law: Legal Principles and Public Policies' (1984) 100 LQR 376.

PART VI

Third-party rights

Introduction

In this part we move on to look at the major third-party rights in land. This group of rights includes mortgages and charges (Chapter 24), easements and profits à prendre (Chapter 25) and covenants affecting freehold land (Chapter 26). As you have already seen (2.3 to 2.7) these rights are capable of existing as interests in land and you should already be familiar with the rules relating to the question of whether such rights will bind any later acquirer of an estate or interest in the land. However, in each chapter, as well as explaining the nature of the rights in great detail, we will also explain how the rules as to later acquirers operate in relation to each interest. As you will see, in some cases this can produce quite complex problems, which can be difficult for practitioners and are much beloved of examiners!

24

Mortgages and charges

24.1 Background

Very few individuals or companies have sufficient liquid assets to pay for the purchase of property outright. The normal method of financing such a purchase is to obtain a loan from a bank, building society or finance house. Since large sums of money are involved, the lender will seek security for the money advanced and this will normally take the form of a mortgage of the property to be purchased. Accordingly, a large proportion of real property in this country is mortgaged. In addition to such mortgages for purchase, it is also common to offer a mortgage of land as security for any sizeable loan. Such a loan might be taken in order to improve the land (e.g., to install central heating) or for purposes unconnected with the land (e.g., to finance the owner's business ventures or re-finance other debts).

Thus far, we have mentioned only mortgages. 'Mortgage' is the traditional name for the arrangement by which property becomes security for a debt but, as we shall see, the correct modern term is normally 'charge'. In practice, however, the two terms are often used interchangeably. You should also note that land is not the only form of property that can be used as security. It is not at all uncommon for valuable chattels also to be used as security for a debt and thus chattel mortgages are perfectly possible. Ships, aeroplanes, fleets of cars, and large pieces of factory equipment are often mortgaged as a way of financing their acquisition. The rules for chattel mortgages are not identical to those for mortgages of land or interests in land, though there are similarities. However, we deal here only with mortgages that relate to land.

In this chapter we examine the types of mortgages or charges of land and interests in land which may be created. We also consider the rules regarding their administration and their protection against later acquirers of interests in the land. At some points the rules are complex and many readers may not need to know all the intricacies of the rules (for example, priority rules in relation to unregistered land and the recent case-law relating to undue influence). However, others may need or wish to know more and thus in these areas we give an outline of the law here in the text and provide further information in the Online Resource Centre linked to this book (referenced as 'W.24' i.e., 'W' plus chapter number): **www.oxfordtextbooks.co.uk/orc/landlaw14e/**.

24.2 Introduction

When they purchased 1 Trant Way, the Armstrongs were able to pay their own removal expenses and legal fees, and provided 10 per cent of the purchase price of the property from their own resources. They obtained the remaining 90 per cent of the house price by way of a loan from the Double Gloucester Building Society (DGBS). As security for the loan, the society took a charge by deed over 1 Trant Way. This charge was registered at the same time as the transfer to the Armstrongs.

James Harding, who is buying a 99-year lease of the maisonette at 2 Trant Way, also needs to raise money by way of a mortgage. He plans to borrow 95 per cent of the price from his bank, the Wensleydale Bank plc.

Mildred Mumps wishes to borrow a large sum of money from her bank (the Royal Windsor Bank), in order to start her own business. The bank has insisted on security for the loan. 8 Trant Way is already mortgaged to the Red Leicester Building Society but Mildred has offered her bank a second mortgage on the property, as security for her business loan. Mildred has not told Henry Mumps of her plans.

Nigel Neep, the owner in fee simple of 14 Trant Way, has asked his bank manager for overdraft facilities for one month. The bank manager has said that this is possible, but has suggested that the bank take Mr Neep's title deeds and hold them as security for the loan. Mr Neep bought the property in 1989, raising the bulk of the purchase price by a loan secured by a mortgage. He finished repaying that debt in 2005. He is happy to deposit the title deeds (which are normally stored for safe-keeping by his solicitor) with the bank as suggested.

24.3 What is a mortgage or charge?

In *Santley v Wilde* [1899] 2 Ch 474 a mortgage was described as 'a conveyance of land...as security for the payment of a debt or the discharge of some other obligation'. The purpose of a mortgage or charge is to provide a lender of money with security for the debt. If the borrower fails to repay the debt, the lender can use the property to recover the sum lent and any interest payable. This is usually achieved by the lender taking the property that has been used as security and selling it. The lender is then able to deduct the sums owed from the proceeds of sale.

24.3.1 Terminology

It is worth stopping here for a moment and considering the terminology that is used in relation to mortgages and charges, since it often causes confusion. In a mortgage the mortgage is granted by the property owner (the borrower), who is thus called the *mortgagor*. The lender, who receives the benefit of the security provided by the mortgage is called the *mortgagee*. It is thus not the building society or bank that grants the mortgage, although in common parlance we often speak as though this is the case.

In the case of a charge, the correct terms are *chargor* (the owner who borrows) and *chargee* (the lender) but the terms 'mortgagor' and 'mortgagee' are often used even where the arrangement is technically a charge rather than a mortgage. The diagram below may help you to remember these rules.

PROPERTY OWNER	BANK, BUILDING SOCIETY etc
BORROWER	LENDER
Mortgagor	Mortgagee
or	or
Chargor	Chargee

24.3.2 Types of mortgage or charge

There are a number of different types of mortgage or charge that can be created, although in modern times, with the registration of title, one form has come to be by far the most common. That form is usually called the 'registered charge' and we will look at it in more detail below. Some of the older methods of creating mortgages are no longer commonly used, particularly those that relate only to unregistered land but we will note them because in relation to mortgages an understanding of how the forms of mortgage or charge developed can make some of the modern rules easier to follow.

24.3.3 Can be legal or equitable

As is the case with many interests in land, mortgages and charges can be either legal or equitable, although modern changes to the law have made equitable mortgages or equitable charges of legal estates much less common. It is also possible to use nearly any interest in land as security and not just a legal estate. The holder of an equitable lease could mortgage or charge his or her equitable interest as security for a loan. However, as this is a mortgage of an equitable interest, the mortgage or charge can only take effect in equity. Thus, while a legal estate or interest can be the subject of a legal or an equitable mortgage or charge, an equitable interest can only be the subject of an equitable mortgage or charge. In the past, it was not at all uncommon for an heir to a large settled estate to mortgage his equitable future interest in the property. However, in modern times, equitable mortgages of equitable interests are much less common.

24.3.4 The traditional method of creating a mortgage

The traditional form of mortgage is no longer possible in relation to a legal estate but it is nonetheless important to understand how it operated, both in order to see why some of the modern rules developed and also to understand some of the older cases. This method was abolished in 1926 (as a consequence of ss. 85–87 of the LPA 1925).

Originally, a mortgage was created by the mortgagor (the borrower) transferring his (in those days the owner was usually male) legal estate in the land to the mortgagee (lender) as security for the loan. If the mortgagor defaulted on his debt (failed to pay) the mortgagee could sell or let the property in order to reimburse himself. He could do this because he owned the estate in the property. The agreement made between the parties did, however, provide for the estate to be re-conveyed to the mortgagor if he repaid the loan in full (usually on a specified date).

There were a number of problems with this arrangement. One that arose early in the history of the mortgage was that lenders often tried to prevent the mortgagor being able to repay on the contractual date. This abuse was dealt with by equity developing the principle that the mortgagor has an equitable right to repay ('redeem the mortgage') after the contractual date. Another flaw was that it was impossible for the mortgagor to create two mortgages over the same piece of property because the first mortgage conveyed the whole legal estate to the mortgagee. This problem was circumvented by the mortgagor granting a mortgage over his equitable right to redeem. However, because that mortgage was of an equitable interest, the second mortgage itself had to be equitable. These are just two illustrations of how the pre-1926 rules caused unnecessary complications, which became unacceptable in a modern commercial world.

24.3.5 The LPA 1925 reforms

The LPA 1925 replaced the older form of legal mortgage with new forms that did not involve the conveyance by the mortgagor of his estate to the mortgagee. Instead, security was provided by either granting the mortgagee a long lease of the premises (LPA 1925, ss. 85 and 86) or by the mortgagor creating a charge over the property that gave the mortgagee the same rights as if he had been granted a long lease (s. 87, LPA 1925). Over time the s. 87 charge became the form used by most banks and building societies. It is also, since the coming into force of the LRA 2002, the only form of mortgage or charge of a registered legal estate that is possible. The ss. 85 and 86 mortgages are technically possible in other instances but are relatively rare. We will now look at the legal mortgages in more detail and then consider the equitable forms of mortgage.

24.4 Legal mortgages

24.4.1 Legal mortgage of a fee simple under LPA 1925, s. 85

Under the provisions of LPA 1925, s. 85, the mortgagor, instead of transferring the fee simple, grants a long lease of the property to the mortgagee. This lease will be expressed to be terminable when the loan is repaid: it is said to be subject to 'cesser on redemption'. This method has the advantage that the mortgagor retains his estate in the land, but the mortgagee also has an estate (the lease) which gives him certain rights in relation to the land. In order to ensure that the lease will not end before the debt is repaid, it is normal to grant an extremely long term of years. Indeed the statute provides that, should one try to create a mortgage by the old method of transferring the fee simple as security for a loan, this will automatically be converted into a grant of a lease for a term of 3,000 years from the date of the mortgage (s. 85(2)), and those drafting mortgages in accordance with s. 85 usually adopted a similar period of lease.

The s. 85 method of creating a legal mortgage had an advantage over the older form of mortgage. It allowed the creation of a second legal mortgage over the same land, by giving the second mortgagee a lease which is longer than the lease of the first mortgagee. This creates a leasehold reversion in the second mortgagee, giving him the landlord's rights in relation to the first tenant (mortgagee). (As we have already explained, it is possible to grant several leases which take effect at the same time in the same piece of land—see 10.10.5.) It would not, in fact, matter if the leases given to the various mortgagees were all the same length, but it was usual to give a slightly longer term to each successive mortgagee.

24.4.2 Legal mortgage of a term of years under LPA 1925, s. 86

Before 1926, mortgages of leases were also created by assigning the whole term of years to the mortgagee. However, LPA 1925, s. 86, provided for such a mortgage to be created by granting a sublease to the mortgagee. Again, the mortgagee was thereby given an estate in the land, while the mortgagor retained his own estate. Should an attempt be made to use the old method of mortgaging, the disposition would be converted into a sublease. The period of the sublease would be the unexpired period of the mortgaged lease, less 10 days (s. 86(2)). The 10-day gap allowed the creation of a second mortgage of the same lease, made by granting a sublease that is a day longer than the first sublease. Once again this allowed for the creation of two or more legal mortgages of the same term of years.

24.4.3 Charge by deed by way of legal mortgage under LPA 1925, s. 87

The third method of creating a legal mortgage is the method in normal use today. Instead of granting a lease or sublease to the mortgagee, the mortgagor merely executes a deed which declares that he is charging his land by way of legal mortgage with the repayment of the loan (plus interest). This form of 'charge' may be used for both freehold and leasehold estates. LPA 1925, s. 87, provides that the effect of such a mortgage is to give the mortgagee 'the same protection, powers and remedies' as if the mortgage had been made by lease or sublease (whichever is relevant). Thus, the mortgagee is treated as though he had a lease or sublease, although in fact no such estate is created.

The effect of this provision is illustrated by *Grand Junction Co. Ltd v Bates* [1954] 2 QB 160, in which leasehold property had been charged by way of legal mortgage under s. 87. Later, the landlord began forfeiture proceedings under s. 146 for breach of covenant by the tenant. Had he succeeded, the mortgagee's security for the loan would have been totally destroyed, for the lease ceases to exist on forfeiture. If the mortgage had been made by sublease, the mortgagee would have been able to apply for relief as a subtenant under s. 146(4) (see Chapter 13), but the question arose whether a chargee could do this since he had no legal estate in the property. However, the court held that the provisions of s. 87 gave him a right to apply for relief, just as though he held a mortgage by sublease.

The charge by way of legal mortgage does have several advantages over the other methods of creating a legal mortgage. It enables an owner to mortgage his freehold and leasehold property in one document and, in the case of leasehold property, has the further advantage that, since no actual sublease is created, the grant of such a charge will not amount to breach of a covenant against subletting (see *Grand Junction Co. Ltd v Bates* per Upjohn J at p. 168).

As a result of its simple form (a brief example is given in LPA 1925, Sch. 5, form No. 1), and the fact that it can be used to mortgage both of the legal estates, the legal charge has become in modern times the most usual method of mortgage. The mortgages of both 1 and 2 Trant Way are likely to take this form. The sample format of such a charge given in the LPA 1925 does not, however, give a true picture of the type of document which one would expect to see today. Most modern charges add a long list of covenants between the mortgagor and mortgagee (e.g., preventing the mortgagor from granting leases or taking lodgers). There will also be detailed provisions concerning repayment of the sum advanced, together with interest, usually by instalments (and normally spread over a period of 20–25 years in the case of domestic mortgages). The modern mortgage is accordingly a very much longer document than the Act might suggest.

24.4.3.1 Registered land

The legal charge is also used when one is dealing with registered land. Section 23(1)(a) of the LRA 2002 expressly says that the powers of an owner in relation to a registered estate include the power to make any disposition permitted by the general law except a mortgage by demise or subdemise (see above 24.4.1 and 24.4.2), thus the legal charge is the form of mortgage to use for registered land. In line with the general policy applying to registered land, the completion of the deed does not, by itself, create a legal mortgage. It is the registration of the charge which perfects it (LRA 2002, ss. 4 and 27). In the absence of registration the charge can only have effect in equity.

Note that in relation to registered land a legal charge may be created (subject to the necessary formalities, such as the need for a deed) by the simple use of words that make it clear that the land is to be regarded as charged with the repayment of a loan. Thus, in registered land, it is not necessary to include the words 'by way of legal charge' in the deed, if the intention to charge is clear. This position in relation to the wording used in the LRA 1925, s. 25(2) was confirmed in *Cityland and Property (Holdings) Ltd v Dabrah* [1968] Ch 166, 171 and now is governed by s. 25 of the LRA 2002 and r. 103 of the Land Registration Rules 2003. Since r. 103 says that 'A legal charge of a registered estate may be made in [the form provided]', rather than that it must ('shall') be made in that form, it would appear that any wording that is clearly intended to create a legal charge will do.

24.4.3.2 Islamic mortgages

The methods of creation of mortgages set out above do not satisfy the need for the increasingly popular 'Islamic mortgage' because they are really designed for repayment mortgages that bear interest. The simplest method of providing finance without using the form of an interest-bearing loan is for the financial institution to purchase the property and grant a long lease (at a rent) to the intended acquirer, who also pays an additional monthly sum to acquire the estate in the property at a later date. In such cases there is no charge or mortgage under ss. 85–87, LPA 1925.

24.4.4 Grant of legal mortgage as a trigger for first registration

The creation of a legal mortgage or charge of an unregistered estate may itself trigger a requirement to register both the estate charged and the mortgage or charge. Under

s. 4(1)(g) LRA 2002, the creation of a 'protected first legal mortgage' of a qualifying estate gives rise to the requirement of registration. The 'protected first legal mortgage' is defined by s. 4(8) as follows:

> (8) For the purposes of subsection (1)(g)—
> (a) a legal mortgage is protected if it takes effect on its creation as a mortgage to be protected by the deposit of documents relating to the mortgaged estate, and
> (b) a first legal mortgage is one which on its creation, ranks in priority ahead of any other mortgages then affecting the mortgaged estate.

You will recall from our earlier discussion of land charges (see 6.4) that, in unregistered land, only mortgages that are not protected by deposit of title deeds can be protected as land charges. The effect of s. 4, LRA 2002 is that the creation of a legal mortgage in which the title deeds *are* deposited will lead to a requirement to register the estate charged, unless the mortgage is not a first mortgage (which is very unlikely because the first mortgagee normally takes the deeds). Section 6(2) makes it quite clear that it is the charged estate that must be registered and not just the mortgage or charge. Thus, the land will become registered land and then all charges must be protected in accordance with the land registration provisions.

Thus, if Mr Neep, the owner of 14 Trant Way, has to create a legal mortgage of his property as security for his bank loan, rather than using the informal method suggested by the bank manager, he will have to register his fee simple estate and the charge.

24.4.4.1 Registration of charges

Once the estate is registered, any legal mortgage or charge over that estate must itself be registered (s. 27(2)(f)). Once registered, the mortgage or charge will take effect as a charge by deed by way of legal mortgage, even if originally created as a different type of legal mortgage (s. 51, LRA 2002). Thus, if Mr Neep did create a new legal mortgage of his premises but incorrectly used the s. 85 LRA 1925 method (the grant of a lease), the effect would be that the s. 85 mortgage will be transformed into a charge by deed by way of legal mortgage (the s. 87 form) once it is registered.

24.4.4.2 Registration not triggered

All of this produces a constant movement towards all estates being registered and all legal mortgages of those estates becoming legal charges. However, even in future, there will still be cases in which registration is not triggered. Notably, these include the creation of a second legal mortgage of unregistered land and the creation of an equitable mortgage of unregistered land. Equitable charges of registered land are, of course, also possible but unlike legal charges are not protected by registration of the charge itself. We will look at this in more detail once we have considered how equitable mortgages and charges can arise.

24.5 Equitable mortgages

24.5.1 Contract to create a mortgage

Under the principle that 'Equity regards as done that which ought to be done', a contract to create a legal mortgage will be regarded as giving rise to an equitable mortgage from the date of the contract. Of course, due to s. 2 of the Law of Property (Miscellaneous

Provisions) Act 1989, the contract itself must be made in writing. Reliance on the equitable rule is also dependent upon the contract being one which the courts would enforce by an order for specific performance (*Tebb v Hodge* (1869) LR 5 CP 73). A defective legal mortgage (e.g., one which has been signed but not witnessed) will be similarly treated, as long as specific performance is available. This is similar to the rule for defective leases (see *Walsh v Lonsdale* (1882) 21 ChD 9 and Chapter 10). However, specific performance will not be available in any of these cases unless the mortgage money has actually been advanced, for traditionally equity has declined to force someone to make a loan. In such cases, the mortgagor could fall back on his common law remedy of damages.

24.5.2 Informal mortgage by deposit of deeds

In the past, the willingness of equity to recognise and protect any transaction in which it was clear that an estate owner had intended to charge his property with the repayment of a loan meant that many informal arrangements were regarded as equitable mortgages because equity regarded what had taken place as evidence of a contract to grant a mortgage. The classic example of the protection afforded by equity arose where an estate owner deposited his land certificate (when these were issued) or title deeds with the lender in return for the loan. This was recognised as creating an equitable mortgage of the property in *Russel v Russel* (1783) 1 Bro CC 269, and continued in modern law under the saving provisions of LPA 1925, s. 13. For this type of mortgage, until 1989, no written record of any kind was necessary, for the deposit of title deeds was regarded not only as constituting the contract to make the mortgage, but also as amounting to part performance for the purposes of LPA 1925, s. 40(2). Moreover, the deposit and receipt of the deeds were regarded as part performance by each party respectively, so whichever side wished to rely on the doctrine might do so. Despite this, however, a written record was desirable in order to provide clear evidence of the nature of the transaction. These mortgages were convenient and cheap where a short-term loan was envisaged.

24.5.2.1 Need for writing

The law relating to these informal mortgages was, however, changed by the Law of Property (Miscellaneous Provisions) Act 1989, s. 2, because that provision relates to:

> A contract for the sale or other disposition of an interest in land...

Accordingly, for an equitable mortgage to be enforceable it is now necessary to show that the agreement was made in writing. It will not do merely to have a later deed which states that the agreement exists (as was previously common practice) because that deed would merely purport to record an existing contract which would not satisfy s. 2, and accordingly would not amount to a contract at all. This effect of s. 2 (which may well have been unforeseen) was confirmed by the Court of Appeal in *United Bank of Kuwait plc v Sahib* [1997] Ch 107. This prevents the creation of the most informal old type of mortgage, in which deposit of deeds was used without anything more being done. Therefore, Nigel Neep's bank will be wise to insist that his mortgage is, at least, made by a written agreement which satisfies s. 2. If a mortgage is ineffective due to s. 2, the loan will become immediately repayable because the security has failed. However, old informal mortgages created before the 1989 Act are not affected by s. 2 and thus a few may still exist.

The one exception to this rule will be cases in which one of the parties (probably the intended mortgagee) can rely on the doctrine of constructive trust, as happened in

Kinane v Mackie-Conteh [2005] EWCA Civ 45 (see 5.5.3.1 for a more detailed consideration of this case). However, it would appear that commercial lenders, like banks and building societies, will not normally be able to rely on this doctrine because of the need for belief in the existence of a mortgage relationship, because such organisations will be clear as to the need for a written contract compliant with s. 2.

24.5.3 Equitable charge

An equitable charge arises when a chargee 'appropriates' specific property to the repayment of a sum of money in such circumstances that a legal charge does not arise. This type of arrangement is rare and would normally require a written document. For an old example see *Matthews v Goodday* (1861) 31 LJ Ch 282.

24.5.4 Equitable mortgage of an equitable interest

One obviously cannot grant a legal mortgage of an interest that is recognised only in equity. This rule dates from the days of separate courts with separate jurisdictions. Common law did not recognise the equitable interests developed in the Chancellor's courts, and accordingly would not enforce any dealings with them. Therefore, any mortgage of an equitable interest in land had to be equitable in character. The method of creating such mortgages was not changed in 1925 and thus they continue to be made in the old-fashioned way by a transfer of the entire interest to the mortgagee, subject to an agreement that it will be returned to the mortgagor on repayment of the loan. The transfer must be made, at the least, by writing, in order to pass the equitable interest to the mortgagee under LPA 1925, s. 53(1)(c). (Note that this is a transfer and not an agreement to transfer.) Normally thereafter, the mortgagee should give notice of the transfer to the trustees of the trust under which the interest exists—usually the legal owners (see 24.13.2).

24.6 Rights of the mortgagor

Having examined the methods of creating a mortgage we must turn our attention to the position of the parties after a mortgage has been made. We will look first at the rights of the mortgagor (the borrower).

24.6.1 Right to redeem

The primary right enjoyed by the mortgagor is the right to redeem the mortgage on repayment of the loan and payment of any interest provided for by the charge. This brings the mortgage to an end.

24.6.1.1 Right to redeem at law

At law the right to redeem is a matter of contract: the mortgagor can redeem on the date or dates and in the manner provided for in the mortgage. Thus, should the agreement provide that the mortgage should be redeemed on a particular date, the mortgagor has, at law, a right to redeem on that date only. The legal rules do not allow him to insist on redeeming the mortgage either before or after the contractual date: see the discussion in *Kreglinger v New Patagonia Meat & Cold Storage Co. Ltd* [1914] AC 25 at p. 35. At common law, if he did not pay on the contractual date, the mortgagor at one time forfeited the land to the mortgagee and could still be sued in contract for the repayment of the debt. Accordingly the legal right to redeem was, and is, very limited.

24.6.1.2 Right to redeem in equity

Fortunately, equity took a very different view of the situation, particularly as there were examples of mortgagees hiding, so that it became impossible for the mortgagor to repay on the contractual date. Equity took the view that, as long as the advance and any interest was paid, the mortgagee should not be able to object to redemption because the purpose of the agreement was merely to provide the mortgagee with security for the loan. Originally equity intervened only in cases of fraud by the mortgagee but soon came to recognise a general right to redeem in all cases (*Salt v Marquess of Northampton* [1892] AC 1). Thus, equity allows the mortgagor to redeem even after the date fixed by the mortgage agreement for repayment has passed. Of course, since this right is enforceable in equity only, it is subject to the general principle that equitable remedies are discretionary in nature and all the equitable maxims (particularly the 'clean hands' doctrine) will apply. Furthermore, in deciding whether redemption is possible, equity will look at the substance of the agreement, not its form. Accordingly, a mortgage which is drafted to look like an outright transfer of the property, rather than the creation of an interest by way of security, will still be subject to the equitable right to redeem, if the facts are such as to indicate that only a grant by way of security was intended (*Darby v Read* (1675) Rep t Finch 226).

24.6.1.3 Instalment mortgages

So far, we have spoken as though the full sum owed becomes payable on one date. The modern mortgage is more likely to provide for repayment by instalments, spread over a number of years. However, it usually will contain a provision that if the mortgagor defaults on the payment of one instalment the whole sum will become due. In law, the mortgagor will then have to redeem the mortgage or lose his property for ever, but equity will moderate the rigour of this in the way already described.

24.6.2 The equity of redemption

Obviously a legal mortgagor retains his legal estate in the land but subject to the rights of the mortgagee (see 24.7). In equity the mortgagor is described as owning the 'equity of redemption'. This must be distinguished from the equitable right to redeem which is mentioned above. The equity of redemption is the mortgagor's equitable interest in the property and it consists of the sum total of the mortgagor's rights in relation to the land (including the right to redeem). The equity of redemption is therefore an interest in land (*Pawlett v Attorney-General* (1667) Hardres 465, at p. 469) and can be dealt with like any other equitable interest.

24.6.3 No clogs on the equity of redemption

Equity is so protective of the mortgagor's equity of redemption that it will not tolerate any arrangement which either prevents or deters the mortgagor from exercising his right to redeem. Similarly, any burdens imposed by the mortgage on the mortgaged property that may continue after the date of redemption are generally regarded with disfavour. They derogate from the principle that the mortgage should provide security only, and that on redemption the mortgagor should recover the property without further fetter. In restricting the contents of mortgage agreements in this way, equity recognised the fact that the mortgagor is often unable to dictate the terms of the mortgage because of his need for the mortgage advance. It was therefore appropriate that the mortgagor should be afforded some protection by the courts. However, in some cases this approach has been taken to undesirable lengths.

Equity's approach is summed up in the rule that there must be no clogs (restrictions) on the equity of redemption. This is applied to a number of situations, some of which we must now consider.

24.6.3.1 **Prevention of redemption**

Any provision in a mortgage which would operate to prevent the mortgagor from redeeming will be disregarded by equity and will be void. Thus a mortgagee cannot include in a mortgage a term that, should a specified event occur, the land would become his absolutely (*Toomes v Conset* (1745) 3 Atk 261).

This rule has, however, been taken to extremes, so that it is not possible to give a mortgagee a valid option to purchase the estate as part of the mortgage transaction. The option, if exercised, would extinguish the mortgagor's right to redeem and is accordingly void. The original rationale for this rule was sound. As Lord Henley put it in *Vernon v Bethall* (1762) 2 Eden 110 at p. 113:

> there is great reason and justice in this rule, for necessitous men are not, truly speaking, free men, but to answer a present exigency will submit to any terms that the crafty may impose upon them.

However, in *Samuel v Jarrah Timber & Wood Paving Co. Ltd* [1904] AC 323 the House of Lords applied (albeit reluctantly) the same rule to an 'arm's-length' commercial transaction. Lord Linley referred to the old axiom, 'Once a mortgage always a mortgage' (meaning that the agreement could not covertly become something greater), and said (at p. 329):

> The doctrine... means that no contract between a mortgagor and a mortgagee made at the time of the mortgage and as part of the mortgage transaction, or, in other words, as one of the terms of the loan, can be valid if it prevents the mortgagor from getting back his property on paying off what is due on his security. Any bargain which has that effect is invalid, and is inconsistent with the transaction being a mortgage.

It was suggested that granting the option in a separate document might avoid the rule, but it seems that even this may not avail the mortgagee, unless the option is granted some time after the mortgage (this gives the mortgagor a chance to refuse an unfair agreement once he has received his loan): *Lewis v Frank Love Ltd* [1961] 1 WLR 261; but see also *Reeve v Lisle* [1902] AC 461 in which an option was upheld. The issue of whether a transaction made later could be acceptable was further considered by the Court of Appeal in *Jones v Morgan* [2002] 1 EGLR 125 and, in the particular circumstances of that case, a later transaction was nonetheless held to be a clog on the equity of redemption and thus invalid, probably because a transaction carried out three years after the initial creation of the mortgage amounted to a complete reconstruction of the debt arrangements, rather than being a separate transaction. The judgment of Chadwick LJ usefully provides a short history of the doctrine (see paras. 50–73). However, the case is perhaps chiefly notable for the acerbic comment of Lord Phillips MR that, '... the doctrine of a clog on the equity of redemption is, so it seems to me, an appendix to our law which no longer serves a useful purpose and would be better excised' (para. 86).

24.6.3.2 Postponement of redemption

Any provision in a mortgage that attempts to postpone redemption to such an extent that the right to redeem becomes illusory may also be rendered void. The equitable right to redeem arises only once the contractual, legal date for redemption has passed. There is no general right in equity to redeem earlier (but see the Consumer Credit Act 1974, ss. 94 and 173, for rare cases of small mortgages which may be redeemed at any time and, if the mortgagor is a consumer, the Unfair Terms in Consumer Contracts Regulations may also assist). Accordingly, one way by which a mortgagee may try to obtain an irredeemable mortgage is to postpone the contractual date for redemption.

1. *Freehold cases*

In *Knightsbridge Estates Trust Ltd v Byrne* [1939] Ch 441 a company had mortgaged its freehold property to an insurance company on terms that the mortgage would be repaid over 40 years. Later the mortgagor wished to redeem the mortgage before that period had expired, but the mortgagee objected. The court held that the term postponing redemption for 40 years was valid. The agreement was a commercial one made by businessmen and the mortgaged property was a fee simple. Due to the great duration of the freehold estate (effectively it is perpetual), the company would recover an estate of equivalent worth when it did redeem the mortgage. The effect of this case is not, however, to make any postponement for a similar period valid. Were a domestic mortgage to be made irredeemable for such a long period, the court might still regard the bargain as oppressive and unconscionable. In fact most modern domestic mortgages expressly allow for early redemption, usually on payment of an extra sum.

2. *Leasehold cases*

Postponement of the date of redemption is rather more serious when one is concerned with a mortgage of leasehold property, because a lease is inherently of finite duration and therefore a wasting asset. In *Fairclough v Swan Brewery Co. Ltd* [1912] AC 565 the residue of a leasehold term of 20 years was mortgaged; the agreement being that the mortgage was not to be redeemed until a date six weeks before the lease was to end. Three years later the mortgagor sought to redeem early and the court upheld his right to do so. In this case, had the postponement been valid, the mortgagor would, on redemption, have recovered an estate which was nearly valueless and very different in character from the property mortgaged. Accordingly, in the case of leases, postponement of the contractual date for redemption is likely to be rather more objectionable, even where the mortgage is a commercial bargain made between businessmen.

24.6.3.3 Collateral advantages for the mortgagee

The final type of clog on the equity of redemption that is commonly encountered is the creation of further advantages for the mortgagee, which are collateral to the mortgage. These are common in certain types of commercial mortgage. Thus, breweries will often advance money on mortgage to the licensees of public houses, provided that the mortgagors agree that they will buy their beer from the mortgagee-brewery. Similar arrangements are made between petrol companies and garage owners (on this see the discussion in relation to similar provisions in leases at 11.2.2.3).

Such collateral advantages, if they are not unconscionable or contrary to competition law, are valid whilst the mortgage continues (*Biggs v Hoddinott* [1898] 2 Ch 307). They will not, however, normally endure once the mortgage is redeemed (even if the mortgagor has accepted a term that they shall continue beyond redemption), for otherwise the mortgagor would recover an estate encumbered in a way the estate mortgaged was not (see also *Bradley v Carritt* [1903] AC 253). An advantage will not, however, invariably end once the mortgage is redeemed. In *Kreglinger v New Patagonia Meat & Cold Storage Co. Ltd* [1914] AC 25 a meat company mortgaged its property to a wool-broker (the mortgage was in the form of a floating charge, a special type of mortgage granted by companies). It was a term of the mortgage that the mortgagor would, for five years, offer its sheepskins (a by-product of its meat business) to the mortgagees for purchase. The mortgage was redeemed after two years but the House of Lords held that the mortgagor was obliged to continue to offer the mortgagees first refusal on the skins for the full five-year period. The option was regarded as being reasonable in its terms (it was for a short period and at the best price) and was to be regarded as a separate agreement not really forming part of the mortgage. It was also, of course, a commercial transaction which had been agreed to by businessmen with 'open eyes'. It seems unlikely that such a collateral advantage could validly continue after redemption of a domestic mortgage.

Collateral advantages may also be held to be invalid, even during the continuance of the mortgage, if they are unconscionable or oppressive. Thus in *Cityland & Property (Holdings) Ltd v Dabrah* [1968] Ch 166 an agreement which imposed an extremely high premium, rather than requiring payment of interest, was rewritten by the court. In this case the mortgagor was allowed to redeem on repayment of the loan together with interest at a rate approved by the court. It is not, however, sufficient to show that the terms are unreasonable (certainly in a commercial bargain), even if they are extremely advantageous to the mortgagee. The agreement must be 'unfair and unconscionable' and imposed by the mortgagee 'in a morally reprehensible manner, that is to say, in a way which affects his conscience' (see *Multiservice Bookbinding Ltd v Marden* [1979] Ch 84, p. 110 per Browne-Wilkinson J).

The issue is not, however, confined to commercial mortgages and charges. The extension of the range of services provided by lenders has led to concerns that mortgagors may be forced into agreements which require them to use a prospective mortgagee to provide, for example, removal vans or estate agency services. The mortgagor might be told that unless he took such other items from the mortgagee the rate of interest on his mortgage would be higher. This problem was addressed by the Courts and Legal Services Act 1990, ss. 104–107 ('tying-in provisions'). These provisions have never been brought into force, but could be were 'tying-in' to become common. Another approach some mortgagees have adopted is to apply unduly heavy rates of interest imposed if the mortgagor is ever late in making payment. The Office of Fair Trading has issued guidance to banks and building societies as to the rates of interest that properly can be charged to those who are 'locked into' mortgages (usually by means of high charges made on early repayment of the mortgage). Institutions that lend on mortgage security are also regulated by the Financial Services Authority, under the Financial Services and Markets Act 2002 (see Sch. 2, paras. 23 and 23A).

24.6.4 Right to grant leases

Having already granted a lease or sublease (or being in a similar position in the case of a charge by way of legal mortgage), the mortgagor would be unable, on general principles, to grant further leases of the same property which could bind himself and his mortgagee. Any further lease he did create would operate as a lease of the reversion, and would not give the tenant any right to possession of the land which he could assert against the mortgagee. However, this caused difficulty, particularly in the case of large estates, where the mortgagor remained in possession of the land and continued to manage it, needing to grant new leases to, for example, tenant farmers and estate workers. The mortgagor is therefore given a statutory power by LPA 1925, s. 99: where he is still in possession of the land he may create both leases and contracts for leases which will be binding on the mortgagee. Section 99 sets out a number of detailed requirements for the form and content of such leases, but we do not propose to consider them here, for in practice most mortgages will exclude the mortgagor's statutory power of leasing altogether, unless the mortgage is security for a business loan designed to allow the acquisition of a property for the purpose of letting it. This is because, in general, the mortgagee does not want the land to be burdened with a sitting tenant, for this will reduce its value if the mortgagee needs to realise his security (obviously different arrangements are made for the management of large estates and in commercial cases where the plan is to let the property).

The statutory power of leasing will almost certainly be excluded in any domestic mortgage, such as that of the Armstrongs at 1 Trant Way, though mortgagees do sometimes agree to waive this exclusion in the case of approved tenants. Interestingly, in *Citibank International plc v Kessler* (1999) EGCS 40 a mortgagor tried to argue that such an exclusion was contrary to Article 48 of the Treaty of Rome as inhibiting the free movement of workers. However, unsurprisingly this claim failed even in that instance, in which a German worker had returned to Germany and could not sell the house in question because it had structural defects that would prevent anyone else obtaining a mortgage on the property.

Should the right to grant leases be excluded, any lease granted will nonetheless bind the mortgagor and tenant (a lease by estoppel) but will be void as regards the mortgagee and his successors (*Iron Trades Employers Insurance Association Ltd v Union Land & House Investors Ltd* [1937] Ch 313). In *Starling v Lloyds TSB Bank plc* [2000] 2 EGLR 101, a mortgagor tried to argue that, where permission to lease had been sought, the mortgagee should be under a duty to consider that request properly. However, this claim was dealt with robustly by the Court of Appeal, who struck out the cause of action because there was no suggestion in the papers that the mortgagee had acted dishonestly or due to any improper motive. The court regarded as impractical the argument that the bank should, on receiving such a request, indulge in a balancing exercise between the interests of the mortgagor and the bank's interests.

24.6.4.1 Surrenders

The mortgagor has power under LPA 1925, s. 100, to accept surrenders of leases as well. This may be done, however, only in order to replace the surrendered lease with a fresh lease and the new lease must be made within one month of the termination of the old.

24.6.5 Right to sue

In some cases the rights of the mortgagor to sue in relation to the land might be hampered by the fact that his estate is subject to the rights of the mortgagee. Any such problems are remedied by LPA 1925, s. 98, which allows a mortgagor in possession, who has not been notified that the mortgagee intends to take possession, to sue in a number of situations in which there might otherwise be difficulties. Generally, therefore, the mortgagor is free to bring any necessary action in relation to the land.

24.7 Rights of the mortgagee

24.7.1 Rights to title deeds or charge certificate

24.7.1.1 Unregistered land

Under the pre-1926 type of mortgage the mortgagee (the lender) necessarily had a right to hold the title deeds to the property, since the grant of the mortgage conveyed the legal estate to the mortgagee. Under the modern system, however, the mortgagee at most has only a lease or sublease and it is not normal for a tenant to hold his landlord's deeds. It is nonetheless desirable for the mortgagee to take any deeds, since this will usually prevent the creation by the mortgagor of later interests in the same property without the knowledge of the mortgagee (see 24.12). Accordingly, ss. 85(1) and 86(1) specifically provide that a first mortgagee has the right to take the title deeds from the mortgagor. A mortgagee under a charge by way of legal mortgage is expressly given similar rights (s. 87(1)). LPA 1925, s. 96(1), gives the mortgagor the right to inspect the deeds and make copies, as long as this is done at a reasonable time and any costs incurred by the mortgagee are paid.

The equitable mortgagee has a similar equitable right to the deeds but, since the most common form of equitable mortgage was that which involved deposit of the deeds, this was rarely a problem.

24.7.1.2 Registered land

In the case of registered land a legal charge is created only when the charge is substantively registered. Section 27(2)(f), LRA 2002, provides that the grant of a legal charge is a disposition that is required to be completed by registration. On the application being made, the registrar will enter the chargee in the register as the proprietor of the charge. Before the 2002 Act, such a registration would then have led the registrar to issue a new certificate in relation to the charged estate: a Charge Certificate. This was held by the chargee (rather like holding the title deeds of unregistered land). Now, however, such certificates are no longer issued, though you may still encounter old ones. All that matters is the content of the register itself.

24.7.2 Right to possession of the land

Since a legal mortgagee has a lease or sublease (or is treated as though he had) he has a right to possession of the land from the moment that the mortgage is created (see *Four-Maids Ltd v Dudley Marshall (Properties) Ltd* [1957] Ch 317 at p. 320 and *National Westminster Bank plc v Skelton* [1993] 1 WLR 72). This right may well be restricted by a term in the mortgage deed that possession will not be taken whilst the mortgagor makes regular payments (see, e.g., *Birmingham Citizens Permanent Building Society v Caunt* [1962] Ch 883).

Usually, the taking of possession is only normal as a preliminary to the remedy of sale and is not otherwise generally exercised. However, at some points in recent years, it became more common for lenders to seek possession of a property in order to let it. This may cause problems for a mortgagor because the interest under the mortgage will continue to mount. In *Palk v Mortgage Services Funding plc* [1993] Ch 330, the Court of Appeal said that where sale was preferable in the mortgagor's interests a sale would be ordered instead (see further 24.8.1.1, on foreclosure, for the court's power to order sale). The taking of possession must, in any event, be exercised peaceably (e.g., one may not break into premises) and this may necessitate an application to the court. However, if peaceable re-entry is possible without resort to the court this is perfectly acceptable (see *Ropaigealach v Barclays Bank plc* [1999] 1 QB 263 but note that the case proceeded on the assumption that the bank had taken possession peacefully but without those facts ever being established). In practice it may be difficult or impossible to regain possession peacefully in the absence of an application to the court. Where it is possible, it will be attractive to the mortgagee because it is a means of avoiding the protection available to the mortgagor when a court order for possession is sought (see 24.8.1.5). See also 13.3.1 for a discussion of potential human rights issues in relation to peaceable re-entry.

24.7.3 Insuring at the mortgagor's expense

Normally, the mortgagee will wish to ensure that the property is properly insured, since should it be damaged the value of the mortgagee's security will be diminished. Accordingly, most mortgages include express terms concerning the maintenance of insurance. If there is no express agreement, LPA 1925, s. 101(1)(ii), implies into every mortgage made by deed a term allowing the mortgagee to insure the property against loss or damage by fire. The premiums paid become a charge on the property in addition to the mortgage advance. The amount of the insurance and the mode of application of any sums arising from the policy are further regulated by LPA 1925, s. 108.

24.7.4 Right to lease

A mortgagee who has taken possession has always had a right to grant leases. These, however, would be subject to the rule that there must be no clog on the equity of redemption and so would not survive redemption by the mortgagor, were it not for the statutory power to lease under LPA 1925, s. 99(1), which gives rights similar to those of the mortgagor described above. Any lease created under the statutory power will also bind the mortgagor. Since possession by the mortgagee was normally only a preliminary to sale, such leases used to be rare but have occurred on occasion in recent years.

24.7.5 Right to tack further advances

This right is relevant only when there is a dispute about priorities, and so we will consider it in the section on priorities (24.16).

24.7.6 Right to consolidate mortgages

This right applies when one mortgagee has vested in him two or more mortgages which were both made by the same mortgagor. This might occur if Henry Harding (2 Trant Way) had already granted a mortgage of, say, his business premises at 15 High Street, Mousehole to the Wensleydale Bank plc. The Bank would have the right to consolidate the two mortgages if, as is normal, this is expressly provided for in the mortgage (LPA 1925, s. 93).

The effect of the right is to allow the mortgagee to refuse to allow the mortgagor to redeem one of the mortgages without also redeeming the other. In the case of Mr Harding's mortgages, this right might prove important to the bank should the value of 15 High Street fall below the sums outstanding on the mortgage of that property. If Mr Harding chose to redeem the mortgage on 2 Trant Way, rather than the mortgage of his business premises, the mortgagee bank would be left with a mortgage for which the security is defective. By consolidating, the bank can insist that Mr Harding redeems both mortgages.

The right to consolidate is an equitable one, and is an unusual example of equity permitting a clog or fetter on the equity of redemption. It may be seen as the 'price' which equity exacts for allowing the mortgagor to redeem the mortgage when he could no longer do so at law. Accordingly, the mortgagee has this right only after the contractual date for redemption has passed, when the mortgagor is relying on his equitable right to redeem. If the mortgagor should in fact repay the debt on the contractual date, the mortgagee would not be able to require him to pay off the other debt as well.

The doctrine can affect subsequent purchasers if they buy land subject to the mortgage. Thus, if someone bought 2 Trant Way from Mr Harding subject to the mortgage and then sought to redeem it, he or she would find that the bank's right to consolidate still applied, and that the mortgage on 15 High Street would also have to be redeemed. Fortunately, it is extremely rare for estates to change hands without any mortgages first being discharged.

We have tried to give a relatively simple account of the doctrine of consolidation, illustrating it with a situation in which both mortgages are granted to the same mortgagee. This is not in fact an essential requirement: provided the mortgages are granted by the same person it does not matter that they are granted to different people. The rules governing the various different situations which may arise as a result of this are complicated, and beyond the scope of this book, but if you are interested you will find them fully discussed in Megarry and Wade, paras. 25–055–25–069.

24.8 Mortgagee's remedies

The whole purpose of a mortgage is to provide security which the mortgagee can realise if the mortgagor fails to repay the loan. Obviously the mortgagee, like any lender, can always sue in contract for the repayment of the loan, but this may be a long process in which enforcing payment, even once judgment is obtained, can be difficult. The advantage of the mortgage is that it allows the mortgagee to use the charged land to repay the loan, sometimes without the need for any court proceedings at all. At one time the special remedies available to a mortgagee were of such importance that it was rare in the extreme for mortgagees to bother to sue for repayment as a simple matter of contract. However, fluctuations in property prices have made it more common, in appropriate cases, for mortgagees to seek a money judgment (since in cases of 'negative equity' the price realised by enforcement against the property will not repay the loan in full) or to use this remedy in addition to the special remedies available to a mortgagee. Despite this change, the additional protection provided by the security of a charge on property still makes mortgagees' remedies of crucial importance.

24.8.1 Remedies available to a legal mortgagee

24.8.1.1 Foreclosure

Foreclosure was the traditional remedy by which a mortgage was enforced. However, today it is rarely used.

Although equity would allow a mortgagor to redeem after the contractual date, there would come a time in many cases when it was obvious that the mortgagor would never have the means to repay the debt. Foreclosure proceedings in equity were therefore the means whereby 'the court simply removed the stop it had itself put on' (*Carter v Wake* (1877) 4 ChD 605 at p. 606) and enabled the mortgagee to realise his security. For this reason foreclosure cannot be sought before the contractual obligation to repay has been broken (*Williams v Morgan* [1906] 1 Ch 804). A court order is required for foreclosure (*Re Farnol Eades Irvine & Co. Ltd* [1915] 1 Ch 22) and its effect is to vest the mortgagor's estate in the mortgagee in full settlement of the debt (LPA 1925, ss. 88(2) and 89(2)).

Should the property be worth more than the debt, the mortgagee is not liable to pay the balance in value to the mortgagor. Since this is normally the case, foreclosure is a remedy which is often unfair to the mortgagor (and to any subsequent mortgagees, who lose their security). Accordingly, on hearing an application for foreclosure, the court will give the mortgagor a period in which he can redeem the mortgage (and will allow later mortgagees the chance to protect their security by redeeming the prior mortgage).

Generally, the mortgagor is in financial difficulties and is unable to repay the loan and redeem. Accordingly he is given the right to ask for an order for sale instead of foreclosure (LPA 1925, s. 91(2)). This is an advantage because on sale the mortgagee may keep only the portion of the proceeds that represents the debt, plus interest and costs. The balance must be returned to the mortgagor, or paid to anyone else entitled, such as later mortgagees. Sale may also be appropriate in any case in which it produces a better financial result for the mortgagor (see *Palk v Mortgage Services Funding plc* [1993] Ch 330).

Another reason foreclosure is an unpopular remedy (but this time from the mortgagee's point of view) is that even once a foreclosure order has been made the court may reopen the whole situation and allow the mortgagor to redeem the property after all. *Campbell v Holyland* (1877) 7 ChD 166 (in which an order for foreclosure was reopened three months after it had been made absolute) sets out the various matters which the court will take into account in considering such an application. These include: the speed of the mortgagor's application; his reasons for failing to redeem before foreclosure; and the nature of the property.

As might be expected, the court would be less willing to reopen foreclosure if the mortgagee had already sold the property to someone else, although even in that case this is, in theory, still possible.

24.8.1.2 Possession and sale

We have already discussed the basic rules relating to possession. Generally this right of the mortgagee is only used as a remedy and normally is a prelude to sale. The mortgagee might, however, take possession so that he can repay his debt from the income produced by the premises (e.g., if the premises are let to a tenant). However, in such cases it is more common to appoint a receiver instead so that, as we shall see below, the mortgagee is not personally liable for any mismanagement of the land. The chief purpose of taking possession is therefore to ensure that on a subsequent sale the mortgagee will be in a position to give vacant possession to the purchaser. The power for the mortgagee to sell the land is implied into every mortgage made by deed by LPA 1925, s. 101(1)(i). This power arises when the mortgage money has become due (for instance, on the contractual date of redemption) but does not become exercisable until one of the conditions prescribed by LPA 1925, s. 103, has been met. These are that:

(a) a notice requiring payment has been served on the mortgagor and the default has continued for three months thereafter; or

(b) some of the interest payable is at least two months in arrear; or

(c) there has been breach of a covenant in the mortgage deed (other than that relating to the payment of money) or of some provision of the LPA 1925.

A purchaser must satisfy himself that there is power to sell under the mortgage (that is, that it was made by deed and that the power has arisen), but he does not have to check that one of the conditions for exercise of the power ((a) to (c) above) has been met (see *Bailey v Barnes* [1894] 1 Ch 25 at p. 35).

Sale has the advantage over foreclosure that it is generally not necessary to apply for a court order. The sale may be negotiated in any suitable manner (e.g., by auction or by private contract) and may be made subject to such conditions as the mortgagee sees fit (s. 101(1)(i)). As we shall see, the mortgagee may be liable to the mortgagor, and others, for any loss caused through his negligence in conducting the sale.

However, an order for possession (as a prelude to sale) may be delayed for a time if the court believes that the mortgagor may obtain a higher price if he sells himself. (See *Target Home Loans Ltd v Clothier* [1994] 1 All ER 439.)

This possibility was also explored in *Palk v Mortgage Services Funding plc* [1993] Ch 330 and in *Barrett v Halifax Building Society* (1995) 28 HLR 634, and in these cases the courts seemed to take a generous approach to the use of the power under LPA 1925, s. 91(2) to direct sale of the property 'on such terms as it thinks fit', in order (for example) in the *Barrett* case to enable the mortgagor to carry out the sale himself. The reasoning was that the mortgagor is likely to get a better price for the property than the mortgagee (in practice this is almost inevitably the case). However, this approach was criticised in *Cheltenham & Gloucester plc v Krausz* [1997] 1 All ER 21, in which the Court of Appeal said that these powers and those under the Administration of Justice Act 1970, s. 36 (see 24.8.1.5) should not be used unless it is clear that the result will be that the mortgage debt will be repaid in full. Where the mortgagor is still faced by a debt greater than the value of the property (a 'negative equity' in common parlance) the mortgagee will still be entitled to immediate possession and sale. (See also Kenny, 'No Postponement of the Evil Day' [1998] Conv 223.)

When considering the possibility of sale, you should also bear in mind that where the land in question is held under a trust of land (which will be the case in all co-owned property which is not the subject of a SLA 1925 settlement) the mortgagee can also apply for sale under TOLATA 1996, s. 14, because the mortgagee has an interest in the property subject to the trust. For an example of this (in which sale was ordered despite the existence of a pre-existing overriding interest) see *Bank of Baroda v Dhillon* [1998] 1 FLR 524. However, in the cases since TOLATA 1996 the courts have expressed differing views as to the weight to be given to the interests of the mortgagee when carrying out the balancing exercise under ss. 14 and 15. See the cases discussed at 17.8.5.1.

It is worth noting when reading these cases that the mortgagee's remedies are cumulative and that, as a last resort, the mortgagee can also sue for repayment of the debt and (if necessary) make the mortgagor bankrupt. Due to the interaction of the various different legal principles and rules, such as s. 36 of the Administration of Justice Act 1970, the effects of TOLATA 1996, the possibility of undue influence (on which see 24.17.2 below) and the law of insolvency (which allows the trustee in bankruptcy to obtain a charge over the bankrupt's home—see s. 313, Insolvency Act 1986 and s. 261, Enterprise Act 2002), the law in this area is complex. A wise mortgagee takes great care before deciding on the exact approach to the issue in any case that is not entirely straightforward and most certainly in any case in which the sale of the property is unlikely to repay all the sums due under the mortgage.

24.8.1.3 **Effect of sale**

On sale, the mortgagee will convey to the purchaser a good estate or interest (for example, the fee simple) free of the interests of the mortgagor and of any estates, interests or rights to which the mortgage has priority, but subject to any estates or interests having priority to the mortgage (LPA 1925, s. 104(1)). Thus, if 1 Trant Way were subject to two mortgages:

(a) to the Double Gloucester Building Society; and
(b) to the Mousehole Bank plc

then on a sale by the DGBS the purchaser would take a title free of the second mortgage to the MB plc, but on a sale by the MB plc the purchaser would take an estate subject to the first mortgage to the DGBS.

It is perhaps worth emphasising that on sale the purchaser obtains the full estate belonging to the mortgagor, not just the long lease or sublease which was granted to the mortgagee (LPA 1925, ss. 88(1) and 89(1)).

As the purchaser takes the estate free of the mortgage, he or she can obtain an order for possession against the mortgagor, if the mortgagor is still in occupation. This became important in *Horsham Properties Group Ltd v Clark* [2009] 1 WLR 1255. Here the mortgagees appointed a receiver, who sold the property relying on a clause in the mortgage document but without obtaining possession. The purchaser then sought possession against the mortgagor, claiming that the mortgagor's rights had been overridden by the sale. The mortgagor claimed that the sale, whether under s. 101 or the terms of the agreement, conflicted with its rights under Art. 1 of Protocol I of the European Convention on Human Rights and the Human Rights Act because there had been no court order and thus no due process of law. The High Court rejected this view, saying that possession by the mortgagor is always contractually at the mercy of the mortgagee, who has a right to possession due to the leasehold estate or equivalent rights granted to the mortgagee by the mortgage. The judge also took the view that the deprivation of possession after default was in the public interest and proportionate, resting as it did on 200 years of history. Accordingly, the mortgage and s. 101 were ECHR compliant. This case confirms the approach in *Ropaigealach v Barclays Bank plc* [2000] QB 271–2, in which (before the HRA) it was accepted that no order for sale is needed (in that case re-entry had, it seems, been effected peaceably without a court order).

Despite this authority (which would always allow sale without a court order), the Association of Mortgage Lenders has agreed that their members will always seek a court order for possession or sale in the case of a domestic mortgage. The Ministry of Justice has proposed that the law should be changed in order to require a court order before sale (whether an order for possession or for sale) in the case of all residential owner-occupier mortgages. This is perhaps desirable because the Horsham case illustrates how little protection a mortgagee currently has. However, legislating may prove difficult, as it will be necessary to define what constitutes a residential owner-occupier mortgage. For example, what if another member of the family is living in the property? On the proposed reforms see the Ministry of Justice Consultation paper: *Mortgages. Power of Sale and Residential Property*, CP 55/09. The consultation has closed but, at the time of writing, no further announcement has been made.

24.8.1.4 **Disposition of proceeds of sale**

The selling mortgagee becomes a trustee of the proceeds of sale of the property (LPA 1925, s. 105), and should apply the proceeds in the following order:

(a) in payment of any sums needed to discharge any encumbrance prior to the mortgage and to which the sale was not made subject;

(b) in payment of the costs, charges and expenses properly incurred in arranging the sale;

(c) in discharge of the mortgage debt, including interest and other sums due; and

(d) any balance should be paid to the mortgagor or the other person 'entitled to the mortgage property'.

Thus, in the example given in 24.8.1.3, were the DGBS to sell 1 Trant Way, it would first pay the costs of sale (e.g., legal expenses), and then would pay its own mortgage debt, interest and costs. Thereafter, the balance of the proceeds of sale should be paid to the MB plc, which at the time of sale was next entitled to the property (*British General Insurance Co. Ltd v Attorney-General* (1945) 12 LJNCCR 113). The MB plc will in turn become trustee, and after repaying itself, should (if anything remains) pass the balance of the proceeds of sale to the mortgagors.

Should the sale not realise sufficient funds to repay the mortgagee, it may still sue in contract for the balance of the debt (*Rudge v Richens* (1873) LR 8 CP 358). Since the property itself may well have been the mortgagor's only valuable asset, it may prove difficult to obtain satisfaction of any judgment but in recent years there have been cases in which mortgagors voluntarily 'handed back' their property to permit sale by the mortgagee but were then sued some years later for sums not recovered on sale. Recent examples of this are to be found in *Bristol and West v Bartlett* [2003] 1 WLR 284, *Scottish Equitable plc v Thompson* [2003] HLR 48 and *West Bromwich Building Society v Wilkinson* [2005] 1 WLR 2303, which establish that any such action is subject to a 12-year limitation period. See also the article by Griffiths at [2005] Conv 469 on the complications in such actions.

24.8.1.5 Protection for the mortgagor

There are circumstances in which it would be unfair for the mortgagee to be allowed to sell the property. Thus, if the mortgage interest is only a few months in arrears and the mortgagor can show that he will be in a position to pay his debts very shortly it would be undesirable to allow the mortgagee to insist on sale. Accordingly the following means of protection is provided for the mortgagor.

As we have seen, the first step towards sale is usually for the mortgagee to obtain possession. The mortgagee may not do this by means of any force (e.g., by breaking a window) since this would constitute a criminal offence (Criminal Law Act 1977, ss. 5 and 6). Normally, therefore, an application to the court for possession will have to be made. This in itself will give the mortgagor extra time to pay and the court has inherent jurisdiction to postpone possession, although this power will be exercised sparingly (see *Cheltenham & Gloucester plc v Krausz* [1997] 1 All ER 21).

If the land is or includes a dwelling-house, further protection is given to the mortgagor by the Administration of Justice Act 1970, s. 36. Under this provision the court may, on hearing an application for possession of a dwelling, adjourn the proceedings, stay or suspend judgment or postpone the date for delivery of possession, if it appears that 'the mortgagor is likely to be able within a reasonable period to pay any sums due under the mortgage'. This permits the court to give the mortgagor a 'second chance' to pay but will not be exercised where the mortgagor cannot make payments which will clear the debt within a reasonable time (whilst continuing to pay current instalments: see *First National Bank plc v Syed* [1991] 2 All ER 250).

As originally drafted, these provisions proved unsatisfactory when dealing with instalment mortgages, in which it is normal to provide that should one instalment be unpaid the whole sum becomes due. If the mortgagor has to pay 'any sums due' in such a case this would include the whole advance and few mortgagors could comply with this requirement (see *Birmingham Citizens Permanent Building Society v Caunt* [1962] Ch 883). Accordingly, an amendment was introduced by the Administration of Justice Act 1973, s. 8, and now in the case of instalment mortgages the 'sums due' are only those payments which are in arrear and a clause requiring repayment of the whole loan can be disregarded by the court when exercising its discretion under s. 36 of the 1970 Act. The 1973 Act also extends the powers of the court to foreclosure actions even where possession is not also sought: s. 8(3). However, if peaceable re-entry can be effected without the need for an order for possession (if, for example a dwelling is standing empty), s. 36 does not come into play: *Ropaigealach v Barclays Bank plc* [1999] 1 QB 263. Nor will s. 36 help if sale takes place while the mortgagor remains in occupation. In such a case the mortgagor's rights are overridden and the purchaser can obtain an order for possession: *Horsham Properties Group Ltd v Clark* [2009] 1 WLR (this was a commercial mortgage but the principle remains the same).

The court's powers under s. 36, Administration of Justice Act 1970, are also not available if the mortgagor has voluntarily given up possession but later realises that it would be in his or her best interests to delay sale. This is illustrated by *Barclays Bank plc v Alcorn* [2002] All ER (D) 146, in which the court said that in such a case it had no jurisdiction to exercise its discretion under s. 36(2). The case was also one in which, even had the court had powers under s. 36(2) it would not, on the facts, have exercised those powers in favour of the mortgagor because the mortgagor had failed to establish that she would be likely to pay the debts within a reasonable time.

The question of what is a 'reasonable period' to allow the mortgagor is a matter which is determined in the light of the circumstances of each case: see *National and Provincial Building Society v Lloyd* [1996] 1 All ER 630. In the case of a domestic instalment mortgage, the Court of Appeal indicated in *Cheltenham and Gloucester Building Society v Norgan* [1996] 1 WLR 343 that it would, in assessing what was a reasonable period, be appropriate for a court to take as its starting point the whole of the outstanding term of the mortgage. Indeed that is an arrangement which had often been proposed voluntarily by mortgagees, where arrears were not too great.

At one time it was thought that the mortgagee owed no duty to the mortgagor when exercising the power of sale (other than the duty not to act fraudulently). However, it is now clear that the courts do consider in such cases that the mortgagee is under a duty to 'obtain a proper price'. This is a duty that arises in equity rather than in contract but is analogous to a duty of care in negligence (see *Raja v Lloyds TSB Bank plc* (2001) Lloyds Rep Bank 113). For this reason, a mortgagee may elect to appoint a receiver rather than sell itself because then the duty of care will fall on the receiver, provided that the appointment itself is not unreasonable. (See para. 24.10 for more on the duties of receivers and mortgagees.)

24.8.1.6 **Protection for tenants of the mortgagor**

In the past, an order for possession granted against a mortgagor could produce a real problem for a tenant of the mortgagor, if the lease had been granted in breach of the terms of the mortgage. In such a case, the mortgagor's tenant could be obliged to leave the property immediately and without prior notice of the risks. Losing any rights to the property without any warning was obviously of grave concern to the tenant, who could be rendered homeless 'at a minute's notice'. Limited reforms of this position have now been made by the Mortgage Repossessions (Protection of Tenants, etc) Act 2010. The new rights apply only to leases of a dwelling-house. The Act requires service of a notice, in every case, before the mortgagee or chargee seeks to enforce an order for possession of such premises, whether or not there is a tenancy. This prevents the lender arguing that no notice was served because it did not know of the tenancy. The tenant may then apply to the court, which may postpone execution of the possession order for a period not exceeding two months. This is hardly generous but will allow a tenant unauthorised by the mortgagee a little time to find alternative accommodation.

24.8.1.7 Power to appoint a receiver

A receiver is a person who is appointed to take charge of the mortgaged land and either manage it (in order to produce an income to repay the debt) or sell it. Receivers are not commonly appointed in respect of mortgages of domestic property but are very frequently used in commercial mortgages.

The power to appoint a receiver may be granted expressly by the mortgage but in addition, provided the mortgage is created by deed, the right to appoint will be implied by LPA 1925, s. 101(1)(iii). The power arises and becomes exercisable in exactly the same way as the statutory power of sale.

The receiver is appointed by a written document executed by the mortgagee (LPA 1925, s. 109). The receiver appointed under the power in LPA 1925, s. 101, becomes an agent of the mortgagor (and not of the mortgagee who appointed him) and thus the mortgagee will not be liable for any negligence of the receiver (but see 24.10). Where a receiver obtains income from the land he should apply it in the following order:

(a) in payment of any outgoings in respect of the land (e.g., rates, and instalments on mortgages which have priority to that under which he was appointed);

(b) in payment of insurance premiums in respect of the land and his own commission (fees);

(c) in payment of interest on the loan;

(d) in payment of capital, if the mortgagee agrees; and

(e) payment of any balance should be made to the mortgagor (or other person entitled to income).

24.8.2 Problems regarding remedies when the mortgage is equitable

In describing the remedies available to the mortgagee we have, so far, concentrated on the position of the legal mortgagee. It is, however, important to note that in a number of ways an equitable mortgagee may not be in such a strong position. In several instances he may, in the end, obtain the same remedy as a legal mortgagee, but he will often do this only after the trouble and expense of obtaining a court order, whereas the legal mortgagee may often make use of such remedies without applying to the court. It must also be remembered that, in any event, remedies given by the court in protection of an equitable mortgagee will always be discretionary in character because of the basic nature of the equitable jurisdiction.

We will now consider each remedy in turn.

24.8.2.1 Foreclosure

This causes little difficulty since it requires a court order in any event and being an equitable remedy applies to equitable mortgages just as it does to legal ones.

24.8.2.2 Possession

There appears to be no reason why an equitable mortgagee should not be regarded as having a right to possession in equity. It has, however, been said that the equitable mortgagee has no such right (see *Barclays Bank Ltd v Bird* [1954] Ch 274 at p. 280). By contrast, other authorities suggest that he may be so entitled (see *Ex parte Bignold* (1834) 4 Deac & Ch 259 and the article by Wade (1955) 71 LQR 204 and the decisions discussed in it).

The weight of academic opinion certainly seems to be that an equitable mortgagee does have the right to possession (see Megarry and Wade, para. 25-046–25-048).

It should be noted that the issue under discussion here is whether an equitable mortgagee has the right to take possession without a court order, for it is certainly possible for him to do so on an order from the court (*Barclays Bank Ltd v Bird*). These days, few mortgagees would risk taking possession without a court order, even when they are entitled to do so and so the whole question, although interesting, does seem largely a theoretical one.

Finally, it seems to be the case that a chargee under an equitable charge will have no right to possession, since he cannot be regarded as having a contract for a lease or sublease, as can other equitable mortgagees (*Garfitt v Allen* (1887) 37 ChD 48). However, even this might be questioned if the equitable charge is regarded as a contract to create a charge by deed by way of legal mortgage, under which the chargee certainly does have a claim to possession.

24.8.2.3 Sale

The statutory power of sale under LPA 1925, s. 101(1)(i), applies only to mortgages made by deed, and therefore an equitable mortgagee will have no automatic power of sale unless he can rely on such a deed. In consequence, an equitable mortgagee normally required execution by the mortgagor of a memorandum under seal evidencing the transaction, which would be sufficient to satisfy the statutory requirements. Today it is more likely that such a mortgage will be made by deed (at which point one might as well opt for a legal charge).

Even if the mortgagee has obtained such a deed he may still experience problems, since it has been held that he is not able to convey the legal estate because he has only an equitable interest in the property (*Re Hodson and Howes's Contract* (1887) 35 ChD 668). Although this view may be supported by the principle that no one can give more than he has, the same argument might appear to apply to the legal mortgagee, who has only a lease but is enabled by statute to convey the full estate (LPA 1925, ss. 88(1) and 89(1)). It is difficult to see why the equitable mortgagee, selling in exercise of the statutory power, cannot rely on these provisions in the same way, and in *Re White Rose Cottage* [1965] Ch 940 Lord Denning MR expressed the view that there was no reason why he should not be able to convey the legal estate (at p. 951).

In order to avoid any difficulties, it has become usual to include in the deed a declaration of trust or grant of a power of attorney. Either will confer a separate power of sale.

However, these issues were recently considered further in *Swift 1st Ltd v Colin* [2012] 2 WLR 186. In this case a charge of a registered estate was made by deed by way of legal mortgage in favour of the claimant but the charge was not registered. It was, however, entered in the register as an equitable charge. There were two subsequent charges. Later, the claimant exercised the power of sale under s. 101 but the Land Registry declined to register the purchasers as proprietors because the claimant's charge was not registered. The court held that the claimant did have the power of sale under ss. 101 and 104, and sale extinguished the subsequent charges by virtue of s. 88. The court held that the lack of registration made no difference in the case of a charge by deed by way of legal mortgage. Furthermore, the court was of the view that, even had the charge only been equitable due to lack of registration, the power to sell and convey the legal estate would still be available.

In the case of an equitable mortgage created without the formality of a deed the mortgagee may still apply to the court for an order for sale under LPA 1925, s. 91(2).

24.8.2.4 Appointing a receiver

The statutory power to appoint a receiver under LPA 1925, s. 101(1)(iii), applies only to equitable mortgages which are made by deed. However, any equitable mortgagee may apply to the court for the appointment of a receiver (Supreme Court Act 1981, s. 37).

24.8.3 Disadvantages of equitable mortgages

From what we have said above, it can be seen that a mortgagee who accepts an equitable mortgage not made by deed may find the remedies available to him less satisfactory than those of a legal mortgagee. To some extent, although not entirely, these disadvantages may be overcome by the use of a deed.

Given the need for a deed to enable the equitable mortgagee to take advantage of the statutory remedies, a lender may regard it as being altogether easier to create a charge by way of legal mortgage (using a deed), and thereby avoid all the problems. In the case of the planned mortgage by deposit of deeds by Mr Neep of 12 Trant Way, his bank manager may well feel, on consideration, that, following the decision in *United Bank of Kuwait plc v Sahib* [1997] Ch 107, the best course as far as the bank is concerned will be to insist on taking a legal charge, rather than adopting a more informal method of creating a mortgage: writing will now be necessary to create an equitable mortgage and very little more effort is required to produce a deed. The bank is most unlikely to be able to rely on the doctrine of constructive trust (see *Kinane v Mackie-Conteh* [2005] EWCA Civ 45) because it will be aware of the requirements of s. 2 of the Law of Property (Miscellaneous Provisions) Act 1989, and thus will know that it is essential to make the mortgage in the prescribed manner. However, the grant of a legal charge will trigger a requirement to register the fee simple: s. 4(1)(g), LRA 2002. Accordingly, Mr Neep may be able to persuade the bank to accept an equitable mortgage made by means of a written contract.

24.9 Right of certain third parties to redeem

The mortgagor and the mortgagee are not the only people who may have rights in respect of a mortgage, for others may be entitled to exercise the right to redeem. This arises because any person who has a right in the equity of redemption is also allowed to redeem (of course by repaying the sums secured by the mortgage) (*Peace v Morris* (1869) LR 5 Ch App 227). Thus, if Henry Mumps manages to establish that he has an interest in 6 Trant Way, he will be entitled to redeem any mortgage of the property should he choose to do so. A spouse who has a right to occupy the matrimonial home has also been held to have a sufficient interest in the equity to allow him to redeem under this rule (*Hastings & Thanet Building Society v Goddard* [1970] 1 WLR 1544). This rule is expressly recognised in the case of married couples and civil partners by the Family Law Act 1996, s. 30(3), in favour of a spouse or civil partner with a right to occupy a dwelling.

24.9.1 Subsequent mortgagees

A second or later mortgagee is also a person who has an interest in the equity of redemption and he may also claim to redeem a superior mortgage. This reference to 'later' and 'superior' mortgages brings us to the notion of priorities, which we must briefly explain. Where there are several mortgages of the same property, those mortgages are ranked in order, with the mortgagees being entitled to receive the money owed to them according to their place in that ranking. Thus, if the property is not worth the full amount of the debts secured on it, those ranking first take their money in full and those coming later may receive nothing. The rules which determine the order of priorities will be explained later but for the moment it is enough to know that mortgages are ranked in this way.

Where a later mortgagee wishes to redeem an earlier mortgage and this can be arranged by agreement, there is no difficulty. It may be, however, that the earlier mortgagee refuses to accept payment, either because there is a dispute about what is owed or because he is relying on his right to consolidate. In this case, the person wishing to redeem will have to seek a court order, and in doing this will find that he is subject to the rule that he should 'Redeem up and foreclose down'. This is best explained by reference to the following illustration.

24.9.2 Redeem up, foreclose down

Assume that land is subject to mortgages in favour of different lenders, A, B, C, D and E, the mortgages ranking for priority in that order. If D wishes to redeem the mortgage to B by court action, he is obliged to redeem also the intervening mortgage to C (redeem up). He does not have to redeem A's mortgage which simply keeps its priority. He is also required to bring foreclosure proceedings, which will extinguish the rights of E and the mortgagor. This apparently harsh provision comes about because B will be required to account for any payments he has already received and show what is still owed to him. The later mortgagees and the mortgagor are all interested in this, because if D redeems B's mortgage he will take over B's position, and be entitled to recover that amount of money from the value of the property in priority to all those who rank after B. They must be made parties to the action between D and B, so that they can protect their own interests and be bound by the court's decision about the amount owed to B. However, it was felt to be unreasonable to put all these people to the expense of coming to court simply to watch the proceedings, and therefore the rule developed that, while they were there, their claims on the property must be dealt with as well. Therefore, as well as redeeming B's mortgage, D must take the opportunity to quantify and pay off the debts due to any intervening mortgagees (here, C), and must also take foreclosure proceedings to vest the property in himself, free from the rights of later mortgagees (here E) and the mortgagor. Of course, if E or the mortgagor can pay off the debt owed to D, one or other of them can prevent his foreclosing. If neither of them has the resources to do that, it may be worth their while asking the court to order sale instead of foreclosure in the hope that sale will produce enough money to pay off all the earlier mortgages and still leave enough for E and the mortgagor.

24.10 Liability of mortgagees, receivers and valuers for fraud or negligence

As we have seen, a mortgagee has extensive powers to enter the property and to dispose of it. Alternatively, he will often choose to appoint a receiver to take charge of the property and conduct any disposition. Inevitably, over the years the issue has arisen as to what liability the mortgagee or receiver has to the mortgagor, should the property be mismanaged or should the sale price be lower than expected. In some instances, the question of the liability of a valuer employed by the mortgagee or receiver has also arisen and whether a mortgagee or receiver who has innocently relied on a negligent valuation is liable to the mortgagor for any loss. The slump in the property market in the 1990s led to many cases in which sale of a property either did not repay the entire debt or realised far less than the mortgagee had expected. Unsurprisingly therefore, there have been a number of important developments in the law in this area in recent history.

The leading case is now the Court of Appeal decision in *Silven Properties v Royal Bank of Scotland plc* [2004] 1 WLR 997, in which in giving judgment Lightman J summarised nearly all the case law on this issue. The case involved 34 properties owned by two family property companies, all of which had been charged to the bank to secure extensive borrowing by the companies. In 1996 the total debt was nearly £5 million and the bank in that year appointed receivers in relation to all the properties, which were then sold over an 18-month period. The mortgagors complained that many of the properties were sold at an undervalue, though by the time of the appeal the issue was restricted to complaints in relation to only six of the sales, in relation to which the complaints were that—

(1) in some cases, a far better price would have been obtained had the receivers or mortgagees first obtained planning permission for development (initially permission had been sought but the receivers later decided to sell without waiting for it to be granted); and
(2) in other cases, a better price would have been obtained had possible leases of vacant property been completed before sale.

In some instances the properties were sold by the receivers and in some cases by the mortgagees. Thus, helpfully, in giving judgment the court considered the duties of both. We will now look at each in turn.

24.10.1 The duties of mortgagees

24.10.1.1 Mortgagee can elect not to exercise powers

In Silven Lightman J first restated the basic principle that a mortgagee is under no obligation to exercise any of his powers: 'He is entitled to remain totally passive.' Thus, the mortgagee cannot be forced to take possession or sell, even if the mortgagor would benefit were this to happen.

24.10.1.2 Mortgagee in possession must take reasonable care of premises

If, however, the mortgagee chooses to take possession of the property, he becomes its manager and thereby assumes a duty to take reasonable care of the premises: on this see *Downsview Nominees Ltd v First City Corporation Ltd* (No. 1) [1993] AC 295 at p. 315A. See also the older cases, *White v City of London Brewery Co* (1889) 42 ChD 237 and *Hughes v Williams* (1806) 12 Ves Jr 493, which show that this concept is far from new.

24.10.1.3 Mortgagee is not a trustee of his powers

Secondly, Lightman J reiterated the time-honoured expression 'A mortgagee is not a trustee of the power of sale for the mortgagor' (which also applies to the mortgagee's other powers). This means that the mortgagee may sell when he chooses and may select the time of sale without regard to whether a different time may be more beneficial to the mortgagor: see *Raja v Austin Gray (a firm)* [2002] EWCA Civ 1965 (which also contains a useful summary of the basic rules), *China & South Sea Bank Ltd v Tan Soon Gin* [1990] 1 AC 536 and *Tse Kwong Lam v Wong Chit Sen* [1983] 1 WLR 1349 at p. 1355B. This principle can be traced back at least as far as *Nash v Eads* (1880) 25 Sol J 95 and *Warner v Jacob* (1882) 20 ChD 220, but note that these older cases proceeded on the basis that a mortgagee could only be liable for fraud (see also, for example, on the older approach, *Davey v Durrant* (1857) 1 De G&J 535). In *Silven*, Lightman J. expressly rejected the suggestions made (*obiter dicta*) by Lord Denning MR in *Standard Chartered Bank Ltd v Walker* [1982] 1 WLR 1410 at pp. 1415G–H and 1416A that there might nonetheless be some restriction on the mortgagee, such as not being able to elect to sell at the worst possible time.

In *Meretz Investments NV v ACP Ltd* [2007] Ch 197, in a case in which it was alleged that a mortgagee had a range of motives for selling, including some that might be improper, Lewison J was called upon to consider what the implications were (if any) in a case in which the mortgagee might have had both valid and invalid reasons to wish to sell. After considering a number of earlier decisions (including *Nash v Eads*) he concluded that even where there are several motives for sale, as long as one reason is to enforce the security given by the mortgage, the sale is lawful, even if the mortgagee also had other motives. This, once again, underlines the strength of the right of a mortgagee to rely upon and enforce the security. The case, while a heavy read, is worth looking at, if only because it demonstrates how complex some modern property cases can be. It also provides a useful analysis of the case law in this area. A more detailed note about the case can be found in the Online Resource Centre, at W.24.1. Lewison J's reasoning is not affected by the subsequent appeal case (see [2008] 2 WLR 904).

24.10.1.4 The mortgagee may sell the property as it is

Thirdly, in relation to the claims that the mortgagees should have taken steps to improve the position before selling, Lightman J said, 'The mortgagee is entitled to sell the mortgaged property as it is. He is under no obligation to improve it or to increase its value.' While accepting that there was a duty to preserve the property (see the first point above) the Court of Appeal in *Silven* declined to extend this to a duty to *improve*, whether by obtaining planning permission, granting leases or in any other way. The mortgagee is free to take such steps if he so chooses but is not even obliged to continue with any steps that he has started to take.

You may wonder what protection the mortgagor has. Lightman J indicated that should the mortgagor wish to impose any such obligations on the mortgagee he should do so when entering into the mortgage or charge as part of its terms. This is, save in commercial transactions and perhaps not even there, likely to be impossible because the lender is likely to be in the position of dictating the terms of the agreement to the borrower. Thus, except in rare cases, this possibility is theoretical rather than practical. Lightman J also says that it is open to the mortgagor to redeem the mortgage, should he feel himself at risk if the mortgagee exercises his rights. Since the issue is only likely to arise in a case in which the mortgagor is already unable to make repayments on the mortgage, once again this is an option that is not likely to be a real one.

24.10.1.5 Duty to obtain market value

However, the mortgagee is not without any duties because, fourthly, the decision in *Silven* confirms that when he does sell, the mortgagee is under a duty in equity to take reasonable precautions to obtain the 'fair' or 'true market value' or 'proper price' for the property at the date of sale. In the conduct of the sale, the mortgagee must not unduly rush the transaction or sell at a low price that will simply cover the mortgage debt: *Palk v Mortgage Services Funding plc* [1993] Ch 330 at pp. 337–8. Lightman J says in *Silven*: 'He must take proper care, whether by fairly and properly exposing the property to the market or otherwise, to obtain the best price reasonably obtainable at the date of sale.'

In the circumstances in *Silven* this would include taking reasonable care to obtain any extra value that would arise as a consequence of drawing the attention of prospective purchasers to the possibility of obtaining planning permission or granting the leases that were under negotiation, but that is the full extent of the duty.

In *Standard Chartered Bank Ltd v Walker* Lord Denning MR seemed to suggest that this was a duty in negligence. The same approach was taken in the modern case that really started the concept of the possibility of liability in negligence for certain matters other than choice of time of sale: *Cuckmere Brick Co v Mutual Finance Ltd* [1971] Ch 949 at p. 969G. In that case the property had the benefit of one planning permission for houses and a second (an alternative scheme) for flats. Subsequently, there was a problem with meeting mortgage payments and the mortgagee moved to sell. The property was widely advertised but the adverts failed to mention that there was planning permission for flats. The mortgagor asked for the sale to be delayed and better details advertised but the mortgagees went ahead with the sale. The property realised £44,000, although the mortgagor had a valuation saying that with permission for flats it was worth £75,000. When the matter came before the Court of Appeal it was held that, while a mortgagee was not a trustee of the power of sale for the mortgagor and, where there was a conflict of interests, he was entitled to give preference to his own over those of the mortgagor (notably in deciding on the timing of the sale), when exercising the power of sale the mortgagee was not merely under a duty to act in good faith but also to take reasonable care to obtain whatever was the true market value of the mortgaged property at the moment he chose to sell it. This was a clarification of the law at the time and the decision appears to be based on the concept of liability in negligence, although a curtailed liability due to the nature of the mortgagee's rights. However, the most recent cases have clearly said that this approach is incorrect and the liability is not in tort for negligence but arises from a duty in equity. Thus, the correct remedy is not damages for negligence but that the mortgagee account to the mortgagor for the sums that would have been raised had the mortgagee complied with his duty. Also, it is a duty owed not just to the mortgagor but also to anyone who has an interest in the equity of redemption. This includes a later mortgagee or indeed a later acquirer of the estate, who takes subject to the mortgage (see *Freeguard v Royal Bank of Scotland plc*, [2002] EWHC 2509).

24.10.2 The duties of receivers

It is normal for a mortgagee to ensure that any receiver who is appointed is appointed as an agent of the mortgagor. This enables the receiver to manage or sell in the capacity of agent but avoids the mortgagee becoming liable for any fault on the part of the receiver (unless the mortgagee 'inter-meddles' with the receiver's actions in some way). However, the supposed agency relationship has over the years given rise to a suggestion that the duties of the receiver to the mortgagor may differ from those owed by a mortgagee who elects to act in person. This issue was also discussed in *Silven*, in which it was argued that as agent of the mortgagors the receiver should have acted in their interests when selling.

24.10.2.1 Duty of receiver same as that of mortgagee when selling

In *Silven* the Court of Appeal confirmed the long line of cases that establish that a receiver when selling property owes the same equitable duty to obtain the market value as does a mortgagee. On this point see also the Court of Appeal decision in *Medforth v Blake* [2000] Ch 86.

24.10.2.2 Receiver may not be passive

Since the receiver is appointed to manage or sell, he or she is under a duty not to remain passive, if to do so would be damaging to the mortgagor or anyone else interested in the equity of redemption. The receiver must be active in the protection and preservation of the property.

24.10.2.3 Otherwise duties are the same as those of a mortgagee

In *Silven* the Court of Appeal recognised that, while the receiver may, due to the terms of appointment, be an agent, the agency in question is very unusual in form. The main differences are:

(1) the mortgagor does not appoint the receiver and cannot give instructions to or remove the receiver;
(2) there is no contractual relationship and no duty in tort between mortgagor and receiver but only a relationship in equity;
(3) the receiver also owes a duty to the mortgagee and thus the relationship is tripartite;
(4) the duty owed to the mortgagor is in fact a duty to the whole class of persons who have an interest in the equity of redemption;
(5) the receiver's primary responsibility is to produce a situation in which the mortgage debt is repaid, rather than just to manage the property; and
(6) really the receiver is managing the security that is the property of the mortgagee for the mortgagee's benefit (in *Silven* this is regarded as a separate point but really seems to be an element of point (5)).

After reviewing all the case law, and considering a very influential article by the then Peter Millet QC in which he pointed out that the so-called agency was not really a true agency (see *The Conveyancing Powers of Receivers After Liquidation* (1977) 41 Conv (NS) 83 at p. 88), Lightman J concluded that the duties of receivers in respect of the exercise of the power of sale were the same as those of mortgagees. Accordingly, in *Silven* the receivers were not liable for not having obtained planning permission or granted leases prior to sale.

24.10.3 Setting aside sale in cases of fraud

While the remedies of a mortgagor are restricted in cases of negligence, the position is very much better where a sale of property is conducted fraudulently. In such a case the sale can normally be set aside, allowing a further sale to take place in a proper manner: see *Farrar v Farrars Ltd* (1888) 40 ChD 395. However, it is frequently difficult to establish fraud and, as we have seen above, a mere sale at an undervalue will not suffice, since it may arise simply due to negligence or the choice of the time of sale. Furthermore, not even the existence of some deception coupled with a sale at an undervalue will necessarily suffice. In *Corbett v Halifax Building Society* [2003] 1 WLR 964, a sale to the uncle of an employee of the Society at an undervalue and subsequent sub-sale to the employee, in breach of the terms of his employment, did not suffice to allow the transactions to be set aside. In this case the mortgagor was left to his remedy in damages.

24.10.4 Valuers

One of the ways in which both mortgagees and receivers endeavour to ensure that they comply with the duty to sell for the market value is to ensure that they take an independent valuation of the property before selling. It had been assumed that provided that reliance had been placed in a competent, qualified valuer the receiver or mortgagee would have done all that was necessary. However, the Court of Appeal decision in *Raja v Austin Gray* (a firm) [2002] EWCA Civ 1965 demonstrates that this is not the case, essentially because the liability of either receiver or mortgagee is not in the tort of negligence but is an equitable duty.

24.11 The end of a mortgage

24.11.1 Formalities

Obviously, apart from a termination by use of one of the remedies set out above, a mortgage normally ends when the mortgagor repays his debt. At that point any estate granted to the mortgagee will terminate automatically (cesser on redemption). However, the mortgagor will require evidence that he has repaid the mortgage sums, so that future purchasers can be assured that the land is free of any encumbrance.

In the case of registered land, the aim will be to remove the registered charge from the register, so that it is clear that the title has been freed of the charge. The procedure is governed by rr. 114 and 115 of the Land Registration Rules 2003 and the accompanying forms (which include an acknowledgement by the lender that the property is no longer charged as security for the repayment of sums due under the registered charge). The registrar will on receipt of the appropriate documents then exercise his wide power under Sch. 4, para. 5, LRA 2002, to bring the register up to date by removing the entry relating to the registered charge.

In unregistered land the necessary evidence of discharge is provided by asking the mortgagee to execute a memorandum of discharge, which is usually endorsed on the back of the mortgage deed itself.

24.11.2 Passage of time

Ashe v National Westminster Bank plc [2008] 1 WLR 710 is a reminder that a mortgage can also be brought to an end by prolonged inaction on the part of the mortgagee. In this case the mortgagee bank had made a formal demand for the money in June 1992, but took no further steps to enforce its security and matters dragged on for some 14 years, during which time the mortgagor continued to live in the mortgaged house. The bank regarded the mortgage as continuing throughout this period and wrote to the mortgagor on several occasions reminding him that it would require full repayment when the property was eventually sold.

In 1993 the mortgagor had been declared bankrupt and all his property, including the right to redeem the mortgage, vested in his trustee in bankruptcy. The mortgaged property was the debtor's only asset; if it had not been subject to the mortgage it could have been sold by the trustee in bankruptcy and the proceeds applied towards paying debts owed to other creditors. In the case before the court the trustee therefore sought a declaration that the mortgage over the property had been extinguished by the provisions of the Limitation Act 1980.

As we explain in Chapter 8, the Limitation Act 1980 provides that rights of action are extinguished after prescribed periods, and a 12-year period is specified for actions to recover possession of land (s. 15) and to recover money secured by a mortgage (s. 20). In the case before the court, the mortgagor had made no mortgage payments for over 12 years and also had done nothing to acknowledge the mortgagee's rights under the mortgage. The bank claimed that the limitation provision did not apply here, because the mortgagor had been allowed to remain in possession of the property with the bank's permission; he was therefore not in 'adverse possession' (see 8.2.2) and time did not run against the bank.

The Court of Appeal held that the mortgagors' rights to possession accrued, in the case of this mortgage, as soon as the mortgage was granted. Failure to require repayment meant that the contractual right to the sums due under the mortgage were time barred. Further, the court held that despite the fact that occupation of the premises by the mortgagors was within the intention of the mortgagees and arose from the mortgagors' legal title to the property, it was nonetheless 'adverse possession' due to the particular wording of para. 3 of Part I of Sch. 1 to the Limitation Act 1980. Therefore, more than 12 years having passed, the mortgagee could not enforce its right to possession of the premises. Time would stop running and the limitation period would begin again if the mortgagor made any payment after the money became due or acknowledged the mortgage in some way (i.e., acknowledged his indebtedness and legal liability to pay—per Kerr J in *Surrendra Overseas Ltd v Government of Sri Lanka* [1997] 1 WLR 565, at 575 (see ss. 29 and 30 of the 1980 Act)).

However in *Ashe* there had been no payment and no acknowledgement. Accordingly the Court of Appeal held that the bank's right to take possession of the property was statute-barred and that the mortgage itself was extinguished by s. 17 of the Limitation Act, which provides that:

> ...at the expiration of the period prescribed by this Act for any person to bring an action to recover land...the title of that person to the land shall be extinguished.

Accordingly, in such a case the mortgagor could apply to the Land Registrar to have any registered charge removed from the register.

24.12 Priorities

Often, when a person is asked to lend money on the security of a mortgage, or when he later comes to enforce that mortgage, he will discover that there are a number of people who have interests in the property. When Mildred's bank is considering her request for a loan secured by a mortgage of 8 Trant Way, it will have to take into account the claims of: (a) the first mortgagee, the Red Leicester Building Society (see 24.2); (b) Laura Lymeswold's lease/licence (see Chapter 22); and (c) Henry Mumps' possible rights arising from contribution (see Chapter 22). The bank will be concerned with these other rights, because it wants to be sure that if Mildred fails to repay the loan it will be able to sell the property (or exercise its other remedies) without any difficulty, and that the proceeds of sale will be sufficient to repay the debt. The bank therefore will need to consider the following issues.

- The amount of the loan secured by the first mortgage. If the property was sold, and the debt to RLBS discharged first, would there be enough left to repay the bank?

- The nature of Laura's interest. If she has a lease, this would decrease the value of the property, because a purchaser is unlikely to pay as much for a house with a sitting tenant as he would for one with vacant possession. If Laura has a licence enforceable against third parties, this would, of course, decrease the value of the property in the same way.
- Whether Henry Mumps has any rights arising from contribution, such as an irrevocable licence or an interest under a resulting or constructive trust. Either of these might give him a right to remain in the property, which would effectively prevent sale; and if he had an interest under a trust, the bank might find that the mortgage attached only to Mildred's share of the beneficial interest.

The existence of other interests in the property is therefore of considerable importance to mortgagees. The mortgagee needs to know which interests he can largely ignore because they are postponed to his rights, and which interests he must take into account because they have priority to his mortgage.

The rules on priorities are in the main merely a practical application of the rules on the enforceability of legal and equitable interests against third parties, which we discussed in Chapters 6 and 7. However, these rules might appear rather confusing when applied to mortgages, because there are so many rules and there seem to be so many different situations to consider. In fact, if you can work out which situation is presented by the facts before you, you should find that applying the relevant rule is not too difficult.

24.12.1 Start with chronological order

We suggest that when dealing with a question of priorities, you begin by arranging the competing mortgages in chronological order, that is, according to their date of creation. The final order of priorities may be very different from this, but it at least provides a starting-point and a basis from which to apply the rules. Having done that, we think you will find it helpful to ask yourself a series of questions, in a prescribed order, which we work through in the following pages, and which are set out in Figures 24.2–24.5. Figure 24.5 provides a diagrammatic representation of the rules as a whole but you will find greater detail in the separate Figures 24.2–24.4, which contain elements of Figure 24.5.

24.12.2 Application to other interests

In what follows, we usually refer to competing *mortgages*, but in general the same principles will apply where questions of priority arise between a mortgage or charge and any other interest (such as that of a purchaser of the fee simple).

24.12.3 What has been mortgaged?

Begin by asking yourself:

> What is the nature of the property which is subject to the mortgage: is this a mortgage of the legal estate or of an equitable interest (such as a beneficiary's interest under a trust)?

We will deal with mortgages of the equitable interest straight away, because the rules can be stated relatively shortly, and we can then concentrate for the rest of the chapter on mortgages of the legal estate.

24.13 Priorities of mortgages of an equitable interest

24.13.1 Where the equities are equal

We have already seen that any dealing with an equitable interest must itself be equitable, so we are concerned here only with successive equitable mortgages. Where there is a competition between equitable interests, the general rule is expressed in the maxim: 'Where the equities are equal, the first in time prevails'.

Therefore the interests will rank chronologically, according to the date of creation, provided each mortgagee has, in equity's view, acted fairly in regard to those who come after him.

24.13.2 The rule in *Dearle v Hall*

However, where the property which is mortgaged consists of a beneficial interest under a trust, questions of priorities are regulated by special rules.

Competing assignments of the beneficial interest are regulated by the rule in *Dearle v Hall* (1823) 3 Russ 1, as applied to trusts of land by LPA 1925, s. 137. This rule applies to all successive assignments of the beneficial interest, and provides that priority of competing assignments (which include mortgages) depends on the order in which notice of the assignments is received by the trustees. Therefore, in the following situation:

(a) mortgage to A,

(b) mortgage to B,

(c) B gives notice,

(d) A gives notice,

B would normally gain priority over A. However, since one is dealing with the equitable jurisdiction, B is not allowed to gain priority by giving notice first if he knew of the existence of A's mortgage when the second mortgage was created, for to allow this would be patently unfair. Thus, only a second mortgagee without notice can improve his priority under the rule (*Re Holmes* (1885) 29 ChD 786). If B had no notice at the date when his mortgage was created, but learned of A's mortgage before giving notice, B may still obtain priority by giving notice first (*Mutual Life Assurance Society v Langley* (1886) 32 ChD 460). It is important to note that the crucial time for the operation of the rule is the date at which the trustee receives the notice, rather than the time at which notice is given. Accordingly, a mortgagee who posted a notice through the trustee's letter-box one evening, was held not to have given notice until the following day when the notice was opened and read (*Calisher v Forbes* (1871) LR 7 Ch App 109).

When giving notice under *Dearle v Hall* the assignee of the equitable interest should take care to give notice to the correct persons. Usually the trustees to be served will be the persons, or person, in whom the legal estate is vested. However, in the case of land which is settled under the SLA 1925, notice should be given to the trustees of the settlement and not to the tenant for life, in whom the estate is vested. Great care should be taken to give notice to all the trustees, whatever the type of trust. If this is done, the notice is effective for priority purposes even if later those trustees who received the notice retire, or die in office, and leave their successors without any knowledge of the notice which was given (*Re Wasdale* [1899] 1 Ch 163). However, if, where there are several trustees, notice is given to one only, that notice becomes invalid when that trustee retires or dies, unless that trustee had told the others that he had received notice

(*Timson v Ramsbottom* (1836) 2 Keen 35, but see also *Ward v Duncombe* [1893] AC 369). If giving notice proves unduly difficult or expensive a 'purchaser' (this includes a mortgagee) can require that a memorandum be endorsed on the document which created the trust and under LPA 1925, s. 137(4); this is effective in place of giving notice to the trustees.

LPA 1925, s. 137(3) provides that, 'A notice, otherwise than in writing,...shall not affect the priority of competing claims of purchasers in that equitable interest'. The meaning of this provision is not entirely clear: it may mean that all notices for the purpose of *Dearle v Hall* must since 1925 be in writing, or it may be that an oral notice is sufficient to maintain an assignee's existing chronological priority, although inadequate to give him priority over an earlier assignee.

Where the subject matter of the trust was registered land, the priority of assignments of the beneficial interest used to depend upon the order in which the assignments were entered in a special index called the Index of Minor Interests (LRA 1925, s. 102(2)). Relatively little use was made of the Index and therefore it was abolished by LRA 1986, s. 5: from that time the rule in *Dearle v Hall* has applied to interests in both registered and unregistered land.

The principles for mortgages of an equitable interest are summarised in Figure 24.2.

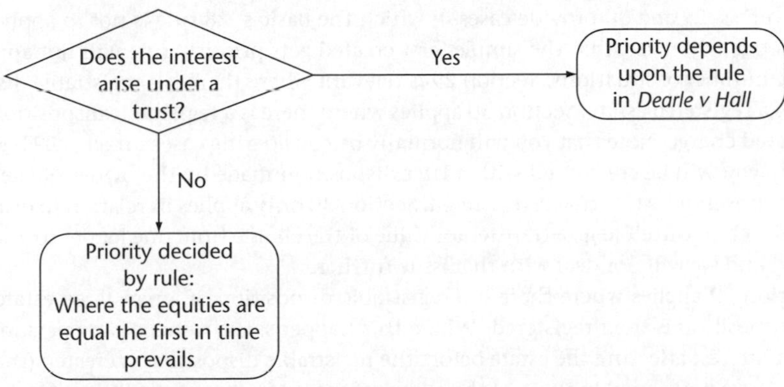

Figure 24.2 Priorities of mortages of an equitable interest

24.14 Priorities of mortgages of the legal estate

Where it is the legal estate which is subject to the mortgage, one begins by asking:

Is title to the estate registered or unregistered?

24.14.1 Registered title

In the case of registered title, the LRA 2002 has codified and, to some extent, modified the various rules relating to the priority of interests in the land. Whereas the LRA 1925 did not cover all these rules expressly, and some not even impliedly, the 2002 Act provides a comprehensive statement of the rules on priority. The result is a general statement of principle in s. 28, LRA 2002 and the provision of modifications that apply in certain cases, which are listed in ss. 29 and 30. The overall result is, in general, to provide a simplification of the rules.

First, however, you should note the requirement in s. 27(1) and (2)(f), LRA 2002 to complete legal charges by registration. The creation of the charge takes effect only in equity until this is done. On registration, the chargee will be entered on the register as proprietor of the charge (Sch. 2, para. 8). This entry is made in the charges section of the register entry for the estate that has been charged. Any *equitable charges* have to be protected by the entry of a notice in the register: s. 32(1). Any notices entered under the provisions of the LRA 1925 continue to have effect for the purposes of LRA 2002.

24.14.1.1 The basic principle

The effect of s. 28, LRA 2002, is that the priority of competing interests in registered land is determined by the order in which they were created. Thus, the section says that a disposition of the registered estate will not affect the priority of an existing interest in that estate. It further says that it makes no difference for the purpose of the section whether or not the earlier interest or disposition has been registered. To apply this rule to two competing charges one therefore simply asks which was created first and that charge has priority even if it was not registered when the second charge was created.

24.14.1.2 The exceptions to the basic principle

However, ss. 29 and 30 provide cases in which the basic s. 28 rule is not to apply and, in practice will mean that the simple 'first created gets priority' rule will not apply in a large number of situations. Section 29 is relevant where there is a registrable disposition of a registered estate. Section 30 applies where there is a registrable disposition of a registered charge. Note that you will normally be considering cases under s. 29 because usually you will be concerned with a later disposition made by the owner of the freehold or leasehold estate that is registered. Section 30 only applies in relation to dealings with the charge itself (e.g., a transfer for value of the charge from one lender to another lender) and we will not deal with that issue further.

Section 29 applies where there is a registrable disposition of a registered estate and that disposition is then registered. Where this happens, the rights of any person who has an interest affecting the estate before the registrable disposition is created (the first interest) are postponed to those of the owner of the interest conferred by the registered disposition (the second interest) unless the priority of the first interest had been protected by the time that the second interest is registered. Thus, if an estate owner creates two registrable charges of the land in the order Charge 1 and then Charge 2, the basic rule in s. 28 is that they will rank for priority in the order: (1) Charge 1; and (2) Charge 2. If, however, Charge 1 is not itself registered when Charge 2 is registered, Charge 1 will lose its priority and they will rank in the order: (1) Charge 2; and (2) Charge 1. This is a simple example involving two registrable charges and in such a case the charges each have to be protected by registration in order to maintain priority. However, this is not the only possibility and s. 29(2) lists the ways in which various forms of interest must be protected. It provides:

> . . . the priority of an interest is protected—
> (a) in any case, if the interest–
> (i) is a registered charge or the subject of a notice in the register,
> (ii) falls within any of the paragraphs of Schedule 3, or
> (iii) appears from the register to be excepted from the effect of registration; and
> (b) in the case of a disposition of a leasehold estate, if the burden of the interest is incident to the estate.

In essence, the effect of this is that in most cases to keep its priority a first interest must be (1) protected by registration where it is a registrable charge (legal charge); or (2) in the case of all other interests must be protected by entry of a notice in the register unless it is (3) in the Schedule 3 class of unregistered interests which override (and has not been the subject of a notice—see s. 29(3)).

Thus, in the case of registered title the first question to ask is:

Is the later disposition for value?

If not, the usual rule is that the disposition will not gain priority over any earlier interest. If the disposition is for value, assume that s. 28 applies. Then go on to ask:

Is any earlier interest (1) a registered charge, (2) protected by a notice or (3) listed in Schedule 3 (overriding)?

If the answer is 'Yes', the earlier interest retains its priority. If the answer is 'No', the earlier interest loses its priority to the later interest (s. 29, LRA 2002).

Under s. 28, time of creation is all that matters and ss. 29 or 30 cannot change the priority. In addition, the complexities in unregistered land in relation to any equitable right arising from estoppel or any 'mere equity' is removed by s. 116, LRA 2002, which treats both as interests capable of binding successors in title.

This approach is designed to produce an admirable simplicity in the rules on priorities in registered land. However, one also needs to consider the extent to which the impact of these rules is changed by other areas of law: see in particular the material below on undue influence (24.17.2).

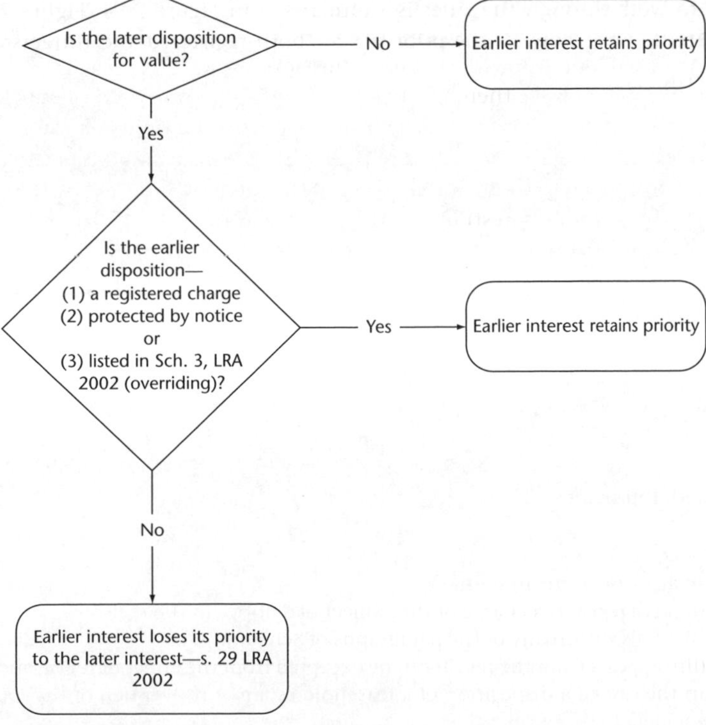

Figure 24.3 Priorities in registered estates

24.14.2 Unregistered title

The rules on priorities in relation to unregistered land are simply a practical application of the material we have already covered in Chapter 6. Accordingly, here we will cover only a few key concepts by way of reminder. However, if you need more detail about any of these matters, you will find a more detailed account of the unregistered land position in relation to priorities and mortgages in the Online Resource Centre linked to this book, at W.24.2.

The basic points to remember are as follows:

(1) If there is a legal mortgage and the mortgagee does not have the title deeds, that mortgage must be registered on the Land Charges Register as a *puisne mortgage*, which is a Class C(i) land charge.

(2) If there is an equitable mortgage and the mortgagee does not have the title deeds, that mortgage must be registered on the Land Charges Register as a *general equitable charge*, which is a Class C(iii) Land Charge.

(3) If there is a legal mortgage and the mortgagee does have the title deeds, that legal mortgage will be good against the world (save in rare cases in which priority is lost due to carelessness with the deeds).

(4) If there is an equitable mortgage and the mortgagee does have the title deeds:

   (a) that mortgage will normally bind any acquirer of a later *legal* estate or interest because the absence of the deeds gives notice of the earlier mortgage;

   (b) that mortgage will normally bind any later acquirer of an *equitable* interest because of the rule that 'Where the equities are equal, the first in time prevails'.

The way to work through the rules is summarised in Figure 24.4. Figure 24.5 gives a flowchart showing how all the priorities for both registered and unregistered land interact.

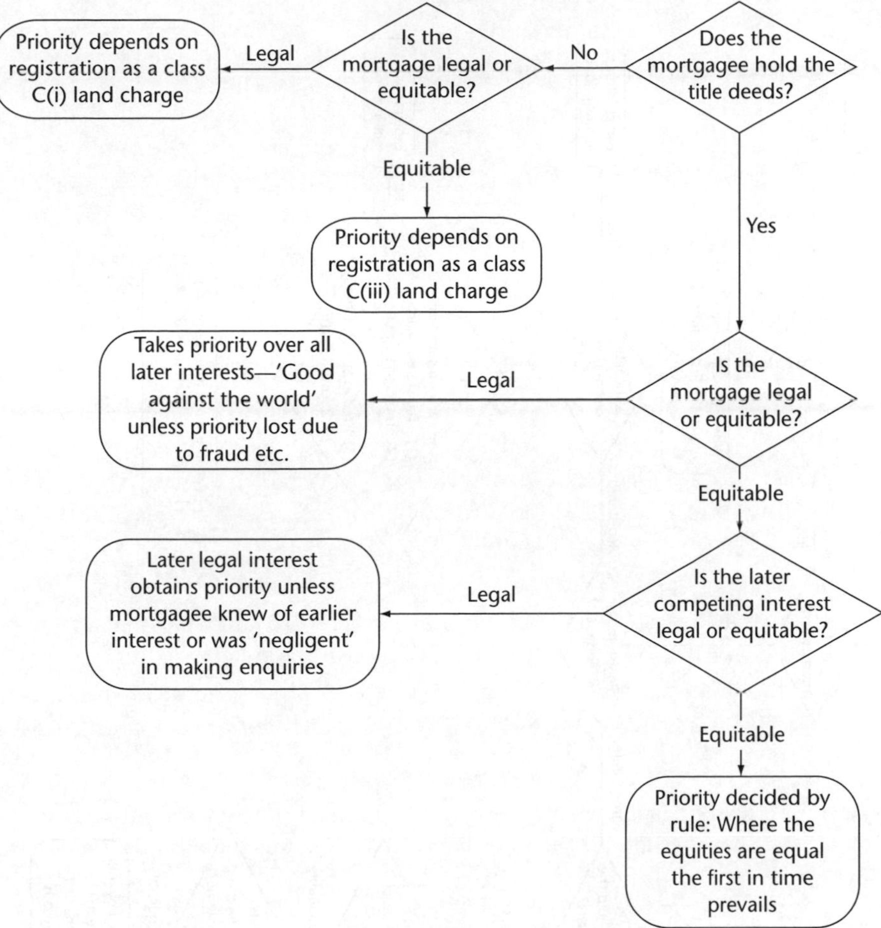

Figure 24.4 Priorities of mortgages of legal estate—unregistered land

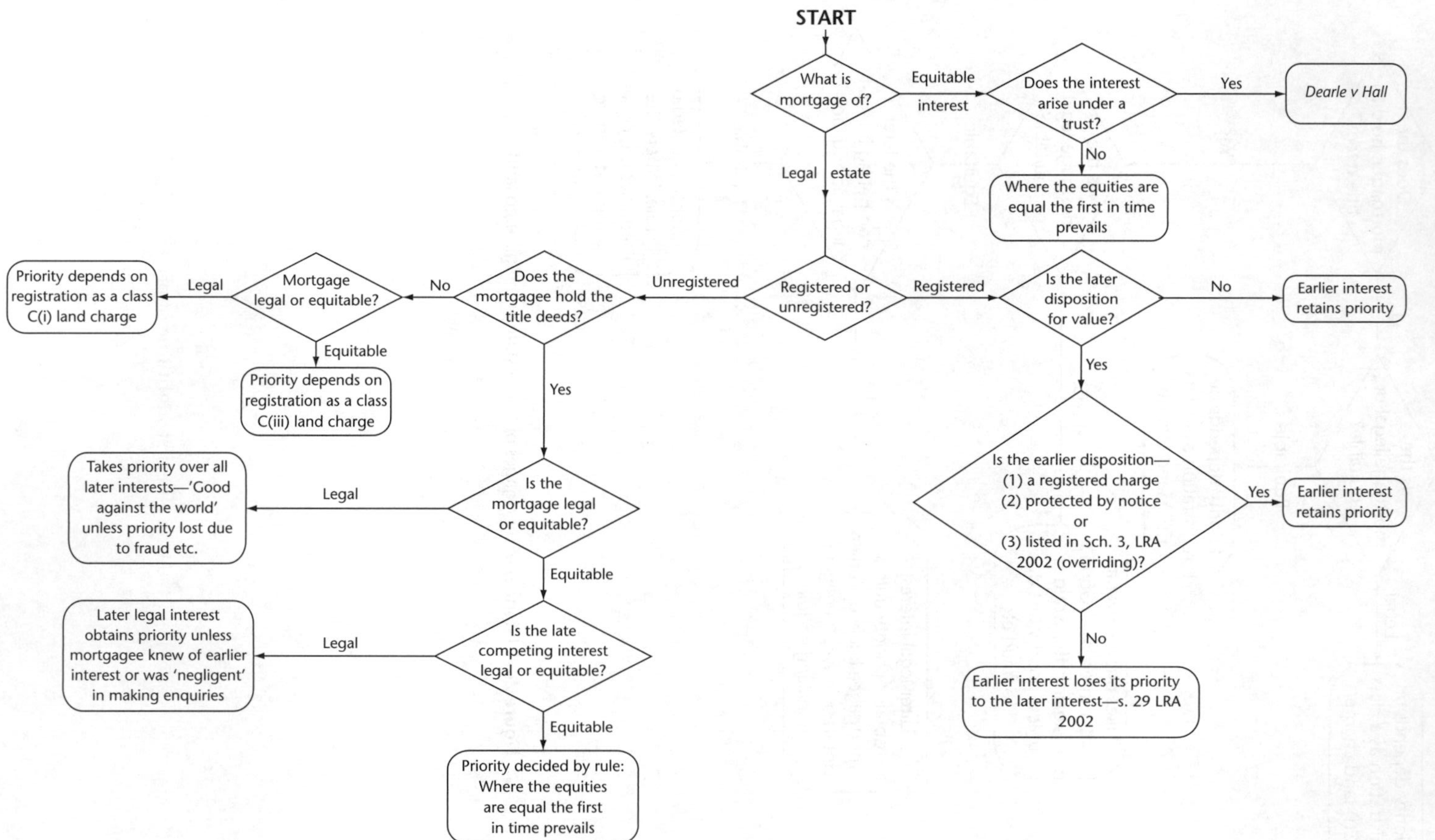

Figure 24.5 Priorities of mortgages in registered and unregistered land

24.15 Priorities of three or more mortgages

So far, we have described the rules about priorities as though we were concerned only with a competition between two mortgages. It is, however, possible to have three or more mortgages of the same estate, and you may therefore have to deal with questions of priorities in such a situation. We suggest that you should continue to apply the approach adopted so far: begin by listing the mortgages according to their date of creation, and then consider the earliest one in relation to each successive mortgage. When you have done this, take the next one to be created, and consider it in relation to each one that follows it. If you proceed in this way, considering each pair separately, you will often find that at the end you can list all the mortgages in order of priority.

24.15.1 A simple example

Take, for example, three mortgages of a legal estate, title to which is not registered, which have been created in the following order:

(a) legal mortgage to A, who takes the title deeds;

(b) legal charge to B, who registers a class C(i) land charge; and

(c) equitable mortgage to C.

Now compare the mortgages in pairs:

(a) *A and B*. A has a mortgage protected by deposit of title deeds, which is therefore not a registrable land charge. He has a legal mortgage, so his right is good against the world, and there is no suggestion of any conduct on his part which would deprive him of his priority.

Result: A before B.

(b) *A and C*. The position is exactly the same as in the case of A and B.

Result: A before C.

(c) *B and C*. B has a legal mortgage not protected by deposit of title deeds. It is therefore a registrable class C(i) land charge, and having been registered as such will bind all those who take a later interest in the property including C.

Result: B before C.

On this occasion, then, this method of approaching the problem produces a clear and simple set of answers:

A before B

A before C

B before C

and the mortgages can be sorted into a neat straight line of priority:

A first

B second

C third

In registered land it should normally be possible to 'sort' charges in a fairly straightforward manner. However, there has historically been a more complex possibility in relation to unregistered land.

24.15.2 A more complex possibility

It is possible to think of cases in which the order of priorities does not resolve itself so readily. For example, after applying the priorities rules to a set of mortgages in pairs (as shown above) you might theoretically come up with the following order of priorities, which produces a circle:

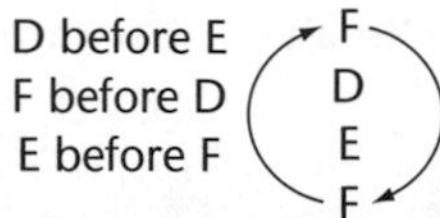

How you break into this circle is unclear, because the point has never come before the courts. Two possible solutions are: (a) that all the mortgagees should bear an equal loss (for there is only a problem if the value of the property is less than the sums outstanding on all three mortgages), or (b) that the mortgages should rank in the order in which they were created. Some authorities have suggested applying the rules of subrogation, but this produces a manifestly unfair result. (See Megarry and Wade, para. 26–034, and Gilmore (1961) 71 Yale LJ 53.) Happily, the circular priority problem is now rarely likely to arise in practice, because, as we have seen above, a mortgage supported by deposit of title deeds will trigger a need for first registration of title. Thus, this possibility, though interesting is very unlikely to occur in future.

24.15.3 Is that the end of the matter?

Once one has sorted out priorities according to the rules given above, it is not the end of the matter because there remain rules which cause the standard pattern of priorities to be disrupted (such as the rules relating to undue influence). We deal with a number of these issues at the end of this chapter, when we look at the position of Henry Mumps in more detail (see 24.17).

24.16 Mortgagee's right to tack further advances

As we have seen, 8 Trant Way is already subject to a first mortgage to the Red Leicester Building Society (RLBS), and a second mortgage may soon be created in favour of the Royal Windsor Bank (RWB). At some later date, after the creation of the second mortgage, Mildred, the owner of No. 8, might return to the RLBS and ask whether it would extend her mortgage to cover an additional advance. If the building society considers doing this, it will wish to know whether the fresh advance is effectively a third mortgage, ranking for priority after the RWB's mortgage, or whether it can 'tack' (add on) this further advance to the first mortgage, so as to gain priority for the later advance.

Again, the need to tack further advances will often arise where a mortgage has been given to a bank to secure the mortgagor's overdraft. As each withdrawal is made from the account, the bank makes a further loan to the mortgagor, but it is obviously desirable, from the bank's point of view, that all these loans should rank for priority with the original mortgage.

The circumstances in which further advances may be tacked are governed by different statutory provisions in the case of registered and unregistered title.

24.16.1 Registered title

Under the LRA 2002, the rules on tacking in relation to registered land changed. LRA 2002, s. 49 provides that the proprietor of a registered charge may make a further advance that ranks in priority to any later charge, if he has not received notice of the subsequent charge from the subsequent chargee. This places the onus on a new chargee to give notice to any earlier chargee of the creation of the new charge. A further advance may also be made with priority over any later charges if the advance is made in pursuance of an obligation and that obligation has been entered on the register (s. 49(3)), or if the parties to the earlier charge have agreed a maximum for which the charge is security and that agreement is entered on the register (s. 49(4)). Section 49(4) was an entirely new provision in 2002. Rules may be made to make certain variations to the position under s. 49(4): see 49(5). However, this power has not yet been used. In any other case, it is only possible to take and gain priority if the chargee of the later charge agrees: s. 49(6).

24.16.2 Unregistered title

The rule is that under LPA 1925, s. 94, a mortgagee has the right to tack further advances in three situations.

(1) *Where all the subsequent mortgagees agree. .*

This is unlikely to happen.

(2) *Where the mortgagee seeking to tack did not have notice of the existence of the subsequent mortgage at the date at which the further advance was made.*

It may be thought that this second category would be of little use to the earlier mortgagee if the later mortgage was registered as a land charge, since registration constitutes notice. However, under s. 94(2), the first mortgagee is not deemed to have notice of the second mortgage merely because it has been registered as a land charge, provided that:

(i) the first mortgage was expressly made for the purpose of securing further advances; and

(ii) the second mortgage was not registered at the date when the first mortgage was created or when the first mortgagee last searched the register, whichever is the later.

Therefore, if a later mortgagee wants to prevent tacking in these circumstances, he must give express notice of his position to the earlier mortgagee.

(3) *Where the first mortgage obliges the mortgagee to make further advances..*

Here he may tack even if he has notice of the later mortgage. Thus, should a mortgagee agree to finance the building of a new estate, it might be agreed that the advance should be paid in stages as each house is finished. In such a case the mortgagee can tack the separate loans together, even if he has knowledge of a later mortgage.

24.17 Interests prior to the mortgage: a cause for concern to the mortgagee

24.17.1 8 Trant Way

Finally, before we leave mortgages, we need to look again at the position at 8 Trant Way. Mildred is seeking a loan from the Royal Windsor Bank (RWB) on the security of a second mortgage of No. 8, and the bank will need to consider the extent to which it will be bound by the existing interests in the property. The title is unregistered.

The RWB must first consider the earlier legal mortgage to the Red Leicester Building Society (RLBS). If the RLBS has the deeds (as is normal) and has not done anything to forfeit its natural priority, it will take priority over any second mortgage to the RWB. Should the RLBS not have the deeds, its mortgage still takes priority if it is registered as a class C(i) land charge. If it does not have the deeds, and its mortgage is not registered when the second mortgage is created, the second mortgagee will gain priority, even if the RWB knew of the earlier mortgage (*Midland Bank Trust Co. Ltd v Green* [1981] AC 513).

SITUATION IF UNREGISTERED LAND

RLBS Legal mortgage or charge	Has deposit of deeds	Does not have deeds. Has registered C(i) land charge	Does not have deeds. Has not registered land charge
RWB If it takes a mortgage or charge	RLBS gets priority RLBS gets paid first	RLBS gets priority RLBS gets paid first	RWB gets priority RWB gets paid first

Accordingly, before making any advance, the RWB should check the situation with regard to the RLBS mortgage. Thereafter, it will need to have 8 Trant Way valued, and should ensure that it does not lend more than the balance of the value after deduction of the sums due to the RLBS.

The RWB needs also to consider the situation of Laura Lymeswold, who has a licence or lease of 8A Trant Way (see Chapter 22). If she has a lease (as is very possible after *Street v Mountford* [1985] AC 809), the RWB will take a mortgage *subject to* the pre-existing legal estate vested in her. It should ensure that its valuation takes account of the existence of a sitting tenant. Should Laura have only a licence, it appears that it will not bind the bank (and a later purchaser on sale by the mortgagee) for the licence would be contractual: see *Ashburn Anstalt v Arnold* [1989] Ch 1 (overruled in *Prudential Assurance Co. Ltd v London Residuary Body* [1992] 2 AC 386, but no criticism was made of the analysis of the position relating to licences).

The greatest problem for the RWB would be the uncertain position of Henry Mumps. If Henry were to have an equitable interest in the property due to his contribution, this will bind the RWB, unless the bank could claim to be a bona fide purchaser for value of a legal estate without notice. Since Henry is in occupation of the premises the bank would be likely to have notice under the rule in *Hunt v Luck* (see 6.5.2.3). If the title to No. 8 were registered, the position might resemble that in *Williams & Glyn's Bank Ltd v Boland* [1981] AC 487, and note the overriding interest which Henry might seek to rely on pursuant to LRA 2002, Sch. 3, para. 2. The existence of such a binding interest would mean that the bank's mortgage would attach only to Mildred's interest in the property and not to Henry's share. Thereafter, since as an equitable co-owner Henry would have a right to reside in the property until sale (TOLATA 1996, s. 12) and as the mortgage would not affect his interest, Henry might be able to prevent the second mortgagee selling the property (see *Williams & Glyn's Bank Ltd v Boland*). This would prevent realisation even of the partial security with which the bank would be left. However, note the decisions in *Bank of Baroda v Dhillon* [1998] 1 FLR 524 and *Bank of Ireland Home Mortgages Ltd v Bell* [2001] 2 FLR 809 which demonstrate that, even where an overriding interest does exist, it may be possible to obtain an order for sale of property held on trust (in the earlier case under LPA 1925, s. 30 but in the latter under TOLATA 1996, s. 14). The possibility of such interests arising has accordingly created a minefield for the building societies and banks. One solution to the problem would be for Mildred to appoint another trustee to join with her in receiving the mortgage money, so that Henry's interest would be overreached and attach only to the mortgage advance (*City of London Building Society v Flegg* [1988] AC 54) and, where no capital moneys (mortgage advance) arise, see also *State Bank of India v Sood* [1997] Ch 276). However, anyone taking on the role of trustee may then have to address any claim to an interest Henry may make and may, therefore, be in a difficult position. Note that any mortgage granted will not trigger registration of the title because it will not be a first legal charge: LRA 2002, s. 4.

24.17.2 **Undue influence**

Of recent years, the professional mortgagees (e.g., building societies and banks) have been increasingly concerned about the position of people such as the mortgagor's family and friends, who occupy the property with him or her at the date of the mortgage and may have rights to the property which can be enforced against the mortgagee. Accordingly the practice has grown up of asking a spouse or anyone else the mortgagee identifies as being resident in the premises to sign a document postponing his or her rights to those of the mortgagee. Also, where there are co-owners the mortgagee will have to seek the signatures of all involved (typically a husband and wife or civil partners or a couple who are living together). However, in recent years, those who have signed such a document have often sought later to argue that they are not bound by the mortgage *despite* having signed the mortgage or some document acknowledging the mortgagee's priority.

The basis on which such claims are made is the equitable concept known as 'undue influence'. This is not a rule which is specific to land law but is a general principle that arose as part of the equitable jurisdiction to see that there was fair play between the parties. Accordingly, it might more properly be regarded as being better dealt with in a text on equity and trusts rather than land law. However, in recent years its importance in the law of mortgages particularly (and in relation to some other interests in land) has become so considerable that we summarise the position here but provide a far more detailed account on the website linked to this book in the supplementary material on the Online Resource Centre—see W.24.3.

The equitable doctrine of undue influence was developed to protect those who had entered into a transaction because of the inappropriate use of influence by a person in whom they reposed a particular level of trust because of the particular nature of the relationship between them. The most common example has therefore been that of a wife who agrees to something (such as signing a mortgage deed) due to the influence of her husband. However, the concept goes beyond the limits of marriage and civil partnership and can cover a far wider range of relationships. Thus it can include cases in which elderly relations act under the influence of young family members on whom they depend, to unmarried couples (like the Mumps) and even other relationships of close trust. For example, in *Allcard v Skinner* (1887) 36 ChD 145, in which a nun made a gift of all her property to her Mother Superior (for the religious order), the relationship was considered to be within the ambit of the doctrine of 'undue influence'. In such cases the transaction will be void as between the person influenced and the person exercising the improper level of influence.

The same doctrine can also affect a third party. The typical modern example is a case in which someone with rights to the property (e.g., a wife) is persuaded by another person (e.g., her husband) to sign an arrangement giving rights to a third party (such as a mortgagee). If this is a case in which there is no clear benefit to the wife (such as where the money raised is applied for something of benefit only to the husband), then as between the husband and wife the transaction might in many cases be set aside. However, really the wife will need the transaction not to bind her as regards the *mortgagee* as well, if she is to protect her rights effectively. Thus, in a number of cases (and increasingly in recent history) people have claimed that the transaction should also not be enforceable by the third party. This is because, in certain circumstances, it can be argued that the third party knew or should have known that the transaction had been effected with use of undue influence. If such a claim succeeds, the transaction is also unenforceable by the third party (e.g., the mortgagee).

The leading case in modern law is *Royal Bank of Scotland v Etridge* [2002] 2 AC 773. In this case, following an absolute flood of claims of undue influence in the last few years of the twentieth century, the House of Lords considered eight conjoined cases in which undue influence had been raised and laid down general principles to be applied in future in such cases. The House of Lords also gave a clear statement of the steps that a third party, such as a mortgagee, should take in order to protect itself from being affected by any undue influence that might have occurred. In doing so, the court moved away from the somewhat convoluted approach to undue influence cases that had developed over the years.

As far as the original parties are concerned (such as the Mumps), Lord Clyde indicated (para. 93) that, where a relationship of trust exists, undue influence can arise in a range of ways. These include coercion, domination, victimisation and also includes more insidious forms of persuasion (which may be harder to identify). In some relationships (such as marriage and civil partnership) it may be easier to infer that some influence has led to the transaction, rather than it being a matter of real free choice by the person adversely affected. However, each case will turn on its own facts and there are no rigid rules as to when undue influence will arise. In each case, one is looking for an element of breach of trust. This is not, however, in the strict legal sense of breach of trust but rather covers the case of someone abusing their position to persuade someone who would not otherwise have been persuaded to act as they did.

Third parties, such as mortgagees, should take steps to protect themselves, if there is anything in the facts to suggest a risk. This will normally be the case where, for example, a spouse or civil partner signs away rights with no advantage to themselves. In such cases, the third party should ensure that the person who may have been influenced is given the chance of having independent advice about the transaction and that she or he has had the full implications explained before deciding to proceed. In essence, normally the third party (usually a lender) will need to be sure that the person in question has had legal advice that is separate from that given to the person who will benefit from the transaction. This usually means a separate firm of solicitors must be instructed to act. Clearly, in some cases, even after such advice is received, in some cases a spouse, civil partner or other person in a close relationship may decide to act in a manner that is not in their own best interests due to love, kindness or a multiplicity of other possible reasons. However, the separate legal advice should ensure that they make this decision freely and in full possession of the facts. Without such advice, the improper 'influencer' and any mortgagee will both be at risk that the transaction will be set aside as against them.

The precise rules are set out in detail in *Etridge* and are covered in greater detail in our website entry. Should you need to know more on this subject, we suggest that you begin by reading those documents and the other cases mentioned in the website entry.

If the RWB want to be sure that any rights Henry may have will not interfere with the RWB's rights to enforce their mortgage they would therefore be well advised to advise Henry to take independent advice and to insist that they have a certificate from his lawyer confirming that the nature and effect of the mortgage have been explained to him. It should also be noted that, in the case of registered land, a signed release from a person in actual occupation may be of limited assistance in any event for reasons which have nothing to do with undue influence: see further on this *Woolwich Building Society v Dickman* (1996) 72 P&CR 470.

FURTHER READING

Bently, 'Mortgagee's Duties on Sale—No Place for Tort' [1990] Conv 431.

Capper, 'Undue Influence and Unconscionability: A Rationalisation' (1998) 114 LQR 479.

Cousins and Clarke, *Law of Mortgages*, 3rd edn., Sweet & Maxwell, 2010.

On the Etridge conjoined cases, see the case note by Thompson, in [2002] 66 Conv 174.

Fisher and Lightwood, *Law of Mortgage*, 13th edn., Butterworths, 2010.

Gilmore, 'Circular Priority Systems' (1961) 71 Yale LJ 53.

Griffiths, 'Mortgages, Repossession and Limitation Periods' [2005] Conv 469.

Kenny, 'No Postponement of the Evil Day' [1998] Conv 223.

Millet, 'The Conveyancing Powers of Receivers After Liquidation' (1977) 41 Conv (NS) 83, p. 88.

Ministry of Justice, 'Mortgages. Power of Sale and Residential Property' CP55/09.

Wade, 'An Equitable Mortgagee's Right to Possession' (1955) 71 LQR 204.

25

Easements and profits à prendre

25.1 Introduction

The title 'easements and profits à prendre' may make you imagine that this chapter is concerned with strange rights known only to land lawyers and having archaic names. In fact both easements and profits are commonly encountered and most of us use such rights every day of our lives: for example, when we walk across the courtyard in the block of flats in which we live, or enjoy the continuing support of our houses that is provided by walls belonging to our neighbours. Once you have read this chapter you can, on your next train journey, play a variant on a childrens' game, and spot from the train windows the situations in which easements and profits are likely to arise. Is the woman driving up a shared driveway exercising an easement (a right of way)? Is the little girl leading her pony into that field exercising a profit (grazing)? Does the path across the back gardens of those terraced houses indicate an easement (right of way on foot)? From this you can see that the interests discussed in this chapter are often quite straightforward and some are essential to our daily life. The common strand to all these arrangements is that they are all rights exercised over land which belongs to another person, and so come into the category of third-party interests in land.

25.1.1 Trant Way

25.1.1.1 14–16A Trant Way

The plan of 14, 15, 16 and 16A Trant Way in Figure 25.1 may assist you when reading this chapter.

In 1947 the then owner of 15 Trant Way decided to install modern drains in the property. The nearest main drain was in Gouda Grove. After discussion, the then owner of

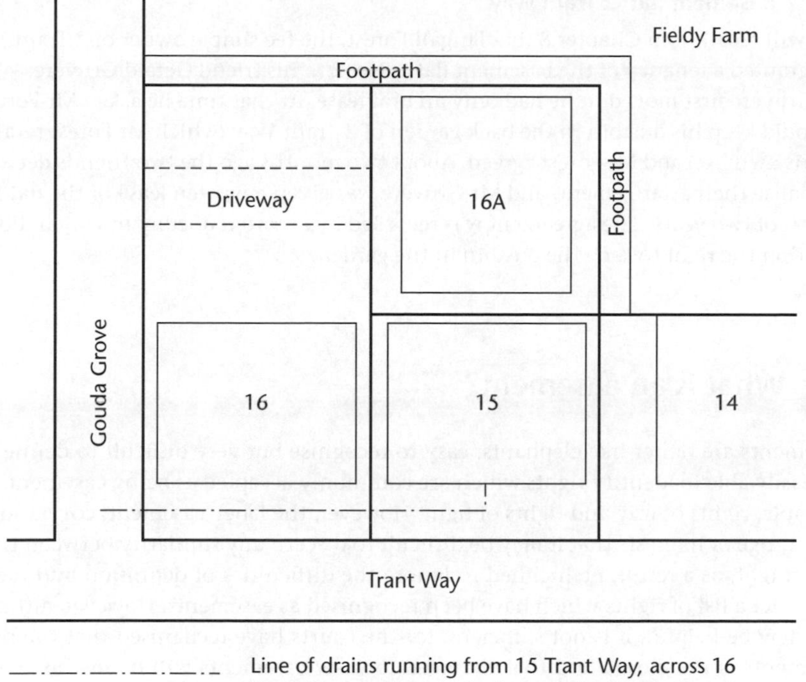

Figure 25.1 Nos. 14, 15, 16 and 16A Trant Way

16 Trant Way agreed that the drains could be laid across his front garden into Gouda Grove. A deed was drawn up which contained the following words:

> The grantor [the owner of 16] as beneficial owner hereby grants unto the grantee [the owner of 15] full right and liberty to use the sewer or drain marked with a dotted line on the plan attached hereto for the passage or conveyance of sewage water and soil from the said 15 Trant Way to the public sewer.

The current owner of 15 Trant Way is Charles Chive.

The current owner of 14 Trant Way (Nigel Neep) keeps a goat which he grazes on Fieldy Farm (to the rear of 14). Fieldy Farm is owned in fee simple by Farmer George.

There is a footpath leading from the back of 14 Trant Way to Gouda Grove. This path runs across Farmer George's land. The path has been in regular use by the owners of 14 Trant Way for many years.

For the last 50 years the fence separating 14 Trant Way from Fieldy Farm has been maintained by Farmer George or his father (who was his predecessor in title).

At one time 16 and 16A formed one plot of land. In 1980 the then owner of 16 Trant Way (Marjorie Marjoram) sold the freehold of the property now known as 16A Trant Way to Basil Borage. The only access to 16A is across the driveway on 16 Trant Way (see Figure 25.1) but this fact was not mentioned in the conveyance to Basil Borage. In 1996 Miss Marjoram sold 16 to Dan Dill (who made a first registration of title). Mr Dill dislikes Mr Borage and wants to prevent his use of the driveway.

At present 16 Trant Way enjoys an uninterrupted view of fields to the rear of the property over Fieldy Farm. Farmer George has just obtained planning permission to erect a corn silo on the farm and Dan Dill believes that this will spoil his view.

25.1.1.2 **Basement flat: 2 Trant Way**

You will recall from Chapter 8 that Fingall Forest, the fee simple owner of 2 Trant Way, has granted a tenancy of the basement flat at No. 2 to his friend Gerald Gruyère. When Mr Gruyère first moved in he had only an oral lease. At that time he asked Mr Forest if he could keep his dustbin in the back garden of 2 Trant Way (which Mr Forest retained for his own use) and Mr Forest agreed. About two months ago the two friends decide to formalise their arrangement, and Mr Gruyère was given a written lease of the flat for a period of two years. The agreement was recorded in a written document which did not mention the right to keep the dustbin in the garden.

25.2 What is an easement?

Easements are rather like elephants: easy to recognise but very difficult to define. We are easily able to identify rights which are commonly accepted as being easements, for example, rights of way and rights of light. However, the label 'easement' covers such a wide range of interests that it may be difficult to discern any similarity between them. One might, as a result, be inclined to ignore the difficulties of definition and merely construct a list of rights which have been recognised as easements. However, although this may be helpful, it is not sufficient, for the courts have recognised that the list of easements is not closed and that the need for new easements will be met as the circumstances of life change (*Dyce v Lady James Hay* (1852) 1 Macq 305). For example, an easement allowing the erection of a satellite dish is obviously a modern addition to the list. We must accordingly address the question of a standard against which a claim to a new right can be tested.

This standard is provided in the judgment of the Court of Appeal in *Re Ellenborough Park* [1956] Ch 131 which, although it does not define an easement, provides rules for its recognition.

25.2.1 The rules in *Re Ellenborough Park*

The original owners of Ellenborough Park also owned the surrounding land, which they sold off in plots for building purposes. Each conveyance granted to the purchasers the right to use the park, subject to an obligation to make a contribution towards the cost of maintaining it. The plaintiffs in the case acquired the park itself from the original owners, and intended to build upon it. The owners of the surrounding plots claimed the right to use the park and to be able to prevent the proposed building. The Court of Appeal upheld these claims, saying that the rights to use the park were legal easements. Since these rights were legal interests in land, they bound the purchasers of the park, and thus prevented them from building upon it. The court approved four rules of recognition for an easement:

(a) there must be a dominant tenement and a servient tenement;

(b) dominant and servient owners must be different persons;

(c) the easement must accommodate the dominant tenement; and

(d) the right claimed must be capable of forming the subject-matter of a grant.

We will now look at these rules and their application in greater detail.

25.2.1.1 Need for a dominant and servient tenement

An easement is a right enjoyed over one piece of land (the 'servient tenement') for the benefit of another piece of land (the 'dominant tenement'). In the case of the easement of drainage given in our practical examples, 16 Trant Way is burdened and is the servient tenement, whilst 15 Trant Way is benefited and is the dominant tenement.

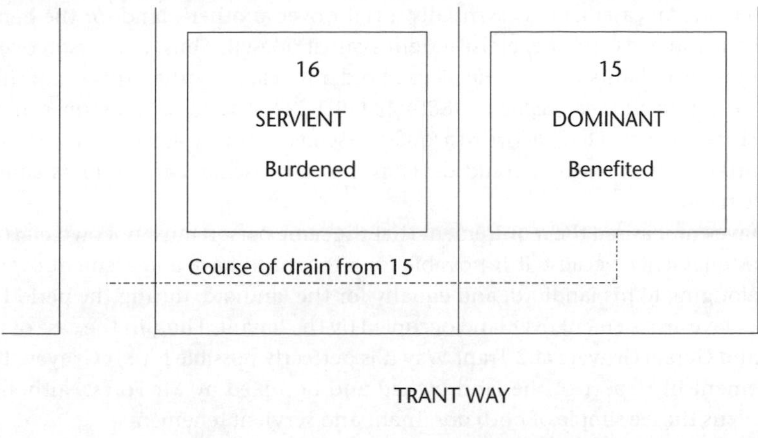

It is essential that there is a dominant tenement, for an easement cannot exist 'in gross', that is, without being attached to a particular piece of land which derives benefit from it. It is this which distinguishes, for example, an easement of way from a public right of way: in the latter, anyone may use the way, whereas the easement is available only to those connected in some way with the dominant tenement.

Accordingly, when a claim is made to an easement, the two pieces of land must be readily identifiable and, therefore, when an easement is being created, care must be taken to ensure that the two properties are clearly identified. This is particularly important in the case of the servient tenement and, in our example of the right to drainage, the burdened land is clearly identified by the dotted line showing the line of the drain as it passes under 16 Trant Way. In a properly drafted document, the dominant tenement should also be clearly defined, thus the use of words such as 'for the benefit of the land known as 15 Trant Way' is desirable. However, it is not fatal if such an express mention is omitted as long as it is clear from the deed which land is to be benefited (see *Thorpe v Brumfitt* (1873) LR 8 Ch App 650).

In recent years there has been an interesting debate as to whether easements have to be appurtenant to land or only to estates in land. In *Wall v Collins* [2007] EWCA Civ 444 the Court of Appeal took the traditional view that easements were appurtenant to land. In this case the benefit of an easement was granted to the owner of a 999-year lease. Later the current leaseholder acquired the freehold of the land and thus the leasehold estate merged into the freehold estate. If the benefit of the easement were only attached to the leasehold estate, it would be extinguished on merger. The court, however, was of the view that it was appurtenant to land but lasted for the period of the lease.

However, in its 2008 Consultation Paper No 186 (see 25.12.1), the Law Commission took the opposite view and proposed that an easement appurtenant to a lease should end when the lease ended. In its 2011 Report No. 327 (see 25.12.1) the Law Commission confirmed its general view, subject to limited exceptions and recommended that

Wall v Collins be overturned by legislation. No bill has yet been introduced in relation to these proposals.

25.2.1.2 Dominant and servient owners must be different persons

This is how the rule is stated in *Re Ellenborough Park*, but it is perhaps easier to understand if one says that the two tenements must not be both owned and occupied by the same person. An easement is essentially a right over another's land for the benefit of one's own, and one cannot exercise a right against oneself. Thus, if a person owns two pieces of land and walks across one piece in order to reach another, this is not the exercise of an easement (*Roe v Siddons* (1888) 22 QBD 224 at p. 236). Sometimes, however, such a situation is said to give rise to a 'quasi-easement': this is, as we shall see (25.7.1.3), a potential easement which could develop into an easement if the plots came into separate hands.

We have emphasised the requirement that the same person must not own *and* occupy the two tenements, because it is possible for a tenant to have an easement over other land belonging to his landlord, and equally for the landlord, during the period of the lease, to have an easement over land occupied by the tenant. Thus, in the case of Fingall Forest and Gerald Gruyère at 2 Trant Way it is perfectly possible for Mr Gruyère to have an easement in respect of the land owned and occupied by Mr Forest, although Mr Forest owns the fee simple of both dominant and servient tenements.

Should one person acquire both the servient and the dominant tenement this will extinguish a pre-existing easement, if at the same time the two properties come into common occupation. If, at some future date, the same person were to buy and occupy both 15 and 16 Trant Way, this would bring the easement over 16 Trant Way to an end. This is because one cannot have rights as against oneself, unless one is acting in different capacities (for example, where the owner of both tenements holds one of them in trust for another person).

25.2.1.3 The easement must accommodate the dominant tenement

This rule requires that the right must confer an advantage on the dominant land. It is not sufficient for the right to confer a merely personal advantage on the current owner. Such a personal right is said to be an interest 'in gross' and it is not possible to have an easement in gross. All easements must be 'appurtenant', that is, they must benefit identifiable land. In *Re Ellenborough Park* the right to use the park was held to benefit the surrounding plots of land because a domestic property is always improved in character by the availability of a garden. Unfortunately it is sometimes difficult to distinguish between personal benefits and benefits conferred on land, though, if it can be shown that the right increased the value of the land or its saleability, this would be sufficient. It may help to consider whether any possible owner of the property would regard the right as advantageous. Obviously any owner would regard the availability of drainage into the main drains as an advantage.

A problem may arise where the right claimed tends to confer an advantage, not on the land itself, but rather on some trade or business which is being carried on upon the land. In *Hill v Tupper* (1863) 2 Hurl & C 121 the right claimed as an easement was the right to put pleasure-boats on the canal which bordered the 'dominant' land. It was held that this right did not amount to an easement, because it did not benefit the land. Rather it benefited the business which Mr Hill happened to be running upon his land. The fact that the right benefits a business is not necessarily fatal, however, to a claim that the right is an easement. In *Moody v Steggles* (1879) 12 ChD 261, a right to hang on neighbouring land a sign pointing towards a public house was held to be capable of being an easement. This may well be because it is common for land used as a public house to remain in such use for prolonged periods, sometimes for centuries, so that the business run on the land and the land itself become inextricably linked.

The requirement that benefit be conferred on the land does, however, mean that the servient tenement and the dominant tenement must be reasonably close together. Normally the two properties will adjoin one another (as is the case in all our practical examples) but this is not absolutely necessary (*Pugh v Savage* [1970] 2 QB 373). The two pieces of land must, however, be close enough to support a claim that the dominant land receives an actual benefit from the right, and thus one could not have an easement exercisable over land at the other end of the country (*Bailey v Stephens* (1862) 12 CB NS 91 at p. 115). The easement does not, however, benefit other neighbouring land not covered by the grant (see, for example, *Peacock v Custins* [2002] 1 WLR 1815).

The requirement for benefit to land has given rise to other issues, notably:

(1) what happens if the benefited land changes its character over time, so that the impact of the easement on the burdened land changes; and
(2) what is the position if the owner of the dominant land tries to use the easement to benefit other land he owns?

1. *Change of character*

This issue was considered in *Attwood v Bovis Homes Ltd* [2001] Ch 379, in relation to an easement of drainage. Here the land having the benefit of the drainage had ceased to be agricultural land and was being developed. It is important to note that here the easement had been obtained by long use (prescription—see below para 25.9) and not by reason of an express grant. Thus, the owner of the dominant land argued that the easement should be restricted to the benefit conferred on land as it had been while the right was being acquired. This argument was rejected. However, as you will see from the decision and the older cases cited in it, a different result might be reached if the changed use of the dominant tenement led to a substantial increase in the burden or changed the nature of the burden (see also *British Railways Board v Glass* [1965] Ch 538). In *Attwood* it was accepted that the drainage had not been increased by the change in use. It appears that the court did consider that it was more likely to be accepted that there was a substantial increase or change in nature where the easement was a right of way. For an example of this, see *Wimbledon and Putney Commons Conservators v Dixon* (1875) 1 Ch D 362. In *McAdams Homes Ltd v Robinson* [2004] EWCA Civ 214 the Court of Appeal held that an easement of drainage granted to benefit a bakery could not endure to benefit two large domestic properties that were later constructed on the same site. The Court of Appeal was of the view that the judge at first instance was entitled on the facts to conclude that at the time of the original creation of the easement the parties could not have contemplated that such a change in the character of the dominant land would come about.

2. *Use to benefit additional land*

In *Peacock v Custins* [2002] 1 WLR 1815 a farmer wanted to use a right of way in order to gain access to a field that was not part of the land expressed to be the benefited land in the conveyance creating the easement but which he farmed with the benefited land. The Court of Appeal held that the right of way could not be used to gain access to the extra field and confirmed that the right was determined by reference to the land mentioned in the conveyance. In *Das v Linden Mews Ltd* [2003] 2 P&CR 4, the same rule was applied to prevent a right to drive across a private mews being used to gain access to a car-parking area that the owners of the dominant properties (houses on either side of the mews) had added by acquiring new land at the end of the mews. You will appreciate that this rule, while generally sensible in order to prevent increase in the burden of an easement, may cause a problem in some cases, if the user of a right of way has a primary purpose of reaching the dominant land but once there may decide to move on to the extra land. This issue was considered in *Macepark (Whittlebury) Ltd v Sargeant* [2003] 1 WLR 2284, in which it was indicated that access to such extra land was acceptable but that the right of way could not be used substantially for that purpose and that the access to the extra land had to be merely ancillary to the proper main use of the easement in relation to the benefited land. The same approach was adopted by the Court of Appeal in *Massey v Boulden* [2003] 1 WLR 1792.

25.2.1.4 The easement must be capable of forming the subject-matter of a grant

Easements are interests in land which can be legal interests, and as such they must 'lie in grant'. This means that a right must be capable of being granted by deed if it is to be recognised as an easement. A number of rules result from this condition, which in *Re Ellenborough Park* (at pp. 175–6) was said to require consideration of whether an alleged easement was:

- too wide and vague;
- inconsistent with the proprietorship or possession of the servient tenement owner (i.e., must not deprive the servient tenement owner of possession); or
- a mere right of recreation and amusement.

The court must consider all these matters when it is asked to recognise a new easement, and we will look at them in more detail, along with some other conditions, in 25.2.3.

The second important consequence of the rule that easements lie in grant is that, at the date at which the right arose, there must have been two persons who were capable respectively of granting and receiving the easement. This is of importance where easements are acquired otherwise than by express grant and will accordingly be discussed later when we consider methods of acquisition.

25.2.2 Some examples of easements

It is not possible for us to list all the rights which have been recognised as amounting to easements, but we will mention some of the most common.

25.2.2.1 Rights of way

The right of way is an easement that you are likely to have encountered frequently in your daily life: it involves a right to pass over the servient land. It can be general (passage by any means) or limited (for example, on foot only, or exercisable only at certain times of the day).

Where one tenement has a right of way over another, questions may arise about which owner should construct or repair any path or road over the route. Should you need material on this, you will find a useful summary of the rules in *Carter v Cole* [2006] EWCA Civ 398 at para. 8. In outline, neither owner is obliged to do the work, but either of them may undertake it if he wishes to do so. Where the dominant tenement owner decides to do the work, he must do it at his own expense and is entitled to enter the servient tenement for the purpose.

25.2.2.2 Right to light

This must be a specific right, so that light is claimed for particular windows or skylights, and there cannot be a general claim for light over the whole piece of land (*Colls v Home & Colonial Stores Ltd* [1904] AC 179).

How much light?

The amount of light which one can claim is that which is necessary according to the ordinary notions of mankind. This rule relates to and in essence is derived from the rule in nuisance that the damage must be such as, 'materially to interfere with the ordinary comfort of human existence': *St Helen's Smelting Co. Ltd v Tipping* (1862) 11 ER 1483 and see *City of London Brewery Co. Ltd v Tenant* (1873) LR 9 Ch App 212.

The amount of light to be expected will also vary depending upon the nature of the property. Thus this right would be infringed were the light so obstructed that in a dwelling the electric light had to be lit all day but this might not be objectionable were the premises in question to be a warehouse (see *Colls* above). However, in *Midtown Ltd v City of London Real Property Co. Ltd* (2005) 4 EG 166 (CS) it was held that owners of an office building could object to a substantial diminution of the light passing to it, even if all the rooms in the office were habitually lit by artificial light whenever they were in use. A mere diminution in the light is not sufficient, nor can one claim extra light because of the activities carried on on the land, unless the special use contemplated was known to the owner of the servient land at the time at which the easement was acquired.

25.2.2.3 Rights to water

One has no general right to water which percolates through the soil, but an easement may exist in respect of water in a defined channel, e.g., a pipe or stream. On this see *Race v Ward* (1855) 4 El & Bl. 702 and *Dickinson v Grand Junction Canal Co. Ltd* (1852) 7 Exch 282 at p. 301.

25.2.2.4 Right to drainage

This is a common and important easement (see the example in para. 25.1.1.1). For a further discussion see *Attwood v Bovis Homes Ltd* [2001] Ch 379 and para. 25.2.1.3(i).

25.2.2.5 Rights to air

Once again there is no general right to the passage of air (*Webb v Bird* (1861) 10 CB (NS) 268) but a claim to air flowing in a defined channel can amount to an easement. This might include, for example, rights in respect of ventilation ducts (*Wong v Beaumont Property Trust Ltd* [1965] 1 QB 173).

25.2.2.6 Right to support

This right is very important where one is dealing with a semi-detached or terraced house. In such a case the boundary frequently runs down the centre of the connecting wall. Were one owner to remove his half, the remaining portion would probably soon collapse. Accordingly, an easement of support is recognised in this, and other similar, cases (*Dalton v Angus & Co.* (1881) 6 App Cas 740); this right is limited, however, so that whilst the servient owner may not pull his wall down he may let it fall down for lack of repair (*Jones v Pritchard* [1908] 1 Ch 630 at p. 637).

The right to support is not, however, confined to walls (see *Jordeson v Sutton, Smithcoates & Drypool Gas Co. Ltd* [1898] 2 Ch 614, which related to quarrying at the bottom of a hill that resulted in part of the land in a neighbouring fruit farm being dislodged). This area of law interacts with the tort of nuisance (see 25.10.2.1 and *Holbeck Hall Hotel v Scarborough BC* [2000] QB 836).

25.2.2.7 Rights to use of facilities

Common examples include the use of a lavatory (*Miller v Emcer Products Ltd* [1956] Ch 304), of a letter-box (*Goldberg v Edwards* [1950] Ch 247) or a kitchen (*Haywood v Mallalieu* (1883) 25 ChD 357).

25.2.2.8 Rights of storage

Claims to rights of storage have given rise to a good deal of case law and academic debate, because they are sometimes said to amount to an unacceptable interference with the rights of the servient tenement owner. We will tell you more about the decisions on this point when we consider the rules for recognition of new easements—see 25.2.3.2(1).

25.2.2.9 Rights of parking

A popular modern claim is to an easement of parking. In a sense this is really only an extension of the easement of storage, giving rise to the same questions about interference with the rights of the servient owner, so we will postpone consideration of the relevant decisions until 25.2.3.2(2).

25.2.2.10 Easement of fencing?

In certain circumstances, a landowner may be under a duty to maintain a fence on his boundary with neighbouring land, and the courts have recognised his neighbour's right to enforce this obligation as being 'in the nature of an easement'. This is unusual, because easements do not usually impose expense on the servient tenement. For example, we have already noted that there is no requirement to make up or maintain a road or track across one's land and that similarly there is no duty to repair a wall which is supporting a neighbour's house. For this reason, the easement of fencing is sometimes described as a spurious easement, but its existence has nevertheless been recognised in at least three decisions of the Court of Appeal: *Jones v Price* [1965]2 QB 618; *Crow v Wood* [1971] 1 QB 77; and *Egerton v Harding* [1975] QB 62.

It should be noted, however, that all these decisions arose in the context of disputes about cattle trespass in which A, the owner of cattle grazing on adjoining land, claimed that his neighbour, B, should have fenced his (B's) land in order to keep out A's cattle. Where this right to require one's neighbour to fence against cattle is found to exist, it has in general arisen through long use (i.e., by prescription) and in *Jones v Price* the Court of Appeal doubted whether it could be acquired in any other way. We shall see later, however, that most forms of prescription are based on a fiction that the right in question was granted at some time in the past, with the consequence that the finding of prescription in *Jones v Price* ([1965] 2 QB 618) compelled Diplock LJ to admit that the right was in theory capable of being granted, although he added:

> There is no precedent in the books for such a grant. I find it difficult to envisage its form.

In the later case of *Crow v Wood* [1971] 1 QB 77, the requirements for establishing prescription were not satisfied, and the Court of Appeal, relying on *Jones v Price*, found that an easement of fencing had been created by implied grant, Edmund Davies LJ saying that 'a duty to fence against trespassers' could arise by express or implied grant and could also pass under LPA 1925, s. 62 (for which, see 25.8). Gray, however, is still of the opinion that it is doubtful whether the obligation to fence can rise other than by prescription (Gray and Gray, para. 5.1.59).

It is important to remember that these decisions were dealing only with the obligation to fence against cattle. We cannot point to any decision on the duty to fence in other circumstances, and interestingly there is still no precedent for the grant of such an easement in any of the precedent books. We are emphasising this point because vendors selling off part of their land often wish to impose obligations to fence on purchasers and their successors in title. In Chapter 26 we will explain why this cannot be done by means of positive covenants, and it would be a mistake to assume too readily (in answering an examination question for instance) that the solution is for the vendor to reserve an easement of fencing. It is, of course worth debating the point—but it is by no means certain that this is the answer.

The types of easements described above merely provide some examples, and reference should be made to C. J. Gale, *Gale on Easements*, 18th edn., pp. 42–45, if you want a more detailed list.

25.2.3 Establishing a new easement

If one wishes to establish a claim to a hitherto unknown easement, one must first show that the right claimed satisfies the four rules of recognition adopted in *Re Ellenborough Park*. Thereafter it is necessary to satisfy the court that the claim to a new type of easement is justified. This is considerably easier if one can show that the nature of the right claimed is analogous to that of some existing easement. Thus, Mr Gruyère might wish to show that his claim to store a dustbin is similar in character to the right to store coal which was accepted in *Wright v Macadam* [1949] 2 KB 744 (see 25.2.3.2(1)).

We have already discussed the first three rules of recognition described in *Re Ellenborough Park* (see 25.2.1), but at that point we postponed any consideration of certain conditions that arise from the fourth rule (that an easement must be capable of being granted). It is now time to tell you about those conditions and to note a number of other requirements which the courts will take into account in considering whether to recognise a new easement.

25.2.3.1 Must not be too wide and vague

The right claimed must be specific and definable, for it would have to be carefully defined if included in a deed. This can be a problem if the right claimed involves issues of taste, since such matters cannot be defined. Thus one cannot claim a right to a prospect (a fair view) as an easement, for one cannot define such a right (*William Aldred's Case* (1610) 9 Co Rep 57b—'the law does not give an action for such things of delight'). Accordingly, Dan Dill at 16 Trant Way cannot complain about Farmer George's silo on the basis of an easement for a view. He should have made his complaints at the stage at which the farmer applied for planning permission (though he might not have been able to prevent the grant of permission).

The vague nature of the right claimed may also result in its failing this test. Thus, in *Dyce v Hay* (1865) 1 Macq 305, a claim to use land for general recreational purposes was held to be too vague to amount to an easement, although a right to use a garden for similar purposes was upheld in *Re Ellenborough Park* itself. In *Chaffe v Kingsley* [2000] 79 P&CR 404, a claim to a right of way failed because the conveyance by which it was alleged the right was granted was insufficiently specific as to the area of land affected. Accordingly, care must be taken when claiming an easement to be as specific as possible about the right claimed.

25.2.3.2 Must not deprive servient owner of possession

The courts will never accept as an easement a right which has the effect of excluding the servient owner from possession of his land. An easement is by nature a limited right, and if the dominant owner seeks to oust the servient owner he is claiming a right that is considerably greater than that conferred by an easement.

Over the years this requirement has received a good deal of attention from the courts, particularly in the context of claims to:

(1) easements of storage; and

(2) easements of parking.

1. *Easements of storage*

It is generally accepted that a right to store goods on another's land can constitute an easement. However, the courts have had some difficulty in rationalising their recognition of this right, because use of a piece of land for storage does appear to involve excluding the owner from it (in practical terms, he cannot use his garden shed if it is full of his neighbour's furniture). However, this problem was not discussed in *Wright v Macadam* [1949] 2 KB 744, and the Court of Appeal accepted without question that a tenant could have a right to store coal in her landlord's shed. The attention of the court focused on the question of how the right had been created, rather than on whether it satisfied the requirements for recognition as an easement.

By contrast, in *Copeland v Greenhalf* [1952] 1 Ch 488, the High Court rejected a claim by the owner of a workshop that he had a right to store vehicles awaiting repair or collection on a strip of land belonging to his neighbour. In the words of Upjohn J (at p. 498), the right claimed was:

> wholly outside any normal idea of an easement... it is virtually a claim to possession of the servient tenement, if necessary to the exclusion of the owner; or, at any rate, to a joint use.

The court in *Copeland v Greenhalf* did not consider the earlier decision of the Court of Appeal in *Wright v Macadam*, and as a result it has been suggested that the judge's decision was *per incuriam* (although it is worth noting that it was referred to with approval by the Court of Appeal in *Re Ellenborough Park* [1956] 1 Ch 131 at 176–7).

The apparent inconsistency between the two decisions was considered by Brightman J in *Grigsby v Melville* [1972] 1 WLR 355. The parties were the owners of two adjoining properties and the defendant claimed a right of storage in the cellar beneath his neighbour's house. The judge did not consider whether the right of storage claimed could amount to an easement, because he decided the case on other grounds. However, he indicated that, if he had been required to deal with that point, he would have followed *Copeland v Greenhalf*, since in his view the right claimed by the defendant amounted to exclusive use of the cellar.

For our purposes, the significance of *Grigsby v Melville* lies in the judge's comments on the supposed inconsistency between *Wright v Macadam* and *Copeland v Greenhalf*. In his view, it might well be that there was no inconsistency: we do not know how much coal was stored nor whether the landlord was prevented from using his shed. As Brightman J put it:

> To some extent a problem of this sort may be one of degree.

Some years later a similar approach was adopted by Judge Paul Baker QC in *London & Blenheim Ltd v Ladbrooke Parks Ltd* [1992] 1 WLR 1278 at 1286:

> The matter must be one of degree. A small coal shed in a large property is one thing. The exclusive use of a large part of the alleged servient tenement is another.

Thus the courts seem to have arrived at a compromise conclusion: it is possible to have a right to store goods on one's neighbour's land—provided one does not try to store too much!

2. *Easements of parking*

In a sense, the right to park is really only an extension of the easement of storage, as can be seen from the words of Megarry VC in *Newman v Jones* (unreported, but quoted by Aldous J in *Handel v St Stephen's Close* [1994] 1 EGLR 70 at 72):

> In view of *Wright v Macadam*...I feel no hesitation in holding that a right for a land-owner to park a car anywhere in a defined area nearby is capable of existing as an easement.

As with the storage cases, however, an alleged right of parking raises questions about exclusion of the servient owner. In *London & Blenheim Ltd v Ladbrooke Parks Ltd* [1992] 1 WLR 1278 at 1288 Judge Paul Baker QC expressed the view that:

> The essential question is one of degree. If the right granted in relation to the area over which it is to be exercisable is such that it would leave the servient owner without any reasonable use of his land, whether for parking or anything else it could not be an easement though it might be some larger or different grant.

The 'compatibility' test

As we have just seen, courts considering a claim of parking or storage have come to apply the test of whether the right claimed is so extensive that it would prevent the servient owner from making any reasonable use of his land or, as Gray and Gray put it (see para. 5.1.65) whether the right claimed is compatible with the owner's use of his land. It may occur to you at this point that this development seems to involve a slight shift in language: the earlier decisions speak of depriving the servient owner of 'possession', but from *London & Blenheim Ltd* onwards we find the courts talking about deprivation of 'use'. (We will return to this point later when considering the House of Lords' decision in *Moncrieff v Jamieson* [2007] 1 WLR 2620—see below.)

The *London & Blenheim Ltd* approach was followed by the Court of Appeal in *Batchelor v Marlow* [2003] 1WLR 764 in which the court rejected a claim by the defendant that he had a right to park up to six cars on the plaintiff's land on weekdays between 8.30am and 6pm. The court considered that such an extensive right would leave the plaintiff without any reasonable use of his land, whether for parking or otherwise (paras. 15 and 18).

This decision by the Court of Appeal seemed to establish the 'substantial interference' test, which until then had been developed in lower-court decisions, and to confirm the limited nature of storage and parking easements. However, the whole question was re-opened by the House of Lords' decision in *Moncrieff v Jamieson* [2007] 1 WLR 2620.

Moncrieff v Jamieson

This case came to the House of Lords as an appeal from the Court of Session in Scotland. The Scots law on servitudes is in many respects similar to that of the English law of easements (paras. 45 and 111), so this case is of relevance to English land law, but if you read the case you should be aware of Lord Neuberger's warning against assuming that the two systems are the same in every respect (para. 136).

There is no need to note the facts of the case in any detail. All you need to know is that the respondent, Moncrieff ('M'), had succeeded at first instance and on appeal in establishing that he had an implied right to park on the land of the appellant, Jamieson ('J'). The appeal to the House of Lords raised a number of issues, but the only ones that concerns us are: (a) J's claim that a right to park did not amount to an easement in law; and (b) that the claim was for an implied right to park.

The speeches of Lord Scott and Lord Neuberger contain interesting discussions of the principle against excluding the servient tenement owner, and its application to easements of storage and parking. Their Lordships emphasised that although the courts often speak of depriving the servient tenement owner of use, the real rule is that he must not be deprived of possession. At para. 55, Lord Scott distinguished between giving the dominant tenement owner 'sole use' of part of the servient tenement (which in his view would not prevent the right being an easement) and giving him 'exclusive possession' of that part, which would not be consistent with the general principle:

> sole use for a limited purpose is not, in my opinion, inconsistent with the servient owner's retention of possession and control or inconsistent with the nature of an easement.

Lord Neuberger agreed with him, saying (at paras. 140 and 143) that he was not satisfied that:

> a right is prevented from being an easement simply because [it] would involve the servient owner being effectively excluded from the property...a right can be an easement notwithstanding that the dominant owner effectively enjoys exclusive occupation, on the basis that the essential requirement is that the servient owner retains possession and control.

Applying this approach to parking claims, Lord Scott (at para. 59) said that he would:

> reject the test that asks whether the servient tenement owner is left without any reasonable use of his land and substitute for it a test which asks whether the servient owner retains possession and, subject to the reasonable exercise of the right in question, control of the servient land.

As a result, both Lord Scott and Lord Neuberger expressed doubts as to whether *Batchelor v Marlow* had been correctly decided by the Court of Appeal (paras. 60 and 143). In the event, however, there is no need for either of them to reach any conclusion on this point, nor to express any final view on the degree of exclusion which is required to prevent a right being recognised as an easement (para. 143). The easement claimed by M was simply that of parking one or two cars somewhere on J's land at the end of a track which led to M's house. The case did not raise any difficult 'borderline' questions: it did not involve parking an excessive number of cars, nor was there any question of excluding the servient owner from any particular parking space. The claim in fact fell clearly within the situation originally envisaged by Megarry V-C in *Newman v Jones*, and their Lordships concluded that M was entitled to an easement of parking.

You will recall that we mentioned above that the second issue in *Moncrieff* was that the claimant was seeking an implied right to park. This issue arose before the Court of

Appeal in *Waterman v Boyle* [2009] EWCA Civ 115. This case concerned a property in relation to which there was an express right of way over a drive and an express right to park in two designated parking places. The owner of the dominant tenement was claiming in addition an implied right for visitors to park on the drive arguing that this was implied as necessary for enjoyment of the property as a dwelling. The Court of Appeal refused to recognise an implied right to park in such a case, saying the fact that a right to park was implied in *Moncrieff* was quite exceptional. Thus it seems now to be the case that while there can be express easements of parking, they will only be implied in very exceptional cases. See 25.7 for the general position on implied easements.

25.2.3.3 **Must not be a mere right of recreation and amusement**

This is the third condition that the court in *Re Ellenborough Park* noted as arising from the requirement that an easement must be capable of forming the subject-matter of a grant. It is derived from statements in *Mounsey v Ismay* (1865) 3 Hurl & C 486, a case concerned with an alleged right to enter land and hold horse races there. The requirement had some relevance to the right claimed in *Re Ellenborough Park* (i.e., that of using a garden), but it is unlikely to affect many claims to new easements, unless of course they involve the use of facilities for sport or other leisure time amusements.

25.2.3.4 **Must be a right**

Any interest claimed must be in the nature of a *right*, rather than a permission (in which case it will amount to a licence). Thus, in *Burrows v Lang* [1901] 2 Ch 502 a claim to an easement to take water from an artificially filled pond was rejected, because exercise of such a right depended on the owner filling the pond and could not be enjoyed without his co-operation. The 'right' was, therefore, too precarious and could not qualify as an easement. In *Green v Ashco Horticultural Ltd* [1966] 1 WLR 889 a claim to a right to park a van failed because the claimant had always moved his van when asked to do so by the servient owner and accordingly exercised his right only as far as the servient owner permitted.

25.2.3.5 **No new negative easements**

Easements may broadly be divided into two categories: positive and negative. In the case of a positive easement the dominant owner must *do* something in order to exercise his right. A right of way is thus positive because the dominant owner must walk, drive or ride on to the servient land in order to exercise his right. A negative easement is a right which is enjoyed without any action by the dominant owner (e.g., a right to light). In *Phipps v Pears* [1965] 1 QB 76 it was said that the courts would not readily accept the creation of new *negative* easements, because they have a tendency to restrict the servient tenement owner and hamper development of his property. Thus, the court rejected a claim to an easement of protection from the weather, which was argued by analogy with the easement of support and which, like that easement, would have the effect of preventing one from demolishing one's own property (on this see further *Rees v Skerrett* [2001] 1 WLR 1541).

25.2.3.6 **Not involving expenditure**

Normally, the courts will not accept an easement which requires expenditure by the servient owner. Thus, in *Regis Property Co. Ltd v Redman* [1956] 2 QB 612 it was held that a claim to the supply of hot water was not an easement. The easement of fencing is an exception to this rule. Another exception arose in the case of *Liverpool City Council v Irwin* [1977] AC 239. Here, the House of Lords, in construing a very incomplete contract between the tenants of a multi-storey block of flats and their landlords, first, implied easements giving the tenants the use of stairs, lifts and rubbish chutes and, secondly, identified a further implied term requiring the landlord to take reasonable care to keep in reasonable repair the common parts over which those easements were exercised. This decision was undoubtedly influenced by considerations of general public policy but it is important to remember that their Lordships were concerned with interpreting the terms of a particular contract and were not laying down rules of general application.

Subject to these general principles the list of easements will continue to expand as circumstances change and the courts seem happy to see new rights arise as and when they prove to be useful or necessary.

25.3 What is a profit à prendre?

A 'profit à prendre' is a right to take something from land which belongs to another person. The 'something' which is removed may either be part of the land itself (e.g., sand), or something growing on the land (e.g., grass) or wild creatures found naturally on the land (e.g., fish, deer or pheasants). There are a number of traditional forms of profit, although others can still arise.

25.3.1 Examples of profits

(a) The *profit of pasture* is an ancient right but still commonly claimed today. It is a profit because the grazing animals take grass and other plants from the land. This cannot exist as a right to graze an unlimited number of animals as this would exhaust the land, and the traditional limit is the maximum number of animals which can be supported through the winter (*Mellor v Spateman* (1669) 1 Saund 339). Mr Neep s right to graze his goat would probably be a profit of pasture.

(b) The *profit of piscary* is the right to take fish.

(c) The *profit of turbary* is the right to cut turf or peat, usually in order to burn it.

(d) The *profit of estovers* is the right to take wood for use as fuel or for domestic or agricultural purposes (e.g., to build fences).

25.3.2 May be appurtenant or in gross

Unlike an easement, it is not necessary for a profit to be appurtenant to land. It may exist in gross, in which case it may be exercised for the personal benefit of its owner. Thus, a profit of piscary in gross would allow the fisherman to take fish in order to sell them, whilst a profit of piscary appurtenant allows fishing only to the extent of the needs of the land to which the right is attached (e.g., to feed those who reside there). Furthermore, profits may exist to the exclusion of the servient owner, as well as in common with the servient owners or other persons. Thus, Mr Neep's right to graze his goat may be for the benefit of 14 Trant Way (appurtenant), or for his own benefit (in gross), and may be to the exclusion of Farmer George (sole) or a right shared with Farmer George (in common).

25.3.3 Profit appurtenant can change character

One might expect that the character of a profit, particularly whether it is appurtenant or in gross, would be set at the point at which that profit is created and could not alter during the currency of the profit. However, despite the hundreds of years over which profits have been important land rights, this point had never been settled until the House of Lords' decision in *Bettison v Langton* [2002] 1 AC 27. When reading this case it is important to be aware that the Commons Registration Act 1965 required the registration of all commons and of all rights over commons. In the case of grazing rights, the Act required that the registration should be for a specified number of animals, thus bringing to an end the old common law limitation to the maximum number that could be supported during the winter (see above).

In *Bettison v Langton*, the land in question enjoyed appurtenant rights of grazing, which had been registered in accordance with the 1965 Act. In 1987 Mrs Langton, the then owner of the land, sold the grazing rights to Mr and Mrs Bettison, while retaining the land. Some seven years later the land itself was sold by Mrs Langton's mortgagee (in exercise of his power of sale—see 24.8.1.2). The purchasers claimed that it was not possible for Mrs Langton to have severed the grazing rights from the land, or, in other words, they claimed that the rights were still attached to the land and had passed to them.

The House of Lords held that, if the scope of a profit appurtenant could be quantified otherwise than by the needs of the property to which it was annexed, that profit could be disposed of separately from the estate to which it had been annexed. Here, the rights had already been quantified on registration, and accordingly the disposal to the Bettisons was valid and the profit had become a profit in gross.

As a result of the Commons Act 2006, s. 9, rights of grazing over common land can no longer be severed from the land they benefit, but *Bettison v Langton* will continue to be relevant where the right is enjoyed over land in private ownership.

25.4 Easements and profits may be legal or equitable

Easements or profits, like other interests in land, may be legal or equitable. In order to constitute legal interests, they must satisfy certain rules concerning the period for which they last and the method by which they are created.

25.4.1 Prescribed period

The first requirement is derived from LPA 1925, s. 1(2), which defines legal easements and profits as being granted for a period 'equivalent to a fee simple absolute in possession or a term of years absolute'. This means that the easement or profit must last either, in effect, for ever, or for a fixed period. Thus, an easement granted 'for 10 years' would be legal, whilst an easement 'for life' cannot be legal because it is not for a period equivalent to a legal estate. Note that, in an interesting article on equitable easements (see (1999) LQR 89), Professor Barnsley argues that it is in fact not likely that an equitable easement for life could exist and we agree that we can think of no example. We agree also with his conclusion that the problem lies with the fact that an easement must be appurtenant to land, whereas an easement for life seems to have personal character. However, the answer here seems uncertain since rights can clearly relate to land while existing only for a lifetime.

Easements which do not satisfy the requirements of s. 1(2) necessarily take effect as equitable interests under s. 1(3) LPA 1925.

25.4.2 Creation by deed

The second requirement, concerning the method of creation, is found in the general rule that all legal estates and interests must be created by deed (LPA 1925, s. 52(1)). If no deed is used, the purported grant is ineffective in law but, provided the requirements of the Law of Property (Miscellaneous Provisions) Act 1989, s. 2 (for which see 3.2) are satisfied, equity may treat the arrangement as a specifically enforceable contract to grant an easement or profit and treat that right as being in existence from the date of the contract.

There is, at present, one apparent exception to the requirement for a deed for the creation of legal easements and profits. As we shall see, these rights can be acquired, without any formal grant, by 'prescription'; that is, by use over a long period of time. No deed is in fact used in such a case but, with only one exception, the various methods of prescription are all based on the fiction that a grant has been made in proper form, so that in this method, too, legal interests are created by deed—even if only by a fictitious one!

The Commonhold and Leasehold Reform Act 2002, s. 31(7) creates a further exception in relation to easements arising under a commonhold community statement, because that provision says that the duties imposed by the agreement will not require any other formality.

For completeness we would point out that Professor Barnsley also identifies two other occasions on which an equitable easement will arise: (1) where the easement is created by an equitable owner; and (2) where the easement arises from an estoppel.

25.5 Enforcement against purchaser of servient tenement

Whether an easement or profit is legal or equitable is of great importance when one comes to enforce it against someone who has bought the servient tenement. We have already dealt in some detail with the enforcement of third-party rights against purchasers and so we will do no more than remind you of the relevant rules.

25.5.1 Registered land

Under LRA 1925, s. 70(1)(a), a legal easement or profit was an overriding interest and accordingly was automatically binding upon a purchaser. Generally, an equitable easement or profit was a minor interest and had to be protected by entry on the register for the servient tenement (but for an exception to this general rule, see *Celsteel Ltd v Alton House Holdings Ltd* [1985] 1 WLR 204).

The position has changed very considerably under LRA 2002. The Act greatly reduced the number of legal easements and profits which can take effect as overriding interests, and ensures that the express creation of these rights results in their automatic protection by notice.

25.5.1.1 Easements and profits which can take effect as overriding interests

1. *On first registration*

All legal easements and profits take effect as overriding interests on first registration (ss. 11 and 12, and Sch. 1, para. 3). This reflects the position in the unregistered system of title, and means that the rights which bound the estate owner in the unregistered system are carried forward and will continue to bind him when his title is registered for the first time. Where the registrar is aware of these encumbrances, they will be noted on the register of title and will continue to bind the estate on any future disposition.

2. *On dispositions of the registered estate*

All legal easements and profits created expressly after LRA 2002 came into force are automatically protected by notice on the register of the servient land, and cannot take effect as overriding interests (for an explanation of how this works, see below).

As a result, an easement or profit will be overriding (under ss. 29 and 30, and Sch. 3, para. 3) only if:

- it is a legal interest; and
- it arises by implied grant or reservation, or by prescription, or under LPA 1925, s. 62; and
- it satisfies one of the following conditions:
  (a) it is registered under the Commons Act 2006 (or its forerunner the Commons Registration Act 1965); or
  (b) the acquirer actually knew of its existence; or
  (c) the acquirer did not know of it but it would have been obvious on a reasonably careful inspection of the land over which it is exercised; or
  (d) even if it does not fall within (a) to (c) above, it has been exercised within the period of one year ending with the date of the disposition in question.

These provisions, depending as they do on factors such as the knowledge of the purchaser or the recent exercise of the right, pose considerable risks to the dominant tenement owner. Accordingly, he would be well advised to take advantage of the fact that any easement or profit may be protected by entry of notice on the title of the servient tenement. Once such a notice is entered, the interest ceases permanently to be an overriding interest (s. 29(3)), but its enforcement against subsequent purchasers is ensured.

25.5.1.2 **Easements and profits which are protected by entry of notice on title of servient tenement**

1. *Legal easements and profits which are expressly created*

As we have already mentioned, legal easements and profits which are expressly created (other than under LPA 1925, s. 62—for which see 25.8) are now automatically protected by entry of notice on the servient tenement's register of title. This is because the express creation of an easement or profit is one of the dealings with registered land that must be completed by registration (s. 27(1) and (2)(d)). When the dominant tenement owner applies for this registration of a newly created easement, details of the easement will be entered in the property section of his register of title, and the registrar will automatically put a notice in the charges section of the register for the servient tenement.

If the new easement or profit is not registered in this way, the requirements for its legal creation will not be satisfied, and it will take effect only in equity (see below).

2. *Legal easements and profits arising other than by express creation*

These may take effect as overriding interests, subject to satisfying the requirements of Sch. 3 para. 3, LRA 2002 but, as we noted above, the dominant owner would still be well advised to protect them by notice.

PROTECTION OF EASEMENTS

REGISTERED LAND		
	Overriding interests	**Must protect by entry on register**
Legal easements and profits	On 1st registration of estate, all legal easements and profits. On later disposition ONLY IF arising by (1) prescription, or (2) implied grant or reservation, (3) or under s. 62, LPA 1925 AND- (a) is registered under Commons Act, or (b) acquirer knew of it, or (c) would have been discoverable on reasonable inspection of land, or (d) exercised in the year before the disposition.	Expressly created easements and profits arising after 1st registration of estate. Expressly created easements which are not protected by entry of a notice on the register take effect in equity only.
Equitable easements and profits	Cannot be overriding	All must be protected by notice.
UNREGISTERED LAND		
Legal easements and profits	Binding on all acquirers because legal rights are good against the world	
Equitable easements and profits	Created on or after 1st January 1926	Must be registered as a land charge to bind acquirer
	Created before 1st January 1926	Apply notice rules to determine whether binding on later acquirer

3. *Equitable easements and profits*
There are no circumstances in which equitable easements and profits can take effect as overriding interests. They must be protected by notice on the register of the servient land and will not bind a purchaser unless this has been done.

25.5.2 Unregistered land

In the unregistered land system, a legal easement or profit is enforceable against any purchaser, under the principle that legal rights bind the whole world.

Equitable easements in unregistered land are registrable as land charges if created on or after 1 January 1926 (LCA 1972, s. 2), while equitable profits, and equitable easements that were created before 1926, are subject to the old equitable rules of notice.

25.6 Acquisition by express grant or reservation

The story of the installation of the drains of 15 Trant Way, given at the beginning of this chapter, shows that an easement or profit can arise by agreement between two owners who already hold separate properties. In such a case, the owner of the land which is to become the servient tenement executes a deed granting the easement to his neighbour.

Very often, however, easements or profits are created when land is divided on sale. The vendor may sell only part of his land, keeping the rest for himself (as happened with 16 and 16A Trant Way), and he and the purchaser may each want to enjoy rights over the other's property. Where the purchaser is to be given easements or profits, they are granted by deed, usually by the same deed which conveys the legal estate to him. Where the vendor wishes to retain certain rights over the land he is selling, he must 'reserve' those rights in the conveyance. The purchaser takes his rights by express grant, while the vendor obtains his by express reservation.

The reservation of an easement requires care because the document will be construed strictly against the vendor/grantor (*Cordell v Second Clanfield Properties* Ltd [1969] 2 Ch 9).

In addition to express grant and reservation, there are three other ways in which easements and profits may be acquired, and we will deal with them in the following sections:

- implied grant and reservation (25.7);
- express grant by virtue of LPA 1925, s. 62 (25.8); and
- prescription (25.9).

25.7 Acquisition by implied grant or reservation

In certain cases in which a conveyance of land makes no mention of the grant or reservation of an easement or profit, it may be possible to say that one arises by implication. As we shall see, it is easier to establish an implied grant, in favour of the purchaser, than it is to set up an implied reservation on behalf of the vendor.

25.7.1 Implied grant

Traditionally, it was said that easements, and in some cases profits, can arise by implied grant in the following cases:

(a) easements of necessity;

(b) intended easements and profits;

(c) easements under the rule in *Wheeldon v Burrows* (1879) 12 ChD 31.

However, *Nickerson v Barraclough* [1981] Ch 426 suggests that the first two of these are not really separate categories, and that easements of necessity are really a form of intended easement.

25.7.1.1 Easements of necessity

An easement of necessity is an easement which is so essential to the enjoyment of the land that the land cannot be used without the easement. The classic example of such an easement arises in the case of 'the land-locked close'. This is land which, like 16A Trant Way, is totally inaccessible, unless an easement to permit access is implied into the conveyance or transfer. On this basis an easement of way would have been implied in the conveyance of 16A Trant Way by Marjorie Marjoram to Basil Borage, as otherwise Mr Borage would have acquired a useless estate.

In many of the cases in which a grant of a way of necessity has been implied, the landlocked close has been completely surrounded by the land of the grantor. In *Adealon International Proprietary Ltd v Merton LBC* [2007] 1 WLR 1604 the Court of Appeal was required to consider whether it would make any difference to the outcome if some of the land surrounding the landlocked plot belonged to a third party. The claimant in this case was in fact claiming an implied reservation, rather than an implied grant, but we are noting the case here because the court also expressed views on implying a grant in these circumstances, although these views are, of course, strictly *obiter dicta*.

The court, differing from the trial judge on this point, considered that it was possible for an easement of necessity to be implied in such a situation. Where a grantee had acquired a landlocked close, there would normally be an expectation that access would be provided over land controlled by the grantor, and so the grant of an easement of necessity might well be implied, despite the fact that alternative access over land belonging to a third party might be a theoretical possibility (para. 16). For the court's views about an implied reservation in these circumstances, see 25.7.2 below.

Basis of the rule

It used to be suggested that the recognition of certain easements of necessity was based on considerations of public policy, because, for example, it was not in the public interest to allow land to become unusable through lack of access. However the public policy argument was rejected in *Nickerson v Barraclough* [1981] Ch 426, in which the Court of Appeal stated that easements of necessity were to be seen simply as a type of intended easement. In the words of Buckley LJ (at p. 447):

> The law relating to ways of necessity rests not upon a basis of public policy but upon the implication to be drawn from the fact that unless some way is implied, a parcel of land will be inaccessible. From that fact the implication arises that the parties must have intended that some way giving access to the land should have been granted.

Thus an easement of necessity could not be implied where, as in the case before the court, the original vendor had expressly stated that no right of access was being granted.

Although this explanation of the basis of the doctrine appears to have been doubted in *Sweet v Summer* [2004] 4 All ER 288, it was quoted with approval and applied by the Court of Appeal in *Adealon International Proprietary Ltd v Merton LBC* [2007] 1 WLR 1604 at para. 11.

Overlap between necessity and intention

The overlap between necessity and intention can be illustrated by the older case of *Wong v Beaumont Property Trust Ltd* [1965] 1 QB 173, in which basement premises had been let upon the express understanding that the property was to be used as a restaurant. Later, after assignment by the original tenant, the assignee was required to improve ventilation if the restaurant business were to continue. The assignee claimed an implied easement for passage of air through a duct to be constructed on the landlord's property, and was successful on the ground that this was necessary if the contemplated use of the premises were to continue. On the facts, one can see that the case might have been similarly decided by implying that the parties intended all rights which permitted the use of the premises as a restaurant.

Another important case in this area of the law is *Liverpool City Council v Irwin* [1977] AC 239 (see 25.2.3.6) in which easements were implied giving the right to use rubbish chutes, stairs and lifts in a multi-storey block of flats. In addition the grant of a flat was held to include an implied right to have the facilities maintained in a reasonable state of repair. Again, is this a matter of intention or is it that a lessee cannot make any real use of a flat at the top of a tall block unless there is a lift, which is kept in working order?

25.7.1.2 Intended easement and profits

As we have seen above, it may be that rights which are necessary for the use of the land are to be presumed to be within the intention of the parties unless expressly excluded. This second category, however, includes more than easements of necessity, for under this heading a grantee may claim a profit or any easement, even though not necessary to the enjoyment of the property, provided he can show that both parties intended that it should be granted. An example of this is found in *Cory v Davies* [1923] 2 Ch 95, where a row of terraced houses had been built with a drive at the front and an exit to the road at each end. One of the owners barred the exit at his end of the terrace, requiring all traffic to go the other way. There was no express grant of an easement in favour of all the house owners over all parts of the drive, but the court found that the original parties had a common intention that the drive should be used in this way, and thus an intended easement was implied.

The decision in *Stafford v Lee* (1992) 65 P&CR 172 shows how the question of the intention of the parties was addressed in a case of 'land-locked' land and which therefore might properly appear to fall into the area of easements of necessity. Here the defendant's predecessor in title had conveyed an area of woodland and a pond to the plaintiffs' predecessors. The land fronted a drive but no right of way over the drive to the nearby highway was conferred. The plaintiffs wished to build a house on part of the land but the defendants said that there could be no right of way over the drive for residential purposes (including construction work). The court accepted that it was appropriate to infer an easement to give effect to the intentions of the original parties, but indicated that this could only be done in cases in which the parties intended that the dominant land should be used in some definite and particular manner. In this case because the plan on the relevant conveyance showed other neighbouring buildings the court was ready to infer that the woodland would be used for similar purposes. Accordingly, the claim to an easement for domestic purposes succeeded.

A recent example of the recognition of intended easements is to be found in the Court of Appeal decision in *Kent v Kavanagh* [2007] Ch 1. A pair of semi-detached houses had been built by a developer early in the twentieth century on 99-year building leases. The boundary between the two plots ran down the middle of a shared pathway, which gave access to the back gardens of both properties. In 2003 a dispute arose between the current owners as to their relative rights over the path. The leases made no reference to its use and as a result the Court of Appeal was required to consider whether they could be said to contain implied grants and reservations of rights of way.

The court noted that the path was only three feet wide, with the result that it would have been obvious when the leases were granted that it could not be used by either tenant without passing over the half that lay on his neighbour's property. It therefore concluded that the original parties to the leases must have intended that the path would be used in this way. As a result Chadwick LJ, citing *Cory v Davies* [1923] 2 Ch 95 as an authority, had no difficulty in inferring that each lease contained the implied grants and reservations of reciprocal rights that would enable the path to be used as intended (para. 63).

25.7.1.3 The rule in *Wheeldon v Burrows*

In order to understand this rule, it is necessary to remind ourselves about quasi-easements (see 25.2.1.2). Although a landowner may derive benefit from one piece of his own land in favour of another, he cannot be said to have an easement, because there are no separate tenements. For example, if he enjoys the uninterrupted passage of light over his garden to his windows, he cannot say he has an easement of light, although, if the garden were in separate ownership he might very well have such a right. This situation is sometimes described as giving rise to a quasi-easement.

1. *The rule*

The rule in *Wheeldon v Burrows* (1879) 12 ChD 31 provides that if, in such a situation, the owner sells that part of his land which is benefited (e.g., the house) and retains the land which is burdened (e.g., the garden), the purchaser may acquire an easement over the land retained by the vendor. Thus, in the example given above, the quasi-easement would become a true easement of light.

In *Wheeldon v Burrows*, Thesiger LJ stated the principle as follows (at p. 49):

> [O]n the grant by the owner of a tenement of part of that tenement as it is then used and enjoyed, there will pass to the grantee all those continuous and apparent easements (by which, of course, I mean quasi easements), or, in other words, all those easements which are necessary to the reasonable enjoyment of the property granted, and which have been and are at the time of the grant used by the owners of the entirety for the benefit of the part granted.

2. *Elements of the rule*

There seem to be three elements of this rule, for the quasi-easement must be:

(a) 'continuous and apparent';

(b) 'necessary to the reasonable enjoyment' of the land sold; and

(c) in use by the owner at the time of the sale.

If all three requirements are satisfied then a grant of a legal easement is implied into the conveyance or transfer of the portion of the land which is sold. There has however always been some doubt as whether it is necessary to show that the quasi-easement is both 'continuous and apparent' and 'necessary to the reasonable enjoyment of the property'. It has been suggested that these requirements should be viewed as alternatives, so that it is only necessary to show that the quasi-easement in question satisfies one or other of them. In *Ward v Kirkland* [1967] Ch 194 at 224, Ungoed-Thomas J put forward the alternative suggestion that each requirement applied to a different type of easement, positive easements (e.g., rights of way) being required to be 'continuous and apparent', while negative easements (e.g., rights to light) must be shown to be 'necessary to the reasonable enjoyment of the property'. However, in *Millman v Ellis* (1995) 71 P&CR 158 (a case involving a claim to a right of way), the Court of Appeal treated the two requirements as separate conditions, each of which had to be satisfied in order to bring the claim within the rule in *Wheeldon v Burrows*.

We will now look briefly at each of these three requirements.

(a) *'continuous and apparent'* Strictly speaking, 'continuous' easements are those which are enjoyed passively, such as rights to drainage, support and light, and are therefore in use all the time (Megarry and Wade, para. 28–016). Although a right of way cannot be said to be in continuous use, the courts accept that it satisfies this test if there is a made-up road or some other clearly defined track (which of course is in place at all times) along which the right can be exercised (see *Borman v Griffiths* [1930] 1 Ch 493 at 499).

The requirement that the quasi-easement should be 'apparent' stems from the principle that underlies all types of implied grant, namely that a grantor must not derogate from his grant. Under the rule in *Wheeldon v Burrows*, a purchaser is to receive the easements that he expected to receive: on inspecting the land he saw visible signs of a quasi-easement and assumed that he would obtain the benefit of such a right if he acquired the property.

In the case of 16A Trant Way, if there was a house on the property when Mr Borage bought it and a driveway across 16 leading to it, the driveway would render apparent the quasi-easement being used by the vendor.

(b) *'necessary for the reasonable enjoyment of the property'* This requirement does not produce a test as strict as that for easements of necessity. All that is needed for *Wheeldon v Burrows* is that the right claimed should facilitate the reasonable enjoyment of the property. However, in *Wheeler v J. J. Saunders Ltd* [1996] Ch 19, a second access route to premises was held by the Court of Appeal not to be necessary for the reasonable enjoyment of the land, even though it was convenient, because the alternative route would 'do just as well'.

(c) *'in use by the owner at the time of the sale'* In considering this requirement, attention has always focused on the fact that the quasi-easement must be 'in use' at the time of the sale. The reason for requiring such use is, as we noted above, that it leads the purchaser to believe that the right will pass with the property.

Recently, however, the Court of Appeal has emphasised the other aspect of the condition: it must be in use by the owner. In *Kent v Kavanagh* [2007] Ch 1, the court rejected a claim under *Wheeldon v Burrows* to an implied grant of a right of way, because at the relevant date the land benefited by the quasi-easement was occupied by a tenant and not by the owner himself. Chadwick LJ considered that it would be 'unnecessary and artificial' to hold that the vendor had been using quasi-easements over part of his land to benefit another part, when the part that received the benefit was in fact no longer occupied by him, but by a tenant (see paras. 44 and 45). Although the judge does not say so, the same argument would probably apply if the benefited land was occupied before the conveyance by a licensee.

It thus appears from this decision that we may need to add a further requirement to the rule in *Wheeldon v Burrows*, namely that an implied grant under this rule operates only where the land conveyed and the land retained were in both common ownership and common occupation immediately before the conveyance.

Simultaneous sales

So far in our explanation of the rule in *Wheeldon v Burrows*, we have assumed that the vendor sells the quasi-dominant piece of land (which has been enjoying the quasi-easement) and retains the quasi-servient land. What happens if, instead, he sells both pieces of land and both sales take effect on the same day (for example, on a sale at auction)? In such a situation, each purchaser acquires any quasi-easements which have been enjoyed with his piece of land and will be entitled to enforce them against the land of the other purchaser (see *Hansford v Jago* [1921] 1 Ch 322 at 335).

25.7.2 Implied reservation

Easements and profits may arise by implied reservation in the following cases:

(a) easements of necessity;

(b) intended easements and profits.

There is, however, no possibility of an implied reservation under the rule in *Wheeldon v Burrows*, for the court in that case rejected the vendor's claim to an easement over the land he had sold. (It is interesting to note that the rule that takes its name from this case is in fact derived from *obiter dicta*, for the court was not dealing with any question about implied grant.)

In general the courts will not readily accept a claim to the acquisition of an easement or profit by implied reservation because of the rule that documents are to be construed strictly against the grantor. This is because it is presumed that the grantor is in a position of strength, and is able to reserve any rights which he chooses to retain. Should he fail to reserve these rights he has only himself (or his conveyancer) to blame. Moreover, it can be said that an implied reservation derogates from the grant, for the grantor has apparently given the grantee an unencumbered estate and is then trying to burden it with an easement or profit.

However, there are a few cases in which claims to have acquired an easement by implied reservation have succeeded. Thus in *Peckham v Ellison* [2000] 79 P&CR 276, a successor to a council that had sold some properties under the 'right to buy' scheme, while retaining other neighbouring property, claimed that the council must have reserved a right of way by implication. Perhaps surprisingly, the Court of Appeal held that on the particular facts of the case, the judge at first instance had been entitled to conclude that there was no other possible explanation of the circumstances other than that the council and purchasers had intended that the council should reserve the easement. The case emphasises that the matter is one to be decided on the facts of each case.

For other successful claims, see *Richards v Rose* (1853) 9 Exch 218 (easement of support), and *Pinnington v Galland* (1853) 9 Exch 1 (right of access to landlocked close). More recently, the Court of Appeal in *Adealon International Proprietary Ltd v Merton LBC* [2007] 1 WLR 1604 (see 25.7.1.1 above) accepted that a right of way to landlocked property could be acquired by implied reservation, even in cases where there was theoretically a possibility of access across adjoining land owned by a third party. The court emphasised, however, the difficulty that faces a grantor who claims an implied reservation. In the words of Carnwath LJ (at para. 16):

> ...the presumption is that any rights [the grantor] requires over the land transferred will have been expressly reserved in the grant, and the burden lies on [him] to establish an exception.

In *Adealon*, there was no evidence of an intention at the time of sale that the vendor would access the retained land by means of a way over the sold land, and thus the presumption that the grantor would expressly reserve any right he required had not been rebutted.

For other cases in which claims to implied reservations have been rejected by the courts, see *Re Webb's Lease* [1951] Ch 808, and *Chaffe v Kingsley* [2000] 79 P&CR 404.

25.8 Acquisition by express grant by virtue of LPA 1925, s. 62

25.8.1 Section 62

LPA 1925, s. 62(1), provides that:

> A conveyance of land shall be deemed to include and shall... operate to convey, with the land, all buildings, erections, fixtures, commons, hedges, ditches,... liberties, privileges, easements, rights, and advantages whatsoever, appertaining... to the land,... or, at the time of conveyance,... enjoyed with... the land.

At first reading the subsection appears to be nothing more than a word-saving provision, designed to make it clear that on the conveyance of an estate in land the grantee obtains the benefit of houses, fences and other things upon the land and any rights, interests and privileges existing for the benefit of the estate, without any express mention of them being made in the conveyance. Express words to this effect used to be included in full in conveyances, but since the end of the nineteenth century statute has provided that such words are deemed to be included in the conveyance. Section 62 thus operates to pass any existing easements or profits that benefit the land conveyed, without any need to mention them in the conveyance.

25.8.2 Interpretation of s. 62

Rather surprisingly, s. 62 has been interpreted by the courts in such a way that it is capable of creating new easements and profits in favour of a purchaser, as well as transferring those that already exist. As a result, any conveyance that does not exclude the provisions of s. 62, will convert into legal easements or profits:

- certain quasi-easements and quasi-profits;
- licences.

It also appears from the decision of the Court of Appeal in *Wall v Collins* [2007] Ch 390 that s. 62 is capable of converting an existing easement for a fixed period into one that is equivalent to the freehold estate (see 25.8.2.3).

25.8.2.1 Conversion of quasi-easements and quasi-profits

We have already explained the nature of quasi-easements in discussing *Wheeldon v Burrows* (25.7.1.3). In order to be converted by a conveyance under s. 62 into full easements binding the land retained by the vendor, the quasi-easement (or quasi-profit) must be 'continuous and apparent' and must have been in use at the time of the conveyance. There is no requirement that the right should be 'necessary for the reasonable enjoyment of the property', as there is in *Wheeldon v Burrows*. (See further, Megarry and Wade, para. 28–029 and 28–030).

25.8.2.2 Conversion of licences

The cases in which the courts have found that a licence has been converted into an easement by virtue of s. 62 all arose in situations in which, before the conveyance, the land to be benefited was already occupied by someone other than the grantor. The occupier was permitted to undertake some activity on other land owned by the grantor, such as using an alternative route of access across it (as in *International Tea Stores v Hobbs* [1903] 2 Ch 165, and *Goldberg v Edwards* [1950] Ch 247) or, for example, storing goods upon it (*Wright v Macadam* [1949] 2 KB 744). The grantor then conveyed the property, either on sale or on the grant of a lease, and the permissive use was converted into a legal easement, binding on the land retained by the grantor.

An examination of the case of *Wright v Macadam* [1949] 2 KB 744 illustrates how this may occur. While in possession as a protected tenant under the Rent Acts, Mrs Wright was given permission by her landlord, Mr Macadam, to store coal in a garden shed, which was retained by the landlord. Later a fresh lease of one year was made (in writing but not by deed, in accordance with LPA 1925, s. 54(2)) which did not refer to the shed. After some time, Mr Macadam tried to charge for the use of the shed and Mrs Wright refused to pay, claiming that she had an easement of storage. It was held, by the Court of Appeal, that the creation of the fresh lease was a 'conveyance' within the meaning of LPA 1925 and that it operated to grant Mrs Wright a legal easement of storage. Thus, by virtue of s. 62, a conveyance had converted a pre-existing licence into a legal easement.

It is not easy to see why s. 62 should have this effect, for the words of the section would suggest that the licence should pass as a licence, rather than changing into a legal right (see Tee [1998] Conv 115). This interpretation was first adopted in nineteenth-century decisions on similar provisions in earlier statutes and it is now well accepted and has been expressly recognised in LRA 2002, s. 27(7). To ensure that new rights are not created in this way, a landowner making a conveyance should either revoke any licences he has previously granted, or include a term in the conveyance that will exclude the operation of s. 62.

25.8.2.3 Conversion of existing easements

In *Wall v Collins* [2007] Ch 390, the Court of Appeal had to consider the question of what happens to easements enjoyed by a tenant over adjoining land belonging to the landlord when the tenant 'buys out' his landlord (i.e., acquires the reversion on the lease and becomes the freehold owner). We will tell you more about this case later (see 25.11.4), but need to note here that the Court of Appeal considered that the conveyance of the freehold to the former tenant had the effect of converting his former easement, granted for a term of years, into one equivalent to the fee simple absolute in possession. Although most of the decisions on the effect of s. 62 have been concerned with activities permitted by licence, the court emphasised that the fact that the right in question here was already a legal easement made no difference:

> ...if at the time of the conveyance the occupier of No. 231 had enjoyed a permissive use of [the passageway] s. 62 would have converted it into a right attached to the freehold. It is hard to see why the occupier of No.231 should be in a worse position because his enjoyment is not simply permissive, but is protected for 999 years (per Carnwath LJ at para.27).

25.8.3 Conditions for successful claims under s. 62

Any claim to be entitled to an easement or profit by virtue of s. 62 must satisfy certain conditions.

25.8.3.1 The right claimed must be capable of being an easement or profit (*Phipps v Pears* [1965] 1 QB 76)

This is, of course, a requirement that applies to all methods of acquisition, and we have already considered the various conditions for recognition as an easement (25.2.1 and 25.2.3).

25.8.3.2 There must be a conveyance upon which s. 62 can operate

The definition of 'conveyance' in LPA 1925, s. 205(1)(ii) in effect requires a written document, other than a will, which creates or transfers a legal estate or interest in land. In general most conveyances are made by deed, because as you will remember dealings with a legal estate are ineffective unless made by deed. A short lease granted informally under LPA 1925 s. 54(2) will amount to a conveyance for the purposes of s. 62 if the grant is made by a written document (as it was in *Wright v Macadam*), but an oral lease has been held not to constitute a conveyance (see *Rye v Rye* [1962] AC 496, in which it was held that the definition of conveyance in LPA 1925, s. 205 requires there to be an 'instrument', i.e., a written document).

The requirement for a conveyance means that s. 62 does not operate upon contracts to grant or transfer an estate in land, despite the fact that such contracts may create equitable interests in the property (*Re Peck's Contract* [1893] 2 Ch 315). An illustration of this is to be found in *Borman v Griffith* [1930] 1 Ch 493, in which it was held that existing easements that benefited a property did not pass to the prospective tenant under a contract to grant a lease. It follows from this that there is no question of quasi-easements or licences being converted into easements by a contract for a lease and, as we mentioned when considering equitable leases (10.3.5.4), this is yet another way in which a contract for a lease is not 'as good as' a legal lease.

25.8.3.3 The conveyance must not express a 'contrary intention'

Section 62 applies only in so far as a contrary intention is not expressed in the conveyance (s. 62(4)), and it is open to the grantor to exclude the section altogether (although this might create some practical difficulties) or to make it clear that there is no intention to grant certain rights.

25.8.3.4 There must be diversity of occupation

In a number of cases, judges have said that new easements and profits arise under s. 62 only where the two properties were separately occupied before the date of the conveyance. This requirement is usually attributed to the decision in *Long v Gowlett* [1923] 2 Ch 177. In this case, the owner of a mill claimed the right to go on his neighbour's land to cut weeds on the river bank which impeded the flow of water to his mill. The two pieces of land had previously been in common ownership, and the owner had cleared and maintained the river banks in this way. The miller claimed that, when the mill was conveyed to him, s. 6(2) of the Conveyancing Act 1881 (the forerunner of s. 62) created an easement benefiting his mill and binding the other part of the land. The court rejected this claim, saying that in such a case there was no 'privilege, easement or advantage' being exercised at the date of such a conveyance, for the owner-occupier of both plots could not be exercising rights against himself. In such a case there were no rights which could mature into easements on the conveyance.

This view is confirmed by *obiter dicta* of Lord Wilberforce in *Sovmots Investments Ltd v Secretary of State for the Environment* [1979] AC 144 (sometimes described as 'the Centre Point case'), in which his Lordship said (at p. 169):

> The reason is that when land is under one ownership one cannot speak in any intelligible sense of rights, or privileges, or easements being exercised over one part for the benefit of another. Whatever the owner does, he does as owner and, until a separation occurs, of ownership or at least of occupation, the condition for the existence of rights, etc., does not exist.

This issue was considered further by the Court of Appeal in *Payne v Inwood* (1996) 74 P&CR 42. This case involved two houses in a terrace of three: No. 1 was the corner house and access to the rear of the house could be obtained by passing up the side of the house; No. 1A was the next house in the terrace and originally access to the rear of No. 1A could only be obtained by passing through the house itself. Both No. 1 and No. 1A had yards at the rear of the house which adjoined one another and in about 1964 the then owner of No. 1 had allowed the construction of a gate between the two rear yards (largely because the owners of the two properties were close friends and this permitted easy access between the houses). Thereafter it was possible to gain access to the rear of No. 1A by walking up the side of No. 1, across the back yard of No. 1 and through the gate into the yard of No. 1A.

In 1971, No. 1 was bought by the then owner of No.1A. She moved into her new property, but retained occupation of No. 1A until she sold it a week later. Some 20 years after this, a dispute arose between the then owners of the two houses, and the owners of No. 1A sought a declaration that they were entitled to a right of way over No. 1. At first instance, the judge rejected claims that an easement had arisen by prescription (i.e., by long use) or under the rule in *Wheeldon v Burrows*, but held that an easement had been created by the conveyance of 1971, which as a result of s. 62 had converted a licence to use the way into an easement.

On appeal by the owners of No. 1, this decision was reversed, the Court of Appeal holding that s. 62 cannot operate to convert a licence into an easement unless there was some diversity of ownership or occupation prior to the conveyance. At the time immediately before the 1971 conveyance, both houses had been owned and occupied by their common owner, albeit only for one week, and this prevented the creation of a new easement under s. 62.

In his judgment, with which other members of the Court of Appeal concurred, Roch LJ considered the case of *Broomfield v Williams* [1987] 1 Ch 602, which appears to conflict with the requirement for diversity of occupation. In this case the plaintiff claimed to have a right of light over adjoining land retained by his vendor. The two pieces of land had been both owned and occupied by the vendor before the conveyance, but the Court of Appeal held that the purchaser had acquired a right to light by virtue of the Conveyancing Act 1881, s. 6(2). In *Payne v Inwood* the court accepted that this earlier decision constituted a genuine exception to the requirement of separate occupation, but considered (at p. 51) that the exception was:

> to be confined to cases dealing with such advantages as light to buildings.

The right to light is often said to be an unusual easement with its own characteristics and so it did not seem unreasonable to distinguish *Broomfield v Williams* in this way. If this could be done, *Payne v Inwood* seemed to provide good modern authority for the requirement of diverse occupation.

So is diversity of occupation an essential requirement?

This question has generated a good deal of academic controversy, and the Further Reading section at the end of this chapter contains references to some of the resulting literature. Although the supposed rule is supported by the *dicta* in *Sovmots* and the decision of the Court of Appeal in *Payne v Inwood*, it must be said that the leading texts on this area of law do not consider that separate occupation is required (see Jackson, *The Law of Easements and Profits*, 1978, p. 100, and Gale, *Easements*, 18th edn., 2008, pp. 3–133).

It may, however, be possible to reconcile these different views if one distinguishes between the effect of s. 62 on:

- continuous and apparent quasi-easements, which can become full easements on conveyance without separate occupation; and
- licences, which are converted under s. 62 only if there is diversity of occupation.

This way of ordering apparently conflicting decisions was suggested not long after the decision in *Sovmots* (see articles by Harpum at [1979] 41 Conv 415 and [1979] 43 Conv 113), and it has now found its way into Megarry and Wade at para. 28–033 (not surprisingly, perhaps, in view of the fact that the current editor was also the author of those two articles). On this approach, the claim in *Long v Gowlett* did not succeed because there was no diversity of occupation and because the common owner's practice of walking along the river bank to cut the weeds was not 'continuous and apparent', there being no track or path which indicated this practice (see [1923] 2 Ch 177 at 199). By contrast, a right to light can be regarded as 'continuous and apparent' (the windows that receive light being a permanent feature of property) and *Broomfield v Williams* can therefore be explained as a case of a continuous and apparent quasi-easement being converted by the operation of s. 62 upon the conveyance.

We have to say that we find this distinction helpful, and accordingly adopted it at the start of our discussion of s. 62. Reassuringly for us, the Court of Appeal appeared to follow this approach in *P & S Platt Ltd v Crouch* [2004] 1 P&CR 18. This case concerned a hotel, situated close to a river, and an adjacent piece of land which provided mooring facilities for guests arriving at the hotel by boat. The claimant bought the hotel from the common owner of both properties but, through failure to exercise an option in time, did not acquire the additional land. As a result, the hotel's customers were no longer able to use the moorings or to access the hotel from the river bank. The purchaser therefore sought a declaration that, on the conveyance of the hotel to him, he had acquired rights of access and mooring over the retained land by virtue of s. 62.

Although both properties had been in common ownership and occupation immediately before the conveyance, the purchaser succeeded in his claim, Peter Gibson LJ stating (at para. 42):

> The rights were continuous and apparent, and so it matters not that prior to the sale of the hotel there was no prior diversity of occupation of the dominant and servient tenements... Accordingly, I reach the conclusion that s. 62 operated to convert the rights into full easements.

25.8.4 **Trant Way**

If we now consider the situation of Mr Forest and Mr Gruyére at 2 Trant Way (see 25.1.1.2), it seems very probable that Mr Gruyére has acquired the legal easement of keeping his dustbin in the garden. The dustbin is unlikely to take up too much space, and so would probably be acceptable as an easement of storage. The recent grant in writing of a two-year lease provides the necessary conveyance for the operation of s. 62 (*Wright v Macadam*) and the magic of s. 62 will therefore have converted what was a mere licence into a legal easement.

25.8.5 Nature of grant under s. 62

Since s. 62 operates by importing certain words into the conveyance, it has the effect of making an express, not implied, grant of the easement or profit (*Gregg v Richards* [1926] Ch 521). It is for this reason that LRA 2002 provides that the requirement to complete an express grant of an easement by registration does not apply to easements arising under s. 62 (LRA 2002, s. 27(7)). Despite this, some textbooks describe easements acquired by virtue of s. 62 as being 'impliedly granted', and there are several recent decisions in which judges have referred to s. 62 as giving rise to 'an implied grant' (although without any discussion of the matter). At present, the question of classification does not appear to be of any great significance, but we mention it here in case you are confused by it.

25.8.6 Comparison of the rule in *Wheeldon v Burrows* and LPA 1925, s. 62

Space does not permit us to make a detailed comparison, and indeed it will be more useful to you to make this for yourself, but we will indicate briefly the main differences.

(a) *Wheeldon v Burrows* relates only to easements, whilst s. 62 applies to both easements and profits (see *White v Williams* [1922] 1 KB 727).

(b) *Wheeldon v Burrows* operates where, before the conveyance, the two pieces of land have been occupied by the same person, whereas, save in the case of continuous and apparent easements, diversity of occupation is required for s. 62.

(c) The types of easements which can pass under *Wheeldon v Burrows* are restricted by the three requirements of the rule, whereas there are no such restrictions in the case of s. 62 (save for the requirement that quasi-easements should be 'continuous and apparent').

(d) *Wheeldon v Burrows*, unlike s. 62, is apparently not limited to conveyances. Thus it seems that a contract to grant a lease may be sufficient to create an easement in favour of the tenant under *Wheeldon v Burrows* (*Borman v Griffith* [1930] 1 Ch 493) although it is not enough to pass even existing easements under s. 62.

25.9 Acquisition by prescription

Both easements and profits may be acquired as the result of long use, as well as by the means of grant and reservation described above. This method of acquisition is called 'prescription', of which there are three forms:

- common law prescription;
- the fiction of lost modern grant; and
- under the Prescription Act 1832.

All these types of prescription have a number of characteristics in common:

1. *Creation of legal interests*
All three forms will give the acquirer a legal easement or legal profit, even although there has in fact been no grant by deed.

2. *Acquisition based on a fiction*
With the exception of one of the forms of prescription under the Prescription Act, all these methods are based on the fiction that a grant of the easement or profit has been made at some time in the past, and long use is regarded merely as evidence of that grant. Some of the rules about prescription that may seem strange will be more easily understood if you remember that they are designed to maintain this pretence.

3. *Acquiescence of servient tenement owner*
In claiming that an easement has been created by any form of prescription, it is essential to show that the owner of the servient land acquiesced in the use during the prescription period. In *Dalton v Angus* (1881) 6 App Cas 740 at 773–4, Fry J stated that in his opinion the whole law of prescription rested upon acquiescence, and summarised the circumstances in which the servient owner can be said to acquiesce as being that:

- he knows of the use
- he has the power to stop it; and
- he does not do so.

In establishing acquiescence, knowledge may be actual or imputed, i.e., the owner will be taken to know facts of which he should have become aware 'as an ordinary owner of the servient land, diligent in the protection of his interests' (per Chadwick LJ in *Williams v Sandy Lane (Chester) Ltd* [2007] 1 EGLR 10). The claimant is not required to prove knowledge on the part of the owner: he is presumed to know of the use and it is for him to rebut this presumption by showing that he did not know (*Pugh v Savage* [1974] 1 WLR 1427 at 1434).

The need to show acquiescence can cause problems when the servient land has been occupied by a tenant for some or all of the prescription period, and we will consider how the requirement operates in these circumstances later (see 25.9.1.2).

25.9.1 Basic rules for prescription

There are three basic rules which apply to all the methods of prescription and we will discuss these first and then consider each of the three forms of prescription in turn.

25.9.1.1 Use must be as of right

It is essential for the claimant to establish that, throughout the period of use, he or she has enjoyed the right claimed 'as of right'. The use (and that of any predecessors in title, if relevant) must be consistent with the fiction that the right was granted at some time in the past, and that the owner of the dominant land has been acting in reliance on this. Any inconsistent behaviour will be taken to show that the claimant does not have such a right. It appears that it is irrelevant that the claimant of the easement has been exercising the right in the mistaken belief that it has in fact been granted (*Bridle v Ruby* [1989] QB 169).

The traditional formulation of the test of whether the use is as of right is that the use must be *nec vi, nec clam, nec precario*.

1. *Nec vi*
This means that the right claimed must not have been exercised by force. Thus, if Farmer George were to have erected a gate blocking access to the footpath on his land, Mr Neep

would be using the path by force if he broke down the gate, or even if he simply climbed over it. Even a protest by the servient owner can prevent user as of right, for ignoring a protest is regarded as use by force (*Eaton v Swansea Waterworks Co.* (1851) 17 QB 267). The rule prevents people obtaining interests in land by use of 'strong-arm' tactics.

It was said at one time that acting illegally also prevented acquisition of an easement: *Hanning v Top Deck Travel Group Ltd* [1993] 68 P&CR 14. However, the House of Lords took the opposite view in *Bakewell Management Ltd v Brandwood* [2004] 2 AC 519, in which their Lordships distinguished between a use that could be or become lawful and a use that could never be lawful. They were of the view that public policy did not require that it be unlawful to acquire an easement by prescription where the use relied upon would not have been a tort or a crime had an easement been granted expressly. Since in *Bakewell Management* the owners of the servient land could have given consent, the right could be acquired by prescription. On this point, see also *George Legge & Son Ltd v Wenlock Corporation* [1938] AC 204 and *Cargill v Gotts* [1981] 1 WLR 441.

2. *Nec clam*

The right must not be exercised secretly, for such use prevents the servient owner from objecting to the acquisition of the right and appears inconsistent with a claim of right. In *Liverpool Corporation v Coghill & Sons Ltd* [1918] 1 Ch 307 a claim to an easement of drainage was unsuccessful because the claimant's drain had entered the general sewer below ground and it was impossible for the corporation to ascertain that one more load of effluent had been added to its general burden. A similar result was caused by secret use in *Union Lighterage Co v London Graving Dock* [1902] 2 Ch 557, in which the claimed easement of support was being exercised secretly, below water level.

Thus, if Mr Neep had used the farmer's path only at dead of night and in a manner designed to conceal his use, he would be regarded as not having exercised an easement of way as of right.

3. *Nec precario*

This means that the right must not be enjoyed precariously, i.e., by permission. If the servient owner has given the claimant permission, the use is by licence, not as of right, and such permissive use is inconsistent with the fiction that an easement was granted at some time in the past. Thus, if Farmer George has given Mr Neep permission to use the path, his use is not made 'as of right', and he will not be able to acquire a legal right of way by prescription. In some cases, of course, permission may have been given so long ago that it may be deemed to have lapsed, so that the more recent use may be regarded as not being by permission (*Arkwright v Gell* (1839) 5 M & W 203).

At this point, we must emphasise that some claims under the Prescription Act are subject to special rules about permission, and we will consider these later (see 25.9.5.2(1)).

Implied licence

In *R (Beresford) v Sunderland City Council* [2004] 1 AC 889, the House of Lords indicated that, even in the absence of express permission, a claim to acquire by prescription can theoretically be displaced by evidence of implied permission. When you look at the case you will see that it did not concern an easement but was about public rights to use a recreational area. However, this is an area of law in which the same concept of user as of right applies and thus the case is also useful in relation to easements and profits. Lord Bingham said (at para. 5):

> I can see no objection in principle to the implication of a licence where the facts warrant such an implication. To deny this possibility would, I think, be unduly old-fashioned, formalistic and restrictive.

Here it was argued that because the Council had mown the grass and provided seating it had impliedly consented to the use being made (and thus given permission). The House of Lords did not, however accept this view of the facts and held that the public use during the statutory period had not been by permission and thus was user as of right.

Distinguishing between acquiescence and permission

We have told you that acquiescence by the servient owner is an essential element of prescription, and yet we are now saying that permission from that owner will prevent time running against him. You may find this confusing, but the courts emphasise that the two concepts are completely different. An owner who acquiesces does nothing: he merely tolerates or 'puts up with' the use of his land. By contrast, permission requires some positive act: the giving of oral or written consent, or the doing of some act from which permission may be inferred. Such permission cannot be inferred from the mere inaction of a landowner with knowledge of the use to which his land is being put (per Lord Bingham in *R (Beresford) v Sunderland City Council* [2004] 1 AC 889 at para. 6). However, permission bars acquisition by prescription even if the dominant owner did not ask for permission: *Odey v Barber* [2008] 2 WLR 618.

25.9.1.2 **The right must be acquired by a fee simple owner against a fee simple owner**

Again, this rule originates in the pretence that the right has been properly granted at some time in the past, for the only way to explain its continuance is that it was granted in fee simple, rather than for a limited period of years. This implies a grant by a fee simple owner to a fee simple owner.

Prescription by a tenant

Even if the use in question is by a tenant, any easement or profit acquired as a result will attach to the fee simple in the dominant land, rather than to the tenant's lease (though of course the tenant will still have an interest in claiming).

As a result, it is never possible for a tenant of dominant land to acquire rights by prescription against his own landlord (*Gayford v Moffat* (1868) LR 4 Ch App 133), for such a tenant can only claim to acquire an easement on behalf of the landlord, and the landlord cannot have rights against himself (*Ivimey v Stocker* (1866) LR 1 Ch App 396). It is emphasised that what we are saying is only that a tenant cannot acquire easements against his landlord by prescription, for we have already seen that he may acquire such rights by express or implied grant. Similarly it was held in *Simmons v Dobson* [1991] 1 WLR 720 that a tenant could not obtain by prescription against another tenant of the same landlord (see also on this point *Wheaton v Maple* [1893] 3 Ch 48 and *Kilgour v Gaddes* [1904] 1 KB 457).

Prescription against a tenant (i.e., where the servient land is occupied by a tenant during the prescription period).

Where an easement is acquired by prescription it binds the fee simple estate in the servient land. If that land is let to a tenant during the prescription period it seems unfair to allow the dominant owner to claim the acquisition of an easement or profit by prescription. The tenant on the servient land may well not be concerned about the exercise of the right, whilst the fee simple owner may not be aware of the user since he has given exclusive possession of the land to his tenant. In these circumstances it would not really be true to say that the owner has acquiesced in the prescriptive use and, as we have noted, such acquiescence is an essential requirement. As a result, some claims under the Prescription Act are subject to special rules, which provide for periods of occupation under leases for more than three years to be deducted from the prescription period (see

25.9.5.2(3)). In all other forms of prescription, the matter is regulated by case law, and the relevant rules have recently been reviewed and restated by the Court of Appeal in *Williams v Sandy Lane (Chester) Ltd* [2007] 1 EGLR 10.

This case involved claims to rights of way said to have been acquired by prescription over the defendant's land. Two different routes were involved. One, the 'secondary route', was held by the trial judge to have been abandoned and we will consider this aspect of the case later (see 25.11.3). The claim to use the 'primary route' raised several issues about acquiescence, one of them being the claim that acquiescence by the freehold owner could not be established because part of the primary route lay on land occupied by a tenant during the prescription period. This argument was rejected by the Court of Appeal, because the rest of the route lay over land still occupied by the owner, who could have prevented the use. As a result, the court's observations on the rules relating to acquiescence in respect of tenanted land are *obiter dicta*, but are still well worth noting.

As summarised by Chadwick LJ (at paras. 22–24) the position is as follows:

(i) *If the use began before the grant of the lease* and the owner knew of it before making the grant, he can be said to have acquiesced in the use, and the prescription period will run against him, despite the fact that the land is occupied by a tenant for part of the period. Thus, in *Pugh v Savage* [1970] 2 QB 373 an easement was acquired by prescription even though the servient land had been let for 10 years in the middle of the prescription period.

(ii) *If the use begins when the land is already let* the general rule is that the prescription period will only start when the fee simple owner re-enters at the end of the lease (*Daniel v North* (1809) 11 East 372; although note that there is some uncertainty in the case of certain claims under the Prescription Act see 25.9.5.2(2)). However, Chadwick LJ suggested (at para. 24) that despite the lease, the owner could be said to acquiesce if he:

> does have knowledge [actual or imputed] of the user and could (notwithstanding the tenancy) take steps to prevent that user, but does not do so.

In these circumstances, the prescription period would run despite occupation by the tenant.

It is therefore the rule that there should be no tenancy of the servient land at the start of the prescription period. If, however, the fee simple owner is in possession when the use begins, he has the opportunity to discover what has happened and, if he subsequently lets the land, can make enquiries of his tenant in order to ascertain whether the use is continuing. Thus, in *Pugh v Savage* [1970] 2 QB 373 an easement was acquired by prescription even though the servient land had been let for 10 years in the middle of the prescription period. If, however, the land is let when the use began, the prescription period will only start when the fee simple owner re-enters (*Daniel v North* (1809) 11 East 372).

25.9.1.3 The use must be continuous

The infrequent use of a right is not sufficient if one is claiming an easement or profit by prescription. Thus, if Mr Neep had used Farmer George's path on only three occasions in the last 12 years this would not support a claim to an easement by prescription (see *Hollins v Verney* (1884) 13 QBD 304). As we have mentioned previously, the exercise of a right of way can never be continuous in a literal sense, but for the purposes of prescription regular usage will suffice. Also the right exercised should not generally be varied during the period for prescription, although in the case of *Davis v Whitby* [1974] Ch 186 it was regarded as acceptable if a minor variation was made for the sake of convenience (here the alteration was to the exact path used in the case of a right of way).

25.9.2 Prescription at common law

In order to establish a claim to an easement or profit by prescription at common law, it is necessary to establish that the interest has been enjoyed, as of right, since *time immemorial* or, to use the traditional phrase, 'from time whereof the memory of man runneth not to the contrary'. You may, however, be amused to discover that lawyers have a very definite view on when the 'memory of man' started. Under the Statute of Westminster the First (1275), c. 39, the date of legal memory is 1189 and this date has never been amended. Therefore this method of prescription requires that the right in question was in existence before that date.

You will appreciate that it is practically impossible to establish positively such a long period of use. Accordingly, the rule has developed that proof of use during living memory will raise a presumption that the right has been enjoyed since 1189. Originally user during living memory was established by asking the oldest inhabitants of the area whether the right had been exercised as long as they recalled. Today all that is needed is evidence that the right has been used for at least 20 years (*Darling v Clue* (1864) 4 F & F 329).

However, the presumption raised by the 20-year use is a rebuttable presumption, and the claim to prescription at common law can be destroyed by evidence which shows that the right claimed must have begun later than 1189. Thus if the claim were to an easement of light, proof that the building on the dominant tenement had been built after 1189 would destroy the claim at common law (*Bury v Pope* (1588) Cro Eliz 118). Similarly, if the dominant and servient tenements have been in common ownership at any time since 1189 this claim at common law will fail because even if the right had been granted before 1189, it would have come to an end when the two pieces of land came into the same hands (see 25.2.1.2), and any grant when they separated again would be after the date of legal memory (*Keymer v Summers* (1769) Bull NP 74).

Thus, were Nigel Neep to claim his right to use the footpath on Farmer George's land by common law prescription, he would be able to raise the presumption of use since 1189 if he and his predecessors in title had used the path for 20 years, but his claim would easily be defeated if Farmer George could prove that 14 Trant Way and Fieldy Farm were once owned by one person (which is very likely to be the case). As a result claims by prescription under the pure common law rule are rarely successful today, although, as we shall see, some assistance is provided by the Prescription Act 1832.

25.9.3 Lost modern grant

Because it was so difficult to obtain an easement or profit under the general common law rules, the courts eventually developed a second method of prescription at common law, known as the fiction of the lost modern grant. This requires that the claimant should first establish user during living memory (for at least 20 years). Once this has been established the court is prepared to presume that the right is being exercised as the result of a modern grant by deed, but that the grant has been lost (see *Dalton v Angus & Co.* (1881) 6 App Cas 740).

25.9.3.1 Rebutting the presumption that a grant was made

It appears that the presumption cannot be rebutted by proving that no grant has been made but it will destroy the claim if the servient owner can show that, at the date at which it is alleged the grant occurred, there was no person capable of making the grant (for example, because the land was subject to a SLA settlement, under which no grant could be made). Similarly the claim may be opposed by showing that at the relevant time the dominant and servient tenements were in common ownership (see *Neaverson v Peterborough Rural District Council* [1902] 1 Ch 557).

25.9.3.2 Continued existence of this form of prescription

This method of prescription, based on a blatant fiction, was disliked in the nineteenth century, and it was hoped that the changes introduced by the Prescription Act 1832 would make it unnecessary to use it. However, as we shall see, this Act has proved to be most unsatisfactory, and although it had been thought that present-day courts would be unwilling to accept a claim based on such a fiction, the doctrine was revived by the Court of Appeal in *Tehidy Minerals Ltd v Norman* [1971] 2 QB 528 (see 25.9.7 for an account of this decision). Since *Tehidy*, this method of prescription has been relied upon in a number of modern cases.

The extent of the fiction is well illustrated by *Bridle v Ruby* [1989] QB 169. There a developer built and sold a number of houses. Originally it was intended that the purchaser of plot 12 was to be granted an express right of way over a drive. In fact the relevant clause was deleted from the conveyance so that the grant of the right was never made. The purchaser and his successors, in the mistaken belief that they had the right to do so, used the driveway for 22 years. Here the Court of Appeal held that the right could be claimed on the basis of lost modern grant. The fact that the relevant clause had been deleted from the original conveyance did not prevent the operation of the theory that, at a later date, a grant had been made. It was even irrelevant that the owners of plot 12 had used the right believing that the right to do so arose from the original conveyance. This case clearly demonstrates that the legal fiction is alive and well in the modern age. For a further illustration see *Mills v Silver* [1991] Ch 271, in which the Court of Appeal considered at length the issue of permission in relation to the doctrine of lost modern grant.

25.9.4 Prescription Act 1832

The Prescription Act 1832 may very well have the dubious honour of being the worst drafted Act of Parliament on the statute book. Indeed it is even generally presumed that there is a serious misprint in s. 8 of the Act and lawyers have accordingly adopted the habit of reading the section as though the misprint did not exist (thereby substituting the word 'easement' for the word 'convenient' where it appears in s. 8). The Act was intended to remove the difficulties which arose with the common law forms of prescription; however, it did not abolish the common law forms, so that the three forms now exist alongside one another. Furthermore, the Act introduced fresh complexities of its own.

The Act divides the easement of light from all other easements and profits and deals with it separately. Furthermore it creates two different prescription periods (a 'short period' and a 'long period'), with different effects, for profits and easements other than light. The provisions relating to the short period merely assist a person claiming under the common law rules, but those relating to the long period introduce a form of statutory prescription, which does not depend on any fiction.

25.9.5 Profits and easements other than light under the Prescription Act 1832

25.9.5.1 Short period

The short period for easements is 20 years (Prescription Act 1832, s. 2), and for profits is 30 years (s. 1). The Act provides that, where use can be shown for the appropriate period, no claim to prescription at common law shall be defeated by showing that the right 'was first enjoyed at any time prior to such period'. The effect of this provision is quite simple but understanding why the statutory words have this effect is not so easy. The explanation is as follows. Legal memory does not go back before 1189, so, if the right was first enjoyed before that date, it would not be possible to show when it started. Thus the fact that one can show when it started means that that beginning must be after 1189, which would be fatal to a claim at common law. Therefore the Act is saying, in a roundabout way, that once the period had been completed, common law prescription cannot be defeated merely by showing that the use began after 1189.

The claim can still be defeated in any other way that would defeat common law prescription, such as showing that the use is not as of right, or that the right claimed lacks the characteristics of an easement or profit.

Deductions

In order to provide some protection for a servient owner who is subject to a legal disability, s. 7 of the Act provides that certain periods should be deducted when one computes the 20- or 30-year short period. The effect of these provisions, as modified by later reforms of the law, is that one should deduct any period during which the servient owner was:

(a) an infant;

(b) a patient under the Mental Health Act 1983 (or the Acts which preceded it); or

(c) a tenant for life.

Thus, if Nigel Neep had exercised his right of way for 35 years but for 20 of those years the owner of Fieldy Farm had been incapable (e.g., Farmer George's father had suffered from dementia for 20 years before his death) Mr Neep can only claim 15 years of user for the purposes of the short period. He can, however, add together the use before the old man's illness overcame his mental capacity and the use after Farmer George inherited on his father's death. He does not have to restart the period once the disability is removed (*Pugh v Savage* [1970] 2 QB 373).

25.9.5.2 Long period

The long period is 40 years for easements (s. 2) and 60 years for profits (s. 1). The benefit of proving use for the longer period is that the right claimed

> shall be deemed absolute and indefeasible, unless it shall appear that the same was enjoyed by some consent or agreement expressly given or made for the purpose by deed or writing.

This is the statutory form of prescription, and does not depend on the common law rules, although use does still have to be as of right. It may also be the case that the long period does not rely upon any fiction that there must have been a grant at some time. This is the view we have always taken and our view is shared by a number of others. However, in *Housden v The Conservators of Wimbledon and Putney Commons* [2008] 1

WLR 1172 the Court of Appeal considered this point (without deciding it) and drew attention to the difference of opinion on the point.

1. *Consents*

It is clear from the statutory provisions we have quoted that written consent can destroy a claim under the long period, whether it was given before the period started or during the period. At first reading this may seem to imply that purely oral permission cannot destroy the claim. However, this is not the case for it is still necessary for the dominant owner to show that his use of the easement or profit during the 40- or 60-year period has amounted to use as of right. As we have seen already, if the servient owner has given oral permission the use is precarious and not as of right. Accordingly oral permission given during the long period will destroy the claim but oral permission given before the period can be ignored.

2. *Does the use have to start against a fee simple owner?*

As we have said, at common law the prescription period could not start at a time when the servient land was let to a tenant. In *Davies v Du Paver* [1953] 1 QB 184 the Court of Appeal appeared to apply the same rule to a case brought under the Prescription Act 1832. However, in the earlier case of *Wright v Williams* (1836) 1 M & W 77 (which was not cited in *Davies v Du Paver*) it was held that the common law rule did not apply because of the positive wording of the Act. It would appear that the better view is that the rule does not apply, particularly as in s. 8 special provision is made for deduction of periods during which the servient land is subject to a lease (see Megarry (1956) 72 LQR 32).

3. *Deductions*

Deductions from the long period are governed by s. 8. It should be noted that these rules bear no real relation to the deductions from the short period prescribed by s. 7. Assuming that the word 'convenient' in s. 8 is a misprint for 'easement', s. 8 provides for the deductions from the long period of any term during which the servient land was:

(a) held by a tenant for life;

(b) held by a tenant under a lease for more than three years.

However, the s. 8 deductions may only be made if the servient owner resists the claim to acquisition by prescription within the three years following the end of the life interest or lease.

4. *Application of rules*

The following example may make this clearer:

1 January 1970	The then owner of 14 Trant Way started to use the footpath on Fieldy Farm.
1 January 1998	Lease of Fieldy Farm for 10 years granted.
31 December 2007	Lease ends.
31 December 2009	40 years' use of right of way.

In this example, if Mr Neep had claimed under the longer period on 1 January 2010, Farmer George would have been able to claim a deduction from the period of use, under s. 8. For in these circumstances the servient tenement, Fieldy Farm, would have been subject to a lease for more than three years (10 years) and that lease would have ended less than three years before the date of the action. (Action started on 1 January 2010 and lease ended two years earlier on 31 December 2007). If, however, the use continues, but no action were brought until 2011, more than three years would have elapsed since the end of the lease, and Farmer George would accordingly not be entitled to make any deduction. Thus, if the matter came to court in 2010 Nigel Neep would only have a claim based on 30 years' use (40 years' actual use, less 10 years during which the servient land was let), whilst if the case started in or after 2011 Nigel Neep can claim 41 years' use (no deduction is permitted). This result may seem odd at first sight but one should remember that the purpose of s. 8 is to provide limited protection for the reversioner who takes action swiftly on recovering the land. This may be particularly important to the freehold reversioner or a remainderman, following on after a tenant for life under an SLA settlement, who should accordingly make immediate enquiries about such matters as soon as his interest vests in possession.

25.9.5.3 Rules common to both short and long periods

Certain rules are common to both the long and the short periods.

1. *User as of right*

We have already seen that the Prescription Act 1832 does not exclude the common law requirement that the user relied upon must be as of right during the period claimed, and this has been held to mean not only that the use should be *nec vi, nec clam,* and *nec precario,* but also that use must be by and against fee simple owners (*Kilgour v Gaddes* [1904] 1 KB 457).

2. *Period must be 'next before some suit or action'*

Under s. 4, the period relied upon must be

> next before some suit or action wherein the claim or matter to which such period may relate shall have been or shall be brought into question

Thus, a period of use which ceased some time before the commencement of an action cannot be relied upon for the purpose of statutory prescription, although it may be effective to support a claim to prescription at common law. Thus, in *Tehidy Minerals Ltd v Norman* [1971] 2 QB 528 claims based upon user which had ceased in 1941 (when the land was requisitioned by the army) were ineffective under the Act, although some claimants succeeded in establishing their rights under the principle of lost modern grant (see further 25.9.7).

Another effect of s. 4 is that no right to the easement or profit can exist under the statutory rules until some action is started, regardless of the length of use involved (*Hyman v Van den Bergh* [1908] 1 Ch 167). Of course, in order to secure his interest in the land, the dominant owner has only to apply to the court for a declaration that an easement or profit has been secured under the Act.

3. *There must have been no interruption*

A claim based on either period may be destroyed by proof that there has been some 'interruption' to the claimed interest and that the dominant owner has acquiesced in that interruption for the period of one year.

An 'interruption' is any action which interferes with the right claimed. In the case of the footpath on Fieldy Farm, Farmer George could create an interruption by erecting a gate, or other barrier, preventing access to the path. Thus, in *Davies v Du Paver* [1953] 1 QB 184, the servient owner erected a fence in order to exclude the dominant owner's sheep and thereby to prevent the acquisition of a profit. This case illustrates, however, that there must not only be an obstruction but that the obstruction must be acquiesced in for one year by the claimant. In *Davies v Du Paver* the dominant owner immediately protested at the erection of the fence, but did not issue proceedings to establish his claim to a profit until 13 months later. The Court of Appeal found that he had not acquiesced in the interruption for one year because his initial protest must have been effective for some period (at least a month) in which case at the start of the action there had been less than one year's acquiescence. However, mere discontent which is not sufficiently communicated cannot amount to sufficient action to indicate a lack of acquiescence (*Dance v Triplow* [1992] 1 EGLR 190).

As a result of this provision about acquiescence, an interruption that begins during the last year of any of the statutory periods will not prevent the claimant succeeding under the Act. For example, if an interruption were made, for example, to an easement after it had been used for 39 years and one day, the dominant owner could still issue proceedings 364 days later, as soon as the 40-year term is up, and claim that he had not acquiesced in the interruption for a year. By protesting at the interruption, he can extend the time still further. Thus, once usage has entered the last year of one of the periods, a servient tenement owner who objects to the use should commence proceedings immediately for trespass, for until the period is completed his opponent will not be able to rely on the existence of an easement or profit by prescription by way of defence.

25.9.6 Right to light under the Prescription Act 1832

25.9.6.1 One period only

The right to light is dealt with by the Prescription Act 1832 in a different way from its treatment of all other easements. There is only one period (not a 'short' and a 'long' period) and that requires use for a period of 20 years. Section 3 of the Act provides that if the 'use of light' to 'any building' has been

> actually enjoyed . . . for the full period of 20 years without interruption, the right thereto shall be deemed absolute and indefeasible

There are a number of differences between this provision and those relating to other easements and profits. In particular s. 3 does not require the satisfaction of the common law requirements for prescription. Accordingly, the use need not be as of right, nor is it necessary for the use to be by a fee simple owner against a fee simple owner. Thus, a tenant can acquire an easement of light by prescription against his landlord, or against a fellow tenant holding from the same landlord.

25.9.6.2 Interruption

The rules on interruption, however, do apply to easements of light in the same way as they apply to other rights claimed under the Act, and it has also been held that the 20-year period relied on must be next before suit or action, even though s. 3 does not specifically mention this (*Hyman v Van den Bergh* [1908] 1 Ch 167).

25.9.6.3 Preventing acquisition of right

It can be seen that it is far easier to acquire an easement of light than any other easement or profit. Accordingly, a 'servient' owner may well wish to take action to prevent his neighbour acquiring such a right. Unfortunately, in order to do this he or she would need to interrupt the use of the right, and the erection of some structure (e.g., a hoarding) in order to do this will probably be contrary to the planning regulations applicable to the property. As a result, the Rights of Light Act 1959 was passed in order to provide a simple means by which a claim to light can be interrupted. Under this Act, instead of building a hoarding, a servient owner may, after taking certain preliminary steps, register a notice in the Local Land Charges Register specifying the size and position of the obstruction which he would otherwise have erected. The entry upon the register operates as though a real obstruction had been built and therefore if the dominant owner takes no action for a year he will be deemed to have acquiesced in the interruption.

25.9.7 How to apply the three forms of prescription

We have now looked at a bewildering variety of rules, and you must wonder how they fit together and which method to use.

There are three main methods to consider, and it appears that they should be applied in the following order. Begin with the long period under the Prescription Act 1832. If there is not a sufficient period of use, or it is not 'next before the action', or for some other reasons that method does not succeed, apply the common law rules, assisted if possible by the short-period provisions of the Act. If that is not successful, as a last resort you should apply the doctrine of the lost modern grant. This is in effect the order in which the various forms of prescription were considered in *Tehidy Minerals Ltd v Norman* [1971] 2 QB 528. This judgment of the Court of Appeal does provide a very good example for anyone who has to deal with a problem of this kind and so we will end this section with an account of that case.

The plaintiffs owned an area of downland on which local farmers had grazed their animals since the nineteenth century. For some time during and after the Second World War the down was requisitioned, and when grazing was resumed it appeared to be by permission. The plaintiffs fenced the down and tried to exclude the farmers, but they broke the fences. The plaintiffs alleged trespass and the defendants claimed that they had a profit of grazing.

It was not possible to make the claim under the long period of the Act, because user had ceased in 1941, when the land was requisitioned, and therefore the period of use was not 'next before the action', as required by s. 4. The long use, dating back to the nineteenth century did, however, enable some farmers to raise a presumption that the right had existed from time immemorial, and they succeeded at common law. The other defendants, however, could not rely on the common law, because their farms and the down had been in common ownership at some time after 1189. They were not assisted by the shorter period under the Act because, again, it was not 'next before the action'. They were, however, able to show over 20 years' use before the war, and the Court of Appeal held that this was sufficient to raise a presumption of a lost modern grant and found that they had acquired a profit by this means.

For another case in which a claim under the short period in the Act failed but the claimant won by relying on lost modern grant, see *Smith v Brudenell-Bruce* [2002] 2 P&CR 4.

By now you will have realised that the rules for identifying and acquiring easements and profits are quite complex in structure (though probably not in themselves difficult to understand). Figure 25.4 provides a basic summary of the structure of these rules and Figure 25.5 provides a summary of the methods of acquiring easements by grant (or reservation), implied grant (or reservation), prescription or contract.

Note that this figure does not set out exceptions or details (see the text for these) and that the right must also satisfy the other requirements for acquisition set out in Figure 25.4.

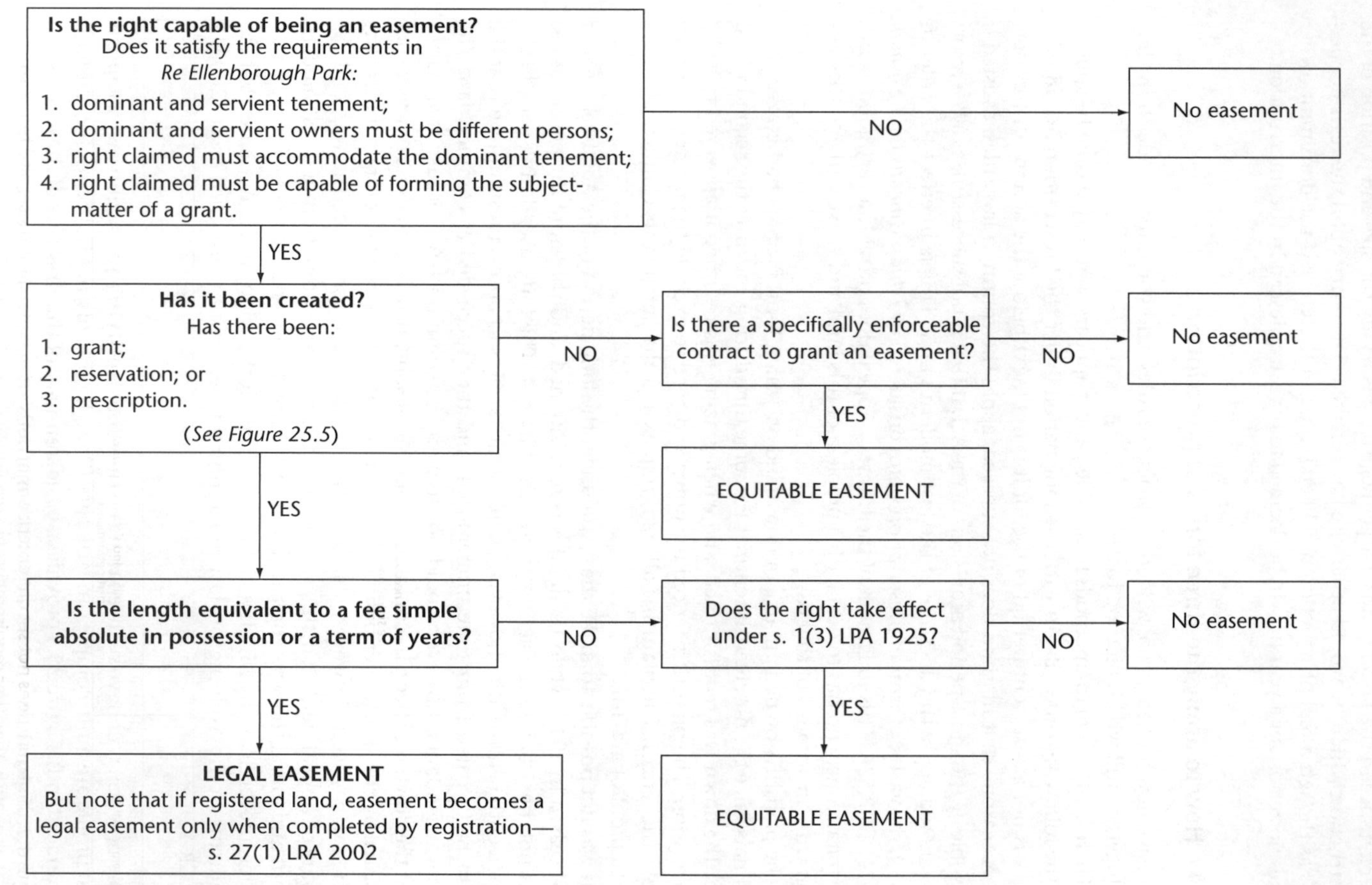

Figure 25.4 Acquisition of an easement

METHOD	REQUIREMENTS	RESULT
	EXPRESS GRANT OR RESERVATION	
Deed	A deed complying with s. 52(1) LPA 1925 (plus, in the case of registered land, completion by registration—s. 27(1) LRA 2002).	Legal easement
Section 62 LPA 1925	Conveyance or transfer may carry with it existing rights (licences) and convert them into easements—see *Wright v Macadam* *Note: This applies to grant only - not relevant to reservation*	Legal easement
	IMPLIED GRANT OR RESERVATION	
Easements of necessity and intended easements	Court will look at the intention of the parties—see *Nickerson v Barraclough*.	Legal easement
Rule in *Wheeldon v Burrows*	Must be: 1. continuous and apparent; 2. necessary to the reasonable enjoyment of the land; 3. in use at the time the land was sold. *Note: This applies to grant only - not relevant to reservation*	Legal easement
	PRESCRIPTION	
Common law prescription	Must be: 1. use as of right; 2. acquired by a fee simple owner against a fee simple owner; 3. continuous use; 4. possible to presume right has existed since time immemorial (1189)—a rebuttable presumption arises after 20 years' use. *Note: The presumption after 20 years is rebutted by evidence which establishes that an easement cannot have existed since 1189 or that tenements have been in common ownership after 1189.*	Legal easement
Common law prescription plus the benefit of the Prescription Act short period *(rights other than light)*	Must be: 1. use as of right; 2. by a fee simple owner against a fee simple owner; 3. without an interruption that has been acquiesced in for one year; 4. for 20 years next before a suit or action; 5. no evidence of express or implied consent either during or before the 20 year period. *Note: The short period under the Act 'assists' acquisition at common law by removing the possibility that the presumption after 20 years can be rebutted by evidence which establishes that an easement cannot have existed since before 1189.*	Legal easement
Prescription Act— long period *(rights other than light)*	Must be: 1. use as of right; 2. by a fee simple owner against a fee simple owner; 3. without an interruption that has been acquiesced in for one year; 4. for 40 years next before a suit or action; 5. no evidence of written consent either during or before the 40 year period or oral consent during the 40 year period.	Legal easement
Prescription Act—rights to light	Must be: 1. used for 20 years; 2. before some suit or action; 3. without an interruption that has been acquiesced in for one year. *Note: There is no need for use as of right and the acquisition need not be by a fee simple owner against a fee simple owner.*	Legal easement
Lost modern grant	Must be: 1. use as of right; 2. by a fee simple owner against a fee simple owner; 3. continuous use; 4. during living memory (20 years' use); 5. no evidence that a grant was impossible at the time any 'lost' grant must have been made.	Legal easement
	CONTRACT	
Contract made on or after 27 September 1989	Must be made in writing—s.2 Law of Property (Miscellaneous Provisions) Act 1989.	Equitable easement
Contract made before 27 September 1989	Must be: 1. recorded in writing and signed by servient owner—s. 40 LPA 1925; or 2. evidenced by part performance.	Equitable easement

Figure 25.5 Methods of creating an easement

Note that this figure does not set out exceptions or details (see the text for these) and that the right must also satisfy the other requirements for acquisition set out in Figure 25.4.

25.10 Remedies

We will now consider briefly the remedies which may be used to protect an easement or profit.

25.10.1 Abatement

Theoretically if any obstruction to the lawful exercise of a profit or easement is erected, the dominant owner may exercise a 'self-help' remedy and may simply 'abate' (remove) the obstruction. This may be done without informing the servient owner (*Perry v Fitzhowe* (1846) 8 QB 757) but the right should be used with care. The dominant owner must not use unreasonable force, nor may he injure any person in attempting to enforce his rights. It would, however, be permissible to break down a fence or gate. A self-help remedy may also be appropriate in the case of an easement of support. As we noted in 25.2.2.6, such an easement does not require the servient owner to maintain his property in order to provide adequate support, and he can in fact allow it to collapse, if that is what he wants to do (see *Jones v Pritchard* [1908] 1 Ch 630 at 637). However, the dominant owner is not obliged to leave the servient property to collapse, thus depriving his own premises of support. He can, instead, enter his neighbour's land and carry out such repairs as are necessary to ensure that the support of his property is maintained (see *Bond v Nottingham Corpn* [1940] Ch 429, per Greene MR at 438–9).

In general, however, it is inadvisable for the dominant owner to rely upon self-help, and indeed in *Lagan Navigation Co. v Lambeg Bleaching, Dyeing & Finishing Co. Ltd* [1927] AC 226 at p. 245 Lord Atkinson indicated that the law preferred that a remedy be sought through the courts, and that abatement should only be used in cases of extreme urgency.

25.10.2 Action

Normally, a person claiming that his or her easement or profit has been infringed will apply to the courts for a suitable remedy. Obviously, it is possible to seek a *declaration* to clarify the rights of the parties (useful where a right is claimed by prescription). The claimant may, however, go further and seek *damages* to compensate for any loss caused by the infringement but, if this is done, must establish some serious interference with the rights, rather than some trivial incident (*Weston v Lawrence Weaver Ltd* [1961] 1 QB 402).

Generally, the remedy which will be sought is that of an *injunction* restraining the interference of which the dominant owner complains. Once again, the courts will not intervene where the act complained of is only a trivial interference with the dominant owner's rights (*Cowper v Laidler* [1903] 2 Ch 337). However, there is no right to alter the terms of an easement even where the dominant owner could not reasonably object to the change. Thus, it would not be a defence to a complaint of interference with a private right of way that a reasonable substitute had been provided (*Greenwich Healthcare National Health Service Trust v London and Quadrant Housing Trust* [1998] 1 WLR 1749). The relevant question is not whether the use left to the person with the benefit of the right is reasonable, but whether it was reasonable for that person to insist on all he or she had bargained for: see *Celsteel Ltd v Alton House Ltd* [1985] 1 WLR 204 at p. 217.

Even if the court considers that the applicant deserves a remedy, it has power under the Supreme Court Act 1981 to award damages in place of an injunction if it considers that this would be a more appropriate remedy. When this power was first introduced in the nineteenth century, there was considerable discussion as to the principles which should guide the court in its choice of remedy. In *Shelfer v City of London Electric Lighting Co. Ltd* [1895] 1 Ch 287, at 322–3, Smith LJ said that in his opinion damages in lieu of an injunction may be given if:

- the injury to the plaintiff's legal rights is small; and
- is capable of being estimated in money; and
- can be adequately compensated by a small money payment; and
- the case is one in which it would be oppressive to the defendant to grant an injunction.

These conditions have recently been considered and applied by the courts in two cases involving interference with easements of light: *Tamares (Vincent Square) Ltd v Fairpoint Properties (Vincent Square) Ltd* [2007] 1 WLR 2148 ('*Tamares*') and *Regan v Paul Properties Ltd* [2007] Ch 135 ('*Regan*'). In both cases the interference complained of resulted from development work on the servient land, which was already well advanced by the time the cases came to court. In *Tamares*, the judge considered that it would be oppressive to require the demolition of a major part of a new building, and awarded damages in lieu of an injunction, while in *Regan* the Court of Appeal held that damages would not be an adequate remedy and required the developer to reduce the height of the building. These cases turn very much on their own facts and we are not suggesting that you should study them in any detail. All you need to note is that the court has the power to award damages in place of an injunction and that the decision as to whether to exercise that power is a matter for the court's discretion.

25.10.2.1 Claim in nuisance

One must also note that the inability to enforce an easement may not mean that a complainant has no remedy at all, because in some cases a claim in nuisance may be available. This may be particularly important in cases which, at first, seem to involve the easement of support. We noted above that, where support is not being maintained, the dominant tenement owner may enter and repair the servient property. However, *Bradburn v Lindsay* [1983] 2 All ER 408 suggests that another right may be available even where abatement has not been practicable. The case concerned two semi-detached houses, separated by a party wall, which were owned respectively by Mrs Lindsay (No. 53) and the Bradburns (No. 55). In 1972 Mr Bradburn complained that dry rot had taken hold in the party wall between the properties. Over the next few years, No. 53 became derelict and eventually the council ordered it to be demolished, because of its dangerous condition. The house was accordingly pulled down, save for its half of the party wall.

The Bradburns, whose half of the house was thus left unsupported, brought a claim in nuisance and negligence. A claim based on the easement of support should not in this case (at least theoretically) have succeeded since Mrs Lindsay had merely allowed the dereliction to occur and the pulling down of the house had been carried out by the council under statutory powers. However, the court held that the Bradburns' claim could succeed. The decision appears to be based in part in nuisance and in part in negligence. Judge Blackett-Ord V-C said that the considerable dry rot at No. 53 constituted a nuisance, that Mrs Lindsay should have appreciated the risks to No. 55 and accordingly should have taken steps to prevent the damage. Accordingly the Bradburns were able to recover the costs of works to strengthen and support No. 55.

It may be that this case does not conflict with the traditional view of the easement of support because, on a careful reading of the case, it seems that the decision is based on the principle that allowing spread of dry rot falls within the ambit of nuisance and goes further than simply allowing a structure to fall down. However, in practice the two may typically run together and thus nuisance may provide a useful alternative when the law relating to easements fails to provide a remedy (see also *Nuisances* by Gordon Wignall, 1998 (Sweet & Maxwell)).

There are two other cases that adopt this approach. In *Holbeck Hall Hotel v Scarborough BC* [2000] QB 836, it was said that a duty may arise in tort but this extends only to damage that is reasonably foreseeable. In *Holbeck* it could only have been foreseen had there been geological investigation and the defendant was not obliged to carry out such an investigation.

Rees v Skerrett [2001] 1 WLR 1541 concerned two terraced houses, one of which was demolished. As a consequence the party wall between the properties became unstable and it also was exposed to the weather. The instability was clearly a breach of the easement of support and the court held so. However, the owner of the affected (dominant) property had suffered additional loss due to the penetration of rain through the wall, which had caused damp in his house. This loss was not attributable to the loss of support. It was accepted that no easement could be claimed in relation to protection from the weather (*Phipps v Pears* [1965] 1 QB 76). However, the court held that the servient owner did owe an additional duty to take care when demolishing his house, to the extent necessary to prevent consequential damage to the dominant property. Thus a claim in relation to the damp could succeed.

25.11 Extinguishment of easements and profits

Once easements and profits have arisen they will, as interests in land, endure through successive ownerships of the land. Indeed they may well endure for very long periods. We must therefore consider the means by which such rights are brought to an end.

25.11.1 Dominant and servient tenements coming into the same hands

Because a person cannot have rights against him or herself, an easement, or a profit appurtenant to land, will be extinguished if the dominant and the servient tenements come into common ownership and possession. It is essential that both ownership and possession become common, and that both tenements are acquired for an estate in fee simple (*R v Inhabitants of Hermitage* (1692) Carth 239). Thus if the fee simple owner of one tenement takes a lease of the other this does not extinguish the easement or profit. All that happens is that the exercise of the easement or profit as a right is suspended for a period of the lease and will revive when it ends (*Simper v Foley* (1862) 2 John & H 555). If, however, the two tenements do come into common ownership the easement or profit will be completely extinguished and will not revive if the plots are separated again at a later date.

25.11.2 Release

An easement or profit may be 'released' (given up) by the dominant owner at any time. Obviously, at law such a release should be effected by deed, but equity will recognise an informal release if it would be inequitable to allow the releasing owner to go back on his word (e.g., *Waterlow v Bacon* (1866) LR 2 Eq 514). The effect of a release is to return the easement or profit to the servient owner, at which point it merges with his or her estate and is thereby extinguished.

25.11.3 Implied release: abandonment

In general the mere lack of use of an easement or profit, once it has been acquired, will not lead to the extinguishment of the right (*Seaman v Vawdrey* (1810) 16 Ves Jr 390), for one is never obliged to exercise the rights which one may have. However, a prolonged non-use may be adduced as evidence that the dominant owner has impliedly abandoned a right.

It should, however, be noted that if the dominant owner explains the non-use he or she may still be regarded as not having abandoned the right. Thus, in *James v Stevenson* [1893] AC 162 a right was not lost due to a long period of non-use because the dominant owner explained that he had simply had no occasion to exercise the right (but presumably might wish to in the future). In *Benn v Hardinge* (1992) 66 P&CR 246 the Court of Appeal said that non-use, even for 175 years, was not enough on its own to indicate an intention to abandon. The court also commented that the abandonment of such a right would not be lightly inferred. In *CDC 2020 plc v George Ferreira* (2005) 35 EG 112 this approach was again confirmed by the Court of Appeal, as was the fact that the dominant owner must make it clear that he was abandoning the right for himself and his successors and not just for himself.

If, however, the dominant tenement has been altered in such a way that the right claimed becomes unnecessary or impossible to exercise, then the alteration may be regarded as evidence of an intention to abandon the right. This presumption may be rebutted by evidence that the original character of the land may be restored in the future and that the need for the easement or profit would revive. Thus, in the case of a right to light, the easement will not be extinguished merely because the house on the dominant land is destroyed, as long as it is intended to erect another building in its place (*Ecclesiastical Commissioners for England v Kino* (1880) 14 ChD 213).

The most recent consideration of the rules about implied abandonment are to be found in the Court of Appeal decision in *Williams v Sandy Lane (Chester) Ltd* [2007] 1 EGLR 10. In this case, the servient tenement owner accepted that an easement over his land had been acquired by prescription, but he claimed that the right, over a path described in the case as 'the secondary route', had been abandoned when the claimant began to use a different route to access the dominant property.

At first instance, the trial judge had inferred an intention to abandon the right, relying among other matters on 30 years' non-use and various developments on the dominant tenement (fencing, creation of a bank of earth and growth of vegetation) that made it difficult to use the path to gain access to the property. The Court of Appeal considered that none of the developments made the use of the route impossible (para. 57) and reversed the trial judge's decision, holding that he had taken into account matters which did not support an inference of the intention to abandon (para. 58).

25.11.4 Do easements benefiting a leasehold property end on the merger of lease and reversion?

We explained in Chapter 10 that, when a lease and its reversion come into the same hands, the two estates merge and the lease comes to an end (see 10.5.2.4). In *Wall v*

Collins [2007] Ch 390, the Court of Appeal considered the effect of such a merger on an easement granted by the lease over the landlord's adjoining land. Did it come to an end along with the lease, or did it survive for the period for which it was already granted and thus benefit the owner of the freehold estate?

The properties in *Wall v Collins* were two houses that had been built by a developer on a 999-year building lease. In 1911, he sold No. 231 (i.e., assigned the lease to the purchaser), while continuing to own No. 233. The assignment of No. 231 included the grant of a right of way along a passageway situated on the retained land. The freeholds of both properties were subsequently acquired by their respective lessees, that of No. 231 being bought in 1986 and that of No. 233 some years later in 1995. For some time the Land Registry maintained separate registers for the leasehold and freehold estates in the two properties, but by the time the litigation began the leasehold registers had been closed and the leasehold estates were regarded as having merged with their respective freeholds.

The case before the Court of Appeal arose from a dispute between the current owners of the two properties about the use of the passageway, and Wall (owner of No. 231) sought a declaration that he was entitled to a right of way over No. 233. At first instance, this claim was rejected, the trial judge holding that the easement granted in the assignment of the lease was attached to that lease and ceased to exist when the lease merged with the freehold.

This decision was reversed by the Court of Appeal, which rejected the view that the easement was attached to the lease and ended when the lease came to an end. An easement must be attached to a dominant tenement (i.e., attached to the piece of land that it benefits), but it is not necessarily attached to any particular interest in that land. The fact that a legal easement can be created for a 'term of years' (LPA 1925, s. 1(2)(a)) does not mean that it has to be attached to a leasehold estate of the same length. Consequently the ending of the leasehold estate through merger with the freehold does not destroy the easement, which will continue to exist for the rest of the period for which it was granted. As a result, the easement granted in the 1911 assignment had survived the merger and Wall was entitled to a right of way along the passageway for the rest of the 999-year period (paras. 13–19).

You may remember that we have already mentioned *Wall v Collins* in connection with s. 62 (see 25.8.2.3). In case you are confused by what appear to be two different decisions, we should explain that the court had heard argument on s. 62 as an alternative ground of appeal, and so gave judgment on this point as well. Thus, although the 999-year easement was accepted by Wall as 'amply sufficient for his purposes' (para. 19), the court also held that, by virtue of s. 62, the conveyance of the freehold to Wall's predecessor in title had converted the existing easement for a term of years into one equivalent to the freehold estate.

25.12 Law reform

25.12.1 The need for reform

By this point you may well have concluded that the law relating to easements and profits is sadly in need of reform. It may be of some comfort to know that the authors agree with this conclusion. The existence of three methods of prescription is in itself an unnecessary complication and the nightmarish quality of the Prescription Act 1832 has been a cause of complaint for generations. Indeed in 1966 the Law Reform Committee recommended that all the existing rules on prescription should be abolished and replaced by one simpler method of prescription providing for a single period of 12 years (14th Report, Cmnd 3100) In addition, in 1971 it was recommended that a more far-reaching reform be contemplated in order to bring the law relating to easements and freehold covenants in line with one another (Law Commission Working Party, Working Paper 1971, No. 36). In March 2008 the Law Commission published a further consultation paper: *Easements, Covenants and Profits à Prendre* CP No. 186. In June 2011 the Law Commission published a final Report on the need for reform in the areas of freehold covenants, easements and profits à prendre, following extensive consultation on its earlier consultation paper: *Making Land Work: Easements, Covenants and Profits à Prendre* (2011) Law Com No 327. The Report is long (257 pages) but well worth reading because it considers in a very clear fashion all the difficulties of the law relating to easements and profits and those relating to freehold covenants (on which see Chapter 26). It also provides, in Part 2 of the Report, a useful summary of the law relating to estates and interests in land, which you may find helpful.

The consultation paper identified the following problems with the law on easements and profits. First, those arising from the practicalities of the extent of use rules and the requirement that the servient owner should not be excluded from using his own land (see the cases on parking). Secondly, the fact that easements can be acquired relatively easily and they can be acquired by multiple means (including implied easements and those obtained by prescription). Thirdly, that the law on prescription is unduly complex and that it seems unnecessary to have three separate forms of prescription operating alongside one another. Fourthly, that, although long use can allow the acquisition of an easement, long-term failure to use an existing easement will not lead to it being lost. Fifthly, even if the factual background circumstances change considerably, the court has no power to modify or discharge a profit or easement (which is possible in the case of freehold covenants).

The Law Commission said that its aim was to have a law of easements and profits which is as coherent and clear as possible and that as far as possible the law relating to these rights and freehold covenants should be brought into line and that overlapping and alternative doctrines (such as the three forms of prescription) should be rationalised or eradicated.

25.12.2 The 2011 recommendations

The 2011 Report makes a wide range of recommendations in relation to easements and covenants and it really is best to read them in full. The Report includes a draft bill, which is also well worth study. However, below we summarise the main proposals in the Report. Here the paragraph numbers refer to paragraphs in the Report.

25.12.2.1 Creation of profits

The Report recommends that it should in future only be possible to create profits à prendre by express grant or reservation or statute. On this see para. 3.9 and clauses 18 and 19 of the draft Bill. Thus, implied profits and those arising by prescription would cease to be possible. The Law Commission was of the view that profits are usually commercial agreements and therefore little would be lost by requiring that they be formally created, and that this would also provide certainty as to the extent of the profit.

25.12.2.2 Implied easements

In para. 3.30, it is recommended that, in determining whether an easement is implied, it should not be material whether it takes effect due to implied grant or implied reservation. At present the courts are more likely to imply an easement where there is a grant rather than a reservation but the Law Commission felt that implied easements usually dealt with cases of inadvertence or mistake, which were just as likely in either case.

The Law Commission takes the view that there should be a single statutory test for implication, to replace all existing methods. The proposal is that an easement should be implied as a term of a disposition if at the time of the disposition it is *necessary for the reasonable use of the land* bearing in mind:

(1) the use of the land at the time of the grant;

(2) the presence on the land of any relevant physical features;

(3) any intention for the future use of the land which is known to both parties at the time of the grant;

(4) so far as relevant, the available routes for the easement sought; and

(5) the potential interference with the servient land or inconvenience to the servient owner.

(See clause 20 of the draft Bill.)

The Law Commission recommends that it should remain possible to prevent implied easements by express exclusion: para. 3.49. Thus express drafting will be possible in order to prevent their creation.

The proposals are not intended to have an impact on ancillary easements (e.g., a right of access to a pipe to repair it, which is ancillary to an easement to use the pipe). These arise from construction of the grant and really relate to the scope of the grant: para. 3.51.

25.12.2.3 Section 62 LPA 1925

The Commission views the effects of s. 62 LPA 1925 as better regarded as an aspect of the express creation of easements rather than as a form of implication: para. 3.11. To us this is unsurprising. We have always been of the view that s. 62 gave rise to wording being implied into a grant and thus produces the creation of an express easement, arising from the wording implied into the document.

Para 3.64 recommends that s. 62 LPA 1925 should no longer operate to transform precarious benefits into legal easements or profits on conveyance: clause 21(1) of the draft Bill. This would prevent licences becoming easements on conveyance and would overrule, for example, *Wright v Macadam* [1949] 2 KB 744.

The Report proposes that it should remain possible for s. 62 to upgrade leasehold easements to freehold easements: para. 3.66. However, this should not in future apply to leasehold profits: para. 3.68.

25.12.2.4 Prescription

Most consultees were against abolition of prescription, even though it can sometimes prove burdensome to the generous, who simply allow adverse conduct to continue over time without objection: para. 3.76. The Law Commission advises the abolition of the *present* law of prescription and its replacement by a new statutory scheme for prescription. See clauses 16, 17 and 18 of the draft Bill for the detailed provisions.

In formulating new rules, the Law Commission had the following objectives (see para. 3.116):

(1) simplicity;

(2) avoidance of litigation;

(3) compatibility with land registration principles; and

(4) ensuring the scope for prescription is not extended.

The proposed scheme is that an easement will arise:

(1) on completion of 20 years' continuous qualifying use;

(2) if the qualifying use is without force, without stealth and without permission; and

(3) if that use is not a use that is contrary to the criminal law, unless the use can be rendered lawful by the dispensation of the servient owner.

See para. 3.123 and clauses 16 and 17 of the draft Bill. This provides one period for prescription and retains the traditional requirement that exercise of the right should have been *nec vi, nec clam, nec precario.*

The intention is that qualifying use must be by and against a freehold owner: para. 3.150. Use is not to be qualifying use at any time when the freehold is vested in a person who, or body which, is not competent to grant an easement over it: para. 3.168.

Where land is let, it is recommended that use is not qualifying use as against the freeholder at any time at which the servient freeholder:

- does not have power to prevent the use during the currency of the lease; or
- does not know of the use or could not reasonably have discovered it.

Two exceptions to this approach are proposed:

(1) if the use began before the lease was granted; and

(2) if, when the lease was granted:

  (a) the landlord knew about the use; or

  (b) could reasonably have discovered it.

25.12.2.5 Prescription and rights to light

No special rules are proposed as to the right to light, in order to maintain consistency: para. 3.130. The proposed new rules should apply in the same way to all easements. Thus the old distinctions between the right to light and other rights would be abolished and one common system introduced. However, it should be noted that the Law Commission is continuing to work on the whole issue of rights to light and a further report on this particular right is promised.

25.12.2.6 Transitional provisions for prescription

The main recommendation is that the new rules should apply to cases in which the use started before any new Act comes into force: you would not apply the old rules to the earlier period of use. However, to cover the oddity that under the 1832 Act, interruption must be for at least a year and thus no interruption is effective once 19 years and one day have passed, it is proposed that the 1832 Act should remain in force for a year in order to allow potential claimants under these provisions to obtain an easement if they bring their claim promptly.

25.12.2.7 Interaction with proposals on land obligations

One of the important proposals in the 2011 Report is the creation of a new system of interests in land called 'land obligations'. We deal with this issue in more detail in Chapter 26 because, in the main, land obligations would replace rules relating to covenants in relation to freehold land. However, the proposals do have a read-across to the law on easements and profits, so we will deal with those issues here.

As we have mentioned above, the easement of fencing is an anomaly and para. 5.94 therefore recommends that in future an obligation to fence should only have effect in the form of a land obligation and not as an easement. This would prevent for the future any confusion as to whether the easement or land obligation rules should apply. This would be the case however the obligation was worded.

There are four easements that may be regarded as 'negative' because they prevent the servient owner from doing something. Those easements are the easements of:

(1) support;

(2) air;

(3) water; and

(4) light.

An easement of support prevents, for example, removal of a wall, whereas the other three negative easements prevent obstruction of the flow of air, water or light. For the future any attempt to create any negative easement would have effect as a new 'land obligation' because no formal wording is to be required in order to create such an obligation. However, the Law Commission recognises that negative easements would continue to be capable of arising by means of prescription or as implied easements (para. 5.99) and makes no recommendation to change this situation.

25.12.2.8 Extensive use

In recent years there have been many cases in which a key element of a case was whether the use being made of land was too extensive to be an easement. (See *Dyce v Hay* (1852) 1 Macq 305.) This has been particularly an issue in cases involving a claim to a parking space. Currently, to be an easement the use must:

- not amount to exclusive possession;
- not prevent the servient owner making reasonable use of the land.

The Law Commission proposes the abolition of the second possibility, leaving only the requirement that an easement does not give exclusive possession. This would reverse the decision in *Batchelor v Marlow* [2003] 1 WLR 764. Thus, for example, an easement granting an exclusive right to park would become possible.

25.12.2.9 Extinguishment by abandonment

At present this is often difficult to establish. In *Benn v Hardinge* (1993) 66 P&CR 246 an easement not used for 175 years was nonetheless not regarded as abandoned because it might be of use in future.

The Law Commission proposal is that where title is registered and an easement or profit has been entered on the register then abandonment should not be able to cancel the right. Where title is unregistered or the easement or profit has not been entered on the register of the servient title, it should be possible to claim abandonment. In such cases, where there has been no use for 20 years there should be a rebuttable presumption of abandonment.

25.12.2.10 Termination of the estate to which the interest is appurtenant

The recommendation is that the decision that an easement that benefits a lease should survive merger with the freehold should be reversed (*Wall v Collins* [2007] Ch 390). However, it is proposed that a statutory right be created that allows the person who would have obtained the benefit to elect to do so.

25.12.2.11 Reform of registered land rules

Four reforms are proposed in relation to easements and profits where title is registered.

(1) *Statutory magic and registered interests*

Section 58 of the LRA 2002 provides a guarantee of validity of registered estates and interests. The Report recommends that it should be made clear that this does not apply where an entry is made on the register due to an instrument that purports to create an easement, if the right it purports to create does not in fact accommodate and serve the dominant land. This is because in principle an easement cannot exist in such a case (paras. 4.11–4.18).

(2) *Unity of seisin*

One of the basic rules for an easement or profit is that the dominant and servient tenements must not be both owned and occupied by the same person. This causes problems in some cases in which properties are temporarily in common ownership and some other cases (paras. 4.25–4.40). The Report recommends that this rule should be abolished if title to both the dominant and the servient land is registered.

(3) *Express release of registered interests*

Oddly, there is currently no requirement to enter on the register an express release (discharge) of a registered easement or covenant. Thus a deed of release is effective, even if the register still shows the right as existing. It is therefore recommended that an express release should become a registrable disposition (para. 4.57).

(4) *Use of short forms for creation of easements*

The Report proposes that the Land Registry should make Rules determining the wording of some easements (which easements being for the Registry to decide). The Rules should then allow these forms of easement to be adopted by registrable instruments. The aim is to produce standard forms of popular easements that *may*, but not must, be adopted by those drafting registrable dispositions.

25.12.2.12 Jurisdiction of the Lands Chamber of the Upper Tribunal

The 2011 Report also recommends changes to the powers of the Lands Chamber, in order to facilitate the removal of barriers to the use of land that have become redundant over time. It is proposed that the jurisdiction of the Lands Chamber should in future extend to any new easements and profits created after the introduction of the new rules and to all of the proposed new land obligations: para. 7.35. Jurisdiction should also be extended to include powers in relation to leasehold land of any term: para. 7.38.

The grounds for modification or discharge should be those currently in s. 84 of the LPA 1925: para. 7.55 of the Report and see also Chapter 26 (26.7.2). However, it is recommended that it be made clear that, where several people can enforce the benefit, an order may be made even if differing grounds under s. 84 apply to each of them (para. 7.87). Thus an applicant would not have to show the same ground or grounds against all the benefited persons.

The Lands Chamber should only modify an easement or profit if it is satisfied that the modified interest will not be materially less convenient to the benefited owner and will be no more burdensome to the land affected: para. 7.60.

It is proposed (para. 7.83) that the power to modify easements and profits should include power to change the *nature* of the interest, if:

(1) the change appears reasonable; and

(2) the applicant seeking the modification does not object to the change.

This might, for example, allow the Lands Chamber to substitute a land obligation for an easement, if this appeared to be appropriate.

Having looked at proposed reforms of the law, we will look briefly at two, limited, reforms which have already been made.

25.12.3 Access to Neighbouring Land Act 1992

In the absence of an easement giving access, in the past there has been no right for a neighbour to gain access to his neighbour's premises in order to enable the carrying out of maintenance work to his own premises. Thus, if one bought an estate in premises which were built right up to the boundary of the land concerned, it was essential to check that express rights had been provided in order to allow access to neighbouring property for the purpose of pointing brickwork, repairing windows or doing any other work which could only be carried out from the neighbour's premises. A limited change in the law was made by the Access to Neighbouring Land Act 1992, which does give some rights to access in order to carry out works but only on grant of a court order. Further details can be found in the Online Resource Centre (see W.25.2).

25.12.4 Party Walls Act 1996

A further limited but important reform has been made by the Party Walls Act 1996 which gives certain special rights in relation to 'party walls' and 'party structures'. Party walls are walls which either separate buildings in different ownership or which are part of a building and which stand on lands in different ownership. The commonest examples are likely to be the central walls which separate the properties in semi-detached or terraced houses. Party structures are things like floor partitions or other structures which separate buildings or parts of buildings which are approached by separate staircases or separate entrances. More on the 1996 Act can be found in W.25.2 of the Online Resource Centre.

FURTHER READING

Equitable easements

Barnsley, 'Equitable Easements—Sixty years On' (1999) 115 LQR 89.

Easements of storage and parking

Gray & Gray, *Elements of Land Law*, 5th edn., Oxford University Press, 2009, paras. 5.1.62–5.1.67.

Hill-Smith, 'Rights of Parking and the Ouster Principle After *Batchelor v Marlow*' [2007] Conv 223.

Zif and Litman, 'Easements and Possession: An Elusive Limitation' [1989] Conv 296.

LPA 1925, s. 62

Harpum, 'Easements and Centre Point: Old Problems Resolved in a Novel Setting'. [1977] 41 Conv 415.

Harpum, '*Long v Gowlett*: A Strong Fortress' [1979] 43 Conv 113.

Jackson, 'Easements and General Words' [1966] 30 Conv NS 342.

Smith, 'Centre Point : Faulty Towers With Shaky Foundations' [1978] 42 Conv 449.

Tee, 'Metamorphoses and Section 62 of the Law of Property Act' [1998] Conv 115.

Thompson, 'The Acquisition of Easements' [1997] Conv 453 (case note on *Payne v Inwood*).

Prescription

Burns, 'Prescriptive Easements in England and Legal Climate Change' [2007] Conv 133.

Dixon, 'Prescriptive Easements: Acquisition, Abandonment and Leasehold Land' [2007] Conv 160 (case note on *Williams v Sandy Lane (Chester) Ltd).*

Land Registration for the Twenty-First Century A Consultative Document, 1998, Law Com No. 254, Part X: Adverse Possession and Prescription, paras. 10.79–94.

Reform

Francis, 'Tinkering really won't do the trick' [2007] EG 28 July 2007 (No. 0730) 125.

Law Commission, 'Easements, Covenants and Profits à Prendre, A Consultation Paper', 2008 (Consultation Paper No. 186) (available on: **www.lawcom.gov.uk**).

Law Commission, 'Making Land Work: Easements, Covenants and Profits à Prendre', 2011, Law Com No. 327 (available on: **www.lawcom.gov.uk**).

Lyall, 'What are Easements Attached or Appurtenent to?' [2010] Conv 300.

Reference

Bickford Smith and Francis, *Rights of Light: The Modern Law*, 2nd edn., Jordans, 2007.

Gale, *Easements*, 18th edn., Sweet & Maxwell, 2008.

Murphy, *The Law of Nuisance*, Oxford University Press, 2010.

26

Covenants relating to freehold land

26.1 Introduction

We saw in Chapter 11 that it is usual for covenants to be included in leases. Similarly, covenants are quite commonly made in respect of freehold property, particularly if land is divided and the person selling part of the land wishes to ensure that his or her new neighbour does not behave in an inconvenient or disturbing manner. In the case of a new estate, the developer may well wish to impose covenants upon all the purchasers, in order to ensure that the estate is maintained in good order. Thus, covenants are frequently imposed upon freehold estates. However, while the covenants made will be binding between the original parties as a matter of the law of contract, once the land burdened with the covenant is sold, the question will arise whether the covenant is binding upon the purchaser of the property. Over the years, special rules have developed in order to settle the question of which covenants can run with freehold land. These rules have some links with the rules governing covenants in leases but the two systems are not the same and should not be confused with one another. In many cases a covenant by a freehold owner will not bind a purchaser from him, although a similar covenant, if contained in a lease, would bind the tenant's assignee.

26.2 Trant Way

26.2.1 17 and 18 Trant Way

In 1988, Nos. 17 and 18 Trant Way were both owned in fee simple by Olive Orange. Miss Orange occupied 17 Trant Way, whilst No. 18 was let to a tenant. When the tenant left the property at the end of the lease, Miss Orange decided to sell 18 Trant Way. She sold the fee simple estate in the property to Robert Raspberry and, because she was concerned that her new neighbour should not inconvenience her, or alter the character of the neighbourhood, she insisted that Mr Raspberry should enter into a number of covenants in the conveyance. The covenants were:

(a) not to use No. 18 'for business purposes';

(b) to keep the exterior of No. 18 in good repair;

(c) to contribute one-half of the cost of maintaining the driveway shared with No. 17; and

(d) not to sell No. 18 to a family with children (Miss Orange was elderly and found the noise of children at play disturbing).

When she made these arrangements Miss Orange wanted to ensure that her neighbour at 19 Trant Way (Daniel Date) was also protected, in so far as was possible. Accordingly, she made Mr Raspberry covenant 'for the benefit of the owners for the time being of land abutting 18 Trant Way' and told Daniel Date about the arrangements she had made. Figure 26.1 shows 17–19 Trant Way at that point.

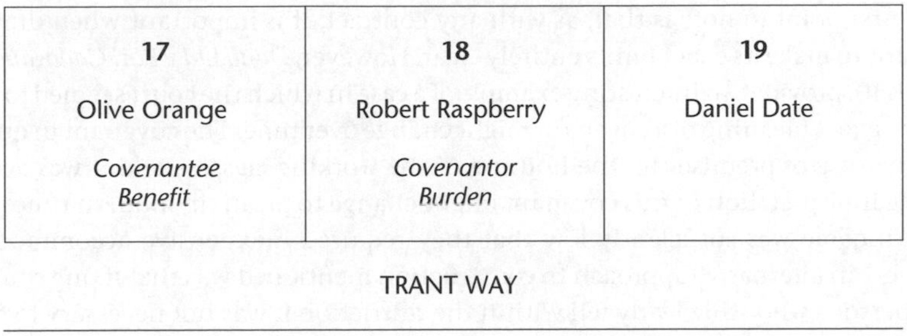

17	18	19
Olive Orange	Robert Raspberry	Daniel Date
Covenantee *Benefit*	*Covenantor* *Burden*	

TRANT WAY

Figure 26.1 17–19 Trant Way

In 1995, Miss Orange died, and her executors sold 17 Trant Way to Paul Peach.

In 1998, Mr Raspberry sold 18 Trant Way to Silvia Strawberry. In the last year Mrs Strawberry has proved to be rather a difficult neighbour to Mr Peach and causes him considerable trouble. She has started to give piano lessons at home and the noise of children playing their scales throughout the day and early evening disturbs Mr Peach greatly. Furthermore, Mrs Strawberry has failed to repair the outside of No. 18, which has become something of an eyesore, and when Mr Peach had repairs made to the joint driveway she refused to contribute to the cost.

26.2.2 20 Trant Way

20 Trant Way was the old rectory, which had a very large garden and an orchard. In 1999, a development company, Big Builders plc, bought the old rectory, demolished it and built a new crescent of six bungalows. The gardens of the properties were landscaped and are 'open plan' in style. The six bungalows have now been sold, and the new owners of the fee simple estates have been registered as proprietors at HM Land Registry. The crescent is called Rectory Crescent, and the bungalows have been numbered 1 to 6, and were sold in that order. 1 Rectory Crescent was bought by Alfred Alpha, and 6 Rectory Crescent was bought by Oscar Omega. On each sale, the purchaser covenanted with Big Builders plc not to fence the garden of the plot being purchased. See Figure 26.5 on p. 548 for a plan of Rectory Crescent.

We now need to consider the extent to which the covenants we have just described are enforceable, not only between the original parties but also between their successors in title.

26.3 Enforceability of covenants: original parties

26.3.1 Covenantor and covenantee: burden and benefit

When Olive Orange sold 18 Trant Way to Robert Raspberry in 1988, the covenants contained in the conveyance to Mr Raspberry constituted a contract between the parties. We have already explained that a covenant is a promise by deed (2.5.5). Here, Mr Raspberry is the 'covenantor', and assumes the 'burden' under the covenant, and Miss Orange is the 'covenantee', and takes the 'benefit'. If Mr Raspberry had broken a covenant, Miss Orange could have sued for damages for breach of contract or sought an injunction restraining the breach. In this situation, the basic rules of the law of contract apply.

The first point to note is that, as with any contract, it is important when drafting a covenant to make its exact limits entirely clear. However, *Dano Ltd v Earl Cadogan* [2003] 2 P&CR 10, provides an interesting example of a case in which the court seemed to accept that the exact meaning of a covenant might change over time. The covenant in question restricted use of premises to 'the housing of the working classes', and it was accepted that the interpretation of this covenant might change to mean (in modern times) those whose income was sufficiently low that they required inexpensive accommodation. However, an alternative approach to construction mentioned was that if one could find some persons who still clearly fell within the restriction it was not necessary to be able to identify every person who did so. (However, in a later Court of Appeal decision on another issue in the same case (see *The Times*, 2 June 2003) it was held that since the document creating the covenant, when read as a whole, envisaged that the covenant lasted only as long as the benefited land remained settled and that had ceased to be the case, the covenant was not in fact enforceable.)

26.3.2 LPA 1925, s. 56

It is easy enough to see that Miss Orange and Mr Raspberry had a contractual relationship with one another, for both executed a deed which contained their agreement. However, it is possible for someone to take the benefit of such a covenant, even though he or she was not a party to the deed or perhaps did not even know that the contract had been concluded. In the case of 19 Trant Way, Daniel Date was not an express party to the deed which included the covenants made by Mr Raspberry. However, you will recall that Miss Orange included in that deed words which indicated that any owner of land abutting No. 18 (which is the case with No. 19) should also benefit from the covenant. This wording may have an important legal effect and may indeed allow Mr Date to sue on the covenant as if he had been a party to the deed. However, as we will see, this result depends upon the case law interpreting the effect of LPA 1925, s. 56(1), which provides that

> A person may take ... the benefit of any condition, ... covenant or agreement over or respecting land, ... although he may not be named as a party to the conveyance or other instrument.

In *Re Ecclesiastical Commissioners for England's Conveyance* [1936] Ch 430, it was held that the effect of s. 56 was that a person, expressed in the conveyance to be one for whose benefit the covenant was made, was to be regarded as an original covenantee, even though he was not a party to the deed. As a result, the covenant may confer enforceable benefits on other persons, even though they may have been unaware that such a covenant had been made! Accordingly, *Re Ecclesiastical Commissioners for England's Conveyance* seems to suggest that if Mr Raspberry broke the covenants Mr Date could sue him for breach of contract, provided that he could satisfy the court that the covenant did purport to be with him as covenantee, although he was not a party to the agreement (*Re Foster* [1938] 3 All ER 357 at p. 365).

However, in *Amsprop Trading Ltd v Harris Distribution Ltd* [1997] 1 WLR 1025, Neuberger J said that s. 56 was only effective in a case in which the covenant purported to be made with the person seeking to enforce and not where the covenant merely purported to be made for the benefit of that person. This appears to produce results that vary depending upon the exact wording used in the covenant in the case but this may be unsurprising in a situation in which a statutory provision appears to be being stretched beyond what would appear to be its intended ambit. It may also be of importance that the case involved an attempt to circumvent the standard rules relating to covenants in leases. You may recall that we considered this case in Chapter 12 (12.9.2) and that it concerned a covenant in a sublease which the head landlord, rather than the tenant/landlord of the sublease itself, was seeking to enforce. The head landlord could not use the leasehold rules to enforce the covenant because there is no privity of estate or contract between the head landlord and the subtenant. However, the covenant in the sublease was expressed to give the head landlord power to enforce the covenant and thus he claimed to be able to enforce the covenant under the general covenant rules because the covenant was clearly intended to benefit the head landlord. Neuberger J held that, on the construction of the sublease in question, the covenant was not expressed to be made with the head landlord, although it was clearly intended to benefit him. In such a case, it was held that s. 56 did not operate to permit the head landlord to enforce the covenant.

One reason for the decision may have been that, were this interpretation not to be adopted, it would be easy to circumvent the standard leasehold rules and to allow enforcement of covenants by persons who have no privity of estate or of contract with the tenant in question. Unfortunately, however, the effect may be merely to make the result in such cases depend entirely upon the particular words used. If *Amsprop* is confined to its facts and Mr Date can rely on s. 56, the position would now be as shown in Figure 26.2.

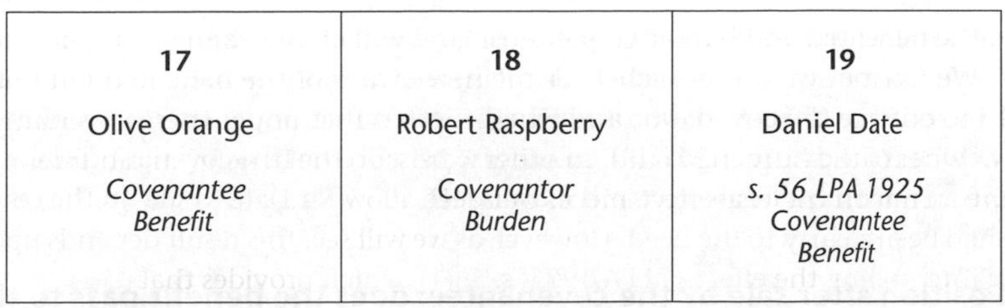

Figure 26.2

26.3.3 The 'mischief' addressed by statute

In trying to decide what s. 56 will or will not do, it may be helpful to consider the mischief that the statutory provisions appear to have been addressing, even if to do so does require a short historical digression. The 'mischief' was the effect of the common law rule that a person could not sue on a deed unless he was actually named in that deed: a description which identified the person in question but did not name him would not do. Accordingly, if in an old deed one described one of the parties as 'the owner for the time being of 21 Trant Way', that would not have sufficed to enable the owner of that property at the time the deed was made to enforce the covenants in that deed. This was true even though the actual person involved was readily identifiable and there was no doubt as to who was intended by the description given. This rule was first modified by s. 5 of the Real Property Act 1845 and then by s. 56. Accordingly, courts might have been expected to view s. 56 as only removing the problem created by the common law rule, so that a person who was described in a document as a party but not named and who clearly was a contracting party could benefit. However, as can be seen from the discussion above, the courts have in fact gone further than this in their use of s. 56. The main limitation on s. 56 seems to be simply that the persons covered by the description in question can only benefit if they are existing and identifiable at the date that the covenant was made. The statutory provision does not (as some originally suggested) have the effect of setting aside altogether the principles of privity of contract (see the discussion in *Smith and Snipes Hall Farm Ltd v River Douglas Catchment Board* [1949] 2 KB 500 at p. 514 and *Beswick v Beswick* [1966] Ch 538 at p. 556).

26.3.4 An alternative

In addition to s. 56, it may be possible to rely on the general contractual provisions in the Contracts (Rights of Third Parties) Act 1999, which were designed to relieve some of the problems connected with the rules on privity of contract. The benefits and obligations conferred by that Act are in addition to those provided by s. 56 (see s. 7(1) of the 1999 Act), but are similar in many ways and normally use of s. 56 will suffice for land cases. However, you should remember this as a possible alternative approach.

26.4 Enforceability of covenants: successors of the original parties

In time, the benefited and burdened pieces of land will change hands, and pass to new owners. We must now consider whether the new owner of the benefited land obtains the right to enforce the covenants, and whether the duties under these covenants bind the new owner of the burdened land. In other words, do the benefits and burdens of the covenants run with the respective pieces of land?

26.4.1 Position after sale by the covenantee: does the benefit pass to the new owner?

In 1995 Olive Orange, the original covenantee in relation to the covenants burdening 18 Trant Way, died and her executors sold her fee simple estate in No. 17 to Paul Peach.

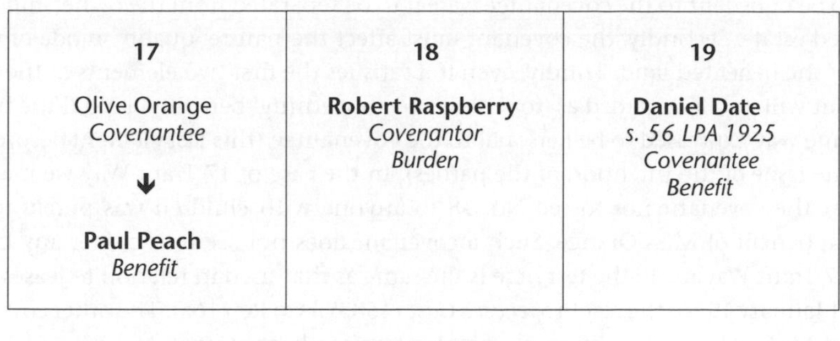

Figure 26.3

At this time, the original covenantor, Robert Raspberry, was still the owner of 18 Trant Way. If Mr Raspberry had broken one of the covenants contained in the 1988 conveyance to himself, could Mr Peach have enforced the covenant against him? At that point the arrangements at 17–19 Trant Way were as shown in Figure 26.3.

Obviously there is no privity of contract between Mr Peach and Mr Raspberry, but common law does allow the benefit of such a covenant to pass to a successor in title of the original covenantee, if four conditions are met:

(1) the covenant must 'touch and concern' the land of the covenantee;

(2) at the time when the covenant was made, it must have been the intention of the parties that the benefit of the covenant should run with the land to the covenantee's successors in title;

(3) at the time when the covenant was made, the covenantee must have held the legal estate in the land to be benefited; and

(4) the claimant must derive his title from or under the original covenantee (this is the common law rule as amended by LPA 1925, s. 78).

We will look at each of these requirements in greater detail.

26.4.1.1 'Touching and concerning' the land of the covenantee

Common law rules do not allow the successor of the original covenantee to claim the benefit of a covenant unless, at the date when the covenant was made, the covenantee had land which was benefited by the covenant. This emphasises the fact that only the benefit of covenants which are appurtenant to land can be claimed under these rules, although no such connection is required where the original contracting parties are concerned.

In addition, the covenant must 'touch and concern' the covenantee's land. The purpose of the rule is to distinguish between covenants which confer a benefit upon land and those which confer a purely personal benefit upon the covenantee. In *P. & A. Swift Investments v Combined English Stores Group* [1989] AC 632 at p. 642, Lord Oliver of Aylmerton provides a useful working test designed to ascertain whether a covenant 'touches and concerns' land. We have already told you about this in connection with leasehold covenants (see 12.5.2.2) but think that it is useful to note it here as well. The first element of the test is that the covenant must benefit the estate owner for the time being and that it would cease to be of benefit to the covenantee were it to be separated from the ownership of the benefited estate. Secondly, the covenant must affect the nature, quality, mode of use or value of the benefited land. Thirdly, even if it satisfies the first two elements of the test, a covenant will not be regarded as 'touching and concerning' benefited land if the benefit is in some way expressed to be personal to the covenantee (this last element accordingly raises the issue of the intention of the parties). In the case of 17 Trant Way we may well feel that the covenant not to sell No. 18 to anyone with children was purely for the personal benefit of Miss Orange. Such a covenant does not seem to confer any benefit upon 17 Trant Way itself: the test here is the same as that used in relation to leases made before 1 January 1996 (the test in *Spencer's Case* (1583) 5 Co Rep 16a). The other covenants made by Mr Raspberry do, however, appear to confer a benefit upon No. 17.

26.4.1.2 The parties must have intended the benefit to run

This condition requires proof that, when the covenant was made, the parties intended that it should run to benefit successors of the covenantee. Evidence of such an intention can be provided by the covenantor expressly covenanting with 'the covenantee, his successors in title, and those deriving title under him'. These words are, however, now deemed to be contained in the covenant, by virtue of LPA 1925, s. 78(1):

> A covenant relating to any land of the covenantee shall be deemed to be made with the covenantee and his successors in title and the persons deriving title under him or them, and shall have effect as if such successors and other persons were expressed.

26.4.1.3 At the time when the covenant was made, the covenantee must have held the legal estate in the land

At common law, covenants attach to the legal estate and pass with it, and so it is essential that, at the time the covenant was made, the covenantee was the owner of the legal estate in the land on which the benefit is to be conferred (*Webb v Russell* (1789) 3 TR 393).

26.4.1.4 The successor claiming to enforce the covenant must derive title from or under the original covenantee

At one time, a successor claiming the benefit of a covenant at common law had to show that he had acquired the same estate as had been held by the original covenantee, for common law regarded the covenants as attaching to the estate, so that only a person who took the estate could obtain the benefit of the covenants. Thus, a purchaser of the fee simple from the covenantee could enforce a covenant, whilst a tenant acquiring a term of years (even if it were for 999 years) could not do so. Today, however, a tenant may claim the benefit of a covenant which is attached to the freehold estate in the land of which he is a tenant, because in *Smith and Snipes Hall Farm Ltd v River Douglas Catchment Board* [1949] 2 KB 500 it was held that LPA 1925, s. 78, has the effect of extending the right to enforce a covenant to such a person. In this case the original owner of the benefited land had sold it to a purchaser and that purchaser had granted a lease of the premises to a tenant. The Court of Appeal took the view that the effect of s. 78(1) was that the benefit of the covenant was enforceable not only by the successor in title to the freehold estate but also by the tenant, who derived title under that freeholder. Section 78 appears to have been intended to be merely a word-saving provision, but here and elsewhere has been held to create important substantive changes in the law. In this instance it was said that, because the section refers to persons 'deriving title under' the covenantee, it extends the benefit of such covenants to tenants, who derive their title under the covenantee (or his successors). Were the intention that such persons remain incapable of obtaining a benefit under the legal rules, the inclusion of the reference to them in s. 78 would be meaningless. Therefore the section has been interpreted as creating an amendment to the law.

The benefit of a covenant amounts to a chose in action and thus it is possible for the holder of the benefit to assign it to any third party in accordance with the ordinary rules of law. Under LPA 1925, s. 136, any such express assignment should be made in writing and notice of it should be given to the covenantor.

26.4.1.5 Application of the rules

One can see from these rules that, when Miss Orange's executors sold 17 Trant Way to Paul Peach, he would have obtained the benefit of all Mr Raspberry's covenants; except perhaps that of the covenant not to sell No. 18 to a family with children, which appears to be purely personal in nature. Apart from this, the benefit of all the covenants, both positive and negative, would pass with the estate to the new owner, for at common law the benefit of both types of covenant can run to a successor of the covenantee.

26.4.2 Position after sale by covenantor: does the burden pass to the new owner?

In 1998, Mr Raspberry sold the fee simple in 18 Trant Way (the burdened land) to Silvia Strawberry, and it appears that Mrs Strawberry is in breach of a number of the covenants originally made between Mr Raspberry and Miss Orange. The current owner of the benefited land, Mr Peach, needs to know whether Mrs Strawberry is in fact bound by these covenants. Mr Peach wishes to establish, if possible, that the position at 17–19 Trant Way is now as is shown in Figure 26.4. Can he do this?

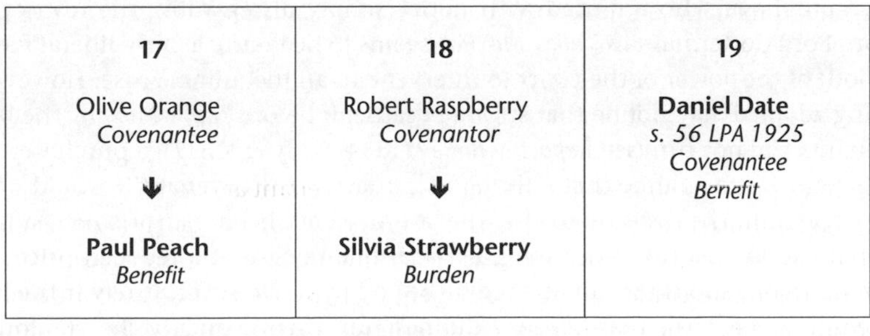

Figure 26.4

26.4.2.1 Burdens do not run at common law

Unfortunately for Mr Peach, the basic rule is that the burden of covenants does not run at common law. Common law dislikes restraints being placed on your use of your own estate, and accordingly applies the strict rule of privity of contract in such cases. The leading decision on this issue is *Austerberry v Corporation of Oldham* (1885) 29 ChD 750, in which it was held that, at common law, the obligation to make up a road and keep it in good repair could not pass to the successor in title of the original covenantor. This position was re-affirmed by the House of Lords in *Rhone v Stephens* [1994] 2 AC 310, in the case of a covenant to maintain a roof. Thus, Mrs Strawberry will not be liable at law for breach of any of the covenants made in respect of 18 Trant Way. This is in line with the general principles of the law of contract, which allow the benefit of a contract to be transferred to a third party but not the burden. The rule arose principally because of the concerns at law to keep land freely alienable and to prevent it becoming burdened with incumbrances which might hinder sale. However, in the increasingly complex modern world, such a rule can be inconvenient since in many cases it may be quite reasonable to wish to impose restrictions when one sells, for example, part of one's property and to wish to ensure that those restrictions apply to anyone subsequently acquiring the part sold.

26.4.2.2 The burden of certain covenants can run in equity

The common law rule caused considerable inconvenience, because the owner of benefited land could find that covenants became unenforceable merely because the burdened land changed hands. Equity took note of this difficulty and, through applying general equitable principles, arrived at the conclusion that where a purchaser acquired the burdened land with knowledge of the covenants it was quite fair that he should be bound to observe them. The enforceability of the burden of certain covenants against a successor in title to the covenantor was settled finally in the famous case of *Tulk v Moxhay* (1848) 2 Ph 774. In this case, the burdened land formed the centre of Leicester Square in London, and the original covenantor had covenanted with the owner of adjacent property that he would maintain the square as an ornamental open space. Later the square was sold, and the purchaser, relying on the common law rule that burdens do not pass on sale, intended to build on the property. It was held that the owners of the neighbouring benefited land had a right in equity to enforce the covenant against the purchaser of the burdened land, because he had known of the restriction when he acquired his estate.

In taking this view of the position the court attached great importance to the inequity of a purchaser who acquired with notice simply disregarding the restriction in question. Lord Cottenham in *Tulk v Moxhay* seems to be taking a fairly liberal view (for the period) of the power of the court to intervene in an inequitable case. However, the reasoning adopted may not be that strong because, if before *Tulk v Moxhay* the burden of covenants had not run (see *Keppell v Bailey* (1834) 2 My & K 517), a purchaser would surely be entitled to assume that although he knew of the covenant it would have no impact upon him. The decision to alter the law may have been a surprising result. Lord Cottenham seems also to have thought that if one bought at a reduced price due to the covenant, one should in conscience be bound by it. However, surely if the law (or rather equity) were clear that burdens did not run, then normally the vendor could sell at a higher price because he would know that the purchaser would not be bound by the covenant. If the vendor failed to claim a higher price in this way, the loss is the vendor's and that of the owners of the benefited land: the vendor loses solely due to his ignorance of the law. It is difficult to see in such a case how the purchaser's conscience is affected. Accordingly, while the decision in *Tulk v Moxhay* proved to be an essential step towards the introduction of a more modern approach to the planning of land use, one wonders to what extent the reasoning in the case stands up to close scrutiny. In essence the decision is an early example of an attempt to introduce land-use planning by non-statutory means. (The Leicester Square covenants were again the subject of litigation in *R v Westminster City Council, ex parte Leicester Square Coventry Street Association* (1989) 87 LGR 675.)

Since 1848 the courts have, in later cases, identified the rules which must be satisfied before equity will regard the burden of a covenant as passing under the *Tulk v Moxhay* doctrine. These rules are derived from *Tulk v Moxhay* but are not (apart from the last of them) expressly mentioned in the case. To a certain extent the rules step back from the very liberal and reforming approach taken in *Tulk v Moxhay*. In their modern form, they may be stated as follows:

(1) the covenant must be negative;
(2) at the date of the covenant, the covenantee must have owned land which was benefited by the covenant;
(3) the original parties must have intended that the burden should run to bind successors; and
(4) as the rule is equitable, general equitable principles (and the need for notice or its modern equivalent) apply.

(1) *The covenant must be negative*

This rule may seem odd when one remembers that the covenant in *Tulk v Moxhay* was to maintain Leicester Square as an ornamental open space, which sounds like a positive obligation. However, it is the substance of the covenant which matters, and not the form in which it is expressed. Thus, the effect of the covenant in *Tulk v Moxhay* was that the owner should keep the square in an open state and not erect buildings. In the case of the covenants relating to 18 Trant Way, the covenants to keep the exterior in good repair and to contribute to the cost of maintaining the driveway are both positive, and thus cannot run to bind Mrs Strawberry under the rule in *Tulk v Moxhay*. This can produce rather inconvenient results, and reform of the law has been recommended (see 26.8.3). Indeed, some writers have argued that *Tulk v Moxhay* makes no mention of such a requirement, and that in the past positive covenants had been enforced against the covenantor's successors (see Bell [1981] Conv 55). However, this limitation on the rule has been accepted since the case of *Haywood v Brunswick Permanent Benefit Building Society* (1881) 8 QBD 403, in which Lindley LJ said that 'only such a covenant as can be complied with without expenditure of money will be enforced' against a successor in title. Thus, a covenant 'not to allow the premises to fall into disrepair' would be regarded as a positive covenant, even though it is worded in a negative form, because compliance with the covenant will require action, and expenditure, on the part of the owner of the burdened land.

The difference between positive and negative covenants was summarised by Cotton LJ in *Austerberry v Corporation of Oldham* (1885) 29 ChD 750 at pp. 773–4 in a passage in which it was explained that a covenant requiring someone to 'lay out money':

> . . . is not a covenant which a court of equity will enforce: it will not enforce a covenant not running at law when it is sought to enforce that covenant in such a way as to require the successors in title of the covenantor to spend money, and in that way to undertake a burden upon themselves. The covenantor must not use the property for a purpose inconsistent with the use for which it was originally granted: but in my opinion a court of equity does not and ought not to enforce a covenant binding only in equity in such a way as to require the successors of the covenantor himself, they having entered into no covenant, to expend sums of money in accordance with what the original covenantor bound himself to do.

This principle was reaffirmed by the House of Lords in 1994 in *Rhone v Stephens* [1994] 2 AC 310. In that case a large single property had been divided into two parts ('the house' and 'the cottage') and the cottage had been sold. The vendor retained the house. Due to the design of the properties the roof remained part of the house but protected both the house and the cottage. Accordingly, on sale, the vendor covenanted that he would maintain the roof for the benefit of the cottage. Over the years both the house and the cottage had been sold on and the current owner of the cottage sought to enforce the covenant to repair the roof, which had fallen into disrepair. The House of Lords was urged to overturn the rule which prevented such positive covenants binding successors and the many criticisms of the rule were argued against it. However, the traditional rule was reaffirmed and it appears now that it can only be overturned by legislation. Lord Templeman said (at p. 321):

> For over 100 years it has been clear and accepted law that equity will enforce negative covenants against freehold land but has no power to enforce positive covenants against successors in title of the land. To enforce a positive covenant would be to enforce a personal obligation against a person who has not covenanted. To enforce negative covenants is only to treat the land as subject to a restriction.

Thus, in a situation like that in *Tulk v Moxhay*, in equity a successor to the covenantor can be prevented from putting the open space to an alternative use but cannot be forced to maintain it in good order, since the latter requires expenditure whereas the former merely prevents the successor taking certain types of action. This was one of the reasons for the introduction of commonhold.

(2) *At the date of the covenant the covenantee must have owned benefited land*

Equity will not enforce a covenant unless it confers a benefit upon land. This involves two requirements: (a) that the covenant touches and concerns land; and (b) that, at the date of the covenant, the covenantee must have retained land which was benefited by the covenant. In *London County Council v Allen* [1914] 3 KB 642 a builder covenanted that he would not build on a particular piece of land. The covenantee was the council, which did not own land in the neighbourhood. Mrs Allen bought the plot with knowledge of the covenant, but was held not to be bound by it, because it was not made for the benefit of land owned by the council. This decision emphasises the fact that equity will protect only covenants which are appurtenant to land: see also *Morrells of Oxford Ltd v Oxford United Football Club Ltd* [2001] Ch 459, in which a covenant was construed as being personal only.

There are, however, a number of exceptions to the rule that the covenantee must retain land which is benefited by the covenant:

(a) If you think of the situation in Rectory Crescent, you will realise that Big Builders plc, after selling plot 6 to Mr Omega, did not retain any land in the Crescent, and so, on the basic rule, the burden of the covenant would not run with that plot to any new owner. However, if it can be established that the development of Rectory Crescent constituted what is known as a 'building scheme', the burden will run with the last plot, despite the fact that the developer did not retain any land in the area. We will explain how building schemes work later in this chapter (at 26.4.3.6).

(b) There are also statutory exceptions to the rule, for example in favour of local authorities or the National Trust. These exceptions allow such bodies to enforce covenants on behalf of the whole community (for example, to ensure that an area of natural beauty is not disturbed: National Trust Act 1937, s. 8).

(c) The rules relating to restrictive covenants in leases require a special mention in this context. Such covenants are capable of amounting to restrictive covenants binding under the rules of *Tulk v Moxhay*. This is of little importance where assignees of the tenant are concerned, for most of the covenants in the lease may be enforced against them under the rule in *Spencer's Case* (see 12.5.2.2) or pass under the Landlord and Tenant (Covenants) Act 1995. However, covenants which fall within the *Tulk v Moxhay* principle are binding on anyone who derives title from or under the covenantor, or one of his successors, and thus such covenants can be enforced against a subtenant, with whom the enforcing landlord has no privity of estate. You may remember that we mentioned this in the chapter on leases, while saying that in general the head landlord cannot enforce covenants in the lease against the subtenant (see 12.9.1). Where the restrictive covenant is contained in a lease, it is not necessary to show that the landlord has retained other neighbouring land which is benefited. It is enough to show that a benefit is conferred on the landlord's reversion (which is normally the case) (*Hall v Ewin* (1887) 37 ChD 74; *Regent Oil Co. Ltd v J. A. Gregory (Hatch End) Ltd* [1966] Ch 402).

(3) *The parties must have intended the burden to run*

It is essential that the parties should have intended the burden to pass to later owners of the affected property. Normally this intention will be expressly evidenced by the covenantor covenanting on behalf of himself and his successors in title, and those deriving title under him or them. In the absence of an express provision, the covenantor is deemed to have covenanted in these terms by virtue of LPA 1925, s. 79. However, this provision may be excluded from the agreement by an express term to the contrary: for a case in which the court construed the document as a whole when deciding whether such an exclusion existed, see *Morrells of Oxford Ltd v Oxford United Football Club Ltd* [2001] Ch 459. If the document creating the covenant is silent on the matter, the parties will be presumed to intend that it will bind later owners. Section 79 only deals with the need for intention. Suggestions that its positive wording ('shall have effect') rendered the other traditional rules on running of burdens redundant have been disapproved by the House of Lords in *Sefton v Tophams Ltd* [1967] 1 AC 50 at pp. 73 and 81 and in *Rhone v Stephens* [1994] 2 AC 310 at p. 322. Thus, s. 79 on its own will not make the burden run to bind a successor.

(4) *The application of equitable principles, and the need for notice or its modern equivalent*

If Mr Peach is to enforce the covenants relating to 18 Trant Way against Mrs Strawberry, he will be obliged to rely on the assistance of the equitable jurisdiction of the court. As we have seen above, in *Tulk v Moxhay* Lord Cottenham regarded the decision of the court as being primarily based upon conscience operating as an equitable principle. As a result, the general equitable principles and maxims will apply to any action which he brings. The most important of these is that 'He who comes to equity must come with clean hands'. This may be of importance where there are reciprocal covenants between neighbouring owners (as we shall see, this is the case in Rectory Crescent), if the owner seeking to enforce is also breaking any of the covenants. In such a case, it would be inequitable for the court to assist the person who is in breach of the agreement.

More importantly, the fact that the burden of the covenants runs only in equity means that one must bear in mind the need to protect the right to the covenant by entry on the register in the case of registered land or registration of a land charge in unregistered land. As we have seen, *Tulk v Moxhay* was decided primarily on the basis that the purchaser of Leicester Square bought with notice of the covenant restricting the use of the land.

26.4.2.3 Unregistered land

Where one is dealing with unregistered land and with restrictive covenants created *before* 1 January 1926 the old equitable doctrine of notice will still apply. You should not assume that such old covenants can be ignored, for they are still frequently encountered and can still be enforced where the rules in *Tulk v Moxhay* are satisfied. Where the title to the land is unregistered, and the covenant was created on or after 1 January 1926, it requires registration as a class D(ii) land charge (LCA 1972, s. 2(5)). If such a covenant is not registered, it will be void against a purchaser of a legal estate for money or money's worth, regardless of notice (LCA 1972, s. 4(6)). The date by which the covenant must have been registered is the date on which the burdened land was conveyed to the purchaser. In the case of 18 Trant Way, Mrs Strawberry will not be bound by the restrictive covenants relating to the property unless they were registered as land charges before she bought the fee simple in 1998 (the land has not been sold since Mousehole became an area of compulsory registration in 1990).

26.4.2.4 Registered land

When she acquired the property, Mrs Strawberry was obliged to register her title to the land with HM Land Registry (see Chapter 7), because Mousehole became a compulsory registration area on 1 December 1990 (see 4.2.3.1). On any such registration, the purchaser must tell the registrar of any pre-1926 covenants of which he or she has notice and present to the registrar a land charges search, which will reveal any registered covenants made after 1925. When the estate is registered, the registrar will also enter on the register notice of any such encumbrances. At the time Mrs Strawberry purchased, this requirement arose from the Land Registration Rules 1925, r. 40; LRA 1925, s. 50(1). Today the requirement on the registrar arises from the Land Registration Rules 2003, r. 35. These burdens on the land will affect a purchaser only if entered on the register relating to the burdened land. Usually the registrar will insert a full copy of the terms of the covenant in the charges section of the register.

Any covenants created after the title becomes registered must also be entered against the burdened estate. Most new covenants are created on transfer of the estate, and in the transfer deed. These covenants will be entered automatically on the register by way of notice. In the case of a covenant created at another time, the person with the benefit of the covenant should apply to have his interest noted on the register of the burdened land (under LRA 2002, s. 32) by way of notice.

26.4.3 Where the burden runs in equity, the benefit must be made to run in equity

Having established that Mrs Strawberry may be bound by certain covenants burdening 18 Trant Way, it must still be established that Mr Peach has a right to enforce the covenants. Where he has to argue that Mrs Strawberry is bound in equity by the covenants, he must also establish that he has obtained the benefit of the covenants according to equitable rules: it is not enough to show that the benefit passes at common law. However, in general the equitable rules are more generous to the person claiming the benefit and thus one would not wish to use the legal rules.

In equity, there are three ways in which a purchaser of the benefited land can acquire the right to enforce the covenant:

(1) by annexation (which may be express, implied or statutory);
(2) by express assignment of the benefit of the covenant; and
(3) under the special rules relating to building schemes.

26.4.3.1 Express annexation

Where 'words of annexation' are used, the benefit of the covenant is annexed or attached to the land, so that forever afterwards it passes automatically with the land to the new owner. In order to achieve express annexation, it is necessary that the words of the covenant should show that the original parties intended the benefit to run, and one way of doing this is to state expressly that the covenant is made 'for the benefit of' named land (*Rogers v Hosegood* [1900] 2 Ch 388). Another method which will have the same effect is for the covenant to be made with the covenantee as 'estate owner', that is, describing him as the owner of the land to be benefited. For example, Mr Raspberry covenanted with Miss Orange as 'for the benefit of the owners for the time being of land abutting' No 18 and that included Miss Orange. These words would have the effect of attaching the benefit of the covenants to No. 17. It is not enough, however, for the covenant to be made with the covenantee and his 'heirs, executors administrators and assigns' (or any similar set of words), for such a phrase does not link these people with the benefited land (*Renals v Cowlishaw* (1878) 9 ChD 125).

Where a claimant seeks to establish express annexation, a problem will arise if the wording of the deed creating the covenant purports to annex it to an area of land which is so large that it cannot reasonably be said that the covenant confers actual benefit on the whole property. In *Re Ballard's Conveyance* [1937] Ch 473, a covenant was said to be for the benefit of the whole of a large estate (approximately 690 hectares). In fact, the covenant could confer a benefit on only a small portion of that estate. Here the court said that, since the covenant did not confer a benefit on the whole estate, it could not run on a sale of the estate. Nor would it run when a part of the estate which was benefited was sold, because the court would not sever the covenant and attach it to parts of the land where the express wording of the deed did not allow for this (but see also *Earl of Leicester v Wells-next-the-Sea Urban District Council* [1973] Ch 110 and *Small v Oliver & Saunders (Developments) Ltd* [2006] 3 EGLR 141). As a result, when one drafts a covenant and wishes to attach it to a large area of land, it is wise in order to avoid any disputes to say that the covenant is for the benefit of 'the whole or any part of' the named land. This will allow the covenant to run with any part of the large estate which is actually benefited, and will also allow the benefit to be divided between several plots if the estate is ever sold off in that way (*Marquess of Zetland v Driver* [1939] Ch 1; and see *Morrells of Oxford Ltd v Oxford United Football Club Ltd* [2001] Ch 459 and below at 26.4.3.4(2)).

26.4.3.2 Implied annexation

Where words of express annexation are lacking, some cases suggest that it may still be possible for the court to identify the benefited land by looking at the circumstances. Where the facts are held to indicate with reasonable certainty the land which is to be benefited, the benefit will thereafter run with that land. This way of proceeding has been called 'implied annexation'.

The notion of implied annexation is usually said to be derived from two decisions: *Newton Abbot Cooperative Society Ltd v Williamson & Treadgold Ltd* [1952] Ch 286 (the '*Devonia*' case) and *Marten v Flight Refuelling Ltd* [1962] Ch 115. The first of these cases was in fact concerned with assignment of the benefit, rather than with annexation, but it was welcomed as 'a useful guide' in *Marten v Flight Refuelling Ltd* (at p. 133). Here there had been no assignment of the benefit, and the court looked at the burdened land and the surrounding area, and came to the conclusion that the covenant had been taken for the benefit of land retained by the vendor. Wilberforce J mentioned with approval (at p. 132) that there seemed to be support for the view 'that an intention to benefit may be found from surrounding or attending circumstances'.

It has to be said that this decision stands very much on its own, and, further, that it has been suggested that the issue of annexation was not relevant (Ryder (1972) 36 Conv NS 26). The covenant was made with the executors of the previous owner, who were holding in trust for an infant beneficiary, and it was these executors and the former beneficiary, now absolutely entitled to the property, who sought to enforce the covenant. Thus, there was no transfer and the benefit did not need to run. The decision has also been criticised as tending to increase the general uncertainty about the enforceability of covenants, for while questions of express annexation can in general be decided from a study of the documents, a claim of implied annexation cannot be decided without an application to the court (*Report of the Committee on Positive Covenants Affecting Land* (Chairman: Lord Wilberforce) (Cmnd 2719, 1968), para. 15).

26.4.3.3 **Statutory annexation**

These rather complicated rules about express annexation, and the uncertainty about implied annexation, may be of less importance since the decision of the Court of Appeal in *Federated Homes Ltd v Mill Lodge Properties Ltd* [1980] 1 WLR 594, which introduced the idea that in certain cases statutory annexation may be effective. The case before the court concerned a covenant by the defendant not to build more than a certain number of dwellings on the burdened land. It was clear from the wording of the document that the land to be benefited was neighbouring land retained by the covenantee, but there were no express words annexing the benefit of the covenant to that land. Later the covenantee sold this land and eventually it became the property of Mill Lodge Properties Ltd. In the case of part of the benefited land no problem about annexation arose, because the benefit of the covenant had been expressly assigned (see below). In respect of the other portion of the land, however, there had been no assignment, but the court held that this did not matter because it was clear which land was intended to benefit, and accordingly the covenant was annexed to that land by LPA 1925, s. 78. In the words of Brightman LJ (at p. 605):

> If, as the language of section 78 implies, a covenant relating to land which is restrictive of the user thereof is enforceable at the suit of (1) a successor in title to the covenantee, (2) a person deriving title under the covenantee or under his successors in title, and (3) the owner or occupier of the land intended to be benefited by the covenant, it must, in my view, follow that the covenant runs with the land, because *ex hypothesi*...every other owner and occupier has a right by statute to the covenant. In other words, if the condition precedent of section 78 is satisfied—that is to say, there exists a covenant which touches and concerns the land of the covenantee—that covenant runs with the land for the benefit of his successors in title, persons deriving title under him or them and other owners and occupiers.

One strange feature of this case, which should be noted, is that the defendant was the original covenantor. There was no need, therefore, to show that the burden had run with the land in equity, and accordingly one would have thought that the court would have been concerned only with whether the benefit ran at common law. Consideration of the equitable requirement of annexation was, strictly, unnecessary for the decision of the case, and it would therefore be open to a later court to treat the statements about statutory annexation as *obiter dicta* (but see the discussion in *Roake v Chadha* [1984] 1 WLR 40). However, since that time it seems to have been accepted that s. 78 does have this effect in any case in which it is clear which land was intended to benefit. Also it appears that the statutory annexation is to every part of the benefited land since the court assumed that every successor or derivative proprietor could claim under s. 78. If this is the effect of s. 78, it renders obsolete many of the traditional difficulties associated with express annexation, including the need to annex to the 'whole or any part' of the benefited land (if such a need exists—see 26.4.3.4(2)).

You should note, however, not everyone accepted that the decision in *Federated Homes* was correct. See particularly two articles by G. H. Newsom on this subject in (1981) 97 LQR and (1982) 98 LQR 202, in which it is argued that the decision is wrong. What is clear is that there are arguments that suggest that the decision is problematic. These include:

(1) The fact that a consequence is that covenants created before 1926 have to be treated in a different way. However, that is normally true with reforming legislation because it does not normally have retrospective effect.

(2) This interpretation took until 1980 (54 years) to be applied and it is easily possible to interpret the provision in a more limited way, to cover the points mentioned earlier in this chapter. A similar provision actually originated in 1881 and this extends the period of judicial blindness to almost 100 years. It is also notable that s. 79 has not been applied in the same way, despite the similarity of wording. It should, however, be noted that the provision in the Conveyancing Act 1881 has been said by some to give clearer evidence of an intention to annex.

(3) One might have expected the legislature to use clearer language to make such a marked change. The wording of ss. 76(6) and 77(5) show that where the legislature intended annexation to arise or be recognised, it uses clear language to produce that effect. Similarly, in s. 80(3) clear language is used to dispense with an old requirement for technical language in documents.

(4) In *Federated Homes* two members of the Court of Appeal said that they agreed entirely with the comments made on annexation by Hall V-C. in *Renals v Cowlishaw* (1878) 9 ChD 125 at p. 130. Yet that reasoning does not seem to tally with a subsequent owner of the benefited land being able to take the benefit of the covenant even though he may not have known of it and perhaps could not even be sure that it benefited his land, because this would not be clear from the documents creating the covenant.

26.4.3.4 Developments after *Federated Homes*

1. *Crest Nicholson*

In *Crest Nicholson Residential (South) Ltd v McAllister* [2004] 1 WLR 2409, the Court of Appeal returned to the issue of statutory annexation and affirmed it as a possibility but also gave rise to some further issues about when s. 78 can be relied upon. The case also provides an interesting discussion of the differences between ss. 78 and 79 of the LPA 1925 and whether s. 78 produces 'statutory annexation' where the benefited land is not identified in the documents creating the covenant.

The case involved an estate which had been sold off in plots in the early 1930s by two brothers and their company (the company had a beneficial interest in the property arising from a contract with the brothers). The conveyance of each plot said that the covenants in the conveyance were given by the purchaser 'to the intent that [the covenants would] be binding in so far as maybe on the owner for the time being' of the plot sold. The covenants were substantially in the same terms in the case of each plot and were as follows:

> The premises shall not be used for any purpose other than those of or in connection with a private dwellinghouse or for professional purpose.
>
> No dwellinghouse or other building shall be erected on the land hereby conveyed unless the plans drawings and elevation thereof shall have been previously submitted to and approved of in writing by [the brothers' company] but such approval shall not be unreasonably or vexatiously withheld.

Some time after the plots had all been sold, the brothers' company had been dissolved and therefore no longer existed as a legal person.

The claimant and the defendant were successors in title to the original purchasers of two of the plots of land. The owner of one (a property called 'Redruth') was Crest Nicholson, which wished to demolish the house on Redruth to build a new house and an access road to new houses on other plots also now owned by the same party. Mrs McAllister was the owner of another plot ('Newlyn'), at least part of which had been one of the original plots and which was sold after Redruth, and she contended that the development proposed by Crest Nicholson was in breach of the covenants mentioned above and that she had the benefit of those covenants. Crest Nicholson brought the initial action in order to determine the effects of the covenants. On appeal the issue of whether the covenants had been annexed to the benefited land was raised. There had been no express annexation in the documents relating to some of the potentially benefited plots, including Newlyn.

At first instance there was no issue taken as to annexation but in the Court of Appeal the issue was raised. The Court of Appeal followed the 'statutory annexation' approach it had adopted in *Federated Homes v Mill Lodge Properties*. However, it concluded (see Chadwick LJ at para. 33) that the land intended to be benefited still had to be so mentioned or defined in the documents creating the covenant that it was easily ascertainable (the requirement in *Marquess of Zetland v Driver* [1939] Ch 1). It was insufficient, in the view of the Court of Appeal, for the benefited land to be identifiable from the surrounding circumstances. As the documents relating to the property that had come into Mrs McAllister's hands contained no references that could be relied upon to identify benefited land, the covenants were not annexed to Newlyn by operation of statute and could not be enforced by Mrs McAllister.

Indeed, such references as existed in any of the documents relating to the string of transactions (when one included documents relating to all the plots sold) only suggested annexation to such land as the company retained from time to time (suggesting that on a sale by the company it was intended that the annexation ended). The Court of Appeal was content that s. 78 gave way to anything in the documents that indicated that enduring annexation was not intended.

Thus *Crest Nicholson* is authority for at least two propositions: (1) the land benefited must be identifiable from the documents creating the covenant and not just from extraneous facts; and (2) the effect of s. 78 gives way to anything in the documents that suggests that it was not intended that the benefit should be annexed so as to run with the land after sale.

It should be noted, however, that the court accepted that it might be possible to assign the benefit of the covenant expressly. However, we wonder whether this can work in a case like this, in which the intention of the original parties appears to have been to create a personal and non-assignable right for the company.

As to the differences in wording between ss. 78 and 79, the court concluded that, although different drafting techniques were used in the two sections the different wording in each section actually achieved the same end result. (This is a slightly surprising approach to statutory interpretation when applied to adjoining provisions in the same Act.) Section 79(1) imposes two qualifications: (i) the land must be land to which the covenant relates; and (ii) there must be no expression of contrary intention. An alternative method of expressing this would be to describe the land as 'land of the covenantor (or capable of being bound by him) and which is intended to be burdened'. If the parties did not intend that land, burdened while in the ownership of the covenantor, should continue to be subject to the burden in the hands of his successors (or some of his successors), they could say so. Accordingly Chadwick LJ (with whom the other Lord Justices agreed) concluded that there is no difference in result between the two sections.

This approach, which results in annexation but only while certain circumstances exist, is interesting. In *Crest Nicholson* itself, the real issue was really whether the covenant was intended to run with land at all or whether it was a covenant purely for the personal benefit of the covenantor company. The overall message is, of course, the need for accuracy in drafting any covenants.

Even had there been annexation, the second issue would have been whether the first covenant prevented more than one building being erected or simply restricted the use that might be made of any such building as was erected. Although one might imagine that the covenant produced the former result, in *Crest Nicholson* at first instance it was held that the covenant only covered use and not number of buildings, and the Court of Appeal indicated it would have agreed, had it had to consider the issue. Once again, the message is that one needs to draft a covenant carefully. If you mean 'a single dwelling-house', you should say so expressly.

2. *Small v Oliver & Saunders (Developments) Ltd*

More recently, the whole issue of whether annexation to the whole of an estate included annexation to every part even prior to s. 78 has arisen again. It has been suggested that the reasoning of the Court of Appeal in *Federated Homes* applies equally to all covenants, whenever made and is not restricted to covenants made after 1925 and that can therefore have implied into them the s. 78 wording. In *Small v Oliver & Saunders (Developments) Ltd* [2006] 3EGLR 141 the covenant in question was a covenant made in March 1925 and thus before the 1925 legislation came into force at the start of 1926. The claimant owned only a portion of the land that had been retained by the covenantee at the point that the covenant was made. The covenant was expressed to be for the benefit of the retained land and was worded to be made 'to the intent that such covenant shall enure for the benefit of and be annexed to the remainder of the Beech Hill Park Estate'. However, the 'magic' wording 'for the whole or any part of' was missing. One issue was therefore whether these words or, perhaps more accurately, this intention, could be implied prior to s. 78 coming into force. Mark Herbert QC, sitting as a Deputy Chancery Division Judge, relied on statements of Brightman LJ and Megaw LJ in *Federated Homes v Mill Lodge Properties* [1980] 1 WLR 594, at p. 606 and p. 608 respectively) to the effect that a covenant annexed to the whole of land must necessarily be annexed also to every part of that land. He concluded that those statements were:

> '. . . statements of principle that, in the absence of any contrary intention, annexation to identified land of the vendor, whether statutory or express, enures for the benefit of every part of the land' (para. 31).

If this is correct, then the impact of s. 78 was less extensive than once had been suggested. It seems annexation to parts as well as the whole may apply even in relation to pre-1926 covenants, provided that there is nothing in the documents to suggest that the annexation was only intended to be to the whole of the retained property.

26.4.3.5 Assignment

Even where the benefit of a covenant has not been expressly annexed to land, it has always been the case that the covenantee could transfer that benefit by express assignment. The benefit of a covenant, like the benefit of any other contract, is a chose in action and can be assigned at will. If one relies on this method it is, however, necessary to show that there is an unbroken chain of assignments, so that on each sale of the benefited land the benefit has been passed to the new owner and has finally come to the person who now seeks to enforce the covenant (*Re Pinewood Estate* [1958] Ch 280). It is also essential that the right should be assigned to the purchaser of the estate at the time of the conveyance to him: an assignment made after the estate has been transferred is not acceptable (*Re Union of London & Smith's Bank Ltd's Conveyance* [1933] Ch 611 at p. 632).

26.4.3.6 Building schemes

Some of the rules discussed above would cause difficulty when applied to the development of a new estate, such as Rectory Crescent. As we have seen, each purchaser entered into covenants with the developer, but now the estate is completed Big Builders plc has sold all of its plots in the area and will move on to work elsewhere and will not be concerned with enforcing these covenants. What the purchasers want is to be able to rely on a sort of 'local law' for the area (*Re Dolphin's Conveyance* [1970] Ch 654 at p. 662), which each householder can enforce directly against all the others. To a large extent, this could be achieved by the ordinary rules for freehold covenants, but this would be complicated and would depend on knowing the exact order in which the plots had been sold.

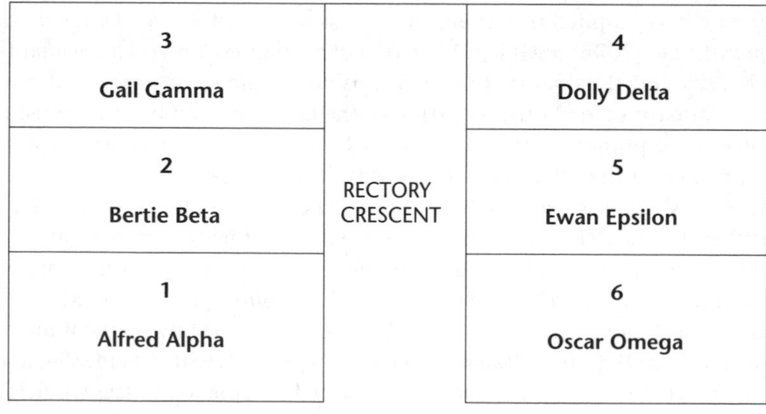

Figure 26.5

Once the new properties built on the old Rectory land had been built and sold the position in Rectory Crescent was as shown in Figure 26.5.

1. *Rectory Crescent: the position without a building scheme*

In our example, plots 1 to 6 Rectory Crescent were sold in that order. If some time in the future, the successor of the original purchaser of No. 3 should fence the garden in breach of the covenant, those holding plots sold after No. 3 (i.e., 4 to 6) could claim that they held land retained by the developer at the time of the sale of No. 3. The benefit of that purchaser's covenant would be annexed to the retained land, assuming of course that the covenant had been drafted correctly. Therefore it would have passed to them, or their predecessors in title, when the later plots were sold. Those who bought before the sale of No. 3 (i.e., 1 and 2) might be able to rely on LPA 1925, s. 56, if the covenant purported to be with the owners of those plots and provided that, if they are not the original purchasers, they can show that the benefit has passed to them under the usual rules.

Proceeding in this way may not seem too difficult, but that is because we have simplified matters by saying that plots 1 to 6 were sold in that order. In real life, the houses on a new estate may be sold in no particular order, as purchasers make their choices. 50 years or so later it could be quite difficult to know, in respect of a particular breach, who could proceed under s. 56 and who could rely on annexation.

There is, further, the problem we mentioned earlier that, because Big Builders plc retained no land when the last plot was sold, an essential rule for the running of the burden is not satisfied on the sale of that plot. Therefore, the successor to the original purchaser of No. 6 would take free of the covenant.

However, all these difficulties are avoided if it can be established that the development satisfies the legal requirements of a 'building scheme'.

2. *Requirements for a building scheme*

The traditional requirements for a building scheme were established in the Edwardian case of *Elliston v Reacher* [1908] 2 Ch 374, in which a building society had laid out an area for development in separate plots and had sold these using identical conveyances and imposing identical covenants upon each purchaser. The court held that the covenants were enforceable against all the successors to the original covenantor and set out four rules to be satisfied in order to establish a building scheme (sometimes called a 'scheme of development'):

(a) the purchasers must derive their titles from a common vendor;

(b) before selling, the vendor must have laid out the land in lots (or plots);

(c) on sale, the same restrictions must be imposed on all the plots, and it must be clear that those restrictions are intended to be for the benefit of all the plots sold; and

(d) each purchaser must have acquired a plot on the understanding that the covenants were intended to benefit all the other plots in the scheme.

3. *Developments after* Elliston v Reacher

In later cases, however, it has been established that these four rules provide only guidance, and that what is crucial is the intention of the parties to create a building scheme. Accordingly, a scheme was found in *Baxter v Four Oaks Properties Ltd* [1965] Ch 816, even though the whole area had not been divided into lots in advance of the first sale. In this case the developer had wished to allow purchasers to choose lots of varying sizes. Again, in *Re Dolphin's Conveyance* [1970] Ch 654, a single scheme was established, even though the purchasers had not acquired from a common vendor. The first sales were made by two co-owners, but later the land came into the hands of their nephew, who continued the sale of plots and imposed covenants identical to those imposed by his aunts. The court considered that this satisfied the essential requirement, since it was quite clear that the various vendors did intend to create a local law for the area. If, however, a common intention cannot be established, for example because the covenants vary between the plots of land, a building scheme will not exist (see *Emile Elias & Co. Ltd v Pine Groves Ltd* [1993] 1 WLR 305 and *Small v Oliver & Saunders (Developments) Ltd* [2006] 3 EGLR 141).

4. *Advantages of establishing a building scheme*
Rectory Crescent would appear to be a clear example of such a scheme. Once a scheme has been established, it is necessary to consider what benefits will accrue. Although it is still necessary to establish that the rules in *Tulk v Moxhay* have been satisfied, the first benefit of a building scheme is that these rules are modified slightly in one respect, so that the burden will run with the last plot sold (here, No. 6). This happens despite the fact that the developer does not retain any land capable of being benefited. With this exception, all the other basic rules have to be observed: so there is no question of the burden of positive covenants being enabled to run under a building scheme, and the usual registration or protection by entry on the register is needed if successors of the covenantors are to be bound.

The second benefit of a building scheme is that all purchasers of plots in the scheme are enabled to enforce the covenants between themselves, irrespective of the date on which they, or their predecessors in title, bought their plots. There is thus no need to distinguish between the earlier purchasers, proceeding under s. 56, and the later purchasers, who rely on express annexation. Earlier purchasers will be able to obtain the benefit of later covenants, and that benefit will run with their plots automatically, provided that they can establish that a building scheme has been created.

The third advantage of a building scheme is that in equity it will ensure that the benefit of the covenants imposed on other plots will automatically run to all successors of the original purchasers, without the need for express annexation or for assignment (although this may be less important since *Federated Homes Ltd v Mill Lodge Properties Ltd* [1980] 1 WLR 594).

Besides the three advantages of the building scheme described above, such a scheme appears not to be subject to some of the other general principles relating to covenants. In *Brunner v Greenslade* [1971] Ch 993, it was established that both the benefit and the burden of covenants in a building scheme will run to affect someone who acquires only part of the original plot. Thus, where a plot is subdivided, the purchaser of one part may enforce the covenants against the purchaser of the other part and against all the other owners of plots forming part of the scheme. This rule was accepted because the aim of the scheme is to create a type of local legal system, and this aim would not be fulfilled if 'islands of immunity' developed in which covenants could not be enforced (as would happen if the owners of subplots could not enforce the covenants between themselves).

Similarly, it appears that should two plots come into common ownership and then later be divided again, the original covenants will revive automatically between the subsequent owners (*Texaco Antilles Ltd v Kernochan* [1973] AC 609). In general law this would not occur, for the common ownership would extinguish the covenants as between the two plots and the rights and duties created by the covenants would not revive when the plots were once more separated. The only way in which the covenants could be revived would be for the common vendor to require fresh covenants from each purchaser. However, when a building scheme can be established, the rights and duties under the original covenants will spring up again automatically when the plots are separated. Thus, the building scheme provides a useful exception to the ordinary rules on this point.

Another interesting issue is what happens if the covenants cannot be shown to benefit the whole of the area described as falling within the scheme. In *Whitgift Homes v Stocks* [2001] 48 EG 130 (CS) the claimants were owners of 55 properties on an estate built in the 1920s. The defendants were owners of two properties, which they proposed to develop in a manner that was in breach of some of the covenants imposed by the original developer. The Court of Appeal accepted that s. 78 LPA 1925 would be effective to annex the benefit of the covenants to all the plots on the estate. However, it was also held that in this case the building scheme tests could not be passed for the estate as a whole. At first instance it was held that this did not prevent it being possible to establish a scheme in relation to part of the whole estate. However, the Court of Appeal pointed out that it was necessary for the scheme to apply to a defined area (*Reid v Bickerstaff* [1909] 2 Ch 305), and said that here this was not possible because one could not clearly identify which of the properties on the estate formed part of the scheme.

26.4.3.7 Letting schemes

At this point it is worth noting that the building scheme rules are also capable of application to leasehold properties that are let as a scheme and in such cases allow the tenants to enforce some of the covenants in their leases against one another. An example is *Williams v Kiley (trading as CK Supermarkets Ltd)* [2003] 1 EGLR 47, in which five shops in a shopping parade had been leased and one tenant claimed that it was able to enforce a covenant against another tenant on the basis of a letting scheme. Here each lease dovetailed with the others to ensure each business did not compete with the others and this was held to demonstrate a sufficient reciprocity of obligation for a scheme to exist and thus for one tenant to enforce against the others. In *Hannon v 169 Queen's Gate Ltd, The Times*, 23 November 1999, it was held that where a block of flats that was covered by a letting scheme was extended upwards, the scheme could stretch to cover that development. The court said that there was only a limitation in the horizontal plane. Thus, it should be borne in mind that the letting scheme can change in area over time but only upwards or, presumably, downwards.

26.5 The problem of positive covenants

The fact that the burden of a covenant will not normally run at law, and that equity declines to enforce a positive obligation against the successor of the original covenantor, can prove decidedly inconvenient. You will recall that when 18 Trant Way was sold originally to Mr Raspberry he undertook to contribute towards the cost of the maintenance of the driveway which is shared with No. 17. Undoubtedly, the same conveyance gave him an easement of way over the same drive. When Mrs Strawberry bought No. 18, she will have acquired the benefit of the legal easement, but may claim that she is not obliged to contribute to the maintenance of the drive, as the burden of positive covenants does not run to the covenantor's successors. This would produce an unfair result, and over the years conveyancers have developed a number of ways in which positive obligations can be made to bind successors. In addition, the common law has recognised one exception to the basic rule that it will not enforce burdens on later owners of the covenantor's land. These methods of avoiding the disadvantages of the basic rules can accordingly be of considerable importance, and we will now consider them individually.

26.5.1 The exception to the rule: *Halsall v Brizellt*

In the case of *Halsall v Brizell* [1957] Ch 169, the purchaser of a plot of land on an estate had been given various easements including an easement of way over the estate roads, and in return had covenanted to contribute to the cost of maintaining the roads, walls and other facilities from which he derived a benefit. A successor of the original purchaser claimed the benefit of the easements affecting the property but denied that he was obliged to make any payment, on the basis that the burden of a positive covenant would not run at law or equity. The court refused to accept this argument, holding that the successor in title could not take the benefit of an agreement unless he was also prepared to accept the related burdens (see also *E. R. Ives Investment Ltd v High* [1967] 2 QB 379, and *Tito v Waddell (No. 2)* [1977] Ch 106 at p. 290). For the rule to apply, the burden and benefit do have to be related to one another in some way. Comments by Megarry V-C in *Tito v Waddell (No. 2)*, which suggested that the benefits and burdens did not have to be inter-related provided that they were part of the same transaction, were expressly disapproved by the House of Lords in *Rhone v Stephens* [1994] 2 AC 310, in which Lord Templeman said (at p. 322):

> It does not follow that any condition can be rendered enforceable by attaching it to a right nor does it follow that every burden imposed by a conveyance may be enforced by depriving the covenantor's successor in title of every benefit which he enjoyed thereunder. The condition must be relevant to the exercise of the right. In *Halsall v Brizell* there were reciprocal benefits and burdens enjoyed by the users of the roads and sewers.

Accordingly, under this rule only related burdens can be enforced and, where there is no necessary relationship between the benefit exercised and the burden for which enforcement is sought, the courts will not act. The problems that this approach can produce when dealing with modern estate housing are illustrated very clearly by *Thamesmead Town Ltd v Allotey* (1998) 37 EG 161. Here the original covenantor had covenanted to pay a service charge to maintain roads, sewers and landscaped and communal areas on an estate. Mr Allotey acquired a property from the original covenantor and was held not to be liable to make payments in relation to the landscaped and communal areas because he had obtained no entitlement to benefit from these areas. He did, however, have to pay the service charge in relation to the roads and sewers, which he had a right to use and did use. The possible arguments that may arise where someone argues that they never use a facility and thus are not going to pay for it can be imagined. However, if they have a right but simply do not choose to use it, this argument should fail.

The principle in *Halsall v Brizell* may assist the current owner of 17 Trant Way, in compelling Mrs Strawberry to contribute to the cost of the repairs recently made to the shared driveway. The rule is also frequently of considerable importance when one is dealing with a building scheme in which positive covenants for the maintenance of shared facilities may be necessary.

26.5.2 Evasion of the rules by techniques of drafting

There are a number of ways in which the burden of a positive covenant can be imposed on a later acquirer of burdened land.

26.5.2.1 Granting leases

Where a lease is granted, covenants in the lease which fall within the rule in *Spencer's Case* or pass under the Landlord and Tenant (Covenants) Act 1995 will bind the tenant's assignees (see Chapter 12). In such cases, the law makes no distinction between positive and negative obligations, and covenants to contribute to the cost of maintenance or to an insurance premium are common. As a result, a vendor may well choose to grant a long lease of property, rather than selling the fee simple estate. In the case of blocks of flats, where the enforcement of positive obligations may be crucial, it is exceptionally rare for the flat owners to hold estates in fee simple, and leases are the norm. In such cases, the purchaser may well pay as much as he would have paid to acquire a freehold estate, but will obtain only a wasting asset. In addition his ownership will be subject to the landlord's rights of re-entry and to a continuing obligation to pay ground rent. He may also encounter the difficulty that mortgagees may be less willing to lend money on the security of a leasehold property. All this is quite a high price to pay to enable the vendor to ensure that the burden of positive covenants passes to the successors in title of the covenantee. The new commonhold system was designed to meet these problems but it has not proved popular in practice.

26.5.2.2 Indemnity covenants

Another method of circumvention is to impose upon the covenantor an obligation to require an indemnity covenant from his successor. Should the covenant be broken, the covenantee can then sue the original covenantor, who remains liable on the covenant; he will sue his successor, and so on down the line. This method is not, however, very effective, because it is dependent on the maintenance of an unbroken chain of indemnity covenants. In the case of *Thamesmead Town Ltd v Allotey* (26.5.1) this approach broke down on the first transfer. In addition, after some years it may prove impossible to find the original covenantor in order to enforce against him.

26.5.2.3 Creating estate rentcharges

Another possible method is for a vendor to require the purchaser to grant him an estate rentcharge over the land. You will remember that a rentcharge imposes a duty on the current estate owner to make regular payments of money to the person entitled to the charge (see 2.4.2), and so a rentcharge can be useful where it is wished to impose an obligation to contribute to the cost of maintenance; it might, for example, have been used in relation to the shared driveway at 17 and 18 Trant Way. However, in addition to this, the rentcharge can be used to enforce other positive obligations beyond the mere payment of money, for the owner of the charge has a legitimate interest in maintaining the value of the land, and so can require the estate owner, when he grants the rentcharge, to enter into covenants for repair and maintenance. The rentcharge, and its associated obligations, run with the land to bind successive owners. The right of re-entry which supports the rentcharge enables the owner of the charge to enter on the land and do the work himself, if the estate owner fails to do so.

The estate rentcharge was exempted from the general bar on the creation of rentcharges imposed by the Rentcharges Act 1977 (see s. 2), and so may still be created. It takes effect as a legal interest in land. In the case of registered land, the rentcharge must be substantively registered in order to be legal. Where a rentcharge is granted in relation to a registered estate its creation does not operate at law until the registration requirements are met: LRA 2002, s. 27. If the rentcharge is granted for a term of years of up to and including seven years' duration, the requirement is to enter a notice on the register of the burdened land (LRA 2002, s. 27(4) and Sch. 2, para. 7). In the case of any other rentcharge the person granted the charge must be registered as proprietor of the rentcharge and a notice must be entered against the register relating to the estate that has been charged (LRA 2002, s. 27(4) and Sch. 2, para. 6). In the case of unregistered land, it is good against the world (LPA 1925, s. 1(2)).

The decision in *Orchard Trading Estate Management Ltd v Johnson Security Ltd* [2002] 18 EG 155 illustrates the use that may be made of the estate rentcharge. The court considered the application of the tests in the Rentcharges Act 1977 for a valid estate rentcharge and the decision indicates how they will be applied in practice. It concerned a rentcharge enabling the recovery of 'all . . . expenditure incurred by [the respondent] in or about the maintenance and proper or convenient management of the estate'. The appellant argued that the rentcharge failed to comply with the requirements of the Rentcharges Act 1977 because payment of rates in respect of the common parts of the estate were not for the benefit of the land charged and there was no limitation to reasonable sums. The court was, however, content that the payment of rates was necessary to enable holding of the common parts for the benefit of all the properties on the estate and the reasonableness requirement did not have to be expressly stated, particularly as here the sums covered were only actual expenditure. The latter point does not, however, seem to deal with the possibility of the person who is spending the money on the maintenance of common parts not doing so in a reasonably cost-effective manner.

26.5.2.4 Creating long leases which are then converted to freehold estates

A long lease with more than 200 years to run, which satisfies the other requirements of LPA 1925, s. 153, may be converted by the tenant into a freehold estate. On such conversion, any obligations on the tenant, including positive covenants, will become burdens enforceable against the freehold estate. This method is rarely used as it is very cumbersome, and, in the main, untested, but it is usual to include it in the list of devices enabling positive covenants to run with the land.

26.5.2.5 Covenants restraining sale of registered land without consent of the original vendor

Under LRA 2002, s. 40, a vendor of registered land may place on the register a restriction preventing the transfer of the registered estate to any person without the vendor's consent. The use of this provision would enable the vendor to require an intending purchaser from the 'covenantee', to enter into fresh positive covenants with the original vendor before he will consent to the sale.

26.5.2.6 Fencing

It should be remembered that, in some circumstances, an obligation to maintain a fence may constitute an easement of fencing, rather than a positive covenant, and the obligation will then run with the servient tenement (*Crow v Wood* [1971] 1 QB 77). However, see 25.2.2.10 on the 'spurious' nature of such an easement.

26.5.2.7 Commonhold

In cases involving a number of units, such as blocks of flats, the use of a commonhold scheme will enable positive covenants to be enforced against successors of the original owners. However, these schemes may prove unduly complex where only two or three units are involved and thus far commonhold has not been a popular option.

26.5.3 Statutory powers of local authorities

Local authorities are able to impose positive obligations and to enforce them against successive owners, under the provisions of a number of statutes. For example, under s. 72

of the Town and Country Planning Act 1990, a local planning authority, on granting planning permission, may impose conditions and these will be enforceable against future owners of the land. For this reason, it is advisable to check when purchasing a property that all planning conditions have been observed because planning authorities have quite Draconian enforcement powers available to them.

26.6 Remedies

26.6.1 Contractual remedies

Should a covenant be broken, the normal contractual remedies of damages for breach, or an injunction restraining breach may be sought. However, where one is dealing with a successor in title to the original covenantor a claim to damages cannot be brought in contract because of the lack of privity (see *Rhone v Stephens* [1994] 2 AC 310). However, it is possible to seek an injunction and/or damages under the Supreme Court Act 1981. (See also *Surrey County Council v Bredero Homes Ltd* [1993] 1 WLR 1361, which emphasises that the covenantee's claim is for his actual loss and not for the profit that the covenantor will make as a consequence of the breach). In many cases the resulting damages may be surprisingly low (see *Small v Oliver & Saunders (Developments) Ltd* [2006] 3 EGLR 141 and the discussion at 25.10.2 above).

In cases in which a positive covenant has been broken, an order for specific performance or a mandatory injunction may be the most suitable remedy. In the case of a negative covenant, the court is unlikely to order demolition of property built in breach of covenant: *Wrotham Park Estate Co. v Parkside Homes Ltd* [1974] 1 WLR 798 and see also *Small v Oliver & Saunders (Developments) Ltd* on this point. *Surrey County Council v Bredero* was discussed by the House of Lords in *A-G v Blake* [2001] AC 268 (a case unrelated to land law, being about the breach of a duty of confidentiality owed by a former member of the security services) and Lord Nicholls indicated that he preferred the approach in *Wrotham* to the assessment of damages. In *Wrotham*, while refusing an injunction to remove buildings, the court awarded damages at a rate of 5 per cent of the developer's expected profit. In *Bredero*, only nominal damages were given, because the value of the benefited land had not been reduced.

26.6.2 Need to avoid delay

Where an equitable remedy is to be sought it is essential not to delay in seeking the appropriate remedy. This is particularly true where the owner of the dominant estate is aware that the servient owner is expending money (for example, by carrying out building work in breach of covenant). Indeed in an appropriate case the dominant owner who has remained silent about breaches for a prolonged period may be regarded as having acquiesed in the breach and thus as having lost his right to relief for breach of covenant.

These possibilities are well illustrated by *Gafford v Graham* (1998) 77 P&CR 73, in which the servient owner, in breach of covenant, between 1986 and 1989 constructed and ran, on the servient land, a riding school. The covenants binding the land permitted only certain buildings and prohibited other building without the consent of the dominant owner (which had not been obtained). The covenants were broken. The first complaint of the breaches had been a solicitor's letter, written three years after the first of the breaches commenced. Nourse LJ held that in relation to most of the construction the delay (three years) in making a complaint was such that the dominant owner's rights to any relief for breach were entirely barred. The complaint in relation to the construction and operation of a riding school was much closer to the events of which complaint was made and in relation to these the dominant owner was not taken to have acquiesced. However, the dominant owner had not sought an immediate (interlocutory) injunction to prevent the building work continuing but had waited until the full hearing of the action and sought there a final injunction (which would have required the removal of the riding school). Nourse LJ concluded that in these circumstances it was not appropriate to grant the injunction sought in relation to the riding school. However, he did award £25,000 damages for the breach of covenant involved in its construction and operation. The sum awarded as damages was to be calculated by reference to the amount that might reasonably have been expected in payment for an agreement to relax the covenant permanently in relation to the riding school.

The message for the aggrieved dominant owner is accordingly not to be tolerant of breaches and to seek a remedy swiftly, obtaining interim relief as appropriate. In such a case, where the servient owner acts flagrantly in breach of covenant and ignores warnings, the court may require any building constructed to be demolished (*Wakeham v Wood* [1981] 43 P&CR 40) but will not do so as an invariable principle (see 26.6.1). In *Mortimer v Bailey* [2005] 2 P&CR 9, the Court of Appeal even granted a mandatory injunction requiring demolition a year after a building had been completed and even though no interim injunction had been obtained to prevent building works continuing. For an older example of acquiescence defeating a claim see *Sayers v Collyer* [1885] 28 ChD 103, where a complainant lost his case in respect of a beershop that had been constructed in breach of covenant because of evidence that he had made regular use of the premises!

26.6.3 Declaration under LPA 1925, s. 84(2)

In many cases, the real problem with a covenant is not in enforcing it, but in establishing whether it is binding on a particular person, or whether the person seeking to enforce it is entitled to do so. Suitable relief in the case of such a dispute is provided by LPA 1925, s. 84(2), as amended by LPA 1969, s. 28(4), which allows an applicant to ask the court to declare whether or not land is affected by 'a restriction imposed by an instrument' and 'the nature and extent' of the restriction. In addition, a declaration may be sought 'whether the same is or would in any given event be enforceable and if so by whom'.

For an excellent summary of the remedies available and some of the difficulties encountered in enforcement, see the article by Professor Martin on this subject in [1996] Conv 329.

26.7 Discharge of covenants

26.7.1 Common ownership

A covenant will be extinguished automatically should the burdened and benefited land come into common ownership and occupation (*Re Tiltwood, Sussex* [1978] Ch 269) but remember the special rule relating to plots within a building scheme (*Texaco Antilles*

Ltd v Kernochan [1973] AC 609). Otherwise it is open to the parties affected to agree to discharge the obligation (the discharge itself being made by deed). Apart from these methods, a covenant would continue to affect land in perpetuity, under the rules of common law and equity. This causes considerable inconvenience, where after the passage of many years the covenant has become redundant or unreasonable. As a result, a statutory method has been provided whereby certain covenants may be discharged or varied.

26.7.2 Application to Lands Chamber

Under LPA 1925, s. 84, as amended by the LPA 1969, an application to discharge or modify, 'any restriction arising under covenant or otherwise as to the user [of land] or the building thereon' may be made to the Lands Chamber of the Upper Tribunal (formerly the 'Lands Tribunal'), which may modify or discharge the restrictive covenant in whole or in part. The party who is applying must establish one of four grounds on which he seeks discharge or modification of the covenant.

First, he may show that the restriction has become obsolete due to 'changes in the character of the property or the neighbourhood' or to other relevant circumstances. This would apply, for example, to a covenant to use premises only as a dwelling, if the surrounding area had come into business or mixed use. Second, it may be established that the covenant impedes a reasonable user and either does not provide any practical benefit of substantial value to any person or is contrary to the public interest and, in either case, money would be adequate compensation for the loss or disadvantage (if any) that would be suffered due to the discharge or modification. Third, it may be established that those entitled to the benefit have agreed, expressly or impliedly 'by their acts or omissions' to the discharge or modification. Finally, the claimant may succeed if he can establish 'that the proposed discharge or modification will not injure the persons entitled to the benefit of the restriction'. In considering applications for discharge, the Lands Chamber must take into account the development plan for the area and any declared or ascertainable pattern for the grant or refusal of planning permission (s. 84(1B)). *In re University of Westminster* [1998] 3 All ER 1014 indicates the approach that should be adopted by the Lands Chamber on any application made under s. 84 and in *Dobbin v Redpath* [2007] 4 All ER 465 it was indicated that the existence of a building scheme would be a material factor if an amendment were sought in such a case.

If the Lands Chamber agrees to discharge or modify a covenant on any ground, it may require the payment of compensation to the owners of the benefited land. It should be noted that the wording of s. 84 is such that the powers of the Lands Chamber do not apply to positive covenants.

26.7.3 Housing Act 1985, s. 610

A further statutory power to discharge a covenant requiring property to be kept as a *single* dwelling exists under Housing Act 1985, s. 610. This permits a county court to authorise an alteration of the property in breach of a covenant (for example, into several flats) if the property cannot be disposed of readily as one unit due to a change in character of the neighbourhood. The aim of this provision is to prevent land falling into disuse because of a limitation imposed by a covenant, and thereby to prevent a diminution in the number of dwellings available for occupation.

26.8 Reform of the law

After reading the last two chapters, you may well be left with the impression that the rules relating to covenants and freehold are in considerable need of reform. This is a generally accepted opinion.

26.8.1 Some proposals for reform

The rules relating to the running of covenants have been particularly heavily criticised and have been the subject of three major reports over the years: (a) the Law Commission, *Report on Restrictive Covenants* (Law Com No. 11, 1967); (b) the Wilberforce Committee, *Report on Positive Covenants Affecting Land* (Cmnd 2719, 1968); and (c) the Law Commission, *Report on the Law of Positive and Restrictive Covenants* (Law Com No. 127, 1984). The last of these reports was a detailed attempt to make some sense of the confusion of the rules relating to easements and covenants. The position regarding positive covenants was particularly criticised, since such covenants do not run to bind a subsequent owner, and accordingly the original covenantor, who remains liable on his contract, can find himself being held responsible for the acts of some later owner long after his own interest in the land has ceased (para. 4.3 of the Report). This problem has now been addressed in relation to covenants in leases (see 12.3) but no reform has yet been made of the law in relation to freehold covenants. In 1998 the Lord Chancellor announced that the Law Commission Report of 1984 (No. 127) would not be implemented but said that the issues it raised would be considered further by the Law Commission in the light of other proposals for reform. With the intention of producing a coherent scheme that is compatible with the LRA 2002, the rules on commonhold and the position in relation to easements, the Law Commission published a Consultation Paper in 2008 (Law Com No. 186: *Easements, Covenants and Profits à Prendre*) and a new 'final' Report in 2011 (Law Com No. 327: *Making Land Work: Easements, Covenants and Profits à Prendre*). For more on these recent developments see 26.8.4.

26.8.2 Problems of the current rules

The horrors of the rules regarding restrictive covenants were cogently summarised in para. 4.9 of the 1984 Law Commission Report:

> The burden of a restrictive covenant does not run at all at law, but it does run in equity if certain complicated criteria are met. The benefit, by contrast, runs both at law and in equity, but according to rules which are different. These rules are, if anything, more complicated than the rules about the burden, and some of them are particularly technical and hard to grasp: as examples one may cite the rules about 'annexation' and those about 'building schemes'.

For some years now there has been further pressure to reform the rules about covenants, as part of a wider campaign for changes in the law to facilitate the sale of flats as freehold rather than as leasehold properties.

26.8.3 Past proposals for reform

26.8.3.1 Land obligations

The 1984 Law Commission Report took the view that the existing rules on covenants should be abolished and a new class of rights, 'land obligations', should be created to replace them. Such rights would be subject to rules similar to those applying to easements (which the Commission regarded as more satisfactory), and should subsist as legal interests in land, binding on successive owners under normal rules. After sale, the original parties would lose their contractual rights and obligations, thus destroying the present continuing contractual liability of the original covenantor (see para. 4.22 of the 1984 Report). Under such a scheme, no distinction would be made between positive and negative covenants.

26.8.3.2 Easements

The 1984 Report accepted that in general the law relating to easements is preferable to the rules on covenants. Whilst this may be true with respect to expressly created easements, the law on implied grant, the provisions of LPA 1925, s. 62, and the law on prescription are also sorely in need of reform. In 1971, the Law Commission Working Paper, *Transfer of Land: Appurtenant Rights* (Working Paper No. 36), recognised the difficulties in this area, and made a number of recommendations. In particular it was suggested that certain important easements (for example, the right to support) should become automatic statutory rights (para. 50 of the Paper) and there is now legislation on 'party walls'. Further recommendations were made in relation to acquisition of easements by other methods. In particular, it was suggested that the prescription period should be reduced to 12 years in order to bring it into line with the limitation period for actions in respect of land (para. 101 of the Paper). In 1966 the Law Reform Committee, when considering easements and profits (Cmnd 3100), had been divided on whether prescription should be abolished in its entirety, but was unanimous in agreeing that, if retained, the law required drastic reform.

26.8.3.3 Commonhold

The various suggested reforms were, to some extent, drawn together in the consultation paper on 'Commonhold' presented to Parliament in November 1990 (Cmnd 1345 (1990)). Thus far, the reforms discussed in Chapter 14 are the only changes that have been made.

26.8.4 Law Commission Report 2011

As we explained in Chapter 25, in March 2008 the Law Commission published yet another paper (Consultation Paper No. 186) dealing with the law relating to covenants. This followed a very serious review of the law relating to easements, profits and covenants and the Report is well worth reading, even if it is rather long. The Report concluded that the law on covenants relating to freehold land is seriously in need of urgent reform and their recommendations build on the earlier consideration of the possibility of creating new 'land obligations'. Following consultation, a final Report was published in June 2011: *Making Land Work: Easements, Covenants and Profits à Prendre*, Law Com No. 327. This Report, while long, is well worth study for the detailed analysis of the problems in this area of law and proposals for a solution. The Report includes a draft Bill, which is also worth attention. Below we identify the areas of difficulty and give a short summary of the proposals.

The Law Commission identified the following important flaws in the current law on freehold covenants:

(1) the burden of positive covenants will not run with land unless complex drafting devices are employed, which do not always work satisfactorily;

(2) burdens can run but only in equity and only if complex and technical conditions are met;

(3) while the benefit of covenants can run with land in both law and equity, different rules apply to law and equity and the rules are even more complicated than those applying to burdens;

(4) there is no need for the document creating an easement to describe the benefited land without doubt, as extrinsic evidence can be introduced in the case of conflict in order to establish what vague wording means. This reduces certainty;

(5) there is no need for benefits to be registered in any way, which makes it difficult to establish at a later date what benefits do attach to land;

(6) the original parties to a covenant remain contractually bound and benefited even after they have disposed of the affected land because they are bound to one another in a contractual agreement. This can leave a covenantor who has disposed of the burdened land at risk of being sued if there is a breach of covenant by the new owner.

The availability of commonhold is noted in paras. 5.16 and 5.17 of the Report but it is said that commonhold is designed for truly interdependent developments with shared facilities and structures. No mention seems to be made of the fact that commonhold has not been widely adopted, even in cases in which it might be appropriate. The Report does, however, point out that commonhold does not cover all possible cases (see above, Chapter 14).

The Law Commission's conclusion is that there should be a fairly extensive reform of the law relating to freehold covenants, both positive and negative.

26.8.4.1 Land obligations

The main proposals are to be found in paras. 5.69 and 5.70 of the 2011 Report. The key intention is to create a new type of interest in land. In the earlier Reports from the Law Commission this new interest was called a 'land obligation', but the Bill attached to the latest Report merely calls them 'obligations'. However, the Report acknowledges that it is easiest to call the new rights 'land obligations' and we adopt this approach here. We anticipate that, if the new rights are introduced, this will become their usual name, in order to distinguish these new rights in land from other types of obligation that can be enforced.

26.8.4.2 Land obligations may be negative or positive

The first detailed proposal is that an estate owner should be able to create both negative and positive land obligations, to take effect as legal interests appurtenant to another estate in land and which are registrable interests under the LRA 2002, provided that:

(1) the benefit of the land obligation touches and concerns the benefited land;

(2) the land obligation is:

(a) an obligation not to do something on the burdened land; or

(b) an obligation to do something on the burdened land or on the boundary between the burdened and benefited land; or

(c) an obligation to make a payment in return for the performance of an obligation of the type mentioned in (b); and

(3) the land obligation is not a covenant between lessor and lessee relating to the demised premises (this excludes leasehold covenants).

It is proposed that land obligations should not operate as covenants but as legal interests in the burdened land, which are appurtenant to the benefited estate in land. Land obligations would replace entirely the existing law on the enforceability of covenants in relation to any new obligations over freehold land (whether worded as covenants or land obligations): see paras. 5.70–5.73 of the Report.

26.8.4.3 **Abolition of old rules on freehold covenants**

Paragraph 5.89 of the Report proposes that following the introduction of the new land obligations it should no longer be possible to create freehold covenants enforceable under *Tulk v Moxhay*.

26.8.4.4 **Creation of land obligations**

Paragraphs 6.1–6.53 rehearse in more detail the manner in which land obligations will operate. Key points are that, as legal rights, they must be granted by deed and, if the estate is registered, the grant must be completed by registration. Para. 6.57 proposes that where title to the burdened land is unregistered the burden of the land obligation should be registrable as a land charge under the LCA 1972 (as a new Class G land charge).

The Commission advises that the new land obligations should arise only expressly. They should not be capable of arising by implication or prescription and s. 62, LPA 1925 should not operate to create a land obligation or to convert one from a leasehold to a freehold interest (para. 6.62).

26.8.4.5 **Land obligations and registered titles**

It is proposed that land obligations will be registrable interests in registered land. They are not to be overriding interests (para. 6.68). Normally, they will have been registered as land charges if created in relation to unregistered land and will be automatically entered on the register on first registration of the title.

26.8.4.6 **Enforceability of benefit of land obligations**

As the land obligation is to be a legal *interest* in land, it will pass to an acquirer of any *estate* in the benefited land to which it is appurtenant. However, the Commission proposes that it should not be transmitted with derived interests: para. 6.98. Therefore, a land obligation cannot be transmitted as appurtenant to another land obligation. This would prevent the decision in *Re Salvin's Indenture* [1938] 2 All ER applying to the new land obligation. In that case a water company had rights over the dominant land but no estate in it. Nonetheless an easement claimed by the water company to lay a pipe over the servient land was regarded as possible and transmissible because it was appurtenant to the other rights that the water company had, even though the water company had no estate in the dominant land.

It is possible that a number of dominant owners may have the right to enforce an obligation. Therefore the Report proposes that where the land obligation is to contribute to the cost of something, only the owner who has incurred expenditure is to be able to enforce the obligation. Thus if landlord A and his tenant B have an obligation to repair a fence and the neighbour C has an obligation to pay half the cost, if tenant B carries out the repairs only he can obtain compensation from C. A cannot claim. (Para. 6.99.)

26.8.4.7 **Enforceability of burden of land obligations**

It is indicated that the proposed registration provisions will deal with any issues of whether the burden of a land obligation runs with the land when the burdened estate is disposed of as a whole. Thus, where a burdened estate is sold to a purchaser of the whole estate, the purchaser takes the land subject to the burden provided the disposition creating the burden has been registered on the register of the burdened land (registered land) or as a Class G land charge (unregistered land). (Para. 6.101.)

The situation is not so straightforward where an estate is *derived from* a burdened estate (e.g., if a lease is created out of the burdened estate). In such a case should the lessee be bound by the land obligation—or more correctly, is the leasehold estate to be bound?

Similarly, if only part of the burdened land is disposed of, should the burden run to bind the part of the land?

(1) *Restrictive obligations*

In both these cases the Law Commission proposes replicating the current law where the land obligation in question is *restrictive*: para. 6.103. This will perpetuate the need to distinguish between negative and positive interests.

Therefore, para. 6.104 proposes that the burden of a restrictive land obligation should pass onto all estates and interests derived from the burdened estate and to all occupiers of the burdened estate. The exceptions would be:

(1) where the derived estate or interest has priority to the land obligation;
(2) where the occupier is authorised by the owner of an estate or interest that has priority to the land obligation (e.g. a licensee of such an owner); and
(3) where the derived estate or interest is a mortgage and the mortgagee is not in possession of the land.

(2) *Positive obligations*

Different rules are proposed in relation to the passing of the burden of *positive* land obligations. This is because of the particularly onerous nature of such obligations, which require expenditure to be made. Thus, for example, the Law Commission would not regard it as right for a weekly tenant of the burdened land to be obliged to pay a large sum for the maintenance of a driveway.

Thus it is proposed that, while generally a land obligation should pass down with any estate derived from a burdened estate, there should be an exception where the derived estate is a lease granted for a term of seven years or less. The burden should also pass to mortgagees when they come into possession of the burdened estate. On all this see paras. 6.106—6.116.

Some protection is to be provided to lessees who do have to take the burden of a land obligation. Where a lessee suffers loss due to the lessor's breach of covenant, the lessee is to be able to recover from the lessor, unless the lease expressly provides otherwise: para. 6.116 and clauses 5 and 6(3) of the draft Bill. It is, of course, likely that leases would, in future, be drafted to cover this point.

(3) *Transmission of part of the burdened land*

The Commission started from the point of view that there should be no difference between dealings with the whole or with a part of the land: para. 6.118. However, they recognised that this approach might cause problems where the acquirer of part could not comply with the obligation. This might arise with an obligation to repair a fence in a case in which the part of the burdened land disposed of provides no access to the fence. With positive covenants, it may also be necessary to apportion the obligation to pay money.

Accordingly, in para. 6.126, it is recommended that where burdened land is divided, the resulting estates should be jointly and severally liable in relation to the obligation. However, liability as between the burdened estates should be apportioned relative to the area of land covered by each burdened estate, unless an express apportionment has been made. Where an express apportionment is agreed, the obligations between the various burdened estates are themselves to be land obligations: para. 6.131.

(4) *Burdens and adverse possession*

Taking account of the changes made to the law relating to adverse possession by the LRA 2002, the proposal is that any adverse possessor of land should be bound by any land obligations that bound the estate of the dispossessed estate owner: para. 6.144.

26.8.4.8 **Remedies**

Breach of a land obligation is to be enforceable by action: para. 6.148 and clause 7 of the draft Bill.

A person bound by a *negative* land obligation is to be in breach if he or she does something it prohibits or if he or she permits or suffers someone else to do so. *Positive* obligations are breached when the obligation is not performed. See para. 6.154.

The normal remedy will be an injunction or an order to perform a positive obligation. In some cases damages may be an appropriate substitute: para. 6.160 and 6.165.

Normal contractual principles should apply to calculation of any damages: para. 6.166.

The limitation period for bringing any action is to be the 12 years that is normal in relation to land: para. 6.171.

It is to be possible to draft 'self-help' remedies into land obligations (such as a right to enter the servient land and do repairs). Where this is done, the Commission advises that failure to exercise the rights should not reduce any damages payable for breach. Where such rights are used, the costs are to be recoverable from the dominant owner, in so far as the costs are reasonable and the work is done to a reasonable standard (para. 6.176 and 6.177).

26.8.4.9 **Powers of the Lands Chamber of the Upper Tribunal**

The Lands Chamber of the Upper Tribunal (formerly the 'Lands Tribunal') already has an important jurisdiction in relation to the release of old rights that provide a bar to proper use of land. However, these powers are subject to restrictions. The Law Commission recommends that the powers of the Lands Chamber should be extended and enhanced and that the jurisdiction of the Lands Chamber should extend to all land obligations: para. 7.35.

Jurisdiction should be extended to include powers in relation to leasehold land of any term: para. 7.38.

The grounds for modification or discharge should be those currently in LPA 1925, s. 84: para. 7.55. However, it is recommended that it be made clear that where several people can enforce the benefit an order may be made even if differing grounds under s. 84 apply to each of them (para. 7.87). Thus an applicant would not have to show the same ground or grounds against all the benefited persons.

The Lands Chamber should have power to modify or discharge a *positive* land obligation if, as a result of changes in circumstances, performance of the obligation (para. 7.69.):

(1) has ceased to be reasonably practicable; or

(2) has become unreasonably expensive by comparison with the benefit it confers.

Where a positive land obligation is modified or discharged the Lands Chamber should be able to modify or discharge any reciprocal financial obligation (e.g., to pay towards the expense of performance) and to re-arrange apportionments between those subject to obligations (paras. 7.70, 7.71 and 7.75).

As you can see, the proposed changes would be quite extensive. We wait now to see whether a Bill will be introduced.

FURTHER READING

Bell, '*Tulk v Moxhay* Revisited' [1981] Conv 55.

Dixon, 'Is There Any Value in Restrictive Covenants? Enforceability and Remedies' [2007] 71 Conv 70 (case note on *Small v Oliver & Saunders (Developments) Ltd*).

Gravells, 'Enforcement of Positive Covenants Affecting Freehold Land' (note on *Rhone v Stephens*) (1994) 110 LQR 346.

Hayton, 'Revolution in Restrictive Covenant Law?' (1980) 43 MLR 445.

Law Commission Consultation Paper No. 186 on *Easements, Covenants and Profit à Prendre*, 2008.

Law Commission Report, *Making Land Work: Easements, Covenants and Profits à Prendre*, Law Com No. 327, 2011.

Newsom, 'Universal Annexation' (1981) 97 LQR 32 (see also Newsom (1982) 98 LQR 202).

Martin, 'Remedies for Breach of Restrictive Covenant' [1996] Conv 329.

Report of the Committee on Positive Covenants Affecting Land (Cmnd 2719, 1968) 583.

Ryder, 'Restrictive Covenants: Problem of Implied Annexation' (1972) 36 Conv NS 26.

Todd, Case note on *Roake v Chadha* [1984] Conv 68.

Todd, 'Annexation After *Federated Homes*' [1985] Conv 177.

Wade, Case note on *Halsall v Brizell* [1957] CLJ 35.

Wade, 'Covenants—A Broad and Reasonable View' [1972B] CLJ 157 (see pp. 171–5: 'What is wrong with section 78?').

PART VII

In conclusion

27

The family home

27.1 Introduction

The purpose of this chapter is to pull together some matters about the family home which we have mentioned at various points in the book, and to give you a little more information about certain statutory rights which members of a family may have in respect of their homes.

27.1.1 Family relationships

Throughout this chapter we will be concerned with three different family relationships, each of which gives rise to different rights in respect of the family home.

27.1.1.1 Marriage or civil partnership

These are both formal relationships, recognised by the State, which create legal rights and duties for each party.

27.1.1.2 Cohabitation

Many couples live together as though they were husband and wife or civil partners. A cohabitant has some statutory rights in respect of property belonging to the other partner, but is not as well protected as a party to a marriage or civil partnership. As we shall see, this can cause major difficulties for both opposite-sex and same-sex couples if their relationships break down. In recent years the Law Commission has undertaken two major projects about the legal position of cohabitants, and in July 2007 published recommendations for a statutory scheme of financial relief on the breakdown of a relationship (*Cohabitation: The Financial Consequences of Relationship Breakdown*, 2007, Law Com No. 307 Cm 7182). We will tell you more about these proposals in 27.4, but must note here that in March 2008 the Ministry of Justice announced that, for the time being, it would not be taking action to implement the recommendations.

27.1.1.3 Other homesharing

Family members (and sometimes friends) may share a home together for a variety of reasons, including the provision of care for the old or infirm. This may well involve one person living in property belonging to the other and can lead to hardship when the arrangement comes to an end. Although these relationships may be of considerable social importance, there is very little legal recognition of them and the government is currently under pressure to review the situation.

27.1.2 Trant Way

There are three inhabitants of Trant Way who are particularly relevant to this chapter:

- Sally Mould, who lives with her husband Mark at No. 11 (20.4.2);
- Henry Mumps, who cohabits with his partner Mildred at No. 8 (p. 392); and
- Bob Bell, who has moved in with his daughter, Barbara, at No. 3 so that she can look after him in his old age (p. 391).

Although the circumstances of each person may be very different, they all have one thing in common. Each of them is living in a house owned by another member of the family; none of them has the legal title to the property he or she regards as home. This can give rise to a number of problems if things go wrong, and this is what we want to focus on in this chapter. We will not concern ourselves with Mr and Mrs Armstrong, although they too occupy a family home, because they are both registered as legal owners of 1 Trant Way (see 16.1.2), and the position of legal joint tenants has been explored sufficiently in Chapter 16.

27.1.3 What might go wrong?

It is always possible that relationships may break down, ending in divorce or dissolution if the parties are married or in a civil partnership, or in separation if they are cohabiting. Similarly, home-sharing arrangements between different generations within a family sometimes become unhappy and are no longer workable. We need to consider the position which Henry, Sally and Bob would find themselves in if this happened to them. Could they go on living in their homes if they wanted to, and, even more important, could they claim a share in the capital value of the property which they could use to acquire alternative accommodation?

Even if all these characters are lucky enough to enjoy successful relationships (and Henry is already worried about his—see p. 392), a further possibility we have to consider is that their families may encounter financial problems. We do not know how the Moulds and Barbara Bell financed the purchase of their houses (although they may very possibly have had to borrow money to do so), but we do know that Henry's home is already mortgaged to the Red Leicester Building Society, and that his partner, Mildred, is planning to create a second mortgage to raise money for her business (see 24.2). If Mildred was unable to meet repayment obligations under a mortgage, the mortgagee would have the right to seek possession of the house and to sell it. We need to consider therefore what rights Henry might have in such a situation, and whether his position would differ in any way from that which Sally and Bob would face if their homes were subject to repossession by a mortgagee.

27.2 Right to a share in the value of the property

27.2.1 Rights against the other partner at the end of the relationship

27.2.1.1 Spouses and civil partners

When a relationship comes to an end, a spouse or civil partner is in a much better position than a cohabitant. On divorce or dissolution, the courts are empowered to make property adjustment orders, and can take into account a wide range of matters, including the needs of the respective parties and the contribution which each has made to the marriage (see 20.4.2.1). If Sally Mould's marriage were to end in divorce, she could rely on these provisions, so as to receive a fair share of what she probably regards as the 'family assets'. If there are children of the marriage, she might well be allowed to remain with them in the family home until they are grown up.

27.2.1.2 Cohabitants

By contrast with spouses and civil partners, there are no legal provisions governing arrangements when a relationship between cohabitants comes to an end.

Cohabitation contracts

These days, couples planning to live together are advised to discuss in advance what would happen if their relationship ended, and to draw up formal cohabitation contracts which would provide for matters such as the division of property. It used to be thought that such contracts were illegal, as encouraging immorality, but it seems that the judges have kept pace with social change, and it is unlikely that any court today would adopt such an approach. This view received support from *obiter dicta* in *Sutton v Mishcon de Reya, The Times*, 28 January 2004, in which Hart J stated that there was nothing to prevent cohabitors from entering into perfectly valid legal relations concerning their mutual property rights:

> Such a contract would not be a contract of cohabitation [that is, a contract for sexual relations outside marriage, which would be void] but a contract between cohabitors.

However, there is as yet no precedent for the enforcement of such a contract. In 2007, in its report on the financial consequences of relationship breakdown (Law Com No. 307 Cm 7182 at paras. 5.5–5.10) the Law Commission recommended that:

> legislation should provide, for the avoidance of doubt, that, in so far as a contract ('a cohabitation contract') governs the financial arrangements of a cohabiting couple during their cohabitation or following their separation, it should not be regarded as contrary to public policy.

The Commission suggested that this free-standing recommendation could usefully be implemented by itself, even if the rest of the recommendations in the report were not accepted, but so far this has not happened.

In any case, couples at the start of a relationship are understandably unwilling to contemplate that it may not succeed. As Waite LJ commented in *Midland Bank plc v Cooke* [1995] 4 All ER 562 at p. 575:

> for a couple embarking on a serious relationship, discussion of the terms to apply at parting is almost a contradiction of the shared hopes that have brought them together

and it is likely that in practice most couples will give no thought to such matters until it is too late.

Henry and Mildred were probably not even aware of cohabitation contracts when they set up home together in 1984. If they have not made any specific arrangement, any claim which Henry might want to make to a share of the property would succeed only if he could establish the existence of a constructive trust or, possibly, proprietary estoppel.

Constructive trust

As explained in Chapter 20, Henry would have to show a common intention between himself and Mildred that he was to have a share in the house. Until the decision of the House of Lords in *Stack v Dowden* [2007] 2 AC 432, we would have said that Henry was unlikely to be able to establish such an intention, because it seems that he has not made the sort of direct contribution to the cost of acquisition that the courts would require. However, as we have seen at 20.5.5, *obiter dicta* in *Stack v Dowden* have raised doubts about Lord Bridge's classic statement of those requirements in *Lloyds Bank v Rosset* ([1991] 1 AC 107 at 132), and this may result in some relaxation of the current rules, from which Henry could benefit. It is certainly true that in *Stack v Dowden* the House of Lords was willing to consider a much wider range of contributions (see, for example, Lord Walker's observations about manual labour at para. 36), but it must be remembered that their Lordships were concerned to discover the parties' intentions about the size of their shares under the trust, and were not dealing with the preliminary intention that Henry would have to show in order to establish such a trust (i.e., that he should have a share in Mildred's property). As we suggested at 20.8.1, it seems very likely that a similar more relaxed approach to establishing intention at this earlier stage may now be adopted by the courts, but there is as yet no authority on this point.

Our inability to predict Henry's chances of making a successful claim to a share in the house illustrates very well the uncertainty which *Stack v Dowden* has created. At present, all we can do is to indicate his position under the present rules, while noting that they may be subject to change in the future.

(1) *Contribution to the family* At present, it is clear from *Burns v Burns* [1984] 1 Ch 317 that Henry's years of devoted 'house husbandry' would count for nothing. As the decision in that case shows, where an unmarried couple is involved in a separation, only financial contributions are effective, and long-term commitment to the family and its welfare count for nothing. By contrast, where a marriage ends in divorce, or a civil partnership in dissolution, the court considering applications for property adjustment orders is specifically authorised to take into account the contributions which each party has made to family life (see 20.4.2.1).

(2) *Improvements to the property* However, as well as running the household, Henry has made considerable DIY improvements to the property, and these may well have increased the value of the house. Could they entitle him to a share? Again, he will find himself at a disadvantage compared with a spouse or civil partner.

Under s. 37 of the Matrimonial Proceedings and Property Act 1970 a husband or wife who contributes in money or money's worth to the improvement of real or personal property belonging to the other spouse may claim a share (or an increased share) in that property. The contributions must be 'of a substantial nature'. A similar provision in respect of civil partners is to be found in the Civil Partnership Act 2004, s. 65. You should note that these provisions apply only to contributions to improvements and not to purchase. Where such a contribution is made it will be presumed that the parties intended the contributor to obtain a share, or an enlarged share, in the premises. This presumed intention may be displaced by express agreement to the contrary. The court is given a general discretion to assess the amount of the share thus obtained.

The improvements which Henry Mumps has made to 8 Trant Way might have allowed him to claim under s. 37 were it not for the fact that he is not married to Mildred. This emphasises once again that cohabitants are at a disadvantage in this type of situation. However, Henry's improvements, if more than routine maintenance which either party might do on the house (*Pettit v Pettit* [1970] AC 777), could help him to establish the agreement necessary to give rise to a constructive trust (if, that is, the more liberal approach of *Stack v Dowden* prevails).

Estoppel

The only other way in which Henry might succeed in claiming a share would be through the doctrine of proprietary estoppel (see Chapter 21). If he could show that Mildred, by words or conduct, had led him to believe that he would have a share, and that in reliance on this he had acted to his detriment, this would, by analogy with *Pascoe v Turner* [1979] 1 WLR 431, give rise to an equity which the court could satisfy by requiring Mildred to hold the legal title in trust for herself and Henry, or by awarding any other remedy which the court considered to be appropriate.

27.2.2 Against a mortgagee on a claim for possession

When a claim to a share in the beneficial interest is being asserted against a mortgagee, it makes no difference whether the parties to the relationship are married or in a civil partnership, or are cohabiting. Both Sally and Henry would have to establish their claims by virtue of a common intention trust or proprietary estoppel: the rights of a spouse or civil partner on divorce or dissolution have no application against a third party during the course of the relationship.

If the claimant's interest arose under a trust, its enforceability against the mortgagee would depend on the usual rules: notice in the case of unregistered land (*Kingsnorth Finance Co. Ltd v Tizard* [1986] 1 WLR 783), and entry on the register or enforcement as an overriding interest by virtue of actual occupation in the case of registered land. You should remember, however, that in practice the beneficiary may have waived these rights expressly in order to enable the owner to obtain a mortgage; where there is no express waiver, the court may yet imply one where the beneficiary knew that a mortgage advance was needed in order to purchase the property (see 7.10.4.7(2) and (3)).

If Henry or Sally based a claim on proprietary estoppel, rather than on a common intention trust, the position would most probably be the same, since it now appears reasonably certain that an equity arising from estoppel will be enforced against purchasers of both registered and unregistered land (21.7.1 and 23.3.4).

From what we know about Bob's story, it seems unlikely that he would be in a position to claim a share in his daughter's house, but he might very well need to assert a right to remain in occupation if Barbara tries to bring their arrangement to an end, and we will consider this in the following section.

27.3 Right to remain in occupation

27.3.1 As a beneficiary under a trust

If Henry or Sally could establish a claim to a share in the beneficial interest, he or she would, as a beneficiary under a trust of land, have a right to occupy the property (TOLATA 1996, s. 12—see 17.7.3). This right would be enforceable against both the legal owner (Mildred or Mark), and against third parties such as mortgagees, on the principles we have noted above. However, as we have seen in *Mortgage Corporation v Shaire* [2001] Ch 743 and *Bank of Ireland Home Mortgages Ltd v Bell* [2001] 2 FLR 809 (see 17.8.5), the secured creditor (and, indeed, the owner) has the right under s. 14 of the Act to apply to the court for an order for sale, and the beneficiary may be ordered to give up occupation so that the property can be sold and the proceeds divided between those entitled. Further, even if the court refuses to order sale, the creditor may adopt the alternative route of suing for the money owed and bankrupting the debtor if he cannot pay, so that eventually the property will be sold under the provisions of the Insolvency Act 1986.

27.3.2 Under a contractual licence or by proprietary estoppel

In Chapter 23 we noted a variety of ways in which the courts have intervened to prevent licensors from revoking licences which arise from family arrangements. We will not repeat what we said there, except to remind you that, in Lord Denning's day, Henry Mumps might have been advised to try to establish an implied contractual licence (by analogy with *Tanner v Tanner* [1975] 1 WLR 1346), but that today both he and Bob Bell would be better advised to rely if necessary on the doctrine of proprietary estoppel.

Spouses are not usually regarded as occupying the matrimonial home as licensees (see *National Provincial Bank v Ainsworth* [1965] AC 1175 at pp. 1223–4), and Sally has in fact a statutory right to occupation, which would serve her better, provided she takes the necessary steps to protect it (as to which, see below).

27.3.3 Under a statutory right of occupation

This is another area of the law in which a spouse or civil partner is in a very much better position than a cohabitant or anyone else seeking to remain in occupation of the family home.

27.3.3.1 Home rights

In 1965 the House of Lords held in *National Provincial Bank Ltd v Ainsworth* [1965] AC 1175 that a wife who had no proprietary interest in the matrimonial home had no occupation rights which she could enforce against a purchaser. She did have a common law right to be supported and provided with a home, but this was a personal right enforceable against her husband only. Thus a husband could desert his wife and family, and sell or mortgage the house in which they lived, leaving them homeless.

The decision in *Ainsworth* brought to an end an interesting development associated with Lord Denning MR, who had pioneered the concept of the 'deserted wife's equity', i.e., a right to remain in the matrimonial home which bound purchasers from her husband.

Although the House of Lords was unable to accept the existence of such a right, the earlier decisions by the Court of Appeal which had developed the concept had drawn attention to the wife's need for protection. Following the House of Lords' decision, new statutory rights of occupation were created in 1967. These rights were renamed 'matrimonial home rights' by the Family Law Act 1996, and have recently been renamed yet again as 'home rights' and made available to civil partners as well as to spouses by the Civil Partnership Act 2004. As their name suggests, home rights apply only to premises which have been a matrimonial home or a civil partnership home of the couple or were intended to be such a home.

The effect of s. 30 of the Family Law Act 1996 (as amended by the Civil Partnership Act 2004, s. 82 and Sch. 9, Part 1) is that where one spouse or civil partner ('A') owns the family home, the other spouse or civil partner ('B') has:

- a right not to be evicted or excluded if already in occupation; and
- a right, with the leave of the court, to enter and occupy if not already in occupation.

B's rights last as long as the marriage or civil partnership continues: that is, until one of the parties dies or the legal relationship is ended by divorce (in the case of marriage) or dissolution (in the case of a civil partnership).

Enforcement against a purchaser

Under s. 31, B's home rights constitute a charge on the estate or interest of A and will bind a later purchaser of the legal estate in the property for valuable consideration provided they are protected:

- *in the case of registered land*, by a notice on the register of title (they cannot take effect as overriding interests even if B is in actual occupation—see 7.10.2.1); or
- *in the case of unregistered land*, by registration of a Class F land charge (see 6.4.2.5).

Occupation orders

Where B has home rights, s. 33 gives the court the power to make an 'occupation order', which can be used for various purposes including requiring A to let B into the premises, regulating the occupation of the premises or even excluding A from the property. The order can last for a fixed period or indefinitely.

Accordingly, Sally does have a statutory right to remain in occupation of 11 Trant Way, but she should be advised to protect it by entering a notice on Mark's registered title, and should be warned as to the consequences of not doing so.

27.3.3.2 Cohabitants' occupation rights

The Family Law Act 1996, s. 62(1)(a) defines cohabitants as:

> two persons who are neither married to each other nor civil partners of each other but are living together as husband and wife or as if they were civil partners.

As a cohabitant, Henry has certain rights of occupation under the Act, but they give him much less protection than those enjoyed by Sally as Mark's wife.

Section 36 of the Act permits the court to make an order against a cohabitant who owns the family home, giving the other cohabitant:

- a right not to be evicted or excluded if already in occupation; or
- a right to enter and occupy if not already in occupation.

An order may also be made excluding the owning cohabitant from the property.

This sounds very similar to the protection given to a spouse or civil partner, but it is in fact very much more limited. An order under s. 36 can be made for a period of six months only, subject to one extension for another six months. Accordingly, the maximum period of security provided by s. 36 is one year. However, from Henry Mumps's point of view, even this limited protection would be of value if Mildred told him to go.

27.3.3.3 Associated persons

Bob, as a father living in his daughter's house, has no right to an occupation order under the Family Law Act 1996. A few provisions of the Act apply to what it terms 'associated persons', who are defined (in s. 62(3)) as including not only spouses, civil partners and cohabitants, but also relatives and those who live or have lived in the same household.

The Act confers a limited range of rights on associated persons (in the case of spouses, civil partners and cohabitants these are, of course, in addition to those we have noted above). Under s. 42 the court may make a non-molestation order, which prevents a person from molesting another associated person or a child living with either of them. These provisions replace and extend the earlier provisions of the Domestic Violence and Matrimonial Proceedings Act 1976, which applied only to couples who were married or were living together as man and wife.

Accordingly, if family relationships deteriorate seriously, both Henry and Bob could seek protection from domestic violence under s. 42 of the Act, but this by itself will not help them to deal with the very real problem of losing their homes.

27.4 Reform

The provisions of the Family Law Act which we have noted take a step in the right direction by giving limited rights of occupation to cohabitants and by extending protection against domestic violence to a wider range of people who are likely to be sharing a home. However, there is still a great difference between the position of spouses and civil partners, with their long-term statutory rights of occupation and the opportunity to seek an adjustment of property on divorce or dissolution, and of a cohabitant like Henry, who has only a limited right of occupation under the Family Law Act, and who has to satisfy strict property law rules if he is to obtain a share in the family home. If his relationship with Mildred does break down and she tells him to move out, he will find himself in a very difficult position. As Waite J noted in *Hammond v Mitchell* [1991] 1 WLR 1127, the lack of any legal process to deal with the ending of a relationship can, due to property disputes, create even greater stress than that which arises on the breakdown of a marriage.

27.4.1 Law Commission reviews

In 1994, the Law Commission embarked on a review of the property rights of home-sharers, a move which was welcomed by members of the judiciary who have to deal with the very difficult problems created by the present law (see Waite LJ in *Midland Bank plc v Cooke* [1995] 4 All ER 562 at pp. 564–5, and Peter Gibson LJ in *Drake v Whipp* (1995) 28 HLR 531 at p. 533). The project was an ambitious one, the aim being to develop a scheme applicable to all home-sharers, irrespective of whether they were sexual partners, members of a family or simply friends. However, the Law Commission was eventually compelled to admit that it was unable to devise any scheme that would be regarded as fair in its application to all home-sharers. For an account of the difficulties which made it impossible to formulate any recommendations, see *Sharing Home: A Discussion Paper*, Law Com, July 2002.

In 2006, the Law Commission embarked on a more limited project, publishing a consultation paper: *Cohabitation: The Financial Consequences of Relationship Breakdown* (Consultation Paper No. 179), which was followed in the next year by a report with the same title (Law Com No. 307 Cm 7182 July 2007).

27.4.2 Law Commission recommendations

The 2007 Report outlined the case for reform (Part 2), and recommended the introduction of a new statutory scheme for financial relief when a relationship ended on separation. The scheme would be of general application, and would enable couples who satisfied certain eligibility criteria to apply for financial relief from each other when their relationship came to an end, unless they had made a valid opt-out agreement. It is important to realise that the proposals related only to financial relief for partners; they did not deal with financial support for any children of the relationship, because there is already statutory provision for child support.

27.4.2.1 Eligibility criteria

The scheme would apply to couples who had cohabited for a prescribed minimum period and to those who had a child of the relationship, irrespective of how long they had been together. The report did not recommend a specific minimum period, since the Commission considered this to be a topic that required political decision.

27.4.2.2 What relief would be available?

The Commission emphasised that it was not proposing a system of relief similar to that which operates on divorce or dissolution of a civil partnership. Thus there was no question of dividing the former partners' property equally between them, nor of one partner being obliged to maintain the other. The Report commented there is no obligation on one cohabitant to maintain the other during the relationship, and that accordingly such an obligation should not be imposed on separation (para. 4.20). Instead, the scheme, summarised at paras. 4.32–4.42, would seek to identify the 'economic impact' that the relationship had had on the former partners and to redress any resulting imbalance. Thus a former cohabitant applying for relief would have to show that, as a result of a contribution to the relationship made by the applicant:

- he/she was now under *an economic disadvantage*; or
- the former partner had acquired *a retained benefit.*

A typical contribution leading to the *economic disadvantage* of the applicant would be the giving-up of paid employment to look after home and family, with the resulting economic disadvantage of lack of savings, inadequate pension provision and poor prospects for future employment.

The most obvious example of a contribution to a *retained benefit* would be the making of direct or indirect contributions to the acquisition of an asset, such as the family home, but it could include many other contributions, such as, for example, supporting a partner during training for a qualification, which created the retained benefit of improved earning power.

Where such a contribution, and the resulting benefit or disadvantage, were established by the applicant, the court would have a discretion to adjust the retained benefit, and/or to share the economic disadvantage equally between the former parties. A number of remedies would be available for this purpose, including the making of lump sum payments, property transfers, orders for sale and pension sharing.

Some responses to the consultation on these proposals expressed concern about 'the potential complexity' of the proposed scheme (see para. 4.29). The Commission recognised that any scheme it devised would need to be capable of use without litigation (para. 4.3), but its proposals gave the court such wide discretion that it seemed unlikely that parties would be able to resist the temptation of 'trying their luck' in court, at least in the early years of such a scheme.

27.4.2.3 Further research

Shortly before the publication of the Law Commission Report in 2007, a scheme similar in many respects to that proposed by the Report had been introduced in Scotland (by the Family Law (Scotland) Act 2006) and research was to be undertaken to assess its cost and efficacy. In March 2008 the Ministry of Justice announced that it proposed to wait for the result of this Scottish research before taking any action on the Law Commission's recommendations for England and Wales. Thus hopes for any statutory reform in the immediate future were dashed again.

In this connection you may like to look at the report published by the Centre for Research on Families and Relationships at the University of Edinburgh, and in particular at Chapter 9, which considers the implications of the Scottish experience for England and Wales (for details, see Further Reading section at the end of this chapter).

27.4.3 What next?

In the past the courts have emphasised that any change in the law affecting the rights of cohabitants on separation must be introduced by Parliament, saying that it was not for the judges to bring about reform in such a politically sensitive matter. However, comments in *Stack v Dowden* [2007] 2 AC 432 suggest that the courts may be ready to take a more proactive approach. Referring to the fact that the Law Commission had been unable to devise a scheme suitable for all home sharers, Lady Hale commented (at para. 46) that:

> [w]hile this conclusion is not surprising, its importance for us is that the evolution of the law of property to take account of changing social and economic circumstances will have to come from the courts rather than Parliament.

At the time this comment was made, it was thought that there was a real chance that the Law Commission's recommendations about financial relief for cohabitants would be implemented (para. 47), but now that this appears unlikely, the ball seems to be back in the judges' court. Perhaps there is hope yet for Henry Mumps!

FURTHER READING

Deech, 'The Case Against Legal Recognition of Cohabitation' [1980] Int. Comp. Law Quart 480.

Jackson, 'People Who Live Together Should Put Their Affairs In Order' (1990) 20 Fam Law 439.

Thompson, 'Home Sharing—Reforming the Law' [1996] Conv. 155.

Law Commission

Sharing Homes: A Discussion Paper, July 2002.

Cohabitation: The Financial Consequences of Relationship Breakdown, 2006, Law Com, Consultation Paper No. 179.

Cohabitation: The Financial Consequences of Relationship Breakdown, 2007, Law Com No. 307 Cm 7182 (available at: www.lawcom.gov.uk).

Research on Scottish cohabitation provisions

Legal Practitioners' Perspectives on the Cohabitation Provisions of the Family Law (Scotland) Act 2006, October 2010, Centre for Research on Families and Relationships, University of Edinburgh (available at: www.crfr.ac.uk/reports/Cohabitation%20 final%20report.pdf).

CRFR Briefing 51: No longer living together: how does Scots cohabitation law work in practice? (available at: www.crfr.ac.uk/reports/Briefing%2051.pdf).

28

What is land?

28.1 The statutory definition

Thus far we have said very little about the definition of land. At first it may seem odd that there should be any question about the matter at all: surely everybody knows what land is? However, as we will see, the word 'land' to a lawyer means far more than it does when the word is used in normal speech. As well as defining 'land', we will also consider some of the other terminology which is applied to estates and interests in land, as this is relevant to the rather complex statutory definition of land.

28.1.1 LPA 1925, s. 205

'Land' is defined in LPA 1925, s. 205(1)(ix), as follows:

> 'Land' includes land of any tenure, and mines and minerals, whether or not held apart from the surface, buildings or parts of buildings (whether the division is horizontal, vertical or made in any other way) and other corporeal hereditaments; also . . . a rent and other incorporeal hereditaments, and an easement, right, privilege, or benefit in, over or derived from land . . .

This definition is, of course the one that is used in the LPA 1925. The SLA 1925 has the same definition in s. 117(1)(ix) and the same words appear in s. 68(6) of the TA 1925 and s. 3(viii) of the LRA 1925. Accordingly, this provides the general rule when you are dealing with the 1925 legislation.

Section 25(2) of TOLATA 1996 adopts the LPA 1925 definitions but you should note that Sch. 4 to TOLATA 1996 repealed some words that used to appear at the end of s. 205(1)(ix) ('but not an undivided share in land'). Those words are no longer relevant after the introduction of the new trust of land rules and the changes made to the doctrine of conversion by s. 3 of the 1996 Act, because a beneficial interest under a trust of land is an interest in land, unlike an interest under a trust for sale, which was in money.

As a consequence of all these provisions, when you are dealing with any of the main property statutes mentioned in this book you will be using the same definition of land.

28.1.2 Interpretation Act 1978

If, however, you are construing other legislation you may need to refer to the definition in Sch. 1 to the Interpretation Act 1978 (but note that this only applies to statutes passed on or after 1 January 1979):

> 'Land' includes buildings and other structures, land covered with water, and any estate, interest, easement, servitude in or over land.

Note that both the LPA 1925 and the Interpretation Act definitions are merely inclusive and not exclusive and thus it would remain theoretically possible for other things also to constitute land (if one could think of an example of such a thing).

You can see that there is a relationship between the two definitions given above and both contain similar terms. Here, because we are primarily concerned with the property legislation, we will concentrate on the LPA 1925 definition. That definition requires some thought and so we will now consider its individual parts.

28.1.3 Other definitions

Were you to be construing a document other than an Act of Parliament you would, of course, have to look to see whether a special definition had been provided for that document and in drafting any such document yourself you might need to provide a definition (perhaps by expressly adopting the LPA 1925 definition).

28.2 Earth, minerals, buildings and fixtures

28.2.1 The basic rule

It is easy to accept that 'land' includes the earth beneath our feet and any minerals contained therein. However, the legal definition of land goes further and includes in the definition plants growing on the land *and* any other thing which is actually fixed to the land. 'Buildings' and 'parts of buildings' are actually mentioned in s. 205(1)(ix), and, after a moment's thought, it is not altogether surprising that they are included in the term 'land'.

It is perhaps more surprising, at first thought, when one discovers that any item affixed to the land becomes land itself. Thus in *Buckland v Butterfield* (1820) 2 Brod & Bing 54, it was held that a conservatory which was attached to a house by eight cantilevers, each 9 inches long, formed part of the land. This is important, because should one wish to retain and remove such a fixture when selling the freehold estate in the land, one must specifically contract to exclude the fixture from the sale. Thus, should a vendor intend to remove the rose bushes from the garden of a house when selling, this should be provided for when the contract is made.

Buckland v Butterfield also illustrates the point that since the house is land, because it is fixed to the earth, anything fixed to the house also becomes land. However, something which is merely placed upon the land, and not fixed to it, will not be regarded as forming part of the land, however heavy it is and even if it would be very difficult to move it. In *Berkley v Poulett* (1976) 242 EG 39, a large statue, made of marble and weighing nearly half a ton, was not regarded as part of the land, because it was not fixed down in any way.

The basic rule is therefore that anything annexed to land is land. However, the courts have long accepted that something which is affixed merely to facilitate its display, or in order to steady it, is not to be regarded as becoming part of the land. Thus in *Leigh v Taylor* [1902] AC 157, a tapestry tacked to strips of wood, which were then affixed to the wall, was not regarded as being part of the land. The degree of annexation in this case was merely that which was necessary for the display of the tapestry. In *Hulme v Brigham* [1943] KB 152, printing machines weighing between 9 and 12 tons were not regarded as fixtures, even though they were attached to motors which were fixed to the floor. In this case the degree of annexation was slight and was necessary merely to render the motors stable.

28.2.2 Items not fixed to the land

In rare circumstances something which is not actually fixed to the land but which appears to form an integral part of it, may be regarded as forming part of the land for legal purposes.

The best example of this is *D'Eyncourt v Gregory* (1866) LR 3 Eq 382, in which stone statues, seats and garden vases were held to be part of the land, even though they were free-standing, as were certain tapestries and pictures hanging upon the walls. The basis of the decision is that the ornaments formed an integral part of the architectural design of the house on the property. Thus it appears that the existence of a 'master plan' concerning the property may render items part of the land, even though there is no real annexation.

Another illustration was supplied by Blackburn J in *Holland v Hodgson* (1872) LR 7 CP 328 at p. 335, when he explained that a pile of stones lying in a builder's yard would obviously not form part of the land upon which it lay. However, were the same stones to be constructed into a drystone wall (which uses no mortar and no method of fixing the wall to the ground) on a farm, the wall obviously would form part of the land of the farm.

A more recent example is provided by *Elitestone Ltd v Morris* [1997] 1 WLR 687, which concerned a chalet bungalow, which had been placed on concrete blocks but which was not attached to them in any way. The blocks were attached to the land. The land was occupied by the defendants under an agreement which purported to be a licence but which the court of first instance held to be a lease. However, for the defendants to have Rent Act protection the bungalow itself had to be land and the landlord argued that this was not the case because the building was not fixed to land in anyway but merely rested on the blocks. The case was finally decided in the House of Lords, who concluded that in this instance the bungalow was land despite the absence of annexation. Lord Lloyd of Berwick said (at pp. 692–3):

> Many different tests have been suggested, such as whether the object which has been fixed to the property has been so fixed for the better enjoyment of the object as a chattel, or whether it has been fixed with a view to effecting a permanent improvement of the freehold. This and similar tests are useful when one is considering an object such as a tapestry, which may or may not be fixed to a house so as to become part of the freehold.... These tests are less useful when one is considering the house itself. In the

> case of the house the answer is as much a matter of common sense as precise analysis. A house which is constructed in such a way so as to be removable, whether as a unit, or in sections, may well remain a chattel, even though it is connected temporarily to mains services such as water and electricity. But a house which is constructed in such a way that it cannot be removed at all, save by destruction, cannot have been intended to remain as a chattel. It must have been intended to form part of the realty.

This decision emphasises that what is of primary importance is the 'intention' involved. However, Lord Clyde (at p. 698) indicated that the use of this word may be misleading because it is the purpose which the object in question is serving which matters and not the intention or purpose of the person who put it there. Thus, Lord Clyde said that the test was objective and not subjective. The relevant issue is whether the object is 'designed for the use or enjoyment of the land or for the more complete or convenient use or enjoyment of the thing itself'.

Although this may sound complicated, the case in fact indicates that the courts are really applying a common-sense test, rather than relying on technical arguments about the degree of annexation. These principles were applied in *Chelsea Yacht and Boat Club Ltd v Pope* [2000] 1 WLR 1941 in which the attachment of a houseboat to pontoons, and to the river bed and banks by means of an anchor and rings, were held to be insufficient to make the boat real property, rather than a chattel. However, by way of contrast see also *Cinderella Rockerfellas Ltd v Rudd* [2003] 3 All ER 219, in which a permanently moored vessel was regarded as forming part of a hereditament for the purposes of rateable valuation. You should, however, note that in giving the judgment of the court Potter LJ appears not to be saying that the vessel in question was land but that it was a chattel which was, for rating purposes, sufficiently connected to the land to be capable of being regarded as part of the rateable property. Accordingly, the apparent conflict with the *Chelsea* case is not a real conflict: the vessel is a chattel but can be taken into account in assessing the rates payable in respect of the land (which includes the water above the land on which the vessel floats as well as the bank to which it is moored).

28.3 Hereditaments

28.3.1 LPA 1925 definition

Before 1926, 'hereditaments' were those rights which were capable of passing to heirs by way of inheritance. The term is defined in LPA 1925, s. 205(1)(ix), as 'any real property which on an intestacy occurring before the commencement of thisAct might have devolved upon an heir'. This includes the estates and interests in land which we have discussed in this book, and which are not purely personal rights. Thus a licence is not a hereditament because it is a personal permission and not an interest which would have passed to an heir.

28.3.2 Corporeal and incorporeal hereditaments

Having defined 'hereditaments' as 'inheritable interests', the common law went on to distinguish between 'corporeal' and 'incorporeal' hereditaments. Corporeal hereditaments are physical objects: the physical land and its attachments. Incorporeal hereditaments are rights, not things, and there is a fixed list of such hereditaments, which includes rentcharges, easements and profits.

This traditional classification may cause you some surprise, for the two groups, corporeal and incorporeal, seem strangely unrelated, though they are supposed to be subdivisions of one category. To paraphrase Austin (*Jurisprudence*, 5th edn., vol. 1, p. 362): one class consists of intangible rights over objects (incorporeal), and the other of physical objects over which rights may be exercised (corporeal). Further, the notion of corporeal hereditaments seems to conflict with the basic principle of English land law, which we emphasised in Chapter 1, that one cannot own the land itself, but only an estate in it. No provision for estates in land seems to be made in this classification: they are certainly not within the accepted list of incorporeal hereditaments, but one cannot describe them as corporeal because they are intangible rights rather than tangible objects.

This is a classification which has always caused difficulty and debate and we would not trouble you with it if it were not for the fact that you will see references to 'hereditaments' in the statutory definition of land. It is also important that you should realise that easements, profits and rentcharges are not merely interests in land but are themselves 'land' within the statutory definition. We suggest, though, that it is enough to note the meaning of the terms and that you should not spend too much time on this rather difficult point until your studies of land law are very advanced.

The statutory definition of 'hereditaments' includes the term 'real property' and this leads us to the next set of technical terms.

28.4 Real and personal property (or, realty and personalty)

28.4.1 The meaning of 'real'

Often you may see references to 'real property' which suggest that this term is synonymous with 'land' (e.g., in the book title, *Cheshire and Burn's Modern Law of Real Property*). This is not, however, entirely true, for, as we shall see, some interests in land do not amount to real property.

The distinction between real and personal property is an ancient one and is still of importance today. The term 'real' property refers to that property which the early courts would protect by a 'real' action (an action *in rem*). In this context the adjective 'real' does not have its usual modern meaning of 'genuine' but is used in a technical sense. The word 'real' derives from the Latin word *res* (thing). A 'real action' was one in which the court would order that the property itself (the *res*) be restored to an owner who had been dispossessed, rather than giving the defendant the choice of returning the property or paying damages to compensate for the loss. If someone takes your table, a remedy in damages will usually suffice, for you may take the money and buy another table. However, land is unique in its character and, at a time when status in society depended upon one's relation to land, it was felt that where land was lost it was essential that it should be recovered. Thus, there was a distinction between 'real' property (where the property could be recovered by an action *in rem*) and 'personal' property, so called because it could be protected only by an action *in personam* (an action against the person of the wrongdoer). Where an action *in personam* was concerned the wrongdoer would in general pay damages rather than return the property. Thus the history of English forms of action has led to a labelling of property which is still used today.

28.4.2 Exceptions

Most of the rights considered in this book amount to real property because they are rights in land which would have been subject to an action *in rem*. There have been, however, two main exceptions.

28.4.2.1 Rights of beneficiaries under trusts

The first of these was the right of a beneficiary under a trust for sale. Since the doctrine of conversion notionally transformed the trust property into money (a form of personal property) the beneficiaries' interests under the trust were seen to be interests in personalty. The doctrine of conversion was abolished in relation to trusts for sale by TOLATA 1996 and now the interests of beneficiaries under the trusts of land, which replaced trusts for sale, *are* interests in land.

28.4.2.2 Leases

The other exception is not so obvious and results once again from the manner in which the law has developed. When leases first came into common use, they were regarded as commercial contracts creating rights *in personam* between the parties. Unlike freehold estates they did not affect the tenant's position on the feudal ladder, and were not subject to one of the real actions. If the tenant were dispossessed by his landlord, he could not recover the land but would only be awarded damages for breach of contract. Since it was protected only by an action *in personam* the lease came to be regarded as personal property. After a time, the tenant was enabled to recover the land by action, whether he was dispossessed of the land by his landlord or by some third party, but by this time it was too late to alter the classification of the lease. A lease was therefore a 'chattel' (another name for personal property, derived from a French word from which 'cattle' is also derived, livestock being an important form of personal property). However, recognition of the rather special nature of the lease led to the rather paradoxical nomenclature of 'chattel real', which emphasises its hybrid nature.

Leases remain personal property to this day and the distinction can sometimes prove to be of importance. Thus if a testator were to make the following disposition in his will: 'All my real property to my son Alfred and all my personal property to my son Bernard', Alfred would receive any freehold property owned by his father, but Bernard would be able to claim any leasehold property, together with all his father's chattels. In this case the freehold property is obviously an estate in land. It should be recalled, however, that the lease, whilst being personal property, is also an estate in land (LPA 1925, s. 1(1)).

28.5 Flying freehold

28.5.1 The extent of ownership

It is often said that a freehold owner owns the land up to the skies and down to the centre of the earth. This theory is usually expressed in the Latin maxim *Cuius est solum eius est usque ad coelum et ad inferos* (which colourfully refers to the heavens and the depths). However, in practice this theory is far from true and in any event lawyers throughout the centuries, while espousing this theory, appear to have had problems with some of the logical consequences.

You will realise that there must be some restrictions on this theory, as otherwise every plane that passes over an owner's land would be committing a trespass, whereas this is not the case. Also, while the title to the land may be vested in the freehold owner, this does not mean that all the elements of the physical land are his or hers to use. One example will suffice to illustrate this point but in fact there are many others. While there are limited cases in which it is possible for a land owner also to own the title to the coal in his land, normally the freehold title to coal is vested in the Coal Authority, regardless of who owns the freehold to the surrounding land (see the Coal Industry Act 1994, s. 7(3)).

The law recognises that the general theory set out above can be disrupted in some cases and also that land can be owned in layers. Thus, it appears perfectly possible for the freehold title to land to be vested in A down to a certain depth and for the title to the land below that depth to be vested in B. This is confirmed in s. 205(1)(ix) of the LPA 1925 (see 28.1.1) which expressly says that both horizontal and vertical division of land is possible. Accordingly, it should follow that it would be possible for layers above ground level to be similarly divided and thus for a freehold to be conveyed, for example in a flat above ground level, without the owner also having to own the fee simple in the land at ground level. Surprisingly, however, this seems to be a concept that lawyers have over the centuries found hard to accept, although it should follow logically from the maxim given above.

28.5.2 The problems of a 'flying freehold'

One could argue for a long time over why the concept of what is usually called a 'flying freehold' has given problems. However, one explanation is that, despite the theory of estates, early land law was very much centred upon physical land, the control of physical land and the relationships within society that were built upon the foundation of tenure of land. Interestingly, the idea of a leasehold estate in a stratum above the ground does not appear to have given the same problems. The reason for this may be rooted in the fact that early leases were viewed solely as commercial agreements that did not give rise to the same tenurial incidents as the freehold estate or have the same impact upon the owner's place in society. Accordingly, while many seem to have struggled with the possibility of a freehold estate in 'thin air', the law of leases accepted that if a tenant had a lease of a upper floor and the building burned down, the lease continued and rent had to be paid: *Cricklewood Property and Investment Trust Ltd v Leighton's Investment Trust Ltd* [1945] AC 221 (but see above at 10.6.1 for the modern rule as to frustration and leases). It is this reasoning, as well as the benefits of a lease in relation to the running of positive covenants (see Chapter 12), that has made it standard practice for the estate granted in flats to be a leasehold estate rather than a freehold estate, with the freehold of the whole property being vested either in the owner of the ground floor flat or in some other person (sometimes to be held upon trust for all the leaseholders but often as a commercial investment in its own right).

This approach to the freehold estate seems, however, to be an unnecessary complication and it has been pointed out for centuries that there is no real justification for the view that there is some difficulty involved in creating a flying freehold. The same approach does not apply elsewhere; for example, Scottish law appears to have no difficulty with the concept of the Scottish equivalent to freehold in a flat and this can prove beneficial to the owner, since a major defect of a lease is that it is a time-limited estate. Although the disadvantage of the time limitation can be overcome by giving the leaseholder the right to renew the lease when it expires, the wish to avoid the use of the flying freehold has, in recent history when tenurial relationships are unimportant, probably arisen solely from the practical problems that can arise because of the freehold rules on running of covenants (see Chapter 26). If the difficulty of ensuring compliance with suitable covenants, including positive covenants where necessary, could be overcome, there seems to be no genuine reason for English law not to accept that a flying freehold can be a useful concept in practice.

One of the very real problems in the past has been that there has been no means of requiring a freehold owner to maintain his building in a proper state of repair. While it is a nuisance if your neighbour allows his house to become derelict (and may even affect the value of your neighbouring property), the problem is not severe if your property does not depend upon his for support. Where support was crucial, the law developed a limited right to support by means of an easement (see 25.2.2.6) but still did not oblige the neighbour to keep his property in good repair. This difficulty becomes acute if the safety of your own property depends upon that neighbour keeping his own premises in good repair (which would be true if his property were a lower flat and yours an upper flat) and thus there was a tendency to adopt the known path of granting leaseholds, with the benefit that, in a lease, positive covenants could be imposed that would bind later acquirers of the estate.

However, even in the past, in particular circumstances, this issue was found not to be impossible of solution and it is perhaps amusing to note that one example of the use of flying freeholds has been in relation to some of the properties forming part of Lincoln's Inn in London. It appears that barristers were less troubled by the concept than other lawyers, or perhaps that they were happier to rely on the careful drafting of agreements in order to ensure that the flying freeholds did not cause insuperable problems. Away from legal London, they are also occasionally found in other places, including in at least one small terrace of country cottages where, as one of us has discovered from personal experience, a bedroom 'flying' over the next-door property is not regarded as unusual.

Having said that flying freehold should not cause insuperable difficulties to the careful, it is perhaps worth looking at a case that illustrates how things can go wrong if insufficient thought is given when a flying freehold is created. In *Abbahall Ltd v Smee* [2003] 1 All ER 465, a house had been separated so that the upper two floors constituted a flying freehold owned by Miss Smee, while the ground floor was owned by Abbahall Ltd. Miss Smee had allowed some parts of the property to fall into disrepair and water thus leaked onto the ground floor and there was a danger of falling masonry. Abbahall therefore obtained a court order allowing it to enter Miss Smee's premises in order to repair the roof. It then brought further proceedings to recover the costs of the repairs from Miss Smee, on the basis that the roof must form part of her premises. The Court of Appeal agreed that both parties were responsible for the roof but that their liability to pay depended on the extent of the benefit to each. On the facts of the particular case, they determined that the parties should each be responsible for half of the costs of the repairs. The case therefore leaves much room for dispute in any future case in which it is not clear to what extent each party benefits from the element of the property in question.

28.5.3 Commonhold

Interestingly, the concept of commonhold advanced by the Law Commission in its Report *Commonhold: Freehold Flats and Freehold Ownership of Other Independent Buildings* (Cm 179, July 1987) decided not to build solely upon the idea of flying freeholds but on an adaptation of the existing model used for flats, where each flat owner has a lease of the flat and is a member of a management company, which owns the freehold. The commonhold scheme provided by the Commonhold and Leasehold Reform Act 2002 involves each flat owner owning the freehold estate in his or her flat and being a member of a company, the commonhold association, which owns the freehold of the common parts of the building. Bear in mind that there can be no 'flying commonhold', thus the issues mentioned in 28.5.2 cannot arise.

28.6 A practical approach to land law

This whole area of law provides an excellent example of how lawyers are affected by both society and custom (the early influence of tenurial incidents and relationships) and practicalities (making covenants work) rather than by absolute theories. The practising lawyer, while being a person who has to understand and apply concepts and theories that are often extremely complex, is mainly driven by the need to find a practical solution to a problem. Where there is doubt, the lawyer will usually prefer a proven solution to the risks of experimenting with uncertainties. The push for growth or reform comes when existing approaches no longer meet all the practical needs of those affected.

We said at the start of this book that it was our intention to avoid a discussion of purely historical matters. However, you will have found that historical issues have intruded rather often into this last chapter. The reason for this is that modern land law is still, to a certain extent, tied to its past. The 1925 property legislation was not a complete break with the past but rather reformed and built upon the existing law, which had developed over the centuries. The relationship between land law ancient and modern is particularly noticeable when dealing with the technical definition of 'land' because in this area the 1925 statutes attempted no radical reforms. Accordingly, we feel that, although a knowledge of the historical development of land law is not essential to the modern student, it may be of interest and assistance to those who wish to deepen their understanding of the subject. We hope that this book has shown you that land law is a fascinating and lively subject and that we have encouraged you to extend your reading into such areas.

FURTHER READING

Cheshire and Burn's Modern Law of Real Property, 18th edn., 2011, pp. 172–83 (The Meaning of Land).

Gray and Gray, *Elements of Land Law*, 5th edn., 2009, pp. 8–55

Lawson and Rudden, *The Law of Property*, 3rd edn., 2002, Chapter 2 (The Classification of Things).

Smith, Property Law, 7th edn., 2011, pp. 3–10 (Basic Property Principles).

Gray, 'Property in Thin Air' [1991] CLJ 252 (on flying freeholds).

BIBLIOGRAPHY

Austin, *Jurisprudence*, 5th edn., Murray, 1885.

Cheshire and Burn, *Cheshire and Burn's Modern Law of Real Property*, 18th edn., Oxford University Press, 2011.

Cooke, *Land Law*, Oxford University Press, 2006.

Fry, A *Treatise on the Specific Performance of Contracts*, 6th edn., Stevens, 1921.

Gale, *Gale on Easements*, 18th edn., Sweet & Maxwell, 2008.

Gray and Gray, *Elements of Land Law*, 5th edn., Oxford University Press, 2009.

Hanbury and Martin, *Modern Equity*, 19th edn., Sweet & Maxwell, 2012.

Lawson and Rudden, *The Law of Property*, 3rd edn., Oxford University Press, 2002.

Maitland, *Equity*, Cambridge University Press, 1936.

Megarry and Wade, *The Law of Real Property*, 8th edn., Sweet & Maxwell, 2012.

Morris and Leach, *The Rule against Perpetuities*, 2nd edn., Stevens, 1962.

Oakley, *Constructive Trusts*, 3rd edn., Sweet & Maxwell, 1997.

Pawlowski, *The Doctrine of Proprietary Estoppel*, Sweet & Maxwell, 1996.

Pearce and Stevens, *The Law of Trusts and Equitable Obligations*, 5th edn., Oxford University Press, 2010.

Preston and Newson, *Restrictive Covenants Affecting Freehold Land*, 9th edn., Sweet & Maxwell, 1998.

Ruoff and Roper, *Registered Conveyancing*, Sweet & Maxwell, looseleaf edn.

Smith, *Property Law*, 7th edn., Pearson Longman, 2011.

Woodfall, *Law of Landlord and Tenant*, Sweet & Maxwell, looseleaf edn.

GLOSSARY

abatement A 'self-help' remedy by which the owner of the dominant tenement may remove an obstruction to the exercise of an easement.

absolute interest An interest which is not determinable or conditional (see 9.3), i.e., it is not granted on such terms that it is liable to end prematurely on the occurrence of some specified event.

Adjudicator to the Land Registry See 7.8.1.3.

administrators See 'personal representatives'.

adverse possession (acquisition of title by) The process of acquiring title to land by dispossessing the previous holder and occupying the land until: (1) the owner's right to recover it is time-barred under the Limitation Act (unreg.land); (2) the adverse possessor is registered as proprietor (reg.land).

alienation The act of disposing of one's property, i.e., passing it from one owner to another.

annexation The procedure of attaching the benefit of a restrictive covenant to the land of the covenantee, so that it will run automatically with that land, without any need for the benefit to be assigned (transferred) to the new owner when the land changes hands.

appurtenant See 'profit à prendre'.

assent A disposition by personal representatives, by which property is vested in the person entitled under the deceased's will or on his intestacy.

assignment A transfer of property (used particularly in respect of the transfer of a lease or a reversion).

barring the entail See 'disentailing'.

base fee The interest created when the holder of an entailed interest tries to transfer it to another person, without satisfying the requirements for 'disentailing' (converting the interest into a fee simple). The recipient takes only a base fee, which lasts as long as the entailed interest would have lasted, and ends when the original grantor becomes entitled to enforce his reversion.

caution, inhibition, notice, restriction Methods of protecting interests in registered land by entry on the register under LRA 1925; under LRA 2002 only notices and restrictions are used.

caveat emptor Let the buyer beware.

cesser on redemption The process by which a mortgage automatically comes to an end when the obligation which it secures is performed.

charge An encumbrance securing the payment of money.

charge by way of legal mortgage See 2.4.3 and 24.4.3.

chattels real Leases—see 2.8.2.3 and 28.4.2.2.

choses in action See 2.8.2.2.

choses in possession See 2.8.2.1.

clog (on the equity of redemption). Any restriction imposed by the mortgage on the mortgagor's right to redeem the mortgaged property.

commonhold See Chapter 14.

conditional interest See 9.3.1.

consolidate (right to). The right of the mortgagee to refuse to allow the mortgagor to redeem one mortgage unless some other mortgage is redeemed at the same time.

co-ownership A form of ownership in which two or more people are entitled to possession of the property at the same time. See 'joint tenancy' and 'tenancy in common'.

concurrent lease See 'lease of the reversion'.

conversion A change in the nature of property, from realty to personalty, or vice versa. Actual conversion of this kind occurs when land is sold, so that the purchaser's property changes from money into land, and that of the vendor changes from land into money. Under the equitable doctrine of conversion, this change notionally takes place at an earlier stage, as soon as the contract to sell is concluded (see 5.7.3). This doctrine was abolished by TOLATA 1996 in relation to trusts for sale.

conveyance An instrument (other than a will) which transfers property from one owner to another.

corporeal hereditament See 28.3.2.

covenant A promise made by deed.

covenantee The person with whom a covenant is made, who takes the benefit of the covenant and has a right to enforce the promise.

covenantor The person who makes a covenant, and has the burden or duty of performing the promise.

deed A document which is signed in the presence of a witness as a deed and is then delivered (see 2.5.4.1).

deed of discharge See 17.9.3.1.

determinable interest See 9.3.2.

disentailing (or 'barring the entail') The procedure by which an entailed interest is converted into a fee simple.

disponee A person to whom a disposition is made.

disponer A person who makes a disposition.

distress (to levy distress, to distrain). The legal seizure of chattels in order to satisfy some debt or claim; in particular, may be used by the landlord against the tenant in respect of unpaid rent.

dominant tenement A piece of land which is benefited by some right (see 'easement').

easement A right enjoyed over one piece of land (the 'servient tenement') for the benefit of another piece of land (the 'dominant tenement'), e.g., rights of way, rights of drainage, rights of light. See also 'quasi-easement'.

encumbrance A liability burdening property.

entail See 'entailed interest'.

entailed interest An interest in land inheritable only by the issue (child, grandchild, etc.) of the original grantee; existed only as an equitable interest after 1925 and can no longer be created after TOLATA 1996.

en ventre sa mère Literally, 'in one's mother's womb', i.e., conceived but not yet born.

equity of redemption The mortgagor's interest in the property during the continuance of the mortgage.

estate An interest in land which entitles its owner to exercise proprietary rights over that land for a prescribed period.

estate contract A contract to sell or grant an estate in land. Both parties are bound by the contract, so that either can enforce against the other. The statutory definition of estate contracts which are registrable as class C(iv) land charges (LCA 1972, s. 2(4)(iv)) includes two further rights, the option to purchase and the right of pre-emption, but these do not create the reciprocal rights and duties of the full estate contract.

An option (to purchase an estate or to renew a lease) gives the person entitled the right to compel the owner to sell or grant the estate, but does not impose on him any duty to buy. He is free to exercise the option or not, as he chooses.

A right of pre-emption (or right of first refusal) gives the person entitled a right to be offered the property if the owner decides to sell, but does not impose any duty to sell on the owner, nor any duty to buy on the person entitled.

estate rentcharge A rentcharge (q.v.) created to ensure that the owner of the land, subject to the charge, contributes to maintenance costs or performs some other positive obligation (see 26.5.2.3).

executors See 'personal representatives'.

fee simple absolute in possession The larger of the two legal estates in land (the other being the term of years absolute: LPA 1925, s. 1) which will last indefinitely, as long as there are persons entitled to take the property under the will of the previous owner or on his intestacy.

fee tail See 'entailed interest'.

fine A premium, sometimes payable on the grant or assignment of a lease.

fixed-term tenancy See 10.1.2.

foreclosure The procedure by which a mortgagee asks the court to extinguish the mortgagor's equitable right to redeem, and his other rights to the property, and to permit the mortgagee to take the property in satisfaction of the debt or other obligation for which it is security.

freehold estate Fee simple absolute in possession.

hereditament See 28.3.

incorporeal hereditament See 28.3.2.

infant A minor; a person who has not attained the age of majority, being under the age of 18.

in gross See 'profit à prendre'.

inhibition See 'caution'.

in possession Denotes that an interest so described gives a right to present enjoyment of the property, rather than to enjoyment that will not commence until some time in the future.

instrument A legal document whereby a right is created or confirmed or a fact recorded.

intestacy The condition of dying without having made a will.

inter vivos Literally, 'among the living'; the phrase denotes that a disposition so described takes effect during the lifetime of the grantor, rather than under his will (which takes effect at death).

joint tenancy The form of co-ownership in which each owner is entitled to the whole property, rather than to an undivided share in it. The right of survivorship (*jus* *accrescendi*) applies here, so that the last surviving tenant becomes solely entitled to the whole property, while those joint tenants who predecease him have no share in the property to pass with their estates. (Compare 'tenancy in common'.)

land obligation A right in land proposed by the Law Commission as a replacement for covenants in freehold land and some easements (see Chapters 25 and 26).

lease The second legal estate in land ('term of years absolute', LPA 1925, s. 1(1); an interest which gives the person entitled exclusive possession of the land for a fixed period of time, usually but not essentially in consideration of the payment of rent. The term 'lease' is used to describe both the estate and the document creating it. (See also 'tenancy'.)

leasehold estate The term of years absolute.

lease of the reversion (or concurrent lease). A lease which is created where a landlord grants a second lease in respect of property which is already subject to a lease granted by him (distinguish 'reversionary lease').

lessee Tenant under a lease.

lessor Landlord under a lease.

licence Permission (in this context, usually permission to use land).

limitation of actions The procedure whereby the right to bring an action is barred after the lapse of a prescribed period of time.

mesne profits The profits lost to the owner of land by reason of his having been wrongfully dispossessed of his land.

minor interest An interest in registered land which required protection by an entry on the register (LRA 1925). The term is not used in LRA 2002.

mortgage The grant of an interest in property as security for the payment of a debt or the discharge of an obligation.

mortgagee The person to whom a mortgage is granted and the interest in the mortgaged property conveyed (see 'mortgage').

mortgagor The person who creates the mortgage and conveys an interest in his property as security for the payment of a debt, etc. (see 'mortgage').

nec vi, nec clam, nec precario Literally, 'not by force, nor by stealth, nor by permission'. The phrase describes the way in which one who claims an easement or profit by prescription must have acted during the prescription period.

notice 1. See 'caution'. 2. Knowledge. (a) actual notice—real knowledge; (b) constructive notice—knowledge which a person is deemed to have, usually because he failed to make the necessary enquiries and is taken to know what they would have revealed; (c) imputed notice—notice belonging to an agent which is ascribed to his principal.

notice to quit The method whereby landlord or tenant may end a periodic tenancy.

option See 'estate contract'.

overreaching The statutory procedure which enables a purchaser to take the legal estate free from certain equitable interests (arising, for example, under a trust of land or a Settled Land Act settlement), provided the purchase money is paid to two trustees or a trust corporation.

overriding interest An interest in registered land, which does not require protection by entry on the register and binds the registered proprietor and all who acquire later interests in the land (LRA 2002).

overriding lease A concurrent lease, which a landlord may be required to grant under the Landlord and Tenant (Covenants) Act 1995. See 10.10.5 and 12.4.2(3).

partition The physical division of land between several co-owners, so that each becomes the sole owner of a separate plot.

periodic tenancy See 10.1.2.

perpetually renewable lease See 11.2.1.3.

personal property (personalty). See 2.8 and 28.4.

personal representatives Persons authorised to administer the estate of a dead person. There are two types: executors, who are appointed by will; and administrators, who are appointed by the court in cases of intestacy (i.e., where the deceased leaves no will), or where there is no executor willing or able to act.

personalty See 'personal property'.

possibility of reverter The right of a grantor to recover the land if a determinable interest comes to an end (see 9.3.2).

pre-emption (right of). See 'estate contract'.

prescription A method of acquiring easements or profits by long use.

profit à prendre The right to take something (such as sand, wood, pasture) from land belonging to another. A profit may be appurtenant to a piece of land, that is, it may benefit that land and run with it; or it may be in gross, that is, it may belong to an individual without being attached to a specific piece of land which is benefited by it.

puisne mortgage A legal mortgage of unregistered land which is not protected by the deposit of the title deeds with the mortgagee, and so is registrable as a class C(i) land charge (LCA 1972, s. 2(4)).

purchaser A person who takes an estate or interest by act of parties rather than by operation of law (2.6.3.2). When used as a technical term, the word does not have its colloquial meaning of 'buyer', and so one who buys has to be described as 'a purchaser for value'.

quasi-easement A potential easement. The term is used to describe the situation in which land, which is owned and occupied by one person, is used in a way which would constitute an easement if the land was divided into two tenements which were separately owned or occupied (see 25.2.1.2).

real property (realty). See 2.8 and 28.4.

registered proprietor The person registered as the owner of a legal estate in registered land.

remainder An interest in land granted under a settlement to take effect after some previous interest (e.g., to A for life, remainder to B in fee simple). A remainder gives a right to possession of the land in the future and so, since 1925, exists only in equity.

rentcharge A right entitling the holder to receive a periodic sum of money from the owner of land charged with that payment. Provision may be made, for example, for the payment of annuities in this way. See also 'estate rentcharge.' A rentcharge should be distinguished from rent service—the rent due from a tenant to a landlord under a lease.

rent service Payments (generally in money, although sometimes in goods or services) made to a landlord by a tenant holding under a lease.

reservation A method of creating an easement or profit, whereby a grantor retains these rights over the land which he conveys to the grantee.

restriction See 'caution'.

reversion The right remaining in a grantor after he has granted some interest shorter in duration than his own. The term is used in respect of both settlements and leases. 1. Settlements: the owner of a fee simple, for example, who grants a life interest or (before they were abolished by TOLATA 1996) an entailed interest, has not disposed of his full estate, and therefore retains a right to the land when the interests he has granted come to an end (the property will 'revert' to the grantor). A reversion gives a right to possession of the land in the future and so, since 1925, exists only in equity. 2. Leases: an estate owner who grants a lease retains his own legal estate in the land (fee simple or superior lease) throughout the duration of the lease. This interest in the land, which includes the right to receive rents and profits, if any, during the lease, and to recover the physical possession of the land at the end of the term, is called the 'landlord's reversion'.

reversionary lease A lease creating a term which will begin at a future date (distinguish a 'lease of the reversion', which arises where a landlord grants concurrent leases of the same property).

rights *in personam* Rights enforceable against only certain categories of persons, e.g., the right of a beneficiary under a trust.

rights *in rem* Rights in respect of a piece of land which are enforceable against any person who acquires an estate or interest in that land, e.g., in the case of unregistered land, a legal easement or a legal lease.

seisin Possession (historically, the type of possession enjoyed by the holder of a freehold estate).

servient tenement A piece of land which is burdened by some right (see 'easement').

settlement A disposition of property, made inter vivos or by will, whereby the settlor (the estate owner making the settlement) creates a series of successive interests in the property, e.g., a grant to A for life, remainder to B in fee simple.

severance The procedure by which a joint tenant converts his relation with the other co-owners into that of a tenant in common, so that he has a notional undivided share in the property and is no longer affected by the right of survivorship. Distinguish 'words of severance'.

socage The surviving form of tenure, by which land in England and Wales is held of the Crown.

statutory owner A person who acts where there is no tenant for life of a Settled Land Act Settlement (18.1); if no express appointment by settlor, role is assumed by trustees of settlement.

sublease A lease granted by a landlord who is himself a tenant of a superior estate owner.

tack (right to). The right to add a further advance (i.e., a later loan) to an earlier debt secured by a mortgage, so that the additional loan shares the priority of the earlier debt and thus takes priority over any intervening mortgages.

tenancy A lease; the two terms, 'tenancy' and 'lease', are used interchangeably throughout the book.

tenancy at sufferance See 10.10.2.

tenancy at will See 10.10.3.

tenancy by estoppel See 10.10.4.

tenancy in common The form of co-ownership in which each owner has a notional, although undivided, share in the property, which passes with his estate at his death; the right of survivorship does not apply to this form of co-ownership. Compare 'joint tenancy'.

tenant for life The beneficiary under a Settled Land Act settlement who has the right to present (current) enjoyment of the property. Under the Act, the tenant for life holds the legal estate and has statutory powers of management over the settled land.

tenure The set of conditions on which a tenant held land from his feudal lord; today all land is held in 'socage' tenure.

terms of years absolute A lease.

title A person's right to property, or the evidence of that right.

transfer The deed used to pass the legal estate in registered land from one owner to another.

trust corporation The Public Trustee or a corporation either appointed by the court in any particular case to be a trustee or entitled by rules made under Public Trustee Act 1906, s. 4(3), to act as a custodian trustee (LPA 1925, s. 205(1)(xxviii)).

trust for sale A trust which imposes a duty to sell the property. Under TOLATA 1996 this form of trust now takes effect as a trust of land.

trust of land The new form of trust relating to land introduced by the Trusts of Land and Appointment of Trustees Act 1996. Any trust in which some or all of the trust property is land constitutes a 'trust of land'.

undivided shares in land The interests of tenants in common; sometimes used as another name for tenancy in common.

usual covenants A term of art, denoting a fixed list of covenants to be included to a lease (see 11.3.3).

volunteer A person who takes property without giving value for it.

waste (liability for). The liability of a limited owner, such as a tenant under a lease or a tenant for life of settled land, for any act or omission which alters the state of the land whether for better or worse.

words of severance Words in a grant of property to co-owners, which indicate an intention that the grantees should hold as tenants in common and not as joint tenants.

INDEX